International Business Information
How to Find It, How to Use It

Second Edition

by
Ruth A. Pagell
and
Michael Halperin

Oryx Press
1998

The rare Arabian Oryx is believed to have inspired the myth of the unicorn. This desert antelope became virtually extinct in the early 1960s. At that time several groups of international conservationists arranged to have 9 animals sent to the Phoenix Zoo to be the nucleus of a captive breeding herd. Today the Oryx population is over 1,000 and over 500 have been returned to the Middle East.

© 1998 by The Oryx Press
4041 North Central at Indian School Road
Phoenix, Arizona 85012-3397

Published simultaneously in Canada
Printed and Bound in the United States of America

∞ The paper used in this publication meets the minimum requirements of American National Standard for Information Science—Permanence of Paper for Printed Library Materials, ANSI Z39.48, 1984.

Library of Congress Cataloging-in-Publication Data

Pagell, Ruth A.
   International business information : how to find it, how to use it
/ by Ruth A. Pagell and Michael Halperin.—2nd ed.
      p.   cm.
   Includes bibliographical references and index.
   ISBN 1-57356-050-2 (alk. paper)
   1. Business information services—Handbooks, manuals, etc.
2. Business—Bibliography—Handbooks, manuals, etc.   I. Halperin,
Michael, 1940–   . II. Title.
HF54.5.P33   1998
016.33—dc21   97-31548
                                                                                    CIP

Contents

List of Exhibits

List of Tables

Preface

"The emerging global economy," "transnational corporations," "the world marketplace": these phrases will define the business environment into the 21st century. The practical impact of the new world economic order is seen in a quote from former U.S. Labor Secretary Robert Reich.

> A sports car is financed in Japan, designed in Italy and assembled in Indiana, Mexico and France, using advanced electronic components invented in New Jersey and fabricated in Japan.
> (*Wall Street Journal*, 5 July 1991: A6)

The globalization of the economy has required librarians and business researchers to learn about new sources of information, as well as to expand their understanding of international business subjects. From any national perspective, much international business information is truly foreign. The sources are different, the language is different, the coding is different, the definitions are different. This book is designed to help you overcome the obstacles to finding and understanding international business information.

International Business Information: How to Find It, How to Use It not only describes key international business publications and databases, but more importantly, it provides the subject background needed to understand them. The book is designed to be a practical guide for a business researcher, information professional, or librarian. Many of the print and electronic sources we describe are available in medium-sized or large libraries and information centers worldwide. Although written by U.S. authors, the information and sources we describe should be of value to anyone performing international business research.

Users of Michael Lavin's *Business Information: How to Find It, How to Use It* (The Oryx Press, 2nd ed., 1992) will see its form, approach, and title reflected in this volume. We are great admirers of Lavin's approach to writing about business topics.

International Business Information is not a bibliography. We have been highly selective in the sources included. No publication or database is highlighted that we have not examined or searched. We have attempted to examine a wide range of sources and to acquire or access newly released sources. We have attended several international business conferences to examine sources not yet available in the U.S. and to obtain a broader perspective on the uses and application of non-U.S. products. Because both print and electronic sources are necessary for comprehensive business research, we have described a mix of these formats. Our emphasis is on what we consider the core of business research: companies, industries, markets, and finance. Most of the print sources we describe are serial publications.

In screening the vast number of possible international business sources for inclusion, we looked for materials that were authoritative, available, and affordable. Most of the sources are in English or have at least partial English translations. We recognize that English-language business sources may not be the most complete or authoritative for non–English speaking countries. Many countries have their own prominent business publishers or information providers. An example is Hoppenstedt in Germany. As a practical matter, we have focused our presentation on English-language directories, yearbooks, reports, and electronic files.

Each chapter of the book consists of subject background followed by a description of the subject's information sources. We occasionally stray from this plan when it seems appropriate to describe a source while discussing a business subject. Most of the chapters stand alone and can be consulted as needed. While we recommend that you read the introductory information in each chapter, you can use this book simply to identify sources.

Inclusion of a source in this book should not necessarily be seen as a recommendation for its use or purchase. We occasionally describe a source with a recommendation that it *not* be purchased. The prices we give for publications are approximate and are designed as a general aid for purchase decisions.

In our description of sources, we have presented extracts of entries, tables, and records to display what a particular entry includes or to illustrate a particular concept. Seeing an actual record, or even a partial record, often will give a better sense of the contents of a source than will the most elaborate description. Although entries change with each edition of a title or reload of a database, the concepts represented do not change as frequently. Therefore, we have kept exhibits from the first edition that continue to serve as good examples.

We believe that it is important for publishers of business information to give dates for the information they describe. For this reason, we include the dates of the editions we examined and the electronic information we extracted. Most of the sources we describe provide data. The indexes, abstracts, and full text databases we describe should be adequate to identify material that treats theoretical or conceptual issues.

We use "electronic" as the umbrella term to describe CD-ROMs, online products, and locally loaded databases. We use "online" when discussing networked distribution of information. Access can be via telnet, modem, or the World Wide Web (WWW). International business sources in all formats are proliferating. Printed sources may be available in one or more electronic versions. We have attempted to list, and in many cases to describe, the electronic versions of key print sources.

We realize that electronic publishing is in such a state of flux that our descriptions may date quickly. WWW sites are particularly prone to change and disappearance. Although the WWW is becoming the access method of choice to commercial and local time-sharing systems, it will continue to coexist for some time with traditional ASCII interfaces and client/ server Windows software. We describe the Internet when its use is appropriate for access to commercial international data sources. We describe other WWW sites that we believe offer content of value to a business researcher. Finally, we provide the WWW sites for the publishers and information suppliers we feature in the book, as places to find more information about these organizations and their products.

The names of products and providers may appear in a variety of ways both in publisher literature and in other sources. When several forms of a name were in use, Oryx Press chose one for use throughout the book. When in doubt, Oryx based the name and its styling on text in the company's WWW site.

Throughout the book, we emphasize the need for care in the use and interpretation of international business data. Business vocabulary often changes meaning when it crosses a border. Terms and concepts familiar in the U.S., such as CPI, current ratio, SIC number, and disclosure, may not be used or may have different definitions in other countries. Something as apparently simple as comparing the GDP of two countries has pitfalls.

An important goal for us has been to provide the reader with the information and techniques needed to evaluate and select information products for international business research. We believe that identifying and explaining the problems in relation to existing international business sources will help the reader evaluate new sources that will appear after this book is published.

While writing the first edition of this book, the map of the world changed dramatically. Thankfully, there has been more geographic stability during the writing of the second edition. However, the trend toward fewer independent major information providers has continued. The Thomson Corporation, a Canadian company, purchased IAC, the new owner of Predicasts. Thomson also owns Investext, Gale Research, and Securities Data Corporation (SDC). Reed Elsevier added LEXIS-NEXIS Services to its information portfolio, along with National Register, Kompass UK, and Bowker-Saur. University Microfilms (UMI) purchased the newspaper databank DataTimes. Primark now owns Datastream and Disclosure. The information industry has become an international industry, and any distinction between U.S. and non-U.S. sources refers to content, not ownership.

Between the time the book was originally written and the time it was finalized for publishing, in fall 1997, there were several significant events affecting our content:

- Knight Ridder is finalizing the sale of its Information Services division, which includes DIALOG and DataStar. The most likely buyer is Profound.

- NewsNet died in September of 1997 and there was no buyer for the content.

- Reuters has discontinued Reuter Textline as an updated database on all systems except FT Profile and has added the Textline content to its own Business Briefing.

- Dow Jones Interactive Publishing, Knight Ridder Information Services, and Financial Times Information created the *World Reporter* Database, released in September 1997. It will be available on DIALOG, DataStar, Dow Jones, and FT Profile. The database includes sources from each of the three publishers, plus additional news sources from around the world. All articles are indexed, and non–English language sources include English abstracts.

- The Big Six accounting firms are in the process of becoming the Big Five, with the merger of Coopers & Lybrand and Price Waterhouse.

This second edition of *International Business Information* includes many of the sources from the first edition, with new examples. More databanks are described, coverage of NAFTA (the North American Free Trade Alliance) is increased, and descriptions of WWW sites are interwoven throughout the chapters. Many of the titles and publishers we featured in the first edition, especially in emerging markets, are no longer available; they have been replaced with a new set of niche publications.

Research guides are, by their nature, incomplete. New editions of publications continually appear with new information, additional company listings, and changes in structure. Business researchers need infor-mation that ranges in complexity from single facts to grand theories. The accessibility of the information they want varies from common knowledge to state secrets. Secondary sources can describe only a portion of this universe of information. Sometimes the answers to apparently simple and plausible questions are nowhere to be found. Having said this, it is important to note that the scope, availability, and currency of published business information has never been greater. Despite the volatility of publishing, many of the core titles in international business have been in existence for decades. We believe that our selection and description of sources in *International Business Information* will serve you well as the foundation for international business research.

Acknowledgments

Our thanks to all the people who have helped us in writing this book. We thank Michael Lavin for allowing us to model this book's form and title after his guide to U.S. sources *(Business Information: How to Find It, How to Use It)*. We thank him, as well, for demonstrating how a guide to business literature should be written.

The help of the staff of the Lippincott Library was crucial for the book's completion. We drew heavily on the entire staff's reference experience, technical processing skills, detailed knowledge of sources, computer skills, and published articles. Several of our colleagues read portions of the manuscript. Our thanks to Steven Bell, Marie Bridy, Linda Eichler, Carol Hartranft, Janet Lentz, Jean Newland, and Oi-Fan Peters. Their comments and suggestions were invaluable. We thank, too, John Ganley of the New York Public Library, Ray Lester, formerly of the London Business School Library, and David Mort of Information Resource Network (Interstat) for sharing their knowledge and their collections with us.

Publishers and database producers were generous in providing review copies, test CD-ROMs, and access to time-sharing systems. They were generous, as well, with explanations of their data gathering and data processing techniques. We owe special thanks to the following information providers:

- Bureau van Dijk
- Datastream
- Disclosure
- Dun & Bradstreet
- Economist Intelligence Unit
- Ernst and Young and Arthur Andersen in Atlanta
- Euromonitor
- FT Extel
- Gale Research
- IAC
- DIALOG/DataStar
- LEXIS-NEXIS Services
- Questel-Orbit
- Responsive Data

We also owe a special thanks to Victor Rosenberg, former owner of Procite, whose database software was used for this publication.

Finally, these acknowledgments would not be complete without recognizing the exceptional editing skills of Oryx editor Elizabeth Welsh and Oryx's typesetter Linda Vespa, who miraculously found ways to fit in our various tables and exhibits.

PART I
Introduction

CHAPTER 1
General Sources for
International Business Research

TOPICS COVERED

- Sources of International Business Information
- Bibliographic Sources of Regional Business Information
- Online Full Text Sources
- General Finding Aids
- Searching the World Wide Web
- Searching for New International Subjects
- International Conferences

MAJOR SOURCES DISCUSSED

- IAC (Predicasts) Publications
- *Business & Industry Database*
- *ABI/Inform*
- *Business Index* and *General Business File*
- *Business Periodicals Index*
- *PAIS International*
- *Index to International Statistics*
- STAT-USA
- *Directory of International Sources of Business Information*

In this chapter, we describe the use of several standard sources of business information for international research, and we discuss the use of general finding aids for a variety of international business sources and subjects.

Michael Lavin devotes the first chapters of *Business Information: How to Find It, How to Use It* to describing sources and forms of business information, including guides for locating people, organizations, and publications. Although Lavin's emphasis is on U.S. business, his explanations and many of the sources he describes are equally appropriate for international business research. Rather than repeat Lavin's descriptions of many standard U.S. sources, we refer the reader to the appropriate sections of his book.[1]

SOURCES OF INTERNATIONAL BUSINESS INFORMATION

Despite the globalization of business and the development of the transnational corporation, the individual nation-state is still the paramount political and economic entity. International business research frequently has a national point of view. Consequently, sources for national and international business research often overlap. For example, the U.S. researcher might be interested in the following topics:

- Japanese investment in the U.S. chemical industry
- Availability of German company stocks in the U.S.
- The effect of EU regulations on U.S. trade with Europe

Many sources for U.S. business and news also have international information. For example, standard U.S. business indexes and abstracts, while emphasizing U.S. business and U.S. publications, often include bibliographic information about international issues. Listed below are examples of standard business sources useful for international research.

- *ABI/Inform*
- *Business & Industry Database*
- *Business Periodicals Index*
- *Business Index*
- *PAIS International*
- IAC *PROMT*
- STAT-USA
- *Wall Street Journal Index*

Some U.S. business sources have international companion volumes. Often these sources have the same publisher. Many of these parallel sources are described in this volume and a few pairs are listed below.

U.S. Business Source	Companion International Business Source
Encyclopedia of Associations	*Encyclopedia of Associations International Organizations*
American Statistics Index	*Index to International Statistics*
F&S Index	*F&S Europe* and *F&S International*
Brands and Their Companies	*International Brands and Their Companies*
Market Share Reporter	*World Market Share Reporter*
D&B Million Dollar Directory	*Dun's Principal International Businesses*
Best's Life/Health and *Best's Property/Casualty*	*Best's Insurance Reports (International Edition)*
Moody's Industrial Manual	*Moody's International Manual*
Encyclopedia of Business Information Sources	*Encyclopedia of Business Information Sources: Europe*

U.S. government publications are often an excellent and inexpensive source of international business information. In later chapters, we describe the international research value of several U.S. government publications. They include the *Survey of Current Business, Country Commercial Guides, Foreign Labor Trends, Monthly Labor Review,* and *National Trade Data Bank.* The *Statistical Abstract of the United States,* described in this chapter, is a useful finding aid to a wide range of international data.

Indexing and Abstracting Services

There are several indexing and abstracting services useful for international business research. Some of the more important are discussed below. All the print publications that are discussed in this section have at least one electronic version. The electronic sources have increasingly been adding full text of articles to supplement indexes and abstracts.

IAC Predicasts publications (published by Information Access Company)

The Predicasts publications, now published by IAC, have the largest set of international articles. The print F&S indexes are divided into three parts: U.S., Europe, and International (which includes Canada and Mexico). All three parts appear online as one database.

IAC *PROMT* (an acronym for Predicasts Overview of Markets and Technology) is available both in print and electronically. It includes fewer publications than the F&S indexes, but all entries have abstracts. The IAC *PROMT* file online may also have extracts or full text. *PROMT* is available on the following databanks:

- DataStar
- DIALOG
- NIFTY Corporation, NIFTY-Serve Japan
- LEXIS-NEXIS Services
- Thomson Financial Networks Inc., Investext/Plus Direct

- Profound
- Questel-Orbit
- FT Profile
- GENIOS
- STN
- BIOSIS Life Science Network

IAC produces a CD-ROM that combines aspects of the F&S indexes and *PROMT.* Called *F&S + Text,* it is composed of separate U.S. and International files. Each file has two CD-ROMs, a backfile from 1990, and a set of current material. The discs, using SilverPlatter software, are sold to public and academic libraries in the U.S. and to most types of libraries in developing countries. IAC also has a subset of *PROMT* on its own CD-ROM product, *IntelliSeek.* Finally, IAC delivers *PROMT* directly through its subscription WWW product, *Market Insite.*

The definition of "international" in Predicasts was where the activity took place. For example, a description of a U.K. company in the *Wall Street Journal* is an international record; a description of a U.S. company in the *Financial Times* is a U.S. record. About 1,000 publications, including magazines, newspapers, and trade publications, are indexed. *F&S + Text International* will provide a German view of Europe or a Japanese view of Asia. Exhibit 1.1 presents an extract of a sample record from *F&S + Text International.*

Many of the publications indexed in *F&S + Text* are not in English, although an English abstract summarizing the article is provided. In addition, many of the sources indexed in *F&S* and *PROMT* are not readily available in print, although all articles contain at least an abstract. Some contain excerpts, portions selected verbatim, that characterize the major points of the articles. Very short articles contain the full text. As seen in Exhibit 1.1, the abstracts include relevant data; therefore, not having access to the full text is disappointing but not fatal. What is more disappointing is that in 1994 *PROMT* stopped including tabular data in most of its articles.

TI: SVENSKA TOBAKS FIMPAR ESTLAND
Svenska Tobaks: Will close down mfg plant of Eesti Tubakas & move operations to Malmoe in Sweden
SO: Dagens-Industri. April 26, 1996, page 13
IS: 0346-640X
LA: Swedish; NONENGLISH
TX: Svenska Tobaks has decided to close down the manufacturing plant of Eesti Tubakas (AET). Some 145 workers will leave the company, and the manufacture will be moved to Malmoe in Sweden. The reason is the change in the Estonian tax policy on cigarettes. Earlier, imported cigarettes were taxed by 3 EEK per pack, while domestically produced cigarettes were taxed by 1 EEK per pack. Now, the difference between imported and domestic brands has been abolished, and sales for the Estonian affiliate of Svenska Tobaks have decreased in a marked way. Market shares have reputedly fallen from around 70 to 35 percent. Svenska Tobaks is the only Western company to have set up a production unit in any of the Baltic states. It owned around 67 percent of the shares in AET, while the Estonian Government controlled the rest. Svenska Tobaks had invested 105 million SEK (around 15,6 million US$) in new machinery for its Estonian plant, equipment which now will be removed from the country.
CO: Svenska-Tobaks
PN: Tobacco Products (2100000)
CN: Sweden (5SWE)
EN: Facilities & Equipment (44)
TA: YES
AN: 4629771

RECORD FROM *F&S + Text International*

EXHIBIT 1.1

Source: Record from *F&S Text International.* Reprinted with permission of Information Access Company.

These IAC *Predicasts* files feature a useful coding system with hierarchical codes for products, events, and geographic areas. Event and product codes were modified on January 13, 1997, to incorporate additional business concepts and new lines of business. Geographic codes were changed to bring uniformity to coding across all IAC information products and to add new countries. The most noticeable difference is in geographic coding on DIALOG, where not only the geographic codes but also the fields are changing. There will be mapping from the old geographic codes to the new ones. Table 1.A presents the changes in geographic codes, reflecting the western hemisphere emphasis of IAC.

TABLE 1.A

CHANGES IN GEOGRAPHIC CODES IN *PROMT* AND F&S INDEXES

	Files 16 and 18	
	Prior to January 13, 1997	After January 13, 1997
Geographic Code Field	CC	GC
Geographic Name Field	CN	GN
Numeric Range		
1	U.S.A. (cc=1usa)	U.S.A., Canada, and Mexico
2	Canada	Central America, exc. Mexico
3	Latin America, incl. Mexico	Latin America
4	Europe—EU 4EU—European Union 4EX—Europe exc. EU	Europe
5	W Europe exc. EU	Caribbean
6	Eastern Europe	Africa
7	Africa	Middle East
8	Middle East	Australia and New Zealand
9	Asia, incl. Australia & NZ	Asia

TABLE 1.B

PROMT GEOGRAPHIC CODES

No of Records	Code	Definition	1997 Code	No of Records	Code	Definition	1997 Code
1,109,232	4 ALL	EUROPE	4 Europe	697,266	9	(ALL ASIA)	90ASI Asia
37,527	4 EC	EUROPEAN COMMUNITY	4 EU Eur. Union	1,554	9 11	(FAR EAST)	
32,804	4B			427	9 2A	(ASEAN)	
891	4BEJ	BENELUX		1,537	9 2T	(SOUTHEAST ASIA)	90SOU Southeast Asia
30,659	4BEL	BELGIUM	4 EUBL Belgium	1,005	9 50	(OCEANIA)	80OCE Oceania
17,468	4DEN	DENMARK	4 EUDE Denmark	20,715	9 THA	(THAILAND)	9THAI Thailand
80,369	6USS	USSRª	4 EXRU Russia 9UZBE Uzbekstan				

a USSR was used for all former Soviet Union countries, except the Baltics

Source: DIALOG File 16, January 1997.

The first quarter of 1997 was the transition period. To find information on Russia in IAC's update File 12 on DIALOG, a searcher would enter *gc=4exru,* and to continue the search back in *PROMT,* the searcher would enter *cc=6ussr.* Table 1.B presents the number of records for selected geographic areas, using DIALOG File 16 as the source.

Business & Industry Database

Business & Industry Database (B & I) provides direct competition to IAC *PROMT. B & I* combines abstracts and full text of articles from 600 sources with exceptionally detailed indexing. The file coverage concentrates on leading trade magazines, newsletters, general and regional newspapers, and international business dailies. Coverage begins in July 1994 with more than 800,000 records available at the beginning of 1997. About half the articles are full text. Tabular data are sometimes included. The database is presently available through DIALOG, DataStar, FIRST SEARCH, and as a DIALOG OnDisc CD-ROM. It has also been added to the WWW product PointCast and will be part of a WWW news service from OneSource.

ABI/Inform (UMI/Data Courier, Inc.)

ABI/Inform was one of the first online business databases, dating back to mid-1971. There is no print equivalent. *ABI/Inform* is available on many systems, including DataStar, DIALOG, LEXIS-NEXIS, and FT Profile. It is also produced as a CD-ROM. Most of the over 1,000 journals indexed and abstracted by UMI/Data Courier are published in the U.S. Some 200 non-U.S. English language management publications were added to the file in 1993. The full text of selected articles has been added to the online database. *ABI/Inform* does not index journals cover-to-cover. How-

ever, UMI/Data Courier has a CD-ROM image product, *Business Periodicals on Disc,* that contains complete image facsimiles of about half the journals abstracted in *ABI/Inform.* A WWW subscription version of this product, called ProQuest Direct, is also available from UMI. *ABI/Inform* is also distributed by OVID and FIRST SEARCH, with WWW access.

ABI/Inform has both geographic descriptors for countries and regions and a numeric classification system that has codes for geographic regions.

Business Index and General Business File
(Information Access Company)

Business Index is available as a microfilm loop, on CD-ROM (under the name *InfoTrac*), or as the *Trade and Industry* online database. None of these forms have identical contents. IAC now has an expanded CD-ROM, *General Business File,* that includes *Business Index* and investment bank reports from *Investext.* It is also available on the WWW as *General Business File,* a subscription service directly from IAC.

Business Index has been adding abstracts to its file and making changes to its CD-ROM software. Unfortunately, the changes have made the product more difficult to use. It is still a good source for locating company information.

IAC makes the full text of some of the articles it indexes available in two formats, online and in microfilm. Selected articles are available online on several databanks such as LEXIS-NEXIS Services, Dow Jones News/Retrieval, DIALOG, and DataStar. Articles are available as well in *Business Collection,* a microfilm system that is linked by a numeric code to *Business Index* citations.

IAC is adding abstracts of European journals to its databases. *Trade and Industry* (File 148 on DIALOG and INDY on DataStar) added titles as diverse as *Bank of*

England Quarterly and *Electrical Contractor*. Few of IAC's new titles are duplicated by *ABI/Inform*.

Business Periodicals Index (H. W. Wilson)

Business Periodicals Index was the original business index. *BPI* is available in print, online direct from Wilson, and on Wilsondisc CD-ROM. A companion product, *Wilson Business Abstracts*, is available on CD-ROM and online. *BPI* has been a standard index in many small and medium-sized libraries. *BPI* is known for the quality of its indexing and its sensitivity to users' collections. However, *BPI* does not have broad coverage of international business topics.

PAIS International (Public Affairs Information Service)

PAIS is another multiformat bibliographic source. It is available in print, online, and on CD-ROM. Many of the sources indexed in *PAIS* are written in French, German, Spanish, Italian, or Portuguese. Though more a social science than a business database, *PAIS* indexes many business-related articles.

Economic Literature Index (American Economics Association)

Economic Literature Index contains international business articles of interest to academic researchers. Again, this *Economic Literature Index* is in print and online as DIALOG File 139. Its CD-ROM equivalent is *EconLit*, from SilverPlatter.

BIBLIOGRAPHIC SOURCES OF REGIONAL BUSINESS INFORMATION

Management and Marketing Abstracts (published by PIRA International, U.K.)

A European competitor to *ABI/Inform, Management and Marketing Abstracts* is available both in print and online in DataStar (MMKA). The focus of the database is on management issues and case studies. Finance is covered only as it relates to management. Only 175 publications are abstracted, the majority from the U.K. About 10% of the entries are non-English and approximately 20% are from North America. Many of the English-language titles in MMKA were added to *ABI/Inform* in 1993.

HELECON (Helsinki School of Economics and Business Information, Helsinki, Finland)

HELECON produces two CD-ROM products with citations and abstracts. *HELECON International Databases on CD-ROM* includes nine international databases covering worldwide economics and business management information. The scope of the CD-ROM includes journal articles, working papers, dissertations, research reports, conference papers, and publications of the International Labor Organization (ILO). While most articles are in English, German, French, and Spanish are also used.

Databases on *HELECON International* have changed since 1994. Sample database titles are listed below.

SCIMA	Abstracts to articles and books in management and marketing
EMD	Multilingual database from European Business Schools Librarians Group
FONDS QUETELET	Belgian business database from the Ministry of Foreign Affairs

Other European databases come from the ILO, Cologne University, and the University of Warwick in the U.K. *HELECON* now also includes ACPICE, a South American business database, and CHINA, which has references to Chinese economics journal articles.

HELECON CD-ROM Nordic databases are based on the collections of six Nordic business libraries. User interfaces are in English, Swedish, or Finnish, and the databases are a combination of Scandinavian languages, French, and German.

Institute of Management International Database Plus (published quarterly by Bowker-Saur)

IMID Plus, the *Institute of Management International Database Plus*, is a CD-ROM collection of management resources produced in conjunction with Bowker-Saur. The disc, which was first released in December of 1992 and has been updated quarterly since then, contains six databases:

- Journals: Over 35,000 abstracts selected from over 300 U.K., U.S., and European journals.
- Books: Details and abstracts of 30,000 English language management books, reports, and cases.
- Management: Abstracts and indexes to 4,000 research papers, working papers, and studies from 720 institutions worldwide.
- Audiovisual Material: Over 1,300 abstracts and indexes to training videos.
- Company Practice: Over 600 examples of company policy and practice.
- Training Exercises: Details of over 400 training exercises for managers.

Bowker-Saur UK maintains a document delivery service that supplies the materials listed on the disc.

According to the Institute, the goal of the product is to serve as an aid rather than as a substitute for coursework, attending conferences, or reading books. The system should save time that otherwise would be wasted in choosing the wrong seminar or book. The disc costs £799 (£699 for Institute members).

ONLINE FULL TEXT SOURCES

Full text business sources online are in great demand. Many business researchers will gladly trade the breadth of coverage and depth of indexing of bibliographic files for the convenience of having the complete text of an article for immediate use. Full text newspapers are often online on the day of their publications, and newswire services are usually updated continuously. Bibliographic files, in contrast, often lag the publications they index by several months. We describe full text sources more extensively in Chapter 6. The availability of full text journals online can be established from *Full Text Online*, published by BiblioData.

GENERAL FINDING AIDS

Most of the finding aids we describe are included in chapters dealing with specific subjects. The general finding aids we describe in this section will help you locate books, serials, periodicals, and data sources on all international business subjects. Several of the sources we mention, such as *Ulrich's International Periodicals Directory* and the *OCLC Online Union Catalog,* are described in detail in Lavin's *Business Information.*[2]

Locating Books, Serials, and Periodicals

Union catalogs of library holdings, such as the *OCLC Online Union Catalog* and RLIN (Research Library Information Network), are useful for establishing ownership of particular books and serials. When used for subject searching, they may overwhelm us with detail. Often, a subject search of the holdings of one strong collection is more productive. The availability of many individual library catalogs on the Internet has made them easily accessible. We have found the online catalog of the New York Public Research Library particularly valuable for business materials (http://www.nypl.org). The following WWW sites are useful for their collection of library links.

- ARL Member Libraries' Information Servers: //arl.cni.org/members.html
- RLG Members with World Wide Web Servers: //www.rlg.org/memweb.html
- Libweb: Library Servers via WWW: //sunsite.berkeley.edu/libweb/

Ulrich's International Periodicals Directory and *Books in Print* use general subject headings, which in the printed versions are too restrictive. These two aids can be used more effectively in their online versions on DIALOG, Files 480 and 470, respectively. With DIALOG's *Journal Name Finder* (File 414) you are able to search DIALOG bibliographic files to identify journal names. The file allows quick identification of files that include a particular journal or have the most comprehensive coverage of a journal. It is useful if you have abbreviations or an incomplete title. The form of the journal name is as it appears in the original database index including abbreviations, punctuation, and spelling variations. Two other DIALOG Name Finder files (*DIALOG Company Name Finder*, File 416, and *DIALOG Product Name Finder*, File 413) are also useful as online finding aids.

SEARCHING THE WORLD WIDE WEB

It has been said that the wonderful thing about the World Wide Web (WWW) is that everyone can publish, and that the terrible thing about the WWW is that everyone can publish. It is easy and inexpensive to create a Web site. It is much more difficult and expensive to maintain one. This has resulted in thousands of abandoned sites.

Finding information on the WWW poses the same problems as finding information in any electronic database, but it is made more complicated by site and content instability and inadequate search engines.

There are dozens of Web search engines. They are much less sophisticated than the best telnet commercial online search systems, such as DIALOG. Although many will search the complete text of Web documents, they usually lack such features as set creation and limits. This is unfortunate, since the chaotic conditions of the Web, with its lack of controlled vocabulary and potential for irrelevant retrieval, requires all the search power we can get. We assume that the comparative weakness of Web search engines will be corrected as the technology develops and as the major commercial databases migrate to the WWW. See Greg R. Notess's site (http://imt.net5/~notess/compeng.html) for a current comparison of Web search engines. Below, we describe a few of the popular ones.

Web Search Engines

Alta Vista (//www.altavista.digital.com)

Alta Vista is one of the few engines that lets you use a proximity operator (NEAR) and a title search to narrow your choices. It also allows limit by date and can sort and display results based on which keywords you want to see first. In 1997, Alta Vista boasted of having access to 31 million pages from 476,000 servers. It has mirror sites in Europe and Australia. The European site (//www.altavista.telia.com) asks you to indicate the country from which you are accessing, and it supports searching in 17 European languages.

Yahoo! (//www.yahoo.com)

The indexers at Yahoo! group Web sites by category. The number of sites is smaller than available through a general search engine such as Alta Vista, but the sites tend to be of higher quality.

Metacrawler (//www.metacrawler.com)

Metacrawler is a "meta-engine"—it searches multiple Web search engines. This type of search is useful for obscure topics when you need to search as much of the Web as possible.

Examples of special-purpose Web search engines include the University of Michigan Directory of Scholarly Discussion Groups (//www.lib.umich.edu/chhome.html); CyberHound (//www.cyberhound.com), which rates Web sites; and the Internet Sleuth (//isleuth.com), which searches some 1,500 "free" database sites.

Web Sites for International Business Information

We describe hundreds of specific Web sites throughout this volume. Below, we list a few international business "metasites" (sites that have as their primary purpose listing other sites).

International Business Resources on the WWW
(http://www.ciber.msu.edu/busres.htm)

Maintained by the Michigan State University Center for International Business Education and Research (CIBER), this site maintains hundreds of links to sources of information on countries, international trade, statistical data, news, and periodicals.

VIBES: Virtual International Business and Economic Sources (http://www.uncc.edu/lis/library/reference/intbus/vibehome.htm)

VIBES is the home page of Jeanie M. Welch, international business subject specialist at the University of North Carolina at Charlotte. It provides links to sources of international business information including full text files (in English), statistical tables, and graphs available on gopher sites and Web sites. VIBES is distinguished by its practical usefulness, organization, and currency.

Worldclass Supersite (http://web.idirect.com/~tiger/)

Worldclass Supersite links to 600 sites from 70 countries. This well-organized site includes links to sources for news, reference, education, trade, and networking. The heading "Business Magazines by Country," for example, will quickly lead you to the site for the *Albanian Times—Business Weekly*.

EUROPA, Information from the European Union (http://europa.eu.int/)

Europa is maintained by the European Commission for institutions. It includes information on the European Union (EU) history, institutions, policies, and news of the EU. Some useful links include Eurostat (statistics), ECHO, and CORDIS (R&D Information); EUR-OP (office for EU official publications); as well as sites for individual governments in the EU.

The following list includes a few more specific sites that we often find useful for international business research:

- United Nations (UN) Web site locator: http://www.unsystem.org/
- Organization for Economic Cooperation and Development (OECD): http://www.oecd.org/
- United Nations Trade Point Development Centre: http://www.unicc.org/untpdc/welcome.html
- The World Bank (international finance and the world's economies): http://www.worldbank.org/
- World Trade Organization: http://www.wto.org/
- Asian Development Bank: http://www.asiandevbank.org/
- Inter-American Development Bank: http://www.iadb.org/

Statistical Sources

Business research questions often center on finding numbers. Many of the sources we discuss in this book are statistical sources for a particular subject area. Described in the following section are general sources of statistics. In addition, several of the guides appearing in Lavin's book, such as *Statistics Sources* (Gale Research Inc.), are useful for international research.

Index to International Statistics (published monthly by Congressional Information Service)

IIS is the one general index to the publications of international organizations. It indexes and abstracts the publications of about 100 intergovernmental organizations. It includes the statistical publications of the United Nations, UN affiliates such as the International Monetary Fund (IMF), as well as the EU and the OECD. Virtually all the publications indexed are published in English. Updated monthly, with quarterly, annual, and multiple-year cumulatives, *IIS* has been published since 1983. *IIS* is arranged by issuing agency. It has five separate indexes:

1. Subjects, names, and geographic area
2. Categories
   Age
   Commodity
   Country
   Individual company or enterprise
   Industry
   Sex
3. Issuing source
4. Title
5. Agency publication number for EU, UN, and OAS (Organization of American States) publications

In addition to its indexing, *IIS* has several additional useful features:

- Membership lists for major international organizations such as the OECD and the EU
- Addresses and phone numbers for the sources of the publications
- Outlines of selected standard classification codes such as the SITC and NACE (see Chapters 14 and 15)

The full text of publications identified in *IIS* are available on microfiche from the publisher.

IIS has been available since 1989 on CD-ROM, updated quarterly. The print version of *IIS*, although detailed, does not usually index to the level of the individual economic series appearing in the publications *IIS* covers. For example, using *IIS* print indexes, you will not be able to determine that IMF credit ratios to exports for Mexico are reported in the World Bank's annual *Trends in Developing Economies*. Searching the CD-ROM version of the *IIS* for "Mexico and IMF credit ratios" would retrieve the appropriate record, a truncated version of which appears in Exhibit 1.2.

Statistical Abstract of the United States (published annually by the U.S. Bureau of the Census)

In *Statistical Abstract of the United States,* the section on "Comparative Economic Statistics" contains more than 50 tables giving figures for the world as a whole and for many countries on a comparative basis with the U.S. The tables often give several years of data. The tables in *Statistical Abstract* are a useful index to more detailed information. For example, a table on

health expenditures gives these two sources: *OECD Health Data* and *OECD Health Systems Facts and Trends.*

The Appendix to the *Statistical Abstract* lists the sources used for the tables. A separate "Guide to Foreign Statistical Abstracts" presents recent statistical abstracts by country, noting the language of the publication. Examples of data on comparative economic statistics in *Statistical Abstract* include:

- Central bank discount rates/money market rates
- Civilian employment
- Communications (number of telephones, newspapers, televisions)
- Consumer prices
- Demographics statistics (population and vital statistics)
- Energy consumption and production
- Foreign trade
- Foreign exchange rates (20-year time series of 30 currencies)
- GDP per capita
- Gross national product in constant dollars
- Growth rates of GDP
- Health expenditures
- Hourly compensation for production workers in manufacturing
- Industrial production
- Labor force participation rates
- Mineral commodities (world production)
- Public debt
- Reserve assets and international transaction balances
- Tax revenues

Statistical Abstract is available on CD-ROM and from the Census Bureau's Web site, //www.census.gov/ stat_abstract/.

STAT-USA (//www.stat-usa.gov)

STAT-USA is one of the U.S. government's premier Internet distributors of business and economic information. About 300,000 reports and statistical series from 50 federal agencies are available. Although primarily about the U.S., the site has extensive international coverage. A subscription is necessary to access most of STAT-USA's material. Important international files include:

- NTDB (National Trade Data Bank)
  Country Commercial Guides
  Market Research Reports
  International Contacts
  Export Yellow Pages

- Economic Bulletin Board
  Trade Opportunity Leads
  International Market Insights
  Market Research Reports
- GLOBUS (Global Business Opportunities Service)
  Commerce Business Daily Leads
  Defense Logistics Agency Procurements
  Trade Opportunity Leads

- Bureau of Economic Analysis Economic Information
  Survey of Current Business
  International Foreign Direct Investment
  International Transactions
  Trade Opportunity Program (TOP)

IIS MAIN NO: 1995 4530-S45
TITLE: Trends in Developing Economies, 1995
PUB. DATE: 1995. <0/95>
PERIODICITY: Annual.
COLLATION: vi+584 p.
ISSUING SOURCE: International Bank for Reconstruction and Development
LANGUAGE: En
LC CARD NO: 90-640763
ISSN: 1014-7004
ISBN: 0-8213-3281-3
AVAILABILITY: IBRD (Washington DC; Paris; Tokyo), $28.95.
MICROFICHE STATUS: IIS/MF

Annual report on economic and social trends in developing countries, varying periods 1980-94 or undated. Includes data on GDP, by expenditure item; GNP; trade; investment; savings; national income; inflation; population; labor force; balance of payments; currency exchange rates; national budget; and external debt, with **IMF credit ratios to exports** and GDP; by country. Also includes data on poverty; life expectancy; infant mortality; child malnutrition; access to safe water; per capita energy consumption; adult illiteracy; and educational enrollment.
    Data sources: IBRD sources.
    Format and data presentation: Foreword, contents listing, and introduction
(p. iii-vi); 114 country or economic grouping sections, each generally with
8 charts and 1 table (p. 1-576); and notes (p. 577-584).
    Monetary values are expressed in US$. Trade data include imports by
product group, and exports by major commodity. Selected GDP data are shown
by sector. Not all data are shown for each country.
    Note: Report complements World Development Report (covered in IIS under
4530-S3).
        MAIN TERMS (and Content Notations):
        Subjects and Authors
        -ECONOMIC.INDICATORS
         (Developing countries basic econ and social indicators, by country,
         1980s-94, IBRD annual rpt)
        -INTERNATIONAL MONETARY FUND
         (Developing countries basic econ and social indicators, including IMF
         credit ratios to exports and GDP, 1980s-94, IBRD annual rpt)
        -AFRICA; ALBANIA; ALGERIA; ANGOLA; ANTIGUA AND BARBUDA; ARGENTINA;
         •
         •
         •
        -MANUFACTURING
         (Trade of developing countries, by product group and commodity,
         1980s-94, IBRD annual rpt)
        Category Breakdowns
        -BY.FOREIGN.COUNTRY
         (Econ and social basic indicators, by developing country, 1980s-94,
         IBRD annual rpt)
        -BY.COMMODITY
         (Trade of developing countries, by product group and commodity,
         1980s-94, IBRD annual rpt)

RECORD FROM *INDEX TO INTERNATIONAL STATISTICS* (CD-ROM)

EXHIBIT 1.2

Source: Index to International Statistics.

Business Information Sourcebooks

Encyclopedia of Business Information Sources: Europe (edited by M. Balachandran, published by Gale Research, 1994)

This is a comprehensive bibliographic guide to sources of industry and other business data. The work is arranged by subject, with subdivisions first by country and then by format (e.g., directories, handbooks, periodicals, and statistics). In addition to published materials, the work includes addresses of research centers and trade associations. No electronic sources are listed.

International Directory of Business Information Sources & Services (published by Europa Publications, 1996)

This 500-page directory has individual chapters on 46 countries. Within each chapter are address listings at national, regional, and city levels for chambers of commerce, government organizations, research organizations, independent organizations, foreign trade organizations, sources of statistical information, and business libraries. Brief descriptions of organizations are often included.

Data Sources for Business and Market Analysis (4th ed., by John Ganly, published by Scarecrow Press, 1994)

While predominantly U.S. in its coverage of business providers and sources, this book does have a section on "Foreign Sources" from national and intergovernmental organizations. It includes non-U.S. publishers within its subject category entries. For example, under "Services—Consumer Behavior," there are entries for U.K. and Japanese market research publishers. Entries are limited to one-sentence annotations.

World Databases of Business Information Sources (published by Euromonitor)

World Databases is a compilation of sources from many Euromonitor print publications described later in this book. The resulting CD-ROM has over 12,000 organizations, 13,000 publications, 2,000 exhibitions, and 700 online databases.

Book Reviews

Some of us rely on book reviews to select titles for our collections. Especially when we are spending several hundred dollars for one title, we want to be careful that the book has been evaluated by a knowledgeable reviewer.

There are, however, several caveats when relying on reviews. In the fast-changing environment of inter-

national business, waiting for a review might lose your organization its competitive advantage. Not all reviewers are knowledgeable in this field. Reviewers may read little more than the publisher's brochure or spot-check a couple of chapters. Many reviewing sources are targeted for academic and public library collections, not specialized business collections. Most reviews that are published are positive. Therefore, throughout this book, we have listed factors to use in evaluating a new source for the specific needs of your organization.

Current Awareness Publications

Several newsletters and journals provide updated information on electronic and print business sources. They include articles on new titles or on changes to existing titles. Listed below are a few recommended publications.

Information Today (Medford, NJ: Information Today; http://www.infotoday.com) and *Information World Review* (Oxford: Learned Europe Ltd.; http://www.learned.co.uk)

These two publications have been the staples on either side of the Atlantic for providing product updates and industry news.

Access: Asia's Newspaper on Electronic Information Products and Services (Knowledge Share International, 90 Tanjong Kalong Rd., #04-01, Singapore, 1543; fax: 65-741-8821; selected articles at http://sunsite.nus.sg/bibdb.bibdh.htm/)

Access is the closest publication to *Information Today* or *Information World Review* available in the Asian market. It tracks the information products available to Asian information professionals and also has articles on finding Asian information.

The Information Advisor: Tips & Techniques for Smart Information Users (FIND/SVP)

Each month, this newsletter offers practical comparisons of databases and directory sources.

Business Information Review (Bowker-Saur, Maypole House, Maypole Rd., East Grinstead, RH19 1HU, UK; e-mail bir@bowker-saur.co.uk)

Formerly published by Headland Press, this journal contains articles that are more research-oriented than newsy. A recent issue included such titles as "Business Information in Denmark" and "Business Information from Central and Eastern Europe: Czech Republic, Hungary and Poland."

Online/CD-ROM Business Sourcebook (Headland Business Information, Bowker-Saur)

Online/CD-ROM Business Sourcebook is one of several Pam Foster–edited titles that Bowker-Saur purchased from Headland Press in 1995. The Headland titles have been standard sources for U.K. special and academic libraries. Online, CD-ROM, diskette, and Internet sources are covered. *European Business Intelligence Briefing*, another former Headland title, focuses on one business information issue each month.

Sources on Conducting International Business

Management

Throughout this book, we will be discussing materials such as statistical sources, directories, and handbooks. The information we provide and the sources we include do not cover the management of international business. Many of the management books are written for the practitioner and have very short shelf lives and limited value in a research library collection. Standard library book review tools should help identify which books of this genre are worth purchasing.

Behavior

One area of international business of importance to business people, business researchers, and academics is personal conduct. Roger E. Axtell has written a series of inexpensive books published by John Wiley that cover all aspects of business protocol, the basic one being *The Do's and Taboos Around the World: A Guide to International Behavior* (1993). Axtell also has written guides on hosting international visitors, cultural barriers to international trade, and understanding international body language.

Another work on international personal conduct is *Kiss, Bow, or Shake Hands: How to Do Business in Sixty Countries*.[3] It contains brief descriptions of the culture, behavior styles, negotiating techniques, and business practices of 60 selected countries including the U.S. The book's authors are the owners of a software and training firm for international travelers called Getting Through Customs. Their Web site is //www.getcustoms.com/.

SEARCHING FOR NEW INTERNATIONAL SUBJECTS

Political changes affect the way we search for business information. The political changes in Eastern Europe have scrambled the controlled vocabularies of all social science databases. It is instructive to see how business databases have reacted to these changes. The Berlin Wall fell in November of 1989. However, database producers, the journals that constitute the databases, and the authors that write for those journals, continue to use both pre- and post-Wall vocabulary. We use examples of Europe, Eastern Europe, and Russia to demonstrate how databases incorporate new or changing subjects.

It takes time for indexers to integrate changes in vocabulary into a thesaurus. New vocabulary appears first in titles and in the text of articles. If the changes in terminology appear significant and permanent, they will be adopted as descriptors (indexing terms). New indexing terms often have appeared online or on disc before they are used in print indexes. The subject vocabularies of institutions such as the Library of Congress are the slowest to change. How have the business databases handled the changing world geography?

Table 1.C lists various identifying terms for Europe as a region on *ABI/Inform*. In the fall of 1988, "EC" was added as a descriptor, and in 1994 "EU" was added as well. This reflects the change in terminology from *European Economic Community* to *European Community,* and then to *European Union*. All the abbreviations and terms still appear in article titles and text and can be retrieved with free text searching.

Researchers are interested in efficient ways to identify records about Eastern Europe, the newly emerging nations, and countries that have changed their names. By the beginning of 1992, *ABI/Inform* had created descriptors for all the newly independent countries from the former Soviet Union, based on the forms used by the Associated Press.

- Armenia
- Azerbaijan
- Belarus (formerly Byelorussia)
- Georgia
- Kazakhstan
- Kyrgyzstan (formerly Kirgizia)
- Moldova (formerly Moldavia)
- Russia
- Tajikistan (formerly Tadzhikistan)
- Turkmenistan (formerly Turkmenia)
- Ukraine
- Uzbekistan

While it is easy to retrieve some articles on geographic areas, you often must use more than one term to find all articles. Because geography is changing rapidly, it is helpful to know when free text words became descriptors.

TABLE 1.C

SEARCHING FOR EUROPEAN TERMS ON *ABI/INFORM*

	FREE TEXT	DESCRIPTOR [and FIELD]	
EUROPEAN COMMUNITY	10,859	0	
EC	15,714	6,558 (DE)[a]	
EUROPEAN UNION	7,454	2,298 (CO)	
EU	6,178	635 (DE)	
EUROPEAN ECONOMIC COMMUNITY	2,243	0	
EEC	2,629	0	
EFTA	657	0	
EUROPEAN FREE TRADE ASSOCIATION	465	0	
EUROPE	76,969	25,853	(GN)
9175 [Code for Europe]	133,616		(CC)
EASTERN EUROPE	11,434	3,036	(GN)
9176 [Code for Eastern Europe]		16,732	(CC)
9175 OR 9176		148,266	(CC)
CROATIA	834	166	(GN from 1989)
SLOVENIA	783	165	(GN from 1986)
BOSNIA-HERCEGOVINA	463	435	(GN from 1992)
BOSNIA?	2,066		
MACEDONIA	342	0	
SERBIA	589	0	
YUGOSLAVIA	2,241	356	
included for comparison:			
ASIA	29,746	7,207	(GN)
9179 (Asia and the Pacific)		72,973	(CC)
LATIN AMERICA		2,320	(GN)
9173 (Latin America)		15,872	(CC)
9190 (United States)		578,454	(CC)

a Added October 1988; both EC and EEC still appear in articles

Source: DIALOG, October 27, 1996.

IAC Predicast files had taken a conservative approach to adding new codes. They had not wanted to change codes constantly, and they have no mechanism for retroactively changing codes. Taking this approach to its extreme, *6yug* was still the code for Slovenia, Croatia, and Yugoslavia at the end of 1996. As noted earlier in this chapter, this approach is changing with the introduction of new IAC geographic codes in 1997.

Textline has handled the name changes by incorporating new terms into its geographic index, but keeping the same code, so that "USSR" remains a code while "Commonwealth of Independent States" is now the term. The same approach allows a user to trace the European Union from its beginnings as the EEC through its change to the EU. Exhibit 1.3 is an example from *Textline* that has European Union, EC, and EEC in the descriptor field, in addition to EU in the title. Notice how *Textline* has continued to use "EEC" as its code to keep the continuity from the EEC through to the EU.

TI BELGIUM: One million could die in Zaire,*EU*says. SO Reuter-News-Service, REUTR; . . .

DE GOVERNMENT-SOCIAL,(GCAT);*EC-EXTERNAL-RELATIONS,* (G158); EUROPEAN-COMMUNITY, (G15); RELATIONS, (G13); RAPID-NEWS- YDB-CODE, (8YDB); RAPID- NEWS-RSK-CODE, (7RSK); COUNTRY- REPORTS-POLITICAL, (1POL). EUROPEAN-UNION,*(EEC); *BELGIUM,

EXTRACT FROM *TEXTLINE* RECORD

EXHIBIT 1.3

Source: Reuter Textline (TXCO) on DataStar. Reprinted with permission from Reuters.

PAIS has always had strong European coverage. Its commitment to worldwide coverage of social, economic, and political activities resulted in the merging of its two paper products—*PAIS Foreign Language Index* and *PAIS Bulletin*—into *PAIS International in Print* in 1991. Because *PAIS* covers social science and historical topics, the "new" nations were already used as subject headings. For example, "Slovenia" appeared in the descriptor field as early as 1980, and "Russia-

Federative-Republic" has been in use for the entire time span of the CD-ROM, although few articles were given this description until recently. Exhibit 1.4 shows a *PAIS* record using the "Russia (Federative Republic)" descriptor.

PAIS's strength as an academic product is a weakness in a business library setting. Many of the articles are in foreign languages. For example, more than 60% of the articles coded European-Economic-Community are not in English. Records include only abstracts or notes.

What terms do you use to search for current information about business in Russia? Searches done in DIALOG in six databases using free text and controlled vocabulary revealed the variation in terms. The six databases are *ABI/Inform, PAIS, Trade & Industry, Textline, Business & Industry,* and *PROMT.* As Table 1.D illustrates, databases have always handled the USSR in different ways and continue to do so. Generally, the term "Russia" is used to refer exclusively to the nation Russia, while the term "Commonwealth of Independent States" refers to the group of states making up the former USSR. *Textline* uses *Commonwealth-of-Independent-States* as its country term and *USSR* as the code. *PAIS* has a unique term,

Russia-Federative-Republic which does not appear in the other databases. Geographic field codes are an important feature when we use standard indexes, abstracts, and full text databases for international applications. Controlled vocabulary for geographic areas allows precise retrieval. Table 1.D compares vocabulary and number of records among business databases for "Russia."

Chistiakov, E.; Teplukhina, T. Gross domestic product of the constituent regions of the Russian Federation. Problems Econ Transition 39:21-5 O 1996, table(s)

In the absence of official figures, estimates gross domestic product for oblasts, krais, and republics in absolute and per capita terms...

Subject Headings: Russia (Federative Republic) - Economic conditions; Gross national product - Russia (Federative Republic); National accounting - Russia (Federative Republic)

PAIS RECORD

EXHIBIT 1.4

Source: Reprinted with permission from Public Affairs Information Services, Inc.

TABLE 1.D

VOCABULARY FOR SEARCHING "RUSSIA"

	ABI/ INFORM	PAIS	TRADE & INDUSTRY	TEXT- LINE	BUSINESS & INDUSTRY	PROMT
Geographic Code	(GN)	(DE)	(GN)	(CN)	(GN)	(CC,CN)
USSR	5,144	995	9,330	431,483	498	94,555
USSR (index)	**2,456**	**0**	**92***	**413,010*** 88,867**	**0**	**78,341**
COMMONWEALTH INDEPENDENT STATES	985	622	4,549	417,381	352	3,536
COMMONWEALTH IND ST (index)	**0**	**588**	**1,714***	**413,010**	**0**	**0**
SOVIET UNION	7,901	10,959	66,358	179,198	1,686	30,669
SOVIET UNION (index)	**0**	**9,866**	**0**	**11,577****	**0**	**0**
RUSSIA	12,424	3,053	42,638	300,589	16,671	51,333
RUSSIA (index)	4,926	2,051	202,767	12,740 148,069**	0	
FORMER SOVIET UNION	4,121	400	9,283	34,064	1,290	8,076
CIS	1.591	104	5,874	27,411	1,328	8,489
CIS AND (RUSSIA OR SOVIET)	618	64	2,106	15,847	654	4,137
FORMER USSR	682	18	1,135	6,103	363	2,894
UNION SOVIET SOCIALIST	49	71	185	364	0	42

PAIS does not have a separate descriptor field for geographic entities
* Term is a descriptor (DE) not in the country name field (GN or CN)
** *Textline* uses a geographic designation in the title

Source: DIALOG, October 27, 1996.

INTERNATIONAL CONFERENCES

One way to keep on top of all the changes in international business information and the sources supporting it is to read as much as possible—the daily newspapers, the business literature, and the information literature. Also helpful, though expensive, is to attend an international business information conference.

One such conference is the European Business Information Conference (EBIC) organized by TFPL, Task Force Pro Libra (London). This conference is held each spring in a major European city. The speakers include representatives from the business community, academia, and the information industry.

The International Online Meeting in London each December (Learned Information Ltd.) is an excellent source for European electronic products. Many products are displayed at this show that are not readily available in the U.S. or that become available later.

NOTES

1. Michael Lavin, *Business Information: How to Find It, How to Use It, Second Edition* (Phoenix: The Oryx Press, 1992). We found the following chapters especially useful: Chapter 1 ("Sources and Forms of Business Information"), Chapter 2 ("Locating Experts"), Chapter 3 ("Finding Reference Materials"), Chapter 4 ("Finding Books, Documents, and Statistical Reports"), Chapter 5 ("Searching Journals, Newspapers, and News Services"), and Chapter 13 ("Introduction to Statistical Reasoning").

2. See note 1.

3. Terri Morrison, Wayne A. Conaway, and George A. Borden, *Kiss, Bow, or Shake Hands: How to Do Business in Sixty Countries* (Holbrook, MA: Bob Adams, 1994).

PART II
Company Information

CHAPTER 2
Accounting Standards and Practices

TOPICS COVERED

- Multinational Issues
- Role of the European Union (EU)
- Accounting Practices in Selected Non-EU Countries
- Emerging Markets
- International Accounting Bodies
- Solutions to Accounting Differences
- Resources
- Using Indexes and Online Databases to Find International Accounting Information
- Accounting Information on the World Wide Web

MAJOR SOURCES DISCUSSED

- *TRANSACC: Transnational Accounting*
- *International Accounting and Reporting Issues*
- *International Accounting and Auditing Trends*
- *Handbook of International Accounting*
- *European Accounting Guide*
- *Accounting and Tax Index*

The purpose of accounting is to provide *information* on business activities in order to facilitate decision-making by users of financial statements.[1]

Accounting provides the tools, rules, and language of communication for financial disclosure. The information published as an outgrowth of accounting standards and practice affects the decision-making of shareholders, potential investors, workers, consumers, host and partner governments, and the general public.

Accounting standards grow out of the economic and legal infrastructure of a nation's business. Within a country, sources of finance, relative importance of shareholders and creditors, the role of government, and taxation all influence accounting standards. Financial statements of companies from different countries, therefore, have major variations.

A researcher trying to compare three companies—Amstrad, IBM, and DEC—questions why Amstrad's performance based on "net income" varies greatly from its American counterparts.

This apparently straightforward question brings up a host of problems. What is net income? How is it measured? Is net income reported for Amstrad in the U.S. the same as net income reported for the company in the U.K.? Which line of the British financial statement is the "right answer"?

Familiarity with accounting standards is essential for business research. We might not all need to know that the price-earnings ratio for a Japanese company understates stockholder earnings or that the French value costs at replacement value. However, we should all be aware of potential differences in standards, practices, filing, and language in our own research or when presenting data to a client.

U.S. accounting standards, for example, provide a uniform platform for company and industry analysis. The regulations that accompany accounting and auditing principles and procedures provide the basis for internal managerial decision-making, investor analysis, bank lending, and client-supplier relationships. In the U.S., accounting standards and U.S. Securities and Exchange Commission (SEC) disclosure requirements are the rules for preparing financial statements. Because companies follow the same set of accounting regulations, we can make reasonable assumptions about the comparable performance of Ford, General Motors, and Chrysler by analyzing their financial statements. But can we make the same assumptions about Daimler Benz, Volvo, Renault, Fiat, and Toyota?

Pressure from international investors and the European Union has increased the availability of company information worldwide and is slowly increasing the comparability of that information. Despite the movement for international harmonization of accounting standards, country differences in accounting standards, filing formats, and disclosure requirements directly affect the financial information presented in published and online sources.

There are also country differences between accounting standards and accounting practices, and between accounting standards and public disclosure of financial information. However, the growth of cross-border trading increases the need for disclosure for three reasons:

- To maintain confidence in capital markets
- To protect investors
- To increase the supply of reliable information from a central source

MULTINATIONAL ISSUES

In order to be listed in the United States, Daimler Benz produced accounting under U.S. Generally Accepted Accounting Principles (GAAP). Its DM 168m profit under German accounting standards translated into a DM 949m loss under U.S. GAAP.

Which country's accounting rules take precedent for a company operating in more than one country or within the EU? In preparing reports, companies have a range of choices of action to accommodate international users. These choices include:

- Doing nothing
- Preparing convenience translations
- Preparing convenience statements
- Restating on a limited basis
- Preparing secondary statements
- Preparing statements according to world standards[2]

Convenience translations are statements translated from a filing language into another language, usually English. They retain all the original accounting principles and the original currency. It must be understood (as illustrated below) that "American English" accounting terms are different from the terms used in "British English."

U.S.	U.K.
Sales or revenues	Turnover
Income statement	Profit and loss account
Common stock	Ordinary shares
Preferred stock	Preference shares
Inventories	Stocks
Treasury stock	Own shares
Receivables	Debtors
Reserve for doubtful accounts	Provision for bad debts
Included in equity	Taken to reserves
Leverage	Gearing
Par value	Nominal value
Stock dividend/ stock split	Bonus/script issue

Not all translations from another language are reliable. Many accounts translated into English are different from the original language and are basically marketing brochures. A statement issued for informational purposes in a second language in other than its home country does not have to obey any disclosure rules.

Convenience statements not only translate the language but convert the currency. However, they still maintain local standards. For example, a convenience statement from a Korean company for the U.S. investment market will be written in English and present financials in U.S. dollars, but maintain Korean accounting standards and definitions. It is difficult to identify a convenience statement.

Restatements modify net income and balance sheet figures to meet another country's requirements. The language may be translated, but the figures are in the original currency. A company needs two sets of accounting records to issue restatements. Disclosure of restated financials appears in footnotes.

Secondary statements completely restate the annual accounts for the foreign reader. The Japanese have adopted this approach. All non-U.S. companies traded on U.S. exchanges (20-F filings) must follow this format.

World standards reporting is a rare approach for industrial countries. A company adopts one set of statements to meet all user needs. Many countries newly adopting accounting standards are using this approach.

If you request an annual report directly from a company that is not traded on your country's exchanges or if you access an annual report off the World Wide Web, you will not be able to tell in advance what form of translation has been used.

ROLE OF THE EUROPEAN UNION (EU)

Much of the focus of this chapter is on the European Union (EU). It is within the EU that legislated harmonization is required. The EU has harmonized company filing requirements and accounting standards for its member countries through a series of directives, some of which are discussed in more detail in Chapter 3.

EU Directives and Harmonization Standards

EU member states have been required to incorporate these directives into their own legal frameworks. However, each state also has flexibility in exactly how the laws are enacted. No additional accounting standards will be drafted. An overview of the EU situation will give a sense of the complexity of the accounting issues researchers and investors are facing. Even where standardization has occurred, dates of implementation differ greatly, making time-series analysis for the same company risky. Three of the most important EU Company Law Directives are the Second, Fourth, and Seventh.

The *Second Directive* addresses public companies, including naming of companies and setting minimum capital requirements. It is discussed in detail in Chapter 3.

The *Fourth Directive* applies to public and private companies. It sets standard accounting formats, provides exemptions for small companies, and introduces accounting principles based on the U.K. Company Law principle of "true and fair value." It defines small, medium, and large companies and specifies what *types* of information each must disclose. The Fourth Directive sets standards for types of information, but not for the actual data items. Article 2 of this directive states:

> 1. The annual accounts shall comprise the balance sheet, the profit and loss account and the notes on the accounts. These documents shall constitute a composite whole.
>
> 2. They shall be drawn up clearly and in accordance with the provisions of this Directive.
>
> 3. The annual accounts shall give a true and fair view of the company's assets, financial position and profit or loss.

Despite the directive, country differences still exist. In the U.K., for example, small companies must be audited; in Germany they are exempt. Other differences arise because the meaning of "true and fair" is not defined.

The *Seventh Directive* concerns "Group Accounting" or consolidated statements. The U.S. has been preparing consolidated figures since the beginning of the 20th century. The U.K. and Netherlands, which have many holding companies, also require consolidated reporting. Other EU countries did not require consolidated statements prior to 1985.

All groups above "medium-sized" must prepare consolidated statements and must include domestic and foreign subsidiaries. However, the directive offers many options, including how to define subsidiaries and which to include. For example, three breweries used different accounting methods for calculating greater than 50% long-term investment (1994 annuals).

BBAG-Oesterreichische Brau Beteiligungs	*No* consolidation; cost basis (parent company only)
Guinness PLC	*All* subsidiaries consolidated
Holsten Brauerei	Consolidation for *significant* subsidiaries; others on cost basis

Chris Nobes, who writes and speaks extensively on the subject of EU accounting, calculates 51 yes/no options for the Seventh Directive alone, which leads to "2 zillion" possible ways to handle group accounting![3]

Table 2.A. shows the year when each EU country adopted the Fourth and Seventh Directives into national law. The dates of adoption vary by as much as a decade.

TABLE 2.A

National Adoption Dates for the Fourth and Seventh EU Directives

	Fourth	Seventh
Drafts Published	**1971, 1974**	**1976, 1978**
Adoption by EU Council	**1978**	**1983**
Adoption by Member Countries		
Belgium	1985	1990
Denmark	1981	1990
France	1983	1985
Germany	1985	1985
Greece	1987	1987
Ireland	1986	1992
Italy	1991	1991
Luxembourg	1984	1988
Netherlands	1983	1988 *
Portugal	1989	1991
Spain	1989	1989
U.K.	1981	1989 *

*Consolidated accounting predated implementation of Seventh Directive

Standardization Problems in the EU

Despite the EU directives and country company laws, there are still unresolved issues:[4]

- Availability of published accounting data
- Language problems
- Extent and type of audit
- Format or presentation of financial statements
- Frequency of reports
- Quantity of data disclosed
- Different currencies
- Biases in the accounting data
- User friendliness of annual reports
- Valuation of assets
- Measurement of profits
- Cultural differences

Publication and Audit

The Fourth Directive provides options for EU member states to exempt small and medium-sized companies from various reporting and auditing requirements. It also requires that the thresholds be revised every five years. Table 2.B shows the upward revision in thresholds.

TABLE 2.B					
SIZE CRITERIA FOR SMALL AND MEDIUM-SIZED COMPANIES					
ECUs (000)	1978	1984	1990	1994	1994 ($US000)
Small					
Balance Sheet Total	1,000	1,550	2,000	2,500	2,175
Net Turnover	2,000	3,200	4,000	5,000	4,350
Employees	50	50	50	50	
Medium-Sized					
Balance Sheet Total	4,000	6,200	8,000	10,000	8,700
Net Turnover	8,000	12,000	16,000	20,000	17,400
Employees	250	250	250	250	
Based on ECU exchange rate on March 21, 1994 ($1.15 per ECU)					

Individual countries handle the exemptions in different ways. There is universal audit in the U.K. for all companies filing with the national registration body, Companies House. In Germany, only large companies are audited. Because banks are major shareholders in Germany and Switzerland, there has been less pressure for public disclosure.

European annual reports are often filed and published many months after the year-end closing date. However, in the U.K., companies must file news releases with the Official Companies Register, an arm of Companies House. Data are then available in sources such as *Extel Cards* or in news databases well before they are available in the annual report.

Format or Presentation

The presentation format for accounts is based on national choice. There is no standard template. Frequency of filing, terminology used, and the quantity of data required also vary among countries, as does the physical layout of reports. French and German company reports are horizontal, while British reports are vertical. The order of presentation also varies. On a U.S. balance sheet, the most liquid assets, current assets, come first. In other countries, they may come last. See Appendix A, at the end of this chapter, for sample U.K. and French balance sheets.

Currency Translation in Accounting Practice

The EU has no directives on currency translation. The U.K., Ireland, and Netherlands have standards but no laws. France and Germany have neither standards nor laws. What exchange rate does a company use to record its international transactions? These transactions can include purchases, sales or subsidiary activities. What do multinational corporations do in practice? There are different approaches for different financial items:

1. Items on a company's own accounts are frozen on the date of purchase. For example, a French company buys a German computer system and records the cost of the asset in francs at date of purchase. This is called the "temporal" exchange rate.
2. Long-term liabilities use fiscal year-end date. A U.K. company with a December 31 year-end date should have translated U.S. debt at 1.87 dollars per pound sterling in 1991 and 1.52 dollars per pound sterling in 1992.
3. Losses usually are translated immediately into profit and loss accounts, as in Item 1 (above), but gains may be handled differently.
4. Balance sheets for the foreign subsidiaries of multinationals use the fiscal year-end rate, as in Item 2, where the pound-to-dollar rate for 31 December 1992 was 1.52. Profit and loss statements for the foreign subsidiaries may apply average or median rates for the fiscal year. For 1992 the exchange rate using the average method was 1.72, the rate using the median was 1.92.

Several questions arise. For example, when using a temporal exchange rate, debits and credits do not balance. The difference is placed in the reserve account. In the next section we will look at valuing fixed assets, but from a currency perspective the question becomes: What exchange rate do you use for fixed assets? U.S. multinationals use the balance sheet date for the balance sheet exchange and a yearly average for the income statement. This is also recommended international practice.

Valuation of Assets and Measurement of Profit

Researchers interested in analyzing European balance sheets and income statements may be unaware of the different methods of valuation of assets and measurement of profits. As Table 2.C shows, fixed asset valuation (property, plant, and equipment) varies from strict historical costs, to revaluation, to current costs.

TABLE 2.C

How European Countries Value Assets

Germany	Historical costs; not revalued; often based on post World War II figures (1946-48; e.g. Daimler Benz)
France	1976 prices
Italy	1983 prices
Spain	1984 prices
Greece	Frequent revisions
U.K., Ireland	Company choice
Netherlands	Some company choice based on replacement costs

The conservative German approach, using historical costs set at 1964 prices, results from the banking sector's use of the lowest figures. Conservatism also affects the measurement of profit. In France, Germany, Belgium, and Italy, companies must set aside about 1% of annual profit in a statutory reserve fund. There are also hidden reserves. For example, most German companies do not account for "goodwill." Knowledgeable analysts will inflate German profit figures when making comparisons.[5]

Other EU Accounting Issues

Segment data for both line of business and geographic segments are generally accepted accounting practice in the U.S. Segment data are still not widely reported outside the U.S. The EU requires that sales be split by sector and market. The 1985 U.K. Companies Act assesses pretax profit by sector, and U.K. accounting practice adds turnover and capital employed as other data items that are reported by segment.

Goodwill is another account item handled in a variety of ways. The valuation of goodwill, especially in mergers and acquisitions, affects the balance sheet, shareholders' equity, and income statement. Anyone interested in an in-depth analysis of goodwill, with examples of different accounting practices, should consult Brunovs and Kirsch, "Goodwill Accounting in Selected Countries and the Harmonization of International Accounting Standards."[6]

Unique European disclosure components, which do not appear on statements of companies from other regions, include a value added statement, employees, and environmental or social issues. Flow of funds and earnings, however, are sometimes excluded.

Inflation is another important accounting issue, although it does not affect the EU as much as other parts of the world. Accounting based on historical costs is obviously distorted in times of inflation. One approach to accounting for inflation is general price level or constant dollar accounting. In this method, assets and liabilities reflect the currency's purchasing power, and the balance sheet is reported in units. A second approach is the current value method, in which assets and liabilities are changed to current dollars. South America and Israel have used the former approach and it has been recommended for international practice.[7]

Financial Culture

The underlying financial culture in a country affects financial statements, accounting principles, and disclosure practices. Legal systems and tax law both have an impact on accounting and disclosure. All discussions of accounting standards describe the dichotomy between countries whose legal systems are based on common law and those whose systems are based on Roman law. Common law countries generally include the United Kingdom, members of the British Commonwealth, and the United States. Most of the European continent uses Roman law. Table 2.D categorizes a number of countries by their legal systems. This categorization will be referred to in discussing other regulatory issues throughout this book.

TABLE 2.D

Categorization of Countries by Type of Legal System

Common Law	Roman Law, Codified
United States	Germany
United Kingdom	France
Ireland	Italy
Canada	Spain
Australia	Netherlands
New Zealand	Japan (commercial)
	Switzerland

Source: Accounting: An International Perspective (Burr Ridge, IL: Business One Irwin, 1994).

Common Law

Common law is English in origin and is grounded in the concepts of the "reasonable man" and "true and fair view." The financial culture in common law countries has been shaped by company demands and a principle of "true and fair value." "True and fair value" has been incorporated into EU law. In theory, it means that firms go beyond the legal requirements in presenting their accounts. There has been a history in common law countries of widespread share ownership and separate financial and taxation accounting. Theory is unimportant, however. Enforcement is only through court action, after a complaint is filed. Accounting standards, which act as regulations, are prepared by professional bodies. There is a limited amount of government control.

Roman Law

Roman law systems are based on detailed, codified law, rather than common practice. Countries with legal systems based on Roman law, such as France or Spain, depend on extensive government involvement. Government-run committees prepare accounting regulations. Banks drive the financial culture in Germany and Switzerland. Banks, rather than individual investors, are the primary sources of corporate funding.

Other Systems

Two additional models are now in use: the Latin American model, which reflects accounting for inflation, and the mixed economy model, into which the new market economies of Central and Eastern Europe are placed. Two other models are under development, the Islamic model and the international standards model.

Reporting for Taxation

Reporting for taxation is a description of past performance necessary to compute tax obligations. It differs from financial reporting, which is both a description of present conditions and an aid to future decision-making. There are three models of tax regulations relative to financial disclosure:

- Uniformity of reporting, where tax rules and accounting regulations are the same
- Separation of reporting (the U.S. model), where reporting for taxation is separate from financial reporting
- Adjustment in reporting where one set of rules is modified to apply to taxation and financial disclosure

Table 2.E categorizes countries by those in which tax rules have little influence on accounting, as in the U.S., and those in which tax rules have a heavy influence on accounting, as in Germany.

The tax rules for the EU are well documented. Publications are available in depository libraries and in many online databases.

TABLE 2.E	
TAX RULES AND ACCOUNTING	
U.K. MODEL (Little direct influence of tax rules on accounting)	*CONTINENTAL MODEL* (Heavy influence of tax rules on accounting)
U.S.	Germany
U.K.	Japan
Ireland	Belgium
Canada	Italy
Australia	Spain
New Zealand	Portugal
Hong Kong	Switzerland
Singapore	Sweden

Source: Baring Securities Guide to International Financial Reporting (London: Basil Blackwell, 1991): 11.

ACCOUNTING PRACTICES IN SELECTED NON-EU COUNTRIES

Europe

Switzerland has not required full disclosure. Swiss accounting regulation is derived from Napoleonic Code and is designed to protect creditors. Switzerland is not a member of the EU and is not controlled by EU company directives. In addition, full disclosure is not required because Switzerland is a country in which there is more reliance on bank financing than on individual shareholder equity. However, disclosure requirements have changed as the result of a revision in Swiss company law in July 1992. Multinational corporations are preparing statements that conform to the International Accounting Standards, and some have adopted the EU's Fourth and Seventh Directives.

Switzerland's largest companies have significantly improved the standard of their financial reporting. Nevertheless, Switzerland's corporate leaders have yet to adopt some of the latest trends in international reporting practices, according to an annual survey of the country's accounting practices. The standard now is to use uniform principles for valuation, currency conversion, and the layout of the financial statements. The "true and fair" approach is now used by 90% of the companies surveyed. Only 41% percent disclosed goodwill in 1988 but almost all did in the most recent survey. More than 90% of the companies in the survey now publish their results in accordance with recognized international standards. They may use International Accounting Standards (IAS), European Union directives, or Switzerland's FER guidelines (from the Swiss association for accounting and reporting recommendations), which are based on IAS.[8]

Norwegian companies comply with a 1976 Companies Act and a 1977 Accounting Act. All companies with control exercised by voting shares prepare consolidated accounts, based on historic costs. Companies file accounts with the Central Registrar of Companies, and the accounts are available for public inspection.

Japan

Japanese accounting standards are hybrid. They derive from medieval double-entry bookkeeping, borrow from German and French commercial codes of the late 19th century, and incorporate U.S. post–World War II securities legislation. Table 2.F categorizes the origins of Japanese accounting standards.

TABLE 2.F

ORIGINS OF JAPANESE ACCOUNTING STANDARDS

From the German Style	From the U.S. Style
Accounting controlled by government	Special rules for public companies
Uniform formats like Fourth Directive (EU)	Full consolidated accounts for public
Dominance of tax rules in depreciation	Balance sheet
Historical cost valuation (also U.S.)	Amortisation of goodwill
Form over substance	U.S. terminology
Requirement for legal reserve	Disclosure of earnings per share

There are three forms of government influence on accounting practice in Japan: the Commercial Code, the Securities and Exchange Law, and the tax law.

1. The Commercial Code, under the Ministry of Justice, applies to the country's one million joint stock companies, the *kabushiki kaisha* (KK). While these companies must file statements to the ministry, the statements are generally not available to the public.

2. The Securities and Exchange Law (SEL), from the Ministry of Finance, applies to the less than 2,000 companies that issue securities to the public and whose securities are valued at 500 million yen or more, or who have total liabilities equal to or greater than 20 billion yen. The SEL is based on U.S. practice. Independent audit, public filings, and consolidated accounts are all required. These filings are available to the public. The Commercial Code favors protection of creditors over shareholders while the SEL favors the protection of the investor. Because the largest companies are under the jurisdiction of the SEL, it is powerful in shaping accounting practice in Japan.

3. Tax law is another government influence on accounting practice, especially in the area of depreciation. Japanese companies, unlike U.S. companies, do not prepare separate filings.

The BADC, Business Accounting Deliberations Council, is another factor in Japanese accounting regulation. The BADC prepares the *Financial Accounting Standards for Business Enterprises*, comparable to U.S. GAAP. The BADC advises the Ministry of Finance and has sole responsibility for establishing accounting and financial reporting standards.

Japanese companies trading in the U.S. follow U.S. SEC guidelines; other English-language accounts may be convenience translations. Many companies do produce reports in "American English," in dollars as well as yen, and adjust for either GAAP or IAS. However, convenience translations are not always accurate translations of statutory accounts.[9]

Table 2.G lists the financial items that Japanese companies are required to file.

TABLE 2.G

REQUIRED JAPANESE FILINGS

Commercial Code Parent: Kabushiki Kaisha	Securities and Exchange Law Parent: Stock Exchange Company
Balance Sheet	Balance Sheet
Income Statement	Income Statement Including Cost of Goods Manufactured
Business Report	
Proposal for Appropriation of Retained Earnings	Statement of Appropriation of Retained Earnings
Supporting Schedules	Supporting Schedules
Consolidated Accounts	

Source: Frederick D. S. Choi, *Handbook of International Accounting*: 5.12–5.13.

The BADC has prescribed a set of standards for foreign currency translation, short term transactions, long term transactions, and foreign branches and foreign subsidiaries. There is no reporting required for either business or geographic segments.[10] *TRANSACC*, described later in this chapter, contains detailed information on Japanese accounting practices.

Australia and New Zealand

Australia and New Zealand are part of the common law accounting model. These two countries have adopted a policy of consultation over accounting standards and conceptual framework.

Australian companies follow the rules introduced in 1991 by a revised Corporations Law and the ongoing standards set by the Australian Accounting Standards Board. The Corporations Law now requires consolidated accounting and compliance of financial accounts with accounting standards in order that balance sheets have some "connection with reality" and with "true and fair value." The new law proved to be so difficult to comprehend that a "plain English" consultant was hired in 1994 to work with the Corporations Law Simplification Task Force.[11]

The Australian Accounting Standards Board issued the "Accounting for the Revaluation of Noncurrent Assets," which revised the method for revaluing noncurrent assets to reflect their recoverable amount.

The effect of all these ongoing changes and the inconsistent manner of their adoption is that comparison with past statements or with other Australian companies is, as the *Australian Financial Review* says, "not straightforward."[12]

January 1, 1993, marked the date of major revisions to New Zealand's financial reporting and accounting standards based on the Company's Bill, first introduced in 1990. The Accounting Standards Review Board (ASRB) was established. New standards, applying to private and public sector entities, have been drafted under a new name: Financial Reporting Standards. In addition, the Accountants' Society has issued exposure drafts dealing with differential reporting for small entities (companies with under 1.5 million in sales and less than 10 employees). Despite the efforts of the ASRB, it has been noted that New Zealand company accounts "leave much to be desired."[13]

NAFTA

NAFTA, the North American Free Trade Agreement, does not have mechanisms to issue or regulate accounting standards. However, efforts are underway to increase the comparability of standards among NAFTA

members to help researchers and investors evaluate company performance. Three organizations are involved: the Canadian Institute of Chartered Accountants (CICA), the most important professional accounting body in Canada; the Mexican Institute of Public Accountants (MIPA), the only Mexican organization issuing accounting statements; and the U.S. Financial Accounting Standards Board (FASB).

Canadian GAAP is comparable to U.S. GAAP but not as extensive. Even with comparability, one Canadian corporation reported an earnings growth of 26% under Canadian GAAP and a decline of 97% using U.S. GAAP. The CICA's Accounting Standards Board (ACSB) publishes the *CICA Handbook*, which contains the conceptual framework, auditing standards, and Canadian GAAP.

Mexico operates under legal and taxation systems that differ from the U.S. and Canada. The country suffers from high inflation, which necessitates different accounting principles. The Accounting Principles Commission of MIPA issues the accounting statements that constitute Mexican GAAP. Most large companies adhere to these statements, and the Mexican National Securities Commission (CNV) requires quoted companies to comply.

Despite the efforts toward harmonization, researchers believe that movement will be slow, especially with Mexico.[14] Table 2.H shows basic disclosure requirements in NAFTA member countries.

TABLE 2.H

BASIC FINANCIAL STATEMENT DISCLOSURES IN NAFTA MEMBER COUNTRIES

	Canada	Mexico	U.S.
Statement of Income	X	X	X
Statement of Financial Condition	X	X	X
Statement of Cash Flows			X
Statement of Changes in Financial Position	X	X	
Statement of Changes in Stockholders' Equity	X	X	X
Notes to Financial Statements	X	X	X
Unaudited Interim Financial Statements (for public companies only)	X	X	X
Inflation-Adjusted Statements		X	
Cost Basis of Financial Statements	Historical Cost	Historical and Current Cost	Historical Cost

Source: Fitzsimons, Levine, and Siegel, *CPA Journal*, May 1995: 42.

EMERGING MARKETS

If there are accounting snares within the well-legislated, well-regulated industrialized countries, there are landmines in the financial accounts from emerging nations. The accounting problems common to new markets include:

- Lax accounting
- Poor liquidity
- Slow and difficult settlement
- Share price manipulation
- Insider dealing
- Scarcity of accurate and timely information[15]

Many emerging nations have not yet developed internal standards or Western accounting and filing systems. One exception is Chile, which has been issuing a series of circulars on accounting and disclosure practices. Circulars No. 869, 922, and 931, for example, stipulate the information to be given to the public.[16] In general, insider trading is both legal and common in emerging markets and in some Southeast Asian markets. Therefore, there is less need or demand locally for reliable public information.

China

Accounting in China had been tax-driven. A "uniform accounting system," based on control through identification of funds, was introduced in 1949. Practices followed those in the Soviet Union. Due to the pressure from rapidly increasing foreign investment in China, the government has been creating an accounting structure integrating existing international standards with Chinese needs and practice. In July 1994, China implemented a conceptual framework document, "Accounting System of the PRC Concerning Foreign Funded Enterprises." The framework applied to accounting information and reporting for wholly foreign-owned entities, economic joint ventures, and cooperative joint ventures. It specified calendar year-end for all enterprises, use of historical cost, and the accurate and timely recording of transactions. In early 1996, the Ministry of Finance issued 32 new accounting standards. A committee composed of representatives from the Hong Kong Society of Accountants, the stock exchanges, and the large accounting firms operating in China reviewed the draft.

State-regulated CPA firms must audit Chinese firms. The large international auditing firms have established joint ventures with Chinese firms to meet the increased needs from a market economy.

For an in-depth discussion of Chinese accounting and the accounting profession in China, see *Perspectives on Accounting and Finance in China* (London: Routledge, 1995).

Eastern Europe

New financial markets and privatized companies in Eastern Europe and the former Soviet Union are trying to cope with Western accounting and filing rules. The reform process underway varies in the individual countries, depending on whether it is being driven by joint ventures, as in the former Soviet Union, or by privatization, as in Poland and Hungary.

In the past, the objective of accounting had been to provide information for the centrally planned economy. Accounting was "bookkeeping," based on detailed instructions from the appropriate ministry. Since the government controlled prices and exchange rates, there was no measurable profit or loss.

By the end of 1992, Russian companies had to prepare accounts based on procedures established by the Ministry of Finance. The latest version appears in the "Instructions on the Use of the Plan of Accounts for Financial and Business Accounting of Enterprises," effective as of January 1, 1992. With the exception of banks and "budget supported agencies," all enterprises using double-entry bookkeeping, including joint ventures and foreign-owned companies, must comply.[17]

The OECD (Organization for Economic Cooperation and Development) created a special information center in Moscow called the OECD Centre for Accounting Reform in the CIS, which opened in January 1996. The OECD's Centre for Co-operation for Economies in Transition (CCET) is the sponsoring body. Representatives of 12 CIS (Commonwealth of Independent States) countries plus Mongolia are involved. To date, the republics have not agreed on the adoption of International Accounting Standards.[18]

An outline of the new Hungarian law was published in the January 1, 1992, *Accountancy*. Hungary is incorporating EU principles and international standards to gain quick acceptance from the West. All economic organizations must prepare annual reports, ranging from consolidated statements to simplified balance sheets for small companies. Some of the accounting laws still use "bookkeeping" terminology and address the form of the books themselves. "Share companies" (public), large limited liability companies, and issuers of bonds must publish annual reports. The new laws went into effect January 1, 1994, for large companies; January 1, 1996, for medium companies; and will become effective January 1, 1998, for the majority of enterprises.

In Poland, a decree issued in January 1991 introduced accounting requirements for profit and loss statements and assets and liabilities. The Ministry of Finance published a sample, but not mandatory, accounts format. The Commercial Code requires that joint stock companies have an annual audit, but the audit had been concerned with adherence to tax regulations, not "true and fair" value. Poland has been phasing in new auditing procedures, meeting international accounting standards.[19]

INTERNATIONAL ACCOUNTING BODIES

In the U.S., a private body, the Financial Accounting Standards Board (FASB), issues accounting standards. A governmental body, the Securities and Exchange Commission (SEC), enforces the standards as they apply to companies required to file with it. Professional associations, such as the American Institute of Certified Public Accountants (AICPA), contribute to the formulation of standards. The U.S. differs from the EU in that only companies filing with the SEC have to be audited and publish reports.

There are many associations concerned with the harmonization of accounting and auditing standards and practices. In addition to the legal approach toward harmonization taken by the EU, the International Accounting Standards Committee (IASC), International Federation of Accountants (IFAC), the Organization for Economic Cooperation and Development (OECD), and the United Nations (UN) are all working both independently and cooperatively to harmonize accounting standards. Listed below are some major accounting organizations and the acronyms by which they are commonly known.

Acronym	Organization
IASC	International Accounting Standards Committee
IFAC	International Federation of Accountants
IOSCO	International Organization of Securities Commissions
ISAR	Intergovernmental Working Group of Experts on International Standards of Accounting and Reporting (UN)
FEE	Fédération des Experts Comptables Européens
IAA	Inter-American Accounting Association
CAPA	Conference of Asian and Pacific Accountants
FASB	Financial Accounting Standards Board
AICPA	American Institute of Certified Public Accountants
SEC	Securities and Exchange Commission (US)
SEL	Securities and Exchange Law (JA)
BADC	Business Accounting Deliberations Council (JA)

International Accounting Standards Committee

The International Accounting Standards Committee (IASC) was founded in 1973, as a result of an agreement by the accountancy bodies in the following countries: Australia, Mexico, Canada, Netherlands, France, the United Kingdom, Germany, the United States, and Japan.

In 1996, this London-based organization was supported by more than 110 professional accounting bodies from 82 countries. These member bodies represent over one million accountants. IASC functions like the FASB in the United States. As stated in its constitution, the objectives of the IASC are:

> (a) To formulate and publish in the public interest accounting standards to be observed in the presentation of financial statements and to promote their world-wide acceptance and observance.
> (b) To work generally for the improvement and harmonization of regulations, accounting standards and procedures relating to the presentation of financial statements.

Therefore, IASC provides a framework for *harmonized* standards that are *non*binding. It issues "world class" standards, which must be approved by three-quarters of the members. It also prepares exposure drafts that must be approved by a two-thirds majority of the IASC board before being distributed to members. The language of approved exposure drafts and standards is English. National members of the IASC are responsible for translating the documents into local languages.

Member bodies agree to support the standards and encourage their local organizations to incorporate them into accounting practice. Some countries such as Malaysia, which had not had standards of their own, have adopted IASC standards as national standards. In general, however, enforcement has been a problem. IASC's goal had been to complete its international standards by the end of 1993. In 1994, the IASC established a Consultative Group of users and preparers of financial statements, standard-setting bodies, and observers from intergovernmental organizations. The International Chamber of Commerce, International Bar Association, the World Bank, and Transnational Corporations and Management Division (UN—observer) were members of the 1995 Consultative Group.

The titles of standards in force as of March 1996 are listed in Table 2.I.

TABLE 2.1

IASC STANDARDS IN EFFECT MARCH 1996

IAS	1	Disclosure of accounting policies
IAS	2	Valuation and presentation of inventories in the context of the historical cost system
IAS	3	(Superseded by IAS 27)
IAS	4	Depreciation accounting
IAS	5	Information to be disclosed in financial statements
IAS	7	Statement of changes in financial position (cash flow)
IAS	8	Unusual and prior period items and changes in accounting policies
IAS	9	Accounting for research and development activities
IAS	10	Contingencies and events occurring after the balance sheet date
IAS	11	Accounting for construction contracts
IAS	12	Accounting for taxes on income
IAS	13	Presentation of current assets and current liabilities
IAS	14	Reporting financial information by segment
IAS	15	Information reflecting the effects of changing prices
IAS	16	Accounting for property, plant, and equipment
IAS	17	Accounting for leases
IAS	18	Revenue recognition
IAS	19	Accounting for retirement benefits in the financial statement of employers
IAS	20	Accounting for government grants and disclosure of government assistance
IAS	21	Accounting for the effects of changes in foreign exchange rates
IAS	22	Accounting for business combinations, includes treatment of positive and negative goodwill and valuing acquisitions
IAS	23	Capitalization of borrowing costs
IAS	24	Related party disclosure
IAS	25	Accounting for investments
IAS	26	Accounting and reporting of retirement benefit plans
IAS	27	Consolidated financial statements and accounting for subsidiaries (superseded IAS 3)
IAS	28	Accounting for investments in associates
IAS	29	Financial reporting in hyperinflationary economies
IAS	30	Disclosure in the financial statements of banks and similar financial institutions
IAS	31	Financial reporting interests in joint ventures
IAS	32	Accounting for disclosure and presentation of financial instruments

The full text of the IASC standards and exposure drafts are published annually in the IASC's *International Accounting Standards: The Full Texts of All International Accounting Standards Extant at 1 January 19— and Current Exposure Drafts*.

Many of these standards were revised or reformatted, effective January 1, 1995. The annual publication includes a "Table of Concordance" from the previous standard to the reformatted one.

The newest standard, IAS 32, addressing financial instruments, was issued in June of 1995 and became operative in January of 1996. It contains the less controversial parts of Exposure Drafts 40 and 48. While IAS 32 is designed to reduce investor risk through improved disclosure, incorporating it into accounts will affect the balance sheet presentation.[20]

Effect of International Standards on Local Practice

The IASC standards, if widely adopted internationally, will present problems for U.S. multinationals. IASC Exposure Draft 32, *Comparability of Financial Statements*, proposed amendments to many standards and would affect the way U.S. companies handle their accounts. Some of these changes were adopted in the reformatted and restated standards.

There are major areas of concern for U.S. firms in three standards. For all three standards listed below, the IASC practice differs from U.S. practice.

- IAS 22 addresses business combinations and the amortization of goodwill as part of mergers and acquisitions.
- IAS 2 addresses "inventory accounting" and disallows the use of LIFO (last in, first out), widely applied in the U.S.
- IAS 9 requires a method of accounting for research and development that is different from U.S. practice.

The new standards will also affect the German practice of hidden reserves and the U.K.'s method of handling goodwill.

We have noted that international companies trading in the U.S. must modify their accounts to meet U.S. standards and that other multinationals may prepare convenience reports to meet U.S. practices. Now

U.S. companies will have to prepare reports to meet international standards when reporting to European or other international shareholders.

Other Accounting Bodies

The International Federation of Accountants (IFAC) was created in 1977 to serve as the professional organization for accountants from IASC bodies. The IFAC is similar to the American Institute of Certified Public Accountants (AICPA). All members of the IFAC are members of the IASC. According to its constitution, the IFAC's broad objective is "the development and enhancement of a coordinated worldwide accountancy profession with harmonized standards."

The IFAC currently sponsors the World Congress of Accountants, which has met every five years since 1962. The IFAC itself was formed after the 11th Congress, as the result of an agreement signed by 63 accountancy bodies representing 49 countries.

The OECD Working Group on Accounting Standards was set up by the Committee on International Investment and Multinational Enterprises in 1979. Its goal is to promote harmonization of accounting practices in OECD countries. It also cooperates with the other multinational accounting bodies, such as the IASC and the Fédération des Experts Comptables Européens. OECD guidelines, which may be more strict than national rules, are not legally enforceable and are not intended to supersede national requirements. Multinational enterprises from OECD countries are encouraged to voluntarily supply any additional information. The guidelines have several objectives:

- To address all categories of companies with "complex structure"
- To focus on *information* in consolidated financial statements
- To set objectives for information disclosure to meet the needs of all categories of users of financial statements[21]

The Fédération des Experts Comptables Européens (FEE) is the coordinating organization for the accountancy profession in Europe. It was founded in 1987 by the merger of two other European accounting bodies. It consists of 34 national accounting bodies in 22 member states, which represent 350,000 members. It has taken on the role of spokesperson for the European accountancy profession in the IFAC.

The Intergovernmental Working Group of Experts on International Standards of Accounting and Reporting (ISAR) was founded by the United Nations in 1977 as part of the United Nations Centre on Transnational Corporations. It now operates through the United Nations Conference on Trade and Development (UNCTAD). Its central role is to develop guidelines for transnational corporations in the area of information disclosure and accounting practices. It participates in discussions on harmonization, writes technical papers, and publishes an annual review, which is discussed below. It does not mandate standards. It studies and makes recommendations on policies and practices to be followed by member standard-setting bodies. Membership in the ISAR is open to any country that is a member of UNCTAD. Membership is on a rotating basis. The United States and Canada are not members.

The International Organization of Securities Commissions (IOSCO), founded in the 1970s and based in Montreal, is another player. It focuses on the free flow of cross-border capital and the harmonization of securities markets. IOSCO has been working with emerging markets. It has been pressuring the IASC to reduce options allowable in its standards, and it will pressure quoted companies to comply with IASC standards. IAS 32 is in response to the IOSCO interaction. For updated information on IOSCO activities, contact their WWW site at http://iosco.org/ios-home.html.

Accountancy Profession

Most countries have accounting and auditing bodies. The number of accountants per country varies. Some differences in numbers are a result of the types of legal systems and sources of funds. Those countries whose accounting standards are based on common law tend to have more accountants than Roman law countries. According to the former *Morningstar Japan*, in Japan "the ratio of accountants to the population is about 1 to 12,000." In the U.S. the ratio is 1 to 800.[22]

The pressure to harmonize international accounting standards has affected the accounting profession. One result of required filings of audited statements has been a need for more accountants worldwide. Another side effect is the issue of reciprocity of licensing.

> *Can a U.S. CPA practice in France?*
>
> *Can a U.K. CPA practice in France?*
>
> *What does a Hong Kong CPA have to do to be able to audit statements in China?*

In the U.S., each state sets its own standards for licensing CPAs. On the other hand, the EU, through EU Company Law's Eighth Directive and the *Directive on the Mutual Recognition of Professional Qualifications,* has transcontinental professional practice.[23] The FEE has proposed supplemental requirements to the EU, including a written or oral exam for candidates wishing to practice in other member states.

The Institute of Chartered Accountants of England and Wales has reciprocal agreements with other Commonwealth chartered accountants, including those in Australia, Canada, Northern Ireland, New Zealand, Scotland, and Hong Kong. The arrangements with Hong Kong will run out in 2001. Now CPAs from Hong Kong are taking the Chinese CPA exam, along with thousands of mainland Chinese, to meet the Chinese target of 200,000 CPAs by the year 2000.

A selected list of countries' reciprocity practices appears in Parveen Gupta's January 1992 article in the *Journal of Accountancy.*[24] He cites as his source various volumes in the Price Waterhouse Series, *Doing Business In ...* A more complete list is published in Jack R. Fay's *Accounting Certification, Educational, & Reciprocity Requirements: An International Guide* (Quorum Books, 1992).

In 1990, the U.K. Accounting Standards Committee (ASC), the British equivalent of the AICPA, was replaced by the Accounting Standards Board and given more power. The Accounting Standards Board issues fewer standards with less detail than did the ASC. The standards apply to all companies. The *Statements of Standard Accounting Practice* (SSAP) are the U.K. equivalent of the U.S. Financial Accounting Standards Board's *Statements of Financial Accounting Standards.* The U.K. Accounting Standards Board intends to use the IASC conceptual framework. Germany and France also have separate state-run auditing bodies whose members act as regulators. Appendix A in Fay's *Guide* has an extensive list of major accounting organizations. Addresses for the major auditing and accounting organizations are included in *International Accounting and Auditing Trends* and *European Accounting Guide*, both described below. Some addresses are also available at the Rutgers University WWW accounting site (http://www.rutgers.edu/Accounting), also described below.

Big Six Accounting Firms

What effect has globalization had on the accounting and auditing profession? Through 1997, the "Big Six"—Arthur Andersen & Co., Ernst & Young, KPMG Peat Marwick, Coopers & Lybrand, Deloitte Touche Tohmatsu, and Price Waterhouse—dominated the international scene.

In non-Western cultures, demand for accountants is increasing with growth in the capital markets and joint ventures. An example is Saudi Arabia, which has about 255 CPA offices, with 15 large firms. The large firms include the international Big Six, whose partners are primarily from the U.S. The Big Six firms account for 75% of the revenue generated by the accounting firms.

Accountancy reported in April 1992 that the "Big Six accountancy firms are establishing themselves in the Commonwealth of Independent States (CIS) at the speed that would impress McDonald's."[25] The first professional organization in Russia, the Moscow Audit Chamber, now called the Audit Council of the Russian Federation, is designed to promote auditing practices and improve training.

SOLUTIONS TO ACCOUNTING DIFFERENCES

Ratios

Ratio analysis is often recommended as a way to circumvent problems created by different languages, currencies, principles, and practices. Unfortunately, ratio analysis has its own set of problems. Ratios are computed on raw data. Accounting definitions vary widely, as do the perceptions of what constitutes a "good" or "bad" ratio. For example, in Japan, a high debt-assets ratio is considered good because it indicates the company is able to get money from a bank. Banks consider a low debt-assets ratio a sign that no one will lend to the company.

As a business researcher, it is important to be aware that you cannot compare the performance of companies from different countries against a uniform standard, even if you use ratio analysis. What is considered acceptable practice in Germany, based either on financial culture or accounting standards and practice, may not be acceptable in Japan or the United States. Sources of ratios are discussed in Chapter 5.

Footnotes to Financial Statements and Company Accounting Practice

As an aid to interpreting financial statements, researchers and analysts need the footnotes from companies' annual statements, as well as knowledge of the accounting standards followed. Access to the footnotes is important to researchers using convenience statements, in order to determine how the company has compiled its accounts. They are also important to researchers using commercial sources of financial information such as Worldscope, which restate data to fit into standardized output formats but do not standardize the data itself or its measurement. Access to the footnotes of financial statements is important for understanding how the data have been standardized. For examples of footnotes on CD-ROM products, see Chapter 5, Exhibit 5.4.

RESOURCES

In conducting research for the first edition of this book, we had to make extensive use of journal and news articles to find information about international and comparative accounting. We relied on four scholars whose research and writing on international accounting proved helpful for the non-accountant: Christopher Nobes, Vinod Bavishi, Gerhard G. Mueller, and Frederick D. S. Choi. Christopher Nobes, a British accounting professor, has written extensively on international accounting standards and practices. Vinod Bavishi began collecting international annual reports when he was a professor at the University of Connecticut and has since established the Center for International Financial Analysis & Research (CIFAR), which conducts extensive research into these accounting and financial issues. Gerhard G. Mueller and Frederick D. S. Choi also have written books and articles that are both informative and understandable. Some of their publications are listed below.

By the mid-1990s, various publishers had recognized the need for both country-level and comparative treatments of accounting and auditing. There are now many new books on the subject. However, some of the titles we featured in the first edition are no longer published.

Sources of Information about Accounting Practices

TRANSACC: Transnational Accounting, edited by Dieter Ordelheide and KPMG Peat Marwick (New York: Macmillan, Stockton, 1995; 2 vols. plus supplement)

TRANSACC is a major new work on international accounting, covering 14 industrial nations, the EU, and the IASC. The countries are:

- In North America: Canada, the United States
- In Europe: Austria, Belgium, Denmark, France, Germany, the Netherlands, Spain, Sweden, the U.K., Switzerland
- In the Asia-Pacific region: Australia, Japan

There are two standard chapters for each of the 16 regions, one on individual accounts and another on group accounts. Each chapter on individual accounts addresses history, forms of business organization, preparation of financial statements, balance sheet and accounting and loss formats, valuation and revaluation, special issues, notes, auditing, filing, and publication and sanctions. Each chapter on group accounts considers such topics as the consolidated group, uniformity of accounting, methods of consolidation, and taxation.

The book begins with a "Reference Matrix" for each set of accounts. The matrix for individual accounts specifies the individual principles of recognition and valuation rules and compares practices among countries, the EU, and the IASC. The second matrix encompasses the principles of consolidation. Each entry indicates whether the accounting method is R (required by law), A (may be used but is not compulsory or is not recommended by the standard-setter), F (forbidden or discouraged), and O (the method does not exist or is not relevant). It also points to the section of the country chapter that discusses the principle. Exhibit 2.1 is a brief extract from the Matrix for Individual Accounts, showing one accounting principle and a country from each of the three regions.

	Australia	Austria	Canada
Overriding Principle(s)	O(III.2)	O(III.2 +VI.I)	Fair Presentation (III.2)
RECOGNITION **Assets side** *Intangible assets*			
Goodwill acquired self-generated arising from application of equity method	A F R (V1.4.2.3)	A F O (V1.4.3)	R F R (V1.5.4)

BRIEF EXTRACT FROM *TRANSACC* REFERENCE MATRIX FOR INDIVIDUAL ACCOUNTS

EXHIBIT 2.1

Source: TRANSACC, Transnational Accounting, edited by Dieter Ordelheide and KPMG Peat Marwick (London & New York: Macmillan, Stockton, 1995): Supplement, 10-11.

The matrices are reprinted in the supplement, which also includes a glossary. The glossary has a definition of terms in British English, and the equivalents in seven other languages: Danish, Dutch, French, German, Japanese (in Japanese and transliterated), Spanish, and Swedish.

This is an expansive and expensive book. It is descriptive, not analytical. It cannot substitute for the equivalent of a local GAAP Guide, but organizations with a frequent need to compare accounting principles should consider purchasing this work. The cost is offset by the time it will save in looking for this information in other sources.

Fundamental Analysis Worldwide (John Wiley, 1996)

Subtitled *Investing and Managing Money in International Capital Markets, Fundamental Analysis Worldwide* is another new title that is targeted for the practitioner as well as for a researcher. The four-volume set plus diskette was published in 1996 and supplements are anticipated. Volume I is an overview of statement analysis and accounting issues. Volumes II–IV are arranged geographically with samples of representative companies, country by country:

Volume II: Canada and the United States
Volume III: Western Europe A–M
Volume IV: Western Europe N–Z (Netherlands, Norway, Portugal, Spain, Sweden, Switzerland, Turkey, U.K.)

Each country-specific chapter follows the same structure: Part 1 contains general information such as reporting requirements, accessibility of reports, reporting practices, accounting standards bodies. Parts 2–6 offer research analysis by sector, covering consumer goods, industrial products, and financial services, with sample reports. Appendixes include financial statement entries in the local language, with an English translation. Exhibit 2.2 is an extract from Appendix 10A, "Sample Financial Statements in Dutch and Their Translation into English: Industrial Company, *Nedloyd Groep."*

Geconsolideerde loss winst -en verliesrekening	Consolidated profit and account
Netto-omzet	Net turnover
Arbeidskosten	Salaries, wages, related expenses
Afschrijvingen	Depreciation
Boekwinst op verkochte materiële vaste activa	Profit on sale of tangible fixed assets
Overige bedrijfskosten	Other operating expenses
Totaal bedrijfslasten	**Operating Costs**

EXTRACT OF SAMPLE DUTCH FINANCIAL STATEMENT FROM *FUNDAMENTAL ANALYSIS WORLDWIDE*

EXHIBIT 2.2

Source: Fundamental Analysis Worldwide, Appendix 10A, Haksu Kim, 1996. Reprinted with permission from John Wiley & Sons, Inc.

International Accounting and Reporting Issues

(Geneva: United Nations Conference on Trade and Development)

International Accounting and Reporting Issues is a record of the annual accomplishments of the Intergovernmental Working Group of Experts on International Standards of Accounting and Reporting (ISAR). An issue reported in the 1994 edition deals with supporting the International Federation of Accountants' call for global accounting qualifications. The pro-posal addresses the development of global qualification standards for accountants and auditors, professional accreditation systems based on the global standards, and a multilingual world dictionary for accountancy.

The annual publication also contains developments in accounting and reporting in about 40 countries. Not all countries are covered in each issue. The coverage varies from a paragraph to a few columns. For example, the 1994 entry for China lists the legal requirements that were adopted during 1992 and 1993. The one-paragraph entry for Cyprus states that the Institute of Certified Public Accountants of Cyprus has adopted the IASC standards in their entirety. At the other end of the procedural spectrum, the 1991 entry for Myanmar states that not only are there no legal requirements or accounting standards but also "no professional body has been given the authority to set corporate accounting or reporting standards." Prior to the 1992 edition, the work was published by the United Nations Centre for Transnational Corporations.

The UN's Transnational Division has a working group that also reviews special topics. A 1990 survey of financial statements of transnational corporations measured the degree of compliance with international accounting standards. Breakdowns for compliance are given by accounting item, by country, and by industry sector. Of the countries surveyed, the United Kingdom and the United States were rated most compliant and Belgium and Switzerland the least compliant.

The 1994 edition has chapters on "Environmental Disclosures: International Surveys of Corporate Reporting Practices" and "Accounting for New Financial Instruments," in response to the IAS Exposure Draft 32, mentioned above.

International Accounting and Auditing Trends, 4th ed., 2 vols. (Princeton NJ: CIFAR, 1995)

In the U.S., the AICPA publishes the annual *Accounting Trends and Techniques,* which examines how publicly traded companies handle various accounting issues. CIFAR publishes *International Accounting and Auditing Trends,* which examines the accounting and disclosure practices of leading international companies. In addition, *International Accounting and Auditing Trends* lists regional and country accounting and auditing bodies, as well as the changes in accounting and auditing standards issued since the previous edition. The volumes, which may be purchased separately, contain primarily tabular data.

Volume 1, "International Accounting Trends," has information based on audits performed on 500 companies in 46 countries. The objective of Volume 1 is to provide an understanding of the differences in accounting standards, reporting practices, and financial disclosure among the world's leading companies. The 4th edition includes a methodology for restating financial statements to global accounting standards. See Appendix B, at the end of this chapter, for a chart of accounting standards in different countries.

How do companies in the food/beverage industry comply to international standards?

Is there an accounting standards board in Mexico?

Do Mexican companies file audited interim reports?

Volume 1 includes "Financial Reporting Practices," a study of 1,000 leading industrial companies from 41 countries, based on 1993 annual reports. Rather than presenting examples of how individual companies handle accounting practices, CIFAR has developed what it calls the *International Financial Reporting Index* (IFRI), which quantifies disclosure of 85 key items, divided into seven categories:

A. General Information
B. Income Statement
C. Balance Sheet
D. Flow of Funds Statements
E. Accounting Policies
F. Shareholders' Information
G. Other Items

Data are presented in tabular format for countries, industries, and companies, by country. Exhibit 2.3 shows average levels of compliance for industrial companies. Exhibit 2.4 extracts data from the "Food and Beverage Industry Table" to show the index for three beer companies. The numbers refer to the degree of conformity to international standards for each of the seven categories.

According to the CIFAR *Index*, the U.K. company Guinness has the highest rate of compliance to international accounting standards of the three beer companies in the comparison.

Volume 1 also contains summaries of accounting standards, reporting practices, and interim reports for the 46 countries. There are tables that present variation in stock and bond price reporting in specific newspapers and a bibliography of research articles recently published worldwide on accounting arranged by topic. Research articles published through 1995 are listed along with a table presenting the number of articles published per journal. According to CIFAR's research, *Accounting Horizons; Journal of Accounting, Auditing, and Finance;* and *Journal of Corporate Accounting & Finance* have the most articles.

Volume 2, "International Auditing Trends," studies the global audit marketplace, including audit fees and clients of major accounting firms. Also included are auditors' liabilities, with recent cases, a bibliography of auditing articles, and tables presenting average number of days elapsed between fiscal year-end date and date of auditors' report, by country, industry, and size of client.

Which are the leading international accounting firms worldwide based on the number and size of clients they audit? Which are the largest in South America?

Who audits Singapore Airlines? What fee did Singapore Airlines pay for the audit?

Information is arranged in tables by accounting firm, country, industry, and company. Information is presented for the Big Six, Middle Ten, and Small Twelve worldwide accounting firms for 1994 or 1995, surveying offices in over 150 countries. The firms are:

Big Six
Arthur Andersen & Co.
Coopers & Lybrand
Deloitte Touche Tohmatsu
Ernst & Young
Klynveld Peat Marwick Goerdeler
Price Waterhouse

Middle Ten
BDO Binder
Grant Thornton International
HLB International
Horwath International
Moore Stephens
Moores Rowland International
Nexia International
Pannell Kerr Foster
RSM International
Summit International Associates, Inc.

Small Twelve
Accounting Firms Associated
ACPA International
Associated Regional Accounting Firms
BKR International
Clark Kenneth Leventhal
DFK International
GMN International
Independent Accountants International
International Group of Accounting Firms
Jeffreys Henry International
Midsnell International
TGI International

COUNTRY AVERAGES OF INDUSTRIAL COMPANIES–TOTAL INDEX

Country	Number of Companies	Compliance Level, Current Study	Compliance Level, Previous Study
United Kingdom	81	85	79
Finland	15	83	74
Sweden	25	83	80
Ireland	10	81	74
Australia	27	80	71
New Zealand	10	80	71
Switzerland	15	80	70
Malaysia	15	79	74
Singapore	16	79	73
South Africa	20	79	72
Chile	7	78	65
France	49	78	74
United States	248	76	72
Canada	40	75	70
Denmark	15	75	66
Norway	15	75	76
Israel	5	74	64
Netherlands	20	74	69
Sri Lanka	10	74	65
Hong Kong	20	73	73
Pakistan	10	73	61
Spain	15	72	65
Zimbabwe	5	72	66
Japan	101	71	70
Mexico	7	71	65
Nigeria	10	70	64
Argentina	6	66	**
Belgium	9	68	**
Korea (South)	8	68	68
Germany	56	67	65
Italy	17	66	65
Thailand	5	66	60
Philippines	10	64	65
Austria	14	62	67
Greece	5	61	58
India	9	61	52
Colombia	6	58	60
Taiwan	5	58	65
Turkey	5	58	60
Brazil	25	56	64
Portugal	10	56	50

COMPLIANCE FROM CIFAR TABLE 7-2A

EXHIBIT 2.3

Source: *International Accounting and Auditing Trends*, 4th ed., vol. 1 (Princeton, NJ: CIFAR, 1995) Chapter 7, 364–65. Reprinted with the permission of the Center for International Financial Analysis and Research, Inc. (CIFAR).

INDUSTRY
Food and Beverages

TI*=Total

Company	A	B	C	D	E	F	G	TI*	CN
CIA Cervejaria Brahma SA	75	82	93	80	25	35	30	60	BRAZ
Guiness PLC	100	100	100	80	90	77	100	92	U.K.
Heineken N.V.	85	82	100	80	95	75	60	83	NE
Industry Average	**87**	**83**	**93**	**76**	**70**	**63**	**62**	**75**	

INTERNATIONAL FINANCIAL REPORTING INDEX FOR INDUSTRIAL COMPANIES, BY INDUSTRY

EXHIBIT 2.4

Source: *International Accounting and Auditing Trends*, 4th ed., vol. 1 (Princeton, NJ: CIFAR, 1995), Exhibit C: International Financial Reporting Index of Industrial Companies by Industry, 417–18. Reprinted with the permission of the Center for International Financial Analysis and Research, Inc. (CIFAR).

Global Register of Leading International Accounting Firms

In 1995, CIFAR published the first edition of *Global Register of Leading International Accounting Firms*, a listing of client, partner, and office data on the 28 firms studied for the second volume of *International Accounting and Auditing Trends*. It lists the worldwide practice offices of the 28 firms by city and country; the audit clients for over 50 selected countries with the fee in U.S. dollars; key partners, arranged alphabetically by country; and the geographic presence in terms of number of partners and offices. Presented below is a sample firm entry for Hanoi:

MP Lenard Tan	No of Ptnrs: 1
ERNST & YOUNG	*Int'l Firm:* EY
61, Trang Thi	P: 84(4)26 55 95
Hanoi	F: 84(4)26 55 96

If the *Register* continues to be published annually or biennially, many libraries might find it more useful than volume 2 of *International Accounting and Auditing Trends*.

The Handbook of International Accounting,
Frederick D. S. Choi, ed. (New York: John Wiley & Sons, 1991, with supplements)

Frederick Choi has published many books and articles on international accounting. The *Handbook* is a more academic approach to worldwide accounting issues than the other sources we have discussed. The first edition, published in 1991, discussed topics such as the world scene of accounting practices, international financial analysis, harmonization, technical issues, and reporting and disclosure. Chapters were written by individual authors who are academics or members of Big Six accounting firms.

Three chapters in the 1991 edition are especially useful to librarians and information specialists coping with international financial statements. One is "Worldwide Regulatory Disclosure Requirements," written by Shahrokh M. Saudagaran of Santa Clara University and Morton B. Solomon of KPMG Peat Marwick. It examines several issues involved with finance and disclosure, presents financial reporting from selected countries (including Japan), and lists "salient" disclosure requirements of major stock exchanges.

Two other key chapters are "1992 and Harmonization Efforts in the EC," written by Gerhard G. Mueller, and "International Accounting Standards and Organizations: Quo Vadis?" by Arthur R. Wyatt. They give a detailed examination of the IASC and the issue of harmonization and standardization. See Appendix C,

at the end of this chapter, for a chart on disclosure requirements.

Supplements updated the first edition. A second edition appeared in mid-1997, too late to be examined for this book.

European Accounting Guide, 2nd ed. (San Diego, CA: Harcourt Brace Jovanovich, 1995)

One of the standard accounting sources in the United States is the Miller GAAP Guide (*Guide to U.S. Generally Accepted Accounting Principles*). The *European Accounting Guide*, edited by David Alexander and Simon Archer, was first published in 1991 as a companion to Miller. As we have seen from our own discussion of European accounting standards, company law—rather than generally accepted accounting principles—determines accounting practice in most European countries. Although there are no generally accepted accounting principles for all of Europe, there are standards within each country and similar issues that need to be addressed.

The *European Accounting Guide* is arranged by country. The second edition covers the EC-12 member countries; other European countries excluding the former COMECON members: Austria, Finland, Iceland, Norway, Sweden, Switzerland, and Turkey; and Eastern Europe: Czech Republic, Hungary, Poland, and the former Soviet Union.

Each chapter has sections on background (which may include information about the accounting profession), form and content of published financial statements, accounting policies and practices, and expected future developments. There also are specimen financial statements. In the spirit of European accounting, the content of each standard chapter varies by country.

The chapters have been written by local experts and are moderately easy to understand. You do not need to be a CPA to read the book. The *European Accounting Guide* is useful for any library that is offering international financial information.

Exhibit 2.5 is a sample financial report from the *European Accounting Guide*, presented to illustrate Polish financial statements.

European Financial Reporting: A History (San Diego: Academic Press, 1995)

European Financial Reporting: A History is described as the first English language source that analyzes the historical development of accounting in different European countries. The countries covered are Austria, Belgium, Denmark, Finland, France, Germany, Italy, Netherlands, Norway, Spain, Sweden, Switzerland, and the U.K., with chapters on international and Western European accounting as well.

```
┌─────────────────────────────────────────────┐
│         Format of Polish Financial Statements │
│                  Balance Sheet                │
│                                               │
│  Aktywa                    Assets             │
│  A. Aktywa zmniejszajace   A. Assets decreasing equity │
│     kapitaly wlasné                           │
│     1. Nalezne wplaty na      1. Subscribed capital │
│        poczet kapitalu           unpaid       │
│  B. Majatek trwaly         B. Fixed assets    │
│     1. Rzeczowe i zrownane    1. Tangible assets │
│        z nimi skladnik                        │
└─────────────────────────────────────────────┘
```

SAMPLE REPORT FROM *EUROPEAN ACCOUNTING GUIDE*

EXHIBIT 2.5

Source: European Accounting Guide, 2nd ed. (1995): 1478. Reprinted with permission from Academic Press, Ltd., London.

Each chapter is written by a different author, which results in a nonuniform approach to the subject. Most chapters include an overview of the evolution of company law as a basis for financial reporting. Some also discuss the growth of accounting and auditing as a profession.

UK GAAP: Generally Accepted Accounting Practice in the United Kingdom, 4th ed. (by Mike Davies, Ron Paterson, and Allister Wilson; Macmillan, 1994) and *UK/US GAAP Comparison: A Comparison Between UK and US Accounting Principles,* 3rd ed. (by Vivian Pereira, Ron Paterson, and Allister Wilson; Ernst & Young, 1994)

Ernst & Young UK publishes two companion volumes on U.K. GAAP. The first is *UK GAAP: Generally Accepted Accounting Practice in the United Kingdom.* The chapters are arranged by Statement of Standard Accounting Practice (SSAP) issued by the U.K. Accounting Standards Board. Many examples from company reports are presented for each practice.

The second title is *UK/US GAAP Comparison: A Comparison Between UK and US Accounting Principles.* This book presents a detailed comparison of U.S. and U.K. standards. It takes specific accounting items and presents the U.S. standard and the U.K. standard on facing pages, for easy comparison. Exhibit 2.6 is a brief extract from the book.

Chapter 9: FOREIGN CURRENCY TRANSLATION UK GAAP
9.1 AUTHORITATIVE PRONOUNCEMENTS
- SSAP 20
- CA 85
- UITF 9

9.3.3 Exchange differences transferred to reserves
SSAP 20 does not specify the category of reserves to which exchange differences arising from the translation of the net investment in subsidiaries etc. should be taken. Common practice is to take such difference to retained profits (see section 36.2) but this is not universally done.

9.3.6 Goodwill on consolidation
SSAP 20.43,53 *SSAP 20 does not appear to regard purchased goodwill as a currency asset. In practice, amounts attributable to goodwill are not adjusted for changes in exchange rates that occur subsequent to the date of acquisition.*

US GAAP

9.1 AUTHORITATIVE PRONOUNCEMENTS
- FAS 52
- FIN 37
- EITF 92-4
COMMENT
The treatment of forward contracts specified in FAS 32 is addressed in Section 36.4

FAS 32.13   **9.3.3 Foreign currency translation reserve**
The translation adjustments resulting from translating the foreign enterprise's financial statements should be accumulated in a separate component of equity.

FAS 52.101   **9.3.6 Goodwill on consolidation**
Goodwill arising on the purchase of a foreign enterprise is a currency asset which should be translated at closing rates. Exchange difference arising upon retranslation are taken to the foreign currency translation reserve.

A BRIEF EXTRACT FROM *UK/US GAAP COMPARISON*

EXHIBIT 2.6

Source: UK/US GAAP Comparison, (UK: Ernst and Young, 1994) brief extract from 142–143; 148–149. Reprinted with permission.

Routledge

Routledge has taken the lead in publishing monographs concerned with accounting and auditing issues. Some have appeared in Routledge's series on International Accounting and Finance, such as *Cash Flow Accounting: International Uses and Abuses,* by G. Douglas Donleavy, 1994. Routledge, in conjunction with the Institute of Chartered Accountants of England and Wales, issued the series European Financial Standards during 1993–94. There is a volume for each of the EC-12 countries. Each volume is organized in the same manner. Part 1, "Business Environment," presents fiscal, legal, and financial background. Part 2, "Accounting, Auditing and Financial Reporting," describes current practice. Each volume includes appendixes with illustrative financial statements; differences in financial reporting among the country, the U.S., and the U.K.; and the manner in which the country has incorporated EU directives. Finally, there is a bilingual glossary and a bibliography.

Routledge has also issued works about accounting that are not part of either series. An example is *Accounting in Transition: The Implications of Political and Economic Reform in Central Europe,* by Neil Garrod and Stuart McLeay, 1996. Routledge Online, http://www.thomson.com/routledge/default.html, has a current catalog.

E. Elgar Publishing Company

E. Elgar Publishing Company's series, The Library of International Accounting, is the newest on this topic. Five volumes were announced in March 1996. Sample titles are *Country Studies in International Accounting: Americas and the Far East*, edited by Gary K. Meek, and *International Harmonization of Accounting,* edited by Christopher Nobes. All Elgar titles are listed on the company's WWW site, at www.e-elgar.co.uk.

Financial Times Professional Publishing

Financial Times Professional Publishing offers several handbooks aimed at practitioners and the monthly accounting journal, *World Accounting Report.*

World Accounting Report is an excellent source for the latest information on changing accounting practices. It costs over $500 in print and is accessible online full text on DataStar in *Financial Times Business Reports* (FTBR). It is also a part of several other databases on a variety of systems: in the IAC's *Newsletter Database* and *PROMT, Accounting and Tax Database*, and in NEXIS NEWS and WORLD libraries as the file WAR. The most complete version of the *World Accounting Report* is in WAR, which contains over 3,300 articles (searched March 1996). The descriptor field in WAR and FTBR includes a region or country, as well as subjects. Numeric codes were added in 1992. The example below is from FTBR.

> (TT) Trinidad-and-Tobago-Caribbean, *Company-law*(P92), (GOVT) Regulations.
>
> (TT) Trinidad-and-Tobago-Caribbean, Accountancy *(P8721),*(GOVT Regulations.

Lafferty Publications

Lafferty Publications, located in Dublin, Ireland, specializes in international accounting and banking markets with publications primarily for the practitioner. In addition to now publishing *The Accountant*, first published in the U.K. in 1874, Lafferty produces several accounting newsletters of its own. Titles include the *European Accountant*, "intelligence for accountants in public practice in the world's largest market," and *Corporate Accounting International*, "the international accounting, reporting, and auditing source," which appears 10 times a year. *International Accounting Bulletin*, "Business Intelligence for Accountants Worldwide" comes out semimonthly. The February 23, 1996, edition included an in-depth survey of South African accounting firms, based on FEE data.

Lafferty publications are available electronically in the *LAFF* database on DataStar, and as *LBI* in FT Profile. Selected articles from selected Lafferty publications appear in *Business and Industry Database*.

In 1992, Lafferty produced the *International Accounting Databank*. The study examined accounting in 17 European countries (the EU plus Norway and Switzerland), 5 countries in the Americas (NAFTA plus Argentina and Brazil), and 12 countries or regions in Asia, Africa, the Middle East, South Africa, Cyprus, and Israel. The study measured the accounting profession worldwide, ranking firms and markets.

Other Selected Accounting Publications for the Specialist

Many of the organizations mentioned previously in this chapter publish works for the specialist. Some of these are listed below, arranged by organization.

United Nations Conference on Trade and Development, Division on Transnational Corporations and Investment (DTCI, Geneva)

This Geneva-based organization is the current name for the former United Nations Centre for Transnational Corporations (UNCTC), which became the United Nations Transnational Corporations and Management

Division. This UN program moved from New York to Geneva in 1993. It has published a series of accounting studies, plus a variety of other titles, under all three authorships. Examples are presented below:

Accounting for East-West Joint Ventures (1992)

Accounting, Valuation and Privatization (New York: UNCTAD Programme on Transnationals, 1993)

Conclusions on Accounting and Reporting by Transnational Corporations, prepared by the Intergovernmental Working Group of Experts on International Standards of Accounting and Reporting (1994)

Joint Venture Accounting in the USSR: Direction for Change, 1990. (UNCTC advisory study, Series B, no. 7, 1990)

Organization for Economic Cooperation and Development (OECD)

The OECD, located in Paris and New York, published two series on accounting and auditing issued through the early 1990s under the authorship of the OECD Working Group on Accounting Standards. Today, discussions of accounting and auditing appear in *OECD Working Papers.* Examples are:

"Environmental Accounting for Decision-Making" (1995). A summary of an OECD seminar, Environmental Accounting for Decision-Making.

"Accelerating Corporate Investment in Cleaner Technologies Through Enhanced Managerial Accounting Systems." *OECD Working Papers* 2, no. 27 (1994).

"Accounting and Auditing Reform in the New Independent States, No. 1" *OECD Working Papers* 2, no. 14 (1994).

Fédération des Experts Comptables Européens (FEE)

FEE publishes a series of works in conjunction with other organizations, including its European Accounting Series, published by Routledge. It also maintains a database with survey data, *FEE European Survey of Published Accounts.* The survey compares company practices by country. The survey gives greater detail than the AICPA survey publication mentioned below. The 1991 survey concluded that there is more variation within countries complying with the EU directives than within those outside the EU. FEE will publish the next survey in 1997, using the 1995 accounts.

Another FEE publication examines all aspects of pensions and early retirement benefits and describes the accounting rules and practices for these benefits in each of the countries surveyed:

FEE Survey of Pensions and Other Retirement Benefits in EU and Non-EU Countries (Routledge, 1995).

The survey concludes that accounting rules and practices concerning pensions are far from harmonized in the EU.

American Institute of Certified Public Accountants (AICPA)

The AICPA issued a survey of its own in 1991, *Survey of International Accounting Practices,* prepared by the SEC, the AICPA, and the Big Six accounting firms. This summary compared U.S. accounting practices with other countries. It concluded that U.S. standards are more complex than those in the other countries. Of all the differences it noted, accounting for goodwill was singled out as one difference with significant impact on earnings.

European Accounting Association

The European Accounting Association in London publishes the quarterly journal *European Accounting,* a good source for up-to-date accounting information.

Institute of Chartered Accountants

The Institute of Chartered Accountants in London has published the quarterly journal *Accounting and Business Research* since 1970, as well as the longstanding accounting journal *Accountancy. Accountancy* started in 1889 under the title *Society of Incorporated Accountants and Auditors and Society of Incorporated Accountants.* The Institute of Chartered Accountants also publishes *Accounting Standards,* the annual full text compilation of all U.K. exposure drafts and accounting standards.

Publications of the Japanese Institute of Certified Public Accountants

The Japanese Institute of Certified Public Accountants, in Tokyo, has published a series of books in English.

- *Corporate Disclosure in Japan: Auditing*
- *Corporate Disclosure in Japan: Overview,* 3rd ed., 1991
- *Corporate Disclosure in Japan: Reporting*
- *Corporate Disclosure in Japan: Accounting*
- *CPA Professional in Japan*

USING INDEXES AND ONLINE DATABASES TO FIND INTERNATIONAL ACCOUNTING INFORMATION

Print Indexes

Accounting and Tax Index (University Microfilms, published quarterly)

Some of the indexes discussed in Chapter 1 have articles about international accounting. For more comprehensive lists of articles and books, use the *Accounting and Tax Index* and its predecessor, the *Accountants' Index. Accountants' Index*, a product of the AICPA, suffered from a lack of timeliness in publishing a print edition, a lack of access to the online file (exclusively on Orbit), and a lack of abstracts. In 1992, UMI/Data Courier took over the index from the AICPA, renamed it *Accounting and Tax Index*, and changed its indexing, its accessibility, and its timeliness.

The print version of *Accounting and Tax Index* continues to include books, journal articles, and reports. The Data Courier thesaurus, used for online databases such as *ABI/Inform*, has replaced the old AICPA Library of Congress–based subject headings. AICPA continues to supply citations for books, but all the indexing is now being done by Data Courier. More accounting and tax-specific subject headings have been added. In addition to the print version, an online version is available on DIALOG. The annual printed version appears about six months after the end of the year. When using *Accountants' Index* for retrospective research, you will find subject headings such as:

> ACCOUNTING—International
>
> ACCOUNTING—Principles and standards— Bulgaria

Accounting and Tax Index introduced more specific terms but has continued to use geographic subheadings such as:

> ACCOUNTING FIRMS—Brazil
>
> ACCOUNTING STANDARDS—Europe

International Accounting Articles Online

Accounting and Tax Database (DIALOG, File 485)

The *Accounting and Tax Database* provides comprehensive coverage to accounting information in journals, books, newspapers, and other business publications. Its international coverage is basically the same as *ABI/Inform*.

While the print index includes only books and journals, the *Accounting and Tax Database* is an amalgam of all accounting and tax information appearing in UMI's other online databases, including:

- *ABI/Inform*—(abstracts and some full text)
- *Accountants Index* (historical citations)
- *Banking Information Source* (former FINIS; full text from 1992)
- *Business Dateline* (full text)
- Dissertation Abstracts
- Newspaper Abstracts
- Periodical Abstracts

Any full text in the original database will also appear in DIALOG File 485. Examples of full text international newsletters are *Australian Tax Forum* and *European Accountant. Accounting and Tax Database* is updated a few weeks after *ABI/Inform* because of the time it takes to pull all the sources together. You should not need to use any other UMI database except DIALOG File 485 for accounting research. Most UMI files have a United States focus. Therefore, the number of articles about non-U.S. subjects in *Accounting and Tax Database* is not great. However, there is more material here than can be found in *ABI/Inform* alone or in other bibliographic sources.

To demonstrate the comparative strength of DIALOG databases in retrieving information on international accounting, we searched all UMI files, the *Textline* files, selected IAC files, and a couple of academic bibliographic files. Table 2.J shows the retrieval results from three searches. It shows the name of the file searched and its DIALOG file number. The first column shows the number of records retrieved with the search of the phrase "international accounting." The second column shows the number of records retrieved when we combined the "international accounting" set (column one) with the words "Russia or USSR or Soviet." We designed the search to emphasize recall rather than precision. Finally, we searched for the phrase "international accounting standard(s)."

The retrieval results indicate the relative strength of the *Accounting and Tax Database* and *Textline* in the area of international accounting. The results also demonstrate the weakness of *PROMT* in this subject. Results were encouraging in the newest file, *Business and Industry,* since it had the most articles from *European Accountancy.* The search also indicates the small amount of material currently available on the former Soviet Union. Finally, it points up the problems with trying to perform the same search across dissimilar databases. We could not use descriptors to perform comparable searches.

TABLE 2.J

INTERNATIONAL ACCOUNTING IN DIALOG DATABASES

	International ( ) Accounting	Russia or USSR or Soviet	International Accounting Standard?
UMI Files			
***Accounting and Tax Database* (485)** 1971-1996/Mar W1	**2,433**	**59**	**1,818**
ABI/INFORM(R)(15)1971-1996/Mar W2	1,116	73	714
Periodical Abstracts Plustext (484) 1986-1996/Mar W1	86	14	40
Business Dateline(R) (635) 1985-1996/Mar W2	377	16	11
Banking Information Source (268) 1981-1996/Mar W1	34	1	22
Textline Files			
1980-1989 (771)	732	12	439
1990-1994 (772)	2,118	87	1,311
1994-3/8/96	822	26	585
IAC Files			
PROMT(R) (16) 1972-1996/Mar 08	603	24	216
Trade & Industry Database (148) 1976-1996/Mar 08	1,657	73	533
Globalbase(TM) 1986-1996	47	2	27
Newletters (636) 1987-1996/Mar 08	814	36	390
Other DIALOG Files			
Business and Industry (9) Jul 1994-1996/Mar12*	117	7	29
Econ. Lit. Index (139) 1969-1996/Mar	114	4	11
PAIS INT. (49) 1976-1996/JAN	48	0	20

All searches were performed March 1996.

Exhibit 2.7 gives examples of records from two of the databases combined for DIALOG File 485.

Textline was a good source for news articles on the status of accounting practices in different countries. It is especially useful for Eastern Europe and the former Soviet Union and emerging markets. A sample article retrieved from *Textline* is "Russia: Finance Minister Simplifies Accounting Procedures" from the June 18, 1993, issue of the publication *Novecom.*

Although the international abstract file *Globalbase* includes fewer records than many of the other files, often has unique articles. An example is "Estonia: Banks Standardise Annual Reports," from the Estonian publication *Stnumileht.*

LEXIS-NEXIS Services

To find current international accounting information in LEXIS-NEXIS Services, use the international li-

braries, or MAGS or NON-US in the NEWS library. A 1990 version of the International Accounting Standards is included in the NAARS and ACCTNG Libraries. Unwary users will not realize that the standards have been reformatted or revised. We ran the search described above for the DIALOG databases in LEXIS-NEXIS Services and retrieved the following results, shown in Table 2.K. The following is an example of a record from the NON-US file.

BBC Summary of World Broadcasts *September 15, 1995, Friday*
SECTION: Part 1 Former USSR; FINANCE; EE/W0401/
WBLENGTH: 73 HEADLINE: TURKMENISTAN;
Turkmenistan to move to international accounting standards
SOURCE: Turkmen Press news agency in Russian, 1405 gmt 5 Sep 95

2.6A: Record from Accountants Index in File 485:
> 00550485
> ** FULL-TEXT AVAILABLE IN FORMATS 7 AND 9 **
> Book reviews: Accounting Education for the 21st Century: The Global Challenges
> Tanju, Murat N
> Issues in Accounting Education v10 n2 PP: 442-443 Fall 1995 DOC TYPE: Journal article LANGUAGE: English
> AVAILABILITY: Fulltext online. Photocopy available from Accounting & Tax
> Database 18572.00
> ABSTRACT: "Accounting Education for the 21st Century: The Global Challenges," by Jane O. Burns and Belverd E.
>> Needles Jr., is the collected papers of the 7th ...

2.6B: Record from Newspaper Abstracts in File 485:

> 00378015 DIALOG FILE 485 Accounting & Tax Database
> Polish Tax Police, Like Taxpayers, Can Be a Bit Evasive
> Newan, Barry
> Wall Street Journal PP: A, 1:4 Nov 6, 1992 ISSN: 0099-9660
> JRNL CODE: WSJ
> DOC TYPE: Newspaper article LANGUAGE: English
> AVAILABILITY:Dow Jones & Co,Inc, 200 Liberty Street, NY ABSTRACT: The methods of Poland's Tax Police, which
>> often skirt the edges...
> COMPANY NAMES:
> Tax Police-Poland
> GEOGRAPHIC NAMES: Poland
> DESCRIPTORS: Police; Law enforcement; Tax evasion; Organizational profiles

RECORDS FROM *ACCOUNTING AND TAX DATABASE*

EXHIBIT 2.7

Source: Reprinted with permission from University Microfilms International (UMI).

TABLE 2.K

INTERNATIONAL ACCOUNTING IN LEXIS-NEXIS SERVICES' DATABASES

	International Accounting	Russia or USSR or Soviet	International Accounting Standard(s)
NON-US Newspapers	1,850	79	993
MAGS	815	72	307
TXTLNE	3,705	12	2,360

Searched March 9, 1996.

Dow Jones News/Retrieval

The newswires on Dow Jones News/Retrieval contain predominately North American articles related to accounting firms. The majority of articles coded "Accounting" in Dow Jones' own text files (*Wall Street Journal, Dow Jones News,* and *Barrons*) are also predominately related to U.S. accounting practices and focus on U.S. accounting firms. For international accounting articles, choose "International Publications," which includes the *Asian Wall Street Journal* and the *Wall Street Journal Europe.* Different Dow Jones codes are necessary to retrieve all relevant information.

Codes for Accounting on Dow Jones News/Retrieval

News/Retrieval Category	*WIRES/ DJINS	DJNEWS	TEXT LIBRARY 18 and 19
Accounting	N/ACC	.I/ACC .N/ACC	ACC.NS. ACC.IN.

* Financial Times *and the Canadian wires used the* .I/ACC *code for accounting. There was no way to access accounting in Japanese or European wires.*

Repeating our previous searches in "International Publications" yielded the following.

international accounting	1,907
and (Russia or Soviet or USSR)	75
international accounting standards	1,055

Dow Jones offers the fewest options for finding international accounting articles of the databases described above.

Online Sources of EU Accounting Information

The databases that provide access to all EU legislation can be used to follow the EU directives and decisions involving company law, accounting standards, and professional qualifications.

Spearhead summarizes all current and prospective EU measures regarding the Single Market or other areas having implications for business. It is accessible on DataStar, FT Profile, and LEXIS-NEXIS. Spicers Centre for Europe Database (SPCE on DataStar) covers all issues discussed by the European Union Institutions. Celex (Computerized Documentation System on European Union Law) is the official database for every area of EU legislation and includes full text. It is available through the EU's EUROBASE. It is also CLXE on DataStar and CEL on FT Profile. Use all three of the files to track EU activities.

ACCOUNTING INFORMATION ON THE WORLD WIDE WEB

There is one premier accounting site on the WWW, maintained by Rutgers University, http://www.rutgers.edu/Accounting. This site is an international forum for accounting in education. The directory listings for both accounting firms and accounting professional organizations as of January 1997 are limited in overall number. There were only 35 non-firms, with 25 located in Canada or the U.K., and there were only 11 non-U.S. associations, most of these in Australia. However, you can use the site's search engine to locate the accounting organizations that do have WWW sites. You can also use the site to locate access to documents, which may either be on the WWW or available for sale. The site is linked to the international accounting network and to the Nordic Accounting Network.

CONCLUSION

An extreme statement of the problems surrounding company comparisons comes from a British expert on European Union accounting: "not only can you not compare companies across countries, you cannot even compare companies within countries"! Although this may be an overstatement designed to make a point, it emphasizes the effect of accounting standards on comparative company analysis.

Researchers performing competitive intelligence, financial analysis, and industry comparisons can use the resources described in this chapter to keep up on the changes in international accounting standards and the move toward harmonization through international standards.

NOTES

1. *Accounting Reform in Central and Eastern Europe*, Organisation for Economic Cooperation and Development, 1991: 11.

2. Gerhard G. Mueller, Helen Gernon, and Gary Meek, *Accounting—An International Perspective: A Supplement to Introductory Accounting Textbooks;* Burr Ridge, IL: Business One Irwin, 1994: 56.

3. Christopher Nobes, "EC Group Accounting: Two Zillion Ways to Do It," *Accountancy* (U.K.) 106 (December 1990): 84–85.

4. *The Baring Securities Guide to International Financial Reporting*, Christopher Nobes, ed.; Oxford: Basil Blackwell, 1991: 3.

5. *Baring Securities Guide:* 74

6. Rudolf Brunovs and Robert J. Kirsch, "Goodwill Accounting in Selected Countries and the Harmonization of International Accounting Standards," *Abacus* 27 (September 1991): 135–61.

7. International Accounting Standard 29.

8. "Truer and Fairer (Survey Finds Swiss Firms Improving Their Financial Reporting)," *European Accountant* no. 63 (February 1996): 8.

9. Christopher Nobes and Sadayoshi Masada, "Japanese Accounting: Interpreters Needed," *Accountancy* (U.K.) 106 (September 1990): 83.

10. *Baring Securities Guide*, Chapter 7, 1108. Frederick Choi, *Handbook of International Accounting;* New York: John Wiley & Sons, 1991: 5.12. Nobes and Masada, "Japan Accounts" 1990: 82–84.

11. Nick Tabakoff, "AASB Bows to Clearer Standards," *Australian Financial Review* (October 12, 1994); LEXIS-NEXIS Services, *Textline.*

12. "The Public Affairs of Private Companies," *Australian Financial Review*, (June 30, 1992): 25; DataStar, *Textline.*

13. "Opinion—Scrap the 'Ride Em Cowboy' Stuff—Corral New Zealand Accounting," *National Business Review*, March 24, 1995, LEXIS-NEXIS Services, *Textline.*

14. Adrian P. Fitzsimons, Marc H. Levine, and Joel G. Siegel, "Comparability of Accounting and Auditing in NAFTA Countries," *CPA Journal* (May 1995): 38–44.

15. Rupert Bruce, "Pitfalls Lurk in Emerging Market Craze," *International Herald Tribune* (January 25, 1992); LEXIS-NEXIS Services.

16. *International Accounting and Reporting Issues,* New York: United Nations Centre on Transnational Corporations, 1990: 36.

17. *World Accounting Report*, "Eastern Europe Update," October 1992; LEXIS-NEXIS Services.

18. "OECD Accounting Agreement," *East European Markets*, December 8, 1995: 6; in *Financial Times Business Reports Business File* on Dow Jones News/Retrieval.

19. "Accounting and Auditing in Poland," *PAP Polish Press Agency*, Business News from Poland (June 6, 1992); LEXIS-NEXIS Services.

20. David Mason, "Learn to Play Your Instruments," *Accountancy* 116 (December 1995): 68–70, 110.

21. OECD, *Accounting Reform*: 134.

22. *Morningstar Japan* (February 28, 1992).

23. Eighth Council Directive 84/253/EEC of 10 April 1984, based on Article 54(3)(g) of the Treaty *Official Journal* Reference L126 of 12 May 1984/.

24. Parveen Gupta, "International Reciprocity in Accounting," *Journal of Accountancy* 173 (January 1992): 46–54.

25. "Accountancy Firms Are Establishing Themselves in the Commonwealth of Independent States at a Rapid Rate," *Accountancy* (April 7, 1992).

APPENDIX A
Sample U.K. and French Balance Sheets

U.K. Company

Consolidated Balance Sheet at Annual Closing Date

	Note	Current Year £000	Current Year £000	Previous Year £000	Previous Year £000
Fixed assets					
Intangible assets	9		104		382
Tangible assets	10		41,940		44,428
Investments	11		27,126		44,574
			69,170		89,384
Current assets					
Stocks	12	188,415		325,155	
Debtors	13	110,692		132,302	
Cash at bank and in hand		30,475		44,681	
		329,582		502,138	
Creditors amounts falling due within one year	15	(81,152)		(276,792)	
Net current assets			248,430		225,346
Total assets less current liabilities			317,600		314,730
Creditors amounts falling due after more than one year	16		(6,500)		(3,920)
Net assets			311,100		310,810
Capital and reserves					
Called up share capital	17		28,211		28,419
Share premium account	18		13,950		13,806
Revaluation reserve	20		8,002		9,848
Other reserves	20		1,429	1,204	
Profit and loss account	20		259,508		257,533
Shareholders' funds			311,100		310,810

French Company

Current Year Balance Sheet (for the Year Ended December 31)

Assets [Actifs]	Gross value [Valeur brute]	Amortization Depreciation of Provisions	Net value [Valeur nette]	Notes
Intangible assets				
Start-up expenses	137	137	0	1
Patents, licences and trade marks	106,828	21,090	85,738	2
Goodwill	0	0	0	
Property plant and equipment				3
Land	84,581	141	84,440	
Buildings	324,868	59,151	265,717	
Technical facilities equipment and machinery	478,638	157,931	320,707	
Other tangible assets	245,269	81,594	163,675	
Construction process	43,919	0	43,919	
Allowances and progress payments	6,809	0	6,809	
Investments and long-term receivables				4
Subsidiaries and shareholdings	909,546	101,073	808,473	
Receivables from subsidiaries and affiliates	300,622	14,343	0 286,279	
Other securities	5,216	0	5,216	
Loans	35,592	1,000	34,592	
Other investments	8,270	9	8,261	
Total I	**2,550,295**	**436,469**	**2,113,826**	
Inventories and work in process				5
Raw materials and components	685,792	47,677	638,115	
Work in process	1,049,941	4,125	1,045,816	
Intermediate and finished goods	132,210	10,856	121,354	
Advances and progress payments and orders	122,952	9	122,943	6
Operating receivables				6
Accounts receivable and related accounts	3,516,869	42,017	3,474,852	
Other receivables	304,393	154	304,239	
Miscellaneous receivables marketable securities	157,381	6,981	150,400	
Other securities	1,401,220	0	1,401,220	
Cash	**136,991**	**0**	**136,991**	
Prepaid expenses	1,945	0	1,945	
Total II	**7,509,694**	**111,819**	**7,395,930**	
Expenses to be shared-out over several fiscal years	69	0	69	
Adjustment accounts	**71,216**	**0**	**71,216**	
Total assets	**10,131,274**	**548,288**	**9,582,986**	

French Company (continued)

Liabilities [Passif]	Before distribution	After distribution	Notes
Capital	1,000,000	1,000,000	
Merger premiums and paid-in surplus	23,435	23,435	
Legal reserve		14,003	
Long-term capital gain special reserve			
Retained earnings	(16)	1,056	
Net income for the year	280,075		
Capital Subsidiaries	0	0	
Regulated provisions	64,248	64,248	
Total I	**1,367,758**	**1,102,742**	7
Provisions for contingencies and expenses	1,707,509	1,707,509	8
Total II	**1,707,509**	**1,707,509**	
Financial debts			9
Borrowings and debts from financial institutions	408,600	408,600	
Miscellaneous financial borrowings and debts	304,722	304,722	
Advances and progress payments from customers	2,951,833	2,951,833	9
Operating liabilities			9
Trade payables & related accounts	1,477,403	1,477,403	
Taxes, pensions & social liabilit	759,754	759,754	
Opther operating liabilities paya	124,167	124,167	
Miscellaneous debts			9
Liabilites to fixed asset suppliers and related accounts	48,236	48,236	
Other debts	416,429	681,429	
Accrued expenses	2,200	2,200	
Total III	**6,493,130**	**6,758,130**	
Exchange adjustments	14,250	14,250	
Total liabilities	**9,582,647**	**9,582,647**	

Source: Company report presented in English on microfiche.

APPENDIX B
Synthesis of Accounting Standards in 48 Countries

INDUSTRIAL COMPANIES

Country	Revaluation of Fixed Assets Is	Consolidated Information Provided by	Inventory Costing Method Used by Majority	Accounting for Goodwill
US	not allowed	80-100%	mixed	C & A
Canada	allowed	80-100%	mixed	C & A
Mexico	allowed	80-100%	cost or equity	C & A
EUROPE				
Austria	allowed	minority	mixed	C & A
Belgium	allowed	40-80%	mixed	C & A
Denmark	allowed	80-100%	FIFO	C & R
Finland	allowed	80-100%	FIFO	C & A
France	allowed	80-100%	mixed	C & A
Germany	allowed	40-80%	mixed	C & A
Greece	allowed	ND	ND	ND
Ireland	allowed	80-100&	FIFO	Taken to reserves
Italy	allowed	40-80%	mixed	C & A
Luxembourg	allowed	80-100%	mixed	C & A
Netherlands	allowed	80-100%	FIFO	Taken to reserves
Norway	allowed	80-100%	FIFO	C & A
Portugal	allowed	minority	ND	ND
Spain	allowed	80-100%	Average cost	C & A
Sweden	allowed	80-100%	FIFO	Taken to reserves
Switzerland	allowed	40-80%	Mixed	Taken to reserves
Turkey		40-80%	Average cost	ND
UK	allowed	80–100%	FIFO	Taken to reserves
ASIA/PACIFIC				
Australia	allowed	80-100%	FIFO	C & A
Hong Kong	allowed	80-100%	Average cost	Taken to reserves
India	allowed	ND	FIFO	C & A
Japan	not allowed	40-80%	Mixed	C & A
Malaysia	allowed	80-100%	Mixed	C & A
New Zealand	allowed	80-100%	FIFO	C & A
Pakistan	not allowed	minority	Average cost	ND
Philippines	not allowed	40-80%	FIFO	ND
Singapore	allowed	80-100%	Average cost	Taken to reserves
South Korea	allowed	40-80%	Mixed	C & A
Sri Lanka	not allowed	80-100%	ND	ND
Taiwan	allowed	minority	Average Cost	C & A
Thailand	allowed	40-80%	FIFO	C & A
AFRICA/MIDDLE EAST				
Israel	allowed	80-100%	Average cost	C & A
Nigeria	allowed	40-80%	ND	ND
South Africa	not allowed	80-100%	FIFO	Expensed/taken to reserves
SOUTH AMERICA				
Argentina	allowed	minority	ND	ND
Brazil	allowed	80-100%	Average cost	C & A
Chile	allowed	80-100%	Mixed	C & A
Colombia	allowed	40-80%	FIFO	ND
Peru	allowed	minority	Mixed	ND
Uruguay	allowed	ND	ND	ND
Venezuela	allowed	40-80%	LIFO	ND

Goodwill: C & A - Capitalizes and Amortized; ND - Not Disclosed

INDUSTRIAL COMPANIES (continued)

Country	Discretionary Non-equity Reserves	Gains or Losses from Foreign Currency Translation	Depreciation Method	Excess Depreciation
US	NU	IS and/or SE	Straight line	not allowed
Canada	NU	SE	Straight line	not allowed
Mexico	SPR	IS and/or SE	Straight line	allowed
EUROPE				
Austria	GPR	ND	ND	allowed
Belgium	GPR	IS and/or SE	Straight line	allowed
Denmark	GPR	IS and/or SE	Straight line	allowed
Finland	GPR	IS	SL or accelerated	allowed
France	SPR	IS or SE	Straight line	allowed
Germany	GPR	IS or SE	SL or accelerated	allowed
Greece	SPR	IS	Straight line	ND
Ireland	SPR	IS and/or SE	Straight line	ND
Italy	GPR	SE	Straight line	not allowed
Luxembourg	SPR	SE	Straight line	not allowed
Netherlands	NU	IS and/or SE	Straight line	allowed
Norway	GPR	IS and/or SE	SL or accelerated	allowed
Portugal	SPR	IS and/or DEF	Straight line	ND
Spain	SPR	IS and/or SE	Straight line	not allowed
Sweden	GPR	IS and/or SE	Accelerated	allowed
Switzerland	GPR	SE	Straight line	not allowed
Turkey	GPR	IS	Straight line	ND
UK	SPR	IS and/or SE	Straight line	not allowed
ASIA/PACIFIC				
Australia	SPR	IS and/or SE	Straight line	not allowed
Hong Kong	SPR	IS and/or SE	Straight line	not allowed
India	SPR	ND	Straight line	allowed
Japan	GPR	IS and/or SE	Accelerated	not allowed
Malaysia	SPR	IS	Straight line	not allowed
New Zealand	SPR	IS and/or SE	Straight line	not allowed
Pakistan	NU	IS	Straight line	ND
Philippines	NU	IS and/or SE	Straight line	not allowed
Singapore	SPR	IS	Straight line	not allowed
South Korea	SPR	IS and/or SE	Accelerated	allowed
Sri Lanka	NU	IS	Straight line	not allowed
Taiwan	NU	IS and/or DEF	Straight line	not allowed
Thailand	NU	IS and/or SE	Straight line	ND
AFRICA/MIDDLE EAST				
Israel	NU	SE	Straight line	ND
Nigeria	GPR	IS	Straight line	ND
South Africa	SPR	IS	Straight line	allowed
SOUTH AMERICA				
Argentina	SPR	ND	Straight line	ND
Brazil	SPR	IS and/or SE	Straight line	allowed
Chile	SPR	IS	Straight line	ND
Colombia	GPR	IS	Straight line	ND
Peru	SPR	IS	Straight line	ND
Uruguay	SPR	IS	Straight line	ND
Venezuela	SPR	SPR	Straight line	ND

Deferred Taxes: GPR - General Purpose Reserves; SPR - Some Specific Reserves; NU - Not Generally Used.
Foreign Currency: IS - Income Statement; SE - Shareholders' Equity; DF - Deferred

Source: Global Company Handbook, 1992.

APPENDIX C
Disclosure Requirements of Major Stock Exchanges

Disclosure Requirement	Toronto	Tokyo	London	NYSE
1. General Information				
(c) Research & Development	No	Yes	Yes	Yes
(f) Corporate social responsiblity	No	Yes	No	Yes
(h) Extent of dependence on major customers	No	Yes	No	Yes
2. Manager and directors				
(a) Salaries of managers	Yes	No	Yes	Yes
(b) Salaries of directors	Yes	No	No	Yes
4. Financial Information				
(d) Interim reports	Q	S-A	S-A	Q
(g) Segment sales or earnings	Both	Sales	Sales	Both
5. Recent developments and prospects				
(c) Profit forecast	Yes	Yes	Yes	No
6. Other requirements for foreign companies				
(a) Differences between accounting principles in country of origin and national accounting principles when former is used	Disclose IAC	Disclose	Disclose IAC	Disclose and Reconcile

Source: Disclosure Differences on Major Exchanges: taken from Choi, 5-28, 5-29 by Ajay Adhikari.

CHAPTER 3
Company Information: Issues

TOPICS COVERED

- Characteristics of Company Information Sources
- Understanding International Company Information
- Identifying Companies
- EU Directives
- Other Country Requirements
- Size of Companies
- Special Cases
- Further Reading

Questions about companies are basic to business research. They can be the most straightforward business research questions, but answering them can often prove to be complex and involved. They range from finding an address to finding "everything" about a known company; from screening a set of companies to meet specific criteria, such as finding gas springs manufacturers in Europe, to ranking the largest food companies in the world. Since there are over 40 million companies for which there is information available, the number of possible company questions is immense.

This chapter provides a framework for our discussion of companies in future chapters. We describe the types of company sources and their applications, and we discuss issues for interpreting their contents.

CHARACTERISTICS OF COMPANY INFORMATION SOURCES

Company information sources fall into several categories, which can be usefully grouped as follows:

- Types of information provided about the companies
- Types of companies included
- Locations of the companies
- Information format or access method

The categories overlap and no clear line divides, for example, a basic directory from a more specialized source. As an aid to understanding the variety of company information sources, we give below examples of sources from each group. An additional checklist of specific data elements appears in Appendix D, at the end of this chapter.

Types of Information

Based on the type of information they provide, company information sources can be categorized as follows:

Basic Directory. Provides name, address, telecommunications numbers.

> *Applications*: To locate the address/phone number/fax of a known company; to find a list of companies in a given location.
> *Example*: *Duns Principal International Businesses.*

Product Directory. Provides a description of the business and its classification codes.

> *Applications*: To identify a company's specific product lines; to determine the companies within a given market segment.
> *Example*: Kompass publications in print and electronic format.

Financial Directory. Provides balance sheet and income statement data.

> *Applications*: To examine the financial performance of a company.
> *Example*: *Moody's International Manual.*
> *Applications:* To screen companies for a set of characteristics; e.g., companies with return on equity >15% and income >$US 500M.
> *Example*: *Worldscope Global* CD-ROM.

Director's Directory. Provides names of company officers.

> *Applications*: To get a list of a company's major officers or board members; to find out what position an individual holds.
> *Example*: *Directory of Directors.*

Rankings Directory. Provides listings of companies arranged by size.

> *Applications*: To see where a particular company ranks in its market; to identify the top companies in an industry or geographic location.
> *Example: Times 1000.*

Types of Companies

Directories use some of the following criteria to select companies for inclusion:

Legal Status. Companies listed on a stock exchange, incorporated, registered nationally.

> *Applications:* To determine if any French company has the name Pagell; To find the addresses of all corporations traded on the Paris Bourse.
> *Example*: *Telefirm* (FRCO) on DataStar.

Size. Large, medium, small, or micro companies.

> *Applications:* To locate companies with less than 100 employees; to identify medium-sized companies.
> *Example*: *Europe's Medium-Size Companies Directory.*

Special Features. Import/export companies, multinationals, members of associations.

> *Applications:* To find a list of potential trading partners.
> *Example*: *Danish Exporters.*

Location of Companies

Geographic location is a special type of criterion for including companies in a directory. Some large publishers, such as Dun & Bradstreet, Moody's, or Gale Research, issue directories covering countries worldwide. In addition, many countries have their own directories, which may be distributed by an international publisher, such as Kompass, or by the local chamber of commerce.

International. May include or exclude U.S. or North America.

> *Example*: *World Business Directory.*

Pan-continental. Includes companies on one or more continents.

> *Example*: *Major Companies of the Far East and Australasia.*

Regional. Includes selected countries within a region.

> *Example: MZM World Business Directory (ex-Socialist World Business Directory).*

National. Includes companies from one country.

> *Example*: *LITCOM '95–'96 Business Directory* for Lithuanian companies.

Format and Access Method

Data Formats

Data formats for directories include print, microform, magnetic disks and tapes, and CD-ROM. Directories in electronic format are accessed through commercial and local time-sharing systems, via the Internet, as well as through stand-alone systems. The trend has been toward increased accessibility to company information in a wide range of formats. Moody's International Manual, for example, is in print and on CD-ROM. FT Extel Research offers company financials on cards, in books, through commercial time-sharing, on CD-ROM, and on locally loaded magnetic disk. Some sources are more exclusive. For example, a Polish company directory, in English and Polish, is presently only available in the United States on one time-sharing database.

Print. All types of directories available.

Microforms. Financial filings from listed companies.

Commercial Time-Sharing. All type of directories available online, via modem or Internet connections.

CD-ROM. A large number of print and time-sharing files are available in CD-ROM versions. Sometimes the CD-ROM version will have more companies than the print version, but far fewer than the commercial time-sharing version.

Local Time-Sharing. Commercial time-sharing files sometimes make their databases available on magnetic tape for local loading.

World Wide Web Sites. Many Web sites refer to themselves as "directories," though at present the number of companies listed at many sites is limited. A growing number of commercial directories may be accessed on the WWW.

Access to Company Information

Most libraries have core collections of national directories. In the U.S., these include Standard & Poor's *Register of Corporations* and Dun & Bradstreet's (D&B's) *Million Dollar Directory. Moody's Manuals and Standard and Poor's Corporate Records* dominate the scene for financial information. D&B's *American Corporate Families* and *National Register's Corporate Affiliations* provide corporate family trees. *Thomas Register* identifies large and small manufacturers.

Business researchers develop tool kits of sources to handle basic reference queries about national companies. They know the limitations of disclosure and the

TABLE 3.A

COMPANY INFORMATION AVAILABILITY CONTINUUM

	WIDELY AVAILABLE In Print/Electronic	GENERALLY AVAILABLE In Print/Electronic	AVAILABLE Electronic	SPECIALIZED Electronic
COMPANY				
Ownership:	Public	Incorporated	Partnership	Single
Size:	Multinational	Large Medium	Small	Micro
Affiliation:	Parent	Subsidiary/Affiliate	Branch	One Location
For Listed Companies:				
Exchanges:	New York	London/FT1000 Nikkei Bourse	Unlisted	
COUNTRY	US EU	Europe/Japan Pacific (non-EU) Rim	Emerging Markets	LDCs
INDUSTRY				
Type:	Manufacturing	Consumer Products	Retail Wholesale Professional Services	
Level:	Industry Sector	Standard Code	Activity	Brand

Copyright 1991 Ruth A. Pagell

resulting public availability of information and have built their information expectations accordingly. For example, a knowledgeable U.S. researcher will not waste time looking for the current ratio of Godiva Chocolate or the current assets of Miller Beer.

Do the same rules of disclosure apply when we are seeking information about U.S., British, or Japanese companies? Is there a core group of publishers prominent on the international scene? The answer to the first question is maybe; the answer to the second is sometimes. Many of the factors that allow us to immediately determine the level of difficulty of questions about our national companies apply to all enterprises worldwide.

There is an information continuum from global parent companies listed on major exchanges to micro enterprises exempted from filing requirements. The level of overall business activity in a country also affects the amount of company information that is available. Obviously, more information is available about more companies in the EU than in most emerging markets.

As Table 3.A shows, we can form reasonable expectations about how much information is available on a given company based on its country of incorporation; its size (multinational, large, medium, or small); if it is listed or nonlisted; if it is a parent or subsidiary, affiliate or branch; and its major industry. We know that we will have an easier time finding in-depth information about Daimler-Benz than about Clear Car Autoservice in Duesseldorf.

We consider next some of the questions researchers may encounter interpreting international company information.

UNDERSTANDING INTERNATIONAL COMPANY INFORMATION

The information needed to answer a question about a company may be found in one of several sources. With some sources, it may be difficult to understand the information once we have found it. These problems of understanding range from the transliteration of a company name to interpreting foreign financial accounts.

Directory Features

There are several features of international company information that may be difficult to interpret. We outline these issues below. We will examine some of these features in more detail in Chapter 4, in relation to specific types of directories.

Company Coverage

The number of companies listed in a source is a fundamental, if obvious, part of our evaluation.

- How many companies are in the source? The more information given about a company in any source, the fewer the companies listed. For example, there will be many more companies in *Duns Principal International Businesses*, a basic directory, than in *Moody's International Manual*. ICC's full text *Brit-*

ish Company Annual Reports (online and on CD-ROM) has the fewest companies but the most information of these three sources.

- What are the criteria for inclusion? Companies may be included in a directory because they fit a certain size category, are in a particular industry group, operate in certain countries, or are willing to fill out a questionnaire to be listed. A key question here is whether the publisher solicits the company for inclusion, or vice versa?
- How is the information compiled? Does the publisher collect information by questionnaire or by phone? Does the publisher use other external sources such as registration records, phone books, or news reports? Is information verified? How long will a company listing remain in the source if the company does not respond to requests for verification?
- How frequently is the source updated? How frequently is a record updated? A printed directory might be published annually and an electronic database updated monthly, but neither of these facts necessarily indicates that each record is updated regularly. Individual records may go unchanged for longer than the publishing or updating cycle.

Product and Industry Classifications

Most sources include at least some basic description of a company's business.

- Is the classification system standard or is it generated by the producer?
- Is the classification numeric, text, or both? Is it in English?
- What is being categorized? The company's primary industry group? An establishment's product line?
- What criteria are used for assigning classifications? Does the company describe its business? Does the publisher assign a code based on sales, income, the description, or a "yellow pages" heading?

Financials

How to understand international financial statements and how to interpret them are discussed in many books and are covered more fully in Chapter 2. Briefly, here are some fundamental characteristics of financial sources to consider.

- Are the companies in a directory "listed" on a stock exchange, privately held, government owned, or of all types?
- What financial items are being reported? For how many years? In what monetary unit?

- What is the fiscal year-end date? The date of the reported financials?
- Has an exchange rate been used to convert local figures to a standard currency? If so, what rate and date were used?
- What are the accounting standards the company follows?
- Are the data "as reported" or "standardized"?

Language

The most appropriate sources may not be in your language. Often, the most detailed information for a company is in a source in the language of the home country. However, many national directories are published in English, even when it is not the language of the country.

- What is the language of the source? Is the source multilingual? Some print sources, such as those from the UN, OECD, or EU have multilingual introductions and data labels. Some computer-readable files can be searched in more than one language. For example, the CD-ROM *Diane* (published by Bureau van Dijk) may be searched either in French or English.
- Is language an obstacle if you are looking only for an address or a provider of a product?
- Are there any standard coded fields? For example, using a standard two-letter country code alleviates the problem of whether to look for "Deutschland" or for "Germany." Knowing that Hoppenstedt's German language publications use U.S. SIC codes may simplify the search for products.
- How are the meanings of key terms translated? It is sometime difficult even to distinguish between British and American financial English. American "stocks" are British "equities" and British "stock" are American "inventories."
- How are non-Roman alphabets handled? Are names translated? Transliterated? For example, the name of the president of a Japanese company is transliterated as Minoru Ohnishi in the Japanese database *Teikoku* but as Minoru Onishi in Hoover.

Quality

A source might list the types of companies you need, cover the countries that interest you, and include the appropriate data items. The publisher may even be well known. However, these facts in themselves do not mean that the information is of high quality.

- To judge the quality of the data, ask yourself a few basic questions: Do the results "make sense"? Is the source free of misspellings and typos? Are data elements dated? Are there references?[1]

Our classic example of results that did not make sense is a search for major food companies in Europe in 1990 that listed Yugoslavian companies as the largest because of discrepancies between the sales figure dates and the exchange rate dates.[2] Another example of poor quality was seen in a regional directory from a well-known publisher that listed companies only in a few industries, clustered in large office buildings.

Publisher Issues

Standard business publishers and databank providers, such Dun & Bradstreet, DIALOG, Dow Jones News/ Retrieval, or LEXIS-NEXIS Services, provide an extensive array of international company information. Non-U.S. publishers, such as Kompass, Graham & Whiteside, FT Extel, and the databanks DataStar or FT Profile often have unique company information. The variety of publishers and formats necessitates another set of decisions.

Multiple Formats, Multiple Systems

If a source is in print, on disc, online via Internet, through a Windows client, or on a WWW site, which format do you use? What is the best way to access these sources?

Moody's International is a standard print source with a "mirror image" on CD-ROM. Its news volume is also available online (through DIALOG). The British Jordan's U.K. company file is a book, an online database on DataStar, and a CD-ROM with enhanced financial analysis software (FAME). The *Teikoku Database* is on DIALOG and LEXIS-NEXIS and there are two versions on DataStar. It is also online on Nikkei, on disc on DIALOG, and as *Jade* from Bureau van Dijk.

Unfamiliar Sources/Systems

- Do you only use the systems you know best?

While many databases appear on multiple systems, some databases are unique to non-U.S. hosts. For example, DataStar specializes in European directories.

Documentation

- Does the printed documentation answer data-related questions?
- Whom do you call for customer service, and how much does that person know about database content?

The print source *D&B Europa* is well documented and will provide answers for many of the questions

relating to its use and interpretation. However, online Dun & Bradstreet files have little or no documentation. When you have a question about international data in the U.S., you may find that the U.S. customer service representative you call does not know the answers to your questions. For example, you may be retrieving German data from a financial database and your client asks for a definition of the data item. You call the database representative in New York, who phones or faxes your question to Ireland for the answer. Your client must wait for Ireland to call Germany and then get back to New York, and for New York to get back to you.

Cost

- What is the purchase price of the directory or CD-ROM compared with the cost of retrieving a company record online?

Because of the number of directories and their expense, it is important that you weigh carefully the benefits of owning a printed directory or its CD-ROM equivalent against accessing individual company records online as needed.

Print vs. Electronic Sources

Commercial online and on-disc company sources are well know for their speed and ability to screen for combinations of variables. Printed sources have their advantages as well. They are usually easier to use than online sources. A printed directory has documentation that tells us basic facts such as how the companies have been selected, how the information has been collected, and inconsistencies the publishers may have encountered. You can also go back to the last edition to see if the data has changed. When we search electronic company files, the documentation is usually sketchy or absent, and the file arrangement is hidden. The complications of searching online files make understanding the data that are presented in the files more difficult.

IDENTIFYING COMPANIES

Companies, like people, have identifying characteristics. We may be interested in a company's name, legal status, and size.

Company Names

Searching for company names may not be straightforward. Companies have legal names and "traded as" names, which are often more familiar. Different companies may have the same or similar names. It can be difficult to tell if they are part of the same corporate family. For example, Sears PLC, the retail chain in the United Kingdom, has no relationship to Sears and Roebuck, the retail chain in the U.S. DIALOG's Company Namefinder (File 416) has over 1,500 companies with Nestle in their name, and no entry appears more than 50 times. There are almost 300 Mitsubishis just in the Japanese *Teikoku* database. Alcatel is another company with hundreds of name variations. Exhibit 3.1 lists a few of the "Alcatels" in the DIALOG files. The location may indicate city, county, state, or country.

	Company	Location
1	ALCATEL	
2	ALCATEL	(AUSTRALIA)
3	ALCATEL	(AUSTRIA)
4	ALCATEL	(BELGIUM)
5	ALCATEL	(BRAZIL)
6	ALCATEL	(CABLE SYSTEMS GROUP)
7	ALCATEL	(CANADA)
8	ALCATEL	(CHILE) SA
9	ALCATEL	(CIE FINANCIERE)
10	ALCATEL	(COLOMBIA)
11	ALCATEL	(COMPAGNIE FINANCIERE)
12	ALCATEL	(F M E CORP) // FRIDEN
13	ALCATEL	(FRANCE)
14	ALCATEL	(FRANCE) // COMPAGNIE FINANCIERE
15	ALCATEL	(GERMANY)
16	ALCATEL	(INDIA)
17	ALCATEL	(ITALY)
18	ALCATEL	(NETHERLANDS)
19	ALCATEL	(NETHERLDS)
20	ALCATEL	(NETWORK TRANSMISSION SYS)
21	ALCATEL	(S A) // TELIC
22	ALCATEL	(SA) // LA TELEPHONIE LYONNAISE TL
23	ALCATEL	(SOCIETE ANONYME)
24	ALCATEL	(SOCIETE ANONYME) // MARS
25	ALCATEL	(SOCIETE ANONYME) // OPUS
26	ALCATEL	(SOCIETE ANONYME) // TELIC
27	ALCATEL	(SPAIN)
28	ALCATEL	(SWEDEN) // RONEO
29	ALCATEL	(THAILAND)
30	ALCATEL	(US)

PARTIAL LIST OF "ALCATEL" COMPANIES IN DIALOG FILES

EXHIBIT 3.1

Source: DIALOG Company Name Finder.

Textline, Reuter's international business news database, has a separate name finder database that is updated weekly. The file contains the names and codes of the almost 300,000 companies appearing in *Textline*. If an article is about an independent company or a subsidiary quoted separately on a stock exchange, the article is indexed with the company's name and a unique code. When the press reports that a company has been acquired by another company, or has changed its name, the *Textline* name finder records these facts with appropriate dates. The file reports names as they appear in the press. It does not attempt to be an exhaustive guide to corporate relationships. Exhibit 3.2 is an example of a search of the name Alcatel on DataStar's *Textline* name finder file (TXCO). Alcatel appeared in 45 records with 15 unique current codes. The same codes are available in the LEXIS-NEXIS "TXTHELP" file.

CO Name:***ALCATEL**-S-T-K-NORW.*
Code: STKNOR.
NT QU.SUBS. OF*ALCATEL*CABLE (FRA), *
ADDED 24/4/95
THIS IS A QUOTED SUBSIDIARY
CABLYN can be used instead of STKNOR
CGE can be used instead of STKNOR
FIRST CODE: STKNOR
SECOND CODE: CABLYN
THIRD CODE: CABLYN

ALCATEL SAMPLE RECORD

EXHIBIT 3.2

Source: Reuter *Textline* (TXCO) on DataStar, January 11, 1996. Reprinted with permission from Reuters.

Other Alcatel companies in TXCO include those listed below.

SEMI-CONDUCTOURS-ALCATEL-FRA
ALCATEL-ALSTHOM-FRA
ALCATEL-S-E-L-AG-GFR
ALCATEL-CABLE-SA-FRA
ALCATEL-TELECOMUNICACOES-BRAZ
ALCATEL-NV-NETH
CEGELEC-FRA
ALCATEL-C-I-T-MAROC-MOROC
ALCATEL-CAVI-ITALY
ALCATEL-CIT-POLSKA-POL

Another difficulty in searching company names is language. Obviously, not all the world's companies have English-language names. Less obvious is that the legal names of companies from countries using the Roman alphabet may be different than the commonly used English-language names.

If you are an experienced DIALOG searcher and *expand* on the French company names RENAULT or AIR FRANCE in the FT Extel database, you will get no hits. However, these companies are in the file. In FT Extel, Renault is listed as "Regie Nationale Des Usines Renault formerly Renault (Regie Nationale des Usines)." Air France's entry is under "CIE Nationale Air France," while in other sources it appears as "Compagnie Nationale Air France" and "Groupe Air France."

D&B Europa for 1996 states in its introduction that all company names are in their local languages—except Greek. Some directories do tell us which form of the name is being used.

The difficulties of searching for company names are magnified if the company is Asian or Russian. Some Asian companies have two names—local and English. Others have to be *translated* or *transliterated*. Dun & Bradstreet uses the romanized name provided by each company.

The Japanese *Teikoku* database on DIALOG (File 502) originally had only those Japanese companies that had "official English-language names" out of approximately 950,000 companies in Teikoku's Japanese databank. For example, the company whose English name is "Stanley Electric Co. Ltd." has the transliterated name "Sutanre Denki KK."

In the DIALOG version of Teikoku, the English name appears in the company field (CO). The transliterated name appears in the romanized company field (RC). *Teikoku* has added over 120,000 companies without English-language names. The names appear in the company field with an asterisk and a note indicating that "* in company name field indicates English name not available." An example is Kokumin Kinyukoko, shown below.

```
KOKUMIN KINYUKOKO *
KOKUMIN KINYUKOKO
9-3, OTE-MACHI 1-CHOME
CHIYODA-KU, TOKYO 100
```

There are international standards for the transliteration of non-Latin characters into Latin characters. An example is "ISO 9:1995 Information and documentation—transliteration of Cyrillic characters into Latin characters—Slavic and non-Slavic languages, edition 2."

How can we guarantee that we have the company we actually want? Various numbering systems and ticker symbols may help us track an individual company. Just as U.S. stock issues are assigned CUSIP numbers, international companies receive numbers such as a SEDOL or VALOR. (These numbering systems are discussed in more detail below).

Standard Numbers

A variety of systems are used for both listed and unlisted companies. One company, Dun & Bradstreet, assigns D-U-N-S numbers to companies worldwide (Dun & Bradstreet Information Services' Data Universal Number System). In January 1996, close to 40 million companies had D-U-N-S numbers. European countries, such as the United Kingdom and France, have central registration systems that assign unique numbers to all companies. More than three million French companies have SIRENE numbers, which are issued by INSEE, the state statistical agency. The company's number must appear in its letterhead. Table 3.B lists company registration systems.

TABLE 3.B

MAJOR COMPANY REGISTRATION SYSTEMS

NUMBER	ASSIGNOR	ASSIGNEE	COUNTRY
Listed Companies:			
CUSIP	American Banking Assn.	Equity issues on U.S. exchanges	U.S.
SEDOL	London Stock Exchange	Securities traded in the U.K.	International
VALOR	Telekurs N.A.	Securities	Swiss & International
ISIN	Telekurs and S&P	Quoted companies	International
Ticker Symbol	Stock exchanges, Information providers	Quoted companies	By Exchange
Publisher:			
D-U-N-S Number	Dun & Bradstreet	Public and Private Companies in D&B files	International
Country Internal Numbers:			
Registration	Companies House	All U.K. Companies	U.K.
SIRENE (Idenfication)	INSEE Institute	French Companies	France
Registrerings Nummer	Danish Government	Companies with Shareholders	Denmark

Other securities numbering systems include: Fondscode by stock exchange in the Netherlands; VPS within ISIN in Norway and Sweden; and ISIN, under adoption, in Turkey.

D&B Europa 1996 includes the local number in its records. Seventeen of the 20 countries in the publication have some national numbering system, including registration numbers, fiscal codes, VAT, and tax codes. Only Germany, Luxembourg, and Switzerland in D&B *Europa 1996* have no numbering systems.

The United Nations has recommended establishment of the D-U-N-S number as one of the standard worldwide identifiers for businesses involved in cross-border electronic data interchange.[3]

Establishment Level Numbers

A D-U-N-S number is given to a business's location at a specific address with a distinct operation. It is a unique 9-digit code, randomly selected within blocks. An example of a D-U-N-S number is 81-197-7859 for the Mexican company Cerveceria Cuahtemoc, S.A. de C.V. The number moves with the business; if the business changes name, address, or ownership, the number remains. If the company ceases operation, Dun & Bradstreet does not reassign the number.

To illustrate the value of a D-U-N-S number, in 1994, the number 30-021-0119 was assigned to the Austrian company 3 Pagen Handels gmbh. In updating this record in January 1997 on DBOS in DataStar, we found no company with that name. By searching on the D-U-N-S number, we found the company under a slightly modified name: 3 PAGEN HANDELSGESELLSCHAFT MIT BESCHRANKTER HAFTUNG SCHATZVITRINE. A D-U-N-S number, according to Dun & Bradstreet, is a social security number for business establishments. D&B assigns a D-U-N-S number when it creates a record or investigates a company. The first two digits of the D-U-N-S number indicate the country; see below.

Austria	30-0	Brazil	89-
Denmark	30-5	Colombia	88-
France	26-,76(1990)	Congo	86-
Germany	31-	Peru	93-
Greece	42-	Venezuela	88-
Ireland	21-, 98(1991)	Zambia	55-
Italy	44-	Zimbabwe	56-
Luxembourg	40-		
Netherlands	40-	Israel	60-
Portugal	45-	Thailand	65-
Spain	46-, 47-	Japan	69-
Switzerland	48-	Philippines	70-
U.K.	21-	Indonesia	79-

The use of D-U-N-S numbers to identify linkages within company families is discussed in Chapter 7.

Listed Companies

While the symbols and codes discussed below are assigned as a way of tracking a company's equities issues, they can also be used as a means of identifying a company. Codes may be assigned to an individual company or to a specific equity issue.

Ticker symbols. We are familiar with the use of ticker symbols to identify companies traded on stock exchanges. Originally, the symbols were the identifying labels for stock prices that came across the ticker tape. In the U.S., companies get to choose their ticker symbols. Many U.S. text database providers, including IAC and UMI/Data Courier, include tickers in U.S. company records.

Use of tickers is not standardized internationally. Symbols may be alphabetic or numeric. We associate the ticker symbol with one company, but the alphabetical ticker symbol is *not* unique to one company. As Table 3.C shows, different companies, trading on different exchanges, may have the same symbol.

TABLE 3.C

EXAMPLES OF NON-UNIQUE TICKER SYMBOLS

Company Name	Country	Ticker Symbol
American Annuity Group, Inc.	United States	AAG
Australian Agricultural Co.	Australia	AAG
Amerada Hess Corporation	United States	AHC
Aikchol Hospital Co., Ltd.	Thailand	AHC
Banco De Credito Balear S.A.	Spain	CBL
Campbell & Armstrong Plc	United Kingdom	CBL
Corroon & Black Corporation	United States	CBL
Carnival Corporation	United States	CCL
Celanese Canada Inc.	Canada	CCL
Coco-Cola Amatil Ltd.	Australia	CCL

Companies that are traded on exchanges outside their home countries may have different symbols on foreign exchanges. For example, the Canadian company "ABITIBI-PRICE INC" is traded as A on the Toronto exchange, but ABY on the New York Stock Exchange. Depending on the commercial source you access, you may get either the Canadian or New York symbol, as illustrated below. ABITIBI-PRICE INC tickers in online databases include:

Database	Symbol	Exchange
EXTEL	A	
DISCLOSURE	ABY	NYS
WORLDSCOPE	A	Toronto, Montreal (NYSE)
CANCORP	A, ABPR	Toronto, Montreal, NY
STANDARD & POORS	ABY	NYS
DOW JONES NEWS	ABY	NYS
RETRIEVAL	T.A	Toronto

REUTERLINK is an online service covering a wide range of exchanges. Depending on the exchange, Reuters uses its own ticker symbols (RICS, Reuters Instrument Codes), the local stock exchange symbols, or FT Extel symbols. For example, when ATTWOODS PLC was trading on the New York Stock Exchange, it had all of the following different tickers in REUTERLINK.

ATTWOODS PLC in REUTERLINK:	
London	A.L
London International (ADR)	ATWLy.L
NYSE (ADR)	NA *
NY (Reuters Consolidated)	A.NY
NY Floor (Reuters)	A.N
*NA is the code; it does not mean "Not Available"	

Japanese companies have numeric ticker symbols assigned by the Securities Identification Code Conference. For example, the ticker for Mitsubishi Corporation is 8058.

Equities Numbers. At the securities level, various numbering systems are used for companies and individual equities; for example, CUSIP, SEDOL, VALOR, and ISIN. A CUSIP is a number assigned to companies and their individual securities by American Bankers Association Committee on Uniform Securities Identification Procedures.

The SEDOL is the Stock Exchange Daily Official List, developed by the London Stock Exchange. Similar to the U.S. CUSIP, it is assigned to individual equity issues. The first digit is a continent designator: all SEDOLs beginning with 0 are U.K. 2—North America, 4—Europe, 6—Asian markets. For example, a SEDOL for Kirin Brewery Co. Ltd. is 6493745, and Hong Kong's AMOY Properties Limited is 6030506.

VALOR is produced by Valor Inform, a Swiss company. There are approximately 300,000 VALORS for Swiss and non-Swiss financial instruments.

The ISIN is the International Securities Identification Number and is a product of ISO, the International Standards Organization. It is designed to help with cross-border identification of international securities. Presently, there are about 200,000 numbers.

The ISIN numbers and the *International Securities Identification Numbers Directory* are a joint product of Telekurs NA and Standard and Poor's, Inc (S&P). Telekurs and S&P participate in the ISO Committee on Global Trading. Telekurs AG is owned by more than 300 Swiss banks and stock exchanges and is chartered to collect and distribute information on securities in all markets around the world. It maintains the Swiss Register of Securities and issues Swiss VALOR numbers to identify securities. S&P is under license from the American Bankers Association to administer the CUSIP number system for the U.S. and Canada.

Telekurs assigns numbers to companies in countries that lack national securities numbering systems or authorities. In the U.S., S&P has adopted the national CUSIP for inclusion in the CINS (CUSIP International Numbering System), a 9-character number that is an extension of the CUSIP. Worldscope and FT Extel (Table 3.D) are companies that use all of these numbering systems in their databases. Note from the highlighted numbers in Table 3.D that the ISIN incorporates the CUSIP for U.S. and Canadian companies, the SEDOL for British companies, and the VALOR for Swiss companies.

Legal Status

Legally, companies may be proprietorships, partnerships, or "limited" corporations. They may also be cooperatives or government-operated enterprises. In the United States, "public" refers to companies that trade stock and are registered with the Securities and Exchange Commission. In international company research, "public" is also used as the designation for government-owned enterprises.

We may find more readily available financial information about non-U.S. "private" companies than for U.S. private companies. Two models for collecting and maintaining company information are the United Kingdom and Italy.

TABLE 3.D

SAMPLE NUMBERS FROM WORLDSCOPE AND EXTEL

COMPANY NAME	CUSIP	SEDOL	ISIN	VALOR
AALBORG PORTLAND HOLDING A/S		4001979	DK0000013616	460403
ABBOTT LABORATORIES	**002824100**	2002305	**US0028241000**	903037
ABITIBI-PRICE INC	**003680105**	2003900	**CA0036801052**	676657
ABERFOYLE LTD.		6003100	AU0008652598	640005
ACCIAIERIE FERRIERE LOMBARDE		4330907	IT0000078003	565642
ACATOS & HUTCHENSON PLC		**0005607**	GB0000056076	368880
ACCOR SA		4112321	FR0000120404	485822
ACERINOX		4005238	ES0132105034	466304
ACHILLES CORPORATION		6496045	JP3108000005	761402
ATTWOODS PLC	000G061261	**0062323**	GB**0000623230**	371003
BASELLANDSCHAFTLICHE KANTONALBANK*		4483016	CH0001**333308**	**133330**
UNION MINIERE SA		4005001	BE0003626372	439007
YEO HIAP SENG LIMITED		6986160	SG0008735854**	824347

*   Berner Kantonalbank in Extel
**   Different ISIN in Extel
    From Worldscope CD-ROM and Extel DIALOG, January 1996

In the United Kingdom, all companies register with Companies House. It holds the records to more than one million companies and registers about four million documents each year. It was first established in England and Wales and separately in Scotland by the Joint Stock Companies Act of 1844. There have been many amendments to the act, the most recent based on EU Directives, discussed below. A new company has 18 months to file an initial Annual Accounts statement. It is the responsibility of Companies House to incorporate and dissolve companies, examine and file the required documents, and make the documents available to the public. Documents include accounts and annual returns, changes to directors' details and registered office addresses, secured loans taken out by a company, and liquidators' and receivers' documents.

In the U.K., two or more persons may form an incorporated company, which can be one of four types:

1. Private company limited by shares
2. Private company limited by guarantee (based on contributions to company assets)
3. Private unlimited company (no limit to liability)[4]
4. Public company with a minimum of £50,000 share capital.[4]

In the U.K., the term "limited" is applied to both listed and private companies that are registered as legal entities. The distinction is that the listed company's shares are sold in a market. A listed company is required by law to include PLC in its name.

In Italy, all companies must register with their local chamber of commerce. The Italian Chamber of Commerce has the legal responsibility to maintain and update all public data on *all* Italian enterprises, both companies and sole traders (of whom there are about 4.5 million). The information is available in electronic form in Italian through CERVED, the Italian Chamber of Commerce Database. Profile information and balance sheets, as well as listings of directorships and defaults, are all part of the databank. Definitions of different terms used to describe companies appear in Appendix E, at the end of this chapter.

EU DIRECTIVES

In the United States, you cannot determine from a company's name whether it is a listed or private company. Either type of company name may end in Corp., Inc., or Co. Within the EU, you can tell immediately by the abbreviation at the end of the enterprise's name whether or not it is listed. Laws for these companies are set down in EU directives.

Table 3.E lists the EU directives on company law. The EU has been moving toward harmonization of company law, based on the EEC Treaty, Article 54(3)g. The Law has been promulgated as a set of EU directives that have then been adopted as law in individual EU countries. A similar approach has been taken toward the harmonization of financial markets. It is important to be aware of the directives that are directly related to company names, size, and disclosure because they affect the availability of information.

A directive, according to Article 189 of the Treaty of the European Community, "shall be binding, as to the result to be achieved, upon each Member State, but shall leave to the national authorities the choice of form and methods." Member States have flexibility in how and when they implement directives.

TABLE 3.E		

EU COMPANY LAW DIRECTIVES

COMPANY LAW	Date Adopted	Notes
First Directive 68/151/EEC *OJ* L65, 14 March 1968 Registration of companies and mandatory publication of specified company documents	1968	In force in all member states
Second Directive 77/91/EEC *OJ* V 20 L26 1977 1 January 1977 Amended 92/101/EEC Safeguards in respect to formation of public companies	1976	Belgium exempt from amendment until 1/98
Third Directive 78/855 EEC *OJ* L295, 20 October 1978 Mergers between two public companies in member states	1978	
Fourth Directive 78/660 EEC *OJ* L222 14 August 1978 Annual accounts of individual companies complemented by the Seventh Directive	1978	Amendments
Proposed Fifth Directive *OJ* C131 December 13, 1972 Structure of Management of PLCs and voting structure		Amended 1983, 1991
Sixth Directive 82/891 EEC *OJ* L378 31 December 1982 Division of PLCs	1982	Not applicable in Germany, Denmark, or The Netherlands
Seventh Directive 83/349 EEC *OJ* L193 18 July 1983 Consolidated accounts	1983	Amended
Eighth Directive 84/253 EEC *OJ* L126 12 May 1984 Qualification of auditors	1984	Exceptions:Italy, Denmark, France Portugal, Ireland
Proposed Ninth Directive Conduct of groups containing PLCs		1984; no action
Proposed Tenth Directive *OJ* C23 25 January 1985 Cross-border mergers of public companies		Little progress
Eleventh Directive 89/666/EEC/*OJ* L395 30 December 1989 Disclosure requirements of branches	1989 for implementation for 1993	Exception: Belgium
Twelfth Directive 89/667/EEC *OJ* L395 20 December 1989 Single member private limited companies	1989	Exception: Belgium
Proposed Thirteenth Directive *OJ* 1989 C64 14 March 1989 amended OJ 1990 C240 Regulation of Public Takeover Bids		Little progress
Directive Amending Scope of Fourth and Seventh Directives 90/605/EEC *OJ* V33 1990 L317 Includes partnerships	1990	
Directive on Exemptions for Small Companies (amends Fourth Directive) 94/8/EC *OJ* 1994 L82 Revises thresholds for "small" and "medium"	1994	Third revision

Another method for implementing harmonization measures in the EU has been through regulations. Article 189 states that a regulation "shall have general application. It shall be binding in its entirety and directly applicable in all Member States. A regulation can supplant or supplement national law." Even though regulations carry with them tighter structure than directives, the anticipated level of harmonization has not occurred:

- Member states, in enacting national law, interpret directives differently.
- It may be difficult to incorporate directives into national law.
- Harmonization requires general agreement on the definition of terms and concepts.
- Directives and regulations rely on company law of member states.
- A range of options may be included in the directive.
- Harmonization in company law depends on harmonization in other areas, which may not be in place.[5]

Proposal *OJ* C262 October 10, 1989 regards the "European company" or "Societas Europaea" (SE). The proposal and its 1991 amendments (*OJ* C138 May 19, 1991; and OJ C176, July 8, 1991) would create a supranational European company subject to Community company law rather than national company laws of the member states. It is designed to facilitate cross-frontier cooperation between firms, especially small and medium-sized businesses that are engaged in joint activities. A European company could be formed by two or more companies through merger, formation of a holding company, or creation of a joint subsidiary. A single public limited company could convert itself into a European company (SE) if it has a subsidiary or establishment in another member state.[6]

As a result of the EU's First and Second Directives, official information about both listed and unlisted EU companies is readily available. We are able to find official registration information and financial information about companies whose shares are not traded on markets.

The First Directive sets down legal requirements for registering listed and private companies in member states. It provides for establishing company registries in the countries. It specifies that companies must publish information on capital, annual accounts, details of directors, registered office, company statutes, and details pertaining to liquidation. The types of repositories for company registration used by EU members is shown in Table 3.F.

TABLE 3.F

EU REPOSITORIES FOR COMPANY REGISTRATION

CENTRAL REPOSITORIES	REGIONAL REPOSITORIES
U.K.: Companies House	Spain (1991): provincial registry
Portugal (based on size)	Luxembourg: local court
Ireland	Italy: (CERVED) Chambers of Commerce
Denmark	Greece (1991)
	Germany, Netherlands, France, Belgium: local courts and Chambers of Commerce

The Second Directive specifies harmonized standards for the formation and maintenance of capital of public companies with a view to protect shareholders and creditors. Standards include naming of companies and setting a minimum capital requirement of 25,000 ECU. Companies must include information on registered office and nominal value of shares. More information about the Fourth and Seventh Directives appears in Chapter 2.

Table 3.G shows commonly used abbreviations to designate legal company type. Many countries use the "Ltd" designation for all corporations that have shareholders, whether they are traded or not.

D&B Europa 1996 identifies 30 legal types of organizations among the 20 countries it covers and gives each legal type a code. It presents a table for each country. Sweden has only one legal type while Italy has 18. Table 3.H is an example, showing the legal status of Belgian companies.

OTHER COUNTRY REQUIREMENTS

Outside the EU, there are no standard regulations for reporting information. It is necessary to check on a country-by-country basis. Although many countries have mandatory filing rules, that does not guarantee that this information must be made available to the public.

Because Scandinavian countries had strict registration and reporting procedures, it was easy for Finland and Sweden to enter the EU. Finland's Company Act and General Limited Partnerships Act of 1988 have been adapted to correspond to EU legislation. Though it has not joined the EU, Switzerland passed a new company law that will primarily affect listed companies.

TABLE 3.G

EUROPEAN COMPANY NAME DESIGNATIONS

Country	Public	Private
Belgium	**SA** (Société Anonyme) or **NV** (Naamloze Vennootschap)	**SPRL** (Société de Personnes a Responsibilité Limitée) or **PVBA** (Personenvennootschap met heperkte aansprakelijkheid)
Denmark	**A/S** (Aktieselskab)	**ApS** (Anpartsselskab)
Finland	**OY** Osakeyhtio	**OY** Osakeyhtio
France	**SA** (Société Anonyme)	**SARL** (Société a Responsibilité Limitée)
Luxembourg		
Switzerland		
Germany	**AG** (Aktiengesellschaft)	**GmbH** (Gesellschaft mit beschrankter Haftung)
Austria		
Switzerland		
Greece	**AE** (Anonymous Eteria)	**EPE** (Eteria Periorismenis Efthinis)
Italy	**SpA** (Societa per Azioni)	**SRL** (Societe a Responsibilita Limitata)
Netherlands	**NV** (Naamloze Vennootschap)	**BV** (Besloten Vennootschap met beperkte)
Portugal	**SA** or **SARL** (Sociedade Anonima de Responsabilidade)	**LDA** (Sociedade por Quotas de Responsabilidade Limitada)* Limitada)
Spain	**SA** (Sociedad Anonima)	**SL** (Sociedad de Resonsabilidad Limitada)
U.K	**PLC** (Public Limited Company)	**Ltd** (Private Limited Company)**
Ireland		

* Also used in overseas territories
** Adopted in Commonwealth countries
*** SA and SpA designations - [anonymous] - companies issue bearer shares and owners are nameless

TABLE 3.H

LEGAL STATUS TABLE FOR BELGIUM

Code	Legal Status	
2	Societe de personnes a responsabilite limitee	SPRL
	Personenvennotschap met beperkte aansprakelijheld	PVBA
3	Societe anonyme	SA
	Naamioze vennootschap	NV
8	Societe cooperative	SC
	Samenwerkende vennootschap	SV
18	Societe en nom collectif	SNC
	Vennootschap onder gemeenschappelijke naam	VGN

Source: D&B Europa 1996. Copyright 1996 Dun & Bradstreet, Inc. All rights reserved. Reprinted with permission.

Central and Eastern European Countries (CEEC)

The Central and Eastern European Countries (CEEC) are trying to bring their company law in line with EU legislation as a preliminary step to their potential entry into the European Union. For example, Hungarian companies will have to make more information about companies public. Hungarian law required pub-

lication of limited financials and little information on share ownership. The Ministry of Justice expects gradual changes to occur during the next few years.[7] Despite its economic problems, another country to watch is Bulgaria, which has expressed interest in EU membership. The positive implication of the interest in CEEC countries in EU membership is an improvement in the company information available from these countries.

Russia introduced a new civil code in 1995 that should provide a framework for commercial law. However, passing laws in the new Russia has not always meant implementing them.[8]

China

China passed company law legislation in 1994. Regulations govern the registration of limited liability companies (LLCs), joint stock companies (JSCs), joint ventures, and foreign-owned firms. According to the law, company registration with the State Industry and Commerce Administration (ICA) is mandatory, along with company name changes, legal representation, and registered capital. The State ICA has overall responsibility for registration but local ICAs almost always have charge of companies within their jurisdictions. Information is recorded in company registries and is open to the public. JSCs have to file an audited financial report.[9] The entire Chinese company law was published in *East Asian Executive Reports* starting in March of 1995.

Australia

In Australia, all companies register with the Australian Securities Commission. Private companies are also to be listed with the ASC. Searches are conducted on company name to ensure a unique name within a line of business. The ASC is maintaining a central databank.

Disclosure Requirement: Sources of Information

The *Directory of World Stock Exchanges* has a summary of requirements for listed companies for individual exchanges. More in-depth coverage may be found in two sources: CIFARS's *International Accounting and Auditing Trends* for listed companies and EIU's *Investing, Licensing and Trading in...* (*IL&T*), which has requirements for listed and private companies. *IL&T* is available in a wide range of electronic sources (see Chapter 9).

Exhibit 3.3 describes disclosure practices for two emerging markets. The information is from the Reporting Practices section of Volume 1 of *International Accounting and Auditing Trends*, 1995. We have included some items that we expect to see in an annual or 10K filing but which are either optional or are not required in these countries.

Investing, Licensing and Trading (IL&T) includes company requirements for all the countries it covers. Exhibit 3.4 is from the *IL&T* report on Argentina. It distinguishes between unlisted (SRL) and listed (SA) requirements.

ARGENTINA: REPORTING PRACTICES

- Product segmentation disclosed by most
- Geographic segmentation disclosed by some
  Exports reported by some
- Earnings per share disclosed by some
- Dividend per share is reported by some
- Major shareholdering is not disclosed
- Subsidiary information disclosed by many
- Number of employees disclosed for parent company
- Management information
  Names and titles of principal officers are reported by many
  List of board members is reported by most
  Company shares owned by directors/officers are not disclosed
  Remuneration to directors/officers disclosed by some
- Research and development expenses is not disclosed

THAILAND: REPORTING PRACTICES

- Changes in shareholders' equity is disclosed by most
- Product segmentation is not disclosed
- Geographic segmentation is not disclosed
  Earnings per share is disclosed by most
- Major shareholding is not disclosed
- Number of employees is not disclosed
- Management information
  Names and titles of principal officers are reported by most
  Company shares owned by directors/officers is not disclosed
  Remuneration to directors/officers is disclosed by some
- Research and development expenses is not disclosed
- Goodwill is not disclosed

EXTRACTS FROM *INTERNATIONAL ACCOUNTING AND AUDITING TRENDS*, 4TH ED.

EXHIBIT 3.3

Source: Reprinted with permission from the Center for International Financial Analysis and Research, Inc. (CIFAR).

	SRL	S. A.
Capital	No minimum	Ps12,000 minimum but may be change
Founders/Shareholders	2–50 partners	Minimum of 2 shareholders
Disclosure	If capital >Ps25,000 an annual report with balance sheet and P&L statement must be submitted for publication in the Official Bulletin	Annual P&L statement and balance sheet submitted to Inspeccion de Justicia, or to provincial authorities, for publication in the Official Bulletin. Annual balance sheets must be adjusted for inflation and audited. There should be one or more independent auditors
	Auditor required	
Types of Shares	Shares or quotes must be of equal peso book value	Shares may be registered or bearer, and either common or preferred.

IL&T REPORT ON ARGENTINA

EXHIBIT 3.4

Source: Investing, Licensing and Trading in Argentina, June 1997: 6. The Economist Intelligence Unit, NA, Inc., 111 West 57th Street, New York, NY 10019.

In Argentina, businesses may be established as sole proprietorships, general or limited partnerships, co-operatives, branches, corporations *(sociedades anonimas—SAs)* or limited-liability companies *(sociedades de responsabilidad limitada—SRLs).* Most foreign companies organize as SAs, but a few are SRLs. The SA is the only entity that may issue shares to the public. The SRL is in effect a partner-ship, but the liability of the partners is limited to their subscribed capital. If one partner is a foreign com-pany, the SRL is taxed in the same manner as a branch. The Argentine affiliates of Abbott Laborato-ries, Miles Laboratories, Ralston Purina, Timken, and Dun & Bradstreet, among others, are organized as SRLs.

Table 3.I shows the abbreviations used for Latin American companies. They are not all specified by law, however, as in the EU.

TABLE 3.I

LATIN AMERICAN COMPANY NAME DESIGNATIONS

Country	Abbrev.	Definition	Type of Company
General Usage:	S.A. Ltda	Sociedad Anonima Limitada	Corporation Limited Liability
Alternatives: Ecuador Venezuela	C.A.	Compania Anonima	Corporation
Dominican Republic	C for A or C x A	Compania for Acciones Compania for Acciones	Corporation

Source: Dun's Latin America (1991: ix). All rights reserved. Reprinted with permission.

SIZE OF COMPANIES

Most companies are small—and the smaller the com-pany, the less information that is available. Therefore, we cannot expect to find much more than an address for the great majority of enterprises worldwide. Within the EU, company size categories are specified by law: large, medium, small, and micro. Over 90% of all enterprises in EU countries fall into the micro cat-egory.

Multinationals

Outside the range of official size categories are com-panies referred to as "multinational" companies. In Chapter 9, we examine the concept of multinationality as it applies to how a company operates abroad. Here, however, we are interested in the definition of a mul-tinational corporation. The multinational is referred

to by a variety of terms: multinational corporation (MNC), multinational enterprise (MNE), or, as used by the United Nations, transnational company/enter-prise (TNC/TNE). The term "global" is also used, along with common references to "international" com-panies.

No standard definition of a multinational corpora-tion exists. An early review of the literature and status of multinationals was written in 1971 by Yair Aharoni in the *Quarterly Review of Economics and Business.*[10] Aharoni credits David E. Lilienthal for first using the term "multinational" in April 1960 when he sug-gested the definition of "multinational corporations" as "corporations which have their home in one coun-try but operate and live under the laws and customs of other countries as well." These first "multinationals" were firms with management operations in more than one country.

In 1982, Richard Caves published a review of the literature of the 1970s about the multinational enter-prise. In it, he defined an MNE as an enterprise that controls and manages production establishments—plants—located in at least two countries.[11]

The definitions that have evolved in the past 15 years have become more complex. The first multina-tional directory, the 1981 *World Directory of Multi-national Enterprises,* listed 500 of the largest industrial corporations with "significant international invest-ments." Companies were included that had manufac-turing or mining activities in at least three foreign countries, 5% of sales attributable to foreign invest-ments, and $75 million sales from foreign manufac-turing operations.

In 1992, John H. Dunning, one of the authors of the *World Directory of Multinational Enterprises,* gave a different broad definition of a multinational enter-prise: one that "owns and controls value-adding ac-tivities in more than one country."[12]

A synthesis of the characteristics that define a multinational includes:

- Number of countries in which a firm is operating
- Number of countries in which a firm makes prod-ucts/services available
- Composition of management operating the firm, both in terms of nationality and outlook
- Financial performance: absolute or relative share of assets, employees sales in a foreign country are "significant portion"[13]

Vinod Bavishi, from CIFAR, suggests three vari-ables as good measures of multinationality: foreign sales, foreign income, and foreign assets.[14] He also suggests using the number of active foreign subsidiar-

	Purely Domestic Enterprises	Multinational Enterprises		
		National Base Enterprises	Joint Venture Strategic Alliance Enterprise Networks	Stateless Global Enterprises
Investor-Owned Enterprises	Canadian Pacific	Nestle SA Union Carbide (US)	Caltex(US) Auto Companies	BCCI Likely ————————————>
Jointly-Controlled Enterprises and Private-Government Combinations	Conrail (U.S.)	British Petroleum (BP)	Union Carbide India Ltd. SAS (Sweden, Norway, Denmark)	Possible ————————>
State-Owned Enterprises	Amtrak(US) Canadian National	Quantas (Australia)	Renault (France)	Unlikely ————————>

MULTINATIONAL ENTERPRISES CLASSIFICATION

EXHIBIT 3.5

Source: Rules of the Game in the Global Economy: 26. Reprinted with permission.

ies, percent of common shares owned by foreign-based shareholders, and number of employees abroad as other measures.

John D. Daniels, author of one of the standard textbooks on international business, *International Business: Environment and Operations*, distinguishes between the multinational and the transnational. For Daniels, the multinational has an integrated philosophy toward home country and overseas operations. Daniels has a narrow view of the transnational, characterizing it as a company that is owned and managed by nationals in a different country.[15]

Lee Preston and Duane Windsor in *Rules of the Game in the Global Economy* suggest a framework in which multinationals are part of a continuum that ranges from purely domestic companies to possible stateless enterprises (see Exhibit 3.5). They also distinguish investor-owned companies from those that are partly or totally state-owned.[16]

Cyrus Freidheim, from the management consulting firm Booz, Allen & Hamilton, suggests that the enterprise of the twenty-first century will be a "relationship enterprise," a network of strategic alliances among big firms from different countries and different industries. Freidheim also notes that today's global companies still have a domestic base, a home-country bias, and are restrained by national laws.[17] Emphasis on relationships and strategic alliances has been the growing theme in business literature. Strategic alliances are relationships between companies involving a sharing of common destinies. The alliances can be intra-industry; for example, the three U.S. automakers

formed an alliance to develop an efficient battery for an electric car. The alliances are often international. The three U.S. auto makers have entered into alliances with non-U.S. manufacturers to sell autos in the U.S.[18] Business reference sources do not systematically capture these alliances.

Forbes magazine has published a special report on U.S. multinationals annually since 1979, using a measure of foreign revenues, income, and assets. Companies are ranked based on total foreign revenue. *Forbes* calculates foreign revenue, profit, and assets as a percent of total revenue, profit, and assets. Exhibit 3.6 includes the data for the top 10 companies listed by *Forbes*. The table as it appears in *Forbes* also has data for total assets. Note that 23 of the top 25 in the 1992 ranking were in the 1996 top 25 as well.

The United Nations actively monitors transnational corporations through its Transnational Corporations and Management Division of the United Nations Conference on Trade and Development (UNCTAD). The goal of the transnational unit is to help developing countries understand and negotiate with transnational corporations. The United Nations defines a transnational corporation as one that owns or controls economic resources in two or more countries. In the mid 1990s, the universe of transnational corporations included over 38,000 parent firms that controlled over 265,000 foreign affiliates worldwide; 34,000 parents were from 23 developed countries. Foreign affiliates' sales were more than $4.8 trillion in 1991, slightly more than the world exports of goods and non-factor services.

Rank 95 91	Company	Revenue			Net profit[1]		
		foreign ($ mil)	total ($ mil)	foreign as % of total	foreign ($ mil)	total ($ mil)	foreign as % of total
1 1	Exxon	83,907	107,893	77.8	4,949	6,470	76.5
2 3	General Motors	49,051	168,829	29.0	3,738	6,933	53.9
3 2	IBM	45,151	71,940	62.8	3,567	4,178	85.4
4 4	Mobil	44,287[2]	66,724[2]	66.4[3]	1,855[3]	2,682[3]	69.2
5 5	Ford Motor	41,884	137,137	30.5	578	4,139	14.0
6 6	Texaco[4]	26,992	48,118	56.1	755[3]	1,091[3]	69.2
7 9	Citicorp	18,802	31,690	59.3	2,005	3,464	57.9
8 10	Philip Morris Cos	18,186	53,139	34.2	1,333	5,478	24.3
9 7	Chevron[4]	17,967	39,363	45.6	1,153	930	124.0
10 13	General Electric	17,832	70,028	25.5	879	6,573	13.4

1 From continuing operations.
2 Includes other income.
3 Net income before corporate expense.
4 Includes proportionate interest in unconsolidated subsidiaries or affiliates.

FORBES 100 LARGEST U.S. MULTINATIONALS

EXHIBIT 3.6

Source: "100 Largest U.S. Multinationals," *Forbes* 15 July 1996. Reprinted by permission of *Forbes* magazine. Copyright Forbes Inc. 1996.

		Top 5 Ranked by Assets and Top 5 Ranked by "Transnationality"		
Ranked by Foreign Assets	Index[b]	Corporation	Country	Index[b]
1	27	Royal Dutch Shell	U.K./Netherlands	63.6
2	80	Ford	United States	28.6
3	26	Exxon	United States	63.8
4	85	General Motors	United States	25.7
5	38	IBM	United States	56.4
60	1	The Thomson Corporation	Canada	92.3
71	2	Solvay	Belgium	92.2
50	3	RTZ	United Kingdom	91.4
17	4	Roche Holdings	Switzerland	90.5
42	5	Sandoz	Switzerland	88.8

b The index of transnationality is calculated as the average of foreign assets to total assets. foreign sales to total sales and foreign employment to total employment.

UNCTAD's TOP TRANSNATIONAL CORPORATIONS 1994

EXHIBIT 3.7

Source: World Investment Report 1996: 30–32. Reprinted with permission from UNCTAD.

The United Nations tracks the performance of transnational corporations in *World Investment Report*, published annually since 1991. Each *Report* includes a list of the top transnational corporations ranked by foreign assets. UNCTAD calculates an index of transnationality, based on the ratio of foreign assets, sales, and employees to total assets, and employees, as shown in Exhibit 3.7.

The *Report* also has a table of the geographical distribution of transnational corporations and analysis of growth and trends. Each report also focuses on one special subject related to transnationals. For example, the 1994 report is subtitled "Transnational Corporations, Employment and the Workplace." Data from the geographic distribution of transnationals is shown in Table 3.J.

TABLE 3.J

TRANSATIONAL CORPORATIONS BY COUNTRY, SELECTED COUNTRIES

Table I.4. Number of parent firms and their foreign affiliates by country, latest available year

Area/Economie	Year	Parent Firms Based in Country	Foreign Affiliates Located in Country[a]
Developed economies (23)		34 199[b]	90 786[b]
Australia	1994	732	2 450
Austria	1993	838	2 210
Canada	1995	1 565	4 708
France	1993	2 216	7 097[d]
Germany	1993	7 003[e]	11 396[f]
Japan	1995	3 967[h]	3 290[i]
Sweden	1995	3 520	5 550
United Kingdom[k]	1992	1 443[l]	3 376[m]
United States	1993	3 013[n]	16 543[o]
Developing economies (24)		4 148[b]	119 765
Bolivia	1990	..	298
Brazil	1994	797	9 698
Mexico	1993	..	8 420
Republic of Korea	1991	1 049	3 671
Uruguay	1994	..	101
Former Yugoslavia	1991	112	3 900
Central and Eastern Europe[w] (11)		400	55 000
Albania	1994	..	118
Hungary	1994	66	15 205
Russian Federation	1994	..	7 793
Ukraine	1994	..	2 514
World		38 747	265 551

a Represents number of foreign affiliates, as reported by country and may not use standard definition; b Total does not include countries for which data is not available; d 1992; e and f Exclusions on some types of holding companies;h and i Includes finance, insurance, and real estate firms collected at different dates; k Assumes numbers are understated; l,m Multi-year data; n,o Banking firms from different date; w Data is estimated

Source: Taken from *World Investment Report 1996*: 8–9. Reprinted with permission of UNCTAD.

The United Nations Transnational Division has been a major source for information about transnationals. Examples of its publications other than *World Investment Report* are listed below.

Transnational Business Information: A Manual of Needs and Sources was published in 1991. Although it is beginning to show its age, it is a simple, clear book that will help researchers better understand and identify information about transnationals. The chapters are organized by the type of information one should know about transnationals and the publicly available sources that provide the information.

Transnational Corporations: A Selective Bibliography 1983–1987, 1988–1990, and 1991–92 are bibliographies published by the Division. About one-third of the titles are for resources in languages other than English. Citations are arranged by broad category, according to the Centre's classification scheme. There are also subject, title, and author indexes.

United Nations Library on Transnational Corporations is a series published by Routledge between 1993 and 1995. The series was published on behalf of the Transnational Corporations and Management Division. John H. Dunning edited the series. It is a definitive review of the extensive literature on transnational corporations.[19] Sample titles in the series include:

- *Transnational Corporations in Services*
- *Transnational Corporations and Regional Economic Integration*
- *Transnational Corporations and Human Resources*
- *Market Structure and Industrial Performance*
- *Transnational Corporations: The International Legal Framework*

World Investment Directory, issued in 6 volumes, is discussed in more detail in Chapter 16. On a country-by-country basis, it includes the legal framework for the operation of transnational corporations and sources of information, and it lists the major transnational corporations in each country.

Size of Enterprises

Enterprises in Europe (Enterprise Policy, European Commission)

In 1986, the European Community began systematic data collection to count the number of establishments within the market by country and by size category. In 1990, there were about 14.2 million enterprises employing 92.1 million people in EUR12 countries.

The EU itself has special programs to encourage a favorable business environment for the creation and development of "small and medium enterprises" (SMEs). Toward this end, the EU's European Commission has collected and published data on the size distribution of enterprises by sector. The first report, *Enterprises in the European Community,* was published in 1990. The Second Report and Third Report, both titled *Enterprises in Europe,* followed in 1992 and 1994.

Official data, similar to the economic censuses in the U.S., had been collected every five years and were limited in scope. The first report used 1983 data and covered only 10 of the 12 EU countries. In 1988, a European Statistical System on SME, a database containing information on the enterprises broken down by size, was created. The Second and Third Reports cover 23 countries: the EU member states, members of the European Free Trade Association (EFTA), the United States, Japan, Australia, and Canada.

The Third Report is in two volumes. Volume 1 is a descriptive analysis at the EU level, country profiles, and the "demography of enterprises." Volume 2 contains data by size-class and sector for the EU-12 and EFTA. The report tries to follow a common format for each country. However, there is variation based on the amount of information available from the different countries.

Data are collected from public and private sources. The first choice for source is a country's national statistics office. The first choice for reporting unit is the enterprise. The classification system is NACE, the official industrial classification of economic activities within the EU, established by Eurostat in 1970. Data are collected for three economic variables: employment (paid and unpaid), turnover (total sales), and value added. Size classification has been based on number of employees. The publications focus on SMEs, which in the Third Report are those enterprises with between 10 and 499 employees. Table 3.K shows the EU classification for enterprise size.

TABLE 3.K	
EU CLASSIFICATION OF ENTERPRISE SIZE	
Classification	*Number of Employees*
Large Business Sectors	500 or more
SME Business Sectors	10–499
Small	10–99
Medium	100–499
Micro Sectors	0–9

In the 1990 count, micro enterprises comprised 92.4% of all enterprises in the EU. SMEs constituted 7.5% and large enterprises made up the difference. Micro enterprises provided 33.3% of all jobs, SMEs 42%, and large enterprises 24.7%. Table 3.L displays the percentages for number of enterprises, employment, and turnover for 1990. A December 1996 "Memo" from Eurostat reported that 99% of EU firms had fewer than 50 workers.

Enterprises in EU-15 1992, Fourth Report, was issued in December of 1996, too late to be examined for this edition.

For comparison, the U.S. defines an SME as an enterprise with less than 500 employees. In 1990, 7% of U.S. enterprises were large; they accounted for 46.6% of employment and 48.1% of turnover. Additional data on company size appear in Appendix G, at the end of this chapter.

SPECIAL CASES

EU law affects the reporting structure of EU companies and therefore the information flow about those companies. Japanese and Korean culture and practice have the same effect.

Japanese Companies

The unique structure of Japanese companies affects Japanese company information, industry analysis, marketing data, and international trade. Major Japanese companies are organized in *keiretsu* (kay-rhet-sue) or company coalitions. The keiretsu are business alliances in which companies have interlocking directors and cross-holdings of debt and equity. Mutual stockholding, two-way flow of capital and personnel, and a predisposition to buy from and sell to one another are characteristics of current keiretsu. The groups may be horizontal or vertical. Six banks control the major horizontal groups: Mitsubishi, Mitsui, Sumitomo, Fuyo, DKB, and Sanwa. How big are they? Studies estimate that the six largest corporate families accounted for about 15 percent of total sales and total

TABLE 3.L

PERCENTAGE OF NUMBER OF ENTERPRISES AND OF EMPLOYMENT BY SIZE CLASS 1990, FOR THE EUR-12

	Micro (0–9)	SME (10–499)	Large (500+)
Enterprises			
All	92.4	7.5	0.10
Industry	79.6	20.0	0.4
Construction	92.6	7.4	2
Distribution	94.9	5.1	2
Rest of Services[1]	94.9	5.0	0.1
Employment			
All	33.3	42.0	24.7
Industry	13.3	46.5	40.5
Construction	43.7	45.9	10.4
Distribution	51.4	37.3	11.3
Rest of Services	40.2	37.4	22.4
Turnover			
All	23.5	47.0	29.5
Industry	9.0	38.6	52.4
Construction	33.5	51.0	14.9
Distribution	31.4	54.8	13.8
Rest of Services	40.3	44.7	15.0

1 Excluding NACE 71,79,81,82 and 9
2 Less than 1%

Source: Enterprises in Europe, Third Report.

assets for all Japanese companies. Expanding holdings to all affiliates, numbers go up to about 25% for total sales. Banks also hold over 40% of all stocks listed on the Japanese stock exchange and other companies hold an additional 30%.

Mitsubishi is a horizontal keiretsu with over 200 affiliate companies and sales of $300 billion. The core membership of its executive council includes 29 companies. Almost all the members of its President's Council *(shacho-kai)* have directors loaned from other member firms. Toyota is a vertical keiretsu, with 175 primary suppliers and 4,000 secondary ones. Toyota is a member of the Mitsui group. Distribution alliances also exist with other manufacturers and retailers. The DKB group comprises Dai-Ichi Kangyo, one of the world's largest banks; Asahi Chemical, one of the world's largest chemical companies; and Fujitsu, one of the world's largest computer companies. It also includes Isuzu Motor.

What distinguishes the keiretsu is the way in which the companies do business together. They differ from U.S. subsidiary or affiliate relationships where the parent company owns a controlling share. Three members of the DKB group are listed as major shareholders in Fujitsu: Dai-Ichi Kangyo Bank Ltd., Asahi Mutual Life Insurance Co., and Dai-Ichi Mutual Life Insurance Co. They hold 4.6%, 6.4%, and 1.3%, respectively.

Some companies are members of more than one group. For example, Nippon Express, a company primarily involved in shipping and transportation, has shareholders from five of the big six keiretsu. The groups have members from the financial services industry, electronics, automobiles, food, construction, real estate, chemicals, industrial equipment, and shipping and transportation. Exhibit 3.8 shows the interrelationships.

NIPPON EXPRESS CO LTD.
MAJOR SHAREHOLDERS in the Company at 31-03-94:
Asahi Mutual Life Insurance Co 92,385,000 (8.6%); The **Dai-Ichi Kangyo Bank Ltd** 50,146,000 (4.7%); The **Sanwa Bank Ltd** 35,329,000 (3.3%); The Koa Fire & Marine Insurance Co Ltd 31,512,000 (2.9%); The Industrial Bank of Japan Ltd 29,356,000 (2.7%); The **Sumitomo Trust & Banking Co Ltd** 28,334,000 (2.6%): The Long-Term Credit Bank of Japan Ltd 28,184,000 (2.6%); Japan Railways Group Mutual Aid Assoc 26,780,000 (2.5%); The **Toyo Trust & Banking Co Ltd** 19,719,000 (1.8%); The Chuo Trust & Banking Co Ltd 19,400,000 (1.8%).

KEIRETSU RELATIONSHIP EXTRACTED FROM *EXTEL* RECORD

EXHIBIT 3.8

Source: Extel Online DataStar, January 12, 1996. Reprinted with permission from Extel Financial, Inc.

Identifying keiretsu relationships is not straightforward. Although the Japanese have changed disclosure requirements to reveal more interrelationships, the Japanese press does not publicize these groupings. Some relationships can be discovered in the *Japan Company Handbook*. For example, the entry in the *Handbook* describes the "Tokyo Sintered Metals" company as a powder metallurgy–based parts maker *belonging to* Toyota Motor group. Using the *Japan Company Handbook* online on LEXIS-NEXIS Services, you can search on "belonging" with a parent name, to retrieve names of group members.

The publishers of the *Japan Company Handbook* publish an annual survey in Japanese, translated as "Overview of the Industrial Keiretsu." Dowdell Marketing Consultants in Tokyo publishes a biannual directory entitled *Industrial Groupings in Japan: Anatomy of Keiretsu* for about $700.

The keiretsu are part of what the U.S. considers Japanese unfair trade practices, and they have been part of the Structural Impediments Initiative (SII). In Japan, however, this is accepted procedure. Japanese companies manufacturing in the United States depend on these affiliated suppliers to provide the parts for products built in the U.S., rather than using U.S. suppliers.

Japanese joint stock companies are referred to as KK—*Kabushiki Kaishas*. There are about one million joint stock companies in Japan. The very large general trading companies are called *sogo shosha*. Examples are Itochu Corporation, Sumitomo, Marubeni, Mitsubishi, and Mitsui & Co. They are some of the largest companies in the world.

Korean Companies

Chaebol are Korean conglomerates that are similar to keiretsu. Like Japan's prewar *zaibatsu*, the four major chaebol, Samsung, Hyundai, Daewood Group, and LG (Lucky Goldstar), began as family businesses. During 1994, the Korean government put pressure on the chaebol to reduce their interlinking holdings, which has also led to more outside management. The sales of all the affiliate companies and the revenues of the top 30 chaebol account for about 75% of the Korean GNP.

Company Structure of Former Soviet Republics

From the few official state trading organizations and state enterprises in existence prior to 1988, many types of business now coexist in the newly independent republics of the CIS. About 30,000 organizations are dealing in international trade. The main forms of business arrangement are:

- State enterprises: Preexisting enterprises run by the government.
- Joint ventures: Started in 1987.
- Cooperatives: Legalized in May 1988, 250,000 were registered as of May 1991; these first nonpublic Soviet enterprises had to be worker-owned.
- Private sector: Small independent entrepreneurs (*malyye predpriyatiya*), legalized in June 1989.
- Joint-stock companies and limited-liability corporations: Legalized in mid-1990.
- State trading companies (FTOs): The limited number of former official organizations for trade have been disbanded.

NAFTA

NAFTA does not include any provisions for harmonizing company law or collecting enterprise data. Chapter 2 discusses company disclosure and accounting issues related to NAFTA.

It is important to remember that while there are similarities between Canada and the United States, the countries have two different cultures and corporate legal systems. Mexico is quite different from the other two NAFTA members. Many of Mexico's major companies are *grupos*, large collections of family-owned businesses similar to keiretsu, but not as integrated.

CONCLUSION

This chapter was designed to provide the background needed to understand the difficulties associated with international company information. It has described characteristics of company information sources that we use to categorize materials in the chapters that follow. It has presented techniques to identify companies. It has introduced concepts such as disclosure, size of enterprises, and country business cultures that influence the amount of information available from secondary sources. We hope that it will provide a basis for sources that we examine in the following five chapters.

FURTHER READING

Selected Reading on Company Law

"Company Law in the People's Republic of China." *East Asian Executive Reports* 17 (March 15, 1995–August 15, 1995).

The entire text of China's company law.

Oiantakanen, Risto; and Jouni Snellman. "Baltic States Overview." *International Financial Law Review* (January 1995): 4–6.

>An overview of strides toward a market economy in Estonia, Latvia, and Lithuania.

Stanbrook and Hooper and KPMG European Headquarters. *Business Guide to European Community Legislation*. Bernard O'Connor, editor. U.K.: John Wiley, 1995.

>A description of all EU legislation, with details, current status. Generally found in law libraries.

Selected Reading on Multinationals

Barnet, Richard J.; and John Cavanagh. *Global Dreams: Imperial Corporations and The New World Order*. New York: Simon & Schuster: 1994.

>For those who do not have time to read the book, read the book review by Thomas A. Hemphill, "Global Dreams: Imperial Corporations and the New World Order," *Sloan Management Review* 33 (summer 1994): 98–99.

Organisation for Economic Co-operation and Development, Working Group on Accounting Standards. *Disclosure of Information by Multinational Enterprises—Survey of the Application of the OECD Guidelines*. 1987.

Pearce, John A. II; and Kendall Roth. "Multinationalization of the Mission Statement." *Advanced Management Journal* 53 (Summer 1988): 39–44.

Porter, Michael E. "Changing Patterns of International Competition." *California Management Review* 28, no. 2 (winter 1986): 9–40.

>Makes a distinction between companies that operate in "multi-domestic" industries (in which competition is independent across countries of operations) or in global industries (in which competition in each country affects competition in other countries).

Riahi-Belkaoui, Ahmed. *Multinationality and Firm Performance*. CT: Quorom, 1996.

>An academic examination of the data from the *Forbes* multinational list.

Stafford, David C.; and Richard H. A. Purkis, eds. *Directory of Multinationals,* 3rd ed. New York: Stockton Press, 1990.

>Includes companies that had $1 billion sales in 1987 with "significant" foreign investments. 450 parents; uses 1987 data.

Sullivan, Daniel. "Measuring the Degree of Internationalization of a Firm." *Journal of International Business Studies* 25, no. 2 (1994): 325–42.

"Survey: Multinationals." *Economist* (March 27, 1993): 5–20.

Selected Reading on Keiretsu and Chaebol

"Japan Keiretsu System Growing Weaker, JFTC Study Finds." *BNA International Trade Daily* (April 30, 1992). NEXIS; CURRNT

>The Japan Fair Trade Commission concludes that the keiretsu relationships are growing weaker.

Kearns, Robert L. *Zaibatsu America: How Japanese Firms Are Colonizing Vital U.S. Industries*. New York: Free Press/Macmillan, 1992.

>The book examines the grip Japanese conglomerates have on American industry. It is in contrast to the report from the Japan Fair Trade Commission.

Montague-Pollock, Matthew. "The Chaebol Adapt." *AsiaMoney* (May 1995, Korean supplement): 18–28.

>The article discusses the chaebol's response to government and political parties to remain viable.

Miyashita, Kenichi; and David W. Russell. *Keiretsu: Inside the Hidden Japanese Conglomerate*. New York: McGraw-Hill, 1994.

>The book illustrates keiretsu structure and relationships and provides hints on how to find keiretsu members in business sources.

"South Korea's Conglomerates: Do or Be Done For." *Economist* 31 (December 9, 1989): 74, 79.

>The conglomerates must restructure to survive. Chaebol need to raise funds on international capital markets. This will dilute family control and cross holdings.

"South Korea's Conglomerates: Spoiled Rotten." *Economist* 31 (June 8, 1991): 76.

>Chaebol dominate the Korean economy. The domination of chaebol in the South Korean economy has become a problem. The companies pursue market share at all costs.

Udagawa, Hideo. "Dawning of a New Age for the Sogo Shosha Traders." *Tokyo Business Today* 60 (January 1992): 54–57.

>Sogo shosha are setting up production subsidiaries worldwide and getting involved in energy and information communications.

Weimer, George. "Keiretsu, Kudzu, Zaibatsu, and You: Are We Japan's New Colony." *Industry Week* (March 16, 1992): 68–.

>Zaibatsu were the 30 giant trading conglomerates that ran most of pre–World War II Japanese industry and were the forerunners of keiretsu and sogo shosha.

NOTES

1. Anne Mintz, "Quality Control and the Zen of Database Production," *Online* 14 (November 1990): 15–23.

2. Ruth A. Pagell, "Sorry Wrong Number," *Online* 14 (November 1990): 20–23.

3. *D&B News* December 1991: 9.

4. *FAME User Manual* (London: FAME, 1991): 9.

5. *EEC Directive on Company Law and Financial Markets* (Oxford University Press, 1991): 2–89.

6. "Company Law—Europe 1995 Topical Report," *Coopers & Lybrand EC Commentary on Company Law Report* (13 October 1995).

7. "Company Law to Be Brought in Line with EU Standards," *MTI-ECONEWS* (29 July 1994).

8. Alexander Crossman, "Practising in the Ultimate Emerging Market," *International Financial Law Review* 13 (December 1994): 11–14.

9. Want Feng, "Company Registration Regs," *East Asian Executive Reports* 16 (15 November 1994): 7–9.

10. Yair Aharoni, "On the Definition of a Multinational Corporation," *Quarterly Review of Economics and Business* 11 (1971): 27–37.

11. Richard E. Caves, *Multinational Enterprise and Economic Analysis* (Cambridge: Cambridge University Press, 1982).

12. Christopher Nobes and Robert Parker, eds., *Comparative International Accounting*, 3rd ed. (Hempel, U.K.: Prentice Hall Ltd, 1991).

13. S. J. Grey, *Handbook of International Business and Management* (Oxford, U.K. and Cambridge, MA: B. Blackwell, 1990).

14. Vinod Bavishi, *Analyzing International Financial Statements: A Systematic Approach* (Princeton, NJ: CIFAR, 1987); presented at SLA Conference.

15. John D. Daniels, *International Business: Environments and Organizations,* 6th ed. (Reading, MA: Addison-Wesley, 1992).

16. Lee E. Preston and Duane Windsor, *The Rules of the Game in the Global Economy: Policy Regimes* (Boston: Kluwer Academic Publishers, 1992).

17. "The Global Firm: R.I.P.," *Economist* (6 February 1993): 6917.

18. Niran M. Vyas, William L. Shelburn, and Dennis C. Rogers, "An Analysis of Strategic Alliances: Forms, Functions and Framework," *Journal of Business and Industrial Marketing* 10, no. 3 (1995): 47–60.

19. V. N. Balsubrasmanyam, "Transnational Corporations and Business Strategy," Book Reviews, *Business History* 36, no. 3 (April 1994): 83.

APPENDIX **D**
Selecting a Company Directory—A Checklist

Listed below are data elements that may be included in a company directory. When evaluating a new source, either in print or in electronic format, use these items as a guide. You may want your source to emphasize the number of data items included or the number of companies described.

You may also be interested in the number of access points; that is, the number of ways you can "get at" the information.

For print sources, the arrangement of the basic text and the accompanying indexes and their organization are equally important. Also evaluate the source on its ability to handle the following questions:

- If you do not know the exact company name, can you still find the company in the source?
- If you are not sure of the product code, will you still find a listing of companies in the lines of business of interest to you?

Electronic sources on commercial services will invariably have more access points than printed sources. However, do not assume that because a data element is available in a computer readable source it automatically is searchable. For example, Disclosure/Worldscope includes standard numbers for companies, such as the SEDOL and VALOR, but they cannot be searched.

When evaluating a new product, be concerned with the data elements provided for individual records and the number and type of individual entries in the publication.

Data Elements

Different directories have few or almost all of the following data elements. Some will be more important to you than others.

- **Company name**
  Legal Name
  "Traded Name"
  Brand Name
  Entire Name or Set Number of Characters
  Name in Local Language, Name Translated into English, or Name Transliterated into English

- **Address**
  Incorporated Address
  Trading Address
  Mailing Address
  Headquarters Location
  Branches
  Country—Text or Code
  Language of Country Name or English

- **Products**
  Standard Numeric Codes
    U.S. SIC, U.K. SIC Codes, other standard country codes, NACE, Harmonized Tariff Schedule, producer derived codes such as IAC Codes or KOMPASS
  Product or Line of Business or Industry
  Language of Country or English

- **People**
  Chief Executive Officer / President / Managing Director
  Board of Directors
  Upper Management
  Trade Contacts

- **Financials**
  Turnover or Sales
  Capital
  Full Financials
  Public Equity / Public Debt
  Annual Date
  Date of Reported Data
  Local Currency / US $ / Standard Currency (ECU)
  Annual Statement Date
  Number of Years of Data

- **Affiliations**
  Parent / Subsidiary / Division
  Mergers & Acquisitions
  Financials—Sales Data for Affiliates

- **Standardized number**
  D-U-N-S Number
  Country Registration Number
  Equity Listing Number

- **Credit ratings**
  Available to Public
  On Request
  Large or Small Companies

- **Ranking**
  Within Industry/Product
  Within Country
  Within Region
  Internationally

- **Import/Export**
  Trading Partner Countries
  Trading Partner Companies
  Contact Names

Directory Scope and Content—Number and Type of Entries

- **What types of companies are included?**
  Legal Status
    Public or Private, Partnerships, State Enterprises, Nonprofit
  Size
    Large / Medium / Small; Largest, i.e., Top 25,000
  Active / Defunct

- **What geographic location is covered?**
  One City
  One Country
  One Country, but Part of a Series
  One Region
  One Continent
  Worldwide
  Industrial Nations
  Emerging Nations Political/Economic Organizations (e.g., EU)

- **How are the financials presented?**
  As Reported or Standardized
  Local Currency of Reporting Country
  Local Currency of Publisher
  Standard Currency
  User's Option

APPENDIX E
Company Definitions—A Glossary

The definitions listed below have been adapted from Dun's Marketing Services Business Definitions and European Union publications.

Branch: A secondary location of a business which reports to its headquarters. Both have the same name.

Company: A general term for all types of businesses.

Corporation: A legal form of business organization in which the company is a separate legal enterprise. Corporations issue shares of equities or bonds to individuals. Most corporations' issues are NOT traded to the public.

Division: A separate operating unit of a corporation. It may have its own officers and name, but it does not issue shares and it is not listed on an exchange.

Enterprise: A legally defined organization which has its own balance sheets, is subject to a directing authority and has been formed to carry out in one or more places one or more activities for the production of goods and services (EC); family of businesses under common ownership and control for which a set of consolidated financial statements is produced (from Statistics Canada).

Establishment: An enterprise or part thereof (whether located separately or not) that carries out a single activity which is characterized by the nature of the goods or services produced or by the essential identity of the production process employed, the activity being defined by a single SIC. (LKAU—local find of activity—EC). In smaller firms, generally under 100 employees, the enterprises and establishments are the same reporting units. Firms having over 500 employees have an average of four establishments each (*Enterprises in the EC*: 1990, p 2.1) In the U.S., a single operating location with at least one employee. Used by the U.S. Bureau of the Census for data gathering.

Headquarters: A business establishment where the executive offices of the corporation are located. In the U.K., this is the "registered office" as opposed to the trade office.

Holding Company: A company that owns or controls others. In the U.K. it implies that the company operates through its subsidiaries.

Listed Company: See "Publicly Held Company."

Partnership: A legal form of business enterprise in which two or more persons are co-owners of the business and share the profit and losses. Partners are liable for the actions of the firm.

Privately Held Company: Generally, a U.S. term to designate those enterprises whose shares are not traded openly to the public. Well over 90% of the world's enterprises are "privately held."

Proprietorship: A legal form of business enterprise in which one individual is the sole owner of the company.

Public Company: A company whose securities may be publicly traded. In the U.K., this is a PLC. There is no direct U.S. equivalent. In countries with state ownership, state-owned enterprises are sometimes referred to as Public Companies.

Publicly Held Company: The U.S. term for companies whose shares are traded on a stock exchange or are available to the public. Often referred to as a "Listed Company" in other countries.

Service Enterprise: Business services are material or non-material functions that are sold to another enterprise in order to contribute directly or indirectly to that enterprise's business activities (EC).

APPENDIX F
Size of Enterprises

Tables F.1 and F.2 emphasize the fact that most of the world's companies fall into the categories of micro or small to medium enterprises.

TABLE F.1

ENTERPRISES IN EUROPE—THIRD REPORT

COUNTRY	Type	Micro	SME	Large	Total	Micro	SME	Large
ALL EUR 12	Enterprises	13202099	1024066	12339	14238504	93	7	0.09
BELGIUM	Employers	156070	28742	470	185282	84	16	0.25
DENMARK	Legal Units	137447	16472	171	154090	89	11	0.11
GERMANY,W	Enterprises	1776436	265487	3512	2045435	87	13	0.17
GREECE	Estblshmts*	8300	64		8364	99		0.77
SPAIN	Enterprises	2142812	114510	850	2258172	95	5	0.04
FRANCE	Enterprises	1826827	146825	2095	1975747	93	7	0.11
IRELAND	Estblshmts*	1636	2973	38	4804	34	62	0.79
ITALY	Enterprises	1539798	50025	988	1590811	97	3	0.06
LUXEMBOURG	Enterprises	13276	2020	25	15321	87	13	0.16
NETHERLANDS	Econ. units	365637	35012	39786	397864	92	9	10.00
PORTUGAL	Enterprises	566198	36746	341	603285	94	6	0.06
U.K.	Enterprises	2459381	197785	2786	2659952	93	7	0.10
ICELAND	Enterprises*	19679	1053	91	20823	95	5	0.44
NORWAY	Enterprises	146948	12947	143	193849	76	7	0.07
AUSTRIA	Enterprises*	4763	9463	247	14473	33	65	1.71
FINLAND	Enterprises	109679	15425	448	125552	87	12	0.36
SWEDEN	Enterprises*	25640	3325	1078	29954	86	11	3.60
LIECHTENSTEIN	Local Units	491	59	0	550	89	11	0.00
SWITZERLAND	Enterprises	238192	37700	447	276339	86	14	0.16
USA	Enterprises	3889547	1422636	35314	5044808	77	28	0.70
CANADA	Enterprises*	755049	65800	1645	822494	92	8	0.20
JAPAN	Enterprises*	1201676	459163	46087	1706926	70	27	2.70
AUSTRALIA	Enterprises*	288720	66406	5774	360900	80	18	1.60

Notes:

Ireland	Nace 1-4; micro 3-9; 157 unreported
Austria	Total does not include 37849 companies which did not report size
Iceland	Micro is 1 to 9; Large is 100 and over
Norway	33811 not reported
Sweden	1991 data; classes are 0-19; 20-99; 100 and over
USA	Micro is 1-9
Canada	Micro is 1-19
Japan	1991 data; large is 100 and over
Australia	Large is 100 and over

Source: *Enterprises in Europe*, Third Report, 1990, vol. 1 and 2.

Duns International Market Identifiers, File 518 on DIALOG, has over 13 million companies. We used these files to approximate how many SMEs there were worldwide. We would expect companies in a commercial database to be generally larger than the population as a whole. Therefore it is interesting to note that in all of the D&B files, large companies comprise less than one percent of the database.

TABLE F.2

SIZE OF COMPANIES IN D&B DATABASES ON DIALOG BY NUMBER OF EMPLOYEES

		WORLD File 518 Number	Percent[2]	EUROPE File 521		CANADA File 520		ASIA-PAC[1] File 518		UNITED STATES File 516	
	NA[3]	4,838,157	36	4,377,053	57	131,820	18	361,866	60	1,874,397	15
Micro	**1-9**	**7,164,232**	**85**	**2,193,325**	**67**	**462,903**	**79**	**83,651**	**34**	**9,183,563**	**88**
SME	**10-499**	**1,136,158**	**15**	**1,046,800**	**32**	**128,809**	**22**	**153,349**	**62**	**1,247,324**	**12**
Small	10-99	972,066	13	939,273	29	118,634	20	127,294	52	1,142,275	11
Medium	100-499	164,092	2	107,527	3	10,175	2	26,255	11	105,049	1
Large	**≥500**	**46,341**	**0.5**	**30,273**	**0.9**	**2,816**	**0.4**	**8,733**	**0.4**	**29,835**	**0.3**
TOTAL	≥1	8,501,328		3,270,398		594,528		245,933		10,456,222	
TOTAL DATABASE		13,339,485		7,647,451		726,348		607,799		12,330,619	

1 Asia-Pacific is no longer a separate file; based on region=Australia/Asia
2 Percent of Micro, SMEs and Large are based on the total number of companies in the database with employee figures (Total - Not Available)
3 Percent of Not Availables based on total in database

CHAPTER 4
Directory Sources

TOPICS COVERED

- Selecting International Directories
- Basic Company Directories
- Industry-Specific Directories
- Product Directories
- Directors and Officers
- Finding Aids
- Company Histories
- Company Information When the Company Is Not Known
- Other Selected Directories
- Further Reading

MAJOR SOURCES DISCUSSED

- *Principal International Businesses*
- *World Business Directory*
- *D&B Europa*
- Graham & Whiteside Series
- Kompass International Editions
- *International Directory of Company Histories*

In Chapter 3, we described the problems of finding and identifying company information. We categorized directories by the types of information they include. A general understanding of the concepts in Chapter 3 should be helpful in evaluating directories. This chapter discusses several categories of basic directories and describes some recent publications, regardless of distribution format. Many of the titles we discussed in the first edition of *International Business Information* either are no longer being published or have not been updated.

Chapter 6 offers an overview of online and on-disc sources by commercial service providers. Check Chapter 6 for lists of electronic directory databases.

SELECTING INTERNATIONAL DIRECTORIES

Until recently, very few company directories offered worldwide coverage. One of the earliest, *Moody's International Manual*, was first published in 1971. Dun & Bradstreet's *Principal International Businesses* (*PIB*) followed in 1974. Publications from individual countries, such as *Kelly's Business Directory* (now titled *Kelly's*) and some Kompass International Editions, were available in libraries that needed detailed

product-level information from individual countries. International organizations such as the United Nations and the World Bank limited their annual publications to statistical sources.

Today, however, there are many company directories, both international and country-specific, from U.S. publishers, non-U.S. publishers, and the international organizations. These publications often are expensive. In emerging market areas, what you order today may be out of date before it arrives.

No single library can own all or even a large fraction of the published directories. No single research guide can discuss all directories in any depth. However, all libraries will need at least a few basic sources for company information. As an aid to decisions about purchasing, we have identified some important questions to ask before choosing an international directory.

- Who is the publisher? Because the market for international business information is now profitable, both new publishers and traditional reference publishers, such as Gale Research, have entered the international directory market. Whatever the size of your materials budget, stay away from unknown publishers and publications unless they are recommended by a reputable reviewer or you get to review a copy before purchase. Non-U.S. sources, are not automatically more accurate than U.S. sources or vice versa. Check the publisher's pricing history and its continuations record.

- What does the book cost? Do your users ask for information about international companies often enough to justify the purchase of a $500 volume, or would it be more efficient to search online for the occasional question?
- How many organizations/companies/people/products/countries are covered? Some directories cost more than others, but the more expensive sources may have more entries and more data items.
- How is the book organized? Most sources have at least three dimensions: country, company, and product/industry. What is the primary arrangement? How are the additional indexes arranged? Can you find what you need?
- If the book contains sales data, are the dates for those figures given? Are sales reported in local currency (e.g., French francs), converted to U.S. dollars, stated in a standard currency (ECUs), or in some combination of these methods? If the local figures are converted, is the exchange rate and date given?
- How well is the book documented? Are the criteria for inclusion presented? Are the methods of collecting the data described? One advantage of printed sources over electronic information is the quality and accessibility of the documentation.
- How timely is the material? How current is the information compared to the date of the publication?
- Who has actually compiled or collected the information? If it comes from other printed sources, are they clearly cited?
- Is there value added? Has the editor included additional information about the countries? Are there summary statistical data?

It is difficult to determine a directory's quality without examining it and using it. Ask the publisher for a 30-day trial. The cost of returning a volume is much less than the cost of buying and processing the wrong directory. Appendix D, at the end of Chapter 3, contains a checklist of directory data items.

BASIC COMPANY DIRECTORIES

Directories should be more than address books. Here are the pieces of information a basic company directory should contain:

- Name: legal or trading name, translated and/or transliterated
- Address: preferably with postal code
- Telecommunications: telephone, fax, e-mail, WWW site
- Principal officers and directors
- Lines of business, using a standard coding system
- Other data: sales/turnover and number of employees

International Directories

Principal International Businesses (published annually by Dun & Bradstreet)

The major provider of directory information worldwide is Dun & Bradstreet (D&B). In 1993, Dun & Bradstreet created one mega-international database worldbase, which serves as the basis of all its products. Information is gathered by non-U.S. affiliates of Dun & Bradstreet. Other D&B products are derived from this database.

The basic international company directory is *Principal International Businesses (PIB)*. Published annually, it includes directory information on more than 50,000 leading enterprises in 140 countries, selected on the basis of workforce size. The directory is easy to use and its layout is familiar to most U.S. users because of its similarities to D&B's *Million Dollar Directory*. The 1996 edition remained one volume, divided into three sections.

Section I: Businesses Geographically (white pages); alphabetically by country, and by company within the country

Section II: Businesses by Product Classification (yellow pages); by U.S. SIC codes and alphabetically by country, city, and then company name within each code with address and all SIC codes

Section III: Businesses Alphabetically (blue pages); one alphabetical listing of all companies, with names and addresses

PIB provides neither the number of countries covered nor a list or index to countries included. Some countries, Albania for example, listed only one company.

D&B selects companies for *PIB* on the basis of size, national prominence, and international interest to businesses outside their own country. No firm solicits a listing. A listing in this directory is not a credit endorsement by D&B. *PIB* is designed for use as a marketing tool.

The range of industries represented includes manufacturing, wholesale and retail trade, construction, mining, communications, power generation and distribution, agriculture and forestry, financial institutions, and other services. Autonomous government enterprises are also included. A sample entry includes as many as 13 data items.

1. D-U-N-S number
2. Import/export designation
3. Business name (complete or "acceptable" abbreviation)
4. Parent company name
5. Business address
6. Cable and telex
7. Telephone
8. Annual sales volume for latest year in local currency (M represents thousands). Note that the year is NOT given
9. Total number of employees
10. Ownership date
11. SIC code(s)
12. Lines of business
13. Chief executive's name and title

Three versions of *PIB* are available on CD-ROM: 70,000 largest companies worldwide based on employee size; 220,000 companies worldwide; or 450,000 companies. Company information is the same as in the print directory.

How is D&B handling the changing international scene and keeping its *PIB* records updated? D&B has added entries for the countries formed following the breakups of the former Soviet Union, Yugoslavia, and Czechoslovakia. Although D&B will acknowledge data collection problems in selected countries, it does not include this information in *PIB's* documentation.

Dun's Europe maintains a WWW site at http://www.dbeuro.com. Other D&B affiliates also have their own sites, linked to that home page. At least two of them, D&B U.K. and D&B Israel, offer free search services, with registration.

D&B U.K. offers a direct mail database, which provides basic information for all companies in their databank. Registration is necessary to search the basic directory. You can search by company name, location, SIC codes (a list is provided), employees, and turnover. Only 25 records are displayed. A record includes company name, contact name, address, legal status, line of business, registration number, telephone number, U.K. SIC, number of employees, and turnover. Additional information may be purchased from D&B U.K.

D&B Israel also has a site (http://www.dandb.co.il/) that is searchable by name, D-U-N-S number, and product classification. Registration is required. Output is a D&B record comparable to a basic electronic D&B record. Additional information is available for some companies.

World Business Directory (published annually by Gale Research Inc.)

The first important competitor to *PIB* appeared in mid-1992, Gale's *World Business Directory (WBD)*. It is compiled in conjunction with the World Trade Centers Association (WTCA). This four-volume set has information on more than 140,000 businesses in over 180 countries. About 25,000 U.S. companies are included in that total. Companies are selected based on their interest in international trade. Businesses in *WBD* are affiliated with World Trade Centers. The number of companies per country is approximately proportionate to each country's participation in world trade. Companies of all sizes are included.

Company information in *WBD* is collected from World Trade Centers, chambers of commerce, and trade officials. Companies respond to questionnaires, and information is gathered or verified by reviewing annual reports and through telephone interviews.

Financial data are presented as reported in the currency in which they are provided to Gale. A warning on differences in financial reporting, which appeared in the introduction to the first edition, is not in the introduction to the 1996 edition.

Volumes 1–3 are arranged by country with companies listed alphabetically within each country. Each entry may have the following information:

1. Company name
2. Alternative company name
3. Complete address
4. Telephone, fax, and telex numbers
5. WTC affiliation and network code
6. Executive officers' names and titles
7. Financial data and year of data
8. Employee figures and year of data
9. Type of organization
10. Fiscal year-end
11. Product lines based on Harmonized Codes
12. Industry activities based on U.S. SIC codes
13. Description of activity
14. Parent

Exhibit 4.1 displays a sample entry from *WBD*.

Hispano Suiza
Rue du Capitaine Guynemer
F-92270 Bois Colomes, France
Tel: 1 47605151 Fax: 1 47 813174
Officer(s): M Raymond Poggi, Director;
M De La Chapelle G Lamy, Mg. Dir; M
Olivier Fagard, Mgr. Dir; M Jean Pa-
raire Mgr. Dir; M Alex Fain, Mgr of
Finance. **Revenue:** 1,924,500,500 Fr
(1993). **Type:** Société Anoyme.**SIC(s):**
Management Services 8741. **Products:**
Aircraft Engines, Propeller Parts.

SAMPLE RECORD FROM *WORLD BUSINESS DIRECTORY (WBD)*

EXHIBIT 4.1

Source: World Business Directory 1996: 1317. Reprinted with permission from Gale Research.

Volume 4 of *WBD* contains three indexes:

1. Alphabetical by product grouping, using 2- and 4-digit Harmonized System codes, with companies listed alphabetically under each code
2. Numerical by 3-digit U.S. SIC codes, with companies listed alphabetically under each code
3. Alphabetical by company name list of companies

WBD is also available on Gale's *Companies International* CD-ROM. Gale will provide customized formats and media, such as magnetic tape or mailing lists. Gale may incorporate *WBD* into its *Gale's Business Resources* file on Galenet, http://www.galenet.com. The World Trade Centers Association maintains a public WWW site, http://www.wtca.org, in which it lists all of its members. It also maintains a members-only WWW site with access to multiple company online databases.

WBD covers more companies than *PIB* and costs less. *WBD* also includes dates for sales figures. This is useful since sales dates may range over at least three years for the same company. However, those figures may be either in U.S. dollars or the currency of the country.

WBD has been a positive addition to the category of international business directories, even though *WBD* does not have the experience of D&B and the D&B staff to back it, nor does it have the huge financial and credit database behind it. D&B, with its worldwide network, has difficulty maintaining the quality of data for all countries. The 1996 *WBD* indicates that Gale is at least aware of the issues necessary to create a quality business directory.

There is very little overlap in the companies covered in *PIB* and *WBD*. For a library that needs one

international company directory, *WBD* will be an alternative to *PIB* if its clientele is more interested in lists of trading partners than in identifying the major companies in a country. Many libraries will find both publications useful. Table 4.A compares features of the two directories, based on 1996 editions.

TABLE 4.A

COMPARISON OF *PIB* AND *WBD*

	PIB	*WBD*
Number of Entries	over 50,000	140,000
Number of Countries	143	180
Size of Firms	"large"	all sizes
Fax Number	No	Yes
Products	SIC	SIC and harmonized codes
Financials —Sales	Most entries	Some entries
Date for Figures	Not given	Given
Currency	Local	Local or U.S. Dollars
No. of Volumes	1	4
Purchase Agreement	Lease	Buy

Regional Directories

Two major publishers of regional international directories are Dun & Bradstreet and Graham & Whiteside Ltd. In addition to *PIB*, Dun & Bradstreet publishes continental directories and directories for individual countries.

Latin America 25,000 (published annually by D&B Worldbase Services)

One example of a regional directory is *Latin America 25,000: D&B's Handbook of Major Companies in the Region.* This is the third title D&B has used for its Latin American directory in the past five years. In 1994, we discussed *Key Business Directory of Latin America,* which had replaced *Dun's Latin America's Top 25,000 Companies.* Information is gathered in the same manner from 35 Latin American countries, but the majority of entries are from Venezuela and Mexico. Criteria for inclusion and industry coverage are the same as *PIB,* but there may be more companies listed per country. Records include the same data fields as *PIB.* The directory is published annually, but not all records are updated regularly due to problems with reporting. This one-volume directory is arranged in three parts:

Section I: Main entry, an alphabetical list by country and businesses within the countries arranged by U.S. SIC code. A company may be listed in as many as six codes.

Section II: Company name, country, and page(s).

Section III: The top 1,000 businesses, ranked by employee size.

D&B acknowledges having difficulty updating individual company records in Latin America. Because of this and the high rates of inflation in some countries, no sales figures are given in this directory. There is also no indication when a record has been updated. We spot-checked some entries in the 1996 edition of the book with DIALOG File 518 (D&B—International Dun's Market Identifiers, September 1996). None of the entries checked had been updated after June of 1994, and some had not been updated in 10 years!

There are two other regional titles in this series, Asia/Pacific and Western Europe. There are also three other directories in this series, a top 25,000 worldwide, and a top 25,000 each for manufacturing and service companies. All six titles are also available on CD-ROM.

D&B Europa (published annually by Dun & Bradstreet International)

Another D&B source is *D&B Europa*, first published in 1989 by International Duns in the U.K. This four-volume set includes approximately 60,000 companies from 19 European countries and Israel.

Volumes 1–3 are listings of companies by country. Countries are arranged alphabetically by European country codes. Volume 4 has European statistics, rankings, and indexes. Separate user guides are available in German, Spanish, French, and Italian.

The number of companies chosen for each country is based on the country's gross domestic product. The largest companies in each country are selected primarily on the basis of annual sales. Total assets are used to select banks, and commissions are used to select insurance companies.

D&B Europa describes more companies per country than sources of listed corporations. It lists fewer companies per country than many country-level directories or online files. For example, *Europa* has 10,400 French companies, while Worldscope CD-ROM has 686 French companies, and the French database, *French Company Full Financial Data,* has 573,000 French companies. Table 4.B displays country codes and the number of companies included per country in *D&B Europa 1996* for the 20 countries it covers.

TABLE 4.B

D&B Europa: Countries Included, Country Codes, and Number of Companies Listed

OS	AUSTRIA	1,520
BL	BELGIUM	1,82
DK	DENMARK	1,196*
FI	FINLAND	857*
FR	FRANCE	10,391*
DE	GERMANY	13,054
GR	GREECE	66
IC	ICELAND	64
IR	IRELAND	515
IS	ISRAEL	638
IT	ITALY	10,010
LX	LUXEMBOURG	101
NL	NETHERLANDS	2,574
NO	NORWAY	908
PO	PORTUGAL	705
ES	SPAIN	4,053*
SW	SWEDEN	2,094
CH	SWITZERLAND	2,524
TK	TURKEY	1,010
UK	UNITED KINGDOM	8,580*

*Indicates a drop in the number of companies from the 1993 edition.

Source: D&B Europa, 1996.

Companies are assigned to one of nine major industry/commercial sectors, with the largest group in manufacturing and the next largest in wholesale. Between 1993 and 1996, there was a slight increase in the percent of companies in construction and services industries, while there was an overall drop in the number of companies in agriculture and retail. Table 4.C shows the approximate number of companies listed for each of the nine industry/commercial sectors in *D&B Europa 1996*.

TABLE 4.C

Industry Sectors in *D&B Europa*

Commercial/ Industrial Sector	Approximate Number of Companies Listed
Agriculture	370*
Mining	415
Construction	2,900
Manufacturing	24,200
Transport/Communication	3,700
Wholesale	12,650
Retail	3,640*
Finance/Insurance	10,280
Services	5,085

*Indicates a drop in the number of companies from the 1993 edition.

Source: D&B Europa, 1996.

The following data elements may appear in a record in
D&B Europa 1996:

1. D-U-N-S Number
2. Importer-Exporter
3. Company name
4. Trading address
5./6. Phone, Fax
7. Telex
8. Company number
9. Legal status code
9A. Year started
10. Executives with function codes
11. Verbal activity
12. 1972 U.S. SIC codes
13. Percent sales export
14. Parent linkage-D-U-N-S number and Parent Name
15. Parent location
16. Nominal capital
17. Net worth
18. Profit or Loss
19. Sales-local currency
20. Sales ranking
21. Number of employees
22. Employee ranking
23. Bankers

Company number, the identifying number assigned within its country, more D-U-N-S numbers for the parent, and net worth are new or expanded fields. SIC codes were still based on the 1972 U.S. codes.

D&B Europa is also available on CD-ROM, through OneSource, and online through Questel, a French-language online system.

Dun & Bradstreet publishes over 50 directory titles. Many of these have corresponding CD-ROMs. Table 4.D shows the number of companies included, when known, in a selection of these directories, along with their prices. D&B has also published individual directories for Australia, China, Hong Kong, Israel, Norway, Taiwan, and most of the EU countries.

In addition to its many print directories, Dun & Bradstreet offers a wide range of electronic alternatives. Both print and electronic products are derived from Worldbase. Individual country data are standardized, and records are matched against worldwide corporate affiliation data. However, the actual database names, records included, and update cycles are not standard across databanks.

There are currently three non-U.S. D&B Market Identifier files on DIALOG: File 518, *International Dun's Market Identifiers (IDMI)*; File 521, *European Dun's Market Identifiers (EDMI)*; and File 520, *Canadian Dun's Market Identifiers*. Former File 522,

Asia/Pacific, has been eliminated as a separate database and the information has been incorporated in File 518. In September 1996, Dun & Bradstreet expanded its *IDMI* records on DIALOG to include additional financial data and the family linkages from Worldbase.

TABLE 4.D		
DUN & BRADSTREET SELECTED INTERNATIONAL COMPANY DIRECTORIES		
Print Title	Number of Companies	Print Price
25,000 Asia-Pacific Directory	25,000	$250*
25,000 Latin America Directory	25,000	$250*
25,000 Western Europe Directory	25,000	$250*
Key Business Series:		
Asia/Pacific Key Business Enterprises		$450*
Canadian Key Business Directory	20,000	$450
India Key Business Directory		$300
Indonesia and Thailand Key Business Directory		$295
Malaysia Key Business Directory		$295
Singapore Key Business Directory		$295
Guide to Canadian Manufacturers	10,000	$425
D&B Europa	60,000	$545*
D&B Europa Central Europe		$450
Key British Enterprises	50,000	$795
Principal International Businesses	50,000	$595*

* Also available on CD-ROM (CD-ROM prices differ from print prices)

Source: Information from Dun & Bradstreet, Inc., November 1996.

DataStar contains individual European country market identifier files and combines these directories into one European file (DBZZ). D&B has additional directory files on DataStar: *D&B Eastern Europe, D&B Canada, D&B Asia-Pacific, D&B Israel,* and *D&B U.S.* Finally D&B has added *European Financial Records,* which will be discussed in Chapter 5.

The D&B databases are loaded on Dow Jones in a menu-driven system. All international companies are in one file. D&B is a library on LEXIS-NEXIS Services. LEXIS-NEXIS Duns includes 42 million businesses from 220 countries from Worldbase. Businesses are arranged into all businesses, U.S. and non-U.S. files, regional files, and over 100 additional country files. There are direct links in the records from a subsidiary to its parent.

All electronic versions now include country-level registration numbers in addition to D-U-N-S numbers. The United Kingdom, France, Spain, Portugal, Turkey, Sweden, Hungary, and the Czech Republic are examples of countries where these unique numbers are available. A complete list of countries with registration numbers is given in LEXIS-NEXIS online guide description of the D&B files.

There are variations in the amount of information presented in different D&B products (see Table 4.E). For companies appearing in both the print *PIB* and in *Europa*, the latter has more data fields. The online records have recently been enhanced with extensive family linkages. The European files on DataStar may have different fields, coverage, and standardization than does *EDMI*. For example, Ireland and the U.K. have both U.K. and U.S. SIC codes, and the French database includes the French APE product codes. Although all of the directory products are based on Worldbase, some companies do *not* appear in all the online versions of *IDMI*.

Major Companies of Europe (published annually by Graham & Whiteside)

Major Companies of Europe is one directory of a "major companies" series published by Graham & Whiteside (formerly Graham & Trotman). The 1996–97 directory is in four volumes, divided alphabetically:

TABLE 4.E

COMPARISON OF D&B PRODUCTS FOR COMPANY PROFILE INFORMATION

	PIB Print 1996	*IDMI* Online 10/96	*D&B Europa* Print 1996	Questel 6/96
Company Name	x	x	x	x
Address				
Street	x	x	x	x
City	x	x	x	x
Region		x		
Country	x	x	x	x
Postal Code	x	x	x	x
Telecommunications				
Telephone	x	x	x	x
Telex/Cable	x	x	x	x
Fax		x	x	x
Business	x	x	x	x
Codes				
Primary Code	x	x	x	x
Secondary Codes	x	x		
Year Started	x	x	x	x
Employees	x	x	x	
Employee Ranking			x	
Financials				
Sales, Local	x	x	x	x
Sales U.S.		x		
Nominal Capital			x	
New Worth		x	x	
Net Gain/Loss		x	x	x
Sales Date		x	x	x
Sales Ranking				x
Conversion Rate Used		x		
D-U-N-S Number	x	x	x	x
Company Number		x	x	
Legal Status			x	
Subsidiary		x	x	
Private		x		
Parent Name	x	x	x	x
Parent City		x		x
Parent D-U-N-S		x	x	x
Ultimate Parent	x			
Officers				
Executives	CEO	10	2	6
Import-Export	x	x	x	x
Export Sales			x	x
Banker			x	

Volume 1: Austria, Belgium, Cyprus, Denmark, Eire, Finland, France

Volume 2: Germany, Greece, Israel, Italy, Liechtenstein, Luxembourg

Volume 3: The Netherlands, Norway, Portugal, Spain, Sweden, Switzerland

Volume 4: United Kingdom

The entire set has more than 20,000 companies and the names of over 150,000 executives. This is fewer companies than in *D&B Europa*, at a higher price. However, the records are enhanced with financial information. You may purchase individual volumes.

Entries are arranged alphabetically by country. Each volume has an alphabetical index to all companies in the volume, companies by country, and companies by SIC code within each country. Professional services such as accountants and lawyers, architecture and town planning, art and industrial design, and developmental agencies—not in the D&B directories—appear in this Graham & Whiteside series.

Companies submit information for inclusion. A company record consists of name, address, telecommunications numbers, chairperson and managing director, board members, principal activities, brand names and trademarks, parent company or subsidiaries (where applicable), and one or two years of brief financial information. The financial information may include: turnover, profits, authorized capital, paid-up capital, total balance, and total assets. Principal shareholders, bankers, date of establishment, and number of employees are also listed.

Table 4.F lists the titles in the series, with companies, prices, and edition dates included for comparison with Dun & Bradstreet publications (see Table 4.D).

TABLE 4.F

GRAHAM & WHITESIDE DIRECTORIES

	Number of Companies	Number of Countries	Price per Volume	Year	Edition	CD-ROM
MAJOR COMPANIES OF EUROPE*	20,000	20		1996–97	16	$2340
Vol. 1: A–F		7	$485			
Vol. 2: G–L		7	$485			
Vol. 3: N–S		6	$485			
Vol. 4: U.K.		1	$485			
MAJOR COMPANIES OF EUROPE SUBSIDIARIES	2,000 8,000		$485	1996	1	
MAJOR COMPANIES OF BENELUX	1,650	3	$380	1995–96		
MAJOR COMPANIES OF SCANDINAVIA	3,300	4	$450	1996–97	2	
MAJOR COMPANIES OF CENTRAL & EASTERN EUROPE & THE COMMONWEALTH OF INDEPENDENT STATES (with D&B)	8.000	23	$765	1996–97	6	$1170
MAJOR COMPANIES OF THE ARAB WORLD	7,000	20	$790	1996–97	20	$1600
MAJOR COMPANIES OF THE FAR EAST** and AUSTRALASIA	12,000	19	$1,350	1996–97	13	$1980
Vol. 1: Southeast Asia		8	$510			
Vol. 2: East Asia		8	$510			
Vol. 3: Australia and New Zealand		3	$330			
MAJOR COMPANIES OF ASIA	4,000	10	$395	1997	1	
MAJOR COMPANIES OF LATIN AMERICA	6,000	21	$665	1996	1	$990
MAJOR COMPANIES OF AFRICA SOUTH OF the SAHARA	4,000	42	$387	1996	1	$630

* $1750 for the set
**$1325 for the set

Source: Distributor's brochure, fall 1996.

For more detail on Graham & Whiteside titles, check the WWW site at http://www.major-co-data.com/direct/.

You may purchase all or any regions on a metered CD-ROM, available in the U.S. from Gale Research.

200,000 Graham & Whiteside companies from 116 countries are part of IAC's Corporate Intelligence database on DIALOG, DataStar, and LEXIS-NEXIS Services. The companies are also part of Business Insite on IAC's own fee-based WWW site, In-Site, http://www.iac-insite.com. Graham & Whiteside also publishes a series of industry titles covering financial institutions, chemical and petrochemical companies, energy companies, telecommunications companies, food and drink companies, and *Major Internet Companies.*

Europe's Medium Sized Companies Directory and Europe's Major Companies Directory (published by Euromonitor)

Better known for its marketing publications, Euromonitor published three company directories, *Europe's Major Companies Directory, Europe's Medium Sized Companies Directory,* and *World's Major Companies Directory.* These differ from the Dun & Bradstreet and Graham & Whiteside titles because they emphasize a company's products. *Europe's Major Companies Directory* includes 5,500 companies while *Europe's Medium Sized Companies Directory* includes 6,500 companies. The one-volume *World's Major Companies Directory* includes North and South America, Africa, the Middle East, Asia, and Oceania, as well as Europe. Arrangement in the directories is alphabetical by country. Companies are selected to represent the main sectors of a country's economy and are ranked by sales converted to U.S. dollars. Criteria varies by country, as illustrated below.

SALES/TURNOVER (Mil US$)		
Major Companies	*Medium-Sized Companies*	*Country*
100 and over	10–100	Greece, Portugal
150 and over	10–149	Austria, Belgium, Denmark, Finland Ireland, Netherlands, Norway, Sweden, Switzerland
150 and over	50–149	Spain
200 and over	50–199	Italy
300 and over	50–299	France, Germany, U.K.

A typical entry includes name, address, communications, activity, ownership, subsidiaries, key personnel, employees, three years of turnover, and profit.

Also included are main products, brands, trading names, and notes covering company news and recent developments. Company reports, financial press and trade journal articles, and direct contact are methods used to compile the information. Listings of top companies per country are also included. Exhibit 4.2 is a sample entry from *Europe's Major Companies Directory.*

Euromonitor claims to have contacted all the companies listed in the directories to ensure that all the information is correct and fully up-to-date.

Hispano-Suiza
Address 333 Bureaux de la Colline, F-92213 Saint-Cloud Cedex
Telephone: +33 1 46027065
Fax: + 33 1 46028373
Activity: aircraft manufacturer
Parent company: Snecma
Key personnel: Raymond Poggi (president and managing director)
Financial information:

FRF(millions)	1991	1992	1993	1994
Turnover			7,500	

EUROPE'S MAJOR COMPANIES DIRECTORY

EXHIBIT 4.2

Source: Europe's Major Companies Directory, 1996. Reprinted with permission of Euromonitor.

Directory of European Business (published by Bowker-Saur)

In 1993, Bowker-Saur published *Directory of European Business*, which combines information on 33 countries with directory information for 4,000 companies. The companies include the top 5 to 10 firms in selected product categories in each country.

There is only one index, an alphabetical listing of all organizations. This directory is a potpourri—a little of this, a little of that, but not much of anything. It is still in print, but Bowker-Saur does not have plans to update it in the foreseeable future.

Eastern Europe / Former Soviet Union Company Information

The breakup of the Soviet Union and the move toward market economies has led to increased interest in this region for business researchers. However, the demand for information and the supply of accurate, reliable information are still far apart.

We hesitate to recommend that any library purchase directories for companies in Eastern Europe. We are unsure about the reliability of the data, the use of translation or transliteration for company names, and even the continued existence of companies once the directories are published. The one directory we recommended in the previous edition, *SBID: The Business Directory for the Soviet Union,* is no longer available because—according to the publisher, FYI—the information is too hard to update and verify.[1] FYI, a consulting firm still active in the former Soviet Union, recommends that clients ask the following questions when researching companies in this region for potential business partners:

- If they are private, why did they become private?
- How independent are they? Do they set their own prices?
- Do they choose their own suppliers?

MZM World Business Directory (compiled by MZM Publishing Co., Sopot, Poland, 4th ed., 1995)

MZM World Business Directory, subtitled *The ex-Socialist World Business Directory,* was first published in 1986. It covers 33 countries, those from the former Soviet Union, Czechoslovakia, and Yugoslavia, as well as Cuba, Mongolia, Vietnam, China, and North Korea. The index is in English and German. The company section is preceded by "General Business Information," a listing of Western organizations involved in trade with the East, along with their founding dates.

Country chapters range from three pages for some of the former Soviet Republics to almost 100 pages for Russia. Entries are very brief, including name, address, and subsidiaries. A sample entry appears in Exhibit 4.3. Within each country, organizations are arranged by topic; these topics relate to trade and business services, not manufacturing. Sample topics are Business Information, Recommended Publications, Foreign Trade Companies, and Advertising Marketing and Publishing Agencies. Banks, insurance companies, forwarders, travel services, and auditing, accounting, and law firms operating in the country are listed.

INSURANCE COMPANIES

RUSSIAN INSURANCE ASSOCIATION (1992)
HO: c/o Rosgosstrakh Inc, 20/21 Petrovka St, 103381 Moscow, Russia; ph: (095) 299-2942

AMERICAN INTERCONTINENTAL LIFE INSURANCE CO.
HO: 8, B. Sadovaya St, 103379 Moscow, Russia; ph:(095) 209-2042

MZM World Business Directory: Sample Entries for Russia

EXHIBIT 4.3

Source: MZM World Business Directory, 1995. Sample provided by publisher.

This publication does not stand up to any of our quality checks. There is no explanation of how companies are selected for inclusion. Information given is minimal. However, it is in a fourth edition, many international trade organizations use it, and it brings together companies in countries for which any print information is difficult to find. Sources given are useful as additional finding aids for company information and also as a source for importing and exporting information, covered in Chapter 12.

Manufacturing & Servicing Companies—Russian CCI Members 1996–1997

Manufacturing & Servicing Companies is a CD-ROM from the Russian Business Cooperation Network Corporation (RBCNET). According to RBCNET's brochure, companies on the CD-ROM are members of the Russian Chamber of Commerce and Industry. An entry includes company names, addresses, contacts, telecommunications, and types of business. Information about the chambers of commerce of CIS countries and statistical and economic data for Russia are also included on the CD-ROM.

Lithuanian Companies and Organizations (LITCOM)

Many new companies are offering specialized directories for countries from the former Soviet Union. One such publication is *Lithuanian Companies and Organizations (LITCOM)*, which contains 4,500 enterprises and organizations. The Lithuanian Information Institute compiles *LITCOM* and John P. Williams & Company in Bryn Mawr, Pennsylvania, distributes it in the United States. The directory is designed for specialists and businesspersons who seek potential partners. The directory includes general information about Lithuania, with contact numbers for local government and transportation organizations. The main section of the book is an alphabetical list (by Lithuanian name) of companies, with address, contact numbers, chief executive officer, legal type, employees, and subsidiaries and assets where available. There is a description of the company's products/services and import/export activities and indexes to these activities using ISIC codes. Below is a sample index entry for imports.

---

36 FURNITURE
3610 Furniture
beds
Belgium, France * 1574

Yellow Pages Moscow (published annually by Claudius Verlagsgesellschaft, commissioned by Telecom Joint Stock Company)

Yellow Pages Moscow is issued in Russian as well as English. It is arranged by products, with an index to advertisers, subject headings, and a section on general Moscow information. No indication is given if the names are translated or transliterated.

An entry includes name, address, and phone and/or fax number. Below is an entry from the 1993/94 *Yellow Pages Moscow,* under the heading, Joint Ventures.

> Formost-Progress (Russia–Canada)..address, phone and fax

Other Print Directories

In addition to *SBID*, several other Eastern European sources we discussed in our first edition have not been updated including Gale's *Eastern European Business Directory*, which is still in print. The two Probus directories, *U.S.-Soviet Trade Directory* and *U.S.-East European Trade Directory: An Invaluable Reference for Conducting Business in Poland, Hungary, Czechoslovakia, Bulgaria, Yugoslavia, Romania, & Albania* are no longer in print. Two individual country directories, *100 Bulgarian Companies* (Sofia, Bulgaria: IS Information Services Corporation, 1991–92) and the *General Trade Index & Business Guide, Poland* (Toronto and Warsaw: Business Foundation Co., 1991) also never had second editions.

Individual Country Directories

Company directories are published for a wide range of individual countries. Sources such as *European Markets, Asian Markets,* and *Latin American Markets,* from Washington Researchers Publishing, list pan-continental and individual country directories.

We used FIND/SVP's slim volume, *How to Find and Use International Business Information,* as a source to locate new titles. The FIND/SVP book is a compilation of articles from its newsletter, *The Information Advisor.* Many of the titles it lists are either no longer being published or have not been updated.

Another source of individual country directories are articles in *Business Information Review;* one example is "Business Information in Denmark," published in the September 1996 issue.

INDUSTRY DIRECTORIES

All the directories discussed so far include companies representing a range of business activities. Other specialized directories are arranged by business activity.

These may include companies within a broad industry grouping or within a specific activity. Coverage may be international, regional, or country specific. Table 4.G lists different types of industry directories with a sample title for each type.

TABLE 4.G		
TYPES OF INDUSTRY DIRECTORIES		
Region/Country	**Industry Sector**	**Activity**
International	*Best's International Insurance Directory*	*Polk's World Bank Directory*
Regional	*Offshore Finance Yearbook*	*European Retailers*
National	*Manufactured Products* (South Africa)	*Wine and Beer* (Australia and New Zealand)

International Industry Directories

Service industry directories predominate in this class. Major titles include *Best's International Insurance Directory, Standard Directory of International Advertisers and Agencies* (described in Chapter 11), and *Polk's World Bank Directory.* One exception to services is D&B's *Top 25,000 Manufacturing Companies.*

Polk's World Bank Directory (100th ed., 1995/96, published by R. L. Polk & Co.)

Polk's World Bank Directory includes known banks and branches worldwide, from the Aaland Islands through Zimbabwe. It also has a section of the 1,000 largest U.S. banks. This book includes advertising displays. Information is derived from the firms themselves, government authorities, or other sources the "publisher regards as reliable." The information has not been verified by the publisher.

Banks are arranged alphabetically by country, and then by city or town. *Polk's* notes that "An effort is made to include the complete bank name (under the English and local title)." Though primarily a finding aid for banks and their branches, *Polk's* has financial information, which was expanded in the 1995/96 edition. Where it is available, the financial data appear under the listing for the head office. The data are nonconsolidated. It has an abbreviated Statement of Condition (Balance Sheet) plus highlights from the Profit and Loss Statement, and key ratios. It is reported in the bank's home currency as originally reported and also in U.S. dollars. An asterisk is used to indicate "not meaningful data" when percentages exceed positive or negative 999.99. All entries include the name, address, communications numbers, SWIFT code, established dates, hours, number of branches, representative offices, officers, and directors. Five years of information on discontinued banks with an explanation of what happened to them is also available. Several other banking sources are discussed in Chapter 5.

Directory of the World's Largest Service Companies (published by Moody's, in conjunction with the United Nations Centre on Transnational Corporations, 1990). Recognized in the first edition of *International Business Information* as an important compilation, this directory is no longer in print.

Regional Industry Directories

Graham & Whiteside's "Major Industry" Directories

In addition to their "major company" series, Graham & Whiteside also have a series of "major industry" publications arranged by region. The chart below shows the different titles in the series and the regions for which there are editions.

	Europe	Far East & Australasia	Arab World
Major Financial Institutions of . . .	X	X	X
Major Petrochemical Companies of . . .	X	X*	
Major Energy Companies of . . .	X	X*	
Major Telecommunications Companies of . . .	X*	X*	
Major Food & Drink Companies of . . .	X	X	

*These titles have about 500 companies; all the rest have about 1,000.

European Wholesalers and Retailers

Two current English language print directories cover the European wholesale and retail industries. Although the coverage of the directories overlaps to some extent, each has unique features. The *European Directory of Retailers and Wholesalers* covers both sectors. *European Retailers* looks at retailers and their worldwide buyers.

European Directory of Retailers and Wholesalers (published by Euromonitor, 2nd ed. 1995; a new edition is scheduled for 1997)

This directory and sourcebook gives as much emphasis to where to locate additional information on the

retail and wholesale industries as on the major companies. It does list 3,000 companies from 25 Western and Eastern European countries. Many of the companies are department stores or retail chains. In 1995, Euromonitor published a companion volume, *World Retail Directory,* which lists 2,000 retailers. Entries include number of outlets, subsidiaries, chief executives, and some financial performance data.

Directory of European Retailers (published by Newman Books, London; 19th biennial edition, 1994–95)

This directory covers major retailers in 21 countries, from Andorra to Yugoslavia. Although the publisher is not well known in the United States, the book has been published for many years. The "How to Use" section is in five languages. The directory includes:

- Trade associations and other professional bodies
- Buying agents worldwide
- Commercial representatives overseas
- Retail journals by country

The publisher claims to include all significant European retail companies. All entries for the companies contain addresses and telephone numbers. Additional data items may be: proprietors, trading names, head office, buying office, type of trade, employees, selling area, chief executives and buyers, and number and location of stores. Towns are given in their native form. See Exhibit 4.4 for a sample entry.

CASA PEREZ SA, (Prop. Family Perez, T/A Grans Magasins Pyrenees. Automobils Pyré nées. Pyrénées Import Export)Avinguda Meritxell 11, P.O. Box 23 Andorra la Vella. **Tel.** 20414; **Fax** 26978 **Telex:** 205; Supermarkets and department stores; **Staff** 1,263 **Ch.**Jacquelline Perez.**Man. Dir.** Philippe Bergeron; **Buyers; Sports, Camping** C. Rondel...**Fancy Jewels** S. Ordoñez. **Grans Magatzems Pyrénées Assoc.** Printemps, Paris; 15,000 sq m... **Other Group Companies: Pyrénées Import-Export** Sole agent... French Forwarding Agent: **Pyretransit...**

EXTRACT FROM SAMPLE ENTRY FOR ANDORRA FROM *DIRECTORY OF EUROPEAN RETAILERS*

EXHIBIT 4.4

Source: Directory of European Retailers 1994/54: 61. Reprinted with permission.

Possible subject headings for types of retail establishments within a country listed in *Directory of European Retailers* include:

- Department & Variety Stores & Large Specialty Shops
- Specialty Chains in Non-Food
- Hypermarkets & Superstore Chains & Groups
- Restaurant & Fast Food Chains
- Mail Order Firms, Home Shopping & Catalogue Showrooms
- Franchising
- Wholesaling of Food & Non-Food (including Cash & Carry Warehouses)
- Voluntary Groups & Chains (Wholesale & Retail)
- Retail Buying & Services Groups
- Consumer Cooperative Societies

Information is collected by questionnaire. There is no charge for inclusion, though there are advertisements. Mailing lists may be purchased directly from the publisher.

European Wholesalers and Distributors Directory
(published by Gale, 1992)

This directory has entries from 20 Western European countries, five former Eastern bloc countries, and countries from the former USSR. Many of the companies are also listed in Gale's *World Business Directory*. The book is still in print but no second edition has been announced.

Euro-RETAILNET (Corporate Intelligence on Retailing)

This source does not fall into the strict category of directory. However, *Euro-RETAILNET*, an online database of information on U.K. and European retailers, has over 3,000 company profiles, with textual information on background and history, sectors, outlets and distribution, foreign activities, and products, in addition to directory information and financial data. *Corporate Intelligence on Retailing in the UK and Europe* is also a database on DataStar. Further information is available at http://www.cior.com.

European Consulting Firms

In 1994, two European titles covered consulting, an activity of interest to many business clients.

European Directory of Management Consultants

This directory, published first by TPFL in 1990 and now by AP Information Services, is in its fourth edition. The AP directory describes 3,500 consulting firms from over 35 European countries. Croatia and Israel are new to the 1997 edition. Each entry lists address, phone and fax numbers, e-mail address, directors, partners, principals and senior staff, date established, languages spoken, major clients, company activities, offices in that country and overseas, up to 25 areas of specialization, and up to 10 industry areas. Main entry is by country with indexes by specialization area, industry area and company name. AP Information Services also publishes directories of management consultants in the U.K. and U.S.

European Consultants Directory and Consultants and Consulting Organizations Directory

In 1991 Gale issued *European Consultants Directory*, with 5,500 consultancies in 34 countries. Although still in print, it has not been updated. *Consultants and Consulting Organizations Directory*, published by Gale for the U.S. market, includes about 500 Canadian consulting firms. The main entry is under broad subject grouping. It includes directory information and a variety of consulting services. There is also a geographical index.

PRODUCT DIRECTORIES

The directories listed above are arranged by broad industry grouping. Often our clients need lists of companies arranged by very specific product grouping.

Who manufactures gas springs in Europe?

Where are the egg producers in the United Kingdom?

While the directories listed below cover a wide range of products, they are organized for the user to find companies in specific product lines.

There is no international equivalent of the *Thomas Register of American Manufacturers,* but there are sources that give detailed lists of a company's products and categorize products by type. It is the detailed product grouping that makes these publications so useful.

Kompass Publications

Kompass, part of Reed Information Services, is probably the most widely known provider of product directories outside the United States. There is no single publisher of Kompass. Publication is coordinated by a holding company in France, which awards the directory franchise to a publisher in each country that is covered. We generally associate Kompass with Reed Information, the primary distributor of the electronic versions of Kompass. There are Kompass directories covering about 12 million companies in 60 countries worldwide. One of the newest editions is Kompass U.S. Each publication has volumes arranged both by product/service with unique charts and by companies.

TABLE 4.H

KOMPASS Registers 1996

COUNTRY	1996 EDITION	NUMBER OF COMPANIES	PRICE
ALGERIA	1st	12,600	$ 225
AUSTRALIA	22nd	30,000	325
AUSTRIA	1st	25,000	440
AZERBAIJAN	1st	1,200	160
BAHRAIN	2nd[a]	2,000	160
BELARUS	2nd	6,000	215
BELGIUM	30th	24,000	425
BRAZIL	1st	NA	NA
BRUNEI	3rd	NA	NA
BULGARIA	1st	6,200	175
CANADA	2nd[d]	30,000	
CHINA	2nd	55,000	475
CROATIA	3rd	12,500	275
CYPRUS	1st	8,300	170
CZECH REPUBLIC	1st	8,000	225
DENMARK	32nd	15,000	225
EGYPT	1st	18,000	340
ESTONIA	2nd	2,500	160
FINLAND	3rd	14,500	295
FRANCE	59th	115,000	550
GERMANY	20th	52,000	450
GREECE	28th	24,000	325
HONG KONG	2nd[a]	7,000	NA
HUNGARY	1st	24,300	250
ICELAND	2nd	NA	NA
INDIA	2nd	60,000	350
INDONESIA	8th	NA	NA
IRAN	*	30,000	360
IRELAND	5th	16,700	325
ISRAEL	6th	15,000	235
ITALY	31st	50,000	445
JAPAN	4th[b]	11,000	NA
KAZAKHSTAN	2nd	4,500	180
KOREA	3rd	15,000	250
KUWAIT	1st	4,000	160
LATVIA	3rd	3,500	160
LIBYA	1st 9-96	1,800	NA
LITHUANIA	4th	5,500	160
LUXEMBOURG	13th	2,050	275
MALAYSIA	15th	23,800	295
MALTA	1st	2,000	195
MEXICO	1st	NA	NA
MOLDAVIA	2nd	1,500	175
MONACO	3rd	2,300	175
MOROCCO	13th	8,000	200
NETHERLANDS	27th	25,000	325
NEW ZEALAND	5th	11,299	250
NORWAY	23rd	16,000	250
OMAN	1st	10,000	195
PHILIPPINES	3rd	14,000	225
POLAND	1st	38,000	350
PORTUGAL	1st	8,500	475
QATAR	1st	2,000	195
ROMANIA	2nd	7,000	195
RUSSIA	1st[c]	10,000	375
SAUDI ARABIA	1st	21,000	295
SINGAPORE	15th	18,300	220
SLOVAKIA	*	16,000	250
SLOVENIA	4th	9,500	275

TABLE 4.H (continued)			
KOMPASS REGISTERS 1996			

COUNTRY	1996 EDITION	NUMBER OF COMPANIES	PRICE
SOUTH AFRICA	3rd	15,000	250
SPAIN	22nd	33,000	325
SWEDEN	25th	17,000	250
SWITZERLAND	42nd	48,000	325
TAIWAN	2nd	25,000	275
THAILAND	4th	20,000	325
TUNISIA	1st	11,000	335
TURKEY	12th	16,000	235
UKRAINE	1st	8,500	225
UNITED ARAB EMIRATES	4th	8,100	195
UNITED KINGDOM	30th	44,000	450
UNITED STATES	1st	55,000	375
VIETNAM	1st	3,200	195
YUGOSLAVIA	3rd	12,000	225
		1224149[e]	17665

a Last updated 1990; b Last updated 1994—no franchisee listed; c WWW site also lists KOMPASS St. Petersburg; d Last updated 1992; e Totals do not include non-updated files.

Many are published in conjunction with sponsors, such as the Export Council of Norway or the Confederation of British Industry. The first Kompass directory was published for France over 60 years ago.

Table 4.H lists the Kompass international editions available through June 1996. Kompass has been adding new editions every year. Most editions are updated annually, although some, like Brunei and Japan, have been updated less frequently. To own the entire series would cost over $15,000.

For the most up-to-date information on individual Kompass titles, with the name and address of the Kompass franchisee, latest and upcoming edition, and number of companies, check http://www.kompass-intl.com/html/worldmap.html.

As an example of a typical Kompass directory, we will describe the *UK Kompass Register* in detail. The present edition of the *UK Kompass Register* is in five volumes, with the first two standard to the series. It is published in conjunction with the Confederation of British Industry. Industrial or industrial service companies with 10 or more employees, doing business nationally, are included in the UK Kompass *Register*.

Volume I Details of 41,000 different products and services offered by British industrial companies

Volume II Corporate information on 42,000 leading companies in British industry

Volume III Latest three years of financial information for 30,000 companies

Volume IV 100,000 parents and their subsidiaries

Volume V Details on 25,000 companies and 100,000 registered trade names

Using a Kompass directory is awkward. First, you must go to the alphabetical product index to find a unique 7-digit code. Second, locate the 5-digit table. The final two digits reference the column in the product grid. Then go to the company index to find more information about the company. Exhibit 4.5 presents a sample entry.

Companies are arranged alphabetically by town, within county. In addition to company name, address, and products, other possible data elements in *UK Kompass Register* entries include:

• Names of ultimate and holding companies
• Employees for the group
• Agents for firm's products
• Trade names
• Locations: Registered, sales, branches, and factory
• Products for which the firm acts as agent in U.K. and overseas
• Group details
• Other information, e.g., type of computer
• Quality assessment awarded

20-26.0 _____ 20.26.0

Egg Products	2 Egg Milk Powder	5 Egg Yolk, Liquid	8 Eggs, Frozen	12 Egg Whites,
	3 Egg White Powdered	6 Egg Whole, Dried	9 Eggs in Shells	Frozen
	4 Egg Yolk Dried	7 Egg Whole, Liquid	11 Custard Powders	

	E I	1 2 3 4 5	6 7 8 9 11	12
*C P C(United Kingdom) Ltd Claygate Hse Esher KT10 9PN				•
Deans Farm Bridgeway Hse Upper Ickneld Way Tring HP23 4JX			•	
>Framptons Ltd Charlton Rd Shepton Mallet BA4 5PD	•	• • • •	• • •	•
Macphie of Glenbervie Ltd Glenbervie Stonehaven AB3 2YB				•
Richlea Eggs Ltd 221 Hillhall Rd Lisburn BT27 5JD	•		•	
Thames Valley Eggs Ltd Membury Newbury RG16 7TX				•

> indicates expanded entry in volume 2   * denotes member of Confederation of British industry

E Export **I** Import

• Manufacturer   • Distributor or agent

UK KOMPASS REGISTER PRODUCT ENTRY

EXHIBIT 4.5

Source: Extracted from *UK Kompass Directory* vol. 1, 1992: 36. Reprinted with permission from KOMPASS.

Exhibit 4.6 shows a company entry for one of the companies in Exhibit 4.5. The electronic record includes additional information in the company record such as the registered office's address, legal status, incorporation date, bank(s), two years of key financials, "additional information," which is often a location, e.g., "2 mins roundabout off A41 in Tring, on Ind Est," and the date of the record change.

Kompass is available from a variety of electronic sources. In 1996, there were six individual Kompass files on DIALOG and one combined file, Kompass.

File Name	File Number	Load Date	Number of Companies
Kompass Western Europe	File 590	May 96	35,9861
Kompass UK	File 591	April 96	132,683
Kompass Asia/Pacific	File 592	March 96	385,429
Kompass Central/ Eastern Europe	File 593	March 96	135,994
Kompass Canada	File 594	1993 2Q	28,941
Kompass USA	File 584	May 1996	53,581
Kompass Middle East/ Africa/Mediterranean	File 585	July 1996	80,000

(searched June and July 1996)

In January 1997, the Canadian file had still not been updated.

Kompass is also available electronically, directly from Reed on REEDBASE. The REEDBASE Kompass covers about 750,000 companies from over 30 countries. The CD-ROMs are listed in Table 4.I.

Tring

Deans Farm,
Bridgeway Hse, Upper Ickheld Way, Tring HP23 4JX
Tel: (0442)891811
Telex: 826916 DEANS G
Facsimile No: (0442)891880
Bank: National Westminster, 15 Bishopgate, London
Directors: P.D. Dean (MD) N Dean (Ops) P D Challands (Mktg) J W Grundy (Sales)
Co Reg No: 672991 **Turnover** £20-£50M
Employees: 990 (Estb)
Product Groups: 20

UK KOMPASS REGISTER COMPANY ENTRY

EXHIBIT 4.6

Source: Extracted from UK Kompass Directory. Reprinted with permission from KOMPASS.

TABLE 4.I

REEDBASE KOMPASS CD-ROMs

	Companies	Countries	Products	Contacts	Search Criteria
Asia-Pacific	400,000	14	40,000	400,000	26
Europe	360,000	15	110,000	950,000	18
Eastern Europe	150,000	15	40,000	198,000	24
UK	200,000	1	45,000	350,000	60
EUREKAA	188,000	10	110,000	38	

Source: Company information, December 1996.

In addition to regions listed in Table 4.I, a Middle East and Africa will be available in mid-1997. REEDBASE CD-ROM tries to maintain the look and feel of the underlying print sources, so the terminal display actually maintains the format of Exhibit 4.5.

REEDBASE has released two other CD-ROMs, BANKbase CD and EUREKAA, European Kompass Accounts and Acquisitions. The CD-ROMs can be purchased once, annually, biannually, or quarterly. They can be networked either by simultaneous user or number of workstations requiring access. The CD-ROM output is metered. The French compiler issues a Kompass France.

What distinguishes Kompass products from other international directories is their very detailed product listings. Kompass has its own coding system, organized at the 2-, 5- and 7-digit level. Note in Table 4.J that the first few categories resemble U.S. SIC codes. Also note the emphasis on the manufacturing sector. Kompass online files also indicate if the company is a producer, distributor, supplier, importer, or exporter for each product; the language spoken; and the date the record was updated.

TABLE 4.J

KOMPASS PRODUCT CODES

Codes	Industry Group
01-09	Agriculture and Fisheries
11-19	Raw material extraction Industries
20-21	Food and Beverages
22-24	Textiles and apparel
25-28	Wood, Paper, and Publishing
29-32	**Rubber, Plastics and Chemicals**
33-36	Metal, Glass, and Ceramics
37-38	Electrical, Electronics, and Optics
39-47	Machinery and Transport equipment
48	Engineering sub-contractors
51-59	Construction and Public Utilities
61-69	Wholesale and Distribution
71-79	Transport services
80-89	Service Industries

30 Plastic Products	
30010	**Synthetic Resins**
30020	Misc. Resins
30080	Pre-processing of plastics
30090	Recycling of plastics
30100	Semi-finished plastics
	...
30950	Plastic Industry Sub-contractors x work
30955	Plastic Industry Sub-contractors x article
3001001	Rubbers, acrylic
3001002	Rubbers, synthetic, Butadiene-Acrylonitrile

Among the different Kompass groups and companies, differences exist in the classification of products and services. While all files now use 7-digit codes definitions, even at the 2-digit level, codes vary among the files. A brief example follows.

Files	Product Code/Product Name
U.S., U.K., and Europe	**36**17054 Springs,wire,coil; helical wire springs
Asia, Canada and Eastern Europe	**35**72002 Wire springs,coil, helical wire springs

Worldwide standardization to a 9-digit level is in progress with a target date of 1998. Because the codes are so specific, it is important for researchers to know their products.

Some individual Kompass franchisees have WWW sites of their own with information. Examples are listed below.

Publishers catalogs	France	http://www.kompass.fr
Company information	Ireland	http://www.kompass.ie
Country wide yellow and white pages	Luxembourg	http://editus.lu/html
Company information registration;some fees	United Arab Emirates	http://www.kompass-uae.com

Europages (Eurédit S.A.)

Europages is a series of pan-European product directories, with a print directory, two CD-ROMs, and a WWW site. All products are available in English, German, French, Italian, Spanish, and some also are available in Dutch. The 14th edition of *Europages Directory* was published in 1997. It is a single volume containing 500,000 companies from 30 countries. The directory is available in each of the six languages, with the largest distribution in German. According to *Europages*, "Companies are listed in *Europages* according to their capacity to export (i.e., export turnover, presence in international fairs, ...).[2] A basic listing is free, but payment is required for an extended listing.

The print directory is now available as *Europages-Direct 500,000* CD-ROM. It covers all EU countries and most other countries from Russia westward. The CD-ROM includes company name, address, and product list, and for some records, turnover and employees. Output is metered and designed for mailing lists. A second CD-ROM is *Europages 150,000 European Suppliers*, covering 25 countries.

For the business researcher who occasionally needs access to European companies, primarily on the basis of product, the *Europages* WWW site, http://www.europages.com, is the place to go. The site is searchable by product or service, activity, or sector, company name, or country. The Web site also offers a limited number of company catalogs arranged by major industry sector. Though this WWW site is no match for full-service databases such as *Kompass, Dun's Market Identifiers*, or *ABC Europe*, it can be used as a starting point for researchers or libraries with limited resources. Other features at this site include daily business news, trade fairs, and economic and sectorial data.

European CD-ROM Product Directories

Thomas Register of European Manufacturers on CD-ROM

While we noted above that there is no international equivalent to *Thomas Register of American Manufacturers*, Thomas International Publishing has produced the *Thomas Register of European Manufacturers on CD-ROM*. This CD-ROM covers 130,000 companies, arranged under 9,500 product groupings, in 12 European countries. The countries in which you can search by native language are France, Germany, Italy, The Netherlands, Spain, and United Kingdom. Also included are companies from Belgium, Denmark, Greece, Ireland, Luxembourg, and Portugal. Unique to this product is the ability to search in either American or British English. Access is only by company name or product. Company record includes name, address, and telecommunications, but no list of products. Therefore, you cannot retrieve a known company and find its competitors. Product listings are very specific. For example, there are 30 entries under "aircraft," from aircraft antenna, cables, and connectors, to aircraft toilets, windows, and wings. Geared toward an end-user market, the software allows the user to pull up a company record, add a note, and print off a form that is ready to be faxed.

Thomas International Publishing also publishes many magazines that cover specific product markets, such as *Industrial Products—Eastern Europe*, first published in 1995, or *Chemical Plant News—Korea*, established in 1994. A complete listing of Thomas International Publishing's titles appears on the Thomas WWW site, http://www.thomaspublishing.com, as does a version of the *Thomas Register of European Manufacturers*.

Country Product Directories

Individual countries have product registers. Two of the major ones in the U.K. are Kompass and *Kelly's*.

Kelly's (published annually by Reed Information Services)

One of the oldest product registers is *Kelly's*. Though it has experienced several name changes, the most recent being from *Kelly's Business Directory* to just *Kelly's* for the 108th edition, the 1996 edition was the 109th edition. *Kelly's* has a classified section and an alphabetical listing by company, with a designation for companies whose entries changed from the previous edition. It also has a Reader Reply section, which has full-color reproductions of some company brochures and brief company descriptions. Almost 90,000 commercial, professional, and industrial organizations in the U.K. are in *Kelly's*. Entries are brief, including address and telecommunications numbers. *Kelly's* is available on CD-ROM from Reed.

The electronic versions of Kompass UK include *Kompass UK Register* and *Kelly's*. They also have additional U.K. sources, such as *Dial Industry*, which covers engineering, electronics, and computing; *U.K. Trade Names*; and *Directory of Directors*, which is discussed below.

Product directories accessible electronically are described in Chapter 6.

FINDING AIDS

Latin American Markets: A Guide to Company and Industry Information Sources (published by Washington Researchers Publishing)

Latin American Markets and the companion *Asian* and *European Markets* are recommended for general collections. They are good choices for small businesses willing to do their own research from the source. The books contain lists of published sources and online and CD-ROM databases for the region. Sources for individual countries also include Internet sites.

Latin America—A Directory and Sourcebook 1993, 1st ed. (Euromonitor, 1993)

This is one of a series of finding aids from Euromonitor that include company and marketing information. They were all published between 1992 and 1994 and are still in print but have not been updated. The Latin American book provides sources of information about eight countries in Latin America: the major markets of Argentina, Brazil, Chile, Mexico, and Venezuela, plus Colombia, Ecuador, and Peru. Other countries or regions in the series are Asia, Eastern Europe, and China. The Euromonitor and Washington Research titles are discussed in more detail in Chapter 9.

Sourceguide to European Company Information and *London Business School Sourceguide to Central and Eastern European Information* (Gale Research, Inc.)

Gale published two excellent sources for company information. The first, *Sourceguide to European Company Information,* 5th edition, was issued in 1993. The second, *London Business School Sourceguide to Central and Eastern European Information* was published in 1994. Neither have been republished. The publications are arranged by country and list print and electronic sources. If you still own these *Sourceguides,* they may still be used as finding aids to other possible directories.

A selected list of other directory titles appears at the end of this chapter.

DIRECTORS AND OFFICERS

Selected Print Country Sources

Questions about companies often concern their officers and directors. What are the international equivalents of the biographical volume of Standard & Poor's *Register* or D&B's *Reference Book of Corporate Managers*? Typical questions are:

> *Who is the CEO of Unilever? Is his biography available?*
>
> *Who are Nestle's general managers?*
>
> *What is the average age of a Japanese CEO?*
>
> *Where are there Wharton alumni working as senior managers outside the U.S.?*

Listed below are biographical sources for selected officers and also sources with extensive lists of officers and directors.

Financial Post Directory of Directors (published annually by Financial Post, Toronto)

The Canadian *Financial Post Directory of Directors* is one national print source of information on officers and directors. The directory has been published for more than 50 years. It is divided into two main sections. Section One is an alphabetical list of directors and executives of Canadian companies who reside in Canada. The basic listing includes name, gender, position, company name, and address. Additional information may include birthdate, home address, and schools attended.

Section Two is an alphabetical listing of almost 2,000 Canadian companies with their boards of direc-

tors and executives, regardless of place of birth. Section Three is a geographical index to the companies listed in Section Two.

Directory of Directors: Key Data on the 60,000 Directors Who Control Britain's Major Companies (published annually by Reed Information Services)

Directory of Directors has been published for over 110 years. Reed took over its publication in 1992. There are two parts. Volume 1 lists directors and Volume 2 lists companies and their board members. Note that this directory does *not* include executives.

Criteria for an individual to be included is based on company size with minimum turnover set at £50,000. Company secretaries supply the initial information. The basic entry in Volume 1 includes name, business address, title, honors, awards, education, and main type of business interest. According to the brochure for the 1993 edition, "three quarters of all entries (are) updated each year."

Volume 2 is arranged alphabetically by company name, with address, main business, corporate family, detailed list of board members, and financial highlights.

The Price Waterhouse Corporate Register (published quarterly beginning in 1995 by Hemmington Scott Publishing)

Corporate Register is subtitled *The No. 1 Source on Decision Makers in UK Stockmarket Companies.* It contains contact details for 20,000 executives, directors, and advisers. Until the 1995 edition, the book was entitled *The Arthur Andersen Corporate Register* and appeared semi-annually.

The main body of the book is arranged by company. Directory information consists of head office address, telecommunications numbers, sector, subsector (group), activities, and ordinary capital. There is then a list of executive directors and non-executive directors, with appointment date, position, and number of ordinary and incentive shares; directors' pay; number of employees and total payroll; names of internal staff such as treasurer, accountant, and personnel officer; and external advisers, such as bankers, auditors, and solicitors.

Following the company entries is an alphabetical listing of directors and officers. A sample entry includes brief biographical information. The biographical entry is shown in Exhibit 4.7.

```
FLEMING, Ian J.,FCA, MA. Wimpey(George)
PLC, 27 Hammersmith Grove, London, W6
7EN. Tel(0181)846 2734  Fax:(0181)846
3303. COMPANIES SECTION:  Wimpey(George)
 (gfc) p575; OTHER COMPANIES: 1994- to date,
Wimpey Homes Worldwide(fd). PAST CAREER:
1993- to date, George Wimpey PLC (gfc);
1988-93 Redland Bricks (fd); 1976-87
Arthur Andersen, London. PROF: FCA;
MA(Oxon)
EDUC:Christ Church, Oxford;
Bromley Grammar School. RECR: Golf,
Football, Theatre. BORN: 27 Sep 1953(41)
MATR:1979, Michelle, 2 sons, 1 dtr.
```

THE PRICE WATERHOUSE CORPORATE REGISTER

EXHIBIT 4.7

Source: The Price Waterhouse Corporate Register, Hemmington Scott Publishing Ltd., Sept., 1995. Reprinted with permission.

Other Directories of Directors and Executives

Bowker-Saur published one edition of *Who's Who in European Business: Biographies of the Top 3,000 Business Leaders in Europe,* in 1993. Entrants come from 35 countries, including Eastern Europe. Information comes from questionnaires. A companion publication, *Who's Who in International Banking,* has not been updated since 1992. Both publications are still in print.

International Corporate Yellow Book: Who's Who at the Leading non-U.S. Companies (Washington DC: Monitor Publishing) has ceased publication.

Electronic Sources

Because of the obvious lack of information in print sources, electronic formats fill in the gaps. Several biographical files are available on LEXIS-NEXIS Services. The PEOPLE library includes the broadest range of biographies, including all the Marquis *Who's Who* publications, a biographical source from Russia, two files covering Canadian biographies, and a European biographical directory.

Marquis *Who's Who* Publications

If your organization owns print copies of Marquis *Who's Who,* these titles can be used to identify known international leaders. However, we do not recommended that you purchase any of these books specifically for international research.

All of the Marquis individual print *Who's Who* publications are loaded in one LEXIS-NEXIS file. The two most important titles to business researchers are *Who's Who in Finance and Industry* and *Who's Who in the World. Who's Who in Finance and Industry* has over 20,000 biographies on business figures

from 100 countries. In addition to being on LEXIS-NEXIS, the Marquis *Who's Who* titles are File 234 on DIALOG, are on CompuServe and Knowledge Index, and comprise *The Complete Marquis Who's Who CD-ROM.*

The Marquis file combines biographical entries from several sources. For example, the biographical entry for the Dutch Sara Lee executive, Cornelis Boonstra, comes from *Who's Who in the World,* 12th edition; *Who's Who in Finance and Industry*, 29th edition and 28th edition; *Who's Who in America*, 50th edition and 46th edition. A standard entry may include personal information such as marital status, gender, birthdate, and address; career information, including occupation and positions held; education information, with degrees and abbreviated references to educational institutions attended; and other information, such as creative works, memberships, and interests.

Who's Who in Russia and the Commonwealth of Independent States (RusData DiaLine)

WHORUS, published by RusData DiaLine in Chicago, Illinois, is a niche biographical source in the LEXIS-NEXIS PEOPLE library. It is a biographical reference to about 2,000 people, primarily from Russia. Biographies are classified into 16 different categories including: National and Public Organizations and Unions, Economics, Industry, and Business. Record segments includes: address, born, career, position, education, family, honors, major works, and hobbies. In November of 1996, information was from August 1995 and loaded in January of 1996.

Who's Who Edition European Business and Industry (published by Who's Who Edition GMBH, Hersching, Munich, Germany)

Last updated in November 1992, *Who's Who Edition European Business and Industry* is available on LEXIS-NEXIS Services as the WHOEUR file in the WORLD, EUROPE, and PEOPLE Libraries. There are about 7,000 entries that consist of name, company, address, position, family, education, career, nationality, birthdate, and may also have recreation, languages, home address, honors, and publications.

Both the Financial Post *Directory of Directors* and Standard and Poor's *Register of Directors and Executives* are available on LEXIS-NEXIS Services. They are in the PEOPLE file and are their own file, EXECDR, in the COMPANY library. Both contain Canadian company directors. As illustrated in Exhibit 4.8, the records of the Financial Post and S&P are very similar. Standard and Poor's *Register* is also on DIALOG File 526.

FPDIR The Financial Post Company *Directory of Directors*	SPBIO Standard and Poor's Corporation *Register of Directors and Executives*
Name — Posluns, David	POSLUNS, DAVID
Position: — Senior vice-president, corporate development and strategic planning, secretary-treasurer and chief financial officer	Senior Vice-President, Secretary, Treasurer & Chief Financial Officer
Company: — Dylex Ltd.	Dylex Limited
Address: — 637 Lake Shore Blvd. W Toronto Ontario Canada M5V 1A8	637 Lake Shore Blvd. W. Toronto Canada M5V 1A8
GENDER: — Male	
DEGREES: — B.S., M.B.A.	
ALUMNI: — Wharton School of Business, U. of Pennsylvania, B.S. U. of Chicago, M.B.A.	Univ. of Pennsylvania (Wharton Sch.), 1982 Univ. of Chicago[sic], 1984
BIRTHDATE: — December 12, 1959	1959, Toronto, Ont., Canada
LOAD-DATE: — January 1, 1993	October 25, 1996

COMPARING *DIRECTORY OF DIRECTORS* AND *REGISTER OF DIRECTORS AND EXECUTIVES* ON LEXIS-NEXIS SERVICES

EXHIBIT 4.8

Source: LEXIS-NEXIS Services, November 1996.

Teikoku

Teikoku, a Japanese database described in detail in Chapter 5, has a small amount of biographical information on the chief executive: birthdate, birthplace, and education. All non-Japanese universities are grouped together as "univ abroad."

Listed Company Reports

Selected company annual reports are another source for selected biographical information about directors and officers. Use SEC filings 20-F for non-U.S. companies that trade on the U.S. stock exchanges and ICC's full-text annual report files for companies that trade on the London exchange. Both these files can be used to search for officers and directors of a company, for an individual, or to screen for specific educational background.

Examples of using the SEC filings *20-F* file on LEXIS-NEXIS Services and ICC *British Company Annual Reports* (ICAC) on DataStar are presented. Exhibit 4.9 displays a record from *SEC-Online* on LEXIS-NEXIS. The same information is on DIALOG File 778, EdgarPlus 10-Ks and 20-Fs.

Example 1:

Q: What Harvard graduates are on boards of directors of foreign companies filing in the U.S.?

A: Search 20-F filings for Harvard.

Company: Teva Pharmaceutical Industries, Ltd.
Filing-Date: 03/15/96   Document-Date: 12/31/95
Jonathan B. Kolber is the President...of Claridge Israel Inc
He received his B.A. from **Harvard** University in 1983.
Mr. Kolber serves as a director of ECI Telecom Ltd., and
Optrotech Ltd.

FROM *SEC ONLINE* 20-F

EXHIBIT 4.9

Source: Reprinted from *SEC Online* on LEXIS-NEXIS, searched November 1996. Reprinted with permission of Disclosure.

The record also tells us that Kolber is 43 years old, has been a director since 1990, and is a member of the executive committee.

The full text ICC annual report files, either online or on CD-ROM, can be used to locate U.K. directors and officers and some background information.

Example 2:

Q: How do I find which Wharton School graduates are presidents or CEOs of U.K. companies?

A: Use ICC British Company Annual Reports.

Biographic information from an ICC record is displayed in Exhibit 4.10.

ICAC
TI WICKES PLC - 1995 Annual Report and Accounts.
SO Wickes PLC
19 - 21 Mortimer Street,
London W1N 7RJ
PUBLICATION DATE: 951231;
TOTAL PAGES OF DOCUMENT: 35._
TX 8 OF 27 DIRECTORS' BIOGRAPHIES
EXECUTIVE DIRECTORS
Henry Sweetbaum (58), Chairman and Chief Executive,
is a graduate of The Wharton School, University of
Pennsylvania. He has been Chairman and Chief Executive
of the Wickes Group since 1982

ICC BRITISH COMPANY ANNUAL REPORTS

EXHIBIT 4.10

Source: Copyright ICC (ICAC) on DataStar, searched November 1996. Reprinted with permission.

DASH

DASH, Directors And SHareholds CD-ROM from Bureau van Dijk, has company and director records covering over one million U.K. companies. It has records for 400,000 "primary" companies and full listings of one million directors associated with those companies. Directors' records include date of birth, home address, marital status, nationality, occupation, qualifications, and appointment date. There are an additional 600,000 "secondary" company records (other companies associated with the one million directors), for which there are summary listings for an additional 8,000 directors. The data are compiled by Dun & Bradstreet. Exhibit 4.11 shows both a primary and secondary director report.

Mr. BRIAN JON KNEZ   **Primary Director**
                                                        Person Identifier:3166562

Home Address: 3 TAMARACK ROAD
                  WESTON MASSACHUSETTS 02193

Biographical data
Date of birth   :10/12/57
Gender   :Male
Nationality   :US Citizen
Qualifications and honors :na
Occupation   : Executive

Directorships
  Current Directorships

1.   BALLIERE TINDALL LTD   Duns Number: 22-520-8537
     Executive position: Director
     Function description: na
     Appointment date: 2/29/93 ...

5.   W.S. Saunders, Ltd.   Duns Number: 21-726-4118

     Previous Directorships:
1.   DRAKE BEAM MORIN PLC   Duns Number: 29-317-49750
     Executive position: Director
     Function description: na
     Appointment date: 8/1/94
     Resignation data: 3/8/96

Director Report   **Secondary Director**

Mr Andrew Peter Clarkson

Person Identifier: 3013547

Directorships:
  1 PEACO SPORT LTD   Duns Number: 78-559-9762
     Executive Position: Director
     Function description: na

SAMPLE DIRECTOR REPORTS FROM DASH

EXHIBIT 4.11

Source: DASH CD-ROM, update November 4, 1996. Reprinted with permission from Bureau van Dijk.

COMPANY HISTORIES

A search for a "company history" often yields little or no results. Some very large international companies have had monographs written about them. However, there is no Library of Congress subject heading that readily identifies all of the histories in a collection, let alone all those in print. The Moody's manuals, including the *Moody's International Manual*, have brief overviews of a company's acquisitions, name changes, etc. *Hoover's Handbook of World Business*, discussed in more detail in Chapter 5, has informal histories for the companies it covers. For a monthly subscription fee, *Hoover's* is also available on the WWW, at http://www.hoovers.com.

International Directory of Company Histories
(published semiannually by St. James)

This is the one comprehensive source. The work was originally published as a five-volume set between 1988 and mid-1992. It had 1,200 companies arranged by industry grouping (see Table 4.K.) However, the publishers began adding semi-annual updates in December 1992. The updates cover additional companies and new information about original companies. By 1996, there were 2,000 companies and 14 volumes. Four new industries in the service sector were added: accounting, engineering & management services, legal services, and personal services. Fewer than 40 companies had been placed in these categories.

Companies are included based on minimum sales of $200 million and influence in their industry or geographical location. State-owned enterprises and subsidiaries that are prominent in their own right are included in addition to their parent firms.

Each entry has directory information, including the company's legal name in English, its native language name, headquarters address, telecommunications numbers, ownership status, incorporation date, employees, and a sales figure in local currency and/or U.S. dollars (with no date). SIC codes have been added to entries in the later volumes. Finally, the entries have a bibliography and the name(s) of the author(s). Each volume has two cumulative indexes, one to people and companies, the other to companies by industry.

Magazines, books, and annual reports, as well as information provided by the companies themselves, are used to compile the histories. Each entry is several pages long.

Although generally a useful source for any collection, the *International Directory of Company Histories* has some shortcomings:

* There is no index by country
* The quality of the entries varies
* There is no index to subsidiaries, only to companies mentioned in the text
* The histories of Asian companies are primarily Japanese
* Emphasis is on U.S. companies

In order to see just how international this source was, we counted the number of companies by region by industry. About half are from the U.S., though distribution varies by industry. Table 4.L shows the geographical distribution of companies by industry in Volume 5. In Volume 13, almost 90 percent of the companies were headquartered in the United States and only two companies were from emerging markets.

TABLE 4.K

Original Industries Included in *International Directory of Company Histories*, as of April 1993

VOLUME 1 & 6	VOLUME 2	VOLUME 3	VOLUME 4	VOLUME 5
Advertising	Electrical & Electronic	Health & Personal Care	Mining & Metals	Retail & Wholesale
Aerospace	Entertainment & Leisure	Health Care Systems	Paper & Forestry	Rubber & Tire
Airlines	Financials: Banks	Hotels	Petroleum	Telecommunications
Automotive	Financials: Non-banks	Information Technology	Publishing & Printing	Textiles & Apparel
Beverages	Food Products	Insurance	Real Estate	Tobacco
Chemicals	Food Services & Retailers	Manufacturing		Transport Services
Conglomerates		Materials		Utilities
Construction				Waste Services
Containers				
Drugs; Pharmaceuticals				

TABLE 4.L

NUMBER OF COMPANIES BY INDUSTRY BY COUNTRY IN *INTERNATIONAL DIRECTORY OF COMPANY HISTORIES* (VOL. 5)

Industry	U.S.	Europe	Asia	Other*	Total	Percent U.S.
Retail	36	21	18	2	77	47
Rubber & Tire	2	3	3	8	25	
Telecommunications	11	11	1	2	25	44
Textiles	8	2	4	14	57	
Tobacco	4	3	1	1	9	44
Transportation	15	9	13	1	38	39
Utilities	41	14	11	2	68	60
Waste Services	2	2	100			
Total	**119**	**63**	**51**	**8**	**241**	**49**

* All other are Canadian

The non-U.S. companies in *International Directory of Company Histories* will be added to Gale's *Business Resource* CD-ROM and database in 1997.

Canadian Company Histories (published by Gale Canada, 1996)

Canadian Company Histories includes 80 Canadian companies, 48 of which are part of the larger series. According to Gale, the entries from the *International Directory* have been updated.

Hoover's Handbook of World Business (published annually by Hoover's)

Though *Hoover's Handbook of World Business* is positioned as a financial source, its more unique contribution to international business literature is the company histories in the 295 company reports that are included in this product. More information about *Hoover's Handbook*, both in print and on LEXIS-NEXIS Services, appears in Chapter 5.

COMPANY INFORMATION WHEN THE COMPANY IS NOT KNOWN

Questions about companies are usually of two types:

1. Finding information about a specific known company
2. Finding a group of companies that meet specific criteria

The second application is used most often for marketing or trade applications, for investing purposes, or for job-hunting. To answer questions of this type, printed directories should have a variety of access points or indexes. Again, our ideal directory will have a listing by industry or product code, a geographical index, and an alphabetical index by company name. In some printed directories, the most information about a company is listed in the alphabetical section. Additional indexes may only list the company name, or give a name and address. D&B's *Principal International Businesses* is an example of this type of directory. In other directories (*Kelly's,* and the Kompass directories, for example) the main information is found in the product index.

Printed directories are useful for finding information about a few companies in a single category. They quickly become impossible to use when we are screening for companies in multiple categories; for example, a list of French companies in computer manufacturing with sales of more than 300 million francs. This type of question must be answered with the directories available through electronic systems or on CD-ROM, which are discussed in Chapter 6.

OTHER SELECTED DIRECTORIES

There are hundreds of company directories in print which we have not mentioned. The list below includes some other major sources. See Chapter 6 for additional online directory sources and Chapter 12 for directories of companies involved primarily in importing and exporting. Appendix D, at the end of Chapter 3, has a checklist of characteristics to use when evaluating other directories.

Regional Directories

Asia's 7,500 Largest Companies (published annually by ELC International)

This directory from a U.K. publisher covers Hong Kong, Japan, Malaysia, the Philippines, Taiwan, Indonesia, South Korea, Singapore, and Thailand. In addition to manufacturing and trading companies, it has banks, insurance companies, investment companies, and privately owned companies. It is arranged in five sections: two rankings of business, an alphabetical index, a trade index, and company directory. Rankings include the 100 largest quoted companies by "profit"; 500 most profitable companies by "profit margin" and money losers; and the largest quoted companies by country and by business activity. *Asia's 7,500 Largest Companies* is also available on LEXIS-NEXIS.

Jobson's Year Book of Public Companies (published annually by Dun & Bradstreet)

Jobson's has more than 2,000 public companies that are listed on the Australian and New Zealand stock exchanges. Entries include corporate structure, five-year financial tables, and operating results. It also has articles and a "Directory of Directors."

Hoover's Masterlist of Major Latin American Companies (1996–97)

A new title in the Hoover series of company publications is the *Masterlist of Major Latin American Companies*, covering 18 Latin American countries. Information came from *AmericaEconomia*, and includes 951 of the largest companies and 486 of the largest commercial banks in Latin America for which existing information was available. Entries are brief, including company name; address; telecommunications; 1994 sales and income in U.S. dollars; employees; president; company status, such as publicly listed or state owned; and a description of the industry.

COUNTRY DIRECTORIES

Brazil

Brazil Dez Mil [Brazil's Top 10,000] (published biennially and distributed by Dun & Bradstreet)

This basic directory, written in Portuguese, covers over 10,000 companies.

Canada

Canadian Key Business Directory (published annually by Dun & Bradstreet, Toronto)

The *Canadian Key Business Directory* lists 20,000 major businesses in Canada, selected from over 1.1 million private and public businesses. The companies meet one or more of the following criteria: $20 million in sales; $1 million of net worth; employ 100 individuals or more, or have branches with more than 500 total employees. Nearly 80,000 officers and managers are included. Unique to a company entry in this directory is a "status indicator" such as headquarters, single location, or branch. The *Directory* is arranged alphabetically, geographically, and by line of business.

D&B also publishes three Canadian regional directories, for Toronto, Quebec, and Vancouver, available separately or as a set.

Financial Post Publications

Financial Post 500, published annually, covers Canada's largest companies in industry and finance. The Financial Post also publishes the annual *Financial Post Survey of Industrials,* which has over 2,000 Canadian public, listed, and unlisted industrials (non-resource) corporations. Entries include names, addresses, telephone numbers, stock symbols, transfer agents, details of operations, management, financial data, and subsidiaries. Access is only by company name. A companion volume to the *Survey of Industrials* is the *Financial Post Survey of Mines and Energy Resources.* This volume has enhanced coverage of 35 companies. Financial Post publications are also available online on LEXIS-NEXIS Services, TELERATE, and Infomart Online.

China

China Business Resources (China Business Resources, Hong Kong)

China Business Resources is an electronic database of Chinese companies, available on diskette, CD-ROM, or as part of two databank services, *Asia Intelligence Wire* and Profound. A directory entry includes name and address, business class, economic class, such as "collective," fiscal date, employees, balance sheet and income statement data in local currency, and production capacity.

United Kingdom

Key British Enterprises (published annually by Dun & Bradstreet Ltd.)

This multivolume set covers 50,000 large and medium-size companies that employ more than one third of the U.K. workforce and account for 65% of U.K. business activity. Included are manufacturers, wholesalers, retailers, distributors, and service companies with minimal sales of £1 million. The set is arranged alphabetically and by line of business. Entries include 30 data items, including name, headquarters, telecommunications, officers, total and export sales, geographic markets, employees, branches, formation date, legal status, registration and D-U-N-S number, description of trading activity, trading styles and trade names, and U.K. SIC code. Information comes from questionnaires, telephone surveys, personal communication, published information, and official sources. Output is available online, off-line, on floppy disk, or by mailing list.

United Kingdom's 10,000 Largest Companies (published annually by ELC, distributed in U.S. by Dun & Bradstreet)

This publication covers companies in manufacturing, distribution, and the service industries. It ranks largest companies by sales, profit, profit margin, money losers, and employees. It is a companion to *Asia's 7,500.*

FURTHER READING

Journal articles discuss regional or country directories. Listed below are a few we recommend. A review article is often more useful than an individual product or book review in a U.S. source, since the latter does not compare the directory with local sources.

Eastern Europe

Kviklys, Danguole; and Mykolas Masiokas. "Tracking a Growing Private Economy: Company Information Sources for the Baltic States." *Business and Finance Division Bulletin* 100 (Fall 1995): 31–35.

Asia

Han, Ying-Shan. "Chinese Business Information Sources." *Business Information Review* 11 (April 1995): 37–42.

Foster, Allan. "Japanese Business Information: A Guide to Sources." *Business Information Review* 10 (July 1993): 12–15.

Israel

Arenstein, Marc. "Israel: A Guide to Business Information." *Business Information Review* 11 (July 1994): 14–28.

Scotland

Reid, Christine; and Keith Webster. "Scottish Business Information: A Guide to Published Sources." *Business Information Review* 11 (October 1994): 24–37.

NOTES

1. Letter from FYI, publisher of *SIBD*, 1996.
2. E-mail from the publisher, January 1997.

APPENDIX G
Company WWW Sources—A Checklist

WWW sites demand the same kind of evaluation as a print source or an online database. Before using a WWW site for reference, research or referral, consider the following issues.

Characteristics of a Directory Site

- **Who has compiled the information?**
  Is this WWW equivalent of an existing directory (Europages)?
  Is this a subset of information from an existing directory (Hoover)?
  Has this been created exclusively for WWW access (Internet Securities)?
  Does the compiler verify the information?

- **How are the companies selected for the site?**
  Already in a producer's directory
  Companies looking for exposure for trade opportunities
  Companies which pay to have a home page with the compiler

- **How often is the site updated? A record updated?**

- **How many companies are included?**
  Many sites which are called "Directories" on the WWW have very limited numbers of companies

- **What types of companies are included?**
  What is their legal status?
  What is their size?
  Is there enough information that you can tell?

- **What geographic location is covered**
  City? Province or State? Country? International?
  Or IP provider's range?

- **How can you access the information?**
  Company name, if it is known; by part of a company name
  By location
  By product
  By sales or employees
  By a combination of charateristics

- **How many data elements are included per company?**
  Many free WWW directories offer little more than yellow pages information

- **What is the cost of the site?**
  Free for all information
  Free with registration
  Free to access and search but a fee to view entries
  Free for basic information; fee for additional information
  Fee to search and access

Characteristics of an Entry

Use Appendix D, at the end of Chapter 3, to evaluate the quality of a directory entry.

CHAPTER 5
Financial Sources

TOPICS COVERED

- Availability of Financial Information
- Sources of International Financial Information
- Sources of Regional Financial Information
- Sources of Financial Data by Industry
- Finding Financial Footnotes
- Sources of International Annual Reports
- Electronic Financial Information for Private Companies
- Text Sources of Company Financial Information
- Finding Aids

MAJOR SOURCES DISCUSSED

- *Moody's International Manual* and CD-ROMs
- Worldscope/Disclosure
- FT Extel Research
- Standard and Poor's
- Bureau van Dijk
- Bankstat and BankScope
- *Best's Insurance Reports, International Edition*

AVAILABILITY OF FINANCIAL INFORMATION

Recent statistics show that one in every five shares traded worldwide involves a foreign share or a foreign investor. This compares to just one in 14 in the late 1970s.[1]

The expanding interest in international investment and trade increases the need for international financial statement information. As discussed in Chapter 3, the amount of financial information available about a company depends on its size and its country of registration, not only on whether it is traded on an exchange. An understanding of what reports a company must file will help you have more realistic expectations concerning what data can be obtained.

In this chapter we will look at specific sources of corporate finance with emphasis on sources of listed company data. Some typical questions about company financial information are:

How is a company performing financially this year? How has it performed financially in previous years?

Is a full financial report (with balance sheet and income statement) available? Does the report contain text?

Is the company profitable?

Chapter 16 contains an analysis of and sources on financial markets.

Registration Requirements

Companies within the European Union have registration and disclosure directives. Disclosure Inc. publishes brochures for its subscribers on U.S., U.K., European, and international filing and disclosure requirements. Requirements may be found in EIU's *Investing, Licensing and Trading in ...* in print, or electronically on LEXIS-NEXIS Services, DIALOG File 627, and other services that provide Economist Intelligence Unit publications. More information about registration can be found in Chapters 2 and 3.

Often, companies listed on exchanges are faced with a set of filing or disclosure requirements. The requirements may not, however, be as frequent, complete, or timely as those required by the U.S. stock exchanges and Securities and Exchange Commission. The average time for European filings for listed companies is six months. There is no international equivalent of the U.S. 10-K or 10-Q reports. Quarterly reports may not be required, nor in many countries are any interim financial statements necessary or forthcoming.

Pressure from the international investor community has increased the amount of information that is disclosed and how it is presented by the companies. Companies, on the other hand, prefer to file on exchanges with the laxest requirements.[2] Providers of international financial filings are continually increasing the number of companies whose financial filings they present.

The form and contents of published annual reports by companies from different countries vary widely. A survey of securities and accounting professionals rated the Swiss, German, and Japanese disclosure levels well below those in the U.S., Canada, and the U.K.[3] CIFAR (Center for International Financial Analysis and Research), ranks countries, industries, and companies on the informativeness of their annual reports. Results are based on an analysis of the annual reports of 1,000 companies, examining 85 variables. Table 5.A lists the top and bottom countries and industries and the top five companies, based on the data reported in the 4th edition of *International Accounting and Auditing Trends* (see Chapter 2). U.S. companies rank very high on financial reporting, but because they do not follow International Accounting Standards, they do not have a high overall ranking from CIFAR.

TABLE 5.A

RATING OF INFORMATIVENESS IN ANNUAL REPORTS

	Most Comprehensive	Below Average
COUNTRY(41)		
	United Kingdom	Portugal
	Finland	Brazil
	Sweden	Turkey
	Ireland	Taiwan
	Australia	Colombia
	New Zealand	India
	Switzerland	Greece
	Malaysia	Austria
	Singapore	Philippines
	South Africa	
INDUSTRY (28 groups)		
Photographic/Scientific Equipment	Utilities	
Cosmetics/Toiletries	Transportation—not air	
Pharmaceuticals	Real Estate Development	
Electronics	Mining/Petroleum	
Hotels	Airlines	
COMPANY (1000)		
Ericsson (L.M. Telefon AB), Sweden		
Inchcape & Co PLC, U.K.		
Thorn EMI PLC, U.K.		
Allied Lyons PLC, U.K.		
Cadbury Schweppes PLC, U.K.		

Source: International Accounting and Auditing Trends, vol. 4, 1995: 364–65; 368, 370.

Quoted companies may be tracked in financial print and electronic sources by their ticker symbols or by using other standard numbering systems (see Chapter 3).

While finding financial information has become easier, interpreting what we find has not. Problems in using company financial reports include the language and monetary unit (e.g., pounds or francs) of the original document, fiscal year-end dates, and delays in publication of reports. Some companies publish a modified report in English for the investment community. See Chapter 2 for a more in-depth discussion of the effects of international accounting standards and practices on financial statements.

Country Coverage in International Sources

Many sources include extracts of listed company filings; a few provide the actual reports themselves. The number of companies for which reports are available has been growing. Table 5.B lists, by country, different international sources and the number of companies with financial balance sheet and income statement data available. Dates and numbers are used for comparison purposes. Every update includes more companies.

We can evaluate our financial sources not only by how many countries or companies they cover, but also on the timeliness of the reports, the breadth and depth of the financial data, the footnoting, and the flexibly of the access tools.

SOURCES OF INTERNATIONAL FINANCIAL INFORMATION

Sources of financial information can be categorized in a variety of ways—by format, financial content, types of listings, and place of publication or coverage. Financial information is published in books, on fiche or cards, online, on CD-ROM, and on the World Wide Web. A report may be in the form of the primary filing, as in *Laser/Disclosure*. It may include extracts from the filing with financials as reported, as in Moody's international products. The report may be a standardized restatement of the financial filing, as in Worldscope products. In countries where non-listed as well as listed companies must file financial statements, sources can be further categorized by whether they include only listed or traded companies, or whether they include unlisted companies as well. Finally, sources can be examined according to their scope: international, pan-continental, regional or single country, or by industry.

TABLE 5.B

COVERAGE OF INTERNATIONAL FINANCIAL STATEMENTS FOR COMPANIES IN MULTI-COUNTRY SOURCES

PRODUCT	FT Extel	Moody's Intl	S&P G V	WSG	S&P	DISC	Hoover's
Format	DIALOG	CD-ROM	CD-ROM	DIALOG	DIALOG	DIALOG	LEXIS-NEXIS
Date	Jan 97	Oct 95	Jan 96	Oct 96	Nov 96	Jan 97	Jan 97
ARGENTINA	6	56	10	30	10	13	1
AUSTRALIA	457	607	459	227	39	29	9
AUSTRIA	106	132	72	82	3		
BAHAMAS	1	8			2	6	
BAHRAIN	23	5	9				
BARBADOS		4					
BELGIUM	167	163	118	145	4	2	1
BELIZE		2			1	1	
BERMUDA	223	261	17		37	44	3
BOLIVIA		5					
BOTSWANA	1	1	1			1	
BRAZIL	7	192	48	119	9	4	1
British V I		5	1			13	
British W I					3	3	
BULGARIA		1					
CANADA	110	1281	540	458	1204	458	40
CAYMAN ISLANDS	69	39	4	13		13	
CHILE	6	73	18	67	8	20	1
CHINA	90	64	2	40	7	6	1
COLOMBIA		37	14	29	2	2	
COOK ISLANDS	2						
COSTA RICA		1					
CROATIA		6					
CYPRUS		2					
CZECH REPUBLIC		5					
DENMARK	107	191	50	185	6	4	2
DJIBOUTI		1					
ECUADOR		9					
EGYPT		3					
FINLAND	65	119	84	119	7	4	1
FRANCE	671	484	618	681	19	17	28
FRENCH GUIANA		1					
GABON			1				
GERMANY	416	504	420	542	15	6	20
GHANA	1	2	1		1		
GREECE		26	15	125	2		
GUYANA		2					
HONDURAS		1					
HONG KONG	398	236	223	202	40	6	6
HUNGARY	36	10	2	9			
ICELAND		3			1		
INDIA	5	260	69	257			1
INDONESIA	241	140	23	97	5	9	
IRELAND	117	96	67	70	13	14	1
ISRAEL	6	69	40	41	64	76	10
ITALY	228	253	155	255	14	13	
IVORY COAST		1					
JAMAICA		6					
JAPAN	1000	705	1224	2228	42	21	53
JORDAN		2					
KENYA	1	9	1				
KOREA (SOUTH)	219	116	33	235	3	4	5
KUWAIT	25	7	15		1		

LIBERIA		2	1				7
LIECHTENSTEIN	5	4	3				
LUXEMBOURG	27	32	7	15	8	7	
MALAWI		1					
MALAYSIA	624	399	238	256	1		1
MALTA		3	2				
MAURITIUS		1					
MEXICO	8	113	50	86	37	30	3
MONACO		3					
MOROCCO		2					
NAMIBIA		2					
NETHERLANDS	234	232	176	202	34	33	15
NETHERLANDS ANTILLES	18	15	3		4	6	
NEW ZEALAND	68	46	58	35	3	7	1
NIGERIA		27					
NORWAY	65	174	79	114	7	7	1
OMAN	5						
PAKISTAN		94	7	82			
PANAMA	2	7	3		1	6	
PAPUA NEW GUINEA	3	7	1			1	
PARAGUAY		1					
PERU	1	34	6	35	5	3	
PHILIPPINES	110	68	12	65	5	4	1
POLAND	27	4		16			
PORTUGAL	20	79	19	79	4	3	1
PUERTO RICO					10		
QATAR	3						
RUSSIA			1		1	1	
SAUDI ARABIA	16	3	5				
SINGAPORE	283	201	173	177	9	5	2
SOUTH AFRICA	102	347	132	205	21	6	1
SLOVAKIA		1					
SPAIN	149	118	143	169	8	7	2
SRI LANKA		35		16			
SURINAME		2					
SWAZILAND		1					
SWEDEN	167	206	121	184	13	10	5
SWITZERLAND	260	238	208	195	8	1	9
TAIWAN	129	109	21	116	3	1	4
TANZANIA		1					
THAILAND	484	260	154	241	3		
TRINIDAD & TOBAGO		4					
TUNISIA		1					
TURKEY		19	23	54	1		1
UNITED ARAB EMIRATES	14	3	1				
UNITED KINGDOM	5419	1709	1439	1588	123	85	54
UNITED STATES	579	38	3463	2985	10018	12063	2488
URUGUAY		13					
VANUATU			1				
VENEZUELA	2	29	3	14	8		1
VIETNAM		3					
VIRGIN ISLANDS					5		
YUGOSLAVIA		1					
ZAMBIA	1	1	1		1		
ZIMBABWE	3	32	3	4	1		
TOTAL	**13,632**	**12,411**	**10,911**	**13,739**	**13,104**	**13,082**	**2,775**
TOTAL NON-US	**13,053**	**12,373**	**7,448**	**10,754**	**3,086**	**1,019**	**287**
TOTAL COUNTRIES	**60**	**101**	**65**	**50**	**58**	**47**	**36**
PERCENT NON-US	**95.8**[a]	**99.7**	**68.3**	**78.3**	**23.6**	**7.8**	**10.3**

a   48% of FT EXTEL companies are from the U.K.

There is no clear distinction between a basic directory and a "financial source" such as *Moody's International Manual*. Most financial sources will include basic directory information, just as many basic directories include sales (or turnover) and income (or profit) and in Europe often a "capital" figure. Financial sources also include detailed company accounts, consisting of

- Balance sheet information, stating assets, liabilities, and shareholders equity
- An income or profit and loss statement
- Stock market performance measures, such as book value, earnings per share, and a price earnings ratio for a given date
- An annual flow of funds statement
- Other performance measures, such as standard ratios

Researchers prefer to have financial accounts for multiples of 3, 5, 10, or even 20 years. In addition to the financial data, the textual footnotes that explain the accounting standards used in presenting the information should be provided. A list of company officers and directors, major shareholders, and subsidiaries is desirable. A description of the company with any corporate structural changes is also welcome.

Ideally, the financial information should be presented in two ways: (1) "as reported" by the company for its domestic exchange; and (2) "restated" to allow us to look at the data items in a standardized format. Having the option of restatement into a familiar accounting standard, using a currency of the researcher's choice, is preferable. Analysts also want the capability to manipulate the data in models of their choosing to predict the growth and performance of companies and their industries.

These characteristics are available with varying degrees of completeness in some electronic products intended for the investment banking community. They consist of CD-ROMs or workstations connected to modems, with special front end software.

Many of us, however, will find that printed sources covering extracts of financial filings for companies in a wide range of countries will be sufficient.

The rules of thumb are the same for financial sources as for basic directories:

- Sources of worldwide information often cover fewer companies than one-country sources.
- The more information given for each company, the fewer companies listed.
- Online time sharing systems cover more companies and may be more timely than print sources.

- Information providers make the same information available in a variety of print and electronic sources.

Moody's Investors Service, Worldscope/Disclosure and FT Extel Research are major compilers and publishers of worldwide financial statement information. These companies distribute their information themselves and also make the information available through third-party providers in a variety of formats and services. Researchers need to determine which data set best meets their needs in which interface. Libraries and information centers catering to financial clientele might require all or most of these sources, including additional more sophisticated services, even though the sources appear to offer duplicate coverage.

Moody's

Moody's International Manual (published annually by Moody's Investors Service)

The major U.S. print source of international extracted financial information is *Moody's International Manual*, first published in 1981. The multivolume *International Company Manual* plus the *News Reports* volume are similar in record content to other Moody's manuals. It has information on almost 9,000 major corporations, as well as national and supranational institutions, from over 100 countries.

Entries in the *Manual* are alphabetical by country. A section for "world corporations" includes regional development banks such as the Asian Development Bank, as well as major international organizations such as the International Monetary Fund and the World Bank (International Bank for Reconstruction and Development). Some of the institutions listed in Moody's are *not* listed companies. For those countries for which Moody's has had unique coverage (see Table 5.B), the listed entities are often banks.

The data are compiled by Moody's Investors Service, which has been collecting company data since 1900. The international company information is derived from the corporations themselves, using stockholders' reports and filing documents. A full entry has a chronological corporate history; a list of corporate changes such as acquisitions, joint ventures, and restructuring; a description of the business; property, such as plant locations, principal subsidiaries, and affiliates; directors; and such facts as the number of employees and the name of the company's auditors. Financial information includes two years of income statements and balance sheet data in the reported currency. Long term debt and the Moody's rating, where available, are also part of a company's record.

Moody's may modify the financial information to achieve *uniformity* among entries, but it has not reworked the numbers. That means that Moody's presents a company's financial statement in the manner in which it appears in the company's own documents. The introduction warns readers that ". . . accounting standards and terminology vary from country to country and that direct comparisons of figures, even when the terms appear to be the same, can be misleading."

There is a special features section in the blue paper insert in the middle of Volume 1. It includes a geographical index, an industry classification index, stock and bond data, and international economic statistics. Companies are divided into more than 100 industry groupings.

Moody's International Company Data

Moody's International Company Data, first released in early 1993, is the CD-ROM version of the *Moody's*

International Manual. It is available in DOS and Windows interfaces. Information on the CD-ROM closely follows the information in the *Manual*. It is the software that makes the CD-ROM interesting. Features include the ability to search and display in over 100 currencies, to compare results in two currencies, and to convert the as-reported balance sheet or income statement to a standard, U.S.-based accounting structure.

The example below illustrates both currency conversion and the use of local financials and cross-border financials. The example comes from *Moody's International Company Data* CD-ROM for the Czech-Slovak foreign trade bank, Ceskoslovenska Obchodni Banka A.S. The local country chart in local currency is the default display. The cross-border chart takes the local income statement and reworks the data into U.S. accounting format. U.S. currency may be selected in place of Czech korunas (crowns) as well.

CESKOSLOVENSKA OBCHODNI BANKA A.S.

Annual income statement in local country charts and local currency
Annual income statement in cross border charts and converted currency

ANNUAL INCOME STATEMENT

LOCAL COUNTRY CHART			CROSS BORDER CHART		
	CZECH REP Korunas Thousands 12/31/94			CZECH REP Korunas Thousands 12/31/94	U.S. Dollars Thousands 12/31/94
EX-RATE TO U.S.->	*0.0358*			*0.035*	
Interest received	15,963,174		Investment revenue	15,963,174	571,482
Commiss rec from fgn exh deals & others	2,106,229		Service revenue	2,106,229	75,403
			Total revenue	16,381,765	584,829
Total earnings	-1,039,173		Other Revenues	-1,039,173	-37,202
Interest paid	8,667,601		Direct Investment Expense	8,667,601	310,300
Commiss paid & other expenses	137,986		Total direct exp	8,667,601	310,300
Salaries	967,042		Selling general & administrative ex	2,208,555	79,066
Depreciation	400,712		Depreciation	400,712	14,345
Material expenses	0		Other s g a ex	6,529,180	233,745
Rates & taxes	0		Total s g a ex	9,182,997	327,156
Net income	1,969,959		Incomes tax	1,560,259	55,867
			Minority Interests	4,700	168
			Net Income	1,969,959	70,525

Note: Order in Local Chart changed to match more closely with Cross Border Chart. Not all lines from Local Chart are included.

MOODY'S *INTERNATIONAL COMPANY DATA* REPORT

EXHIBIT 5.1

Source: Moody's International Company Data, October 1995. Reprinted with permission from Moody's Investors Service.

Moody's Global Company Data

At the end of 1995, Moody's introduced a *Global* CD-ROM for the non-U.S. market only. This product includes a subset of its U.S. companies (those trading on the New York, American, and NASDAQ exchanges) and all of the companies on the international disc. It has over 15,000 companies from 100 countries.

Moody's Corporate News-Intl

Moody's Corporate News-Intl, DIALOG File 557, covers the articles and financial filings that appear in the print news updates. Records in the online file date back to 1983. The file is useful to search for name changes and new ventures. News records also appear on the CD-ROMs.

Inclusion in Moody's is based on size of the company, exchanges on which the company is traded, and importance as an international entity. Some enterprises pay Moody's a fee to have an enhanced entry, "corporate visibility." As in the U.S. manuals, Moody's gives ratings on debt securities, though the number of international companies with a rating is limited. On the October 1995 *Moody's International Company Data* CD-ROM, less than 10% of the companies had a debt rating. The issuers of the securities have paid Moody's a fee for the ratings.

Moody's International Annual Reports

Moody's International Annual Reports on CD-ROM has image-scanned reports for over 10,000 non-U.S. publicly held companies in 100 countries. There are 13 searchable fields. Quality of the image varies. Reports may be in English or the native language. Information about Moody's products may be found at their WWW site, http://www.moodys.com.

Worldscope/Disclosure

In the mid-1990s, Disclosure joined with Wright Investors Services, a Connecticut investment firm, to create Worldscope/Disclosure CD-ROM. The product dominated the U.S. nonspecialist library market for full text international annual reports and extracted financial data products. A chief competitor at the beginning of the decade, CIFAR (Center for International Financial Analysis and Research), sold its international annual report microfiche collection to Worldscope and agreed not to compete in that market for several years. Worldscope is now wholly owned by Disclosure.

In 1984, Professor Vinod Bavishi provided the first U.S. international annual report collection. The re-

ports, based on Bavishi's research interests, were offered in microfiche. As the collection grew, University Microfilms, CIFAR (the company Bavishi established), and finally Disclosure marketed the microfiche collection.

Then, Disclosure entered into a joint venture with Wright Investors to provide Worldscope/Disclosure and ended its venture with CIFAR. The Worldscope products have continued to expand but the microfiche is no longer available. CIFAR, after a brief entrance into the mass business information market, spent several years setting up shop in India and focusing on specialized services.

The first Worldscope/Disclosure disc became available in 1991. In February 1996, Worldscope's database of companies covered 44 countries and over 13,000 companies. Disclosure issued one CD-ROM database, *Worldscope Global,* which folded in the short-lived *Worldscope Emerging Markets*. About 3,000 companies on *Worldscope Global* are headquartered in the United States. Worldscope intends to continue adding more emerging market companies.

Worldscope presents data in standard templates, not as they are reported. There are templates for industrial corporations and banking, insurance, and other financial services. Records are divided into company profile; 10 years of annual accounts, footnotes, flow of funds, growth rates, and ratios; annual and monthly stock information; segment data; and news headlines. On the Worldscope/Disclosure CD-ROMs, almost all fields are searchable, displayable, and sortable. Users can choose DOS, DIALOG-emulation, or Windows interfaces.

Disclosure introduced a new CD-ROM, *Global Researcher,* in 1996. *Global Researcher* runs Worldscope data on the Bureau van Dijk software, discussed below. User-defined ratios, currency conversion, and an Excel add-in option are available. There is also a link to Disclosure's new subscription WWW product, *Global Access,* www.disclosure.com. Full text image annual reports are available from this site.

The distribution strategy for Disclosure is to make the database available on a wide range of hosts. Therefore, Worldscope is on LEXIS-NEXIS Services, enhanced with data for multiple stock issues. It is on Dow Jones News/Retrieval, Companyline on Corporate Profound, DataTimes, Bridge Information Systems, Datastream International Ltd., Randall-Helms International Inc., Vestek Systems, Inc., and abridged on OCLC FIRST SEARCH. It is also on CD-ROM as part of OneSource Information Services.

FT Extel Research

Extel has been an information institution in the U.K. Known for its "annual cards" (similar in concept to microfiche), the company was founded in 1872 as the Exchange Telegraph Company. In 1919, it began disseminating financial data about British companies. In the mid-1990s, it became a wholly owned subsidiary of the Financial Times Information Group of Pearson PLC. Its wide range of products and services now goes under the name FT Extel Research. FT Extel Research tracks more than 11,500 listed companies from about 60 countries. The largest number of companies is from the U.K., and its international strength is in former British Commonwealth countries.

The card service includes cards with financial statements and cards of news information. Because most international companies do not file quarterly reports, the most up-to-date financial information appears in these news cards.

There are 11 card services (see below), each offering the companies' annual reports and accounts, as well as regular news cards updating the service with interim results and major company news. Subscribers may also design their own selections.

Service	1996 Price* £	Service	1996 Price* £
U.K. Quoted	9550	Singapore	1200
Unquoted	4120	Poland	450
Analysts	2150	Thailand	990
Europe	4250	Australia	1580
Matched Bargain	1090	Malaysia	1550
Hungary	450		

* Prices are lower in the U.K. for most products.

FT Extel Research publishes four financial directories. An example is the *European Handbook*, published two times a year. This *Handbook* has more than 2,000 companies from 15 European countries. FT Extel collects information directly from the companies. The *Handbook* provides up to three years of profit-and-loss data, balance sheet, performance ratios, and ordinary share records. Companies are arranged alphabetically by country, with an alphabetical index and an index by broad sector. Rankings by market capitalization and pre-tax profit are calculated across countries, by country, and by market capitalization across industry segments. News services update the U.K. and Asian handbooks. Table 5.C lists four titles in the series. A fifth title is *Emerging Markets Handbook*.

In 1996, FT Extel divided its electronic company services into the following product groupings, but it may change by the time this book is published.

Research Product	No. of Companies
Company Analysis	10,486
Company Research	11,865
Equity Research	25,041

Company Analysis, also referred to as the Structured Database, is a Windows-based service, updated weekly by CD-ROM. There are over 10,000 companies with from 350 to 500 data elements per company available "as reported." Up to 10 years of balance sheet, profit and loss statement, flow of funds, preliminary and interim results, share price and corporate action data, notes to accounts and international exchange rates are presented. The software includes sophisticated analysis capabilities that permit the researcher or analyst to redefine financial information to individual or in-house style which FT Extel refers to as "your view."

Company Research is based on structured presentation of data. Five years of balance sheet and profit and loss accounts, flow of funds statements, segment data, performance ratios, and the chair's statement are included along with market performance data. A report can be 40 pages long. Company Research runs on a Windows platform and has enhanced graphic capabilities. Data are updated daily or weekly via a modem link. This database is also available on magnetic tape. In 1996, FT Extel began to use the name *Company Research* for its Extel Card products.

TABLE 5.C

FT EXTEL FINANCIAL DIRECTORIES

Title	Number of Companies	Number of Countries	Price, £	Frequency
Major UK Companies Handbook	700	1	210	2 x yr
Smaller Companies Handbook	1500	1	265	annual
European Handbook	2000	15	240	2 x yr
Asia Pacific Handbook	1300	7	190	2 x yr

Equity Research focuses on share price data but also has fundamentals, announcements, and news. It has extensive graphing and charting capabilities.

Researchers may also purchase FT Extel data directly from FT Extel on tape or diskette. Weekly and monthly updates are available. Data may also be stored on a hard disk and updated online daily. FT Extel also has an Equity database with seven years of daily stock prices. FT Extel is distributed through third party vendors and distributors. FT Extel is online through FT Profile, Corporate Profound, DIALOG, DataStar, and LEXIS-NEXIS Services; on CD-ROM with OneSource and Wave Systems; on Lotus Notes; and terminal-based with Bridge Information Systems.

FT Profile has made some of the FT Extel information available for free on its end-user Discover WWW site, http://www.info.FT.com/online/discover/sampler. You can screen across about 10,000 companies, using company name, turnover, profit, capitalization, or major industry groups. Up to 10 companies are displayed. The amount of data provided varies from company name, directors, and activities, to basic financials: three years of balance sheet, capital, key financials, and profit and loss. This is *not* a research tool. You cannot search by country, and financials are in local currency.

Worldscope and FT Extel design their products for use by accountants and financial analysts. Files contain the footnotes that accompany the financial data and accounting standards used.

Standard and Poor's

Standard and Poor's Corporation Records

(published by Standard and Poor's Corporation, with daily news)

Standard and Poor's is regarded as the main competitor to Moody's in the U.S. print financial market. However, S&P is keeping a lower profile in the international print market. About 2,800 international companies are now listed in its directory, *S&P Corporate Register*. Over 1,800 non-U.S. companies are included in its print financial reports, *S&P Corporation Records*. However, more than 1,200 of the non-U.S. companies in the *Corporation Records* are Canadian. The only other non-U.S. companies in the *Corporation Records* trade American Depository Receipts (ADRs) in the United States (see Chapter 16 for information about ADRs). Therefore, the selection of companies in this publication does not reflect the size of the non-U.S. companies, nor the size or importance of their home financial markets.

Data are presented as reported by the company. Key data items are also reported as "fielded annual data," standardized for comparisons. Local currency is used in both presentations. Additional information in the *Records* is an extensive business description, company history, property owned, and debt ratings, if any. A daily news update accompanies these looseleaf volumes.

Any library owning this publication will get a substantial amount of information about the companies included. However, given the limited number of companies, you would not buy this product for its international coverage.

The *Corporation Records* are available on DIALOG File 133, Corporation Descriptions plus News. Both S&P titles are loaded together on LEXIS-NEXIS Services in the COMPNY library as SPCO.

Global Vantage

At present, S&P does not have plans to expand its international print coverage. However, Standard & Poor's provides a high-end CD-ROM product, *Global Vantage*, that uses Compustat PC Plus Windows software. The product is designed for financial analysts and academic researchers.

Global Vantage switched primary data providers. Listed below are the sources for data in *Global Vantage*, with the * indicating new sources.

COMPANY DATA	SOURCE
*Industrial Commercial—U.S. and Canada	Compustat
Industrial Commercial—Rest of World	World'Vest Base
*Financial Services—Entire World	Compustat
Equity Pricing	James Capel & Co. (UK)

Companies in *Global Vantage* appear in at least one of approximately 90 indexes:

- Morgan Stanley Capital International Index (MSCII Prospective)
- Financial Times S&P World Index
- Local Market Indexes

S&P will add non-U.S. companies that analysts request. The only additional U.S. companies are those added to the S&P 500.

See Table 5.2 for a list of country coverage. The CD-ROM product has annual data starting in 1983 for 11,000 companies. 3,000 of them are from the U.S. 280 data elements are available for each company, derived from the company's home-country annual report. Each data element has in-context definitions. The data are not restated, but they are classified to fit into standard templates based on a company's industry classification. Companies are divided into two categories, Industrial/Commercial and Financial Services. Most companies fall into the former category. The Financial Services category is further divided into the following formats, each of which has its own set of data elements:

Bank
Insurance
Broker/Dealer
Real Estate
Other Financial Services

Only U.S., Canadian, Japanese, and U.K. companies have flow of funds data. There are extensive precalculated financial and growth rates, with the software capability to create your own ratios and growth rates. There are no product or geographic segment data in the file. The file has extensive footnotes detailing accounting standards, valuation principles, and methods of consolidation. Extensive financial and growth ratios have been calculated.

In *Global Vantage,* 110 currencies are represented, with translation rates available for month-end, monthly average, and 12-month moving average. Translations may be done from a country's native currency to other currencies. There is also a file of more than 12,000 equity issues and 95 indexes in 65 countries, with up to 12 years of prices, dividends, and earnings data.

Added features of the software are the ability to create a report from a library of standard reports or design a custom report. For example, there are five types of income statements and 180 calculated items. Country Overviews, from DRI/McGraw Hill, have also been added to the product. Brief information on the *Global Vantage* product is available on the WWW at http://www.compustat.com.

Other Financial Directories

Hoover's Handbook of World Business (published annually by Hoover's, Inc.; Austin, TX)

Moody's is the standard international print financial directory in the United States. It is required for most medium and large libraries with business clients. For those libraries that need financial information only on major international companies, *Hoover's Handbook of World Business* may be enough. *Hoover's Handbook* contains profiles of about 300 companies worldwide that Hoover's has identified as major. It is one of a growing series of handbooks that Hoover publishes.

Many of the companies listed in *Hoover's Handbook of World Business* are traded in the United States. Hoover's compiles information from a variety of other publicly available sources such as Standard & Poor's for company financials and Economist Intelligence Unit reports for country information. Hoover's makes the following interesting disclaimer in its introduction:

> *Readers should not rely on any information contained herein in instances where such reliance might cause loss or damage.*

A chatty history and a list of competitors are unique features in all Hoover's handbooks.

Hoover's also includes country profiles, rankings, and a plethora of lists. Hoover's applies the following criteria to select companies:

1. Exporters or producers known in the U.S.
2. Businesses that dominate big industries or lead the industry in their countries
3. Representative companies worldwide (e.g., one company from India is included)
4. Representative companies from 24 industry groupings

Hoover's Handbook of World Business uses a standard format for each company entry, with the following headings:

- Overview
- When: A brief history of the company
- Who: Executives, directors, and auditors
- Where: Addresses and general foreign locations
- What: Product information by segment; major joint ventures and subsidiaries
- How Much: Key financials, including 10 years of sales, net income, earnings, stock prices and dividends
- Key Competitors

While Hoover's considers itself a financial source, it is probably more useful for its brief history.

Hoover's Handbook of World Business is on LEXIS-NEXIS Services as part of the HVRDWL, the Hoover's file in the COMPNY library. Internet addresses for the companies with Hoover's records appear in the 1996 entries online; 1996 entries appeared online before the edition was available in print.

Hoover's also has company profiles on its Web site, http://www.hoovers.com. A WWW entry for a company includes directory information (name, address, telecommunications, WWW link, CEO, CFO, and human resource contact) and brief financial information (fiscal year end, date of annual sales figure, latest quarter and annual sales, net income, earnings per share, and shares outstanding). To receive a full report from Hoover's on the WWW, it is necessary to subscribe for about $10 per month.

Should you purchase *Hoover's Handbook of World Business*? At about $40, it looks like a bargain. Obviously, Hoover's handbooks will not substitute for a collection of international company sources; however, for a small high school, company, or public library, this book does give you your money's worth. Note, however, that the cost per company in *Hoover's* is about the same as many of the more expensive directories.

Buyers beware: Another Hoover's publication, *Hoover's Handbook of Emerging Companies,* refers to fast-growing U.S. companies, *not* to companies from emerging markets.

Global Company Handbook (Princeton, NJ: Center for International Financial Analysis and Research, CIFAR, 3rd ed. due 1997)

In 1994, we recommended the second edition of *Global Company Handbook: An Analysis of the Financial Performance of the World's Leading ... Companies* for basic financial data for a maximum number of companies and countries in print form. The third edition of the *Handbook* will be in four volumes. Volume I, "Analysis of the World's 50 Capital Markets," contains company rankings and industry and country averages. Volumes II, III, and IV each will have 4,000 company profiles, organized by continent.

Volume II	Europe/Africa/Middle East	
	Europe	20 countries
	Africa/Middle East	15 countries
Volume III	Asia/Pacific	16 countries
Volume IV	North/South America	
	North America	3 countries
	South America	7 countries

Each volume can be purchased separately. There is a minimum of 25 companies from each country, representing 32 industry groupings. This is an excellent print source, packed full of information in a concise format. However, the publisher's inability to issue the publication in a timely manner is of great concern. CIFAR files are accessible through the LEXIS-NEXIS COMPNY library, but they have not been updated since 1993.

Dow Jones Guide to the World Stock Market

Dow Jones Guide to the World Stock Market has been published annually since 1994 as a joint effort by Dow Jones and Morningstar. The book includes brief financial snapshots of the 2,700 companies from 20 countries that constitute the Dow Jones World Stock Index. Each entry includes a brief description of the business, three years sales, net income and book value, price-earnings ratio, yield, market capital, SEDOL and ADR ticker. This inexpensive book might serve the international financial needs of small libraries. Because Morningstar withdrew from distributing international financial information in late 1996, we do not know if Dow Jones will continue to publish this guide.

Bureau van Dijk

Bureau van Dijk (BVD) is a management consulting and software development firm in Brussels and Paris, with a sales office in New York. It has a series of financial CD-ROM databases that it offers in conjunction with local information supplier's. Examples of Bureau van Dijk discs are *FAME*, with data from Jordan & Sons in the U.K.; *Diane*, the French disc with SCRL data; *Dafne*, the German database with Creditreform data; and *JADE*, Japanese accounts and data on enterprises, with Teikoku data. BVD recently issued *Global Researcher* as a joint venture with Disclosure, using Worldscope data.

All of the CD-ROM products use the same sophisticated statistical analysis package. A description of the Bureau van Dijk CD-ROM financial products appears in the March 1993 *CD-ROM Professional*.[4] *FAME* is one of the most heavily used financial products in the U.K. A Windows version of the software and a debit card system to keep track of use are two enhancements to the product.

BVD also has a product, *Amadeus,* that has several strengths as a pan-European financial CD-ROM product.

- It gives detailed financial information on about 150,000 of the largest companies from 26 European countries: the EU plus Norway, Switzerland, Iceland, and companies in Eastern Europe. Amadeus includes the top companies from other Bureau van Dijk products such as FAME, Diane, and Dafne. In 1996 it contained all companies in the covered countries with turnover above $13 million (U.S.) or total assets greater than $26 million (U.S.) or more than 150 employees.

- Bureau van Dijk uses a financial model to standardize the income statement and balance sheet accounts for 44 financial items plus 20 ratios and 36 growth trends. Historical data are available for 5 years. All Bureau van Dijk databases include private as well as listed companies. Bureau van Dijk software performs peer group analysis across countries or across industries.

- In addition to their national industry codes, the companies in the *Amadeus* database have been assigned one or more activity codes, one of which is a primary code, using the 7-digit system of the British Central Statistical Office. BVD then cross references the code with all popular national and international industry classifications, allowing users to search for companies using the code of their choice.

Amadeus is updated every month. The information is sourced by 23 national information providers, each long-established in the countries they cover. All Bureau van Dijk databases include private as well as listed companies.

In January 1997, Bureau van Dijk was beta-testing a WWW site with free access to directory information and subscription access to the *Amadeus* databases. Searching is by company, country, major industry group, and "operating revenue" in U.S. dollars or percent rate of growth. Five years of balance sheet and profit and loss statement data in the local currency, plus key financials in U.S. dollars, are available as output. One of the strengths of BVD CD-ROM software is its peer group analysis. A peer group report is also available on the WWW site. BVD's home page, with product information, offers access to *Amadeus* as well: http://www.bvd.com.

OneSource

OneSouce (originally, Lotus OneSource) was an early player in the delivery of company information on CD-ROM. OneSource repackages other products and delivers them under one search platform, through Windows interface, Lotus Notes, and now on the World Wide Web. OneSource designs its search software and suite of products for the financial audience. Its international products include "International Public," from the *Extel Financial Card Service*, "UK Private+" and "UK Small Companies" from ICC, Duns *CD/Europa* and "International Equities" from *Worldscope, I/B/E/S* and Morgan Stanley Capital Markets. U.S. public companies from Moody's and U.S. private companies from *Ward's Business Directory* are available using the same search interface. OneSource also distributes a wide range of more specialized products.

U.K. Quoted Companies is its first non-U.S. product available via the WWW. It includes 12 years of fundamentals and 7 years of share price data. It covers all 2,000 U.K. quoted companies. Much of the company information is from Hemmington Scott, discussed below. OneSource is trying to create a WWW

inferface that retains much of the functionality and flexibility of their other interfaces. For a full review of OneSource WWW products, see the "Test Drive" in the December 1996 *Online/CD-ROM Business Information*.[5] OneSource's URL is http://www.onesource.com.

Internet Securities Inc. (http://www.securities.com)

Traditional providers of financial information continue to offer information in formats ranging from print to the Internet. Newcomers to the field are bypassing print and CD-ROM and are delivering directly via the WWW. An example is Internet Securities, a subscription service offering WWW delivery of financial information from emerging markets. Internet Securities was founded in 1994, as an outgrowth of a student initiative at Carnegie Mellon University to locate hard-to-find financial data on emerging market companies and economies. The company recently relocated to Boston to be closer to the financial information provider scene. Its target market is people doing business in these emerging markets.

As of January 1, 1997, Internet Securities covered the Baltic States, Bulgaria, Czech Republic, Hungary, India, Poland, Russia, Ukraine, Central Asia (Kazakhstan, Kyrgyzstan, and Uzbekistan), China, India, and Colombia. Commercial subscribers pay a monthly fee, based on the number of countries or regions selected.

For each country, there is current news, company financial statements, securities pricing, industry reports, and economic data from local providers. There are also links to EIU reports and an additional subscription for Investext industry strategy reports. Most of the sources in Internet Securities are local, unique, and many are in the local language, while others, like EIU, are available everywhere. Internet Securities offers financial filings from emerging markets that are presented as reported by the local company to a local information provider. For example, for Polish companies, the latest monthly, quarterly, and annual reports were available, as well as stock information, major shareholders, and underwriters of recent issues. Polish company information is provided by Polish Press Agency (PAP) and Notoria Serwis. Russian company information comes from Dun & Bradstreet CIS.

The strength of Internet Securities is that it presently offers information available nowhere else and has many more companies per country than our other sources. The weakness of Internet Securities is that much of this information is not available anywhere else because it is not authoritative. Statements have not been standardized, there are no footnotes, statements may not be audited, time series are limited, and the organizations providing the data to Internet Securities are local. Internet Securities is trying to contract with suppliers who are reliable, but the present policy is, "any data are better than no data," and if a supplier proves to be unreliable, Internet Securities will look for another one. It is important that Internet Securities be used by analysts who recognize the limitations to this financial information.

SOURCES OF REGIONAL FINANCIAL INFORMATION

Europe

European 5000 (published in London by Euromoney)

European 5000, formerly the *Price Waterhouse European Company Handbook,* is a pan-European financial source. It contains national companies with securities traded on the stock exchanges in European countries (OTC excluded). The most recent edition, 1994, was issued in four volumes: (1) Northern Europe, (2) Western Europe, (3) Central & Southern Europe, and (4) Indices. The handbook has the top 2,000 companies ranked by market capitalization with a minimum of 25 companies per country. Information is gathered from the local stock exchanges. Entries indicate if the accounts are restated or nonconsolidated. While no date for a new edition has been announced, Euromoney considers this a "live" title.

Asia

Asian Company Handbook (published annually by Toyo Keizai)

Toyo Keizai, publisher of the *Japan Company Handbook*, began publishing the companion *Asian Company Handbook* in 1991. Both directories are now distributed by Moody's. In 1995/96 the *Asian Company Handbook* included information on more than 1,000 selected corporations on stock exchanges in the following countries: Hong Kong, Indonesia, Malaysia, Korea (Republic), Singapore, Taiwan, and Thailand.

According to the introduction, companies are selected based on the recommendations of "acclaimed research organizations in the eight nations."

Companies are listed alphabetically. A Securities Code Number, if the country assigns one, is provided, as are Chinese characters, where applicable. The *Asian Company Handbook* includes the following data items:

- *Establishment date.* Usually the date when a company first registered as a joint-stock company.

- *Head office.* Except Hong Kong, the place that controls the companies' activities and is registered as Head Office NA not available; "-" none.
- *Financial data.* Generally uniform item; some national differences do exist, however, due to terminology or preference of the research agency. (For example, Korea uses "Bank Borrowing" for long- and short-term debt issued by banks and other corporations.)
- *Sales breakdown* (segment data). Ratios.
- *Geographic breakdowns.* Ratio of overseas workers at location/total workers.
- *Subsidiaries and affiliates.* Stockholding ratio of company and its subsidiaries and affiliate companies; not all listed.
- *Special feature.* Export destinations.

SOURCES OF COUNTRY FINANCIAL INFORMATION

Japan

Japan Company Handbook (published quarterly by Toyo Keizai)

The major English-language print source for financial information on Japanese companies is the *Japan Company Handbook,* formerly the *Japan Company Directory.* The source has been published since 1957. Starting in 1987, the *Japan Company Handbook* has been published quarterly in two parts: the First Section, which provides financial information on the more than 1,300 companies on the first sections of the Tokyo, Osaka, and Nagoya stock exchanges; and the Second Section, which provides financial information for 770 companies on the second section of the same and local exchanges.

Companies are arranged by their Japanese numeric stock symbol. Names are in English, Japanese, and transliterated. There is a brief profile and three years of seven financial items, plus two years of forecasts. Other data elements are sales segments, five years of stock prices, with graph, capital changes, and 10 major shareholders, plus percent foreign ownership. There are 11 selected financials from the balance sheet, borrowing, and research and development. Additional information mentioned in the profile includes banks, exchanges, underwriters, the year established and the year listed, number of employees, and group membership.

Japan Company Handbook is also available electronically on LEXIS-NEXIS Services as the file JCH in the COMPNY library. Exhibit 5.2 is a brief extract from a company record.

2503 KIRIN BREWERY FULL-TERM FIGURES			
	Dec 1994	**Dec 1993**	**Dec 1992**
Sales (mil Y):	1,445,033	1,346,368	1,366,105
Operating Profit (mil Y)	84,123	63,076	69,918
Current Profit (mil Y):	95,473	76,939	82,705
Net Profit (mil Y):	44,633	36,284	37,520
Earnings Per Share (Y):	42.4	34.5	35.6
Dividend Per Share (Y):	11	10	10
Return on Equity (%):	7.3	6.3	6.8

Capital Changes from 1977 -

DATE	CHANGE	SHARES (1000)
Feb 1977	20 : 1 Gratis	612,878...

FACILITY INVESTMENT (Y mil):

Dec1995*	90,000
Dec1994	93,658

R&D EXPENDITURE (Y mil):

Dec1995*	17,000

HIGHEST TERM PROFIT (Y mil):

Dec 1994	95,473

EXTRACT FROM *JAPAN COMPANY HANDBOOK*

EXHIBIT 5.2

Source: Japan Company Handbook Spring 1996, search in JCH on LEXIS-NEXIS Services.

Information about both the *Asian* and *Japan Company Handbooks* is available at http://www.mediagalaxy.co.jp/toyokeizai/jch/jch.html.

Teikoku

The most complete source of financials for Japanese companies in the U.S. is the Teikoku database with financials for over 120,000 Japanese companies. This is the file used in the CD-ROM products *JADE*, from Bureau van Dijk, and Japan Company Factfinder, from DIALOG. It is also examined in more detail in both Chapters 6 and 8. *Teikoku* is available on DIA-LOG File 502, on DataStar as TOFF, and on the major Japanese databanks as well.

Teikoku includes many of the same summary data items as *Japan Company Handbook* but much more extensive financials. There are three years worth of data, with up to 98 balance sheet items and 91 income statement data elements. Information about Teikoku products can be found at http://www.teikoku.com.

Morningstar

Morningstar, a U.S. firm known for its publications in mutual funds, published the short-lived *Morningstar Japan.*

France

French Company Handbook (published annually by International Business Distribution in Paris and by the International Herald Tribune, Paris)

The *French Company Handbook* is a multipurpose, single-country directory. It has one page of information on 132 major listed French companies. Thirty-one industry segments are included, with companies listed in more than one segment. The *French Company Handbook* also includes a brief summary of the French economy, industry evaluations, and information about investing in France.

Sample Data Items in the
French Company Handbook

Sample company data includes name, head office, telecommunications, management, major activities, employees at home and abroad, consolidated turnover, breakdown by sector, company background, major brand names, major known shareholders, principal international subsidiaries, exports, research/innovation, strategy and trends, and important developments.

Financial highlights contain 6 years of tabular data for 17 items from the income statement, balance sheet, and price data, and a verbal description of the prior year. For example, the 1995 edition had data for 1990–1994 with a verbal summary of important developments for 1994–95.

United Kingdom

There are many sources of financial data for U.K. companies, in print and electronically.

Company REFS (published monthly by Hemmington Scott, UK)

Company REFS (Really Essential Financial Statistics) is, accorded to its "devisor" Jim Slater, the closest U.K. product to the U.S. investor newsletter, *Valueline. REFS* is a monthly two-part publication that covers the approximately 1,600 companies in the U.K. market indices. The "Tables" volume ranks companies on performance measures such as earnings per share growth rates, price-earnings ratios, and dividend yield, by index grouping. Companies are divided into almost 40 industry sectors. Sector medians and sector-weighted averages are calculated. *REFS* presents insider trades (directors' share dealings) for the year. The "Companies" volume provides a half page of data for each company, with a graph of the company's share price movement and a beta. Additionally, there is a handbook for the investor, *How to Use Company REFS.*

Hemmington Scott also has a free online service, UK Equities Direct, which includes summary company data, contact data, consensus forecasts, and links to annual reports: http://www.hemscott.co.uk/hemscott.

Jordan and Sons

Jordan and Sons offers print directories, online, and CD-ROM company databases, and industry reports. Data come from Companies House. Jordan's has full financials for more than 100,000 U.K. companies out of the over 250,000 companies in the database. Jordan's includes companies with turnover greater than 500,000 pounds, pre-tax profit greater than £25,000, or shareholder funds of more than £25,000.

ICC Information Group

ICC Information Group is another major U.K. provider of company and industry information. Access ICC information online either directly to ICC or through the major timesharing systems. The range of products includes British company financials, from the same Companies House source as Jordan's. ICC has full text annual reports from the U.K., industry reports, and brokerage house reports. ICC also provides Sharewatch, on its own system, which tracks share ownership in British quoted companies. The annual reports and ICC KeyNote industry reports are also available on CD-ROM through SilverPlatter and as DIALOG's *UK Company Factfinder.*

At the end of 1996, ICC unveiled new names for its product line. Plum is the name of its new Internet online facility, http://www.icc.co.uk. It will offer company status reports, credit status reports, and overview reports. Juniper is a new Windows client, Blueberry the CD-ROM portfolio, and Damson ICC's traditional direct online database.

ICC is best known in the U.K. for its ratios. At the end of 1996, it launched a new CD-ROM, *ROM:BUS*, subtitled "The Business Ratios plus CD-ROM." The CD-ROM provides ratios on over 500 industry subsectors. Individual print *Business Ratios* plus reports by industry sector are also available for 15 major sectors and from 50 to 150 leading companies within the sector.

Companies House

Companies House itself is accessible online through Mercury Data Network in the U.K. Profile data, including company incorporation date, registered number, date of accounts, and a history screen, are on the online file. Researchers may obtain any document filed with Companies House via post, microform, or by fax. Image files for 3,000 companies are also available. Like the U.S. SEC, Companies House has complete microfiche collections in reading rooms. Types of documents include annual accounts and returns, change in directors, change institution, new companies, mortgage documents, capital, and liquidations.

It has its own CD-ROM, *Companies House CD-ROM Directory,* that contains basic information on all live and recently dissolved companies (about 1.20 million in 1996). The *Directory* will be available as a monthly subscription or a bargain £30 individual purchase.

Canada

Financial Post Survey of Industrials (published annually by Financial Post DataGroup).

Published since 1927, *Financial Post Survey of Industrials* covers more than 2,500 manufacturing, real estate development, forestry, investment, holding, financial management, communications, transportation, banking, retailing, and service companies publicly traded in Canada. A companion volume, *Financial Post Survey of Mines and Energy Resources,* which has also been published since the 1920s, has almost 3,000 listings.

A basic entry includes legal name, address, communications numbers, history, directors, major shareholders, two years of key financials, and five years of operating revenue, net income before taxes, and earnings per common share. Companies with enhanced coverage include a review and outlook provided by the company.

Documentation in the book is very clear, including explanations for data elements, company inclusion, cutoff dates, and accuracy. Financials are standardized, based on industry grouping.

The electronic version of the two *Surveys*, which is updated weekly, is available as a joint venture with Micromedia. *CanCorp Canadian Financials Database* has records for almost 9,000 companies. Each record has 5 years of consolidated accounts, stated in U.S. dollars, explanatory footnotes, and a list of news releases from the *Financial Post. CanCorp Plus,* the file containing the complete records, is on DIALOG File 491, DataStar CNCO, LEXIS-NEXIS Services (CNCORP), and the Disclosure CD-ROM, *CompactD/ Canada. CanCorp* on DataStar (CNCO) does not include the *Financial Post* added data. It is also available in Canada on QL Systems and Infomart. A nice feature of *CanCorp* is that it states the source of information for each section of a company record.

SOURCES OF FINANCIAL DATA BY INDUSTRY

Less prevalent are international financial sources arranged by industry group. Banking is one industry grouping well covered in print and electronically. There is also one international source for insurance.

Banking Sources

Bankstat (Institutional Investor)

Bankstat, a CD-ROM database from Institutional Investor, includes current data and five years of historical data on over 7,000 international financial institutions from 180 countries. As of fall 1996, regional distribution of institutions is as shown below.

Region	Number of Institutions
Africa	361
Asia-Pacific	1,448
Caribbean	144
Eastern Europe	380
Western Europe	3,392
Middle East	267
USA & Canada	649
Latin America	759

Data elements are *all* items and ratios from the balance sheet, income statement, and footnotes, as well as number of employees, shareholder and subsidiary information, and earnings. Credit ratings and

rankings are also provided. Bankstat Windows software offers screening capabilities, report writing, graphs, and peer group analysis. There are at least 35 CD-ROMs issued per year. More information is available at http://www.bankstat.com.

Annuals on CD-ROM is the full-text image companion product to *Bankstat* with reports for about 6,000 institutions. Reports may be both in English and the local language.

BankScope (Bureau van Dijk)

BankScope, formerly called EURA-CD, is a CD-ROM from Bureau van Dijk, containing 8,300 world banks. The data on the disc is produced in conjunction with International Bank Credit Analyst (IBCA), a European banking authority. *BankScope* uses standard Bureau van Dijk analysis software. It has up to eight years of data. It covers the top 4,505 European banks, top 940 North American banks, 185 Japanese banks, 1,645 major banks from other countries, and 15 supranational banking and financial organizations. Each country has its own data template to allow for differences in reporting and accounting.

There are two years of Reuter Textline articles related to banks with online access to recent news. IBCA ratings, Moody's and S&P ratings, Capital Intelligence Ratings and Reports, and BREE Ratings and Reports all are on the CD. There is also shareholder data. *BankScope* is issued 18 times per year.

Two new bank CD-ROMs are coming on the market, both from prestigious U.K. sources. One is from *The Banker* journal, the other derived from *Bankers' Almanac.*

BANKbase (Reed Information Services)

Bankers' Almanac, published for over 150 years, is a directory of international banks. The multivolume print publication has 4,000 international banks arranged alphabetically, including address and telecommunications details, names of directors and senior officials, correspondent banks in all major financial centers, history and ownership, two years' abridged balance sheets in local currency, abridged comparable profit and loss statements and performance ratios, long and short term credit ratings, plus details of more than 7,000 international branches. There is geographic access, by country, to over 174,000 individual bank branches, representative offices, and agencies worldwide. Finally, it includes a further 23,000 banks and some 600 law firms active in banking law, a shareholders section detailing the main shareholders of the international banks, plus a unique section of bank name changes and liquidations since 1750.

Reed is introducing *BANKbase*, a CD-ROM based on *Bankers' Almanac*. It will have additional information from IBCA plus news items and group structure details. According to Reed literature, coverage, in principal, includes "all institutions globally which are recognized as banks by the authorities in their country of incorporation plus nonbanking institutions which either own banks or are owned by them." Over 27,000 registered banks, with almost 180,000 branches from 199 countries, are on the CD. IBCA is supplying five years of full financials for about 8,000 institutions. For the rest, you will find two years of abridged balance sheet and profit and loss data.

The CD-ROM is designed to have the feel of the print publication. The three primary access points to the database are bank name, town name, or country name. The CD-ROM has hypertext links between banks and correspondents, owners, and branches. There are also world ranking tables.

The Banker Directory and *The Banker World Banks Database* CD-ROM (Financial Times)

The Banker, first published in 1926, announced a 1997 release date for a three-volume directory of the top 1,200 international banks and their financial records, and a corresponding CD-ROM. *The Banker Directory* is arranged geographically with volumes for the Americas; Asia, Pacific, Africa and the Middle East; and Europe. Each volume contains a listing of all major banks in each region, a ranking index, and a geographic index. Each entry contains directory information, contact details, historical financials, tier one capital, assets, profits, performance and "soundness" data. The three volumes may be purchased individually, as a set, or on CD-ROM as *The Banker World Banks Database CD-ROM*.

Insurance

Best's Insurance Reports: International Edition
(published annually, with updates, by A. M. Best)

A. M. Best has been publishing U.S. insurance company reports since 1913. In 1985, they issued their first *Best's Insurance Reports International*. We commend Best for the care it has taken in its introductory remarks to remind the user of the pitfalls of using international financial information.

For this edition, we have tried to standardize the reporting headings across countries with the major accounting differences being reported either as headnotes or footnotes. In future years, we plan to work at developing the data on a more comparable basis among countries and companies. The user should take great care when utilizing the material contained in these reports to understand just what differences many exist due to reporting variations, which may arise because of tax environments, legal requirements, and/or accounting practices in the various nations around the world.

("Introduction," 1996 edition)

Best's includes more than 1,100 insurers and reinsurers in 65 countries. Companies are classified in one of 15 size categories from up to $1,000,000 adjusted policyholder surplus to more than $2 billion.

Reports contain the source of information, investment results, taxes, consolidated and group reports, history, management, and operations. There is an "English-Foreign Index" of companies and a "Foreign-English Index," followed by an alphabetical list of rated companies. Company reports are then arranged alphabetically. There is also a country index.

Information comes directly from the company either as annual reports to stockholders or policyholders, or as statements presented to the regulatory bodies having jurisdiction in the various countries in which the companies operate. Reports also may include supplemental information obtained by Best's from questionnaires, examination of other reports, and meetings with company management.

Data items include balance sheet, income, and expenditures data, reported in the currency of country and also in U.S. dollar equivalents. There is an exchange rate table. Entries vary in length but most are at least two columns. Exhibit 5.3 presents excerpts from a sample entry.

International companies are part of Best's CD-ROM. Best's also issues a separate *Life/Health Canada*.

FINDING FINANCIAL FOOTNOTES

When comparing companies across industries and across countries, it is important for researchers to know how the data have been calculated by the company. The footnotes in financial statements provide this information.

**THE NICHIDO FIRE AND MARINE
INSURANCE COMPANY, LTD.**
No. 3-16 Ginza 5-chome
Chuo-Ku, Tokyo 104, Japan
Tel: 81-3-3571-5141   Telefax: 81-3-3574-0646
AMB:85023

CURRENT BEST'S RATINGS/FPR

Based on our current opinion of the company's financial condition and operating performance, it is assigned a Best's Rating of... The company's Financial Size Category is Class XIV... Rating Effective November 21, 1994

Rating Rationale

The financial data of the company has been updated to show 1995 results. However, due to the delay in receiving supplemental company submissions, qualitiative and quantitative analysis to update the Best's Rating for the company is still in progress...

COMPANY OVERVIEW

The company writes the following lines of business: fire, marine, transit, automobile, compulsory auto liability, person accident, bond third party... Domestic business is written through 49 branch officers 291 sub-branch offices and 34,578 agencies located throughout Japan. Foreign business is written through several affiliates...

OPERATING COMMENTS

Fiscal 1993 ended March 31, 1994 continued to be a difficult period for the Japanese insurance industry...
Source of Information: Company Annual Report

Summarized Accounts as of March 31 1995
US$ per Local Currency Unit .011553=1 Japanese Yen (JPY)
ASSETS

	03/31/95 JPY (000,000)	03/31/95 %	03/31/95 US$ (000,000)
Bonds	166,863	10.7	1,055
Stocks	268,167	17.2	1,695
Foreign securities	215,036	13.8	1,359 ...

EXCERPTS FROM *BEST'S INSURANCE REPORTS* (INTERNATIONAL ED.)

EXHIBIT 5.3

Source: Best's Insurance Reports, International Edition, 1996. Copyright A.M. Best Company, used with permission.

Worldscope emphasizes the availability of footnote information on its CD-ROM products and online files. Every significant word in these fields is searchable. For example, on *Worldscope*, you can:

- Search for accounting practices for French companies that use straight line depreciation.
- Search for examples of how U.K. companies handle extraordinary earnings when calculating earnings per share.
- Identify "stock splits" in the footnotes to stock reports, or "reorganizations" in the footnotes to financials.

There is no standardization for footnotes to financial statements. The text comes directly from the company's report. *Worldscope* also includes notes that indicate when the data have been reworked for the database. For example, the French hotel conglomerate ACCOR S.A. does not report current liabilities. Therefore, calculations for the *Worldscope* database are based on other balance sheet data. The footnotes section of *Worldscope* reports the following calculations.

FOOTNOTES TO FINANCIAL STATEMENTS:...
3: 1990, 1989, 1988, 1987, 1986—COMPANY DOES
NOT REPORT CURRENT LIABILITIES; **CALCULATED...**

FT Extel does not report the textual footnotes, but includes footnoted calculations. *Global Vantage* and Bankstat both include footnotes. Extensive footnotes appear in *CanCorp*. Exhibit 5.4 is an example of *CanCorp* footnotes.

FO   (from Annual Report to Shareholders: 12/31/94)
*Alcan*Aluminium Limited
Notes to Consolidated Financial Statements
December 31, 1994 (in millions of US$, except where indicated)

NOTE 2 Differences Between Canadian and United States
Generally Accepted Accounting Principles (GAAP)
DEFERRED INCOME TAXES.
Under Canadian GAAP, deferred income taxes are measured
at tax rates prevailing at the time the provisions for deferred
taxes are made. Deferred income taxes for U.S. GAAP are revalued
each period using currently enacted tax rates.
RECONCILIATION OF CANADIAN AND U.S. GAAP.

	1994	
	As Reported	U.S. GAAP
Net income (Loss) from continuing operations before cumulative effect of accounting changes	$ 96	$ 175
Cumulative effect on prior years of accounting changes	_____	_____

EXTRACT FROM FOOTNOTE REPORTED IN *CanCorp*

EXHIBIT 5.4

Source: CanCorp Canadian Financial on DataStar. Reprinted with permission of Micromedia Ltd.

SOURCES OF INTERNATIONAL ANNUAL REPORTS

We have been discussing financial data. Listed below are the major sources of the text of annual statements in a variety of formats.

Print	*Moody's International Manual* (extracts)
	Standard and Poor's Corporation Records (extracts)
Cards	Extel Card Service
CD-ROM Primary Image Documents	
	Laser D/International (Disclosure)
	Disclosure Select and *Global Access*
	Moody's International Annual Reports (IAR)
CD-ROM Text and Data	
	U.K. Company Reports (ICC on SilverPlatter and DIALOG U.K. FactFinder)
	FT Extel
	Moody's International Company Data
	CIFAR's *Full Text* on CD-ROM (announced too late for examination)
Online	ICC Annual Report file—full text (DIALOG, DataStar, LEXIS-NEXIS Services, ICC Direct)
World Wide Web	
	Use Yahoo! to locate individual companies
	Disclosure *Global Access*

U.S. SEC EDGAR

Companies filing on U.S. exchanges have to file their 10-Ks, 10-Qs, and many other required filings electronically with the Securities and Exchange Commission (SEC). These filings are available, free of charge, at http://www.sec.gov in raw format. Unfortunately for the international researcher, the 20-F form filed by non-U.S. companies trading on U.S. exchanges had not been required, and there were fewer than 20 such filings as of January 1997. Raw EDGAR filings require reformatting before presenting to a client. Only terms appearing in the tagged header are searchable. A sample EDGAR header for the Canadian company Advanced Gravis Computer Technology is presented in Exhibit 5.5.

World Wide Web

The WWW can be an efficient way to retrieve an individual annual report. Some companies place selected annual report data on the WWW. It may be more up-to-date than data in commercial sources. It may include more or less information. For example, the Canadian company Advanced Gravis Computer Technology Ltd. includes more in-depth background and officer biographical material than our commercial sources. It posts its quarterly results as soon as they are released. It also is one of a handful of non-U.S. companies trading on U.S. exchanges to file an EDGAR 20-F. However, it also uses such nontechnical terms as "world leader," "passion," and "revolutionary."

```
y-BEGIN PRIVACY-ENHANCED MESSAGE——
Proc-Type: 2001,MIC-CLEAR
Originator-Name: webmaster@www.sec.gov
Originator-Key-Asymmetric:
 MFgwCgYEVQgBAQICAf8DSgAwRwJAW2sNKK9AVtBzYZmr6aGjlWyK3XmZv3dTINen
 TWSM7vrzLADbmYQaionwg5sDW3P6oaM5D3tdezXMm7z1T+B+twIDAQAB
MIC-Info: RSA-MD5,RSA,
 Ci6JsZBslFlALZZG4b+AMSkk26fEZLwy+RvqMUqahB42U2kWibevuNzgTG0wLA/i
 LGz4bv28TpIVw+uqc9IIJw==
```

```
<SEC-DOCUMENT>0000891020-96-000814.txt : 19960819
<SEC-HEADER>0000891020-96-000814.hdr.sgml : 19960819
ACCESSION NUMBER:               0000891020-96-000814
CONFORMED SUBMISSION TYPE:      20-F
PUBLIC DOCUMENT COUNT:          3
CONFORMED PERIOD OF REPORT:     19960131
FILED AS OF DATE:               19960731
DATE AS OF CHANGE:              19960731
SROS:                 NONE

FILER:
  COMPANY DATA:
  COMPANY CONFORMED NAME:    ADVANCED GRAVIS COMPUTER TECHNOLOGY LTD
  CENTRAL INDEX KEY:                     0000850208
  STANDARD INDUSTRIAL CLASSIFICATION:    3577
  FISCAL YEAR END:                       0131

  FILING VALUES:
    FORM TYPE:            20-F
    SEC ACT:             1934 Act
    SEC FILE NUMBER:     000-17740
    FILM NUMBER:         96602081

  BUSINESS ADDRESS:
    STREET 1:            101 3750 NORTH FRASER WAY
    STREET 2:            CANADA V5J 5E8
    CITY:                BURNABY BC V5J 4M5 C
```

RAW SEC EDGAR 20-F HEADER

EXHIBIT 5.5

Source: http://www.sec.gov, January 1997.

However, there are limitations in using the WWW for research purposes. Given what we know about international financial data, the task of searching for individual reports on the WWW and then trying to recognize what we are viewing is daunting. Other companies are now trying to organize this information, and provide fee-based access to the reports. Disclosure offers *Global Access*, subscription Web-based access to over 4 million global company filings dating back 26 years. Many of the other information providers mentioned in this chapter are creating subscription WWW sites as a method of searching and delivery.

Hemmington Scott's UK Equities Direct, mentioned above, includes financials for many U.K. listed companies. However, there is a limited number of companies providing annual reports and there is no screening capability.

We cannot recommend surfing the Web as an alternative to commercial sources. It is a useful complement to see what a company has chosen to reveal on its home page. However, serious research and comparison *across* companies requires the value added from commercial sources.

ELECTRONIC FINANCIAL INFORMATION FOR PRIVATE COMPANIES

Financial information for hundreds of thousands of European companies appears in databases on databanks such as DataStar and Questel-Orbit. The information is publicly available based on the European Directive requirements discussed in Chapters 2 and 3. That means that most of the records for private companies actually come from company filings, rather than third party credit ratings, such as those collected in the U.S. by Dun & Bradstreet. A listing of these files, arranged by databank provider, and by country, is in Chapter 6.

Dun and Bradstreet's *European Financial Records* on DataStar DEFR and DIALOG File 523 covers Andorra, Belgium, France, Germany, Ireland, Luxembourg, Monaco, Netherlands, Portugal, Spain, San Marino, and the United Kingdom. Information comes from D&B's credit reports. In January, 1997 the database included almost 2.9 million records. About half of them have financial records and most of those are for companies in the United Kingdom and France. Where available, there are three years of comparative data in U.S. dollars, reported in the new "EEC format."

TEXT SOURCES OF COMPANY FINANCIAL INFORMATION

Companies issue annual financial statements. There is often a lag of six months between the end of the fiscal year and the time the statement is released to the international audience. As a practical matter, researchers cannot track changes between reports by reading and clipping the extensive range of text sources about companies in newswires, newspapers, newsletters, business magazines, academic journals, investment bank reports, and market research reports. However, many of these publications are available electronically, are updated daily or weekly, and can be delivered to the desktop via modem, Internet, WWW services, or wireless.

Newspapers and Newswires

Many countries have financial newspapers, similar in purpose to the *Wall Street Journal*. In addition to their native language papers, non-English speaking countries often publish business newspapers and journals in English to reach an international audience. Some of the papers are also available in electronic format.

The British *Financial Times*, the international equivalent of the *Wall Street Journal,* is published in Philadelphia, as well as in England and Frankfurt. It has a printed index and is also widely available online.

The Wall Street Journal includes international coverage and publishes both an *Asian Wall Street Journal* and a *European Wall Street Journal* daily on their continents. There are also weekly editions in the U.S.

FT Extel, in addition to its annual report cards, publishes news cards. McCarthy International Ltd., another U.K. information provider, also has a news card service.

All of the indexing services and online databases we cover in Chapter 1 have articles about companies. Three of the financial CD-ROM products we discussed, Moody's *International Company Data*, *Worldscope*, and FT Extel include brief news items, associated with financial issues, as part of the company records.

Dow Jones News/Retrieval is an efficient way to search across a variety of wires to track the latest financial news for listed companies worldwide. Dow Jones wire services includes all the Dow Jones Wires, Canadian Newswire and Corporate News, Japan Economic Newswire, and European business news from Agence France Presse-Extel.

FINDING AIDS

Information Sources in Finance and Banking
(Bowker-Saur, 1996)

By far the most complete listing of sources, both print and electronic, is Ray Lester's *Information Sources in Finance and Banking*. The book lists over 2,800 titles and 1,300 organizations or information providers. There are brief descriptions of each title, generally taken from the publishers' brochures. This extensive work has chapters on "Corporations," "Financial Institutions and Markets," and "Financial Management and Investment." Organizations and their sources in the latter two chapters are arranged geographically under international, Europe, U.K., and United States. Commercial online services, from those designed just for analysis to the consumer service CompuServe, are also described. Despite its breadth of coverage, the arrangement makes the book difficult to use.

CONCLUSION

Interest in international financial statements will only continue to grow as investment becomes more international. More companies are providing reports in English and using some standard accounting practices. Individual investors could, therefore, try to collect the reports themselves and do their own comparative analysis. A few large information providers compile international company financial data and provide value added text and software while many more companies offer more specialized financial services.

Most libraries will need at least one source of financial information for listed companies and some may need several. Some libraries will need financial data for private companies as well. Given the wide range of products on the market today, each library should carefully evaluate its clients' financial information needs to purchase the right mix of print and electronic financial products.

NOTES

1. Mary Keegan, "Whose Standard Should We Bear," *Independent* (19 July 1994): 30.

2. Shahrok M. Saudagaran and Gary C. Boddie, "Foreign Listing Location: A Study of MNCs and Stock Exchanges in Eight Countries," *Journal of International Business Studies* 26, no. 2 (2nd quarter 1995): 319–41.

3. *Ibid.*

4. Ruth A. Pagell, "European Information on CD-ROM: Part III—Individual Country Financial Information from Bureau van Dijk," *CD-ROM Professional* (March 1993): 107–17.

5. "Testdrive: U.K. Quoted Online," *Online/CD-ROM Business Information* (December 1996): 305–26.

CHAPTER 6
Electronic Sources

TOPICS COVERED

- Databank Overviews
- Online Information by Region
- Company Databases with Product Codes
- Company Data on CD-ROM
- Online Text Sources of International Company Information
- WWW Directories
- Caveat Emptor

MAJOR SOURCES DISCUSSED

- DIALOG
- DataStar
- LEXIS-NEXIS Services
- Dow Jones News/Retrieval
- FT Profile
- Questel-Orbit

No single library owns or would want to own all the published company directories or their CD-ROM alternatives. They are expensive. They are quickly dated; many are often out of date when published. The print directories lack the flexibility to screen for a variety of characteristics. The information in these directories is often available through standard commercial systems that are easily accessible worldwide. This online availability allows us to compare the annual cost of purchasing a specialized print directory with the annual cost of searching an online database for the same information only when needed.

The distinction between types of directories becomes less significant when they are searched electronically. Many of the online and CD-ROM files include basic information, extensive product listings, officers and directors, and one or two financial data items.

Articles in publications such as *Database* in the U.S. and *Online/CD-ROM Business Information* in the U.K. evaluate current databases and address common questions. *Information Today, Information World Review*, and *Link-Up* offer database descriptions. The Washington Researcher and Euromonitor guides, discussed in Chapters 3 and 9, complement the print coverage of sources with a country-by-country listing of online sources as well. Print and online database directories, such as *Online Business Sourcebook* and its monthly newsletter, *Online Business Information*, and *European Business Intelligence Briefing,* former Headland titles now distributed by Bowker-Saur, may be used to generate lists of international company directories. *Gale's Directory of Databases*, in print, online on DIALOG, DataStar, and on GaleNet, lists most commercially available databases. Bowker-Saur published a new book, *World Databases in Company Information,* covering databases with company financials, directory information, products, individuals, and organizations.

Selecting the right source of electronic information is a difficult task in an international environment. There are thousands of databases, on hundreds of hosts, many of which are unfamiliar to us. The numbers keep growing as do the formats.

Remote timesharing, CD-ROM, locally loaded tapes, resident databases, and real-time satellite feeds are all options. Information publishers are becoming databank providers. The WWW is the up-and-coming, though incomplete, delivery medium.

We highlight and recommend certain sources of electronic information throughout this book. However, by the time the book is published, new databases will be available and many more will come along. Others may die or merge. Appendix H, at the end of this chapter, presents guidelines for selecting an international database.

DATABANK OVERVIEWS

There are many online company databases, from the equivalents of standard print sources, mentioned in Chapter 4, to niche databases for individual countries and applications. Detailed descriptions of these databases are provided through databank documentation. The purpose of this section is to organize the many directory titles by presenting them in tables arranged by databank provider. We discuss DIALOG, DataStar, LEXIS-NEXIS Services, and Dow Jones News/Retrieval in detail and provide overviews of other prominent players, such as FT Profile, Questel-Orbit, Profound, Info Globe, Infomart, and Nikkei. Table 6.A provides help in finding online company information from commercial databanks.

DIALOG

Searching for companies and news by geographic region is simplified by DIALOG's Onesearch files, for example, ASIACO and ASIANEWS. Tables 6.B and 6.C list the DIALOG databases in each geographic category at the end of 1996. Dates are given for comparison.

A helpful tip for finding alternative entries for company names when searching across DIALOG files is to use DIALOG *Company Name Finder* (File 416).

DIALOG introduced an end-user Windows-based system called BusinessBase, which is designed specifically for company and market intelligence. The system uses U.S. and international D&B Market Identifiers as its underlying company name base. Other international files are accessed by BusinessBase. International financial data come from FT Extel. Market position and news includes IAC databases, Business and Industry, and ABI/Inform. Investext reports are also accessible. International structure is from Corporate Affiliations. Intellectual property is all U.S. based files, but it does have the U.S. trademarks and patents for international companies. BusinessBase will be replaced by the Web-based DIALOG Select.

DataStar

DataStar, purchased by Knight-Ridder in 1993, presently has the largest number of country-specific databases for Europe. The files include directory files, product files, and financial statements for hundreds of thousands of European companies.

The strength of the databank is the number of databases and companies that are included. A prob-

lem for searchers is that the information is fragmented into many files, each having its own file structure and field codes. Another problem for searchers is that many of the files are in the local language. Searchers can "limit" by sales and other selected financial items, but there is no way to create a spreadsheet with the data. Table 6.D lists company directory files found on DataStar. Table 6.E lists DataStar company files by geographic coverage or region.

In order to determine which DataStar files contain your company, you can use the CROS database, which is similar to DIALINDEX. There are categories for all companies, company directories, or company financials, categories by location (e.g, all company financial data from Japan), and news categories. Exhibit 6.1 is an excerpt from a ranked CROS search in the all companies category.

LEXIS-NEXIS Services

The international company files found in LEXIS-NEXIS Services are listed in Table 6.F. These files are part of the COMPNY library, the WORLD library, and the appropriate individual regional libraries they cover. For example, *Japan Company Handbook* (JCH) is a file in the COMPNY, WORLD, and ASIAPC libraries. All of the files may be searched simultaneously in INTLCO. Also on the menu are a series of files from CIFAR. However, these are not included in Table 6.F since they have not been updated since 1993 and CIFAR at present has no plans to update them.

Non-U.S. companies that trade in the U.S. by filing 20-Fs are in the 20-F library, a subset of SEC Online. Disclosure (DISCLO) has companies filing 20-Fs. ADRs are covered in the LEXIS-NEXIS version of *Standard & Poor's Corporate Descriptions* (SPDESC). The company files are complemented by scores of full text international, regional, and country news and business publications. *Walden Country Reports*, which are found in the geographic libraries, for example WORLD or EUROPE, are an unexpected source of company listings. What is unique in the *Walden* reports are lists of top national companies, in those countries where national enterprises are the most important organizations. For example, the *Walden* report for Ghana lists 17 core state enterprises excluded from privatization that include Ghana Airways, Ghana Oil, and Ghana National Petroleum Corporation. In addition, the report lists the 15 companies on Ghana's Stock Exchange. However, reports have not been updated in two years.

TABLE 6.A

WHERE TO SEARCH FOR COMPANY INFORMATION ON COMMERCIAL DATABANKS

DIALOG: Best general source for manipulating data online
DATASTAR: Best source for European company directory files
LEXIS-NEXIS SERVICES: Best source for full text local news; many international financial files
DOW JONES: Up-to-date newswire and company information; international financial data
FT PROFILE: Major British business information databank; remaining *Textline* source
QUESTEL-ORBIT: Former French databank, with many French company files
PROFOUND: Formerly MAID, known for market research reports, but now has company profiles as well
INFO GLOBE ONLINE: Canadian companies and company news
INFOMART: Canadian companies, news and legal sources
NIKKEI: Major Japanese business information databank

TABLE 6.B

DIALOG COMPANY FILES (XXXXXCO)

File Name	Date	Asia	Canada	Europe	Japan	Latin America*	Mideast Africa*	U.K.
286 BIOCOMMERCE ABS & DIR	81-Oct 96			X				
443 IMSWORLD DRUG MARKET	**			X				
479 COMPANY INTELLIGENCE	96/Nov 14	X		X	X		X	X
491 CANCORP	Nov 96 W2		X					
500 EXTEL	85-96 Nov W2	X	X	X	X		X	X
502 TEIKOKU	1996/Sep	X			X			
505 FBR ASIAN COS	1996/Q3	X						
513 CORPORATE AFFILIATIONS	1996/Q3	X	X	X	X	X	X	X
518 D&B INTL DMI	1996/Sep	X		X		X	X	X
520 D&B CANADIAN DMI	1996/Q3		X					
523 D&B Europe Financials	1996 **			X				
529 HOPPENSTEDT - GERMANY	1996 Q3			X				
533 CANADIAN BUSINESS	Q2 96 **		X					
561 ICC BRITISH CO+	1996 OctW1			X				X
562 ICC BRITISH CO FINANCIALS	1996 OctW2			X				X
585 KOMPASS MID EAST/AFRICA/ MEDITERRANEAN	July 1996 **						X	
590 KOMPASS EUROPE	Apr 1994			X				
591 KOMPASS UK	1996/Apr			X				X
592 KOMPASS/ASIA/ PACIFIC	1996/Oct	X			X			
593 KOMPASS CENTRAL/EASTERN EUROPE	1996 Aug**			X				
594 KOMPASS CANADA	1993/Q2 **		X					
758 ASIA/PAC DIRECTORY	1996/Nov **	X						

* Latinco; Mideastco
** Databases added since the 1st edition of *International Business Information*.
+ All or some of file available on CD-ROM
DIALOG File 521, *European Market Identifiers* is not included as a separate file.
Extel and *Company Intelligence* have companies from company files in which they are not included.

Source: DIALOG searching, November 1996.

TABLE 6.C

DIALOG NEWS FILES (XXXXXNEWS)

File Name	Date	Asia	Canada	Europe	Japan	Latin* America	Mideast* Africa	U.K.
9 BUSINESS & INDUSTRY +	94-96Nov18**	X	X	X	X	X	X	X
16 IAC PROMT	72-96Nov18	X	X	X	X	X	X	X
30 ASIA PACIFIC	85-96Oct	X			X		X	
111 NTL NEWSPAPER INDEX	79-96Nov	X	X	X	X	X	X	X
148 TRADE & INDUSTRY +	81-96Nov18	X	X	X	X	X	X	X
211 NEWSEARCH	96-96Nov18	X	X	X	X	X	X	X
258 AP NEWS	84-96Nov 17**	X		X	X	X	X	X
262 CANADIAN BUSINESS & CURRENT AFFAIRS	82-96 Oct		X					
466 INFO-SOUTH L A NEWS	88-Dec 95 W1 CLOSED					X		
481 DELPHES +	80-96Nov W1			X				
483 NEWSPAPER ABS DAILY	86-96Nov15**		X				X	
484 NEWSPAPER & PERIODICAL ABS	86-96NovW2							X
501 EXTEL INTL NEWS	89-96NovW2	X		X	X			X
545 INVESTEXT +	82-96Nov15	X	X	X	X	X	X	X
563 ICC INTL BROKERAGE HOUSE REPORTS	86-96SepW4							X
564 ICC BRITISH CO ANNUAL REPORTS	84-96Sep W4			X				X
583 IAC GLOBALBASE	86-96Nov W2	X	X	X			X	X
607 ITAR/TASS News	96-96Dec28			X				
609 BRIDGE WORLD MARKET NEWS	89-96 Dec28***	X	X	X	X	X	X	X
611 REUTERS	87-96Nov16	X	X	X	X	X	X	
612 JAPAN ECONOMIC NEWS	84-96Nov15				X			
613 PR NEWSWIRE	87-96Nov17		X	X				
614 AFP-ENGLISH WIRE	91-96Nov15			X				
616 CANADIAN NEWSWIRE	96-96Nov15**		X					
617 SOUTH AMERICAN BUSINESS INFORMATION	96-96Nov16**					X		
618 XINHUA NEWS	96-96Dec28**	X						
622 FINANCIAL TIMES FULL	86-96Nov16			X				X
620 EIU Views	96Nov W3**	X	X	X	X	X	X	X
624 McGRAW-HILL PUBS	85-96Nov14	X		X	X			
627 EIU Country Analysis+	96 NovW3**	X	X	X	X	X	X	X
628 EIU Country Risk & Forecast	96NovW2**		X	X	X	X	X	X
629 EIU Business Newsletters	96Nov W2**	X	X	X	X	X	X	X
635 BUSINESS DATELINE +	85-96NovW3		X	X				
636 IAC NEWSLETTER	87-96Nov18	X	X	X	X	X	X	X
637 JOURNAL OF COMMERCE	86-96Nov15	X		X				
660 FEDERAL NEWS SERVICE	91-96Nov17**	X		X		X	X	X
710 TIMES/SUNDAY TIMES	88-96Nov16			X				X
711 INDEPENDENT (LONDON)	88-96Nov11			X				X
726 SO CHINA MORNING POST	92-96Nov17**	X						
727 CANADIAN NEWSPAPERS	90-96Nov10**		X					
728 ASIA/PAC NEWS	94-96NovW2**	X						
748 ASIA/PAC BUS JOURNALS	94-96Nov16**	X						
749 LATIN AMERICA NEWS	95-96NovW2**					X		
750 MIDDLE EAST NEWS	Oct 1996 **						X	
771 TEXTLINE GLOBAL NEWS+	80-89							
772	90-95							
799	96-96Nov14	X	X	X	X	X	X	X

*   Latinnews;Mideastnews
**   Databases added since the 1st edition of *International Business Information.*
***   Formerly Knight Ridder/Tribune Financial News
\+   All or some of the file available on CD-ROM

Source: DIALOG searched November 18, 1996 (new titles added December 29th).

TABLE 6.D

COMPANY DIRECTORY FILES ON DATASTAR

Database	Label	Type	Geographic Coverage	File Size	Lang	Last Update
ABC EUROPE	EURE+	D	EUROPE	158,862	E	961130
ABC GERMANY	ABCE+	D	GERMANY	72,611	E	961107
BDI-GERMAN INDUSTRY	BDIE+	D	GERMANY	27,965	E	961108
BIOCOMMERCE ABS and DIRECTORY	CELL	D	WORLDWIDE	2,500 profiles	E	961219
CANCORP DATABASE	CNCO	F/D	CANADA	9,292[a]	E	970103
CHEM SOURCES COMPANY DIRECTORY	CSCO	D	WORLDWIDE	12,532	E	960930
CHEMPLANT PLUS	PLAN	D	WORLDWIDE	36,612	E	961125
COMPANY INTELLIGENCE	INCO	D, N	International	42,013 non US	E	961217
CREDITREFORM AUSTRIA	AVVC+	D	AUSTRIA	51,780	G	960927
CREDITREFORM GERMANY	DVVC+	D	GERMANY	753,109	G	960927
CREDITFREFORM: SWISS COMPANIES	CRCH	D	SWITZERLAND	301,177	G	961125
CZECH AND SLOVAK COMPANY DIRECTORY	CZCO*	D	CZECH AND SLOVAK REPUBLICS	1,574,957	E	950925
D & B EUROPEAN FINANCIAL RECORDS	DEFR	F	13 European countries	2,8923683	E	961231
DANISH COMPANIES FULL FINANCIAL DATA	DKFF/ DKEF*	F	DENMARK	81,651	E/D	970108
DISCLOSURE	DSCL	F	Traded in US (20-F and ADR)	881	E	9701
DUN & BRADSTREET ASIA PACIFIC	DNAP+	D	ASIA PACIFIC	224,464	E	9509
DUN & BRADSTREET CANADA	DNCA+	D	CANADA	262,515	E	9612
DUN & BRADSTREET EUROPE	DBZZ	D	EUROPE	3,232,536	E	9608
DUN & BRADSTREET E. EUROPE	DNEE+	D	CEES	61,347	E	9608
DUN & BRADSTREET ISRAEL	DNIS+	D	ISRAEL	32,718	E	9608
DUN & BRADSTREET SWISS COMPANIES	SWCO	D	SWITZERLAND	190,064	E	9602
DUN & BRADSTREET SWISS CO. FINANCIALS	SWFF	F	SWITZERLAND	1,579	E	9602
DUN & BRADSTREET US	DBUS+	E	UNITED STATES	3,697,478	E	9611
ECO REGISTER	ECCO+	D	GERMANY	3,353,273	G	85-970109
ECONOVO-GERMAN COMPANIES IN BUNDESANZEIGER	ECNE+	D	GERMANY	411,9364	G	9701092
ELECTRO/ELECTRONIC BUYERS GUIDE	ZVEE+	D	GERMANY	4,030	E	961111
EXTEL CARD DATABASE	EXTL	F	WORLDWIDE	11,558	E	961228
FIRMIMPORT/FIRMEXPORT	FRIE	I/E	FRANCE	38,263	E	9610
FRENCH COMPANIES FULL FINANCIALS	FRFF FREF	F	FRANCE	658,781	F/E	961204
GERMAN BUYERS GUIDE	E1X1+	D	GERMANY	51,453	E	961119
GERMAN COMPANY FINANCIAL DATA	FINN/ COIN	F	GERMANY	12,738	G,E	9612
HOPPENSTEDT AUSTRIA	HOAU	D	AUSTRIA	9,999	G	961129
HOPPENSTEDT BENELUX	BNLU	D	BELGIUM, LUXEMBOURG, NETHERLANDS	94,216	E,G, FD,S	9612
HOPPENSTEDT GERMANY	HOPE+	D	GERMANY	73,164	G	961217
ICC DIRECTORY OF UK COMPANIES	ICDI	D	U.K.	3,150,585	E	961230

TABLE 6.D (continued)

COMPANY DIRECTORY FILES ON DATASTAR

Database	Label	Type	Geographic Coverage	File Size	Lang	Last Update
ICC FINANCIAL DATASHEETS	ICFF	F	U.K. all Ltd Cos.	883,483	E	961127
ICC BRITISH COMPANY ANNUAL REPORTS	ICAC	F	U.K.	appx 2500	E	87-9701
IMSWORLD DRUG MARKET MANUAL COMPANIES	IPDI	D	WORLDWIDE	4,834	E	961111
IMSWORLD PHARMA COMPANY PROFILES	IPCP	D,T	WORLDWIDE	724	E	961209
INFOCHECK BRITISH COMPANY FINANCIAL DATASHEETS	CHCK	F	U.K.	9484267	E	960110
INFOTRADE BELGIUM CO. DATABASE	BECO	D	BELGIUM	732,051	E,F,D	960101
IRISH COMPANIES AND BUSINESSES	IRFF*	F	IRELAND	368,787	E	961028
ITALIAN COMPANY FULL FINANCIAL DATA	ITFF	F	ITALY	6,306	E	970103
ITALIAN TRADING COMPANIES	ITIE SDOE	I/E	ITALY	105,348	E I	950112
JORDANWATCH	JORD	F	U.K.	345,732	E	970107
KEY BRITISH ENTERPRISES	DKBE	F	U.K.	55,540	E	9612
KREDITSCHUTZVER-BANK VON 1870	KSVA	D	AUSTRIA	175,081	G	9609
DM HUSET NORWEGIAN COMPANIES	NOCO/ NECO	D	NORWAY	281,974	N/E	961016
SCRL	SCRL/ SCEF	F	FRANCE	545,381	F/E	961120
SEMA GROUP SWEDISH COs	SECO	D	SWEDEN	1,340,118	E	970106
TEIKOKU JAPANESE COMPANIES	TOKU	D	JAPAN	227,953	E	961231
TEIKOKU: FULL FINANCIAL	TOFF**	F	JAPAN	122,623	E	961029
TELEADRESON'S DIRECTORY OF POLISH COMPANIES	PLCO PDCO*	D	POLAND	866,463	E G	961129
TELEFIRM	FRCO	D	FRANCE	16474,974	E	960918
UK IMPORTERSCI	UKIM	I/E	U.K.	114,706	E	9611
WER GEHOERT ZU WEM	WGZW	D	GERMANY	12,787	E	9607
WHO MAKES MACHINERY & PLANT	VDME+	D	GERMANY	6,960	E	961205
WHO OWNS WHOM	WHOW	D	WORLDWIDE	384,235	E	961218
WHO SUPPLIES WHAT?	WLWE+	D	GE,AU,SW, NE,BE,LU	208,697	E	961128

TYPES OF FILES ARE:D (DIRECTORY), F (FINANCIALS), I/E (IMPORTERS/EXPORTERS), N (NEWS)

GEOGRAPHIC COVERAGE:Number of companies in database January 1997

LANGUAGES ARE E (ENGLISH), G (GERMAN), F (FRENCH), D (DUTCH), S (SPANISH)

+ Part of the FIZ-Technik German Databank

* Databases added since first edition

Source: Searched January 1997; adapted from Linda Eichler and Jean Newland, "Data-Star: A Galaxy of Databases," *Database* June 1993.

TABLE 6.E

DataStar Company Files by Geographic Coverage/Origin

GEOGRAPHIC COVERAGE	DATABASE	LABEL	TYPE	NUMBER OF COMPANIES
AUSTRIA	CREDITREFORM	AVVC	D	51,780
	KREDITSCHUTZVER BANK VON 1870	KSVA	D	175,081
	HOPPENSTEDT AUSTRIA	HOAU	D	9,999
	DUN & BRADSTREET AUSTRIA	DBOS *	D	58,420[a]
BELGIUM	DUN & BRADSTREET BELGIUM	DBBL *	D	106,166
	HOPPENSTEDT BENELUX	BNLU	D	94,216[b]
	INFOTRADE BELGIUM	BECO	D	732,051
CANADA	CANCORP DATABASE	CNCO	F/D	9,292
	DUN & BRADSTREET CANADA	DNCA	D	262,515
CZECH REPUBLIC	CZECH AND SLOVAK COMPANY DIRECTORY$	CZCO	D	1,228,271
DENMARK	DUN & BRADSTREET DENMARK	DBDK *	D	498,709
	DANISH COMPANIES FULL FINANCIALS	DKEF/DKFF	F	81,651
FRANCE	DUN & BRADSTREET FRANCE	DBFR *	D	205,053
	FRENCH COMPANIES FULL FINANCIALS	FRFF/FREF	F	658,781
	FIRMIMPORT/EXPORT	FRIE	I/E	38,263
	SCRL	SCEF/SCFF	F	545,381
	TELEFIRM	FRCO	D	1.647,974
GERMANY	ABC GERMANY	ABCE	D	72,611
	BDI-THE GERMANY INDUSTRY	BDIE	D	27,965
	CREDITREFORM GERMANY	DVVC	D	753,109
	DUN & BRADSTREET GERMANY	DBWG *	D	502,595
	ECO REGISTER	ECCO	D	3,353,273
	ELECTRO/ELECTRONIC BUYERS GUIDE	ZVEE	D	4,030
	FINF-NUMERIC/COIN-NUMERIC	FINN/COIN	F	
	GERMAN BUYERS' GUIDE	E1X1	D	51,453
	HOPPENSTEDT GERMANY	HOPE	D	73,164
	WER GOHOERT ZU WEM	WGZW	D	12,787
	WHO MAKES MACHINERY & PLANT	VDME	D	6,960
GREECE	DUN & BRADSTREET GREECE	DBHE *	D	28,834
IRELAND	DUN & BRADSTREET IRELAND	DBEI *	D	17,036
	IRISH COMPANIES AND BUSINESSES	IRFF	F	368,787
ISRAEL	DUN & BRADSTREET ISRAEL	DNIS	D	32,718
ITALY	DUN & BRADSTREET ITALY	DBIT *	D	477,004
	ITALIAN COMPANIES PROFILES	ITFF	F	6,306
	ITALIAN TRADING COMPANIES	ITIE SDOE	I/E	105,348
JAPAN	TEIKOKU JAPANESE COMPANIES	TOKU	D	227,953
	TEIKOKU FULL FINANCIALS	TOFF	F	122,623
LUXEMBOURG	DUN & BRADSTREET LUXEMBOURG	DBLU *	D	6,650
	HOPPENSTEDT BENELUX	BNLU	D	[b]
NETHERLANDS	DUN & BRADSTREET NETHERLANDS	DBNL *	D	267,819
NORWAY	DM HUSET NORWEGIAN COMPANIES	NOCO/NECO	D	281,974
POLAND	TELEADRESON'S DIR OF POLISH COS	PLCO/PDCO	D	866,463
PORTUGAL	DUN & BRADSTREET PORTUGAL	DBPO *	D	117,186
SLOVAK REP	CZHECH AND SLOVAK CO DIRECTORY	CZCO	D	346,686
SPAIN	DUN & BRADSTREET SPAIN	DBES *	D	251,374
SWEDEN	SEMA GROUP SWEDISH COs	SEMA	D	1,340,118
SWITZERLAND	DUN & BRADSTREET SWISS COMPANIES	SWCO	D	190,064
	DUN & BRADSTREET SWISS COMPANIES FULL FINANCIALS	SWFF	F	1,579
	DUN & BRADSTREET SWITZERLAND	DBCH *	D	304,663
	CREDITREFORM SWITZ COMPANIES	CRCH	D	301,177
UNITED KINGDOM	DUN & BRADSTREET UNITED KINGDOM	DBGB *	D	391,027
	ICC DIRECTORY OF UK COMPANIES	ICDI	D	3,150,585
	ICC FINANCIAL DATASHEETS	ICFF	F	883,483
	ICC FULL TEXT COMPANY REPORTS AND ACCOUNTS	ICAC	F	approx. 2,500
	INFOCHECK BRITISH CO FINANCIALS	CHCK	F	948,267
	JORDANWATCH	JORD	F	345,732
	KEY BRITISH ENTERPRISES	DKBE	F	55,540
	UK IMPORTERS	UKIM	I/E	114,706
EUROPE/EAST EUROPE	ABC EUROPE:EUROPEAN EXPORT INDUSTRY	EURE	D	158,862
	DUN AND BRADSTREET E. EUROPE	DNEE	D	61,347
6 COUNTRIES	WHO SUPPLIES WHAT	WLWE	D	208,697
WORLD	COMPANY INTELLIGENCE	INCO	D	42,013

TYPES INCLUDED ARE: D (DIRECTORY), F (FINANCIALS), I/E (IMPORTERS/EXPORTERS)

* Part of DBZZ

a Not updated since 1994; b No way to separate Belgium and Luxembourg

Searched January 13, 1997

CROS		1_: HISPANO-SUIZA				
Code		Database Name		Hits for Company		Records in Database
PTDT	F	IAC AEROSPACE/DEF. MKTS TECH '83-		152	OF	409985
PTSP	F	IAC PROMT '78-		58	OF	5424851
EBUS		IAC GLOBALBASE '85-		31	OF	1343300
PTIN		IAC F&S INDEX '78-		24	OF	2116546
FLIG	F	FLIGHTLINE: '88-		23	OF	70914
INDY	F	IAC TRADE & INDUSTRY '92-WK17/'96		18	OF	3596674
DELP		DELPHES EUROPEAN BUSINESS '80-		16	OF	631871
BIDB		BUSINESS & INDUSTRY '94-		4	OF	443763
SDCA		SDC WORLDWIDE M & A: '81-		4	OF	192599
ID91	F	IAC TRADE & INDUSTRY '81-'91		3	OF	2857078
DEFR		D&B EUROPEAN FINANCIAL RECORDS		2	OF	2641301
EXTL		EXTEL INTERNATIONAL CARDS NOV'89-		2	OF	248383
FRCO		TELEFIRM: FRENCH COMPANIES REG		2	OF	1364646

F Full Text

RANKED CROS SEARCH IN DATASTAR

EXHIBIT 6.1

Source: DataStar, April 1996.

TABLE 6.F

LEXIS-NEXIS SERVICES: INTERNATIONAL FILES IN THE COMPNY LIBRARY

Label	Database Name	International Company Reports Number of Companies	Country	Type	Load-Date
ABICAN	ABI Canadian Bus Directory	1.1 mil[1]	Canada	D	961220
CNCORP	CANCORP Plus Database	8,580	Canada	F	970110
CIINTL	Inl Company Intelligence	41,007	Worldwide	D,N	961217[a]
ELC	ELC Largest Companies	50,418	UK, Europe, Asia	D	960822
ESTNCO	Estonian Companies Register	64,120	Estonia	D	960403
FTEXTL	Extel Cards	9.959	Worldwide	F	970108
FPCORP	Fin Post Corp Surveys	5,877	Canadian	F	970114
ALLHOP	All Hoppenstedt	237,983	MultiCountry[b]	D	961014
HOPWOW	Hopp Affiliations	13,361	MultiCountry	A	961008
HOPBNL	Hoppenstedt Benelux	46,674	Benelux	D	990604
HOPBAL	Hopp Bilanzdatenbank	8,384	Germany	F	961014
HOPAUS	Hoppenstedt Austria	9,185	Austria	D	960730
HOPSTD	Hoppenstedt Germany	72,893	Germany	D	960807
HOPTRD	Hoppenstedt Trade Assoc	30,494	MultiCountry	D	961010
ALLVVC	All Credit Reform	622,876[2]	Austria, Germ.	D	960418
VVCACO	Credit Reform Austria	47,867	Austria	D	960418
VVCDCO	Credit Reform Germany	575,000[2]	Germany	D	960418
ICCCO	ICC Company Rpts	2,000[3]	U.K.	F	92-961213
ICCDIR	ICC Directory	"all U.K. live"	U.K.	D	91-961128
ICCLCO	ICC Financial Analysis	all Ltd	U.K.	F	91-9610
JCH	Japan Company Handbook	9,384	Japan	F	960514
LACDB	Latin America Database	333	Argent., Brazil Mexico, Venez.	F	92-95
SOVCO	BizEkon Russian Co Dir	37,694	CIS	D	9601[4]
JPCORP	Teikoku Companies	227,953	Japan	F/D	970106
WLDSCP	Worldscope	20,387[5]	Worldwide	F	961205
WLW	Wer Liefert Was?	98,921	Germany	D	961127

1 - According to GUIDE; 2 - Estimated; new to LEXIS-NEXIS; 3 - About 2,000 reports per year; 4 - Lists a load date of 1996 but April 1994 directory date; 5 - Equities reports in addition to annual data; a Not all companies updated; b All individual Hoppenstedt plus Holland and Switzerland; different load dates by file

Source: LEXIS-NEXIS Services, January 14, 1997.

Comparison of Financial Databases on LEXIS-NEXIS Services

Since so many sources of international financial data exist in electronic form, it is difficult to distinguish among them. For example, Worldscope, FT Extel, Standard and Poor's, and 20-F SEC Filings are all files with international financials in the LEXIS-NEXIS COMPNY library. The individual country files CNCORP, HOPBNL, ICCCO, JCH and JPCORP have financials as well. From the searcher's perspective, this is unfortunate, since LEXIS-NEXIS's software does not lend itself to sophisticated screening, sorting, and report building. Data cannot easily be saved for use in spreadsheets, as they can using DIALOG's report format or on CD-ROM products. Also, each file is constructed differently, using different segment codes for items as basic as the company name!

Listed below are some special features from these files on LEXIS-NEXIS.

- Worldscope: Extracts from annual reports and reports for other securities; standard format for every company; key financials in U.S. dollars; product; and geographic segment data; most useful range of screen and sort segments such as sales, net income, market capital, and earnings per share; extra equity information.
- FT Extel: U.K. terminology and U.K. SIC codes; news cards as well as annual cards in one file, Key-Financials, in three currencies: U.S., U.K., and local; ADR information; text descriptions of business ventures and a chairman's letter; screening and sorting capabilities are *not* usable for this file on LEXIS-NEXIS.
- S & P: News as well as financials in one file.
- SPCO: Limited number of non-U.S. companies, mainly Canadian, that are traded in the U.S.; screening and sorting capabilities are *not* usable for this file on LEXIS-NEXIS.
- 20-F: Multiple years of filings; non-U.S. companies trading in the U.S. with some ADRs; includes Forbes and Fortune numbers; no numeric screening of company data elements.

Financial information in electronic format should offer the flexibility to screen on a series of variables and to download data in a form for processing in a spreadsheet. It is disappointing, therefore, that so many company financial databases are loaded on a system that does not have that capability. We recommend that if you need this type of data frequently you consider purchasing these products in a CD-ROM format and use online databases for updating purposes.

Finally, Dun and Bradstreet's full Globalbase is in the D&B library. Files are arranged as U.S. and non-U.S. and by continent or region. Many of the companies in this version of D&B are *not* found in DIALOG because they have not met the test of containing "marketable" information. Easy links from subsidiary to parent are built into the records.

Dow Jones News/Retrieval

Dow Jones News/Retrieval is one of the key online tools for the U.S. financial researcher. It does *not* play the same role for international company information. Table 6.G displays the international company information found on Dow Jones News/Retrieval.

TABLE 6.G

FILES WITH INTERNATIONAL COMPANY INFORMATION ON DOW JONES NEWS/RETRIEVAL

Database	Type of Data
Worldscope	Financial
Corporate Canada Online	Financial and News
Dun & Bradstreet *	Directory
Standard & Poor's	Limited financial and News
Nikkei Telecom	News with company profiles
Saudi 1000	Directory information with sales

* Menu-driven screening capabilities

Worldscope is the only worldwide financial file on Dow Jones. The Worldscope company reports can only be retrieved by company name. Searching Dow Jones in its Windows version, TRAX software, offers different options than searching it in its older interfaces, but at the end of 1996, screening on Worldscope had not been enabled.

A second source of financial information on Dow Jones News/Retrieval is selected financial and markets information on 2,400 public, private, and government Canadian enterprises, supplied by Info Globe.

A subset of the U.S. and international *Duns Market Identifier Database* is available on Dow Jones. This file is not accessible to academic subscribers. The global file on Dow Jones has over 1.7 million records. This menu driven interface is searchable by geographic unit, size, and line of business characteristics. It also provides family linkages.

The newest addition to Dow Jones company databases is the niche database, *Saudi 1000,* produced by International Information and Trading Service, Al Khobar, Saudi Arabia. Companies can be retrieved by name, by ranking group, or by ranking within industry. Rankings are based on sales. Information includes company name, address, contacts, description of business, and sales in local currency.

Current news information is available in newswires and Dow Jones Text international library. In fact, using the wire services is one of the most efficient ways of keeping up on daily financial changes for listed international companies. The number of international newswire services on Dow Jones keeps expanding. Examples of wire services as of January 1997 are:

- News from 11 Dow Jones wires, including *Asian Equities Report,* and *Australia New Zealand*
- Releases from *PR Newswire, Business Wire, Canada NewsWire* and *Canadian Corporate News*
- *Japan Economic Newswire* from Kyodo News
- Business articles from today's newspapers through Agence France Presse-Extel, Deutsche Presse-Agentur
- Today's *New York Times, Los Angeles Times, Financial Times, Wall Street Journal,* and *Washington Post*

Services from Indonesia and Malaysia are new additions.

Dow Jones includes many other non-U.S. publications in its international text files. For example, it has the following publications with news on China:

AsiaInfo Daily News Service AIDN
Beijing Weekend BEIW
Business Weekly BUWK
China Business Review CBRV
China Chemical Reporter CHCR
China Daily CHND
Free China Journal FCJ
Shanghai Focus SNGF
Xinhua English Newswire XNHN
Xinhua News Agency—CEIS XNHA

Dow Jones has a gateway to Nikkei Telecom Japan News and Retrieval, from Nihon Keizai Shimbun, Inc., Japan's leading business news service. We discuss Nikkei in more detail under the section on "Online Information—Asian Companies."

FT Profile

The primary U.K. business databank is FT Profile, part of the Financial Times Information Group. In addition to its own publications, such as the *Financial Times* and *FT Business Reports,* FT Profile includes many of the standard business databases such as *ABI/Inform, PROMT,* and Investext; a wide range of marketing reports; and the following company files: Extel, Hoppenstedt Germany, ICC Full Text Annual Reports and Jordans Company Reports and D&B European Financial Records. More general news is offered through the *McCarthy* card service. FT Profile also provides gateway access to Kompass. Nikkei, and Infocheck.

A subset for FT-Profile files is available in the end-user package, FT Discovery. Company information is provided by FT Extel and Jordans.

Questel-Orbit

Questel-Orbit is the international online information company formed in 1994 by the merger of Questel with Orbit as part of the Maxwell breakup. Orbit had generally been used in U.S. technical libraries for its strong patent and engineering data. Questel adds European business news, trademarks, and European company databases. Questel-Orbit also has new end-user software and an innovative approach to WWW access of patent information.

Questel has some of the European company databases that are on DataStar plus a few additional ones. French is the basic search language for all the databases. Table 6.H lists the company files on Questel-Orbit.

Profound

M.A.I.D, Market Analysis and Information Database, expanded its coverage, changed its databank name to Profound, and went public in the United States. It no longer wants to be known as a market research supplier but as the "most comprehensive supplier of business information in end-user format." As part of its service, Profound offers Companyline, Company Briefings, and Company Snapshots.

Companyline has reports on over 4 million international companies. Databases accessed through Companyline include the Duns Market Identifiers Files, Duns Europa, FT Extel, ICC, Moody's, Teikoku, and Hemmington Scott Corporate Database. Profound also has three additional files, China Business Resources, China International Business Database, and Korea Investors Service. Company Briefings are two-page overviews from Disclosure and Worldscope.

TABLE 6.H

COMPANY FILES ON QUESTEL-ORBIT

Database	Label	Type	Language	Number of Companies
Belgian Companies	BELGI	D	F	116,000
D&B Britain	DBUK	D	F	290,000
Duns Europa	EUROPA	D	F,G,E	63,000
D&B France	DBFM	D	F	195,000
D&B Germany	DBGR	D	F,G	210,000
D&B Italy	DBIT	D	F	500,000
D&B Spain	DBES	D	F,S	150,000
D&B Switzerland	DBCH	D	F,G	115,000
French Companies SCRL BILAN PLUS	BILAN	F	F	350,000
French Companies & Trade	BODACC	Text	F	2,500,000
French Company Trade Register	ESSOR	D	F	189,000
Hoppenstedt Benelux	BENELUX	D	F,G,D	70,000
Hoppenstedt Germany	HOPGER	D	F,G,E	67,000
Italian Companies Yellow Page Directory	ITALI	D	F,I	290,000
French company bankruptcies	SCRL	D	F	

Numbers from Questel-Orbit documentation

News information on companies comes from the standard newswire services and business databases, such as UMI and IAC databases, KYODO, Reuters, and FT Extel.

Profound is designed for the end-user. It is accessible either through a Windows-based client interface or with a Web browser. Profound uses Adobe Acrobat PDF format to transfer color graphics and images as well as formatted text.

There are several tiers of pricing, all starting with a base access fee. Full reports are segmented into small pieces to allow for selective downloading. The careful, moderate, end-user will find the new Profound pricing reasonable. In January 1997, there was no pricing for the academic market.

Reuters Business Briefing (RBB)

Reuters Business Information Products offer a range of products to the corporate end-user. Reuters Business Briefing is the direct access text service which has supplanted Reuters *Textline*. While *Textline* itself still exists in a scaled-down version (several hundred rather than 1,500 titles) on few databank providers, Reuters has initiated a graphic user interface with over 2,000 sources of information in addition to Reuters' own news. Some of the news stories are in their original languages and others are translations from 17 languages. Company profiles, EIU, reports and market research reports are also included. *Textline* may be eliminated from all databanks except RBB by the end of 1997.

WESTLAW

WESTLAW has long been the competitor to LEXIS-NEXIS Services in the legal information community.

In February 1996, Thomson purchased West Publishing, making WESTLAW part of the Thomson group. As a subscriber to WESTLAW, you can access international company information through DIALOG and Dow Jones. With a WESTLAW subscription to these other databanks, the user gets one monthly bill and the use of WESTLAW's natural language software. As of mid-1996, WESTLAW itself did not have any international directories. WESTLAW's full text newspaper and journal service contains several Canadian business publications.

FIZ Technik

FIZ Technik is one of the major German databanks. Many of the business directories in FIZ Technik are also available through DataStar and there is a gateway from one service to the other. However, separate passwords are required. The directories on FIZ Technik which are not available on DataStar include specialized German environmental services directories, and three Kompass Buyers' Guides, for Germany, Scandinavia, and Finland. All databases are either in German or English. FIZ Technik also has a suite of German language full text business news sources. FIZ Technik is available as a subscription service on the WWW at http://www.fiz-technik.de.

REGIONAL ONLINE DATABANKS

Canada

Canada has its own direct information providers. Two major databanks with business information are Info Globe and Infomart.

Info Globe

Info Globe Online has two current company files. One is the menu-driven Corporate Canada Online, similar to *CanCorp* on Dow Jones. Corporate Canada Online covers over 2,400 major Canadian public, private, and "crown" corporations. Records include financial data, stock market information, industry ratios, officers, and stories from the *Globe and Mail* and *Northern Miner*. Use this database to find information about a known company.

Report on Business Corporate Database (ROB) contains financial information on more than 3,000 Canadian companies traded on the major Canadian exchanges. Search on 300 annual data items. Annual data starts in 1974, and quarterly in 1985.

Info Globe also provides a range of full text Canadian newswires and newspapers such as the *Globe and Mail, Financial Times of Canada*, and *Canada Newswire Online*. Info Globe has a gateway connection to Dow Jones News.

Infomart

Infomart DIALOG Ltd has been a joint venture of the Canadian Southam Inc. and Knight-Ridder Information Inc. Infomart supplies DIALOG databases, enhanced with several Canadian directories, newspapers, and legal information. Databases may be in English and/or French. In addition to the internationally distributed CanCorp database, Infomart offers:

- Canadian Federal Corporations & Directors
- Canadian Trade Index
- Canadian Bankruptcy File
- Canadian Corporate Names
- Dun & Bradstreet Guide to Canadian Manufacturers
- FT Corporate Survey
- Inter-Corporate Ownership
- Kompass Canada
- Scott's Regional Canadian Directories
- Canadian Business is also available.

Japan

Nikkei TELECOM

Access Nikkei TELECOM Japan News & Retrieval directly or as a Dow Jones gateway service. Nikkei is a service of Nihon Keizai Shimbun, Inc., the publisher of Japan's leading economic newspaper. It provides a wide range of English language resources on the Japanese economy and Japanese financial markets. There are three company files on Nikkei. One is Nikkei's Corporate Information, a file of the about 2,000 companies on the eight Japanese stock exchanges. This database includes company profiles and more than 25

years of financials. Also on Nikkei is the Teikoku Databank, found on the other international databanks, and Asian Corporate Profile, a listing of 16,000 companies from China, Korea, Hong Kong, Taiwan, Singapore, Malaysia, and Thailand with Japanese joint ventures.

To update the company financials, Nikkei includes major Japanese business publications in full text such as *Nikkei Industrial News* and *Nikkei Financial Daily*.

The gateway is not available to academic subscribers of Dow Jones.

ONLINE INFORMATION BY REGION

Pan-Asian Databases

Kompass provides a separate company database on DIALOG, File 592, for the Asia-Pacific region. In January 1997 Kompass covered the following Pacific-Rim countries: Australia, Brunei, China, Hong Kong, India, Indonesia, Korea, Malaysia, New Zealand, Philippines, Singapore, Taiwan, and Thailand. There is also direct dial-up via Reednet to Kompass. D&B eliminated Asia-Pacific DMI as a separate DIALOG file and includes the information in File 518. D&B has added a regional code (RG) to File 518. Searchers can retrieve all companies within major regions: Africa; Australia/Asia; Europe; Middle East; and South and Central America. *Duns International Market Identifiers* has entries from more countries than Kompass, including such places as the Christmas Islands and Tahiti. However, at the beginning of 1997, IDMI on DIALOG had very few companies from the ASEAN countries because those records did not meet the update and element standards for the DIALOG file.

Another Asian DIALOG file is Asia-Pacific File 30. The file has both journal abstracts and company records. There are several fields for company location. The indexing in these fields appears to lack authority control. For example, "PO", the field for ultimate parent country, has Bahrain entered with several variations: Bahrain, Bahran and Bahrian. Consequently, it is not possible to give an accurate count of the companies described. Also this obvious lack of quality control makes us wary of the file contents.

Asian companies, from the Graham & Whiteside *Major Company* series, are in *Company Intelligence*. However, there is no way to limit companies to the region. Table 6.I compares the data items available for the same company on D&B Market Identifiers, IAC Company Intelligence, and Kompass Asia/Pacific. An "X" indicates that the data element is included in the company record.

TABLE 6.1

COMPARISON OF A COMPANY RECORD ON THREE DIALOG FILES: 518, 479, AND 592

DIALOG Database Name	D&B Asia Pacific 518	Company Intelligence 479	KOMPASS Asia/Pacific 592
Company Name	X	X	X
Address	X	X	X
Region in Bangkok		X	X
Country	X	X	X
Telephone	X	2 NOS	Multiple
Fax		2 NOS	X
Telex	X	X	X
Description of business	X	X	X
Brand name		X	X
Primary SIC	U.S. SIC		KOMPASS CODE
Secondary SICs	1		11 PRODUCTS
D-U-N-S Number	X		
Year Started	X	X	
Employees Total	2000	2049	2255
Sales—local	20,268,892,000	16,818,927,000(92)	16,894,000,000
Sales—U.S. $	812,217,600	.6 mil	
Exchange rate used	25.45	24.449	
Date of conversion		950803	
Financial Information			
Year		2 yrs (91-92)	
Profits		X	
Dividends per share		X	
Earnings per share		X	
Share capital		X	
Total assets		X	
Status: SF Field, incl Import and Export	X		X
Headquarters	X		
Officers - Chief Executive	MD	ExD	Chair
Other Executives		X	X
Board		X	
Subsidiaries		X	Branch
Principal Shareholders		X	
Bankers		X	
Citations to articles		X	
Languages spoken			X
Date of record change	950223	950807	941015

Source: DIALOG, searched April 21, 1996.

Asia Intelligence Wire

Chamber World Network created the Asia Intelligence Wire, an electronic service with full text of newspapers, newswires, and some directories. In July 1996, FT Profile purchased the Wire and integrated it into FT Profile. A new end-user subscription service, *Asia Exec,* featuring *Asian Intelligence Wire,* was developed by Chamber World Network as part of the FT line of services and is being marketed in the U.S. by Mitsui Comtek. Access is via dial-up Windows client software. The full Wire service is on the WWW at http://www.asiawire.com. Content includes full text articles from 160 Asian publications, 35 newswires, and other information services worldwide. Information available on the *Asia Exec* include the following broad categories:

- General business news
- International trade opportunities and tenders
- Business directories
- Financial information
- Market analysis reports (Marketline, NTDB reports)
- Regulatory update
- Country profiles (Countryline, NTDB reports)
- Trade show information
- Capital markets update

- Economic and industry sector briefs
- Industry newswires
- Publication search

Users can search on these general categories; combine industry, country, and publication categories; or create their own searches and save them in personal profiles.

Specific "Asia News" categories are: Bankruptcies, Contracts and Negotiations, Corporate Debt Ratings, Dividends and Earnings, Environmental News, Joint Ventures, Lawsuits, Layoffs, Mergers and Acquisitions, Patents, Privatisations, Public Offerings, and Strikes.

Industry data are arranged by NACE-1 code. There are seven industry categories which then each have their own submenus:

- Agriculture, Forestry, Fishing, Mining, Oil and Gas
- Food, Tobacco, Garments, Printing, Publishing
- Chemicals, Plastics, Glass, Ceramics, Cement
- Metallurgy, Machinery, Machine Tools, Weapons, Office Machines
- Electrical Components, Automobiles, Consumer Goods
- Telecommunications, Transportation, Banking Services

While some of the titles are unique, much of the information is readily available from newswires and NTDB reports on other services.

Marydee Ojala has written an in-depth examination of electronic information in the Asia/Pacific region in the December 1996 *Database*.[1]

Japanese Databases

Two Japanese databases are on U.S. databanks, Teikoku and *Japan Company Handbook*. The former is available on many databanks; the later, the online version of the book discussed in Chapter 4, is exclusively on LEXIS-NEXIS Services.

Teikoku Databank Ltd. is the largest credit reporting organization in Japan. The companies in the Teikoku databases on DIALOG, DataStar, and LEXIS-NEXIS Services are a subset of the approximately 900,000 companies in Teikoku's COSMOS2 databank. Unique to the Teikoku record are sales rankings within industry, major trading banks, and a credit rating. The sales rankings are based on the entire databank and not just those companies in the file. Teikoku Databank is also available as the DIALOG OnDisc CD-ROM, *Japanese Company Factfinder*, and as the Bureau van

Dijk CD-ROM, *JADE*. Teikoku is also available on Nikkei and on the Japanese databank, G-Search.

Teikoku on its U.S. hosts has more than 215,000 Japanese companies. You can search by English language names or translated names or for the transliterated Japanese names. Only DIALOG has a separate field for the two types of names. Japanese SIC codes of 3 and 4 digits are assigned to each company with an English description of business.

Japan Company Handbook is the standard print source for information on companies listed on the Japanese stock exchanges. The file is on LEXIS-NEXIS Services as JCH. In addition to financials, JCH includes group affiliations in its descriptions. This allows us to track such groups as the keiretsu described in Chapter 3. The extract in Exhibit 6.2 is from a search on "Mitsubishi" as a company and the word "group."

Japan Company Handbook
    3864
Mitsubishi Paper Mills
3-4-2, Marunouchi, Chiyoda-ku,
    Tokyo 100 Japan
    Tel: 03-3213-3751
    Fax: 03-3214-4534
    July 1995
DESCRIPTION:
6th largest paper manufacturer in production, belonging to Mitsubishi group...

JAPAN COMPANY HANDBOOK EXTRACT

EXHIBIT 6.2

Source: Searched on LEXIS-NEXIS Services.

Western, regional and local business databases are available in Japan. They may be in English, Japanese, or Japanese and English. The databases on G-Search Corporation databank include Japanese language company financial files, biographical data on Japanese CEOs, news articles, and a market research database. Another major Japanese databank with business databases is NIFTY Corporation with Japanese business newspapers and newswires, the text of *Economist* in Japanese, financial information from Japanese sources, and other miscellaneous information including movie and restaurant guides and a horse race tip sheet. Japanese databases are promoted in the United States through the Database Promotion Center, which exhibits on behalf of Japanese databases at international online trade shows. Table 6.J lists sources of Japanese online information.

```
┌─ TABLE 6.J ──────────────────────────┐
│                                       │
│  SOURCES OF JAPANESE ONLINE INFORMATION│
│                                       │
│  Database Promotion Center, Japan     │
│  2-4-1 Hamamatsucho, Minato-ku, Tokyo │
│  fax: 81-03-34327558                  │
│  URL: http://www.dpc.or.jp            │
│                                       │
│  G-Search Corporation                 │
│  LOOP-X Bldg., 3-9-15                 │
│  Kaigan, Minato-ku, Tokyo             │
│  108 Japan                            │
│  fax: 81- 3-5442-4391                 │
│                                       │
│  NIFTY Corporation                    │
│  U.S. representative - CompuServe     │
│  500 Arlington Centre Blvd.           │
│  P.O. Box 20212, Columbus, OH 43220   │
│  fax: 614-457-0504                    │
│                                       │
└───────────────────────────────────────┘
```

Korea Database Promotion Center

Korea has established a Database Promotion Center, modeled after the Japanese Database Promotion Center. The Center is attending major online industry shows and has prepared reports on the database industry in Korea along with lists of major information providers and databases available in Korea from both local and international providers. There is no international databank provider from Korea. However, a few Korean news publications have WWW sites. Publications are in Korean.

Central and Eastern Europe / Former Soviet Union Companies

During the past three years, databases that were devoted solely to East Germany have been integrated into their German counterparts, while new databases have appeared for other countries in the former Eastern bloc. Pan-European and international databases which include Central and Eastern Europe and the former Soviet Union include:

- Dun & Bradstreet IDMI, EDMI (Files 518 and 521 on DIALOG)
- ABC Europe—EURE (DataStar)
- Company Intelligence (479)—from Graham & Whiteside's Major Companies Series (DIALOG, DataStar, LEXIS-NEXIS, SEARCHBANK)
- Moody's Corporate News Int (557) and Moody's International Company Data CD-ROM (primarily banks)

Selected databases with only Eastern European companies are:

- DNEE Dun & Bradstreet Eastern Europe: 26 countries, including Turkey and Asian former Soviet Republics (DataStar and Profound)
- Kompass Central/Eastern Europe (DIALOG): 14 European countries
- ESTNCO *Estonian Companies Register* (LEXIS-NEXIS)
- CZCO *Czech and Slovak Company Directory* (DataStar)
- PLCO/PDCO *Teleadreson's Directory of Polish Companies* (DataStar, Internet Securities)
- SOVCO Former Soviet companies (BizEkon Russian Business, part of SovLink) LEXIS-NEXIS and WESTLAW

Searching for companies in Central and Eastern European countries and the former Soviet Union is complicated by lack of consistency among database providers as to what countries constitute this region and how their names are even spelled. There are also the usual problems with how company names are presented. MaryDee Ojala's article in *Online*, "The Companies of Eastern Europe," offers in depth coverage of the databases and the problems.[2]

Exhibit 6.3 is a sample record from *BizEkon* on LEXIS-NEXIS Services. *BizEkon* has over 37,000 companies. The database enhances company profiles with a section on miscellaneous information such as production potential, volume, R&D infrastructure, advertising and reference materials, and number of commercial deals. None of this information is available for the tractor company. However, in the miscellaneous section of the record for the Chemical Foreign Trade Association, BizEcon reports that the organization has 30 percent of world's ammonia and 20 percent of world's carbamide, methanol, and potassium fertilizer, earning 2,368 million foreign-currency rubles. Though the file was updated in 1996, this record has remained unchanged since 1992 and the most recent records are dated 1994. The 1994 load has both translated and transliterated company names.

Date of entry into database: February 6, 1992
Company name: Industrial Tractors Works Production
Association
Alternate name: Cheboksary Industrial Tractors Works
Production Association
Address:
Street: Traktorostroitelei Prospect,
City and Postal Code: Cheboksary 428033,
Region: Chuvash Autonomous Region
Country: Russian Federation
Telecommunications:
TELE: 23-3748
FAX: N/A
Telegraph: TRAKTOR
Telex: 158131 KVANT

COMPANY DESCRIPTION: Industry (Basic Line of
Activity): Tractors, other agricultural machinery,
equipment and tools (18). Basic Lines of Products/
Services: - Tractors, other agricultural machinery,
equipment and tools (18) - Patents,licenses, knowhow
(01)
EXECUTIVE: Mingazov, Khanif Khaidarovich; director
general
CONTACT: Manager for Foreign Markets: N/A,TELE: N/A
WORKFORCE: N/A
BANK:
Foreign Currency Account: VNESHECONOMBANK
of the USSR
Ruble Account: N/A

MISCELLANEOUS:
Production Potential: N/A
Production Volume (total): N/A
Export Oriented: N/A
R&D Infrastructure: N/A
Performance Indicators: N/A
Advertising and Reference Materials: N/A
Statistics Available from: August 20, 1991
External Economic Operations: yes
Foreign Partners (Direct): N/A
Licenses (Short list of products): N/A
Number of Commercial Deals: N/A
Annual Trade Turnover (Export/Import): N/A
Program and Area of Cooperation (Including import): N/A
Specialization: INDUSTRIAL ENTERPRISE
COUNTRY: SOVIET UNION

SAMPLE RECORD FROM BizEkon ON LEXIS-NEXIS SERVICES

EXHIBIT 6.3

Source: Reprinted with permission from Russica Information, Inc.

IN	*PROMTRACTOR* Joint-Stock Production Company.
PS	Tractorostroiteley Prospekt.
RE	RU-428033*Cheboksary,*Tschuwaschien Russian Federation.
CN	RU Russian Federation.
TL	Telephone: (8350) 233748 Telefax: (8350) 233508 Telex: 412627.
PF	Heavy-duty track-type tractors, models T-330P-1-01, T-500P-1, T-25.01BP-1, TT-330, TT-500 (earth moving, stripping, highway construction, open mining of ore and coal, wood and jungle cutting for culture planting, gas and oil pipe laying).
PE	Agricultural tractors. Road tractors.
IM	Imported Products: Foundry equipment, CNC machine tools, lasers, flexible production lines, welding equipment, travelling column CNC machines, precision metering machines, programmable controllers, surface grinders.
IC	Ia <*Construction of vehicles, ships and aircraft*>.
RP	Exports to: Bulgaria, Romania, Poland, Germany, Democratic People's Republic of Korea, Czech Republic, Slovakian Republic, People's Republic of China, Mongolian People's Republic, Italy, Spain, Nigeria, Botswana, Iraq, Jordan, Zambia, Greece, Cyprus, Hungary. Imports from: USA, Japan, Italy, Austria, Germany, France, Sweden, Switzerland, Great Britain and N.I., Democratic People's Republic of Korea. USA, Japan, Italien, Oesterreich, Deutschland, Frankreich, Schweden, Schweiz, Grossbritannien u. Nordirland, Demokratische Volksrepublik, Korea.
MM	General Manager: Khaniff Kh. Mingazov. Sales Manager: George N. Volkov. Import Manager: Eugine Yu. Korsakoff. Export Manager: Eugine N. Trofimoff.
YR	Established: 1972.
EM	Employees: 2300.
CA	Capital: 1.200.000.000.-.
BK	Bankers: Mosbusinessbank, Chuvashcreditprombank.

SAMPLE RECORD FROM ABC EUROPE (EURE ON DataStar)

EXHIBIT 6.4

Source: ABC Europe, November 1996. Reprinted with permission from ABC Europe.

The same tractor company is also in Dun and Bradstreet, in DNEE on DataStar, and File 518 on DIALOG, under the following name, which was its original listing in EURE in 1992 with a third spelling for its region:

CO CHEBOKSARSKY*TRACTOR*PRODUCTION
AMALGAMATION. Chyvashskay Rep.

Searchers can use the *Estonian Companies Register* to identify share ownership by country (see Exhibit 6.5). Therefore, this very specialized database can answer the question:

What U.S. holdings are there in Estonia firms?

Our tractor company is listed under another name in DataStar's ABC Europe, a name that is different from its 1992 entry (see Exhibit 6.4). The ABC Europe record has extensive information on the company's foreign partners and specific information on its product line. Capital rather than revenue or sales is reported. It is interesting to note that the capital and employee data have remained unchanged, the spelling of the general manager's name has changed, but the other officers are new.

Copyright 1996 KREDIIDIINFO AS
Estonian Companies Register
Akbar Eesti AS

COMPANY-NUMBER: 1363070

ADDRESS: Trummi poik 6-4, Tallinn EE0026, Estonia
Tel: (22) 445944
Fax: (22) 6313057

COMPANY-TYPE: Corporation
OWNER-TYPE: Property of Legal Person
FOUNDED: February 3, 1995
MANAGEMENT: Paul Toom
SIC: 5520 Restaurants bars and canteens / 5110 Wholesale on a fee or contract
basis / 7010 Real estate activities with own or leased property / 7499 Other
business activities n.e.c. ...

SHAREHOLDERS:
M.K. Catering Consultants Inc., USA, 800000.00 (EEK)

EXTRACT FROM ESTONIAN COMPANIES REGISTER

EXHIBIT 6.5

Source: Reprinted with permission from Krediidiinfo As Estonia.

The WWW-based Internet Securities, discussed in Chapter 5, has company directories for the Baltic States, Bulgaria, Czech Republic, Hungary, Poland, Russia, and Ukraine, and limited country information on Kazakhstan, Kyrgyzstan, and Uzbekistan. Company coverage varies. There are 1.5 million Czech companies, 5,000 with financials, supplied by Albertina. There are less than 70 Russian companies, all with financials. The system also has current news, equity prices, and industry reports.

Moody's International Manual in print, online and on CD-ROM, has the most financial reports from Eastern Europe. *Moody's* covers Bulgaria, Croatia Czech Republic, Hungary, Poland, and Slovakia. The institutions reported are primarily banks.

LEXIS-NEXIS Services includes the full text of newswires from individual Eastern European countries. *Financial Times Reports: Eastern Europe*, another source of Eastern European news, is available as a database on DataStar and FT Profile. Coverage began in 1992 and updates are weekly. Records are full text and come from FT internal documents plus sources such as *East European Markets* and *Finance East Europe*. The database uses ISO country codes, regional codes, and U.S. SIC codes. The individual publications which comprise the report, such as East European Markets, are available on LEXIS-NEXIS Services, in Dow Jones Text and as part of databases such as *ABI/Inform.*

A few Russian information consultancies are providing information to the international market and have exhibited at information industry shows. An example is Mosvneshinform, Russian Information Specialists, which maintains a WWW site with advertisements and listings for their fee-based products:

http://www.Access-2000.com. The site is actually located in the U.S. Mosvneshinform has over 35 databases containing 375,000 Russian commercial entities and also has published market research reports, available electronically. Another source is Russian Business Cooperative Network, which has business information on Russia on CD-ROM and has a subscription WWW site, http://rbcnet.ankey.ru.

A more complete listing of both online and print resources on Eastern Europe and the Commonwealth of Independent States was provided by Michel Bauwens in the February and March 1993 issues of *Business Information Alert.*

COMPANY DATABASES WITH PRODUCT CODES

Table 6.K lists some of the major databases with product listings and the coding schemes that are used.

In January 1997, ICC reloaded File 562 and introduced 1992 U.K. SIC codes, which are similar to newer NACE-1 codes. U.K. SIC codes in other databases, such as FT Extel, are an earlier version. Notice that "chocolate" changed from 42141 to 15840. Another example is that "manufacture of computers," 300?? has replaced "electronic data processing," 330??

If you are looking for companies in a specific product line on DIALOG, use Product Code Finder, File 413, to find out what codes are being used in the various DIALOG company databases. Table 6.L lists some of the results from a search for "Information Services" on the *DIALOG Product Code Finder*, File 413. In this example, the U.S. SIC codes have no equivalent codes. Notice that the international Dun & Bradstreet files do not use that phrase. *Duns Interna-*

tional Market Identifiers uses 7299, "Misc. Personal Services," 7389, "Business Services, not elsewhere classified," and 7375 for "Information Retrieval Services." Also note that Kompass EUROPE does not have any equivalent code. Closest matches from Teikoku, and the text file *ABI/Inform* are also included in the table.

TABLE 6.K

DATABASES CONTAINING PRODUCT CODES

Database Name or Code	Coding Scheme	Sample Code	Product Name Category
ABCE, EURE	ABC	Vb	Chocolate
BDI- The German Industry	BDIE	43-0103	Chocolate & Chocolate products
CanCorp	US SIC	2066	Mfrs-Chocolate & Cocoa product
DBFR (D & B France)	FR- APE	4031	
	US SIC	2066	Chocolate & cocoa product mfrs
Duns Market Identifiers on DIALOG & DBZZ	US SIC	2066	Chocolate & cocoa
D&B Great Britain (DBGB)	UK SIC	42141	Cocoa and chocolate
D&B Germany (DBWG)	US SIC	2066	Chocolate & cocao product mfrs
	GER SIC	2870	...Schokoladenerzeugnissen
E1X1-German Buyers' Guide	E1X1	36-0571-435	Chocolate & chocolate products
FT Extel	UK SIC	42141	Cocoa and chocolate
FRCO French Companies	NACE	1584	Mfr cocoa chocolate sugar cnfctry
	NAF	158K	Chocolaterie; confiserie
Hoppenstedt Files	HOPE &	2870	Confectionery industry
	US SIC	2066	
ICC files	UK SIC &	15840[1]	Cocoa-chocolate-and-sugar-cnfctry
	ICC	ZCM	Confectionery manufacturers
ITIE/SDOE Italian Trading Companies	HS	HS1806	Chocolate, other food or Confectionery-
	US SIC	SIC206000	type chocolate and cocoa products
KOMPASS EUROPE	KOMPASS	20740	Cocoa & Chocolate products
KOMPASS ASIA PACIFIC	KOMPASS	2074034	Chocolate bars

1 ICC uses 1992 U.K. SICs; the other U.K. SIC databases use the earlier version

Source: Online searches, April 1996, ICC, January 1997.

TABLE 6.L

SELECTED RESULTS FROM A SEARCH FOR "INFORMATION SERVICES" ON FILE 413—DIALOG PRODUCT CODE FINDER

PRODUCT NAME	PRODUCT CODE	FILE	PC RECORD COUNT	TYPE OF CODE
INFORMATION SERVICES	8110016	592	75	KOMPASS
ECONOMIC INFORMATION SERVICES	8834001	591	43	KOMPASS
COMPANY INFORMATION SERVICES	8066002	591	83	KOMPASS
INFORMATION SERVICES	8032005	591	162	KOMPASS
PERSONAL DOCUMENT & INFORMATION SERVICES	729906	516	1,564	SIC-DUNS
MISCELLANEOUS INFORMATION SERVICES	8529	502	219	SIC-JAPAN
RESEARCH AND INFORMATION SERVICES EXCE	8523	502	309	SIC-JAPAN
MEDICAL INFORMATION SERVICES	809912	531	108	SIC-ABI
INFORMATION RETRIEVAL SERVICES	7375	531	428	SIC-ABI
INFORMATION RETRIEVAL SERVICES	7375	518	18	SIC-DUNS

Source: DIALOG File 413 searched April 1996 and individual files searched through June 1996.

COMPANY DATABASES ON CD-ROM

Many directories and financial products are published as CD-ROM databases. We discussed many of these in Chapters 4 and 5. The quality of the search software varies greatly, as does the value added by purchasing the CD-ROM version. Consider purchasing CD-ROMs as a substitute for heavily used print directories if you will get increased flexibility from the CD-ROM product. If your primary clientele uses your international directories primarily to locate companies by name, then purchasing the CD-ROM counterpart is not necessary. Table 6.M lists some CD-ROM company databases.

TABLE 6.M

WHERE TO FIND COMPANY INFORMATION ON CD-ROM—SELECTED PRODUCTS

DISCLOSURE/WORLDSCOPE - Financial
D&B Woldbase Top 25,000
    Latin America
    Asia Pacific
    Western Europe
    Manufacturing
    Service
    Worldwide
OneSource - Financial, Market and Directory
    CD/Investment International Equities (Worldscope)
    CD/Corporate UK (Extel Financial Service)
    CD/Private+ UK (ICC British Companies Database)
    CD/Europa (Dun & Bradstreet)
MOODY'S
    International Company Database - Financial
    Global -Financial (not for sale in the U.S.)

SILVERPLATTER
    UK Corporations CD (ICC) - Financial and text
    COMLINE - (text)
    COIN (from Reuter *Textline*) - text
    F&S Index Plus Text International (also available from IAC)
    Canadian Business, Trade, and Technology -FT
DIALOG OnDisc
    U.K. Factfinder (ICC) - financial and text
    Japan Company Factfinder (Teikoku) directory, financial and credit
    Directory of U.S. Importers & Exporters (including
        Piers data) - directory and trade
GALE RESEARCH *Companies International* (including *World Business Directory* and *Ward's* U.S.)
STANDARD AND POOR'S *Global Vantage* - financial and equity

BUREAU VAN DIJK - Financial
    BNB-NB   Banque Nationale de Belgique
    FAME   Jordan, UK
    DIANE   SCRL, France
    DAFNE   Verband der Vereine Creditreform e.V., Germany
    AIDA   Novcredit SpA, Italy
    REACH   Delwel Uitgeverij BV/Databank NV, Holland
    SABE   Informa SA, Spain
    JADE   Teikoku, Japan
    AMADEUS   pan-European

HOPPENTSTEDT - directories
KOMPASS UK and *EKOD* (Europe) - product directories
BOWKER-SAUR (Reed Intl Group)
Corporate Affiliations, including *International Directory of Corporate Affiliations*
GRAHAM & WHITESIDE - *Major Companies* series

TABLE 6.N

Bureau van Dijk CD-ROMs

Geographic Coverage	Database	Type	Number	Source	Criteria
BELGIUM	BNB-NBB	F,D	200,000	National Bank of Belgium	All Companies
	MASTER	D	700,000	Euro DB	
DENMARK	CD-DIRECT	D	100,000	Kobmandstandens Oplysning	
FRANCE	DIANE	F	470,000	SCRL [1]	Turnover>1.3 m f
	DAFSALIENS	F	120,000	Dafsa	French quoted cos & subs
	SCRL Enter.	Credit	400,000	SCRL	
	ASTREE	D	400,000	SCRL	
GERMANY & AUSTRIA	DAFNE & MARKUS	F D	12,000 700,000	Creditreform	All filing companies
ITALY	AIDA	F	70,000	Novcredit	Turnover>5b L
JAPAN	JADE	F	100,000	Teikoku	Cos with accounts
NETHERLANDS	REACH	D,F	150,000	Deiwel Uitqeverij	Assets>2m NLG
	REACH	D	250,000	Databank	Assets<2m NLG
SPAIN	SABE	F	100,000	Informa SA	
U.K.	FAME	F	260,000	Jordan & Sons	Turnover>.5 m pd
	DASH	Dir	1 mil	D & B	
	EMMA	D	600,000	ICC	
U.K.& IRELAND	HALO	F	2,000	Hemmington Scott; Jordans	OTC ISE companies
U.S.	GLOBAL RESEARCHER	F	11,000	Disclosure	Quoted US
EUROPE 20 Countries	AMADEUS or em>150	F	150,000	Many companies	Turnover>10 m ECU or em>150
EUROPE	CD-EXPORT	T	10,000	Many [2]	
WORLD	GLOBAL RESEARCHER	F	12,800	Disclosure	Quoted cos
	BANKSCOPE	F	9,220	IBCA, etc.	Largest banks

1 Online access to SCRL smaller companies and credit reports
2 France, Italy, Spain, Portugal—from Chambers of Commerce

The most extensive range of individual company CD-ROM products comes from Bureau van Dijk. Individual financial CD-ROM titles are discussed in Chapter 5. Bureau van Dijk also provides the search platform for a series of marketing databases. Individual titles are listed in Table 6.N.

Bureau van Dijk has a WWW site that is a subscription service to *Amadeus*, with the possibility of pay-as-you-go in the U.S. Screening, sorting, and peer group analysis are all features of the site. BVD will also offer access to the one million companies in their marketing databases (http://www.bvd.com).

For an in-depth discussion of many company financials on CD-ROM, read "European Information on CD-ROM Part II: Financial Information (*CD-ROM Professional*, November 1992) and Part III(March 1993). The word "International" can be substituted for "Europe" in Part II for the products from Worldscope and CIFAR. Coin and Comline are discussed in CD-ROM Professional July 1993.[3] Content of the databases has not changed, but CD-ROM information providers have moved to Windows or WWW-based software options.

D&B Europa is a OneSource CD-ROM. The OneSource CD-ROM version includes the information from the print directory plus financial data and credit ratings. For example, with the CD-ROM you can search for companies in France, Germany, or Switzerland who manufacture chocolate and have a top credit rating. All financial information is stated in local currency. The most recent year's key financials are translated into six currencies: U.S. dollars, pounds sterling, French francs, Deutschmarks, Japanese yen, and ECU. Output is in pre-formatted or customized reports. The data can be exported into a spreadsheet. Updates are bimonthly. The same companies are on the CD-ROM as are in the print version. Like all OneSource CD-ROM products, *D&B Europa* is expensive. See Chapter 4 for lists of CD-ROM versions of print directories.

ELECTRONIC TEXT SOURCES OF INTERNATIONAL COMPANY INFORMATION

As mentioned above, news sources are important for keeping updated on company information. There are numerous electronic files that provide real-time, daily, or weekly information about companies. Many of these have been described in Chapter 1. Table 6.O offers a selected list of online sources of international company information. Use BiblioData's *Fulltext Sources Online* to locate the databanks covering international newspapers.

Some of the individual text publications, such as *Agence-France-Press, Economist,* or *Il Sole 24 Ore* are available on CD-ROM from Chadwyck-Healey. A news publication on CD-ROM plays an archival and research function and is not a substitute for the paper or electronic versions.

SilverPlatter includes many of the text-based business databases, such as *ABI/Inform Global,* IAC's *Business ASAP,* the Japanese *Comline,* and *F&S International Plus Text.* ABI is also available on SilverPlatter's WWW site, http://www.silverplatter.com.

Newspapers like *Financial Times, Les Echos,* and *Jerusalem Post* are also available on the WWW. The amount of free information varies from paper to paper. To locate papers on the WWW by country, go to http://www.yahoo.com; select News and Media: Newspapers. You may then select regional and finally countries.

COMPANY INFORMATION ON THE WEB

The WWW has hundreds of thousands of company listings. Some are from traditional publishers, some are in newly created WWW directories, and some are from company provided home pages. Table 6.P lists examples of the different types of directory information now accessible on the WWW.

TABLE 6.O

SELECTED LIST OF ONLINE SOURCES OF INTERNATIONAL COMPANY INFORMATION

Database	Systems
Articles:	
Business & Industry*	DIALOG, DATASTAR, FIRST SEARCH
Promt *	DIALOG, DATASTAR, LEXIS-NEXIS, IAC INSITE, SEARCHBANK
GlobalBase	DIALOG, DATASTAR, FT PROFILE
Delphes	DIALOG, DATASTAR
International Libraries	LEXIS-NEXIS
//DJINTL	DOW JONES News Retrieval
WorldReporter	DIALOG, DATASTAR, DOW JONES, FT PROFILE
Comline *	DATASTAR, LEXIS-NEXIS
Investment Bank Reports:	
ICC Stockbroker Research *	FT PROFILE, DIALOG, DATASTAR,
Investext *	DIALOG, DATASTAR, DOW JONES, Direct to THOMSON, SEARCHBANK
Sample Newspapers	
*Il Sole Ore 24 **	DATASTAR, FT PROFILE, LEXIS-NEXIS
*Jerusalem Post **	DATASTAR, DATATIMES, DOW JONES, LEXIS-NEXIS
Asian and European Wall Street Journals	DOW JONES
International Herald Tribune	DATATIMES, DOW JONES, FT PROFILE, LEXIS-NEXIS
Financial Times	DATATIMES, DIALOG, FT PROFILE, LEXIS-NEXIS, DOW JONES
South China Morning Post	DATATIMES, DIALOG, DOW JONES TEXT, LEXIS-NEXIS

* Subsets also available on CD-ROM

TABLE 6.P

TYPES OF WWW DIRECTORIES

TYPE	EXAMPLE	WWW PROVIDER	NOTES
Versions of Existing Products			
High-End CD-ROMs	Amadeus	Bureau van Dijk	Subscribe; Screening
	U.K. Quoted	OneSource	Subscribe; Screening
Online Databases	Major Companies	IAC Insite	Subscribe
Credit Reports	Duns Access	D & B	Credit card
Subsets of Existing Commercial Products:	Company Profiles	FT Extel	free
	Company snapshots	Hoover's	free[a]
Print Suppliers Directories	Europages	Europages	free
	Yellow pages	Hong Kong, US	free
Exclusively WWW			
Trade contacts	Tradepoint	UNCTAD	free
IP Provider	Business	IndiaWorld	free
Home Pages	Directory		
Company Home Page	Thai Farmers Bank		free

a Fee for full reports

Casual browsers and people unfamiliar with commercial country directories may not recognize that many sites are no more than a collection of home pages. Typically directories of this type do not provide the level of disclosure given by *IndiaWorld* (http://www.indaworld.com/oper/biz/index.html) which reveals that its Business Directory is "Home pages and web sites of leading Indian Companies managed by IndiaWorld."

Depth of information from WWW directories ranges from full annual report filings to "yellow pages" entries, giving names, addresses, and telephones. Authentication of data ranges from what we expect with all subscription commercial services to whatever a company wants to say about itself.

Many of the traditional commercial database producers we have been discussing now have WWW access to their data. In January 1997, database providers and publishers such as IAC, UMI, Disclosure, and Gale Research had subscription WWW access to their company information. At this time, the WWW sites do not have the same level of searching, scanning, and formatting as the CD-ROM products.

Commercial online databanks are rushing to offer some WWW access. Questel-Orbit, FT Profile, and Profound have various versions of their systems as WWW subscription services. DataStar has a beta test running for current subscribers. DIALOG has a set of WWW interfaces. LEXIS-NEXIS is planning specialized WWW products.

CD-ROM providers, such as SilverPlatter, OneSource, and Bureau van Dijk also have subscription sites. The latter two are developing more sophisticated software so that users do not lose the functionality associated with current WWW browsers. Table 6.Q lists the WWW sites for these companies, as of January 1997. Even the subscription sites provide information about their databases for free.

TABLE 6.Q

DATABANK AND DATABASE PROVIDER WWW SITES

Databank	URL—http://	Type of Information	Access
Commercial Online:			
DIALOG	www.krinfo.com	Databank access	Free
DATASTAR	www/kfinfo.com	Databank access	Subscription
LEXIS-NEXIS	www.lexis-nexis.com	Databank access	Free
DOW JONES	www.dowjones.com	Databank access and Links to other DJ products	Subscription, Pay-as-you-go, and Free
FT-PROFILE	www.info.FT.com	News, companies	Registration
PROFOUND	www.maid.com	Databank access	Subscription
QUESTEL-ORBIT	www.questel.orbit.com	Databank access	Subscription
		Patent links	Free
REUTERS	www.reuters.com	News highlights	Free
WESTLAW	www.westlaw.com	Legal product information	Free
FIZ-TECHNIK	www.fiz-technik.de	Databank access	Subscription
INFOMART	www.infomart.ca	Product information	Free
CD-ROM Platforms:			
BUREAU VAN DIJK	www.bvd.com	Company profiles; Amadeus	Subscription
SILVERPLATTER	www.silverplatter.com	Some CD-ROM databases	Subscription
ONESOURCE	www.onesource.com	Some Company CD-ROM databases	Subscription
Database Providers:			
DISCLOSURE	www.disclosure.com	Global Access	Subscription
GALE	www.galenet.com	Print and CD sources	Subscription
IAC	www.iac-insite.com	IAC Databases—commercial	Subscription
	www.searchbank.searchbank.com	IAC Databases—academic	Subscription
UMI	www.umi.com	ProQuestDirect	Subscription

You can locate companies on the WWW using Yahoo's Business subset, selecting directories. Yahoo lists directories in 59 countries. Lycos also has a subset for directories, http://www.companiesonline.com. This is a listing of 60,000 U.S. companies with WWW sites. There is a link to the D&B company reports.

Until more companies upgrade their WWW search engines, use the WWW versions of commercial sources when sophisticated screening is not required. Use free WWW sites as supplements to more traditional sources and evaluate them with the same care you would a paid site. Go to a company's home page to find out what it says about itself.

FINDING AIDS

Many of the Euromonitor and Washington Research publications mentioned throughout this book have lists of primary company databases. The databank providers all have lists of the company databases available on their services. However, in addition to the major company databases we discuss here that appear on the major databank providers, there are close to 2,000 databases worldwide, in all types of electronic format, that can be classified as "company

databases." To find contact and coverage information about a specific databases or to identify company databases with certain characteristics, two finding aids are available.

Gale's Directory of Databases

Gale Research's *Directory of Databases* incorporated the standard Cuadra Directory. It is available in print and electronically as a database on DIALOG and DataStar and as part of Gale's own GALENET online service. There are over 17,000 total entries in the Gale directory. Entries include database name, electronic format, database producer and address, geographic coverage, time span, update cycle, first year available, name of databank provider, and rates.

World Databases in Company Information (Bowker-Saur, 1996)

World Databases in Company Information is one of 11 titles in a series of *World Databases* titles released by Bowker-Saur. The editors, C. J. Armstrong and R. R. Fenton, credit the Gale directory, plus other directories of electronic databases, as sources of their information.

This book includes almost 2,000 databases arranged under the headings Company Profiles, which have financial information, Company Directories, Product Directories, Individuals Directories, and Organizations Directories, covering nonprofits. There is an alphabetical index of database producers' addresses, a subject index, a producer index to the database they produce, and an alphabetical index of database names.

A database entry includes a master record with the database name, producer, type, year started, language, update period, and a description of database elements. There are records for the electronic formats, with the type of format, name of databank provider, if applicable, and rates.

This book is useful if you are trying to identify company databases or the content of known company databases on a daily basis and are willing to go beyond your usual databanks to retrieve niche company information. Other researchers may be better served with the more comprehensive Gale publication or going online for the occasional need.

CAVEAT EMPTOR

While electronic databases offer expanded sources and increased flexibility for company research, they also create a new set of issues concerning data quality. Online and on-disc files allow us to manipulate directory data in ways not envisioned by the database producers. We sometimes retrieve results that do not make sense.

Quality Issue—Exchange Rates

As an example of using a database in a way not expected by its producers, consider the case of ranking food companies by annual sales in an international directory and marketing database. Yugoslavian and then Greek food companies[4,5,6] were listed as the largest in Europe. These rankings were the result of the way the database producer applied exchange rates. Sales figures in the database are in both local currency and U.S. currency. The exchange rate that is applied is the one "current" at the time the database is being loaded. However, the database producer has used sales figures in local currency that may be several years old. This is often the case in countries such as Brazil and the former Yugoslavia, where currency fluctuation is the greatest.

According to U.S. accounting standards, the conversion for annual sales figures should be the annual average rate for the year. The two examples below illustrate the effect of using non-current exchange rates. At the end of the 1980s Argentina experienced a high rate of inflation and revalued its currency. Example 1 presents three years of sales figures for an Argentinean company as reported in *Worldscope*. U.S. dollar sales have been calculated using the average exchange rate for each year.

EXAMPLE 1

THE EFFECT OF EXCHANGE RATE FLUCTUATIONS ON REPORTED SALES

Data Presented in Worldscope:
Income Statement (000's)

Fiscal Year Ending	*12/31/90*	*12/31/89*	*12/31/88*
Net Sales (Local)	169,208	18,234	354
Sales (US$)	32	13	22
Rate Used by *Worldscope*	0.0002	0.0007	0.062

Suppose that in 1992, the sales figure in a company database had not been updated since 1989. The sales figure in local currency would still be 18,234,000 australs. However, using the May 1992 rate of 1.0101 australs to the dollar, instead of the 1989 rate of .0007, the company's sales in U.S. dollars would be given as $18,418,000 instead of $13,000!

EXAMPLE 2

RECALCULATED DATA USING THE PROCEDURE OF SOME DIRECTORY DATABASES

Argentinean Company: 1989 Sales	**Local Currency (000 austral)**	**U.S. Dollars (000)**	**Exchange Rate**
Worldscope	18,234	13	.0007
Directory Database	18,234	18,418	1.0101

Database producers have become more aware of this pitfall. D&B does not include any sales figures on its *Latin America Top 25,000* CD-ROM. The companies are selected by number of employees. In April 1996, users of D&B on DIALOG File 518 would have seen the message that Brazilian sales figures were inaccurate due to inflation and in January 1997 there was a note that sales figures for South Africa were "temporarily incorrect."

Quality Issue—Date of the Data Elements

We often use online databases because they are updated more frequently than print or CD-ROM. However, online directories are not always more current than print or CD-ROM. For example, two of the Kompass files have not been updated for a couple of years. Other company databases may be updated monthly or even weekly. However, updating does not necessarily mean that an individual company record has been changed. In fact, even if a company record has been modified, the change might be only to one data element. The best quality online databases give us the date of the sales figure they are using. This allows us to do our own conversions using the exchange rate we select.

For example, information on a Turkish company had been available in a printed directory and in its online equivalent. By checking back issues of the printed volume, we could see that the local sales figure had not been updated between 1991 and 1995. The same sales figure appeared in the online database until the fall of 1995, when the company was finally dropped from the database. Since many online directory files include only the "most recent" sales figure, the user has no way of knowing what year that is.

The online source for the Turkish company also presents sales in U.S. dollars. The exchange rates changed each update so that the U.S. dollar figure changed accordingly. Listed below are the figures from two print editions and three online updates.

Date of Print Ed.			Date of Online Update		
1992	1993	1995	11/91	10/92	6/95
©1991	©1992	©1994			
Local Sales (000)					
971,000	971,000	971,000	971,000	971,000	971,000
US$ Sales (000)					
NA	NA	NA	200	135	29(est)

Quality Issue—Confusing Answers

Sometimes, using more than one database to verify results leads to confusing answers. In November of 1992, we searched two databases for a list of major Japanese banks. We found Saitama Bank Ltd, Kyowa Bank, and Kyowa Saitama in database A with Saitama Bank Ltd listed as the second largest Japanese consumer bank. Only Kyowa Saitama Bank was listed in Database B. What is the relationship of these banks?

To answer the question, it became necessary to go beyond directory databases. When we checked a Japanese company news file we learned that Kyowa Bank merged with Saitama Bank 18 months before database was A loaded. When it merged, it changed its name to Kyowa Saitama Bank. Taking the search a step further, we checked a newswire file to see if there were any further developments. About two weeks before the Database A had been loaded the bank had changed its name again, this time to Asahi Bank Ltd.

Quality Issue—Using the Web

If judging the quality of standard directories presented by reputable publishers is difficult, imagine the task of trying to evaluate directories that only appear on the WWW; see Appendix G, at the end of Chapter 4.

CONCLUSION

As this chapter has illustrated, there is a wide range of electronic company databases in a variety of electronic formats. The number of companies in these files far surpasses the number of companies in libraries' print collections. Some of these files give the researcher the added capability of screening for companies and downloading this information to disc in spreadsheet format.

Because of the many problems we have discussed regarding company information in Chapters 3 through 6, use international company information with caution. Don't use financial information in an international online directory unless you have a good understanding of the contents and limitations of the database. Online directory information is not necessarily more timely or accurate than a printed source.

Note that the WWW is replacing modem connections to character-based interfaces or client-server software as a means of searching and delivering company data, but company directories and the archival news sources that report on them will remain subscription products.

NOTES

1. MaryDee Ojala, "The Orient Express for Information Tracking the Asia/Pacific Region," *Database* 19 (December 1996): 24–37.

2. MaryDee Ojala, "The Companies of Eastern Europe," *Online* 20, no. 5 (September/October 1996): 44–49.

3. Ruth A. Pagell, series of articles on European on international CD-ROM products in *CD-ROM Professional*, July and November 1992, March and July 1993.

4. Ruth A. Pagell, "It's Greek to Me! Exchange Rate Translations and Company Comparisons," *Database* 14 (February 1991): 21–27.

5. Ruth A. Pagell, "Sorry Wrong Number," *Online* (November 1990).

6. Ruth A. Pagell, "What's for Dinar," *Database* (April 1991).

APPENDIX H
Selecting an International Database—A Checklist

Much of the information we discuss in the book is available from more than one source. There are multiple directory databases, financial filing databases, and text databases. Which should you use? This appendix presents guidelines as to what to look for in an international database. Some of these criteria will be the same as for print sources; some will be the same as for any database.

Checklist

- **Time**

  Currency—How up-to-date is the information?

  History—How many years of data are available?

  Updates—How frequently is the database updated? How frequently is a directory entry updated?

  Loading dates—Does the database indicate when it was reloaded? When an entry was reloaded? When an element was changed?

- **Data**

  Amount of directory information

  How many companies are in the database?

  How many countries are included?

  How many data items (fields) are there per record?

  Amount of textual information

  How many titles of journals, newspapers, etc. are covered?

  Accuracy of information

  Are there many typos? These are often easier to spot when browsing on a CD-ROM. Expand a DIALOG country field and notice the variant spellings. One database has more than 10 entries for "European Community"

  Do your clients question the data?

  Collection of information

  How are the data collected? By phone? Questionnaire?

  How are the data verified?

  How long are non-respondents kept in the database?

  Uniqueness of information—Is this information available in other sources? In other formats?

  Value added—What are the benefits of accessing the information in this format?

  Depth and/or breadth of information—Is this a mega-database *(PROMPT)*? Is it boutique *(Delphes)*?

  Completeness of information

  For text, are you getting abstracts, extracts, selected full text, or cover-to-cover full text or image?

- **Searching**

  Ease of use

  Can you use the database with little training time or preparation?

  Is it suitable for end-users?

  Flexibility

  Are there multiple access points?

  Is there a tradeoff between ease of use and flexibility?

  How many fields are searchable? sortable? reportable?

  Hardware/Software

  Do you need special hardware and software or will this run on any machine?

  Are their versions for DOS, Windows, Mac, and NT?

  If it requires client software, how much space does it require?

  Windows

  Will it run under all versions of Windows (3.1, 95, NT)?

  Networking

  Can this product be networked?

  Is it an appropriate product to network?

  WWW

  Does this databank provider have a WWW interface? Do you use IPs or passwords?

- **Output**

  On-screen presentation

  Are the data presented in a clear manner?

  Report features

  Can you create your own reports?

  Downloading

  If the database is numeric, in what format does it transfer data?

  How easy is it to import the data into a spread sheet? To e-mail it?

- **Database Provider**

  Familiarity

  Have you used other products either in print or online by this provider?

Reputation

What is the reputation of this provider?

Availability

Does the database provider have a local representative? A toll free telephone number? A fax? An e-mail address? A WWW site?

Training and documentation

Does the provider have user manuals, code books, and help sheets or videos?

Will the database provider come to your institution to give training?

Do you have to pay for training?

Knowledge

Does the database provider understand the information?

Access

Does the database producer make this information available electronically directly or through a databank provider?

- **Databank Provider**

Familiarity

Do you use other databases on this databank?

Reputation

What is the reputation of the provider? Innovative? Helpful? Responsive?

Availability

Does the databank provider have a local representative? What hours are help available? Your time zone or the provider's time zone?

Other complementary databases

Are there other databases that you can access at the same time to answer your question? Can you do a multi-file search?

Training and documentation

Does the provider have user manuals, etc.?

What level of training and support does the databank producer provide?

Knowledge

How knowledgeable is the databank provider about the content of the database?

Does the databank representative know when to refer you to the database provider?

Document delivery

Does the databank offer a document delivery service to articles that are not available full text online? Does the provider have a way to handle copyright?

You might want to build up a core group of international databases that will answer most of your routine questions, e.g., company addresses, industry participants, product/market information, financial information, and stock prices. Look for databases that are multi-purpose. These should have field codes for country name or country code, for company name, and for product coding ideally a standard code like the U.S. SIC or NACE. Look for families of databases, such as the Dun & Bradstreet databases, the Kompass databases, the UMI databases, or the IAC databases. If you can search one, you can search them all.

Multiple Databanks, Multiple Databases

- Whose data do you use when more than one database has "similar" data on the same system?

- Which databank do you use if a database is available from several providers?

Read the documentation! Talk to your local representatives. Ask for some free practice time or a trial of a CD-ROM. One of the major problems with electronic databases today is that it is just as difficult for the customer service reps to keep up with the changes as it is for us. Databank representatives, though familiar with how to search the system, are not conversant with the content of the databases. International information is complicated. Many CD-ROM providers are not familiar with database content.

When similar information is available from multiple sources, then cost becomes a factor in your decision. In determining cost, however, consider the following factors:

- Online costs
- Preparation time
- Searching and output format alternatives
- Methods of pricing—pay as you go or fixed rate; pay for all time online; just pay for output

For example, when screening for a list of companies with multiple variables that your client wishes to use in a spreadsheet, DIALOG may be the only online databank to which you have access with these capabilities. However, it might be preferable to retrieve several full text articles from Dow Jones Text during evening hours.

- If the database or databank resides in another country, how much information can your local representative provide?
- What is the turnaround time for a question to be answered?

If you have gone online because your client needs the information now, you need to use a system that can answer the question for you now. According to the U.S. representative for a non-U.S. databank, Americans do not like to make international phone calls, even to the U.K. Can you use e-mail or a fax?

Evaluating Online and CD-ROM

- When do you decide to get the information on CD-ROM rather than going online or using print?

This decision should be made very carefully. All of the usual CD-ROM decisions that you should have been making, but probably haven't been, become much more important when deciding to purchase a specialized international CD-ROM product. Think of all of the possible international questions you are asked and the possible sources you could use to answer these questions.

- Is it advantageous to buy one CD-ROM that will answer one type of question or use the same money to go online to a variety of different systems?

Look at alternative pricing with online systems such as negotiating a fixed price as alternatives to CD-ROM. Consider all of the costs involved in networking CD-ROMs.

- Who is your user group?

Do you want to encourage end-user access? Will your users be better off using one of the menu-driven systems such as Dow Jones, KR BusinessBase, or DataStar's Business Focus? Will the CD-ROM answer the routine questions and leave you free for the more difficult ones?

If you intend to buy an international CD-ROM when you are not familiar with the printed directory or the online equivalent, the documentation and the sales rep are again very important to you.

Human Resource Issues

For not only those of us who are new to business research, but also those of us who have been involved in business research for many years, the wealth of international information and the wide ranging demand for this information is taking us into unfamiliar territory. We are looking at print products from producers who are unfamiliar to us and online systems that originate in countries outside our borders. We must understand international business practice and terminology. We have a responsibility to our clients to know what it is we are offering them, in our print sources and our machine-readable ones. We need to have:

- Knowledge of source content—Are you and your staff familiar with the online source and printed equivalents?
- Understanding the question asked—Can you reasonably answer the question? Is the question reasonable?
- Ability to judge results—Do you know enough about the data, the source, and the topic to evaluate the output?

See Appendix G, at the end of Chapter 4, for a WWW checklist.

CHAPTER 7
Corporate Affiliations and Corporate Change

TOPICS COVERED

- Corporate Affiliations
- Corporate Change

MAJOR SOURCES DISCUSSED

- *Directory of American Firms Operating in Foreign Countries*
- *Directory of Foreign Firms Operating in the United States*
- *Directory of Corporate Affiliations*
- *Mergers and Acquisitions Source Book*
- *Merger Yearbook*
- *Merger & Corporate Transaction Database*
- *Mergerstat Review*

This chapter discusses two specialized and often related aspects of corporate research: corporate affiliations and corporate change. Corporate affiliations are the network of subsidiaries and branches that make up a corporation. Corporate change involves events that significantly alter a company's identity. These changes can be as broad as a total corporate restructuring or as specific as a change in an executive position.

CORPORATE AFFILIATIONS

"Who owns whom?" is the central question concerning corporate affiliations. The question is about corporate parent-subsidiary relationships.

Many other questions are related to these issues of ownership. For example:

What is the corporate hierarchy?

When and from whom were the subsidiaries that now make up the company acquired?

What percentage of the subsidiary's stock is owned by the parent company?

International corporate affiliations also raise questions about the nationality of the parent and subsidiary.

What U.S. companies are subsidiaries of Japanese companies?

Foreign ownership is carefully defined by countries and international organizations as part of the process of estimating foreign direct investment. For example, the OECD benchmark definition of "foreign direct investment" has these components:

Company X is a subsidiary of Enterprise N if, and only if:

1. Enterprise N is either
   A. A shareholder in or member of X and has the right to appoint or remove a majority of the members of X's administrative, management, or supervisory body; or
   B. Owns more than half of the shareholders' or members' voting power in X.
2. Company X is a subsidiary of any other Company Y which is a subsidiary of N.

Ownership is easier to determine than control. For example, assume that Company A in the U.S. owns 100% of Company B in Canada, and that Company B owns 100% of Company C in the U.S. From the U.S. point of view, Company C is foreign owned (owned by a Canadian company) but it is not clear if it is foreign controlled.[1]

Information about corporate affiliations, like information about corporate finance, is usually not volunteered by companies. Disclosure rules, described in Chapter 2, require that certain corporations reveal details concerning their ownership of subsidiaries. However, if a company is intent on concealing its corporate relationships it will often succeed. For example, the Bank of Credit and Commerce International (BCCI) managed to buy a bank in Washington D.C. without revealing its identity.

The secondary sources for corporate affiliations that we describe will not reveal the secret network of holdings of a BCCI, but they will allow you to see the details of corporate structures for many of the larger companies in the world. Exhibit 7.1 lists the terms used by Dun & Bradstreet to describe corporate hierarchies; it will serve as useful background for our description of sources.

COMPONENT	DESCRIPTION
Corporate Family Location	The top-most company of a corporate family
Division	A secondary location of a company reporting to main office (i.e., the headquarters). Usually has a different distinct name or trade name
Headquarters	The main office of a company. Implies the existence of a branch or branches reporting to it and having the same name.
Branch	A secondary location of a company. Reports to a main office. Branches carry the same name as their headquarters.
Parent	A corporation that owns more than 50% of the voting stock of another corporation (i.e., the subsidiary).
Subsidiary	A corporation in which more than 50% of its voting stock is owned by another company

DUN & BRADSTREET TERMS USED IN CORPORATE LINKAGE

EXHIBIT 7.1

Source: *DIALOG Chronolog*, March 1993, 93: 81.

Sources for Corporate Affiliations

The first three sources we describe are helpful if we need basic information on the subsidiaries of large corporations. However, their usefulness is limited by infrequent updates and by lack of comprehensive coverage and description of corporate relationships.

Directory of American Firms Operating in Foreign Countries (Published triennially by Uniworld Business Publications)

The 13th edition of the *Directory* (1994) lists 2,600 U.S. corporations, which have some 19,000 subsidiaries and affiliates in 138 countries. Included are companies in which American firms have a "substantial direct capital investment and which have been identified by the parent firms as a wholly or partially owned subsidiary affiliate or branch." Volume 1 lists U.S. firms that have operations overseas. The entries consist of the company name, address, chief officer, number of employees, and the countries in which the company operates. Volumes 2 and 3 contain listings by country—from Algeria to Zimbabwe—of the American firms' foreign operations. Franchises and non-commercial enterprises are not included. Information for the *Directory* is collected mainly through questionnaires. Exhibit 7.2 displays two sample entries.

ABBOTT LABORATORIES
 Abbott Park, North Chicago, IL 60064
 Tel: (708) 937-6100
 (Pharm & lab prdts)
  Abbott Labs., Ltd., P.O. Box 2633, Bangkok, Thailand
  Abbott Pharma Ltd. (JV), P.O. Box 2633, Bangkok, Thailand

ABERCROMBIE & KENT INTL INC
 1420 Kensington Rd, Oak Brook, IL 60521 210 ,
 Tel: (708) 954-2944
 (Tour wholesaler)
  Abercrombie & Kent (Thailand) Ltd., 4th fl., Silom Plaza, 491-29 30 ilom Rd.
  Bangkok 10500, Thailand

SAMPLE ENTRIES FOR THAILAND IN *DIRECTORY OF AMERICAN FIRMS OPERATING IN FOREIGN COUNTRIES*

EXHIBIT 7.2

Source: *Directory of American Firms Operating in Foreign Countries,* Uniworld Business Publications.

Directory of Foreign Firms Operating in the United States (published triennially by Uniworld Business Publications)

This standard directory has been published every three years since 1969. The eighth edition (1995) lists more than 1,600 foreign firms in 46 countries and 2,800 businesses in the U.S. that they own wholly or in part. Only the American headquarters or one major location of each subsidiary or affiliate is listed. The basic arrangement is by country. Within each country, the foreign firms are listed alphabetically together with the American firms owned wholly or in part. Separate indexes are provided for foreign firms and American affiliates. Exhibit 7.3 displays a sample record.

ENGLAND	
FOREIGN FIRM	**AMERICAN AFFILIATE**
GRAND METROPOLITAN PLC	**BURGER KING CORP** 17777 OLD CUTLER RD MIAMI, FL 33157 JAMES B. ADAMSON, CEO TEL: (305) 378-7011 FAX: (305) 378-7262 EMP: 31000 % FOREIGN OWNED: 100 RESTAURANTS, FAST FOOD OUTLETS **CARILLON IMPORTERS** GLENPONTE CENTRE W TEANECK, NJ 07666-6897 TEL: (201) 836-7799 FAX: (201) 836-3312 TLX: 431329 EMP: 50 % FOREIGN OWNED: 100 IMP/MKTG ALCOHOLIC BEVERAGES

RECORD FROM *DIRECTORY OF FOREIGN FIRMS OPERATING IN THE UNITED STATES*

EXHIBIT 7.3

Source: Directory of Foreign Firms Operating in the United States. Uniworld Business Publications.

Directory of Corporate Affiliations (published annually by National Register)

This five-volume set has information for some 33,000 companies. The volumes are organized so that the subsidiaries, no matter where they are located, will be found in the same volume as the parent company. The basic form of the listings is the same in each volume. Parent company information is given first, with the name, address, and telecommunications data in bold type. These entries are followed by any divisions, subsidiaries, affiliates, and joint ventures of the parent. The five volumes in the *Directory of Corporate Affiliations* set are:

- U.S. Public Companies, Volume 1: Lists U.S. public companies and their subsidiaries
- U.S. Public Companies, Volume 2: Contains geographic SICs (Standard Industrial Classifications) and personnel listings for public companies
- U.S. Private Companies: Lists U.S.-based private companies and their subsidiaries
- International Public and Private Companies: Lists all non–U.S.-based companies, whether they are public or private, and all of their subsidiaries, whether they are located in the U.S. or overseas

- Master Index: Lists all companies alphabetically, both headquarters and subsidiaries; also contains brand name index

In addition to its company listings, the International Public and Private Companies volume contains these features:

- Geographic index arranged by country and by city within country
- SIC Index
- Personnel listing—"Who's Where Internationally"—giving organization name and page reference
- A list of mergers, acquisitions, and name changes for the previous six years
- Addresses of foreign consulates
- Addresses of U.S. embassies
- Addresses of American chambers of commerce abroad
- Addresses of foreign trade commissions and chambers of commerce
- Major international public holidays
- Foreign currency exchange
- Country telephone codes and dialing instructions

Exhibit 7.4 shows a sample record from a company listing that displays subsidiary listings

Sullivan Graphics, Ltd. ———————————————————— Company Name
52 Upper Fitzwilliam Bd. ————————————————————— Company Address
Dublin 12, Ireland
Tel: 000l 568 333 ——————————————————————— Telecommunications Data
Telex: 95421
Fax: 0001 588 334
Year Founded: 1967
SULLI- (DUB LON) ————————————————————— Ticker Symbol & Stock Exchanges
Approx. SIs: $7,498,898,900 ———————————————— Financial Information
Fiscal Year End: 12/31/91
Emp: 10,800 ————————————————————————— No. of Employees, Including Sub-entries
Designs, Manufacturers & Markets ——————————— Business Description
Electronic Design Automation (EDA)
Software & Systems for the IC and
Systems Design Markets
S.I.C.: 3577 —————————————————————————— SIC Codes
Joseph M. McGillivary (Chm. Bd .) ————————————— Key Personnel
Elizabeth Mulloy (Pres. & Chief Exec. Officer)
Kevin B. O'Reilly (Chief Oper. Officer)

Simmons & Fitzgerald (Legal Firm) ————————————— Name and Address of Service Firm
Consheagh Bd.,
Dublin 17, Ireland

Subsidiary:

Ericsson Systems, Inc. (1) ————————————————— Reports to Parent Company
2 Wellington Bd., Killamey,   (Sullivan Graphics)
County Kerry, Ireland
Tel: 1 7183 48
Telex: 96140
Mfr. of Computer Peripheral
Equipment
S.I.C.: 3577
Thomas J. McSweeney (Pres .)

Subsidiary:

Kerngan Co., Inc. (2) ————————————————————— Reports to Level 1 Co.
8 Swords Rd., Dublin 17, Ireland   (Ericsson Systems)
Tel: 01611778 (100%)
Telex: 30472
Emp.: 850
Mfr. of Computer Printers
S.I.C. 3577

Tennant & McDaniel, Inc. (1)
Greenhills Rd., Tallaght, Dublin 24,
Ireland
Tel: 35 3712 6832 (100%) ———————————————————— Percentage of Ownership
Emp: 1200
Mfr. of Computer Peripheral
Equipment
S.I.C.: 3577
Raymond J. O'Sullivan (Chief Oper. Officer)

Non-U.S. Subsidiary:

Padova Systems, Inc. (1) —————————————————— Subsidiary not in Ireland or U.S.
Via Laurentina 449, 1-20097, Milan   Reports to Parent
Italy   (Sullivan Graphics)

Tel: 06 305291
Emp.: 1500
Mfr. of Computer Printers
S.I.C. 3577
Anthony Macaluso (Pres.)

RECORD FROM *DIRECTORY OF CORPORATE AFFILIATIONS*

EXHIBIT 7.4

Source: Directory of Corporate Affiliations. National Register Publishing.

The online version of the *Directory of Corporate Affiliations* is available on DIALOG as *Corporate Affiliations* (File 513) and on LEXIS-NEXIS Services. The file includes more than 100,000 parent companies and their affiliates. *Corporate Affiliations* is also available on CD-ROM from Bowker-Saur.

Corporate Affiliations (DIALOG) has two types of records. The first (parent company record) contains the complete corporate family tree. The second (affiliate company record) contains the portion of the corporate family tree in which a particular company fits. Exhibit 7.5 is the parent company record (trun-

cated) for the U.K. company Grand Metropolitan, owner of several widely known American companies. As the exhibit indicates, the information includes (in addition to a list of subsidiaries) the parent company name, address, and telephone number; ticker symbol and stock exchange; up to 20 SIC codes and descriptions; the number of employees; total assets, sales, net worth, and net liabilities; names of executives; and members of the board of directors. The record also includes a 10-digit NRPC (National Register Parent Company) number that can be used to retrieve all related companies regardless of name.

[4/96]
1932215
Grand Metropolitan Plc
20 St James's Sq
London, SW1Y 4RR
United Kingdom

Telephone: 0171 321 6000

NRPC Number: 020659000
Ticker Symbol: GRM Stock Exchange: NYSE,ASE,PS,LON

Number of NonUS Affiliates: 98
Number of US Affiliates: 22
Total Number of Affiliates: 120

Business: Mfrs, Wholesalers & Retailers of Spirits, Wines & Foods; Opthamalic
 Products & Services

SIC Codes (Primary listed first):
     2041   Flour & other grain mill products
     2045   Prepared flour mixes & doughs
     5813   Drinking places (alcoholic beverages)
     2033   Canned fruits, vegetables, preserves, jams & jellies
     2045   Prepared flour mixes & doughs
     2051   Bread & other bakery products, except cookies & crackers
     2037   Frozen fruits, fruit juices & vegetables
     2086   Bottled & canned soft drinks & carbonated waters
     2091   Canned & cured fish & seafoods
     2096   Potato chips, corn chips & similar snacks
     2099   Food preparations, NEC
     5812   Eating places

Number of Employees: NA

Sales: $12,490,184,000
Total Assets: $15,243,562,000
Net Worth: $5,834,392,600
Total Liabilities: $9,409,169,400

This is a(n) Parent, NonUS, Public Company

ONLINE RECORD FROM *CORPORATE AFFILIATIONS*

EXHIBIT 7.5

Numeric Field(s) Last Updated: 951011
Textual Field(s) Last Updated: 951208
Executives:
    Chairman of the Board
      Lord Sheppard/Chairman of the Board
Chairman of the Board
      RV Giordano KBE/Chairman of the Board
Chairman of the Board, Chief Executive Officer
      DP Nash/Chief Executive Officer
Chairman of the Board, Chief Executive Officer
      JB McGrath/Chief Executive Officer
Chief Information Officer MIS
      WD Brant/Chief Information Officer MIS
Chief Executive Officer
      George J Bull/Chief Executive Officer
Controller
      DB Rickard/Controller
Treasurer
      N Rose/Treasurer
General Counsel, Corporate Secretary
      Roger H Myddelton/Corporate Secretary
Employee Benefits, Pension Administration
      RJ Amy/Pension Administration
Planning & Development
      PEB Cawdron/Planning & Development
Finance Executive-Other
      GMN Corbett/Finance Executive-Other
Real Estate
      DE Tagg/Real Estate
Other
      ML Hepher/Other
Other
      Prof G Hohler/Other
Other
      PJD Job/Other
Vice President - No Function
      Sir Colin Marshall/Vice President - No Function
Other
      Sir David Simon/Other
Public Relations
      Mary Carroll/Public Relations
Personnel Training & Development
      Krishna De/Personnel Training & Development
Public Relations
      Neil Garnett/Public Relations
Investor Relations
      CB James/Investor Relations
Administration/Operations
      V Osborne/Administration/Operations
Human Resources
      Jeff Slater/Human Resources

Board of Directors: Sheppard, Lord; Bull, George J; Cawdron, Peter ER; Corbett, GMN; Giordano, Richard V, KBE; Hohler, Gertrud, Prof Dr; Hepher, ML; Job, PJD; Marshall, Colin, Sir; McGrath, John B; Nash, David P; Simon, David AG; Tagg, David E

Corporate Family Hierarchy:

=>Grand Metropolitan Plc 1932215<=
    GrandMet Foods UK (Subsidiary) 1932214
      Grandmet Foods Europe (Non-US Subsidiary) 1932213
      Grandmet Foods GmbH (Non-US Subsidiary) 1932212
      Grandmet Foods Southern Europe (Non-US Subsidiary) 1932211
    .
    .

ONLINE RECORD FROM *CORPORATE AFFILIATIONS*

EXHIBIT 7.5 (continued)

GW Archer & Co (Non-US Subsidiary) 1932201
Callitheke International Ltd (Non-US Subsidiary) 1932200
.
Justerini & Brooks Ltd (Non-US Subsidiary) 1932191
The Singleton of Auchroisk (Non-US Subsidiary) 1932190
Twelve Islands Shipping Company (Non-US Subsidiary) 1932189
W & A Gilbey (Non-US Subsidiary) 1932188
Carillon Importers Ltd (US Subsidiary) 1932187
Bombay Spirits Company (Non-US Subsidiary) 1932186
.
IDV North America (Non-US Subsidiary) 1932185
IDV Czech Republic (Subsidiary) 1932168
IDV France (Subsidiary) 1932167
IDV Hungaria Impari es Kereskedelmi Kft (Subsidiary) 1932166
IDV Operations Ireland Ltd (Subsidiary) 1932165
IDV Poland (Subsidiary) 1932164
International Distillers South Asia (Subsidiary) 1932163
International Distillers Japan (Subsidiary) 1932162
J&B Scotland (Subsidiary) 1932161
Marqint Marcas Internacionales SA (Subsidiary) 1932160
Metaxa Distillers (Subsidiary) 1932159
Metaxa Greece (Subsidiary) 1932158
Piat Pere & Fils (Subsidiary) 1932157
Sileno SOC Distribuidora de Bebidas (Subsidiary) 1932156
.
Grand Metropolitan Foodservice Inc (US Subsidiary) 1932146
Heublein Inc (US Subsidiary) 1932145
Beaulieu Vineyard (Subsidiary) 1932144
Palace Brands (Subsidiary) 1932143
Lancers (Non-US Subsidiary) 1932142
The Pierre Smirnoff Company (Non-US Subsidiary) 1932141
Pearle Inc (Non-US Subsidiary) 1932140
Pearle Express (Subsidiary) 1932139
Pearle Vision Inc (Subsidiary) 1932138
The Pillsbury Company (Subsidiary) 1932137
Martha White Foods Inc (Division) 1932136
Roush Products Co Inc (Division) 1932135
.
Pillsbury Canada Ltd (Non-US Holdings) 1932107
The Pillsbury Company (Non-US Holdings) 1932106
GrandMet Foods UK (Non-US Holdings) 1932105
Pillsbury GmbH OHG (Non-US Holdings) 1932104
Pillsbury GmbH (Non-US Holdings) 1932103
Pillsbury Japan KK (Non-US Holdings) 1932102
Pillsbury UK Ltd (Non-US Holdings) 1932101
.
.

ONLINE RECORD FROM *CORPORATE AFFILIATIONS*

EXHIBIT 7.5 (continued)

Source: DIALOG File 513.

There are several ways to search corporation relationships in DIALOG File 513. The first six digits of the NRPC number are the same for related companies, so searching on these first six digits will bring together all related companies in the file. You can also search and retrieve companies reporting to the "ultimate parent" (the company at the top of the hierarchy) or companies reporting to an "immediate parent" (the company that owns a subsidiary). The DIALOG file uses the prefix "UP" for ultimate parent and "IP" for immediate parent. More information can be found on individual subsidiaries and plants by searching directly by subsidiary name.

Another use for File 513 is to find the names and characteristics of cross-border subsidiaries (for example, the names of U.S. companies owned by Japanese companies). As Table 7.A shows, DIALOG's report format allows the information to be displayed as columns and rows.

TABLE 7.A

U.S. SUBSIDIARIES OF MAJOR JAPANESE COMPANIES (1996)

Company Name	Japanese Ultimate Parent
Marubeni America Corporation	Marubeni Corporation
Toyota Motor Corporation, Toyo	Toyota Motor Corporation
The CIT Group Inc	The Dai-Ichi Kangyo Bank Limit
Nissan Motor Corporation in US	Nissan Motor Co Ltd
Mitsubishi International Corpo	Mitsubishi Corporation
The Southland Corporation	Ito-Yokado Co Ltd
Heller Financial Inc	The Fuji Bank Limited
7-Eleven Stores	Ito-Yokado Co Ltd
Matsushita Electric Corporatio	Matsushita Electric Industrial
Bridgestone/Firestone Inc	Bridgestone Corporation
Sony Corporation of America	Sony Corporation
Canon USA Inc	Canon Inc
Toshiba Corporation, Toshiba A	Toshiba Corporation
Hitachi America Ltd	Hitachi Ltd
Sony Music Entertainment Inc	Sony Corporation
Omron Systems Inc	Omron Corporation
National Steel Corporation	NKK Corporation
Sharp Electronics Corporation	Sharp Corporation
Mitsubishi Electric America In	Mitsubishi Electric Corporatio
Subaru of America Inc	Fuji Heavy Industries Ltd
Toyota Motor Corporation, New	Toyota Motor Corporation
Sony Pictures Entertainment	Sony Corporation
Kyocera Corporation, Kyocera I	Kyocera Corporation
NEC Corporation, NEC Electroni	NEC Corporation
Union Bank (San Francisco)	The Bank of Tokyo Ltd
Reichhold Chemicals Inc	Dainippon Ink & Chemicals Inc
Fujitsu Computer Products	Fujitsu Limited
Komatsu Dresser Company	Komatsu Ltd
Pioneer Electronics (USA) Inc	Pioneer Electronic Corporation
NMB Corporation	Minebea Co Ltd

Source: DIALOG File 513.

Who Owns Whom (published annually by Dun & Bradstreet International)

Who Owns Whom contains information on the corporate structure of approximately 23,000 parent companies and their 300,000 subsidiaries. Approximately one-third of the companies in *Who Owns Whom* are in the U.K., one-third are in continental Europe, and one-third are in the rest of the world. Information in each full company entry includes name, status as parent or subsidiary, country of incorporation, percentage shareholding (when available), an indication of whether the company is currently active or dormant, and its position within the group.

Parent company entries also include company address, telephone number, and U.S. SIC number. *Who Owns Whom* also includes many companies owned by official bodies (such as governments) that have subsidiaries but are not themselves corporations.

Information is collected by annual questionnaires and telephone interviews with company secretaries (or equivalent authority). Company annual reports, major business newspapers of the world, and selected trade journals are also scanned for information on new groups to be added to the database. The printed version of *Who Owns Whom* is in 6 volumes:

- Australia and Asia (Volume 1)
- North America (Volume 2)
- United Kingdom (Volumes 3 and 4)
- Continental Europe (Volumes 5 and 6)

The *Who Owns Whom* directories present data in two basic arrangements. The first is by country, subdivided by parent company name. The second is alphabetically by parent company name. The information provided includes address, SIC codes, principal officers, and a list of subsidiaries and their countries. The index is by subsidiary name, showing parent company and percentage of ownership when available. The sample record in Exhibit 7.6 is from the online version of the directory, available on DataStar.

```
        1 WHOW
AN      000184234, Duns number: 21-012-4764, D-S Update: 960312.
OC      PARAGRAPH
        CO (1)
CO      Grand Metropolitan PLC.
AD      20 St. James's Square,
        London,
         SW1Y 4RR.
        LONDON.
CN      United Kingdom.
RE      European Union;
        Western Europe.
TL      0171-321-6000.
RN      Registration number: 291848.
CC      US SIC:  6711 HOLDING COMPANY
                 7011 HOTELS, MOTELS, AND TOURIST RESORTS
                 5141 GENERAL GROCERY WHOLESALERS
                 5143 DAIRY PRODUCT WHOLESALERS
CT      Ultimate parent
NU      Number of subsidiaries listed in SU: 538 in 47 group(s).
SU      1    OF 47.
        -    Binehall Ltd. (A) (d), Gibraltar.
        2    OF 47.
        -     Buckingham Restaurants Ltd. (d), United Kingdom.
        3    OF 47.
        -    Bullard & Sons Ltd. (d), United Kingdom.
        4    OF 47.
        -    Burgerking (Holdings) Ltd., United Kingdom
           -   Burger King (U.K.) Ltd. (d), United Kingdom
             - King Foods Ltd. (d), United Kingdom
           -   Haeagen-Dazs UK Ltd. (d), United Kingdom
             - Haeagen-Dazs Ireland Ltd. (d), Ireland, Republic of

[an additional 12 pages of subsidiaries listings]
```

SAMPLE RECORD FROM *WHO OWNS WHOM*

EXHIBIT 7.6

Source: DataStar, *Who Owns Whom.*

D&B Global Corporate Linkages (DIALOG File 522)

D&B Global Corporate Linkages is an online company directory file of 4.2 million companies that links a company to its corporate family, showing the size of the corporate structure, family hierarchy, and key information (including D-U-N-S numbers) for the parent company and its headquarters, branches, and subsidiaries worldwide. Corporate family structure information is provided in one online record.

The firms in File 522 represent all types of industries including manufacturing, retail and wholesale trade, agriculture, mining, construction, financial services, educational institutions, and business and professional services. Public, private, and government-run companies are included. This resource includes businesses from Europe (including Eastern Europe), Africa, Mexico, the Middle East, Asia, Australia, Central and South America, the United States, and Canada. Exhibit 7.7 shows a sample record for Nestle SA.

D&B—Dun's Market Identifiers (Dun & Bradstreet)

D&B—Dun's Market Identifiers may be used to find some cross-border corporate links. The DIALOG version of the file (File 516) lists about 17,000 U.S. companies that have foreign ownership. The records of these companies are tagged "NON-US OWNED." On DIALOG, you can retrieve these companies by selecting SF=NON-US OWNED.

Only the top-most company of a corporate family hierarchy in the U.S. that has foreign owners has this designation. For example, Friskies Petcare is a U.S. company owned by Nestle Food Co., another U.S.-based company. Nestle Food Co. is owned by Nestle Holdings Inc., also U.S. based. Nestle Holdings Inc. is owned by the Swiss company Nestle SA, the ultimate parent.

NESTLE SA
Entre-Deux-Villes
VEVEY 1800
SWITZERLAND

REGION: Europe

TELEPHONE: (0041)   219242111

BUSINESS: Dry, condensed, evaporated products

PRIMARY SIC: 2023   Mfg dry/evaporated dairy products
SECONDARY SIC(S):   2095   Mfg roasted coffee
                     2043   Mfg cereal breakfast food
                     2066   Mfg chocolate/cocoa products
                     2834   Mfg pharmaceutical preparations
                     6719   Holding company

THIS IS:
    An Ultimate Location
    A Headquarters Location
    A Corporation
    An Importer
    An Exporter

DUNS NUMBER: 48-070-8874
PARENT DUNS: 48-070-8874
PARENT NAME: NESTLE SA
PARENT ADDRESS: Entre-Deux-Villes
PARENT CITY: VEVEY
PARENT COUNTRY: SWITZERLAND
DOMESTIC ULTIMATE DUNS: 48-070-8874
DOMESTIC ULTIMATE NAME: NESTLE SA
DOMESTIC ULTIMATE ADDRESS: Entre-Deux-Villes
DOMESTIC ULTIMATE CITY: VEVEY
DOMESTIC ULTIMATE COUNTRY: SWITZERLAND
GLOBAL ULTIMATE DUNS: 48-070-8874
GLOBAL ULTIMATE NAME: NESTLE SA
GLOBAL ULTIMATE ADDRESS: Entre-Deux-Villes
GLOBAL ULTIMATE CITY: VEVEY
GLOBAL ULTIMATE COUNTRY: SWITZERLAND

NUMBER OF FAMILY MEMBERS: 867

CORPORATE FAMILY HIERARCHY
RECORD UPDATE DATE: 12 Sep 1995
FAMILY UPDATE DATE: 18 Oct 1994

RECORD FROM D&B GLOBAL CORPORATE LINKAGES, DIALOG FILE 522

EXHIBIT 7.7

Source: D&B Global Corporate Linkages (DIALOG File 522).

Only the record for Nestle Holdings Inc. (the U.S. ultimate parent) is designated by D&B as "foreign owned." Exhibit 7.8 shows three brief company records. The first two are from the DIALOG version of *D&B—Dun's Market Identifiers* (File 516). They show that the Corporate Family D-U-N-S number for Friskies Petcare links it to Nestle Food Co. The third record is from DIALOG's *D&B—Global Corporate Families*. It illustrates how the D-U-N-S number for Friskies Petcare links to the ultimate parent, Nestle SA in Switzerland.

Record #1
    Friskies Petcare Company Inc

DUNS NUMBER: **87-770-0435**
CORPORATE FAMILY DUNS: **13-148-1657**   Nestle Holdings Inc.

Source: DIALOG File 516

Record #2
    Nestle Holdings Inc.

NON-US OWNED
DUNS NUMBER: **13-148-1657**   Nestle Holdings Inc.
PARENT DUNS: **48-070-8874**   Nestle SA

Source: DIALOG file 516

Record #3
    Friskies Petcare Company Inc

DUNS NUMBER: **87-770-0435**

PARENT DUNS: **00-825-6224**
PARENT NAME: Nestle Food Company (inc)
PARENT COUNTRY: UNITED STATES
DOMESTIC ULTIMATE DUNS: **13-148-1657**
DOMESTIC ULTIMATE NAME: Nestle Holdings Inc
DOMESTIC ULTIMATE COUNTRY: UNITED STATES
GLOBAL ULTIMATE DUNS: **48-070-8874**
GLOBAL ULTIMATE NAME: NESTLE SA
GLOBAL ULTIMATE COUNTRY: SWITZERLAND

NUMBER OF FAMILY MEMBERS: 867

D-U-N-S Number Cross-Border Links

EXHIBIT 7.8

Source: D&B Dun's Market Identifiers (DIALOG File 516).

Wer gehoert zu wem (*Who Belongs to Whom*) (DataStar)

Wer gehoert zu wem (*WGZW*) is the online version of the printed Commerzbank publication of the same name. *WGZW* contains information on the ownership of approximately 11,500 companies located in the Federal Republic of Germany with a capital stock of at least one million marks. The database covers nearly all "AG" companies (public companies) and about two-thirds of the capital of "GmbH" companies (private companies). Exhibit 7.9 is an example of a record.

AN	0105002822 9607, Copyright: COMMERZBANK AG.
CO	Microsoft GmbH.
LO	8044 Unterschleissheim.
CA	DM 5.050 Mio.
LS	GmbH.
CC	30 Manufacture of office machinery and computers,
	31 Manufacture of electrical machinery and apparatus n.e.c.
OS	Microsoft Corporation Redmond, Redmond/Wash, (United States of America), (105012804) - 100.00 %.

Record from Wer gehoert zu wem

EXHIBIT 7.9

Source: DataStar WGZW (August 1996).

Each document contains the exact name, legal status, and location of the company; its industrial sector, amount of capital, major shareholders or partners, and percentage shareholdings; the country of foreign shareholders; and cross-references to shareholders entered elsewhere in the database. Several of the fields can be searched in English or German.

The information in the database is the result of direct written contact between Commerzbank and the companies concerned. The information is updated twice a year by means of official published sources and the companies' own publications.

Although the records in *WGZW* are brief, the database provides the answers required of a corporate affiliation file. You can search the database to find

> *Who owns whom? (e.g., Who owns Union Deutsche Lebensmittelwerke?)*
>
> *Who belongs to whom? (e.g., Which companies does Siemans own?)*
>
> *Corporate links (e.g., How many companies does Siemans own?)*
>
> *Country of shareholders*
>
> *How many companies are located in the former East Germany?*

A useful feature of the database is its ability to be searched for percentage of shareholdings. Exhibit 7.9 is a record retrieved from a search of the file for all companies that were 100% owned by U.S. firms.

CORPORATE CHANGE

Our discussion of sources for corporate change begins with a brief list of key terms and their definitions. The definitions are generally applicable internationally, although many legal, accounting, and institutional details apply to individual countries. Some examples of such country-specific items include:

- Accounting regulations: German companies are not permitted to buy their own shares, which limits their defense against hostile takeovers.
- Anti-monopoly laws: Japanese law (Anti-Monopoly and Fair Trade Maintenance Act) requires a report before a merger is carried out.
- Foreign ownership: Switzerland has restrictions on the foreign ownership of corporate assets.

An overview of the legal and tax issues relating to U.S. cross-border acquisitions can be found in *The Art of M&A.*[2]

Definitions

Acquisition: The acquiring of control of one corporation by another. The acquiring company is often referred to as the "buyer" or "acquirer"; the acquired company is referred to as the "seller" or "target." "Acquisition" is often used to describe a transaction in which both the buyer and seller are willing to make a deal. A "hostile acquisition," in which the seller is unwilling to deal, is usually called a "takeover."

Bankruptcy: The conditions under which the financial position of a corporation are such as to cause actual or legal insolvency. When a bankruptcy is declared, three basic resolutions are possible: liquidation, acquisition, or reorganization.

Consolidation: A combination of two or more organizations into one, to form a new entity. Consolidation, in that it creates a new corporate entity, is similar to both an acquisition and a merger. Consolidation is considered a more friendly, cooperative deal than either a merger or acquisition. It gives equal footing in the new firm to each corporation. However, this defines the classic situation, and in reality a consolidation may be no more friendly than any deal type, nor is there a certainty the two firms have equality in the new entity.

Leveraged Buyout (LBO): The acquisition of a business primarily with borrowed funds that are repaid from the target company's earnings or sale of excess assets. The LBO differs from a typical acquisition in that, along with transfer of ownership, there is also a complete restructuring of the target company's balance sheet. An LBO often transforms a target company's balance sheet from a debt-free condition to a highly leveraged state.

Liquidation: The winding up of the affairs of a business by converting all assets into cash, paying off all outside creditors in the order of their preference, and distributing the remainder, if any, to the owners in proportion, and in the order of preference (if any) of ownership.

M & A (Merger & Acquisition): A phrase that is often applied to a wide range of corporate change activities including: mergers, acquisitions, partial acquisitions, leveraged buyouts, divestitures, exchange offers, stock repurchases, self-tenders, tender offers, and spinoffs.

Merger: The combining of two or more entities through the direct acquisition by one of the entities of the net assets of the other. Mergers usually involve an exchange of stock. Regardless of the format of the deal, a merger is the final legal requirement for its completion.

Recapitalization: Altering the capital structure of a firm by increasing or decreasing its capital stock. In doing so, a firm also may increase its debt or leverage. In a leveraged recapitalization, stock is exchanged for debt securities, and leverage becomes a greater percentage of the total capitalization. Methods of decreasing stock, as a takeover defense or to increase stock value, are referred to as *stock buybacks* or *stock repurchases*. The stocks are bought back from existing shareholders, which shrinks outstanding shares.

Reorganization: The altering of a firm's capital structure, often resulting from a merger, that affects the rights and responsibilities of the owners. In a bankruptcy, the objectives of a reorganization are to eliminate the cause of failure, to settle with creditors, and to allow the firm to remain in business. Alternatively, a company may undergo a nonlegal reorganization that may result only in changes to the organizational chart through a shuffling of subsidiaries and divisions.

Restructuring: A collection of activities designed to increase shareholder wealth by maximizing the value of corporate assets. These activities may include divestiture of underperforming businesses, spin-offs to shareholders, stock repurchases, recapitalization, or acquisitions.

Spin-Off: The separation of a subsidiary or division of a corporation from its parent by issuing shares in a new corporate entity. Shareowners in the parent receive shares in the new company in proportion to their original holding, and the total value of the shares remains about the same.

Accounting rules may affect the price that acquiring companies are willing to pay for acquisitions. Rules affecting goodwill are an example. Goodwill is the purchase price of the acquisition minus the market value of the acquisition's assets. In the U.K., for example, acquiring companies can write off goodwill against shareholders' equity. In the U.S., goodwill must be paid for out of earnings.

In the European Union (EU), all large mergers, acquisitions, and joint ventures are subject to review by the European Commission's Merger Control Task Force. The review applies to all large EU business transactions, as well as to international deals meeting the community's criteria for review.

Cross-Border Transactions

Cross-border deals are M & A transactions in which the target (the company being acquired) and the acquirer (or the acquirer's ultimate parent) are based in different countries. An example of a cross-border M & A transaction is Grand Metropolitan's purchase of Pillsbury in 1988. Grand Metropolitan is a U.K.-based company and Pillsbury is based in the United States. A domestic deal, from a U.S. point of view, is the acquisition of a U.S. company by another U.S. company. As Table 7.B indicates, a combination of a non-U.S. acquirer and a non-U.S. target can be either a cross-border transaction (e.g., a German company acquiring a U.K. company) or a domestic transaction (e.g., a German company acquiring another German company). Companies have several motives for becoming involved in cross-border acquisitions. They include increased access to foreign markets, achieving international brand name recognition, and favorable exchange rates.

TABLE 7.B		
M & A TRANSACTIONS IN RELATION TO NATIONALITY		
	U.S. Acquirer	**Non-U.S. Acquirer**
U.S. Target	U.S. Domestic	U.S. Cross-Border
Non-U.S. Target	U.S. Cross-Border	Non-U.S Cross-Border *or* Non-U.S. Domestic

From a U.S. perspective, it is easiest to find information about M & A transactions in which either or both the parties are U.S. companies.

Sources for Corporate Change Information

M & A Yearbooks. Several important M & A yearbooks are listed below.

Mergers and Acquisitions Source Book (annual cumulation published by Quality Services Company Quarterly)

Although primarily a reference for U.S. mergers, the 1996 edition of the *Source Book* includes a chapter describing foreign transactions. The transactions include completed transactions, negotiations, and terminated deals. Most descriptions (some 400) are brief, giving SIC number; the name, industry, and description of buyer and seller; and the purchase price, if disclosed. A few "Featured Transactions" supply capsule balance sheet, income statement, and market data. The *Source Book* is handicapped by its single index of transaction—by company name only. There is no country index.

Merger Yearbook: U.S./International Edition
(published annually by Securities Data Publishing, Inc.)

Subtitled *Corporate Acquisitions, Mergers, Divestitures, Leveraged Buyouts,* the *Merger Yearbook* will report a deal regardless of whether a U.S. company is a party. It also reports many more cross-border deals in a single volume (some 12,000) than were previously available in a printed source. The information in the *Merger Yearbook* is based on the SDC *Mergers and Acquisitions Database,* described below.

Organized by four-digit SIC number, each record gives basic deal information including the value and current status of the transaction. A useful feature in each *Merger Yearbook* entry is a code for type of deal. These types include such deals as private negotiations, divestitures, spinoffs, and even rumors. Bankrupt companies are included if they are seeking a buyer. The deals are indexed only by company name or investor, making it impossible to identify cross-border deals by the company's country. Despite this limitation, the *Merger Yearbook* is the best single printed source for cross-border and non-U.S. merger information.

Aggregate figures for worldwide M & A are an important feature of the *Merger Yearbook.* The data presented include tables for the following transactions, measured in billions of U.S. dollars:

- Global mergers and corporate transactions
- Global acquisitions
- Hostile acquisitions of global targets
- Acquisitions of global targets valued at $1 billion or greater
- Global LBOs and MBOs
- Global acquisitions of targets with industry breakdowns

Another unique listing is a ranking of targets and acquirers by nation. Exhibit 7.10 is derived from their ranking of targets by nation. The original table included three years of data for 50 countries.

Exhibits 7.11 and 7.12 show the form of the entries from the *Merger Yearbook* and the *Mergers and Acquisitions Source Book.*

Ranking of Targets by Nation (Global Acquirors) in 1995			
	Value ($ Mils)	Mkt. Share	Number of Deals
United States	$422,408.0	57.2	7,064
United Kingdom	$117,198.4	15.9	1,578
Australia	$28,740.5	3.9	481
Canada	$19,575.5	2.7	738
Germany	$17,334.9	2.3	648
France	$16,391.5	2.2	572
Italy	$14,196.7	1.9	333
Sweden	$11,776.6	1.6	239
Czech Republic	$9,546.3	1.3	76
Switzerland	$7,065.4	1.0	121
Netherlands	$4,640.2	0.6	245
Brazil	$4,183.8	0.6	99
Malaysia	$4,048.2	0.5	250
Hong Kong	$3,892.1	0.5	162
Portugal	$3,803.4	0.5	48
Peru	$3,191.0	0.4	46
New Zealand	$3,181.3	0.4	187
Finland	$3,057.4	0.4	141
Singapore	$3,046.7	0.4	127
Spain	$2,674.8	0.4	165
Argentina	$2,528.0	0.3	75
Japan	$2,396.2	0.3	61

EXTRACT FROM *MERGER YEARBOOK*

EXHIBIT 7.10

Source: Merger Yearbook, 1996: 22. Copyright 1996 Securities Data Publishing, Inc., 40 W. 57th St., 11th Floor, New York, NY 10019. Reprinted with permission.

SIC NUMBER	SELLER	BUYER	Purchase Price ($ Millions)
2841	80% of Pollena Bydgoszcz, a Polish detergent maker, owned by the Polish government	Unilever, Rotterdam, Netherlands an Anglo-Dutch food, detergent, and toiletries manufacturer	$20.00

COMMENTS: Unilever said that is has agreed to purchase 80% of Pollena Bydgoszcz from the Polish government for $20 million. The Polish government, which is to retain 20% of the detergent maker, describes the planned sale as the country's largest privatization so far. Unilever said it intends to invest a further $24 million to double the Polish concern's production capacity, upgrade its technology and add equipment to make liquid products. Pollena Bydgoszcz, which employs 430 people, will be renamed **Lever Polska.**

RECORD FROM *MERGERS AND ACQUISITIONS SOURCE BOOK*

EXHIBIT 7.11

Source: Mergers and Acquisitions Source Book, 1992: 6–43. Reprinted with permission.

Elvia Schweizerische 6311	RAS Riunione Adriatica di Sic		
Insurance Company	Insurance Company	$1,164.5	SFR
Zurich	Milano	P/E: 40.4	Acq. Maj. Int.
Switzerland	Italy	Ancd: 09/30/94	Efct: 02/28/95
Credit Suisse First Boston		1,500.0	

RAS Riunione Adriatica di Sicurta, a unit of Allianz AG Holding Berlin und Munchen, (AH) acquired a 59.9% interest, or 383,142 ordinary shares, in Elvia Schweiz Versicherungs-Gessellschaft (EV) from Swiss Reinsurance at 3,915 Swiss francs ($3039.22 US) per bearer share, for an estimated 1.5 bil francs ($1.16 bil). The transaction was subject to approval by the European Commission Cartel Office. Upon completion, RAS planned to launch a tender offer for the remaining 40.1% stake in EV.

CROSS DIVEST PRIVNEG SFDEBT SFCOM

ENTRY FROM *MERGER YEARBOOK*

EXHIBIT 7.12

Source: Merger Yearbook 1996: 823. Copyright 1996 Securities Data Publishing, Inc., 40 W. 57th St., 11th Floor, New York, NY 10019.

Mergerstat Review (published annually by W. T. Grimm & Co.)

Mergerstat Review contains summary data on cross-border merger transactions. It does not report the names of companies involved in transactions but reports only aggregate statistics. The *Review's* statistical tables include a section for both foreign buyers and foreign sellers. A limitation of the *Review's* coverage of cross-border deals is its requirement that a U.S. company be involved in a transaction to be included. The foreign buyers section gives data on both the foreign purchase of domestic companies and purchase of foreign-based subsidiaries of U.S. corporations. The foreign sellers section lists U.S. corporations' purchases of foreign companies and units of foreign companies. Ten years of data are given for most series. The main series for foreign buyers are

- Foreign acquisitions of U.S. companies
- Foreign acquisitions—price paid
- Foreign acquisitions—price offered
- Average premium paid over market
- Average price/earnings ratio paid
- Industries attracting foreign buyers
- Number of transactions by country
- Dollar total by country

The main data series for foreign sellers are

- U.S. acquisitions of foreign business—number of transactions
- U.S. acquisitions of foreign businesses—total dollar value
- Industries attracting American buyers
- Industry dollar totals
- Number of transactions by country
- Dollar total by country

M & A Journals. Journals that provide international coverage of mergers and acquisitions supplement the annual coverage of yearbooks.

Acquisitions Monthly (published monthly by Lonsdale House)

This journal emphasizes U.K. mergers. Each issue contains an "Acquisition Record" for the month. It includes 40 pages of capsule descriptions of domestic and cross-border deals. About half the descriptions involve U.K. companies. The information is presented by company within country. A separate "sector analysis" presents the same information grouped by U.K. SIC numbers. Each issue has a company index. *Acquisitions Monthly* provides the data for the *AMDATA M&A* database. The database runs on a personal computer and is updated with diskettes. It supplies 180 data fields for each transaction. The database covers domestic and cross-border transactions for Europe, Japan, and the United States. Historical coverage varies by country. Most have coverage from 1989 to date.

Mergers & Acquisitions (published semi-monthly by MLR Publishing)

Mergers & Acquisitions includes an "M & A Roster" giving capsule descriptions of deals that took place during the previous quarter. Two sections focusing on cross-border deals are included in the roster. One section covers U.S. deals for foreign firms and the other covers deals for U.S. companies by foreign firms. There is no coverage of deals between two non-U.S. firms. In the "M & A Roster," standard information, such as terms of the deal, is provided for each transaction. There is also an annual index to all deals covered in the roster, but it is an index by company name only. The index always appears in the May/June issue of *Mergers & Acquisitions*, an issue that also includes the "Almanac," a statistical summary of the year's M & A activity. The "Almanac" includes tables titled "Countries most active in U.S. acquisitions" and "Countries attracting U.S. buyers."

M & A Europe (published semi-monthly by MLR Publishing)

This is a companion publication of *Mergers & Acquisitions*. *M & A Europe* focuses on deal activity among European firms. Though articles make up the bulk of the journal, lists of deals and statistical analyses of deal activity are included. *M & A Europe* is also available as a full text database on the LEXIS-NEXIS Service, in the EUROPE Library.

Mergers & Acquisitions International (published monthly by Financial Times Business Information)

This monthly journal provides information on U.K. private and public companies, whether pending, completed, or terminated. There are also detailed sections for areas outside the U.K., and here transactions involving U.S. and European firms are recorded. Deals are indexed by company name and country, both for acquirers and targets.

Multinational Business (published monthly by Economist)

A non-U.S. perspective of deal activity may be found in the center section of each issue of *Multinational Business*. The "Acquisitions and Mergers" report provides a summary of major deals in Europe, the United Kingdom, the U.S., and other major regions (Japan, Canada, the Middle East).

Euromoney (published monthly by Euromoney PLC)

A more specialized annual report on European merger and acquisition activity is found in the February issue of *Euromoney*. The reports in this magazine emphasize advisor activity. A representative table ranks advisors by all completed deals for European countries buying into the United Kingdom. There are also summary statistical tables on cross-border deals by nation, industry breakdowns, and deal values. *Euromoney* does not provide specific information for each transaction.

Japan M & A Reporter (published monthly by Ulmer Brothers Research)

Japan M & A Reporter is a newsletter giving brief descriptions of current acquisitions, joint ventures, and buyouts involving Japanese companies. Useful charts group transactions by geographic region (e.g., Europe/Japan).

World M & A Network (published quarterly by International Executive Reports, Washington, DC)

Companies interested in selling all or part of their business often make their wishes known by informing potential acquirers or by publishing their intention to sell. *World M & A Network* lists companies for sale, merger candidates, and willing buyers. A typical listing is a 100-word description of a business, the terms of the deal, and an asking price. The companies' names are not given. Leads are organized by company size, geographic region, and SIC codes. Although primarily a source of U.S. opportunities for U.S. sellers and investors, *World M & A Network* does include non-U.S. offers.

Electronic Sources for Corporate Change Information

Finding information about cross-border merger and acquisition transactions is made easier by using "transaction" databases. These databases bring together the main facts about individual M & A transactions. The databases take information about M & A activity from newswire stories, the financial press, and company reports. They combine this information in one record. Transaction databases allow you to answer such questions and complete such projects as:

> *Which companies are actively buying into the German electronics industry?*
>
> *How many cross-border U.K./French deals have been made from 1988 to the present?*
>
> *Define the M & A strategy of Grand Metropolitan.*
>
> *Rank U.K. financial advisors by dollar volume of their deals.*

Merger & Corporate Transaction Database
(Securities Data Company)

SDC's *Merger & Corporate Transaction Database* is the most comprehensive source of merger activity information. It is a menu-driven system that is updated daily and available 24 hours a day. The database describes more than 55,000 domestic U.S. transactions dating back to 1980 and more than 40,000 international deals since 1985. Five hundred data items per transaction are provided for screening and reporting. The database covers mergers, acquisitions, partial acquisitions, leveraged buyouts, divestitures, exchange offers, stock repurchases, self-tenders, squeeze outs, tender offers, and spinoffs. The information is updated daily from SEC filings (8-Ks, 10-Ks, and 10-Qs), proxy statements, tender offers, annual reports, major financial publications, and company press releases. Some of the system features include:

- Merger Daily Activity Report: Gives details of all merger-related activity within a given time
- Volume Totals: Provides online calculation of the volume of merger activity for any designated period
- Reports: Allows creation of customized reports including any named variables

Exhibit 7.13 is a brief record of the acquisition of a U.K. company by a German company. It is often difficult to find published information on this type of small, non-U.S. cross-border deal.

Worldwide Joint Ventures & Strategic Alliances
(Securities Data Company)

A unique database that gives details on cross-border and intra-nation joint ventures and strategic alliances. Transactions include new operating units, privatizations, and many types of strategic alliances such as R&D, manufacturing, and technology licensing agreements. Updated daily, the file allows you to monitor global venturing and alliance activities by company, industry, and country: identify potential partners; and evaluate capitalization scenarios.

Date Announced Date Effective Date Unc	Target Name Business Description Financial Advisors(s)	Acquiror Name Business Description Financial Advisor(s)
04/06/88 04/06/88	Bruce Engineers Manufacture automotive parts	Schade Plettenberg Mnfr motor vehicle components
  Value(mil)	Form Status Attitude	 Acquisition Technique(s)
0.8STG Price/Sh	Acq. Maj. Int. Completed Friendly	Divestiture
755,000 British pounds ($1.4 mil US) cash/50% ownership interest		

RECORD FROM SDC'S *MERGER & CORPORATE TRANSACTION DATABASE*

EXHIBIT 7.13

Source: Merger & Corporate Transaction Database. Copyright Securities Data Publishing, Inc., 40 W. 57th St., 11th Floor, New York, NY 10019. Reprinted with permission.

Additional Security Data Company databases are described in Chapter 16. SDC's WWW site (http://www.secdata.com) has descriptions and sample pages from their databases.

Financial Times M&A International (Financial Times)

FTMA provides detailed transaction reports on mergers, acquisitions, buyouts, joint ventures, pre-bid speculative announcements (rumors), and share swaps in all key non-U.S. markets, as well as cross-border bids involving U.S. companies. It covers the period 1990 to date. In addition to the basic bid details, documents contain (where available) names of advisors, related deals, and financial information. For U.K. and European quoted companies, comprehensive interim and 5-year profit-and-loss data, sales analysis, share price history, and company announcements are also included. Information is collected from financial newspapers, public offering documents, and company press releases. As of May 1993, the database held about 24,000 records. Exhibit 7.14 is a brief record of a U.K. purchase of a French company.

---

	1 FTMA
AN	930408000567 930408.
AQ	Williams Holdings.
AA	UK.
AH	Public.
AE	UK SIC: 4836 Plastic Products 6510 Dealer in Motors/Motor Parts 6130 Timber & Building Materials Distribution 4834 Plastic Building Products US SIC: P3080 Miscellaneous Plastics Products, NEC P5500 Automotive Dealers and Service Stations P5030 Lumber and Construction Materials P3080 Miscellaneous Plastics Products, NEC.
DV	ACQUIROR'S ADVISORS: Bidder's financial advisor: None; Bidder's solicitor: Slaughter and May; Bidder's stockbroker: None; Bidder's accountants: Pannell Kerr Forster.
TG	Lecat-Porion.
TA	France.
TE	UK SIC: 4836 Plastic Products 3169 Metal Finished Products/Fasteners/Locks US SIC: P3080 Miscellaneous Plastics Products, NEC P3499 Fabricated Metal Products, NEC.
DI	Bid announcement date: 25 February 93 (930225) Bid status: agrees bid for Bid classification: UK Bids for European & Other Companies Terms: Vendor: Dynaction (France). Products: Target manufactures curtain rails. Trade names: Swish (bidder). Bidder results: to 31/12/92. Target results: FFr 57m turnover annually. Source: LE 26/02/93 p9; LT 26/02/93 p10; FT 05/03/93 p17. Related deals: Bidder acquired THORN EMI's portable fire extinguisher business. Notes: Deal will be transacted via bidder's subsidiary Swish.
DF	Change of status or information: 04 March 93 (930304).

RECORD FROM *FINANCIAL TIMES M & A INTERNATIONAL*

EXHIBIT 7.14

Source: DataStar FTMA Database.

SkyePharma Makes French Acquisition
Marketletter Sep 30, 1996 p. N/A.
ISSN: 0951-3175

SkyePharma of the UK is to acquire a pharmaceutical manufacturing facility near Lyon, France from Wyeth-Ayerst, a subsidiary of American Home Products. The deal will be made through SkyePharma's principal operating subsidiary Jago. Under the terms of the agreement, Jago will acquire a newly-incorporated subsidiary of Wyeth into which a 66,000 square meter consideration of 1 French franc, according to Skyepharma. The site comprises a plant and laboratories providing 17,000 square meters of floor space together with an adjoining administration building covering 2,400 American Cyanamid in 1993 but was never used for its original purpose. The plant was subsequently taken over by Wyeth in 1994 as part of the acquisition of American Cyanamid by Wyeth's parent, AHP. It is currently used by Wyeth for packaging. Jago will assume responsibility for 109 employees, and the net assets of the new subsidiary are estimated to be worth around 46 million francs.

THIS IS THE FULL TEXT: COYPRIGHT 1996 Marketletter Publications Ltd. (UK)
WORD COUNT: 175

COMPANY:
    *Wyeth-Ayerst Laboratories
    American Home Products
    SkyePharma

PRODUCT: *Drugs & Pharmaceuticals (2830000)
EVENT: *Asset Sales & Divestitures (16); Acquisitions & Mergers (15)
COUNTRY: *France (4FRA); United Kingdom (4UK)

FULL TEXT RECORD FROM DIALOG'S VERSION OF *PROMT*

EXHIBIT 7.15

Source: PROMPT (DIALOG File 16).

PROMT (IAC Predicasts)

The online *PROMT* database is a good choice for international news on corporate change. Its controlled vocabulary allows precise retrieval. *PROMT* uses several "event names" to describe corporate change. They include

- Organizational nomenclature
- Organizational history
- Subsidiary to parent data
- Parent to subsidiary data
- Acquisitions & Mergers
- Asset Sales & Divestitures

Exhibit 7.15 is an example of an article retrieved from *PROMT* that combines the event names "Acquisitions & Mergers" and "Asset Sales & Divestitures" with the country names "France" and "United Kingdom."

FirstList (produced bimonthly by Vision Quest Publishing Inc., Lake Bluff, IL)

This merger and acquisition listing service for both U.S. and non-U.S. companies provides descriptive profiles of individual companies seeking acquisition, companies available for acquisition, companies seeking equity or debt financing, and joint venture and licensing opportunities. Most of the companies listed for acquisition are small (sales of less than $20 million). Listings in the "seeking acquisitions" and "available for acquisitions" sections are categorized by two-digit SIC codes. Subscribers receive contact names by referencing a five-digit number assigned to each listing. *FirstList* is available in print and as a WWW site through Knowledge Express (http://www.keds.com).

World M&A Network (Washington, DC)

World M&A Network is a WWW site (http://www.cqi.com/MandA/index.html) for merger and acquisition leads in the U.S. and worldwide. Similar in scope and detail to *FirstList*, it includes 2-digit SIC code classifications for sellers (companies seeking to merge) and buyers (companies seeking acquisitions). This subscription service is updated quarterly.

NOTES

1. Christine Spanneut, "Who Runs European Business?" *The Globalisation Newsletter* (published by Eurostat, no. 2 October 1995): 13–16.

2. Stanley Foster Reed and Alexandra Reed Lajoux, *The Art of M&A: A Merger/Acquisition/Buyout Guide* (New York: Richard Irwin, 1995).

TOPICS COVERED

- International Credit Information
- Regional and National Credit Information
- Bankruptcy
- Rankings and Comparisons
- Sources of Rankings
- Online and On-Disc Rankings

MAJOR SOURCES DISCUSSED

- Dun & Bradstreet
- Global Scan
- SCRL
- ICC British Company Financial DataSheets
- Infocheck
- Teikoku
- *Fortune, Forbes,* and *Business Week*
- *Times 1000*

INTERNATIONAL CREDIT INFORMATION

Finding international credit information is very important to the researcher who is considering doing business with a buyer or seller in another country. The credit worthiness of a potential partner is a vital piece of information. There are international credit services as well as services from individual countries. We will discuss a few of the larger services that make themselves known at international conferences. We cannot guarantee the level of quality of the services we are discussing. More information about obtaining credit, in relation to international trade, is presented in Chapter 12.

Most countries have at least one credit reporting agency. A list of credit agencies is given in Appendix K of the 1992 publication, *The McGraw-Hill Handbook of Global Trade and Investment Financing.* The list is not complete, but it covers a wide range of countries.

International Credit Reporting Services

Dun & Bradstreet

Dun & Bradstreet has an international credit reporting service in addition to its United States credit service.

The international credit reports are collected in the over 200 individual countries Dun & Bradstreet covers.

D&B International uses a two-part rating code in its business reports, for example 5A 4. The first part of the rating, Financial Strength, reflects the company's *tangible net worth,* derived from the latest available audited financial statements. When the net worth figure is unavailable, the financial strength indicator will be based on paid-in or registered capital and signaled by a double letter rating, e.g., 4AA 2.

Standards of financial strength differ from country to country, based on country practices and norms as illustrated in Table 8.A.

The second part of the rating is the Composite Credit Appraisal. It indicates D&B's calculation of the level of risk associated with dealing with the firm. Codes range from 1 to 4, with 1 being the lowest risk. D&B uses a scoring system based on 30 key company data elements to assign the Risk Factor. These elements come from the payment data, financial data, other public records such as court judgments, and special events such as a press release that may affect the company's trading position. D&B provides the definitions in Table 8.B as a guide to interpreting the risk levels.

TABLE 8.A

D&B Standards of Financial Strength

D&B CREDIT RATING Indicator	UNITED KINGDOM Net Worth (£000)	USA Net Worth ($000)	URUGUAY Net Worth (000,000) New Pesos
5A 5AA	35,000 or more	50,000 or more	101,250 or more
4A 4AA	15,000–34,999	10,000–49,999	20,250–101,249
3A 3AA	7,000–14,999	1,000–9,999	3,037.5–20,249
2A 2AA	1,500–6,999	750–999	1,518.8–3,037.4
1A 1AA	700–1,499	500–749	759.375–1,518.7
A AA	350–699		380.7–759.374
B BA	200–349	300–499 200–399	190.35–380.6
C CB CC	100–199	125–299 75–124.9	95.175–190.349
D DC DD	70–99.9	50–74.9 35–49.9	48.6–95.174
E EE	35–69.9	20–34.9	24.3–48.5
F FF	20–34.9	10–19.9	12.15–24.2
G GG	8–19.9	5–9.9	up to 12.149
H HH	up to 7.9		

Source: Key to D&B International Ratings. Reprinted with permission.

TABLE 8.B

Interpreting Levels of Risk in D&B Credit Ratings

Classification	Composite Credit Appraisal	Guide to Interpretation
1	Strong or High	Undoubted standing; minimal trading risk
2	Good	Financially stable, competent trading record; less than average risk
3	Fair	Below average financial standing and trading record; higher than average risk
4	Poor	Known financial weaknesses, unsatisfactory trading record; significant trading risk
0 or -	Not Classified	Difficult to classify within symbols; seek additional information

Source: Documentation from *Understanding D&B's International Reports*, 1996: 28. Reprinted with permission.

Other ratings may be INV, under investigation; N, negative net worth; NB, new business; or NQ, not quoted. Companies that do not lend themselves to a credit rating may receive an Employee Range Designation, from ER1, the highest with 1,000 or more employees, to ER8, one to four employees.

D&B offers a range of reports, from *D&B Select*, where you only purchase one module, to *D&B Comprehensive Report* which includes in-depth financial and performance data, enhanced with public notice information.

D&B Business Information Reports contain more than 20 million records worldwide, including 10 million across Europe and 2.5 million in the U.K. Reports include:

- Financial Information, with the comprehensive report also having up to 18 key ratios
- Unique D&B Rating
- Maximum Credit Figure
- Payment Experiences, which include a payment score for the company and the industry quartiles

- Public Record Information, including court judgments and mortgages
- Background Information, such as legal structure, history, principals, subsidiaries, parents, and branches

Two types of U.K. D&B credit reports are available via Internet at D&B United Kingdom's Web site, http://www.dbeuro.com. A compact report has directory information; a credit evaluation; a summary statement with start and incorporation dates, legal form, turnover and profit or loss, nominal capital, net worth, employees, issued capital and date, and 1972 U.S. SIC codes. Key financials compare current and previous year's annual filing data and the current quarter.

The D&B Report builds on the compact report and is designed to measure the financial strength and risk associated with the business. Financial items include the latest balance sheet and Profit & Loss accounts, together with the latest three years' financial comparisons and performance ratios. County Court Judgments are provided that include the date, company name, amount, court, and plaint number. Also provided are details of mortgages and charges registered, a legal filing summary, special events, and bankers. Payment habits are calculated from trade references. The company's payment score is compared to its industry group for the current quarter. Details are given for operations and premises.

An example of the ratings in a U.K. D&B Report is given in Exhibit 8.1.

D&B RATING:	F3
FORMER RATING:	2A3
CONDITION:	FAIR
AVERAGE DAYS BEYOND TERM:	UP
MAXIMUM CREDIT:	150,000
D&B PAYMENT SCORE:	77
ACCOUNTS INCORPORATED IN REPORT	30-06-96

SAMPLE D&B RATING

EXHIBIT 8.1

Source: Copyright 1996 Dun & Bradstreet, Inc. Reprinted with permisison.

D&B also calculates a payment score for its Payment Trend Report. Scores range from a high of 90+ for companies that prepay to 20 for companies that are four months beyond term.

For subscribers, some reports are available electronically from D&B Access using a Windows interface or on the WWW. Reports can be ordered online with D&B Access, by telephone, speaking computer, facsimile, telex, magnetic tape, and post. D&B Access is also available for individual countries such as France, Australia, and Canada.

Given the wide range of D&B credit information, a new researcher may be best served talking to D&B directly to determine what kind of reports are needed and whether they are available for the country and companies of interest.

Global Scan (Infocheck Equifax)

Global Scan is available online directly from Infocheck Equifax and through Questel, FT Profile, and BT Telecom Gold. Reports are available in the original language of the document as well as in English. Users may search in one of 10 languages. More than 8 million reports from 160 countries are available in the databases. Reports have financial and credit data as well as descriptive summaries. Table 8.C lists the type of information available by country directly from Global Scan.

Other countries for which there are reports include Afghanistan, Algeria, Argentina, Barbados, Bahrain, Bangladesh, Botswana, Brazil, Bulgaria, Cambodia, Colombia, Cuba, Greenland, Iran, New Zealand, Poland, Russia, Vietnam, Zaire, and Zimbabwe.

Sources of information for Global Scan include reports filed with companies houses and chambers of commerce or compiled by business information specialists. Users pay for each report retrieved. Other conditions vary by gateway.

Global Scan has extensive information available through the WWW at http://www.infocheck.uk.co. WWW browsers may register and receive information about Global Scan database coverage in the over 250 geographic regions the database covers arranged by continent. Listed below are the number of countries per region.

Africa	74	Europe—Other	32
Americas	62	Europe—Western	30
Asia	42	Oceania	35

Reports can be bought individually or as part of a WWW subscription.

Credit reports in developed countries are provided by local credit services. The database for developing countries is provided by International Company Profile, ICP. The Developing Nations Database contains over 50,000 credit status reports on companies and businesses in Africa, South and Central America and the Caribbean Islands, Western Europe, the Middle East, and the Atlantic, Indian, and Pacific Ocean Islands. The information includes company legal form and correct style; ownership and capital; date established and history; nature of activity and number of employees; sales turnover, profit, and other available

TABLE 8.C

GLOBAL SCAN REPORT AVAILABILITY

Country	Credit Reports	Balance Sheets	Country	Credit Reports	Balance Sheets
Austria	500		Netherlands	200,000	
Belgium		120,000	Norway	50,000	
Canada	1,500,000		Portugal	50,000	
Denmark		50,000	Sweden	100,000	
Finland	130,000		Switzerland		500
France	2,000,000[1]		United Arab		
Germany	1,900,000	6,000	Emirates	30,000[2]	
Italy	400,000	15,000	United Kingdom	420,000	3,200[3]
India*	1,500		Taiwan*	40,000	
Ireland*	50,000		United States		6,000
Mexico*	NA				

1 Not specified; 2 Market reports; 3 News
* Added since 1994

Source: *Global Scan* documentation, 1996.

financial information; payment record and credit opinion; principal bankers; and associated companies. Most countries covered by the databases have no legal requirement to publish or disclose balance sheets. A sample record, the same for every country with just the address changed, is provided on the WWW site. Payment is per report.

Global Scan is less expensive than D&B. However, it is also not recommended, at this time, for expensive deals.

REGIONAL AND NATIONAL CREDIT INFORMATION

European Credit Services

EUROGATE is an online service, introduced in late 1992 and designed for the European market. It is a partnership of European companies active in credit assessment, debt collection, and marketing information. It was founded by three major credit information agencies in Europe: Graydon Holdings, Bürgel Wirtschaftsinformationen (BW), and SCRL, with backing from major credit insurers. Over 10 million companies from Germany, Austria, Spain, France, the United Kingdom, Portugal, and Switzerland are currently included.

Online searching is by gateway from a local European country. Searchers from non-European countries can still gain access through one of the local gateways. Searching is menu driven. Users may select the language of their choice. EUROGATE's French language informational WWW site is http://www.scrl.com/fr/international/eurogate/index.html.

SCRL is one of the major credit suppliers in France. A standard financial record, available on DataStar or SCRL Bilans in Questel, may include the data items listed in Table 8.D.

TABLE 8.D

DATA ITEMS IN AN *SCRL* CREDIT REPORT

Identification	**Activities**
Siren	Trade class
Address	Position (i.e. manufacturer)
Foundation Date	Activities (i.e. product)
Legal Type	Market
Capital	Franchising
Reg No	Trademarks
Town	Branch(es)
Director(s)	

Financial Details (2 yrs)	**Shareholding**
Turnover	Shareholder(s) and %
Exports	Subsidiaries
Current result	
Net result	**Comments**
Employees	
Real property	**Failures**

Accounts
Balance Sheet
Profit and Loss Account
Additional Data
Detail of fixed assets
P/L Accounts data including subcontracting work and leasing income
Schedule of debts: within 1 year, 1-5 yrs; over 5 years
Sundry information: lease commitments, discounted bills
VAT collected

The report may also include a comment on the credit-worthiness of the company. The example of a comment follows.

> THIS COMPANY OFFERS GUARANTEES BUT DEFAULTS HAVE BEEN NOTED AND ITS FINANCIAL STRUCTURE IS WEAK. THE EVOLUTION SHOULD BE FOLLOWED.

Additional information is available in a credit report. Exhibit 8.2 shows the credit section of an SCRL report. The "Rankings" section is also available in SCRL on DataStar.

SOLVENCY

Registered defaults	:	**UNPAID BIL. 10/91**
Privilege(s)	:	**NIL**
Payments	:	**PRES. REGULAR**
Cial Reputation	:	**GOOD**
Banker (s)	:	**BNP AG. MESSINE_PARIS 8E**
		POMMIER PARIS 8E

SCRL BACKGROUND (over the 12 last months)

CREDIT RATING	:	**STABLE**
Number of requests	:	**12**
Average credit requested	:	**455 000 FRF**
Average credit opinion	:	**230 000 FRF**

SCRL'S OPINION

Credit requested	:	**500 000 FRF**
Credit opinion	:	**300 000 FRF**

**COTEXPERT
(CREDIT RATING)**

2.5

RANKING

Ranking of the company compared to 344 companies.

RATIO year 91		COMPANY	SECTOR	QUARTILE
Debt ratio (financial debts/income)	%	33.03	186.61	3
Shareholders funds/total liabilities	%	17.83	31.37	2
Liquidity ratio (net current assets - stocks/debts)	U	.68	1.36	1
Clients credit period	D	88.89	64.32	1
Suppliers credit period	D	68.55	74.77	2
Self financing capacity	U	0.05	0.02	3
Net profitability (net result/turnover)	%	-4.92	0.75	1
Value added/turnover	%	57.94	50.06	3

ND: NOT AVAILABLE   U: UNIT   D: DAY

CREDIT SECTION OF *SCRL* REPORT

EXHIBIT 8.2

Source: SCRL sample report December 1992. Reprinted with permission from SCRL.

SCRL reports are also available on the Bureau van Dijk CD-ROM, *SCRL Enterprises*. The CD-ROM has 400,000 companies and includes the credit risk class, such as Low, Normal, High; a credit limit; and the date of the most recent inquiry. The CD-ROM only has four financials: turnover, export, operating profits, and profit/loss for the period.

SCRL Defaillances is a Questel database containing judgments, such as liquidation and bankruptcies. The information appears in the database before it is published in Bulletin Officiel des Annonces Civiles et Commercials (BODACC). Information about SCRL is available at http://www.scrl.com.

TELE INFORM 1. is another large French database. It offers descriptive and financial data in French and English on about 2.5 million French firms. Credit data include revenues, profit history, debt statement, a credit rating, and a credit opinion. An annual subscription to O.R. Telematique is required. Reports are transmitted online, by fax, and by mail. This service provides historical data back to 1980. TELE INFORM 2 is a companion database, without the credit information.

Creditreform-Online from Verband der Vereine Creditreform e.V. has credit information on over 1.7 million joint stock and individual trading companies in Austria, Switzerland, and the Federal Republic of Germany. In addition to profile information, company records have dates of formation or re-formation, capital, partners, financial indicators covering capital, obligations, loan payment record, liabilities, and credit rating. Creditreform supplies the German and Austrian credit reports for Global Scan. The Creditreform databases on DataStar and LEXIS-NEXIS do not contain credit information. In January 1997, Web site http://www.creditreform.de was under construction.

United Kingdom Credit Services

ICC provides credit services both online and off line. According to ICC, credit services include:

- Financial Reports for trading U.K. companies with scores, limits, and credit opinion
- Status Reports for smaller companies with credit limits
- Overviews for fast credit checks with scores and ratios
- Special Premium Services with tailored credit ratings for U.K. and non-U.K. companies; also available in print

The online file, ICC *British Company Financial Datasheets*, includes both credit ratios and a credit rating score for a company for up to nine years. The file is available through almost all international databank providers. It can be accessed directly online from ICC and on *Credit Index* CD-ROM for all 1.2 million live British limited companies. The ratios and ratings are on the *U.K. Factfinder* CD-ROM for 1,800 major U.K. quoted companies, and on Bureau van Dijk's *Emma* CD-ROM. ICC's credit ratios and industry comparisons separate this U.K. database from the other U.K. financial products on the market.

Exhibit 8.3 displays portions of a record with credit information.

CO PRESCIENT ENGINEERING LTD

RA RATIOS:		960630	950630	940630
Credit Ratios:				
Stock Turnover	R	7.13	7.57	8.10
Credit Period	Days	99.14	109.37	119.83
Liquidity	R	4.20	4.10	3.52
Current Ratio	R	5.38	5.21	4.45
Current Liabilities/Stock	R	.85	.90	1.08

ICC INDUSTRY COMPARISONS
  SIC Code: 3161 (Hand tools and implements).
CS ICC Scores
  Based on an analysis of the company's financial performance and a comparison with the industry sector represented by SIC code 3161 (Hand tools and implements), the company scored as follows, out of 100, in the following years:

1996:	75
1995:	75
1994:	90
1993:	80

ICC *BRITISH COMPANY FINANCIAL DATASHEETS*

EXHIBIT 8.3

Source: DataStar search on file ICFF, November 1996. Reprinted with permission from ICC.

The sophisticated DIALOG searcher could use this file to answer the question:

What companies in the hand tools and implements industry are most credit worthy in 1996?

ICC just introduced *Business Ratio Plus*, print reports comparing the financial performance of between 50 to 150 companies within 15 major industry sectors. The reports use the individual ratios to rank companies on 26 different key performance and growth criteria.

Infocheck Equifax, the company that offers Global Scan, is another U.K. credit service. Infocheck reports provide full and snapshot credit profiles on about 420,000 limited companies in England, Scotland, and Wales. Credit evaluation is based on company performance and prospects. Sources of data include filings with the U.K. Registrar of Companies, newspapers, and Infocheck's own confidential database of share debtor information.

Infocheck is available electronically by direct dial to Infocheck or by using its WWW site. Infocheck is a database on FT Profile, DataStar, and through the local U.K. MercuryLink. The DataStar version had over 925,000 records in November 1996. Much of the information in the Infocheck record is available on the other U.K. company files on DataStar, such as basic directory and financial data, ratio analysis, and shareholders. What is unique in Infocheck is the credit profile with details of County Court judgments, although most company records will not have court cases. Searching using terms such as "liquidator appointed," "county court," or "judgement" identifies companies that might be in trouble. Of special interest is the "Comments" field in which you can search not only for companies that have been dissolved but also for those companies that file "modified reports" under the Small Company Act. Exhibit 8.4 is an extract from a record in Infocheck, as it is loaded in DataStar, showing both a County Court listing and the comments.

```
    1  CHCK
AN    Company registered number: 02589070 D-S update: 960101
Date report prepared: 10/11/95
Report status: Full report, up to date.
CO    MUNSLOW PRECISION ENGINEERING LIMITED.
AD    WEDNESFIELD
      WOLVERHAMPTON
      WV11 3RG
      UK.
CJ CCJ's Registered:
Information concerning county court judgements is
provided by INFOCHECK in good faith; however
INFOCHECK does not accept responsibility for
accuracy here.
Court:                    BIRMINGHAM
Case number:              9217679
Amount:                   4,732.00
Case status:              Judgement
Registry number:          07122.07637

Court:                    MILTON KEYNES
Case number:              36113570
Amount:                   390.00
Case status:              Judgement
Registry number:          21103.07885

Gazette information:      - None registered -.

CM COMMENTS
─────────
. . . These are modified  accounts as the company is exempt from certain disclosure regulations, including the requirement to file a
profit and loss account, under the 'small company' classification of Sections 246 & 249 of the  Companies Act 1985.
. . . Information is provided in good faith, we do not guarantee the accuracy of this data.
```

INFOCHECK (CHCK) on DataStar

EXHIBIT 8.4

Source: Infocheck on DataStar, November 1996.

Infocheck has partnered with the U.S. credit company Equifax. Infocheck Equifax offers a subscription WWW service for credit reports at http://www.infocheck.co.uk, described in detail above under the discussion of Global Scan. The following types of U.K. reports with credit information are available through the WWW:

- Full Report: Company Identification, Company Capitalization, Financial Analysis, Auditors, Extended Company Ratio Analysis, Infocheck Analyst Report, Credit Profile, Industry Comparison, and list of Directors.
- Full Report Plus: Full Report plus the Equifax Consumer Database for any County Court Judgement Information that may be held against Company Directors.
- Snapshot: Company Identification, a brief Financial Analysis, Extended Company Ratio Analysis, Infocheck Brief Analysis, Credit Profile, and Industry Comparison.

Samples of all reports are available to the viewer. The Infocheck Equifax WWW site also has a "Watch-Out" service to alert the subscriber to changes in status.

Infolink states that it is the U.K.'s largest independent credit information organization. The database has data on 2.5 million organizations in the U.K. Infolink company reports have three-year profit and loss accounts, supplemented with details of credit transactions and defaults. Options for Ltd. companies include a full company search, directors search, and mortgages and charges search, while public notice searches and consumer credit license searches are available for sole traders and partnerships as well. Prices range from £25 for a full search to £4.05 for a consumer credit license search. The data are supplemented by details of credit transactions and defaults. The reports are accessible through Infolink's online service, Automated Credit Inquiry. Infolink's U.K. Consumer Service offers credit searches, voter roll searches, including confirmation of residence against the Election Register, and trade references.

Asian Credit Services

Teikoku, which is also discussed in Chapter 6, includes credit ratings as part of each company record. Teikoku has been providing credit ratings for Japanese companies for almost 100 years. Company records are updated two times a year. Teikoku can be searched on DIALOG, DataStar, LEXIS-NEXIS Services, Profound, and I/PLUS, and on the CD-ROM products *JADE* and *Japanese Company Factfinder*. Custom

reports in English can be ordered for any Japanese company, not only those in the Teikoku database, through DIALORDER.

The companies in Teikoku are a subset of those covered in the Japanese-language database, COSMOS2. The COSMOS2 source has ratings on over 850,000 Japanese companies. It corresponds in part to the Japanese language directory *Teikoku Ginko Kaisha Nenkan (Teikoku Bank and Company Yearbook)*. A third product from Teikoku, also in Japanese, is *Company Credit Reports (CCR)*. This has credit information on 150,000 companies in the Tokyo metropolitan area. It is available through subscription or a per-report basis.

Teikoku scoring is composed of five credit ranges with a full mark equaling 100. Credit ranges are ranked with A (86–100), B (66–85), C (51–65), D (36–50), and E (below 35). The score is given for every credit factor. The credit factors are classified into history, net worth, business scale, profitability, financial condition, chief executive, business vitality, additional marks (if necessary), and demerit marks (if necessary). In the Teikoku database on DIALOG, companies receive an overall rating from A to E. On LEXIS-NEXIS and DataStar, the actual overall credit scores are given. During the last three years, fewer companies have received A or B ratings.

Rating	Number of DIALOG Companies	
	November 1996	*March 1993*
A (86–100)	130	244
B (66–85)	19,700	25,604
C (51–65)	149,044	130,510
D (36–50)	51,029	24,538
E (1–35)	3,025	1,266

Source: DIALOG search File 502, November 23, 1996 and March 23, 1993.

Exhibit 8.5 is a sample report from the Teikoku database on DIALOG created to answer the question:

> *Who are the largest Japanese textile companies with A or B credit ratings?*

Teikoku Database provides the credit information on Japanese companies for Global Scan. Teikoku's WWW site, http://www.teikoku.com, provides information about the credit reports, but no online searching or ordering.

Taiwan On-line Business Data Services from FBR DATA BASE INC. is reported to contain five files of Asian business and corporate information. One file, Credit Reports, has descriptive and financial information on approximately 20,000 of Taiwan's largest corporations with profile information, banking refer-

Japanese Textile Companies with Credit Ratings A or B, Ranked by Sales				
Company Name	Primary Japanese SIC CODE	Sales ($000)	Credit Rating	Sales Rank x SIC
TOYOBO CO LTD	2221	2,735,048	B	2
NISSHINBO INDUSTRIES INC	2221	1,466,481	B	4
KURABO INDUSTRIES LTD	2221	1,186,539	B	5
SUMINOE TEXTILE CO LTD	2292	817,694	B	1
KAWASHIMA TEXTILE MANUFACTURER	2292	528,478	B	2
THE JAPAN WOOL TEXTILE CO LTD	2222	524,239	B	1

REPORT FROM TEIKOKU DATABASE ON DIALOG

EXHIBIT 8.5

Source: DIALOG File 502, Teikoku Databank: Japanese Companies. Copyright 1996 Teikoku Databank. All rights reserved. Reprinted with permission.

ences, and data on facilities, assets, capital, and turnover. Credit reports appear in Global Scan. FBR Asian Company Profiles, with almost 50,000 Taiwanese companies, is on DIALOG as File 505. Over 4,000 of these companies have fields expressing credit worthiness. The fields and typical FBR statements are:

- Banking: The firm maintains no record of bounced cheques with local banks.
- Litigation: The firm has no record of litigation from the time of its establishment to the present.
- Reputation: Reference checking for the purpose of establishing the firm's reputation within the respective industry failed to reveal any negative information.
- Credit Opinion: FBR has received no negative information regarding this firm. However, as per trade practices in Taiwan, FBR suggests initial trade with this firm by newly established clients be conducted on an L/C [letter of credit] basis.

U.S. Credit Services

Equifax is a major player itself in supplying credit information on non-U.S. companies. Equifax owns 50% of Dicom, a Chilean credit system that is planning on investing in the Mexican credit market. Equifax operates credit bureaus in 18 countries and has sales offices in 46 countries.

Dun & Bradstreet is considered the major credit reporting service in the U.S. Use D&B Access on the WWW to purchase individual U.S. reports: http://www.dnb.com.

Credit Ratings for Banks

Standard and Poor's and Moody's, discussed in relationship to their own publications in Chapter 5, rank bonds and banks. The Standard & Poor's ratings are based on fundamental credit analysis and subjective factors such as management depth and quality and business aggressiveness. Ratings are provided for long- and short-term debt and investments.

Moody's Bank Credit Report Service rates long- and short-term debt for banks from 30 countries. There are three listings: alphabetical by company, by country, and region by rating.

A third bank rating service is ICBA, established in the U.K. in 1978. ICBA assesses the risk that a bank or corporation may not meet its unsecured obligations in a timely fashion. ICBA uses financial performance, historical information, and meetings with management to create its ratings. ICBA ratings include ratings for long- and short-term obligations and indicate when a rating was changed and whether it was downgraded or upgraded.

Thomson BankWatch Inc. monitors more than 1,000 banking, securities, and financial firms in more than 60 countries. Thomson BankWatch Inc. is available via print, CD-ROM, Bloomberg, Investext, and FIRST CALL BondCall.

The two bank CD-ROM products discussed in Chapter 5 include credit ratings. Bankstat provides a one-page ratings report for each bank. The report includes Institutional Investor's credit rating for the country and Moody's long- and short-term bonds and bank deposits sovereign ratings for the country. Bank credit ratings come from Thomson's BankWatch, ICBA, Moody's, and Standard and Poor's. Moody's ratings are for long- and short-term bank deposits and debt and commercial paper, preferred stock, and where applicable, financial strength and counter party. The date is given for each rating as well as the rating direction. The Standard and Poor's ratings include long- and short-term certificates of deposit, commercial paper, and senior implied and unsecured debt. Bankstat also has ratings for the banks on assets and equity, for within their home countries and worldwide.

BankScope has long-term, short-term, legal, and individual ratings from ICBA, and long-term and short-term ratings from Moody's or from one of the Cyprus-based rating firms, Capital Intelligence or BREE. BankScope also has a "risk category," with minimum and maximum limits.

BANKRUPTCY

In many of the chapters we discuss searching for supporting information in traditional databases. In general, information about an individual company's credit-worthiness is not going to appear in our textual databases. However, general databases such as the WORLD files on LEXIS-NEXIS can be used to find out information about bankruptcy law and also major companies that file for bankruptcy. Some sample article titles from LEXIS-NEXIS include:

- Russia investigating 2,000 firms for bankruptcy, *Reuters Money Report. Bonds Capital Market* (July 14, 1994).
- Major state enterprise in Sichuan declared bankrupt, *Zhongguo Xinwen She News Agency,* Beijing (March 23, 1994).
- Mongolia adopts laws on privatization and bankruptcy, Ulan Bator, *Xinhua General News Service* (June 24, 1991).
- China's new bankruptcy law to go to parliament, *Reuters Money Report, Bonds Capital Market* (November 14, 1995).
- Bankruptcy law takes effect, *Finance East Europe* (September 22, 1995) [for Romania].
- EU Moves Toward the Creation of a European Convention. *Eurowatch* 8 (April 15, 1996).

The EU has been late in harmonizing bankruptcy law across countries. In 1996, it agreed upon the EU Convention on Insolvency Proceedings. This Convention will offer companies investing in Europe "certainty of risk" through agreed procedures on choice of law and jurisdictional proceedings. The EU has been trying to find a balance between individual country bankruptcy laws and universality. The Convention generally asserts that bankruptcy proceedings will occur in the jurisdiction where the debtor's principal assets are located, and that the laws of that country will be applied. In addition to trying to develop an EU-wide coordinated system of procedures, the EU also attempted to incorporate general principles of international insolvency proceedings.

Documents relating to liquidations in the U.K. are available from Companies House, and the latest 12 months' insolvencies are on the Companies House

CD-ROM Directory, along with the current live companies.

Bankruptcy on the WWW

There is a WWW site devoted to bankruptcy information, Internet Bankruptcy Library Worldwide Troubled Company Resources, http://bankrupt.com. The site includes bankruptcy news, bankruptcy and insolvency resource materials, and a worldwide directory of bankruptcy and insolvency professionals, including law firms, accounting firms, and consulting firms, arranged by continent. There is legal or regulatory information for Canada, Mexico, the Czech Republic, Austria, Denmark, France, Germany, Russia, Switzerland, U.K., Japan, Australia, Singapore, and Israel, in addition to expensive information on the U.S. The site is maintained by Bankruptcy Creditors' Service, Inc. and the Beard Group.

Further Reading on Credit

"Monitoring Financial Markets: Company Financial Information Services." *The Financial Times*, August 22, 1990.

The various credit services available in the U.K. are described.

Cindy Tursman. "Eastern European Credit Issues Made for Top-Notch Conference in Prague." *Business Credit* 94 (January 1992): 18–19.

The article describes the first Foreign Credit Interchange Bureau-National Association of Credit Management's conference in Prague, Czechoslovakia, October 14–15, 1991. The conference had 130 attendees.

Peter Williams. "Who Will You Put Your Money On?" *Accountancy* 114 (October 1994): 36–40.

Describes Infocheck in detail.

Credit Company Addresses

Creditreform-Datenbank-Dienste
Verband der Vereine Creditreform e.V.
Hellersbergstr. 12,
Postfach 10155 D-4040 Neuss-1 West Germany
Phone: 02101 109210; Fax: 02131 109225
http://www.creditreform.de/

Dun & Bradstreet, Ltd.
Holmers Farm Way
High Wycombe, Bucks. HP12 4UL, England
Phone: 44 1 494 422000; Fax: 44 1 494 422260
http://www.dbeuro.com

ICC Information Group Ltd.
Field House, 72 Oldfield Rd.,
Hampton Middlesex TW12 2HQ
Phone: 081 783 1122; Fax: 081 783 0049

Infocheck Group Ltd.
Global Scan and Infocheck
Godmersham Park
Godmersham, Canterbury, Kent CT4 7DT UK
Phone: 44 1 227 813000; Fax: 44 1 227 813100

Global Scan America
67 Arthur Ct.
Port Chester, NY 10573
Phone: 914-939-7400; Fax: 914-939-7400
http://www.infocheck.co.uk

Infolink Ltd.
Coombe Cross, 2-4 South End
Croyden CRO 1DL, England
Phone: 44-081-686 7777; Fax: 44-081-680 8295
http://www.infolink.com

O. R. Telematique
7, rue de Sens
Rochecorbon, F-37210, France
Phone: 33 1 44 08 56 56; Fax: 33 1 44 08 5657

SCRL
5 Quai Jayr, B.P. 9063-69255
Lyon, Cedex 09, France
Phone: 33 72 20 10 00; Telex: 330903 SCRL F
http://www.scrl.com

Teikoku Databank Ltd.
5-20, Minami Aoyama 2-Chome, Minato-ku
Tokyo 107, Japan
Phone: 813 34044311; Fax: 813 34085519
http://www.teikoku.com

Taiwan On-Line Business Data Services
FBR DATA BASE INC.
9-16 Nan Kan Hsia, 15 Lin, Nan Kan Village
Lu Chu Hsiang, Tao Yuan County, Taiwan
Phone: 88 62 87 54355; Fax: 8862 875 4630

RANKINGS AND COMPARISONS

Who are the top 50 companies in the world?

Who are the biggest companies in Japan?

What are the sizes of the leading chemical companies in the world?

Who are the largest food companies in Europe?

Interpreting Rankings

No matter how the question is phrased, rankings of companies and products are frequently requested. Many directories say they include the "Top 1,000" or the "7,500 Largest" companies. But, as we have discussed, using international financial data to make comparisons among companies is risky.

Several years ago, we did some research on company rankings in U.S. sources.[1] We found that data-bases agreed on company rankings only about 25% of the time. This led us to identify a series of factors that affect rankings: type of company, industry/product classification of companies, and ranking criteria. Not only do all these factors apply to international comparisons, but there are additional problems as well.

Type of Company

Is the entity being ranked the parent company, a subsidiary, or both? As we mentioned in our discussion of European Company Directives, consolidated or group accounting is new to many European countries and is not used uniformly throughout the world. Some company rankings may include only the parent company while other rankings may have the parent and its subsidiaries. Some sources rank only those companies listed on stock exchanges while other sources include government enterprises, privately held companies, and subsidiaries.

Industry Classification

Often, we are seeking rankings for competitive or financial analysis in which we compare companies within a specific industry grouping. What categories are being used and how have companies been assigned to these categories? Europe's Largest Companies (ELC), the publisher of a "Largest" series of books, uses very broad categories; e.g., industrial or trade (wholesale/retail) and service. Actual requests for industry rankings are usually much more specific. Therefore, we encounter the coding problems we discussed previously under product listings in Chapter 4.

In most print sources, companies are ranked only by their primary industry or product grouping. If they are major participants in more than one industry, they may be ranked only in the primary industry. For example, a print source may list Philip Morris as the world's largest food company and RJR Nabisco as the world's largest tobacco company. Since Philip Morris was listed as a food company it is not included in the rankings of tobacco companies, although it may be the world's largest tobacco company as well.

Ranking Criterion

A request for a ranking of the "top" companies must include a criterion. Sales or revenue (turnover) is frequently used, but rankings may also be of profit or income, market capitalization, or employees. Many non–North American sources use profit rather than net income. Keep in mind that there are several measures of profit, such as profit before taxes or after taxes. In countries where financial data are unreliable, number of employees is used as the key ranking item.

Date of the Ranking Criterion

How current are the data used for the rankings? We might expect publications copyrighted in the current year to be using year-old data. However, because companies have different year-end dates and information is not always filed in a timely manner, it is possible that the latest filings for a group of companies could be as much as three years old. For example, a book with a 1996 copyright might have 1993, 1994, or 1995 data, or a mix or all three. Some publications, such as those from ELC, generally drop back to the latest year for which most company data are available. Some sources put the dates in footnotes while others provide no dates. In countries with stable currencies and in times of economic and social stability the date effect may not be that important.

Foreign Exchange Conversions

When seeking worldwide rankings, some standard unit of currency has to be used, whether it is the U.S. dollar, the British pound, the Japanese yen, or the pan-European ECU. The information providers have to use some method to convert all the financial figures into the one currency. Several factors should be considered in the calculations:

- Company issues: Date of sales figure (year and year-end)
- Exchange rate issues: Rate used (current rate, year-end rate, average rate)

For meaningful rankings, the rate to use in translating sales, net income (profit), or asset figures is based on accounting practices. U.S. standards require one method for income statement items, such as sales or net income, and another for balance sheet items such as assets. The former use a weighted average for the company's fiscal year while the latter are translated from local to reporting currency using the exchange rate at the balance sheet date of the foreign entity. The objective is to keep the same financial results and relationships as expressed in the local currency.[2]

When ranking companies within the same country and using data as reported (e.g., French franc or Japanese yen), there is no foreign exchange effect. However, we have documented the effect that foreign exchange may have on international rankings.[3]

If you need country-level information, it is better to try to find a source published in that country or a source with extensive coverage of the country with data presented in local currency.

Products from Worldscope, FT Extel, or Moody's, whose intended audience is financial analysts and accountants, use generally accepted accounting practices in their currency translations. However, some directory sources give undated financial information. If they convert financial information to dollars, the rate or date of exchange may not be given.

In the United States, the standard international ranking source is the *Fortune Global 500,* while in the U.K. it is the *Times 1000.* In fact, there is a general sense of agreement about the largest companies in the world. Table 8.I, later in the chapter, illustrates that anyone's "Top 30" list covers everyone's "Top 20." Some sources, such as the D&B International Online Files, should *not* be used to create rankings. These files are designed for company identification and market applications. Attempting to get a "Top" list from D&B *International Market Identifiers* may cause anomalous results.

How do the issues we have been discussing affect the accuracy of rankings? We may be generating a ranking in which the definitions for the characteristics being ranked vary—both for the data item and the product/activity—the date of data collection varies, and the foreign exchange rates do not follow accepted accounting standards. For comprehensive analysis, we recommend using more than one source and reading the notes carefully.

SOURCES OF RANKINGS

Sources may be arranged geographically, such as worldwide, by continent or by country; by industry, for example industrials, service, food and drink; for all companies or just listed companies. Companies are ranked by a variety of different criteria, such as sales or turnover, market capitalization, or even "most admired." Rankings may appear annually in books, such as ELC's "Largest" series, in annual issues of periodicals, such as *Fortune's* "Global 500," as special one-time reports, or as part of journal articles.

Sources from the U.S.

Three popular U.S. business magazines, *Fortune, Forbes,* and *Business Week* all publish "global" rankings in summer issues. *Fortune's* rankings include U.S. companies as well as the rest of the world. *Forbes* does not include U.S. companies in its 500 ranking. *Business Week* ranks the top 1,000 companies in the world but uses market capitalization instead of sales. Table 8.E shows the number of companies by country found in *Fortune, Forbes,* and *Business Week* and changes from 1992.

TABLE 8.E

NUMBER OF COMPANIES BY COUNTRY IN *FORTUNE*, *FORBES*, AND *BUSINESS WEEK* RANKINGS

	Fortune		*Forbes*		*Business Week*	
	96	**92***	**96**	**92**	**96**	**92**
United States	153	296			422	383
Japan	141	232	207	195	227	245
France	42	63	46	44	43	48
Germany	40	77	39	37	35	39
Britain	34[b]	86	63	74	97	110
Switzerland	16	24	17	18	18	12
Italy	12	15	14	11	17	18
South Korea	12	16	15	10	e	
Netherlands	11[a,b]	11	18	14	18	15
Canada	9	31	16	23	25	23
Belgium	6[a]		12	10	11	
Spain	6	16	9	11	12	16
Australia	4	17	12	13	16	20
Brazil	4	s	6		e	
Sweden	3	28	12	14	19	15
China	2	s	4			
Finland	2				2	
Norway	2		1		1	
Argentina			1			e
Hong Kong	1	3	4	3	17	21
India	1				e	
Mexico	1		2		e	
Netherlands Antilles	1					
Taiwan	1				e	
Turkey	1		1			
Venezuela	1					
Austria			2		1	
New Zealand			1		2	
Singapore			1		13	
South Africa		s	3		e	
Denmark					7	
Ireland					3	

92* Total of *Fortune* Industrial and Service 500
a One company also listed in Netherlands
b Two companies also listed in Netherlands
s 1992 Service companies
e *Business Week* emerging market countries; also includes Chile, Greece, Indonesia, Malaysia, Pakistan, Peru, Philippines, Thailand

TABLE 8.F

RANKINGS TABLES IN *FORTUNE*

Ranking	*Criteria*	*Number One*
Top 25 U.S. subsidiaries which disclose revenue	U.S. revenue, % parent's revenue; U.S. employees global parent; parent rank	Shell Oil
Money losers	Rank; amount	Alcatel Alsthom
Biggest Increase in Revenues	Rank, Revenue and % change	First Chicago
Highest Profits	Rank, Profits and % change	Royal Dutch/ Shell
Biggest Increase in Profits	Rank, Profits and % change	Fuji Heavy Inds.
Highest Returns on...		
Revenues with median	Rank, Profits as a % Revenue	Seagram
Assets with median	Rank, Profits as a % Assets	Intel
Biggest Employers with median	Rank, Number of employees	U.S. Postal Service

Source: Fortune Global 500, 1996.

Fortune Global 500 (published annually by Time Inc., Chicago)

Fortune has been publishing an international industrial ranking since 1974. The title of the report has gone through a series of name changes. For a few years, beginning in 1991, *Fortune* published a separate global "Service 500." The 1996 edition is entitled "Fortune Global 500" and appears in the August 5, 1996 issue. The largest 500 companies in the world, based on revenues, that publish financial data and report these figures to a governmental agency make up the list. In the 1996 edition, data are shown for the fiscal year ending on or before March 31, 1996. Average annual exchange rates are used for conversion.

The 500 companies are ranked on revenues, profits, assets, stockholders' equity, and employees. All companies are ranked within countries, with head-quarters address, telephone number, and CEO. There is an alphabetical index. Table 8.F lists the rankings tables in *Fortune* and the number one company in the 1996 edition.

An added feature is a ranking of companies within industry grouping by revenues. Data elements also include profits, and profits as a percent of revenues and assets, with rankings. There are also aggregate data for each industry for revenues, profits, assets, stockholders' equity, and employees, with rankings. Industries are further ranked on revenues, return on revenue, revenues per employee, change in profits, return on assets, and assets per employee. Table 8.G lists the *Fortune* industry grouping used for industrials.

The "Fortune Global 500" is available on the WWW at *Fortune's* home page: http://fortune.com. The lists are also on CompuServe and can be purchased on diskette.

TABLE 8.G

Fortune Industry Groupings for Industrials

Aerospace	Furniture	Publishing, printing
Apparel	Industrial & farm equip.	Rubber & plastics
Beverages	Jewelry, watches	Scientific & photo equip.
Building Materials	Metal products	Soaps, cosmetics
Chemicals	Metals	Textiles
Computers, Office Equip.	Mining, crude-oil	Tobacco
Electronics, Electrical equip.	Motor vehicles & parts	Toys, sporting goods
Food	Petroleum refining	Transportation equip.
Forest Products	Pharmaceuticals	

Source: Fortune Global 500, August 5, 1996.

TABLE 8.H

Rankings Tables in *Forbes*

Ranking	Criteria	Number One
25 largest foreign companies	Company, business, revenues, employees	Mitsubishi
Large foreign companies that are subsidiaries of foreign companies	Parent, country, % owned, revenue, market value, eps, P/E, yield	Telecom Italia
Super Fifty	Business, country, revenue, net income, assets, market value Employees	Royal Dutch/Shell
100 largest foreign investments in the U.S.	Country, U.S. investment, % owned, industry, revenue, net income, assets	Royal Dutch/Shell
100 U.S. traded foreign stocks	Exchange, country, ADR price, eps, P/E 1996e	Alphabetical list

Source: Forbes "500 Largest Foreign Companies" 1996.

Forbes "500 Largest Foreign Companies"
(published annually by Forbes Inc.)

The companies in the *Forbes* "500 Largest Foreign Companies" are all publicly traded as of May 31 of the ranking year and incorporated outside the United States and its territories. The 1996 edition uses fiscal 1995, defined as year running between June 1995 and May 1996. The 1996 edition appeared in the July 15, 1996 issue.

Companies are ranked by gross revenues. The main ranking is by country. Data on the country's business climate precedes each ranking. There is an alphabetical index. Table 8.H lists the rankings tables in *Forbes* and the number one company in the 1996 edition.

There is a separate listing of the U.S. multinationals (see Chapter 3). *Forbes* also identifies the "Super Fifty," based not only on sales but also on profits, assets, and market value, with Royal Dutch Petroleum heading this list. Raw data for the rankings are supplied by Morgan Stanley International. The 1996 issue also includes the world's richest people.

Business Week "Global 1000" (published annually by McGraw Hill)

The *Business Week* "Global 1000" measures how a company performs on the stock market, not in the marketplace. The first issue was 1988. For 1996, rankings are by market capitalization, based on the share price available on May 31, 1996, multiplied by the latest available number of shares outstanding, translated into U.S. dollars using May 31, 1996, exchange rates. Market value may include several classes of stock, price, and yield data and are based on the company's most widely held issue. There is a list of the top 100. The main entries are by country. There is a composite for each data element for each country. There is one alphabetical index.

The "Global 1000" is also compiled by Geneva-based Morgan Stanley Capital International. Additional tables include those shown below.

Ranking	Criteria	Number One
Top 10 by:		
Sales	Sales in US $b	General Motors
Profits	Profits in US $b	Royal Dutch/Shell
Share price gain	% change from 95	Iomega
Return on equity	Percentage	Glaxo Wellcome
Top 100 Emerging-	Same as main table,	Korea Electric
Market Companies	1996 & 1995 rank	Power

To show the relative consistency among the rankings for the world's largest companies based on sales, we have, in Table 8.I, compared the *Fortune* rankings to several other international ranking sources. The *Business Week* "Global 1000" rankings illustrate the difference in rankings by using the company's stock market performance. The *Business Week* rankings are very much a function of the market on which companies trade. Notice that 10 out of the top 20 *Business Week* companies are from the U.S. while only 3 of the top 10 *Fortune* companies are from the U.S. Only 3 of the top 10 *Business Week* companies are in the *Fortune* top 10. Table 8.J compares *Business Week's* market capitalization ranking with *Financial Times,* discussed below, and *Forbes*. Because of the differences in ranking criteria, many libraries may want to own all three publications. Table 8.K compares and contrasts the rankings.

TABLE 8.I

WORLD'S LARGEST COMPANIES RANKED IN 1996

Fortune by Revenue 96	95	92*	Company	Country	Fb (1)	WS (2**)	EX (3**)	GV (4**)	Sales $US000	BUSWEEK (6)	(7)
1	1	4	MITSUBISHI	JP	1	1	1	6	184,365	111	2
2	2	5	MITSUI & CO.	JP	2	2	2	5	181,518	204	3
3	3	1	ITOCHU	JP	3	3	4	2	169,164	301	4
4	5	6	GENERAL MOTORS	US		6	6	3	168,828	36	1
5	4	2	SUMITOMO	JP	4	4	3	1	167,530	251	5
6	6	3	MARUBENI	JP	5	5	5	4	161,054	380	6
7	7	9	FORD MOTOR	US		7	7	7	137,137	33	7
8	11	11	TOYOTO MOTOR (2)	JP	6	8	12	10	111,052	8	10
9	8	8	EXXON	US		10	8	8	110,009e	6	8
10	10	7	ROYAL DUTCH/SHELL	UK/N	7	22/44	9/10		109,883e	2	9
11	9	10	NISSHO IWAI	JP	8	9	11	9	97,886	728	
12	12	31	WAL-MART	US		11	13	11	93,627	19	
13	13	18	HITACHI	JP	9	12	17	13	84,167	62	
14	14		NIPPON LIFE INSURANCE	JP	10	13			83,206		
15	16	25	NIPPON TEL & TEL	JP	14	14	21	14	81,937	3	
16	15	14	AMERICAN T & T	US		17	15	12	79,609	7	
17	20	19	DAIMLER-BENZ	GE	11	21	16	15	67,755	71	
18	21	12	IBM	US		18	22	20	71,940	20	
19	17	24	MATSUSHITA ELECT	JP	12	15	14	16	70,398	50	
20	19	15	GENERAL ELECTRIC	US		19	25	17	70,028	1	
21	18	16	TOMEN	JP	13	16	18	18	69,901	327	
22	22	21	MOBIL	US		22	19	19	66,724e	30	
23	23	33	NISSAN MOTOR	JP	14	20	26	38	62,568	118	
24	34	29	VOLKSWAGEN	GE	15	27	24	22	61,489	259	
25	30	30	SIEMENS (6/95)	GE	16	26	23		60,673	60	
26	26		DAI-ICHI MUTUAL LIFE	JP		25			58,052		
27	31	17	BRITISH PETROLEUM	UK	17	30	28	28	56,981e	25	
31	28	26	PHILIP MORRIS	US		34	20	25	53,139e	9	
32	36		TOSHIBA	JP	19	32	41		53,046	102	
35	24	22	NICHIMEN	JP	20	23	27	23	50,841		
190	186	116	COCA COLA	US		78			18,018	4	
215	210	152	MERCK	US		81			16,681	10	
137	173		BANK OF TOKYO	JP	18	59			22,479	5	

*   Derived combined Fortune Rankings from 1992
** Author derived rankings from databases
1   *Forbes* by Revenue ranked in 1996
2   *Worldscope* Revenue Ranking from May or July 1996 CD-ROM using 1995 year end dates
3   FT EXTEL on DIALOG, May 11, 1996. Year end dates varied from 1993 to 1995, with the majority of even the Japanese companies 1994
4   *Global Vantage* 1996
5   *Fortune* Revenues
6   *Business Week* by Market Capitalization, 1996
7   *Business Week* by Sales, 1996

TABLE 8.J

COMPARISON OF RANKINGS BY MARKET CAPITALIZATION

| | | | Based on *Business Week* Top 10 | | |
Fortune		Country	BW	FT	Forbes
20	General Electric	US	1	2	4
10	Royal Dutch/Shell	NE/UK	2	3	1
15	Nippon Telegraph	JP	3	1	10
190	Coca-Cola	US	4	6	
75	Tokyo Bank -Mitsubishi	JP	5	16	5
9	Exxon	US	6	5	3
16	AT&T	US	7	4	28
8	Toyota Motor	JP	8	9	6
31	Philip Morris	US	9	8	7
215	Merck	US	10	7	
333	Roche Holding	Swi	11	11	
	Microsoft	US	12	14	
176	Johnson & Johnson	US	13	21	
83	Fuji Bank	JP	14	12	17
228	Intel	US	15	15	
99	Sumitomo Bank	JP	16	13	22
56	Industrial Bank of Japan	JP	17	10	13
71	Procter & Gamble	US	18	18	19
12	Wal-Mart Stores	US	19	22	11
18	Intl Bus Machines	US	20	19	8
91	Dai Ichi Kangyo Bk	JP	21	17	24
68	Sanwa Bank	JP	22	20	16
84	Hewlett-Packard	US	23	23	26
89	Pepsico	US	24	26	
27	British Petroleum	UK	25	27	23
353	Glaxo Wellcome	UK	26	25	

FT January 25, 1996

Business Week, July 8, 1996

Fortune, August 5, 1996

Forbes World Super Fifty, July 15, 1996, based on best three out of four rankings for sales, profits, assets, and market value

TABLE 8.K

COMPARISON OF *FORTUNE*, *FORBES*, AND *BUSINESS WEEK* RANKINGS

	Fortune	*Forbes*	*Business Week*
Number of Companies	500	500	1000
Includes U.S	YES	NO	YES
Number Non-US Companies	347	500	678
Primary Ranking Category	Revenue	Revenue	Market Value
Previous Year Ranking	YES	YES	YES
Ranking by Country	YES	YES	YES
Ranking by Industry	YES	NO	NO
DATA ELEMENTS			
Revenues/Sales	US $m	US $m	US $m
Percent Change	YES	NO	NO
Profits/Net Income	US $m (r)	US $m	US $m
Percent Change	YES	NO	NO
Assets	US $m (r)	US $m	US $m
Stockholders Equity	US $m (r)	NO	NO
Employees	YES (r)	YES	NO
Industry Classification	YES	NO	YES
Securities Data:			
Market Value	NO	US $m	US $m
Stock Price	NO	US $	US $
Percent change	NO	NO	YES US$ and local
Earnings per share	NO	95/96e	NO
Yield	NO	YES	YES
Price/Book Value	NO	NO	YES
Price Earnings Ratio	NO	NO	YES

Sources from the U.K.

Times 1000 (published annually by Times Books, London)

The *Times 1000* has been a standard source in the U.K. since 1975. Originally the *Times 300*, this is a listing of the world's "leading industrial and financial companies." In addition to rankings for the U.K., such as the "top 100" and the "top 50 investment trusts," the 1996 edition has the tables listed below, plus a company index.

Location	Number of Companies	Ranking
World	50	Industrial Companies
Europe	1,000	
	50	Profit makers
	50	Market capitalization
North America	100	
Japan	100	
Australia, New Zealand & Southeast Asia	100	

Data are tabulated by FT Extel Financial. Rankings in the 1996 edition are not directly comparable to previous editions, or to any other ranking source. The 1996 edition uses "capital employed" as its means to rank companies rather than turnover. The *Times* believes that this method makes it possible to compare industrial, commercial, and financial companies. It also opens up the rankings to governmental enterprises. However, this is not a model that will suit many of our non-financial users. Capital employed is "Shareholder's funds plus long-term loans (where separately disclosed) plus intra-group payables plus deferred liabilities less (for insurance companies) technical reserves."

The introduction provides users with the definitions of other principal items. For example:

> 2) Exchange rates: At each company's relevant financial end period.

> 4) Number of employees: Where possible the average full-time equivalent number of employees during the latest accounting period. Otherwise, if disclosed by the company, the number of employees as at the latest period.

In addition to capital employed, tables also list turnover, pre-tax profit, number of employees, and equity market capital. Using this new measurement, European Investment Bank and the French bank, Societe General, were ranked numbers one and two in Europe, while British Gas was number one in the U.K. and Nippon Telephone and Telegraph was tops in the world.

FT500 (14th ed., January 25, 1996; published annually by Financial Times)

Financial Times publishes an annual survey on the 500 largest companies in Europe, as well as the 500 largest in the U.K. In 1994, the survey expanded to include the top 100 companies in the United States and Japan, and in 1996 the number rose to the top 500. In 1996, further additions included a list of top Canadian companies; the top 100 Asian-Pacific companies, excluding Japan; the top 100 in Latin America; and the top 50 in Eastern Europe. Other tables include the 50 largest companies in the Middle East, sub-Saharan Africa (excluding South Africa), and South Africa itself. Finally, 1996 marked the introduction of the top 100 companies worldwide, ranked by market capitalization in U.S. dollars. Half the companies are from the U.S., with 27 from Japan and 19 from Europe, and a company each from Singapore, Hong Kong, and Taiwan.

Like *Business Week* above, FT uses market capitalization as its measure for identifying the companies on its top lists. The data used in the January 1996 ranking were current to the close of September 1995. Glaxo, after its takeover of Wellcome, became the number one U.K. company while Nippon Telephone and Telegraph was number one on the world list, followed by General Electric.

Financial Times identifies three factors that affect the market capitalization rankings: performance of the company; movement of the company's national stock exchange; and currency fluctuations. *FT* uses market capitalization instead of sales, however, because it *"avoids the difference between national accounting standards that bedevil rankings based on profitability and avoids the inconsistencies between industries that undermine rankings by revenues."*[4] This method underrepresents French and Italian companies, since many major enterprises are state or family owned. U.S. dollars in October 1995 are used as the currency for the pan-European rankings. Sources for the tables are FT Extel, Datastream International, Standard & Poor's Compustat Services, ING, Baring Securities, MEEDMONEY, Hartland-Peel Emerging Market Research, and local stock exchanges.

The *FT500* is a dated issue of the newspaper and is available for separate purchase directly from the *Financial Times* in London.

1996	1993	Company	Country	Sales ECU mil.	Employees Number	Rank
1	1	NV KON. NEDERLANDSE PETROLEUM	NL	87.394	117000	42
2	4	DAIMLER-BENZ AG	DE	55.784	341905	3
3	10	SIEMENS AKTIENGESELLSCHAFT	DE	45.345	382000	1
4	5	VOLKSWAGEN AKTIEGESELLSCHAFT	DE	42.902	243638	15
5	*	UNILEVER NEDERLAND BV	NL	39.891	9300	1015
5	7	UNILEVER NV	NL	39.891	9300	1015
7	3	THE BRITISH PETROLEUM CO. PLC	UK	39.497	66550	113
8	*	VEBA AKTIENGESELLSCHAFT	DE	38.079	128976	34
9	*	MERCEDES - BENZ AKTIENGESELLSCHAFT	DE	37.903	201977	29
10	*	NESTLE SA	CH	37.544	209755	17

* not in top 10 in 1993

EUROPE'S TOP 5,000 COMPANIES RANKED BY SALES IN ECU (MILLIONS) FROM *D&B EUROPA 1996*

EXHIBIT 8.6

Source: *D&B Europa* 4 (1996): 67. Copyright 1996 Dun & Bradstreet, Inc. All rights reserved. Reprinted with permission.

2-3 MANUFACTURING
20 Food and Kindred Products

Rank	Company	Country	Financial Size	Employees Number	Rank	Vol:Page
1	UNILEVER NEDERLAND NV	NL	39.891	9300	42	3: 180
2	UNILEVER NV	NL	39.891	9300	42	3: 180
3	NESTLE SA	CH	37.544	209755	2	1: 277
4	UNILEVER PLC	UK	35.383	304000	1	1:1146
5	GRAND METROPOLITAN PLC	UK	9.279	64300	5	3: 836

TOP COMPANIES IN EACH MAIN BUSINESS ACTIVITY RANKED BY FINANCIAL SIZE IN ECU (MILLIONS) IN *D&B EUROPA*

EXHIBIT 8.7

Source: *D&B Europa* 4 (1996): 210. Copyright 1996 Dun & Bradstreet, Inc. All rights reserved. Reprinted with permission.

Regional Rankings

D&B Europa, which is discussed in the previous company chapters, includes a list of the top 5,000 companies in Europe ranked by sales in ECUs (excluding banks and insurance companies). Exhibit 8.6 lists the *D&B Europa* top 10. Companies will vary from other lists because non-listed companies and subsidiaries are included.

Other rankings in volume 4 of *D&B Europa* 1996 are:

• Top 500 banks ranked by total assets in ECUs
• Top 5,000 companies ranked by employees
• Top companies in each main business activity ranked by financial size in ECUs

A brief example of Business Activity ranking, by 2-digit U.S. SIC code, is presented in Exhibit 8.7. A cross-country exchange rate table, which also serves as a bookmark, accompanies each volume.

ELC, Europe's Large Companies, publishes three "Largest" lists, which are distributed in the U.S. by Dun & Bradstreet. Titles published in 1996 are listed below with the date they were first published and the number of companies included in the first edition.

Title	Number of Companies	1st Date
Europe's 15,000 Largest Companies	5,000	1975
UK's 10,000 Largest Companies	7,500	1985
Asia's 7,500 Largest Companies	7,500	1985

The European volume covers the EU without Greece, Norway, and Switzerland. Headings are in English, German, and French. There are separate rankings for the largest industrials, trading companies, and service companies. Companies are included based on sales in U.S. dollars. The distribution of companies by sector is listed below.

Industrials	9,700
Trading Companies	3,750
Service	
Banks	300
Transport	300
Advertising Agencies	50
Hotels and Restaurants	100
Miscellaneous	300

Data are presented in spreadsheet format. For each company in the top 15,000 ranking, there are 21 columns of data:

- Rankings: By current and previous years for sales
- Directory Data: Company name, country, headquarters country, ISIC industry codes
- Financial Data: Sales, current and previous years profit, employees, assets, equity capital, and year established
- Percentages: Change in sales in U.S. dollars and local currency; profit as a percent of sales for current and previous years, assets, and equity; equity capital as a percent of assets

For the 1996 edition, "current year" is December 1994, except where footnoted.

There are separate lists of the top 500 companies in Europe ranked by sales, profit, and employees, and lists of up to the top 100 companies for each country. Eight of ELC's top 10 are also *D&B Europa's* top ten.

There is an alphabetical index of companies with their rank and code. The data are also currently available on diskette.

The activity coding system used in this publication is the ISIC, the U.N. International Coding system. The list of codes and exchange rates are included in the publication.

ELC Directories are in the ELC file on LEXIS-NEXIS. However, we do not recommend using them. Rankings are not provided; the August 1996 load date still has 1994 and 1993 data.

Asiaweek 1000

The *Asiaweek 1000*, published annually since 1992 in the November issue, ranks the companies in the region by sales. In the 1996 ranking, 275 companies were Japanese, the same number as in the first edition. The 1996 edition used consolidated sales for its ranking criteria for the first time. The 1996 rankings are based on fiscal year ends between July 1995 and June 1996. Data include net profit, sales per assets, equity, profit as a percent of sales, and workforce. Market capitalization was added in 1995. The top 20 enterprises are listed for each country, with main business, sales, profit, profit as a percent of sales. There is also a list of top enterprises in ASEAN.

Hoover's Masterlist of Latin American Companies (1996–97)

The first edition of *Hoover's Masterlist of Latin American Companies* contains rankings of companies on sales and employees for Argentina, Brazil, Chile, Colombia, Mexico, Peru, Uruguay, and Venezuela. Companies are also ranked by employees for major industry groupings such as automotive, electronics, and retail. There are also "Top 100" lists by sales and employees, based on all companies in the book.

While there is consensus among publications on the largest companies worldwide, there is much more variation among top company lists in Latin America. For example, Hoover's lists 12 Argentinian companies with sales over one billion U.S. dollars while Worldscope has only five. Dun & Bradstreet recommends using employees as the ranking criteria for Latin America. However, only three of the 15 Argentinian employers on Duns *Latin America 25,000* CD-ROM matched Hoover's top employers. What was more disconcerting was the list of top Argentinian employers on Duns CD-ROM was not the same as that in DIALOG File 518.

Country Rankings

British Business Rankings (Dun & Bradstreet)

British Business Rankings is a companion volume to the Dun & Bradstreet directory, *Key British Enterprises*. It ranks the largest 5,000 employers, within counties, by employee numbers, and by sales within SIC codes. There is an alphabetical list of all companies. In addition to employees and SIC codes, addresses and telephone numbers are included in the book.

National business magazines publish their own "500" lists. Some examples are the *Financial Post* "Canada's 500 Largest Corporations" and *Canadian Business's* "Performance 500," *Business Korea's* "Korean Corporation 500," and *Director's* (U.K.) "Director's 1000."

Sector Rankings

Industry Week

May 29, 1996 marks the first edition of the *Industry Week* "World's Top 1000 Industrial Companies." In addition to the worldwide ranking by sales, the article ranks the top 10 companies by categories, country, and industry.

Categories	Data Elements
Performance Measures	
Profit Margin	Overall rank, industry, date for
Return on Equity,	measure, revenue, country
Profit Growth	
Country	
U.S., Japan, U.K.,	Ranking, industry, revenue,
France, and Germany	profit margin
Industries	
Food, chemicals,	Ranking, country, revenues,
electronics, metals,	profit margin
industrial equipment	

323 companies are from the U.S. and 244 from Japan. The format allows for interesting comparisons among the different performance measures, industries, and countries, not featured in the other standard ranking sources. Data are from Moody's Investors Service and Dun & Bradstreet. Listed below is an example of a ranking by a performance measure, profit margin.

Rank	Company	Revenues	Profit Margin
1	General Motors Corp.	168828.6	4.08%
2	Ford Motor Co.	110496	3.75%
3	Toyota Motor Corp.	94203.3	1.62%
4	Hitachi Ltd.	188070.2	1.50%
5	Matsushita Electric Industrial Co.	80598.6	1.30%

Companies are distributed across industrial sectors, with no sector having more than 12% of the companies.

Food	12.1%
Chemicals	11.5%
Electrical/electronic equip.	11%
Metals	9.4%
Industrial equip.	8.9%
Motor vehicles & parts	6.1%
Other industries*	41%

* Other industries encompass 21 industries.

"The Euromoney Bank Atlas," *Euromoney*,
(Euromoney Publications, London; June issue)

Euromoney published the "Euromoney 500," a ranking of the world's 500 largest banks from 1982 to 1994. In 1995, the ranking was renamed "The Euromoney Bank Atlas," a new "improved ranking of the world's most important banks." Rankings are based on total shareholder equity.

In conjunction with EURASTAR division of Sleigh Corporation, *Euromoney* expanded its rankings to include a total of 1,249 banks from 134 countries. Coun-

tries listed for the first time include El Salvador, Macau, Mozambique, and Angola, as well as former eastern bloc states such as Albania, Estonia, Armenia, and Belarus. The 200 biggest banks in the world are ranked in one table and then the total 1,249 banks are ranked within their countries. Number of banks per country range from one for Albania to 50 for Japan. In addition to shareholders' equity, information for each bank includes fiscal date, equity growth, total assets, asset growth, net profit, profit growth, return on average equity and a U.S. dollars differential.

In January 1996, *Euromoney* published a separate ranking of the world's most successful investment banks, based on 70 different polls. The top 20 overall, plus the top 20 by underwriting, trading, and advisory functions are presented.

Institutional Investor

The August 1996 issue of *Institutional Investor* has the 19th edition of "World's 100 Largest Banks." Banks are ranked by total capital, with much discussion in the article on the measurement of total capital. Other data elements include fiscal date, equity, total assets, reserves, pretax profit, the ratio of liquid assets to total assets. Percent change from the previous year is also calculated. Finally, rankings include the Bank for International Settlements data element, tier-1 capital. *Bankstat,* discussed in Chapter 5, helped with the measurement.

Management Today (December 1992)

A listing that interests investors in Europe because of its methodology appeared in the December 1992 *Management Today*. It is a study by a German professor that ranks the 400 largest European quoted companies (by turnover) plus the 50 largest banks and the 50 largest insurance companies on the criteria noted below.

Profitability	Financial Solidity	Growth
• Return on Equity	• Equity as a percent of capital	• Annual % growth of total assets and turnover
• Cash flow as a percent of sales	• Liquid assets as a percent of total assets	

Number one is the U.K. company Glaxco. Other well-known European firms in the listing are Royal Dutch and BP, at numbers 76 and 266, respectively.[5]

Brands

Ranking by brand within country eliminates some of the definitional issues associated with other rankings. While *Advertising Age* and *Brandweek* rank brands by

	Brand	Owner	£m Sales	Agency	Adspend£000*
1	Coca-Cola	Coca-Cola	Over 483	Publicis . . .	28,827.2
2	WalkersCrisps	PepsiCo	295-300	BMP DDB	3772.9
3	Nescafé	Nestlé	250-255	McCann . . .	6356.7
4	Ariel	P & G	220-255	Saatchi	22,495.1
5	Pampers	P & G	195-200	Saatchi	9823.5
6	Persil	Lever Bros.	180-185	J Walter . . .	26,834.1

* Ad spending from Register-MEAL; Survey by ACNielsen

EXTRACT FROM "BIGGEST BRANDS"

EXHIBIT 8.8

Source: Marketing (June 27, 1996): 22.

advertising expenditures, the U.K. periodical *Marketing* ranks consumer brands by sales in its annual "Biggest Brands" issues. The issues list the biggest brands, the parent company, the advertising agency, and the amount spent for advertising. Using this ranking you can say that Coca-Cola is the biggest selling soft drink in the U.K. Using many of the other sources listed in this chapter, Coca-Cola, the leading brand, would not even be included in a list of largest U.K. companies. Exhibit 8.8 is a brief extract from "Biggest Brands." The 1996 Survey appeared in the June 27, 1996, and July 4, 1996, issues of *Marketing*.

Other Rankings

As a follow-up to its top 1,000, discussed above, *Industry Week* published "The World's 100 Best Managed Companies" in August 1996. Companies are drawn from the IW 1,000 manufacturing companies. Inclusion in the 100 is based on a combination of quantitative and qualitative measures, such as financial performance, distribution and logistics, global strategy, and corporation citizenship. Companies are arranged alphabetically, but are not given a rank or a score. These companies represent "best practices" as determined by *Industry Week* for manufacturing companies. Four of the top 10 on the 1000, including number one, did not make this list. There is a 50-word synopsis of each company and an alphabetical table with company name, headquarters, revenues in millions of U.S. dollars, CEO, and business description.

Management Today (U.K., December 1995)

Management Today offers an innovative survey of "Britain's Most Admired Companies," which first appeared in 1989. Cadbury Schweppes was voted by its peers to be Britain's Most Admired Company in 1995. Ten companies in 25 sectors are included in each survey. Senior directors at these 250 companies, together with leading investment analysts in the relevant industry sectors, evaluate the companies in their sector and evaluate each company for an overall ranking.

Companies are given a score of 0 (poor) to 10 (excellent) for their performance on nine equally weighted criteria: management quality; recruiting/retaining staff; quality of marketing; financial soundness; long-term value; use of corporate assets; community and environmental responsibility; product/service quality; capacity to innovate. Three separate analyses were produced: a ranking of the top 10 companies in each sector; a list of all 250 companies, from which the overall most admired are drawn; and the top 10 for each characteristic. The top 10 companies in the full 250 in 1995 are shown below.

1995	1994	Company
1	7	Cadbury Schweppes
2	5	Unilever
3	18	Smiths Industries
4	31	Tesco
5	25	Whitbread
6	12	Vodaphone
7	3	Marks & Spencer
8	9	Shell Transport & Trading
9	16	J. Sainsbury
10	6	Reuters Holdings

Finding Aids for Rankings

There are hundreds of other rankings available in published sources. The researcher needs tools to find the ones that are relevant to his or her project or to confirm that none are available. The following tools can be used as finding aids, or in some cases, for answers in themselves.

World Market Share Reporter (Gale, 1st ed., 1995–96)

In 1992, Gale published *European Business Rankings*, which was similar to its U.S. *Business Rankings Annual*. Instead of publishing a second edition of European rankings, Gale has incorporated worldwide rankings into the *World Market Share Reporter: A Compilation of Reported World Market Share Data and Rankings on Companies, Products, and Services,* discussed in more detail in Chapter 10. There are entries by products and services, companies, and brands. No distinctions are made between a market share entry and a rankings entry. Entries are arranged by U.S. SIC code.

The rankings component of this book has obvious limitations. Many of the rankings are from standard print sources, though there is no index by source. Dates of the rankings vary, and in many cases, the date of publication is given but not the date for the data. The *Reporter* makes no judgment on the quality or reliability of the data. For comprehensive research, this book should be used *only* as a finding aid and not as a source in itself.

Exhibit 8.9 is a sample entry from *World Market Share Reporter.*

253
Food
SIC:2000-ISIC 1500
The 12 leading food companies are ranked by 1992 sales in billions of dollars. Shares of the group are shown in percent.

	Sales ($ bil)	% of (Group)
Nestle	$ 37.6	21.5%
Philip Morris	33.0	18.9
Unilever	22.5	12.9
PepsiCo	13.7	7.8
Coca-Cola	13.1	7.5
BSN	12.4	7.1
Grand Metroplitan	9.7	5.5
RJR Nabisco	6.7	3.8
Sara Lee	6.6	3.8
CPC International	6.6	3.8
Heinz	6.6	3.8
Campbell	6.3	3.6

SAMPLE ENTRY FROM *WORLD MARKET SHARE REPORTER*

EXHIBIT 8.9

Source: Economist, December 4, 1993: 3, from Food Business in *World Market Share Reporter* 1995/96. Reprinted with permission from Gale Research.

Gale Country and World Rankings Reporter (Gale Research, 1995)

In 1995, Gale issued another rankings compendium, *Gale Country and World Rankings Reporter.* The *Reporter* has over 3,000 rankings, by country. It includes a flea market arrangement of rankings:

- "People per McDonald's" for four countries, from an article in *Fortune*

- Office rents for 16 cities worldwide from the *Economist*
- Lipstick prices in Sao Paulo and Frankfurt from *USA Today*

Many of the tables come from the *CIA World Factbook* 1993 diskettes and the *Statistical Abstract of the United States.* While the compilation was obviously a monumental task, the resulting volume is a hodgepodge of numbers, some which are meaningful, many of which are not. Tables may have as few as two countries. Only one table ranks companies. The table is derived from the Morgan Stanley market value rankings used in the *Business Week* rankings described above.

Online Databases

Researchers can find references to published rankings directly by using standard online databases. ABI/Inform has over 10,000 articles indexed as "rankings" or "ratings & rankings," with more than 4,000 not from the U.S. Most of the ABI records do not include the actual rankings. *PROMT, Textline,* and *Trade and Industry* include references to articles with rankings, but there is no guarantee that the rankings themselves will be included in the article. For example, in the case of the *Management Today* article discussed, full text was available in several sources, but only *Trade and Industry* included the tables. Listed below are some typical rankings articles found in these standard sources:

Sample "Top 10" titles in *PROMT* include:

- "Michelin No. 1 brand worldwide," *Tire Business* (August 19, 1996)
- "Japan Loses World Banks' Top Spot-Temporarily" *American Banker* (August 5, 1996)
- "HSBC tops list of most profitable banks in region" (Asia)
- *Business Times* (Singapore) (May 29, 1996)

Top 10 articles in *Textline* include:

- "CHINA: SHANGHAI FIRMS FLY HIGHEST" *South China Morning Post,* (September 4, 1996) (top 10 listed firms)
- "BRAZIL: BCN BANK TOPS IN BRAZIL LEASING—PAPER" Reuters, *Reuters Newswire* Central & S. America, Reuters Economic News (top 10 leasing firms)

Business & Industry specifies "Rankings" as a data type. It has several thousand non-U.S. articles with this designation. *Business & Industry* also includes tables. Both *B&I* and *PROMT* had the *Tire Business* article listed above, but only B&I has the tabular data that accompanied the text. Exhibit 8.10 is an extract of a "rankings" record with tabular data.

DIALOG(R)File   9:Business & Industry(R) Jul
(c) 1996 Resp. DB Svcs. All rts. reserv.

01507525   (THIS IS THE FULLTEXT)
A world of difference: Part II
(Andersen Consulting leads the world consultancy market with 1995 revenues of $4,224.0 mil, vs $3,452.0 mil in 1994)
Management Consultant International, n 81, p 10
June 1996
DOCUMENT TYPE: Newsletter; **Ranking**

Full text tables details 1994-95 revenues, growth rate, effective date, number of consultants, number of partners, total staff and 1995 revenues/consultant; and the top 8 consultancies' fee splits by type. Included in separate records: text article on the world consultancy market and table of the world's largest consultancies' offices worldwide.

TEXT:
THE WORLD'S LARGEST CONSULTANCIES RANKED BY REVENUE

Firm	1995 Revenue ($/million)	1994 Revenue ($/million)	Growth Rate (%)	Effective date
Andersen Consulting	4,224.0	3,452.0	22.4	Dec 95
McKinsey & Co	1,800.0(2)	1,500.0	20.0(2)	Dec 95
KPMG International	1,544.0(3)	1,206.0(4)	28.0	Sep 95
Ernst & Young	1,523.0	1,181.4	28.9	Sep 95
Coopers & Lybrand	1,221.0	1,049.0	16.4	Sep 95
Deloitte Touche Tomatsu International	1,200.0	1,061.0	13.1	Aug 95
Arthur Andersen	1,169.5	832.9	40.4	Aug 95
Mercer Consulting Group(5)	1,056.4(5)	933.1	13.2	Dec 95
Price Waterhouse	964.0	763.0	26.3	Jun 95
Booz-Allen & Hamilton	880.0	783.0	12.4	Mar 96

(1) Or partner equivalents
(2) Estimated by MCI
(3) Total billing to clients
(4) In last year's survey MCI estimated KPMG's 1994 consulting revenue at $875 million. KPMG has since expanded its definition of consulting services and switched to reporting gross fee income (see MCI 76)
(5) Mercer Consulting Group comprises William M Mercer ($802.9 million), Mercer Management Consulting ($200.7 million) and National Economic Research Associates ($52.8 million)

SPECIAL FEATURES: **Table**

EXTRACT FROM RANKING RECORD IN *BUSINESS & INDUSTRY*

EXHIBIT 8.10

Source: Business & Industry Database, reprinted with permission from Responsive Database Services, Inc.

World Economies

A look at the biggest and the best in the world appeared in an article in *Across the Board*, taken from the Conference Board Study "Global Presence and Competitiveness of U.S. Manufacturers." This ranking is of the top 100 "economies," which includes both countries and companies. The ranking was first performed in 1971 by the Library of Congress's Congressional Research Service. In 1981, Congressional Research Service printed an updated version. Between 1981 and 1991, the date of the most recent ranking, more companies have been added to the list. In 1981, 61 countries and 39 industrial companies were listed. In 1991, the number of industrial companies grew to 47.

To make international comparisons, a purchasing power parity method was used for countries; however, countries such as Russia, for which there was no reliable data, are not on the current list. The company list is arbitrarily limited to manufacturers, which leaves out mega-banks and trading companies. Exhibit 8.11 shows the top 46 economies on the list.

THE TOP 100 ECONOMIES

Rankings are based on countries' gross national products and companies' sales.

		(000)				(000)
1	United States	$5,237,707,000		24	Norway	$92,097,000
2	Japan	2,920,310,000		25	Saudi Arabia	89,986,000
3	Germany	1,272,959,000		26	Indonesia	87,936,000
4	France	1,000,866,000		27	Exxon Corp	86,656,000
5	Italy	871,955,000		28	South Africa	86,029,000
6	United Kingdom	834,166,000		29	Royal Dutch/Shell Gr	85,537,900
7	Canada	500,337,000		30	Turkey	74,731,000
8	China	393,006,000		31	Argentina	68,780,000
9	Brazil	375,146,000		32	Poland	66,974,000
10	Spain	358,352,000		33	Thailand	64,437,000
11	India	287,383,000		34	IBM Corp	63,438,000
12	Australia	242,131,000		35	Toyota Motor Corp	60,443,600
13	Netherlands	237,415,000		36	Hong Kong	59,202,000
14	Switzerland	197,984,000		37	Yugoslavia[sic]	59,080,000
15	Korea	186,467,000		38	General Electric Co	55,264,000
16	Sweden	184,230,000		39	Greece	53,626,000
17	Mexico	170,053,000		40	Algeria	53,116,000
18	Belgium	162,026,000		41	Mobil Corp	50,976,000
19	Austria	131,899,000		42	Hitachi Ltd	50,894,000
20	General Motors	126,974,300		43	British Petroleum	49,484,400
21	Finland	109,705,000		44	IRI	49,077,200
22	Denmark	105,263,000		45	Venezuela	47,164,000
23	Ford Motor Co	96,932,600		46	Israel	44,141,000

ACROSS THE BOARD

EXHIBIT 8.11

Source: Across the Board (December 1991): 18.

ONLINE AND ON DISC RANKINGS

When rankings do not exist for the criteria a researcher requires, online and on disc company databases can be used to create individualized rankings. There are, however, several pitfalls.

Annual financial figures are released once a year. Therefore, online databases do not have the same timeliness advantage with rankings as they do with other company issues. Many of the company databases are designed as marketing tools to identify companies participating in an industry and they should *not* be used for ranking applications.

However, company databases that have financial fields, such as sales or profits, and are retrieved on systems that have numeric sorting, such as DIALOG (or, to a limited extent, LEXIS-NEXIS Services and DataStar), may be used to produce customized rankings. It is important to know both the content and structure of the database before creating your own ranked lists of companies.

When using a database for rankings, look for the following:

- Can you select companies based on their fiscal year-end dates?
- Are primary industry codes, such as SIC, assigned? Can you rank on segment data?
- If the financial figures are converted into one currency, is the exchange rate or the exchange rate date provided?

The financial CD-ROM products from Disclosure, Moody's, FT Extel, Bureau van Dijk, OneSource, or Global Vantage are designed for ranking applications. You may use them to produce your own rankings. In Worldscope, the software is easy to use. However, even with Worldscope, you may be retrieving different financial year-end dates and consolidated information for the company. Exhibit 8.12 illustrates a user-defined ranking report from Worldscope. The ranking in yen differs from the ranking in dollars because of different year-end dates and exchange rates.

Y	$	Company Name	Net Sales or Revenues (Y000)	($000)	Annual Date of Filing	Primary US SIC	Calculated Exchange Rate
1	1	HITACHI, LTD.	7,592,266,000	87,690,672	3/31/95	3570	0.01155
2	2	MATSUSHITA ELECTRIC	6,948,159,000	80,251,236	3/31/95	3651	0.01155
3	3	TOSHIBA CORPORATION	4,790,766,000	55,333,347	3/31/95	3575	0.01155
4	4	SONY CORPORATION	3,983,438,000	46,008,709	3/31/95	3651	0.01155
5	5	NEC CORPORATION	3,769,357,000	43,536,073	3/31/95	3570	0.01155
6	6	MITSUBISHI ELECTRIC	3,250,876,000	37,547,618	3/31/95	3621	0.01155
7	**8**	**SANYO ELECTRIC CO.,**	**1,742,286,000**	**17,074,540**	**11/30/95**	**3570**	**0.0098**
8	**7**	**SHARP CORPORATION**	**1,617,620,000**	**18,683,511**	**3/31/95**	**3651**	**0.01155**
9	9	VICTOR COMPANY JA LT	767,217,000	8,861,356	3/31/95	3650	0.01155
10	10	OKI ELECTRIC INDUSTRY	656,989,000	7,588,223	3/31/95	3577	0.01155

Y Ranked by sales in yen.
$ Ranked by sales in U.S. dollars.
Search on companies in electronics industry in Japan.

WORLDSCOPE: A RANKING OF PUBLICLY TRADED JAPANESE ELECTRONICS COMPANIES

EXHIBIT 8.12

Source: Worldscope CD-ROM, July 1996. Reprinted with permission of Disclosure.

Using *Moody's International* CD-ROM to generate a list of top companies based on sales did not capture the largest Japanese trading companies, since Moody's template did not capture the sales data for this type of enterprise. Even switching to total revenues did not capture three of the largest Japanese trading companies. Moody's allows the user to select the currency and the date of conversion. Anomalies still occur with a couple of Croatian companies being ranked in the top 20 using the "year-end" January 1996 disc.

In sources such as these, which contain listed companies, rankings are based on the company's *total* sales or turnover, not on the sales from individual segment groupings. This creates two other ranking issues—consolidated sales and industry groupings. These are both illustrated by a search on FT Extel on DIALOG (File 500), performed in 1996, for the largest tobacco and beer companies in the database. FT Extel includes a series of financials that have been translated into U.K. pounds and U.S. dollars. As we can see in Exhibit 8.13, one company can be ranked first in more than one industry, and the same sales figure is presented. Also, while that company is ranked first in both industries, its primary SIC code is for neither. It is listed as a holding company. Two different user-defined reports have been selected to present the relevant data.

Largest TOBACCO Companies:

COMPANY NAME	(Sales) TURNOVER($000)	TOBACCO SALES
PHILIP MORRIS COS INC	**65,125,000**	<—32,316,000
RJR NABISCO HOLDINGS CORP	15,366,000	
AMERICAN BRANDS	13,146,500	
B.A.T. INDUSTRIES PLC	10,482,000	
BRITISH AMERICAN TOBACCO LT	8,901,000	
GALLAHER LTD	7,209,000	
CIE FINANCIERE RICHEMONT AG	6,574,516	

Largest BEER Manufacturers:

COMPANY NAME	Turnover (Sales) ($000)	Latest Annual Date	
PHILIP MORRIS COS INC	**65,125,000**	31 Dec 94	<- 4,304,000 GRAND
KIRIN BEWERY CO LTD	17,025,000	31 Dec 94	
DANONE	16,246,000	31 Dec 95	
ALLIED DOMECQ PLC	13,826,000	31 Aug 95	
ANHEUSER-BUSCH COS INC	13,734,000	31 Dec 94	

RANKING USING *FT EXTEL* ON DIALOG

EXHIBIT 8.13

Source: FT Extel on DIALOG, November 1996. Reprinted with permission of Extel Financial Inc.

The actual sales figures for the tobacco and beer segments of Philip Morris are reported in *Worldscope* and shown in Exhibit 8.14. Most countries outside the United States do not require companies to disclose the amount of sales and profit derived from different lines of business. The major databases have no mechanisms to search on these figures.

One database designed for ranking applications is the *Teikoku Databank of Japanese Companies*. Each company record has a ranking by sales within its primary Japanese SIC group. Therefore, Teikoku can easily answer questions like the following:

> *Who are the 5 largest software companies in Japan?*
>
> *Which Japanese companies are No. 1 in their SIC group?*

Exhibit 8.15 shows records from the *Teikoku Databank* on DIALOG that can answer these two sample questions.

Product Segment Data—1995 (000s U.S. Dollars)

	Sales	Operating Income	Assets
Food	29,074,000	3,188,000	33,477,000
Tobacco	32,316,000	7,177,000	11,196,000
Beer	4,304,000	444,000	1,751,000
Financial Services	377,00	164,000	5,632,000

PHILIP MORRIS SEGMENT DATA REPORTED IN *WORLDSCOPE*

EXHIBIT 8.14

Source: *Worldscope* CD-ROM June 1996. Reprinted with permission from Disclosure.

Example 1: Top 5 software companies in Japan
Search Teikoku using PC=8521 and SR=1:5

Company
Name

1. NTT DATA COMMUNICATIONS SYSTEM
2. HITACHI SOFTWARE ENGINEERING C
3. NIPPON STEEL INFORMATION $& COM
4. TOYO INFORMATION SYSTEMS CO LT
5. MICROSOFT CO LTD

Example 2: Largest Japanese Companies by SIC Code
Search for sales >10billion and SR=1

Company Name	Roman Company Name	Primary Japanese SIC	Sales (000 $)	Latest Sales Date
THE SANWA BANK LTD	SANWA GINKO KK	502	376,077,798	03/1996
THE NORINCHUKIN BANK	NORINCHUO KINKO	511	334,224,977	03/1995
JAPAN FINANCE CORPORATION FOR	KOEI KIGYO KINYUKOKO	504	181,369,476	03/1995
THE SHOKO CHUKIN BANK	CHUOKINKO SK	5214	165,623,442	03/1995
THE ZENSHINREN BANK	ZENKOKU SI RENGOKAI	5212	160,641,140	03/1995
ITOCHU CORPORATION	ITOCHU SHOJI KK	4011	146,231,414	03/1996
KOKUMIN KINYUKOKO *	KOKUMIN KINYUKOKO	5216	101,961,908	03/1995
JAPAN FINANCE CORPORATION FOR	CHUSHOKIGYO KINYUKOKO	5215	98,248,972	03/1995
TOYOTA MOTOR CORPORATION	TOYOTA JIDOSHA KK	3711	75,109,986	03/1996

U.S.$ are calculated by DIALOG and are for informational purposes only.

Not all companies have English names (see Chapter 3).

TEIKOKU RANKINGS ON DIALOG

EXHIBIT 8.15

Source: DIALOG File 502: Teikoku Databank: Japanese Companies. Copyright 1996 Teikoku Databank. Reprinted with permission from Teikoku Databank America, Inc.

Teikoku on DIALOG, DataStar, and LEXIS-NEXIS can be used to generate a listing of top companies; only DIALOG and the CD-ROM versions on *JADE* and *Japanese Company Factfinder* can create reports.

WEB RANKINGS

The WWW is *not* the place to surf for rankings or credit. As we have mentioned throughout this chapter, however, some of the suppliers of credit and ranking information have WWW sites. Most of the credit sites require subscriptions and are fee-based.

Some of the magazines make their rankings available free on the WWW, without the necessity of subscribing to the journal or the special issue. *Fortune* was one example. Another is *Financial Post Magazine* of Canada. *Financial Post Magazine's* "FP Top 50 Companies" is available at the magazine's WWW site, http://www.canoe.ca/FP-Top50. Information on how companies are selected is included with the rankings; what is not noticeable is the date the article was written.

Companies that are ranked are worldwide operations of Canadian-owned companies and the Canadian operations of foreign-owned firms. Unless otherwise stated, figures are for the fiscal year ending December 31, 1995. Definitions are given for revenue, net income, earnings per share, and all the other data elements that are provided. Bank of Canada's 12 monthly average noon exchange rates for each company's fiscal year are used to convert income statement items (e.g., sales, net income); the Bank's closing rate at a company's fiscal year-end is used to convert balance sheet items (e.g., assets, shareholders' equity). This final statement is something we would like to see in all sources providing financial comparisons. These rankings are not available in commercial online sources of *Financial Post*.

CONCLUSION

In this chapter, we have looked at two special aspects of business information: credit information and rankings. We listed some major international, Euro-

pean, and Asian credit services and identified a source that had a global listing.

Researchers often want lists of companies ranked by some measure of size globally, by geographic region, or by industry grouping. There are many underlying data factors that are considerations in global rankings, such as the measurement used, the date of the data for each company, and the foreign exchange conversion rate. Major business magazines publish rankings of international companies. These sources are discussed along with other sources of international, regional, and country rankings. Finally, we present online and on-disc sources of rankings, and techniques for creating your own ranking.

Reference Hint

Small and medium-sized libraries may be able to answer most of their rankings questions from the *Fortune* international list or the *Times 1000*. Use the Gale's *Rankings* title, despite its limitations, as a finding aid to special issues in your own or other libraries. Be aware of the limitations of all these sources. If you are using ranking sources not mentioned here, be sure to read the introduction of the source to verify that the compiler has addressed the issues we have discussed.

NOTES

1. Ruth A. Pagell and Michael Halperin, "Who's Top 20," *Database* 10, no. 2 (1987).

2. Ruth A. Pagell, "It's Greek to Me! Exchange Rate Translations and Company Comparisons," *Database* (February 1991).

3. Ruth A. Pagell, "What's for Dinar: Foreign Exchange Rate Data Sources," *Database* (December 1990).

4. FT500, *Financial Times* (February 23, 1993): 2.

5. "Europe's Top 500: Why Germans Like the Best of British," (December 1992): 38–52.

PART III
Marketing

CHAPTER 9
International Marketing Issues and Sources

TOPICS COVERED

- Approaches to International Marketing
- Environmental Scanning
- Sources for Country Market Information
- The International Four P's
- International Marketing of Services
- Franchising
- Sources of International Marketing Information
- Selected Articles on International Marketing

MAJOR SOURCES DISCUSSED

- *Social Indicators of Development*
- EIU Publications
- *Country Commercial Guides*
- *European and International Marketing Data and Statistics*
- Euromonitor Marketing Information Sources
- Washington Researchers Guides to Company and Industry Information

---

Companies must learn to operate as if the world were one large market—ignoring superficial regional and national differences.[1]

The 1989 Pontiac LeMans was made in *eight* different countries.

In order to sell ice cream in Hungary, a German company had to give free refrigerators to kiosks and gas stations.

International sales are a vital part of the global economy. Although 70% of all world trade is accounted for by the Triad (the U.S., Western Europe, and Japan), companies in countries all over the world are looking for ways to do business beyond their borders.

All companies require planning and research before embarking on marketing abroad. However, the information needs of a small business trying to sell its product overseas are different from those of the large corporation that is developing an international marketing strategy. Smaller companies and new entrants into the international marketing arena are often concerned with information and issues related to exporting.

Our discussion of international marketing is divided into four chapters:

Chapter 9: International Marketing Issues and Sources

Chapter 10: International Marketing Research
Chapter 11: Advertising, Media, and Direct Marketing
Chapter 12: Exporting and Importing

According to Vern Terpstra, international marketing is finding out what customers want around the world and satisfying these wants better than other domestic or international competitors.[2] International marketing research involves many of the same issues and resources we discussed in previous chapters. In our home countries, research for marketing requires primary as well as secondary sources. Because primary sources are often unavailable outside their country of origin, researchers must rely on the secondary sources discussed in these chapters.

APPROACHES TO INTERNATIONAL MARKETING

Various definitions of the international firm, based on organizational and financial characteristics, are presented in Chapter 3. What constitutes an international firm from a marketing perspective? The list below presents some of the scenarios.

- Export mode: Manufacture at home, use an intermediary to market abroad; manufacture at home, market abroad directly.

- Import mode: Manufacture abroad, sell at home; distribute goods manufactured abroad.
- International mode: Produce abroad, sell abroad.
- Corporate affiliation mode: Joint venture between domestic and foreign company; domestic company invests in a foreign firm; foreign firm invests in a domestic firm; domestic firm licenses a foreign firm; domestic firm issues franchise to foreign franchisee.

An Export Scenario

Described below is an American-Russian export project:

> A Pennsylvania company builds steel-framed modular homes, equipped with American appliances and saunas. It ships the homes to suburban Moscow with all the required parts for assembly. Included with the shipment are three American assemblers. The homes are part of a joint venture between a Connecticut firm and the Russian cooperative Rosinka to provide a planned townhouse community for Western executives working in Moscow.[3]

The mode in which a company produces and distributes its products or services determines how it is described. For example, if a company manufactures in Japan and markets within the U.S., it may be described as "foreign" within the U.S. If, however, it is manufacturing in multiple markets, then it is described as "international."

There are different levels of "international." If a company operates in several countries, adjusting its products and practices to each, it is described as multinational. Michael Porter refers to these companies as "multi-domestic."[4] If a company such as Sony or Rolex offers a standardized product across all markets, it is described as a "global" company. Marketing in the 1990s has taken on a global perspective. "International" marketing has been based on differences among consumers in regional and national markets; "global" marketing assumes similarities among consumers in regional and national markets.

According to marketing theory, a key decision for the larger company is where to operate on the global marketing continuum. In order to make these decisions, the corporation needs to gather a large amount of data. The major steps in information gathering lead from macroeconomic analysis of the world economy to developing a specific marketing plan for the firm. We will look at these steps and the information needed for the decisions.

- Step 1: General Information
  External Environment—World Economy
- Step 2: Country Information
  Economic Environment—Country Economy
- Step 3: Specific Information
  Market Environment—Industry Economy
- Step 4: The Marketing Plan

ENVIRONMENTAL SCANNING

World Economy

The first step for a company should be to perform macroeconomic research. The global researcher is concerned with general issues about the movement of goods between countries and must answer the following questions:

> *What goods does the country trade and to whom does it trade them?*
>
> *What is the country's attitude toward trade?*
>
> *To what international trade agreements is the country a party?*
>
> *How stable is the country's currency?*
>
> *What is the global influence of the company's home country?*

Macroeconomics is concerned with aggregate data for a country, such as total population or national income. It analyzes the overall economic activity of a country, not the activity of individual companies, industries, or segments of the population. The data sources for this macro-level research are described in Chapters 13 and 15.

Economic Environment: Domestic Economy of the Host

The economic and cultural characteristics of the host country have been referred to as "uncontrollables." These are the conditions with which companies planning to undertake international marketing must contend. The company's decision that the country is not suitable as a host, that it requires adaptation, or that it can be addressed with standardized marketing factors will result from collected and analyzed data.

The economic features of the potential host country can be divided into several categories:

- Market size
- Market potential
- Market resources
- Market activity
- Infrastructure
- Urbanization

Market Size: Population Size and Distribution

While the Triad—the United States, Western Europe, and Japan—dominates the world trading market, there are many other potential markets. The U.S. International Trade Administration is focusing on what it calls the "Big Emerging Markets" of Asia and Latin America. The United Nations had 186 members in 1995. The 1996 *U.S. Statistical Abstract* World Population Table listed 193 countries and 35 additional "Areas of Special Sovereignty." A global company such as Singer sells sewing machines in over 150 countries.

Population is the most obvious indicator of market size. According to data from the *U.S. Statistical Abstract*, there were over 40 countries with populations of less than one million in 1995, the smallest country having a population of 10,000. There were under 40 countries with populations greater than the world's largest city, Tokyo. In 1995 more than half the world's population lived in six countries. By 2000, 90% of the world's population will live in 40 countries.

Age distribution is another market indicator. Statistics show that 40% of the population of developing countries is under 15 but only 20% of the population in industrial countries is under 15. Table 9.A illustrates the aging of the population in the EU.

TABLE 9.A

EU POPULATION BY AGE GROUP (%)

	0–19	20–59	≥60
1960	31.8	52.8	15.4
1990	25.5	54.9	19.6
2020	21.6	52.8	25.7

Source: Europe in Figures, 4th ed., published by Statistical Office of the European Communities (1995): 142.

Population density and distribution is a third indicator of market size. There are, for example, 1,750 people per square mile in Bangladesh but only 7 people per square mile in Canada. Most of Canada's population is concentrated along the U.S. border.

Market Potential: Income Factors

Market potential research seeks to discover the data that will tell a company how many people in a country are able to buy its product or service.

Per capita income, such as disposable income or GDP per person, is one way of measuring market potential. Other measures use the family or the household as the unit of measurement. How comparable are such measurements among countries? Countries' statistical definitions of "family" or "household" may differ. The accuracy of official economic statistics become suspect if a country has a large underground economy or if many "free" government services are provided to the population.

In addition to per capita measures, total GNP/GDP and total population are also important for understanding a market. A country with a large population and low per capita income (India, for example) will have a larger number of people in more affluent segments than a small rich country like the United Arab Emirates. Table 9.B compares population and GDP per capita for India and the United Arab Emirates.

TABLE 9.B

POPULATION AND GDP PER CAPITA FOR INDIA AND UNITED ARAB EMIRATES

	India	United Arab Emirates
Population	920 million (1994e)	2.23 million (1994e)
GDP	$294 billion (1995e)	$39.91 billion (1994)
GDP per Capita	$328 (1995e)	$16,549 (1994)
Population per square mile	787 (1993)	82 (1993)

Sources: EIU Reports, 1995/96 on LEXIS-NEXIS Services *Statistical Abstract* CD-ROM.

Income distribution measurements should be used in conjunction with the income figure. A study conducted in many countries on the relationship between the percent of income held by the richest 40% of the population and the country's per capita GDP showed no statistical relationship.[5]

One source of income distribution figures is *Social Indicators of Development (SID),* an annual published by the World Bank. For example, a non-Spanish company planning to market a summer camp to Spanish parents could use *SID* to find income distribution figures for Spain. *SID* shows that the top 10% of Spanish households hold 25% of the income; the top 20% have 40% of the income, while the bottom 40% have only 19% of the income. This leaves the middle class (the middle 40%) with 41% of the income. In 1994 the GNP per household in Spain was $9,150, compared with an EU average of $18,840. Exhibit 9.1 shows that over the past generation a slight movement toward a more equitable distribution has taken place in Spain.

Information about *SID* and other World Bank products may be found at http://www.worldbank.org.

Latin American Market Planning Handbook (published annually by Strategy Research) is a source of income distribution data. In the brief extract in Exhibit 9.2, a "buying power per household figure" is

Social Indicators of Development Spain

	Unit of measure	1970–1975	1980–1985	Most Recent Estimate 1988–93	1995 Same region/income group High Income
INCOME					
Household Income	% of income				
Share top 20% households	"	44	40	37	"
Share bottom 40%	"	17	19	22	"
Share bottom 20%	"	6	7	8	"

EXTRACT FROM *SOCIAL INDICATORS OF DEVELOPMENT*

■ EXHIBIT 9.1

Source: Social Indicators of Development (1995): 319.

3.3 Urban Households & Percent Distribution by Socioeconomic Status—Selected Countries 1996(e)

	Socioeconomic Status A	B	C	D/E	Total Country Households
Brazil—Households	719,250	4,603,200	8,343,300	15,104,250	28,770,000
Distribution	2.5%	16.0%	29.0%	52,5%	
Buying Power per HH	$137,571	$25,518	$10,710	$2,610	$11,998
Brasilia—Buying Power	244,876	47,463	17,564	4,288	63,495
Distribution	17.2%	32.4%	29.0%	21.4%	
Venezuela—Households	52,353	172,018	1,346,230	2,168,926	3,739,528
Distribution	1.40%	4.60%	36.00%	58.00%	
Buying Power per HH	$116,206	$58,238	$12,922	$3,125	10,771
Rural—Buying Power	66,026	37,094	4,751	1,894	5,440

1996(e) buying power per urban household $US

INCOME DISTRIBUTION IN LATIN AMERICA

■ EXHIBIT 9.2

Source: Extracted from *Latin American Market Planning Handbook, 1996,* Strategy Research Corporation. Reprinted with permission.

calculated. The difference in number of households, buying power, and percent for Brazil and Venezuela illustrate differences in countries' income distribution patterns. The top two categories comprise 18.5% of the households in Brazil, while in Venezuela, the same income categories comprise only 6% of the households. Also notice that the income for Group A is over five times that for Group B for Brazil but not quite two times for Venezuela. A brief newsletter, *Inside Strategy,* comes with a purchase of the *Handbook.* Information about Strategy Research may be found at http://205.161.216.531.

Economist Intelligence Unit (EIU) *Country Profiles* and *Country Reports* and the International Trade Administration (ITA) *Market Reports* sometimes include distribution data. A few individual countries publish their own statistics. For example, a rich source of general market-related statistical data is in the annual *Report on the Survey of Personal Income Distribution in Taiwan Area of the Republic of China.* This government source has income distribution and average disposable income by household by quintile, as well as regional data and household ownership of products. In the 1991 edition of the *Report,* for example, there were 136.68 motor bikes owned per hundred households when the head of the household was a laborer from the Taiwan area.

Social Trends, from the U.K. Office of National Statistics, formerly the Central Statistical Office, is another rich source of data. It has an entire section on Income and Wealth. For example, it has income distribution figures by type of household, distribution of wealth, and gross domestic product by region. Further information on ONS and availability of data can be found at http://www.ons.gov.uk.

Finally, the sales of some goods are not related to income, as witnessed in the worldwide appeal of Coke and Pepsi.

Indicators of Market Size has been published for over 30 years, first as an annual publication by Business International and since 1993 as an August issue of Economist Intelligence Unit's *Crossborder Monitor.* The publication calculates Indexes of Market Size, Market Intensity, and Market Growth. According to this measure, the United States has 20% of the world market, followed by China and Japan. The Market Intensity Index measures the richness of the market or the degree of concentrated purchasing power it represents. The world value is set at 1.00. In 1993, the Index for North America was 5.05, for Western Europe 3.21, and for Asia 0.52. Russia had the largest five-year decrease in growth, while EIU's figures gave Mexico the largest five-year growth increase. The 1996 edition included 115 countries.

Market Resources: Economic Geography

Topography, climate, and the presence of natural resources are all important market factors, especially in developing countries. The U.S. Department of the Interior publishes reports on mineral resources worldwide, which are compiled in the *Minerals Yearbook.* Country reports mentioned in Chapter 13 or any encyclopedia provide basic information on a country's economic geography. For example, the *Walden Reports* on LEXIS-NEXIS Services have sections for "Geography and Climate" and "Raw Materials and Natural Resources."

Market Activity: Agricultural vs. Industrial vs. Service

In evaluating a country's potential, the relationship among the three economic sectors and the rate of change that is occurring is another market indicator. The usual pattern of development is agriculture to industry to service.

Infrastructure

The business infrastructure will have serious implications for the distribution of goods or services. Data on the following aspects of the infrastructure are often needed:

* Modes of transportation to move goods
* Communications—telecommunications, fax, Internet
* Energy—supply, cost
* Commercial infrastructure—banks, accounting firms, insurance companies, advertising agencies, market research support services
* Technology—computers, networking, robotics

Urbanization

The degree of urbanization is another measure of a country's potential demand for goods and services. Highly urbanized countries usually have a higher per capita income, and cities have a higher per capita income than rural areas. For example, in Thailand, the 1989 per capita income in Bangkok was $3,700, while in the rural Northeast part of the country, it was $470.[6] According to more recent data from Thai Farmers Bank, incomes in Bangkok are now around 12 times those in the five poorest rural Thai provinces. According to the World Bank, 68% of rural Filipinos live in poverty, double the proportion in urban areas.[7]

The United Nations Department of Economic and Social Information Policy Analysis, Population Division, tracks urbanization and the growth of the world's largest cities in its biennial *World Urbanization Prospects.* Some examples of the movement toward urbanization are presented in Table 9.C. For example, in 1970, 36.6% of the world's people lived in urbanized areas. The figure was 44.8% in 1994 and is projected to be 61.1% by the year 2025. Table 9.C shows selected urbanization patterns by world and regions.

TABLE 9.C			
PROSPECTS OF WORLD URBANIZATION			
	Percent Urbanized		
	1970	1994	2025
World	36.6	44.8	61.1
More Developed Regions	67.5	74.7	84.0
Australia-New Zealand	84.4	84.9	89.1
North America	73.8	76.1	84.8
Europe	64.4	73.3	83.2
Less Developed Regions	25.1	37.0	57.0
Latin America	57.4	73.7	84.7
Africa	23.0	33.4	53.8
Asia except Japan	21.0	32.4	54.0
Least Developed Regions	12.6	21.9	43.5

Source: World Urbanization Prospect, 1994 Revision (copyright 1995): 20, 21, 23.

Cultural and Lifestyle Data

Serious marketing mistakes have been made when companies have failed to consider the lifestyles and culture of the countries to which they market. For example, one U.S. firm introduced cake mix into Japan with an advertising campaign saying it was as easy as making rice. However, Japanese housewives take pride in their rice and do not perceive rice as easy to prepare.

When seeking information about a country's culture and lifestyles, researchers should consider these factors:

- Material culture
- Language
- Education
- Religion
- Ethics and values
- Social organization

Material Culture

Material culture includes technology, manufacturing processes, and durable goods ownership. Manufacturing processes in developing countries are labor intensive. The availability of electricity, refrigeration, and stoves are related to the manufacturing process, with the availability of media, storage facilities, and transport related directly to the marketing function.

Language

Language affects many aspects of marketing; in particular, brand names, packaging, and promotion. It is also a consideration in designing surveys and questionnaires. The importance of language on marketing is discussed throughout the following chapters.

Education

Education levels and systems are indicators of the quality of the potential work force. In many countries, learning is by rote. Some countries have good systems of technical education. Companies were interested in the former Eastern European countries as sites for foreign ventures because of the availability of a well educated labor force. Education is also an important factor in analyzing the potential consumer.

Religion

Religion affects behavior well beyond traditional holidays and well-known consumption taboos. For example, Strohs developed non-alcoholic beer for the Saudi Arabian market, where the large Muslim majority of the population is forbidden by their religion to consume alcohol. Social structure, such as castes and the role of women, is often related to religious

practices. Religion plays an important role in many societies. For example, while U.S. researchers find little readily available government data about religious behavior, researchers on religious behavior in Thailand can use the Thai government's *Report of the Cultural Activity Participation and Times Use Survey 1990*, which contains primarily data about Thai religious activities.

Ethics and Values

Ethics and values vary; many countries, for instance, view selling as a suspect occupation. Companies developing sales forces in these countries have to be prepared to offer incentives to workers. Officials in some countries expect "incentives" to facilitate a deal, a practice that is illegal under U.S. law.

Social Organization

Social organization includes the composition of the family unit, family compounds, neighborhoods, or tribes. In addition, every culture has its special-interest groups, defined by religion, occupation, and recreational lifestyles. Class, still important in many cultures; age; and again, the role of women are all factors that need to be measured.

Political and Legal Environment: Home, Host, and International

Even if the economic and social conditions in a country are right for a venture, certain political issues should be considered. These issues include the general political climate of the country and its prevailing system of laws and regulations.

Political Climate

Political climate addresses such questions as "How compatible is a company's activities with the interests of the host country?" or "How important is national sovereignty?" If a product, such as oil, is too important to national interests, it may not be left in the hands of foreigners and may be nationalized. The *Walden Country Reports* from Walden Publications Ltd. were a good source for lists of the largest nationalized companies in a country and their primary industries. The *Walden Country Reports* are also on LEXIS-NEXIS Services. Privatization rather than nationalization has been the trend in the late 1990s. Researchers now need to know which countries are encouraging foreign activities in privatization and what industries are being privatized.

Another aspect of political climate is the stability of government and the assessment of the *political risk* associated with doing business in the country. Some sources concerned with political risk are described in Chapter 13.

The relationship between the host country and home country is another factor affecting assessment of political climate. Are the two countries friendly? Do they belong to the same treaty organizations? If your home country is Switzerland, your ability to function successfully in the international arena is very different than if your home country is Cuba.

Laws and Regulations

The effect of a country's legal environment on international marketing practice is similar to the law's effect on accounting practice, which we discussed in Chapter 2. Some countries, such as the U.S. and the U.K., are common law countries; the countries on the European continent, such as France or Germany, are code law countries. Legal trade restrictions may take the form of tariffs, currency restrictions, exchange rate controls, and operational restrictions such as percent of foreign ownership or production quotas. Other legal considerations are patents, trademarks, brands, packaging, and labeling.

In the U.S., there are export controls on destinations and products; Internal Revenue Service rulings on transfer prices; and antitrust considerations on acquisitions, joint ventures, or marketing agreements that affect a company's action in the U.S. or abroad.

SOURCES FOR COUNTRY MARKET INFORMATION

Comprehensive publications about individual countries are the best sources for global scanning. Many commercial publishers offer country reports that provide current information about many of the social, political, and legal issues relating to marketing. Other sources for this type of information are the publications of international banks and accounting firms.

Economist Intelligence Unit (EIU)

The Economist Intelligence Unit, since it purchased Business International, has the most extensive range of country products. It established EIU Electronic Publishing to market its products on a variety of electronic media: CD-ROM, online, WWW, LAN feed, fax delivery, and microform from UMI. Some products resemble their print equivalents while others are customized to meet individual user group needs. Though designed for the economist or political analyst, EIU quarterly *Country Reports* and annual *Country Profiles* have obvious applications for the marketer. There are *Reports* and *Profiles* for 180 countries, each

with the same format and content. A sample table of contents, from *Country Report Mexico*, follows:

Table of Contents

Summary: Mexico—Nth Quarter 199X
Political Structure
Economic Structure
Outlook
Political Scene
Economic Policy
The Economy
Agriculture, Oil & Mining
Manufacturing
Foreign Trade and Payments
Appendix: Quarterly Indicators of Economic Activity in Mexico
Appendix: Trade of Mexico with Major Trading Partners
Appendix: Direction of Mexico's Foreign Trade

Annual *Country Profiles* have additional content, with sections on Population and Society, National Accounts, Tourism, and Money and Banking. *Profiles* also contain bibliographies that include newspapers, central bank publications, and publications from international organizations such as OECD.

More specific business applications are found in EIU's *Investing, Licensing and Trading Conditions Abroad.* A list of EIU country products follows (asterisked items are former Business International titles):

*Business Africa**
*Business Asia**
*Business China**
*Business Eastern Europe**
*Business Europe**
*Business Latin America**
Business Middle East
Business Reports
Business Russia
Business South Asia
China Hand
Country Forecasts
Country Profiles
Country Reports
Country Risk Service
*Cross Border Monitor**
EIU ViewsWire
European Trends
*Financing Foreign Operations**
*Investing, Licensing & Trading Conditions Abroad**
World Outlook
World Trade Report
*Worldwide Regulatory Update**

TABLE 9.D

AVAILABILITY OF EIU PUBLICATIONS

System	File	Start Date	Countries	Titles	Update
DIALOG	VW 620	January 1989	180	13	Weekly
	Country 627	January 1989	180	1	Daily
	Risk 628	January 1989	58	4	Weekly
	News 629	January 1989	180	13	Weekly
	Industry 768	October 1996	64		
Lexis-Nexis	WORLD ASIAPC, etc.	January 1987	180	23	Weekly
FT Profile	EIU	1993	180	23/9*	Weekly
	EIU Industry	1985	180	9	Weekly
Corporate Profound		Country 1989	13		
Reuters Business Briefing	EIU	Current	40	1**	As changes occur
Bloomberg	EIU	Current	***	4	As changes occur
MARKINTEL		Industry 1992		9	Weekly
		Country 1992	35	5	
DIALOG OnDisc		Regional Business Intelligence	98	varies	7 discs
SilverPlatter		Country Reports	180	2	6 discs
CDs and WWW		Country Forecasts	58	1	5 discs
		Business Newsletters		8	1 disc

*   Industry research reports also included
++   Extracts from EIU ViewsWire
*** Four special titles: *Economic Overviews* (81 countires); *Foreign Exchange and Trade Controls* (41 countries), *Tax Regulations* (41 countries) and *Currency Consensus Forecasts* (45 countries)

Source: EIU.

Access to EIU is media independent. Whatever your choice of access, EIU is there. EIU titles are available through most major databanks, as shown in Table 9.D. In November 1996, EIU split its one file on DIALOG, File 627, into four files: File 620 *EIU ViewsWire*, daily business news; File 627 *EIU: Country Analysis*, country reports; File 628 *EIU: Country Risk and Forecasts*, providing country risk ratings; and 629 *EIU: Business Newsletters*, the former Business International publications. EIU was added to DataStar in the fall of 1997.

EIU has also loaded tailored packages of databases on the WWW. *TradeWire* is a joint venture with I-Trade, a subscription service at http://www.i-trade.com. Selected EIU publications are also available through Internet Securities, a WWW-based subscription product dealing only with emerging markets (http://www.securities.com).

Investing, Licensing and Trading and *Country Risk Service* are being added to the SilverPlatter lineup. EIU titles are also available through FT's end-user Discovery product. It is delivered to the desktop via NewsEdge, and on Lotus Notes. A niche initiative is adding *Risk Service* to Bureau van Dijk's *BankScope* CD-ROM.

Other Country Services

Other country services are available in print, online, and on CD-ROM as well. Table 9.E lists the range of reports available electronically. Most also have print equivalents.

For a complete discussion of EIU and the other country reports, see "As the World Turns," in *Database* (April 1995). We also describe some of these reports in Chapter 13.

Culturgrams (published annually by the David M. Kennedy Center)

Libraries that need a compilation of cultural characteristics of countries might consider *Culturgrams*, four-page summaries for 143 countries. *Culturgrams* are published by the David M. Kennedy Center for International Studies, at Brigham Young University. They are available in two books, one covering the Americas and Europe, the other covering Africa, Asia, and Oceania. For libraries not requiring the entire set,

TABLE 9.E

ELECTRONIC COUNTRY REPORTS

Provider	Product	Availability
ABC/Clio	*KCWD/Kaleidoscope*	LEXIS-NEXIS
	EXEGY	CD-ROM
Abecor and member banks	*Country Research Reports*	LEXIS-NEXIS
Bank of America	*World Information Services Forecasts, Risk, Outlook*	LEXIS-NEXIS
Business Briefing Pub.	*Business Monitor*	LEXIS-NEXIS
Political Risk Services (IBC)	*Intl Country Risk Guide*	LEXIS-NEXIS, CD-ROM
	Political Risk Letter	Asia Intelligence Wire http://www.polrisk.com
	Country Report Services	DATASTAR http://www.countrydata.com
MarketLine	*CountryLine*	DATASTAR, FT, PROFOUND
Walden Publishing	*Walden Reports*	LEXIS-NEXIS, Asia Intelligence Wire
U.S. Dept of State	*Country Commercial Reports*	NTDB CD, STAT-USA
U.S. CIA	*World Fact Book*	NTDB CD, STAT-USA, LEXIS-NEXIS

Source: Ruth A. Pagell, "As the World Turns: Electronic 'Country' Publications," *Database* April/May 1995.

the *Culturgrams* are also available in loose-leaf format. For smaller libraries needing annual country background information focusing on culture, these publications are a best buy. An entire set, either in loose-leaf or bound format, costs $105 retail and $70 for educational usage. The *Culturgrams* are also on the *Encarta* CD-ROM. Cultural characteristics include religion, general attitudes, personal appearance, greetings, gestures, visiting, eating, family, dating, diet, and recreation. For example, under "Gestures" in the entry on Thailand, the reader is informed that body posture and physical gestures are extremely important, noting that it is offensive to cross one's legs. Information about *Culturgrams* and a sample are available at http://www.byu.edu/culturgrams.

Country Reports from the U.S. Government

The U.S. government has a wide range of sources useful for international marketing. A summary of each is offered in the *Basic Guide to Exporting*. These government sources include export statistics, country reports, and industry reports. Many are available through the Commerce Department's widely publicized *National Trade Data Bank*, accessible on CD-ROM or on STAT-USA, the fee-based Internet site for U.S. government information. Individual reports can be purchased from US&FCS (US & Foreign Commercial Services) District Offices.

The U.S. government had published two country level series used widely by marketers. These were *Foreign Economic Trends and Their Implications for the United States (FET)* and *Overseas Business Reports (OBR)*. These have been replaced by a new series, *Country Commercial Guides*.

Country Commercial Guides (U.S. Department of Commerce, International Trade Administration)

Country Commercial Guides are published for a wide range of countries and incorporate the type of information found in both the *FETs* and *OBRs*. The table of contents from the 1996 *Guide* for China listed the following topics:

- Executive Summary
- Marketing U.S. Products and Services
- Political Environment
- Investment Climate
- Business Travel
- Trade and Project Financing
- Trade Regulations and Standards
- Leading Sectors for U.S. Exports & Investments
- U.S. and Country Contacts
- Trade Event Schedule

A *Guide* will answer many questions relating to a country's marketing infrastructure. In addition, it has specific marketing background and information, including names of local market research firms and the availability of advertising media. Though prepared by a U.S. government agency, the information in the *Guides* is of value to anyone interested in doing business in the country. In addition to print distribution, *Country Commercial Guides* are part of the Market Report series on the *National Trade Data Bank* CD-ROM and through the fee-based STAT-USA on the World Wide Web. They may be purchased in hard copy or on diskette from NTIS, the National Technical Information Service (http://www.stat-usa.gov).

International Organizations

The United Nations, World Bank, and the International Monetary Fund publish a wealth of data and information useful for marketing. An example is the IMF's *Exchange Arrangements and Restrictions*. Other sources of valuable information are publications from intergovernmental organizations such as the Organization for Economic Cooperation and Development (OECD); the European Union (EU); the Food and Agricultural Organization (FAO); the International Labor Organization (ILO); and the World Trade Organization (WTO), formerly General Agreement on Tariffs and Trade (GATT). Many of these sources are described in Chapter 13.

Some of the statistical sources are also available electronically, on CD-ROM, on diskette, or through remote access. At the beginning of 1997, the percentage of data from these organizations available on the WWW was still limited, and the trend seems to be for the organizations to offer fee-based subscription services for in-depth data access.

In addition to compiling data, the United Nations Department for Economic and Social Information and Policy Analysis, Population Division, published a textual analysis of the world's largest cities, *The Challenge of Urbanization: The World's Largest Cities* (1995). Each city profile is two to four pages long and covers demographic characteristics, economy, infrastructure, social services, and planning issues. A bibliography of data sources and articles on each city is also presented.

Additional sources of marketing information can be found in the publications of the following groups:

- Business and trade associations
- Chambers of commerce
- National Foreign Trade Council (an association of American companies doing business abroad)
- Foreign trade associations (at least 50 in the U.S.)
- World Trade Organizations (country-level member of World Trade Association)
- Service organizations—banks, transportation companies, accounting firms, and advertising firms

Two excellent comprehensive articles, "Electronic Sources of European Economic and Business Statistics," appeared in the 1996 February and March issues of *European Business Intelligence Briefing*. The articles, written by David Mort of Information Research Network, which offers a fee-based data service, Interstat, contain an annotated list of sources with contact information. Many of the sources cited here are useful for Chapter 13 as well.

Gale's *World Business Directory* lists World Trade Centers in each country. The World Trade Centers Association Inc. is an international organization of trade service and facility providers with locations worldwide. These centers are designed to encourage international trade and provide information on business opportunities. A list of these centers may be found at http://wtca.org.

Measures of Country Risk

Whether you are doing research for a small business or a large investment bank, country risk is an important parameter in deciding if a country is a suitable partner. A full discussion of country risk appears in Chapter 13.

The annual *World Competitiveness Yearbook* and *Euromoney's* semi-annual report on country risk are two publications that can be used to assess economies for the reliability of their market potential. The *World Competitiveness Yearbook* from the Lausanne International Institute for Management Development and the World Economic Forum (IMD, Geneva, Switzerland) calls international competitiveness the ability of a country "to proportionately generate more wealth than its competitors in world markets." You will find some information from the *Yearbook* at http://www.imd.ch. *Euromoney* ranks countries on nine categories grouped as analytical indicators, credit indicators, and market indicators. Luxembourg was least risky on the *Euromoney* list. The *Euromoney* indicators and list are available on the WWW at http://www.emwl.com.

Table 9.F lists the most stable countries from both sources.

TABLE 9.F		
WORLD'S MOST STABLE ECONOMIES		
World Competitiveness Yearbook 10 Most Competitive Economies (1996)	*Euromoney* Least Risky Countries	
	(March 1996)	(Sept 1991)
1 United States	5	7
2 Singapore	3	13
3 Hong Kong		
4 Japan	4	1
5 Switzerland	2	8
6 Germany	7	11
7 Netherlands	6	14
8 New Zealand		
9 Denmark		
10 Norway	11	9

THE INTERNATIONAL FOUR P's

Once a company has decided *where* to operate (the market), it must then determine *what* (product) to offer to *whom* (the consumer). Although internal company information and policy play the most important role in creating the marketing plan for the four P's (product, price, place, and promotion), secondary data are also consulted. Borden's ice cream and cheese operations in Japan is an example of a company that did not research the four P's, placing too much emphasis on brand name, misjudging the yen/dollar price relationship, failing to maintain its distribution chain, and underspending on advertising.

Product

A product can be described by size, shape, color, special features, and options. Listed below are some of the features most affected by international marketing:

- Adaptation
- Brands and Trademarks
- Patents
- Labeling and Standards
- Warranties
- Service
- Product life cycle

Adaptation

A company can standardize by selling the same product worldwide, adapt by making minor or major adjustments, or localize by developing different products for each country. Coke is as an example of a global brand with minor adjustments to local taste. For example, Thai Coke is sweeter than U.S. Coke, and the international game of football (soccer), rather than U.S. football, is used in non-U.S. Coke commercials. Luxury goods such as Rolex watches are the same worldwide. Some beer, such as Heineken, is available worldwide, but almost every country has its own brand of local beer, such as Singha in Thailand or Zagorka in Bulgaria.

Brands and Trademarks

Brands identify and differentiate a product or service, communicate a message to the consumer, and are a piece of legal property. Brands are treated as assets on balance sheets (goodwill) and are important in merger and acquisitions valuations.

Brands that are successful in one market are increasingly likely to have appeal to consumers internationally because of:

- Improved communications
- Increased travel
- Greater use of English language
- Similarity of consumer tastes
- Impact of television

International brands provide cohesion to international companies. Local brands may fragment the international company. Even companies in niche markets can be successful using a global brand name; for example, Crabtree & Evelyn.

Brands also fall into the category of intellectual property rights along with trademarks, copyright, and patents. Many sources use the words "brand" and "trademark" interchangeably. The trademark is a distinctive word, symbol, design, combination of letters or numbers, or other device that identifies and distinguishes a product or services in the marketplace. The trademark consists of two parts, the name (brand) and the physical design that appears on the product. In the U.S., trademarks are registered with the U.S. Patent and Trademark Office or a state government. Until 1989, a trademark could only be registered in the United States after it had been on the market. Now a trademark may be registered with an "intent to use." In many other countries a brand name itself can be registered, even if it is not used. There is a cost to register a brand in each country.

In an attempt to harmonize trademark law, on October 28, 1994, the Trademark Law Treaty (TLT) was concluded among members of the World Intellectual Property Organization (WIPO). The treaty was signed by 36 states and a further three states signed at the end of 1994. According to Article 2, the TLT applies to marks relating to goods (trademarks) or services (service marks) consisting of visible signs. The treaty must be ratified by each signatory country. In January 1996, the European Union introduced a Community Trade Mark, a single mark that will be protected throughout the EU. More information is available from the EU Office of Harmonization, http://www.europa.eu.int/agencies/ohim/ohim.htm.

Kodak is an example of a trademark that is registered internationally. Kodak machines and processes are patented, Kodak artwork on packages is protected by copyright, and the shape of a container may be protected by design trademark.

The multinational company has to weigh the costs of registering its trademarks in many countries against the threat from pirates who will register it themselves. Before mid-1991, Indonesian companies could legally register trademarks that were well-known outside Indonesia for themselves.

Another important trademark issue is language. Should the brand name be registered in English, translated, or transliterated—or do you even have a choice? For example, in China, trademarks must be registered in the Chinese language. About half are translated, the other half transliterated. Companies are advised to use one name in all Chinese-speaking jurisdictions, including the PRC, Hong Kong, Taiwan, and Singapore. They are also advised to develop a Chinese equivalent of a foreign mark that is phonetically similar to the original mark while, at the same time, descriptive of the function or benefits of the product. Perhaps the best example of this is the Chinese trademark for Coca-Cola. Not only is the Chinese version (pronounced "ke kou ke le" in Putonghua) very close in sound to the original mark, but the characters mean "tasty, happiness producing."[8]

International Brands and Their Companies (Gale, 1995–96)

This is the international companion to *Brands and Their Companies,* formerly titled *Gale Trade Names Dictionary.* First published in 1989 as *International Trade Names Dictionary*, this nonauthoritative source is designed for the personal user. Information comes from other published sources, not government offices. There is at least one brand from each of 130 countries worldwide, including Eastern Europe. Arrangement is alphabetical by brand name with cross reference to the company marketing the product and its address.

The primary role of both *International Brands* and its U.S. counterpart, is to locate the company producing a consumer brand. However, it may serve the international marketer as a preliminary guide to trade names already in use.

An electronic version of *International Brands and Their Companies* and *Brands and Their Companies* is on DIALOG as part of File 116, *Trade Names Database.* An entry includes the trade name, product, company, address and phone number, and the source publication. There were over 80,000 international entries in 1996. The *Trade Names Database* can be used to answer such questions as:

> Are there any products from China with international brands?
>
> What unique toothpaste brands are sold in Southeast Asia?
>
> What company owns the rights to the shampoo Timotei?

World's Greatest Brands (Interbrand, McMillan Business, 1996)

In late 1996, Interbrand published its second edition of *World's Greatest Brands,* rating 350 brands out of an original 1,000 potential brands. Interbrand scored brands against four criteria: brand weight or market dominance; brand length, or extension beyond its original category; brand breadth across demographic markets; and brand depth or customer commitment to the brand. An overall score was computed for each brand. Summary findings are in the *Economist,* November 16, 1996.[9] *Advertising Age's* issues on brands are discussed more fully in Chapter 11.

Electronic Access to Trademarks

Two databanks offer worldwide access to international trademark registrations: Questel-Orbit and DIA-LOG. Both provide software for image retrieval. Questel-Orbit has the most complete set of trademarks and patents. The trademarks are on the Questel system. Compu-Mark is the source for most of the files. Files include image drawings. FMARK, the French trademark database, is produced by the Institut National de la Propriete Industrielle (INPI). The electronic file precedes publication by three weeks. INPI also produces the international file. Questel-Orbit is preparing its own U.S. trademark file for release.

DIALOG has had TRADEMARKSCAN, a trademark of Thomson & Thomson, for many years. Thomson & Thomson is a major supplier of trademark information and research in the United States. Thomson also partners with Compu-Mark for international files and with IntelPro for Canadian files. These files have been added to DIALOG. The Compu-Mark files include the trademarks filed with the World Intellectual Property Organization. DIALOG and Compu-Mark are also adding Madrid Protocol records to the DIALOG databases. Madrid Protocol is an international filing system under the auspices of WIPO. The protocol, which went into effect in April 1996, makes it possible to file a single, national trademark application with an office of origin and to subsequently designate any of the other contracting parties for trademark protection. Presently, 12 countries have ratified the protocol. Table 9.G lists the trademark files available on Questel-Orbit and DIALOG.

The U.S. DIALOG files are also available as a *DIALOG OnDisc* CD-ROM. The databases display, for users with the proper software, the actual design as well as identifying the company. Any trademark that is officially registered in the countries covered by the database, regardless of the home country of the registrant, is listed. TRADEMARKSCAN can answer the following kinds of questions:

TABLE 9.G

TRADEMARK FILES ON QUESTEL-ORBIT AND DIALOG

COUNTRY	FORMAT	COVER-AGE	LANG	START DATE	QUESTEL LABEL	DIALOG FILE
Austria	ST	N,I	E,GE		OSMARK	WIPO 662
Benelux	FT	N	E,F	1971	BEMARK	WIPO 658
	ST	I				
Denmark	FT	N	DA,E	1960	DKMARK	WIPO*659
France	M	N	F	1976	FMARK	WIPO*657
	Legal	N,EPO	F		JURINPI	
Germany	FT	N	EN,G	1894	DMARK	WIPO*672
	ST	I				
	Legal	N	G		JURGE	
Ireland	ST	N	E			676
Italy	FT	N,I	It,E		IMARK	673
Liechtenstein	ST	N	E,G	1973	LMARK	677
	FT	I				
Monaco	ST	N	E,F	1979	MOMARK	WIPO*663
	FT	I				
Switzerland	ST	N,I	E,G		SUMARK	WIPO 661
U.K.	FT	N	E	1876	UKMARK	T&T 126,WIPO*
Intl Register	M	WIPO	F		TMINT	WIPO*671
Canada	T&T	127				T&T 127
U.S. Federal	FT	N	E		USMARK +	T&T 226
U.S. State						T&T 246

* Madrid Protocol records being phased in starting Dec. 1996.
ST = Short Text   N = National
FT = Full Text   I = International
M = Mixed   EPO = European
+ To be added to QUESTEL-ORBIT

Source: QUESTEL-ORBIT, July 1996, and DIALOG, December 1996.

What Thai foods are registered in the U.S.?

What are the registered trademarks for Canadian toothpaste?

In what countries is the brand name Timotei registered?

A record includes the name and description of the design; product classification; status, from pending through abandoned; name and address of the application; registration in the country of origin; dates it was used; where it is used; legal representative in U.K. or Canada; and registration number and type. Exhibit 9.3 displays a record from *Trademarkscan-International Register.*

The International file and the files from Austria, Benelux, Germany, and Switzerland disclose data based on the International Register (World Intellectual Property Organization) records. WIPO records are enhanced with original registration information, current owner name, and location and goods/services description. The latter must be published in French. TRADEMARKSCAN Canada, File 127, added images in 1996.

Thomson & Thomson has an electronic version of *International Guide to Trademarks*, last issued in print in 1994, on its WWW site. The *Guide* covers over 130 countries. Updated information to these countries plus new information is available in print and on the WWW in *ClienT&Times*. Finally, Thomson & Thomson provides links to other information about trademarks and a subscription service (http://www.thomson-thomson.com).

Another electronic source for trademarks is on DataStar through D-S IMSMARQ TRADEMARK Focus. IMSMARQ provides the following country and date coverage:

Canada: 1867 to date
Great Britain: 1876 to date
International: 1893 to date
Denmark: 1880 to date
Sweden: 1985 to date
Finland: 1891 to date
Norway: 1911 to date

IMSMARQ also includes currently used pharmaceutical trademarks. Applications for these files are limited, since many include only the trademark name and number, classification, and type.

```
10389767
TIMOTEI et element figuratif (and Design)
INTL CLASS: 3 (Produits nettoyants, cosmetiques/
      Cosmetics and cleaning preparations)
STATUS: Enregistrement (Registered)
GOODS/SERVICES: 03 SAVONS; PARFUMERIE,
      HUILES ESSENTIELLES, COSMETIQUES,
      LOTIONS POUR LES CHEVEUX; DENTIFRICES.
REGISTRATION NUMBER: 644511
REGISTERED: 05 Octobre 1995 (October 5, 1995)
LAST FULL PUBLICATION: 19 Decembre 1995
      (December 19, 1995)
PUBLISHED IN: LMI 10 page 6530
EXPIRATION DATE: 05 Octobre 2015 (October 5, 2015)
DURATION: 20 YEARS
ORIGINAL REGISTRATION INFORMATION:...

PROTECTION CLAIMED: AL (ALBANIE / ALBANIA),
      AT (AUTRICHE /AUSTRIA)... TJ(TADJIKISTAN /
      TAJIKISTAN), MD (MOLDAVIE / MOLDOVA),
      KG (REPUBLIQUE KIRGHIZE / KYRGYZ
      REPUBLIC) VIENNA CODES: 2705
LAST REPORTED OWNER(S): UNILEVER N.V....
```

EXTRACT FROM *TRADEMARKSCAN—INTERNATIONAL REGISTER* (FILE 671)

EXHIBIT 9.3

Source: Trademarkscan-International Register on DIALOG, June 1, 1996. Reprinted with permission of Compu-Mark N.V.

Patents

Electronic patent files may have worldwide coverage, *Derwent World Patents Index*, for example; regional coverage, such as Questel-Orbit's EPAT; or single country coverage, such as the *Chinese Patent Abstracts* in English.

INPADOC/Family and Legal Status Database (International Patent Documentation Center, Vienna; DIALOG File 345, Orbit File INPADOC)

INPADOC contains patents issued by 55 countries and patenting organizations. *INPADOC* gives the title, inventor, and assignee for most patents. In addition, this file brings together information on priority application numbers, countries and dates, and equivalent patents (i.e., patent families) for patents issued by the same countries and organizations. Also, this file contains the legal status information of patents from eight individual countries, the European Patent Office, and the World Patent Office.

Derwent World Patents Index (Derwent Publications, Ltd.; DIALOG Files 350, 351; Questel-Orbit File WPIL)

Derwent World Patents Index provides access to information from over 12 million patent documents, giving details of over 3 million inventions from 34 patent-issuing authorities. Each record in the database describes a single "patent family" containing the data from the original "basic patent," as well as equivalent patents. Patent coverage begins in 1963 although the dates covered vary by country and by subject.

JAPIO (Japan Patent Information Organization; DIALOG File 347 and Questel-Orbit File JAPIO)

This database is based on the print *Patent Abstracts of Japan* and represents the most comprehensive English-language access to Japanese patents. The file contains approximately 4 million records from October 1976 to the present. Abstracts are provided for applications originating in Japan.

Chinese Patent Abstracts in English (Patent Documentation Service Center, People's Republic of China; DIALOG File 344 and Orbit File CHINAPATS)

Chinese Patent Abstracts in English is produced by the Patent Documentation Service Center of the People's Republic of China. The file includes all patents published in the People's Republic of China since April 1, 1985. Records contain the bibliographic information as well as English-language titles and abstracts where available.

PATENT, the patent library on LEXIS-NEXIS Services, covers U.S. patents. Searching the database can answer the question:

> *What Japanese patents on digital TV are filed in the United States?*

Questel-Orbit specializes in patent databases. The databank has more than 40 patent files and finding aids. Patent offices from the U.S., Europe, Japan, France, and WIPO supply the information. It provides free searching of U.S. patents and a WWW site containing links to international patent information: http://www.questel.orbit.com/patents. The European Patent Office maintains its own site at http://www.epo.co.at/epo/ with both free and fee-based information.

Labeling and Standards

Cultural issues affect product size, shape, and color, but labeling is mandated by local law and regional regulations. The EU has adopted legislation in the area of labeling. EU Directives and Regulations cover labeling of such products as hazardous substances, tobacco and smoking materials, food additives and food nutrition, and footwear. The export compendia discussed in Chapter 12 have general labeling provisions.

Country Commercial Guides (U.S. Department & Commerce, International Trade Administration) each have a chapter called "Trade Regulations and Standards." The chapter includes a section on standards, testing, labeling, and certification. For example, the Mexico *Guide* reports that according to a decree published in Mexico's Federal Register ("Diario Oficial") on March 7, 1994, effective the next day, all products sold in Mexico must bear a label in Spanish prior to being imported to Mexico. Products that must comply with NOMs (Normas Oficiales Mexicanas—product standards) must use labeling language specified in the NOM.

A compilation of standards is provided in a CD-ROM, *Standards Infodisk*. In addition to extensive U.S. standards authorities, the disk includes standards from over 30 international, regional, and country standards authorities. You can freely search for the existence of standards on the WWW at http://www.iso.ch, but there is a charge to actually view a standard. A list of European standards organizations is available on the Europages WWW site, http://www.europages.com.

Warranties

Warranties or guarantees are generally considered part of the product description. For example, the warranties for General Motors vehicles vary internationally from 3 months/2400 miles to 24 months/unlimited miles. Labeling, warranties, and gradings in the U.S. are available in a 1993 book from Gale, *Consumers' Guide to Product Grades and Terms*. This is *not* a legal source and was compiled primarily to provide information for the consumer in anticipation of new 1994 U.S. labeling laws. There is no international equivalent.

Service

There are several alternatives for servicing an international product including offering no service, local service providers, local distributors who may offer training and parts, and direct on-site service.

Product Life Cycle

When introducing a product into another country, companies consider where the product is in its international product life cycle. A product typically goes through a life cycle consisting of introduction, maturity, and decline. Products are usually introduced first in highly industrialized countries and later in less industrialized countries. When a product has saturated its market in one country and is in decline, it may be transferred to another country in a different product life stage. An example is the microwave oven. Microwave ovens dropped in sales value and volume in the U.S. between 1990 and 1994, while increasing in emerging markets.

Price

Pricing an item for the international market is a complex issue. Many of the sources of information required for this decision are internal to the company. There is no comprehensive source that provides prices for specific manufactured and consumer goods and services sold in either the U.S. or the international market. Factors determining the price of an item include consumer behavior based on economic demand and utility curves, competitive structure of the market, the firm's cost structure and profit objectives, and government regulations. The different types of international pricing decisions include:

- Export pricing and terms
- Transfer pricing
- Foreign market pricing

Export Pricing and Terms

A company that is manufacturing at home but marketing abroad incurs additional expenses, including tariffs, transport, packaging, insurance, and taxes. However, increased output from the export sales may result in economies of scale that bring down the unit cost.

Different financing schemes and terms of payment may result in a discount to full cost as well.

Is the quoted price f.o.b., c.i.f., or some combination? (see Table 9.H)

TABLE 9.H

EXPORT PRICE QUOTATIONS

Abbreviation	Term	Meaning
EX	From	Applies only to point of origin; ex factory; ex dock. The seller agrees to place the goods at the disposal of the buyer at a specified place within a fixed time.
f.o.b.	Free On Board	Price includes loading goods into transport vessels at a specified place; f.o.b. Philadelphia
f.a.s.	Free Alongside	Price includes delivering the goods alongside a specified vessel: f.a.s. Merchant Transport
c.i.f.	Cost, Insurance, Freight	Price includes cost of goods, insurance, and freight
c & i	Cost & Insurance	Price includes cost of goods and insurance
c & f	Cost & Freight	Price includes cost of goods and freight

In what currency is the price quoted? The buyer's currency, or the seller's currency, or some standard such as ECU?

How will the deal be financed?

Chapter 12 on exporting has a more complete explanation of export financing alternatives. Table 9.H gives the definitions of standard export pricing terms.

The buyer would like the price to be c.i.f. with long payment terms. The seller, on the other hand, wants the price quoted f.o.b. with immediate payment.

Export pricing is generally higher than domestic pricing but it often does not reflect the full additional costs. A company or its agent needs to know the price range for similar products in the target market and determine if it can operate within that range. This information comes from a representative on-site, not a secondary source.

Exchange Rate Effect on Export Pricing

We discuss foreign exchange as an economic concept, as a part of international financial markets, and as a factor affecting company financial rankings. The fluctuation in the relationships between currencies also has an impact on pricing decisions since a company has to decide whether to price its product in its home currency or the foreign currency.

Ironically, a weak currency (a currency that is losing its value in relation to foreign currencies) is considered good for the home economy. It results in strong exports and an improvement in the home country trade balance. For example, when the dollar is weak, U.S. goods are less expensive for foreign buyers. The reverse is true for imports. A weak dollar makes imports more expensive.

In deciding which currency to use for pricing, a researcher may wish to check time series data to see how the domestic and foreign currencies have been moving against each other, as well as checking forward foreign exchange data to estimate trends.

Here is a simple example of the effect of currency rates on prices. In December 1985, an American importer agreed to buy widgets from a Japanese manufacturer at the cost of $100 per widget through 1994. The American importer is protected from the 50% decrease in the value of the dollar in relationship to the yen over that time period. As seen in Table 9.I, $100 was worth 20,050 yen in 1985 and 9,974 yen in 1994.

Conversely, what if that same importer had agreed to pay 20,050 yen per unit, the exchange rate in 1985? Instead of paying $100 per unit by 1994, the importer would be paying $201.02, an increase of 101% per unit in dollars.

TABLE 9.I		
EFFECT OF EXCHANGE RATE FLUCTUATIONS ON EXPORT PRICING		
Year End December	Yen to buy one unit @ $100	Dollars to buy one unit @20,050 yen
1985	20,050	100.00
1986	15,910	126.02
1987	12,350	162.35
1988	12,585	159.32
1989	14,345	139.77
1990	13,400	149.18
1991	12,520	160.14
1992	12,475	160.72
1993	11,185	179.26
1994	9,974	201.02
% Change in value of dollar	-50%	101%

When the seller's currency is strong, as in our example, it is to the buyer's benefit to have the price quoted in the buyer's currency. When the seller's currency is weak, it is to the buyer's benefit to have the price quoted in the seller's currency.

Transfer Pricing

A company providing goods or services from its home country to a facility abroad, whether it is a manufacturing or a distribution arm, has to charge the receiving unit for the items. This is transfer pricing. If the producing unit is a cost center, then it wants to charge the international unit what it charges anyone else. To be competitive, the international unit only wants to pay the cost of manufacturing.

Foreign Market Pricing

Foreign market pricing is the price that the company sets in another country. The actual price will depend upon:

- Company Goals: Profit (U.S.) or market share (Japanese)
- Costs: Manufacturing, transportation, distribution, and marketing
- Demand: Number of consumers, their ability to pay, and their tastes
- Competition: Price, number of competitors, country, and attitude
- Government: Policy of competition, price controls, taxes and tariffs
- Inflation: Time between production and sale, sale and payment

Place or Channels of Distribution

Many of the issues discussed in Chapter 12 on export deal with the transport and distribution of goods or services that originate in one country and are sold in another. A country's transport infrastructure should have been part of the initial research and decision making. At this point, the distributor needs to identify sources of wholesale and retail trade and direct marketing. There are directories of wholesalers and retailers listed in Chapter 4. Country sources and export guides give overviews of the transportation infrastructure.

Promotion and Advertising

Promotion is the communication by the firm to its audience with a view of informing and influencing the audience. Advertising is paid communication through impersonal media. Advertising as a part of the marketing plan is included here. A fuller explanation of international advertising agencies and regulations is presented in Chapter 11.

A variety of factors make up the international advertising environment: language, economic differences, tastes and attitudes, and local competition. Other factors include agency availability, media availability, and government regulations.

Even if a firm decides to market a global product, that firm must still decide whether to use standard or adapted advertising and promotional campaigns. A firm faces several types of decisions when putting together a global marketing campaign.

- Selecting the agency—international or local
- Choosing the message—high context/low context, language
- Selecting the media—print, TV, satellite TV, etc.
- Determining the budget
- Organizing for advertising

Journal articles that address these issues disagree on how to proceed. Despite the convergence of tastes worldwide, cultural and language differences that may interfere with a global advertising campaign still exist.

Selecting the Agency

International companies often select international agencies (for more information, see Chapter 11).

Choosing the Message

In addition to local standards and tastes, cultural differences are based on the context of a culture. Table 9.J divides countries into high context and low context cultures, where "context" refers to the importance of the social situation.[10]

Product comparisons are illegal in Japan because Japanese culture finds open criticism of others unacceptable. In Thailand, effective advertisements are graphic displays rather than written text.

TABLE 9.J

HIGH AND LOW CONTEXT CULTURES

High Context Cultures	Low Context Cultures
Asia, Africa and Middle East	North America and Western Europe
Interpersonal relations; non-verbal expression; social circumstances	Spoken and written messages; action oriented; analytical
TV commercial drama with product in context	Illustrated lecture; product comparisons

---

There are a variety of language issues beyond the obvious ones of having an incorrect translation, misspellings in the translation, or different meanings for words. Other language issues are illustrated by the following examples.

- Swiss, German, and Japanese people do not believe anything being given away free is of value.
- The number 4 means death in some Asian cultures.
- In judging ad space, the German language takes 20% more space than English.
- Idioms or trendy words do not translate.[11] For example, many countries were unable to translate the name of the logo for the 1996 Olympics.

Some global marketing successes include:

- Coca-Cola's "I'd like to teach the world to sing"
- British Airways' "Manhattan Landing" campaign in 35 countries
- Proctor & Gamble's Pampers slogan: "Even when they're wet they're dry"
- IBM's "Little Tramp"

Some global marketing failures include:

- Imperial Margarine's "Magic Crowns," which was offensive to monarchies
- Chevrolet's Nova (the classic: "No va" means "doesn't go" in Spanish)
- GM's Body by Fisher, which became "Corpse by Fisher" in Flemish
- Kentucky Fried Chicken's "finger lickin' good," (translated as "eat your fingers off" in Chinese)[12]

Sometimes a national campaign can be carried to global markets if it is somewhat modified. For example, Coca-Cola's "Mean Joe Green" campaign substituted local sports figures for the U.S. football player in non-U.S. markets.

Selecting the Media

Publications read by international business persons are obvious places to advertise global products. Such publications include the *Financial Times*, the *Wall Street Journal*, the *International Herald Tribune*, *Le Monde*, and *The Times*. *Reader's Digest* and *National Geographic* are the two most widely read international consumer magazines in Europe. There are problems advertising in local print sources. In some countries, the quality of printed sources is variable, and more important, there is a lack of fixed or published rates and no audited or authenticated circulation data.

In the U.S., published auditing circulation figures come from the Audit Bureau of Circulation, advertising expenditures from BAR LNA, and published rates from Standard Rate & Data Service. The U.K.'s advertising reporting service is MEAL. Chapter 11 discusses the availability of this type of information internationally.

There have been recent changes in broadcast media worldwide with the growth of satellite transmission. Within Europe, deregulation has resulted in new TV stations, new programs, and therefore space for more advertising. There are pan-European satellite systems and worldwide channels. MTV is a strong player in the cable market because it does not face traditional language problems. Other top stations in Europe are EUROSPORT and CNN.

Determining the Budget

How much should a firm budget for advertising in any one country? Theory says put money into advertising as long as the ad dollar returns more than the dollar spent on anything else. Among the different international strategies are:

* Percent of sales in a country: The more you sell, the more you advertise; this depends on whether you are entering a market or expanding, what the competition is doing, and media availability.
* Comparative or parity: Match your competition, but national competition may behave differently from home country competition.
* Objective-and-task: Determine your objectives (e.g., sales, brand awareness, or market share), determine the tasks to reach objectives, estimate cost of the tasks.
* Comparative analysis: The large company, advertising in many countries, uses categories to group countries.

The comparative strategies require access to competitor spending data. This type of information is not widely disseminated.

Organizing for Advertising

In organizing for advertising, the firm determines where the decisions are to be made. Again, there is a continuum from centralization in the home market to decentralization in each market. The decision is not dependent on secondary data sources.

Other Marketing Issues

Personal selling in foreign markets at a national level may be important. Although the sales force may be hired cheaply, sales is often a low prestige job. The challenge is to provide motivation to recruit a quality sales force. The company needs to do an analysis of the market to determine the role of the sales force. There are variations by religion, ethnicity, language, education, and race, even within a country. An alternative is to use a distributor or licensee, but then the company gives up control.

Sales promotions, such as contests, coupons, samples, premiums such as cents off, and point-of-sale promotions account for 60% of the ad dollar in the United States. The use of these techniques in other countries depends on culture, retailer cooperation, and laws that may restrict premiums. The U.S., U.K., France, and Philippines are considered liberal, while Germany, Switzerland, Italy, and Mexico are considered restrictive.[13]

Other promotional techniques include traveling exhibits, videodiscs, and seminars. Financial incentives, referred to as bribery, which is illegal in the United States under the Foreign Corrupt Practices Act, is an accepted form of promotion in many countries. In 1996, the International Chamber of Commerce issued *The ICC Rules of Conduct to Combat Extortion and Bribery in International Business Transactions,* with recommendations for government action. ICC encourages all governments, particularly in developing countries, to implement the recommendations issued in 1994 by the Organization for Economic Cooperation and Development (OECD) on curbing bribery in international business.[14]

Public relations is distinguished from forms of advertising in that it is external relations that involve a company's image and its corporate communications. Press releases, consumer service, and participation on local advisory committees are all forms of a company's PR. The newest form of public relations is use of a WWW site to transmit a positive corporate image.

INTERNATIONAL MARKETING OF SERVICES

The emphasis in the marketing and exporting literature has been on the movement of goods. Services follow goods. The international market for services is fundamentally different from the market in goods; it is more difficult to measure and analyze. In more developed economies, services account for a large percent of GDP. It is estimated by the IMF that at least 25% of the world's trade is in services. Eurostat reported that the European Community was the world's leading exporter and importer of services between 1979 and 1988.

There are fewer alternatives in ways to export services than to export goods. Alternative means to market services internationally include:

- Foreign direct investment (in a service company)
- Licensing (a name, a technique)
- Franchising
- Joint ventures and alliances

Certain service industries lend themselves to internationalization. Improved communications networks have resulted in an international financial service industry. As international marketing expands, so does the internationalization of the advertising industry. Consulting organizations and accounting firms operate on a worldwide basis. There is also an internationalization of sports, movies, retail, airlines, insurance, and real estate (see also Chapter 14).

Sources For International Services

International Trade in Services (Eurostat, 1989–)

Eurostat compiles statistics on trade in services. The most recent edition of *International Trade in Services* was published in late 1995 and covers 1984–1993. International trade in services is included by definition in balance of trade statistics. The statistics are roughly comparable among countries. But, as with all other data we have examined, there are also problems.

- There is no detailed international classification in services; some countries compile branch statistics in banking.
- Valuation methods are not identical; some countries record gross flows, others net.
- There is no agreed method of valuing insurance.
- Certain transactions are not regarded as services in all countries; some countries consider construction of more than one year direct investment.

In addition to overview data, the publication includes estimated data for 12 services, including tourism, transport, advertising, and insurance and for the EU-12 member countries. The U.S. and Japan are included for comparison.

Services: Statistics on International Transactions 1970– (OECD, 1992–)

Services: Statistics on International Transactions compiles and assesses available information on international trade in services for OECD member countries. The 1996 edition covers 1970–1993 and includes data that were available through mid-1995. Balance of payments data are reported.

Section A presents data for the entire OECD area and for travel, trade, government service, and other private services. Other private service categories are communications, construction and engineering, insurance, financial services, computer-related services, consulting, legal services, management services, advertising, and films and television. No OECD subtotals are calculated because no item is reported by all countries.

Section B provides available data on all members with an international compilation, using a standard format. Definitions are provided for all data elements. The publication does not include service trade with nonmember countries.

Individual countries may have their own service data. For example, the United States tracks trade in services as part of its monthly publication FT-900, *U.S. International Trade in Goods and Services.* Service categories are too broad to be of much use to a marketer:

- Passenger travel and fares
- Other transportation
- Royalties and license fees
- Other private services
- Military contracts and government misc. services

FRANCHISING

Another marketing alternative is franchising. It is a legal arrangement in which the franchiser grants to the franchisee not only the right to use the product or service and its trademark, but also the right to use the entire system of the business, including support in site selection, training, advertising, and product supply. A key to franchising success is consistency among outlets.

> The franchise operation is a contractual relationship between a Franchisor and Franchisee in which the Franchisor offers or is obliged to

maintain a continued interest in the business of the Franchisee in such areas as know-how and training; wherein the Franchisee operates under a common trade mark, formation or procedure owned or controlled by the Franchisor, under which the Franchisee has or will make a substantial capital investment in his business from his own resources.

(International Franchise Association)

U.S. franchisers, especially fast food chains, have made their presence known around the globe. By the early 1990s, McDonald's, Kentucky Fried Chicken, and Holiday Inn all had franchises in over 50 countries. In 1995 the International Franchise Association reported that over 800 U.S. franchises had operations abroad with a total of 8,500 franchises worldwide.

The emerging markets of China, Russia, India, and Latin America are now open for franchise opportunities. In 1995, there were almost 140 non-hotel franchises in Indonesia, over 80% foreign-based. In general, however, franchising activities have centered in Western Europe, Japan, and Australia. The Japanese Franchise Chain Association reports that franchising began in the 1960s in Japan, grew rapidly from the mid-1970s to the mid-1980s, and has tapered off. In 1994, there were 714 franchises, the largest group in food services. Local rather than foreign franchises dominate in Germany, where photography is the number one line of franchise business.

Because franchising is a legal agreement, the franchiser has to understand the legal environment and commercial practices of the target country. In 1990, the United States was the only country that had passed a law concerning the sale of a franchise. Since then, more nations have been considering franchise regulations, but few have introduced any legislation. For example, South Africa has a Code of Ethics with statutory support, Canada relies on self-regulation, and the European Franchise Association has a Code of Ethics with disciplinary procedures. France has a pre-contract disclosure law for trademark licenses, which includes most franchises. Similar laws have been introduced in Brazil and Mexico. The World Intellectual Property Organization concluded that since franchising operates on contract law, legally no new legislation should be needed.[15]

The EU addresses franchises in its regulations and defines a franchise and a franchise agreement. EEC Commission Regulation No. 4087/88 November 30, 1988, Article 3(a) and 3(b), states:

'franchise' means a package of industrial or intellectual property rights relating to trade marks, trade names, shop signs, utility models, designs, copyrights, know-how or patents, to be exploited for the resale of goods or the provision of services to end users;

'franchise agreement' means an agreement whereby one undertaking, the franchisor, grants the other, the franchisee, in exchange for direct or indirect financial consideration, the right to exploit a franchise for the purpose of marketing specified types of goods and/or services; it includes at least obligations relating to:

- use of common name or sign and a uniform presentation of contract premises
- communication by franchisor to franchisee of know how
- continual provision by franchise to the franchisee of commercial or technical assistance during the life of the agreement.

International franchising has been fostered by the International Franchise Association, a U.S.-based organization. It participates in the Council of Multinational Franchisors and Distributors, which provides an international network to people and information. Membership is open to franchisers or distributors having operations in more than one country or plans to have operations in more than one country and who also belong to their national franchise organization. By 1996, there were over 25 national franchise associations and the number keeps growing. There is also a European Franchise Federation (EFF), founded in 1972, composed of national franchise groups in Europe and non-European associates.

Sources of Franchising Information

In researching franchises, two major information needs are:

What franchises are located in what countries?

What are the laws and regulations affecting franchising in an individual country?

We have been unable to find what we consider a comprehensive directory of international franchisers. Information on the franchise activities of individual companies or the franchise climate of individual countries can be found through electronic searches. For example, in March 1996, the *Financial Times* published a series of articles addressing franchising in the U.K. in its "Survey on Franchising."

Franchise Opportunities Guide (published annually by International Federation, Washington, DC) lacks an index to those companies that are franchising internationally, although that information is part of the individual entry. The *Guide* is available from the home page of the International Franchise Association, http://www.entremkt.com. Searching is by category, investment required, and an alphabetical list of company names. There is no access to companies operating internationally.

The lack of an international index is also true of *Bond's Franchise Guide*, 1996 edition. This formerly was *The Source Book of Franchise Opportunities,* which does have 400 Canadian franchises. Each entry has a section entitled "Specific Expansion Plans," with U.S., Canada, and Overseas as the choices.

Restaurant Business publishes a report on the "Top 50 Franchisers" in its November first issue. In the 1995 issue, the publication included international sales and units. The top 50 restaurant franchisers had over 18,000 international units, about 10 percent of all units with 22% of their sales coming from the international units. These data did not appear in the 1996 franchise issue.

The *World Franchise Directory: A Guide Offering Details for Comparing Franchises and Franchise Investment Opportunities Around the World,* published by Gale in 1991, had not been republished by the end of 1996. This *Directory* had over 75% U.S. entries.

Survey of Foreign Laws and Regulations Affecting International Franchising (American Bar Association, 1989, 2nd ed.) listed the franchising laws for 24 countries.

International Franchising, by Konigsberg, (Ardsely-on-Hudson, NY: Transnational Juris Publications, 1991) addresses many of the issues discussed above in relation to selecting a country in which to locate franchises. The loose-leaf book is legal in tone and might be useful to the smaller potential franchiser.

International Franchising distinguishes between a license agreement and a franchise agreement. The license agreement is a contractual agreement in which the licenser grants the licensee the right to use the licenser's patents, know-how, and trademarks in connection with manufacturing or distribution of a product but does not affect how the licensee conducts business. Two types are technology transfer and trademark license agreements.

SOURCES OF INTERNATIONAL MARKETING INFORMATION

The sources listed here build on the more general country-level sources listed above. These sources focus more on the consumer and product, though many also have macroeconomic data.

Statistical Compilations

European Marketing Data and Statistics and *International Marketing Data and Statistics* (published annually by Euromonitor)

Euromonitor is one of the leading international publishers of marketing information. It publishes marketing reference books, directories, and market research reports. Two of its most widely distributed publications are *European Marketing Data and Statistics (EDMS)*, annual since 1962, and *International Marketing Data and Statistics,* from 1975. These are compendia of statistical information relevant to marketing in many countries. The data are gathered from large international organizations, such as the United Nations, OECD, and the International Monetary Fund; from national statistical offices; pan-international and national trade associations; industry associations; unofficial research publishers; and from Euromonitor's own statistical databases. As with so many published data sources, the date of the publication does not reflect the date of data. Usually, 1994 is the latest data available in the 1996 editions, which were published in the fall of 1995.

These publications answer general marketing questions. For example, they will tell you how much beer is consumed per capita in Australia but won't tell you which brands of beer are sold in Australia. Twenty-three principal sectors cover 207 countries worldwide. Not all data is available for all countries. The tables in the two publications have been standardized to facilitate comparisons. The sectors are:

Demographic Trends and Forecasts
Economic Indicators
Finance and Banking
External Trade by Destination and Commodity
Labour Force Indicators
Industrial Resources and Output
Energy Resources
Defense Spending and Equipment
Environmental Data
Consumer Expenditure Patterns
Retail Sales Figures
Advertising Patterns
Consumer Market Size
Consumer Prices and Costs
Housing Stock
Health and Living Standards
Literacy and Education
Agricultural Resources
Communications Data
Automotives in Use
Transport Infrastructure
Travel and Tourism
Cultural Indicators

Notice that the sector headings match many of the data items discussed above. The data items are presented in spreadsheet format with up to 18-year trends.

Each volume includes a section titled "Key International Market Information Sources." It contains the names of the principal international and national organizations that publish statistics.

Beginning in 1995, Euromonitor issued *World Marketing Data and Statistics* on CD-ROM, the electronic compilation of both print titles. The 1996 CD-ROM has the same data from the 207 countries, presented in more than 450 tables. The structure of the CD-ROM is based on the print sources, with an 18-year time series, from 1977 to 1994, where available. The CD-ROM runs on a Windows platform and requires a link to Excel for effective downloading of spreadsheets. Exhibit 9.4 is an extract from a table on consumption in *World Marketing Data and Statistics* CD-ROM.

Consumption of Drinks per Head					
Country	Carbonated Drinks	Fruit Juice	Beer	Wine	Spirits
Argentina	66.96	3.1	23.75	41.81	0.16
Australia	103.61	26.5	95.94	17.75	2.46
Brazil	15.9	7.03	39.69	1.89	7.73
Canada	51.68	21.49	73.77	8.22	3.66
Chile	246.38	6.16	26.09	26.16	4.49
China	2.6	0.06	8.2	10.03	14.56
Thailand	25.83	0.92	3.01	0.02	10.00
USA	182.74	48.46	84.09	6.22	7.11
Venezuela	49.29	7.78	80.66	0.94	5.75

EXTRACT FROM *WORLD MARKETING DATA AND STATISTICS* CD-ROM

EXHIBIT 9.4

Source: World Marketing Data and Statistics CD-ROM, 1996. Reprinted with permission from Euromonitor.

Sources for the tables are given. International Sugar Organization, OECD, GATT, International Tea Committee, National Statistical Offices, and Euromonitor estimates had all been listed in the 1993 print edition. Only Euromonitor appears in the 1996 edition. Unlike the *Statistical Abstract of the United States*, where the citations to tables serve as finding aids to more up-to-date and detailed data, the citations to Euromonitor tables only direct users toward general publications or publishers.

Euromonitor also publishes a series of regional handbooks and country handbooks. There have been first editions of a *Directory and Sourcebook* for Eastern Europe, Latin America, Asia, and China. In addition, there are *Advertising, Marketing and Media Handbooks* for Asia and Latin America in print, plus a 1992 edition for Europe. Finally, there is a growing series of *Consumer...* titles, supplemented by the first edition of a CD-ROM, *World Consumer Markets 1995/96*. Table 9.K lists the countries and/or regions for which Euromonitor has a 1995 or 1996 *Consumer*

volume. Earlier volumes also exist for Japan and Southern Europe.

TABLE 9.K

EUROMONITOR *CONSUMER...* TITLES

Location	Date of Publication	Sectors	Countries
Asia	1994	87	12
Canada +	1996	150	1
China	1997	100	1
Eastern Europe	1994	10	
Europe +	1996	242	17
International (no Europe)	1996/7	150	26
Latin America	1994/95	80	8
Mexico +	1996	150	1
South Africa	1994	100	1
USA	1996	150	1
World Consumer Markets CD-ROM	1996/7	230	55
+ includes forecast data			

World Consumer Markets includes the market size data from the Eastern Europe, Europe, and international volumes. It only provides market value and volume, presented in spreadsheet format. With the Windows-based software, the user can display the data in local currency, standard currency, and per capita value and units, and can also create graphs and charts. The CD-ROM presents the per capita data as "apparent consumption."

Euromonitor publications are expensive. However, most libraries with business collections should consider purchasing the two *Marketing Data and Statistics* titles or the equivalent CD-ROM.

Eastern Europe

International marketers immediately recognized the market potential of Eastern Europe, with over 400 million inhabitants and consumer spending of about U.S. $1,000 billion per year. They soon recognized the market limitations both in terms of consumer resources and information resources. Euromonitor estimates the per capita spending power to be no more than $3,000, and a recent EU study showed that even the most prosperous former Socialist country, Slovenia, had a GDP per person (based on purchasing power parity) that was less than the poorest EU country, Greece, and about one-third of the United States.[16]

Consumer Eastern Europe (Euromonitor, 1992–)

Consumer Eastern Europe offers a general overview of Eastern European markets and has individual chapters on the Baltics, Bulgaria, the Czech and Slovak

Republics, Hungary, Poland, Romania, and Russia. The book is primarily statistical as opposed to analytical, with the data drawn from official sources and compiled with "considerable care." The source answers such questions as:

> *What percent of Russia's economy is in the agricultural sector?*
>
> *What was the average annual retail price for a liter of milk in Hungary?*

Euromonitor is careful to warn the user of the limitations of the data, stating that there are still instances of false and misleading figures. The handbook presents "fragmented" data from the states of Eastern Europe, tries to standardize it, and then make its own deductions. For example, official consumption figures in the early 1990s often ignored the free-market stalls. Changes in governmental structure have resulted in changes in statistical collection, which necessitates revisions for time series data. Most of the data are at least two years old, while pan-regional data may be even older. Finally, there has been a problem with exchange rate conversion and inflation. Much of the data therefore appear in local currency; when rates are used, they are average dollar free-market rates from the IMF.

Chapter subheadings for all countries include: demographics, economic indicators, standard of living, advertising and media access, retail distribution, consumer expenditure, consumption rates, transport, service industries, and consumer market size. There may also be tables for consumer expenditure, consumption or apparent consumption, service and consumer market size. Exhibit 9.5 shows extracts from two tables in *Consumer Eastern Europe* for the Russian Federation.

TABLE 11.23 RUSSIAN FEDERATION PRICE INDICES 1989–1992
December 1990=100

	1989	1990	1991	1992 (Sept)
CPI	-	95.6	187.5	3,531.4
RPI	91.4	100	173.9	2,112.9

Source: Goskomstal/Russian Government/Russian Economic Trends

TABLE 11.54 FORMER USSR: RETAIL SALES OF CONSUMER ELECTRONICS 1989-1990

	1988	1989	1990
TV Sets			
Production (000)	9,637	9,938	10,519
of which colour TV Sets	5,700	6,341	7,155
Number owned per 100 households	103	105	107

SAMPLE DATA FROM *CONSUMER EASTERN EUROPE*

EXHIBIT 9.5

Source: Consumer Eastern Europe, 1994. Reprinted with permission of Euromonitor.

Two other titles from Euromonitor are the rather dated *Eastern Europe: A Directory and Sourcebook* (1992) and *The East European Business Handbook* (1993).

Asia

Euromonitor's Asian coverage includes the three regional titles, plus individual consumer volumes for Japan and China and a *Directory and Sourcebook* for China.

Asia: Directory and Sourcebook is a companion to the *Consumer* publications and has more text and analysis, plus company information. The book has five parts:

- Section One: Overview of Asian Markets in the 1990s. Features major Asian economies and is the only section of the book covering Japan.
- Section Two: Accessing Asian Markets, with detailed data for China, Hong Kong, Korea, Malaysia, Philippines, Singapore, Taiwan, and Thailand.
- Section Three: Major Companies in the former eight countries plus India, Indonesia, and Pakistan. The type of companies varies by country.
- Section Four: Sources of Information.
- Section Five: Statistical Datafile.

There is an index to companies and information sources.

NAFTA

There is no organized body of country statistical material focusing on NAFTA. Statistics Canada, known for the quality of its data, has a catalog of its publications and can be accessed via the Web at www.statcan.ca. Data are available on the people, the economy and the land. Examples of the former include tables on Culture, Leisure and Travel; Families and Households; and Population.

The Instituto Nacíonal de Estadistica, Geografía e Informatica (INEGI) provides the Mexican government data. Information is available in print, on diskette, and on CD-ROM. Unfortunately for many of us, most of the information and the *Catálogo de Productos* are in Spanish. There is a very limited amount of data available on the Web site, www.inegi.gob.mx.

The Inter-American Development Bank has aggregated some basic economic indicators, including GDP per capita for NAFTA. The bank also has extensive data for Mexico, but has not made comparable data available for the U.S. and Canada. This information is retrievable through the bank's WWW site, http://iadb.org. A brief extract of NAFTA data, compared to the rest of Latin America, appears in Exhibit 9.6.

PRINCIPAL ECONOMIC INDICATORS BY INTEGRATION GROUP

Group	1991	1992	1993	1994	1995	1996p
Population (Millions)						
MERCOSUR	191.8	194.9	197.8	200.8	203.8	206.9
Andean Group	91.8	93.7	95.6	7.4	99.3	101.3
CARICOM	5.6	5.7	5.7	5.8	5.9	5.9
NAFTA	363.6	368.4	373.3	378.2	383.0	387.8
The Americas	709.4	720.5	731.4	742.5	753.6	764.8
Gross Domestic Product (Billions of 1990 U.S. Dollars)						
MERCOSUR	561.2	574.7	599.7	636.7	648.0	664.1
NAFTA	6,266.3	6,404.9	6,597.5	6,837.2	6,926.0	7,089.0
The Americas	7,080.4	7,243.7	7,470.7	7,758.7	7,873.9	8,061.4
Gross Domestic Product Per Capita (1990 U.S. Dollars)						
MERCOSUR	2,926	2,950	3,031	3,170	3,179	3,210
NAFTA	17,232	17,383	17,672	18,078	18,082	18,280
The Americas	9,981	10,054	10,215	10,450	10,448	10,540

EXTRACT OF AGGREGATE DATA FOR NAFTA

EXHIBIT 9.6

Source: Statistics and Quantitative Analysis, Inter-American Development Bank, http://www.iadb.org, December 22, 1996.

FINDING AIDS FOR MARKET INFORMATION

Other Euromonitor publications, such as the *World Directory of Marketing Information Sources* (1995), the *European Compendium of Marketing Information* (1996), *European Directory of Non-official Statistical Sources* (2nd ed., 1993), and the *World Directory of Non-official Statistical Sources* (1996), include more complete source listings.

The *World Directory of Marketing Information Sources* features general marketing information, contacts, and sources relevant to business needs. Other Euromonitor reference works contain comprehensive listings of sources and business contacts, trade associations, trade journals, and research organizations.

The *World Directory* is divided into nine sections covering as many as 200 countries. There is also an alphabetical and country index.

Section 1: Official Sources and Publications
Section 2: Major Reference Libraries
Section 3: Leading Market Research Companies
Section 4: Private Research Companies (publishers of reports and surveys)
Section 5: Online Sources
Section 6: Abstracts and Indexes
Section 7: Major Business Journals
Section 8: Major Business and Marketing Associations
Section 9: International Business Contacts

While many of the resources are available in other sources, it is convenient for the user to have all of it together in one place.

Euromonitor publishes an index to all its publications in print, *Euromonitor Index*. This is a complete, annotated list of publications and can be ordered directly from Euromonitor at 87-88 Turnmill Street, London EC1M 5QU, Fax: 44 71 251 8024; or 122 South Michigan Ave., Chicago IL 60603, Fax: 312-922-1157. Some Euromonitor titles are also distributed by Gale Research in the United States.

All Euromonitor directories are available on one new CD-ROM product, *World Databases of Business Information Sources*, issued in 1996.

European Markets: A Guide to Company and Industry Information (1983–) (Washington, DC: Washington Researchers)

Asian Markets: A Guide to Company and Industry Information (1st ed. 1988) (Washington, DC: Washington Researchers)

Latin American Markets: A Guide to Company and Industry Information (1st ed. 1993) (Washington, DC: Washington Researchers)

All Washington Researchers Guides have the same basic arrangement. Part 1 lists national and international organizations in the government and private sector. Part 2 lists published sources and databases. Among the three guides, there is a high degree of overlap of information presented in Parts 1 and 2. Part

3 is country data, including U.S. government offices, officials and sources, associations, research and transportation organizations.

The books are complied from a U.S. perspective. The Washington Researchers publications are recommended for a general library that is looking for a U.S. source of European, Asian, or Latin American information for business clients.

A direct way to find statistical information is to use official publications from the central statistical department of individual countries. These departments all produce basic statistical sources that serve as starting points for country-level marketing information. Most European countries publish a statistical yearbook, an annual bulletin of industry data, and manuals that examine imports and exports in detail. There are also family expenditure surveys and retail trade censuses. Some of these statistical agencies have sites on the WWW.

The Future

The successful marketer not only has to understand the present situation but also correctly predict the future. Chapter 13 presents sources of economic forecasts. Up until 1996, researchers used the print and electronic compilations originally published by Predicasts as finding aids for international and U.S. forecast information. The titles in this series, *Worldcasts Product, Worldcasts Regional,* and *U.S. Forecasts,* extracted forecast data from a variety a print sources. As of 1996, these publications ceased. Researchers will have to extract published forecasts on their own from online searches in text files.

In 1997, Euromonitor announced *International Marketing Forecasts, European Marketing Forecasts* and a CD-ROM, *World Marketing Forecasts,* with coverage through 2010. These publications were released too late for us to examine them for evaluation.

CONCLUSION

To succeed in the international marketplace, companies need to research the host country, gathering data on the economy, the culture and lifestyles of the residents, and the political and legal environments. This external data analysis should be combined with internal marketing decisions about the four P's: product, price, place, and promotion. Researchers depend on secondary data sources, such as those described in this chapter. While compilations exist from international, national, and private sources, the data are often several years old.

Sources of current information at the consumer, product, and company level are presented in Chapter 10 on international marketing research. Listed below are a few useful reference tips for using the sources described in this chapter.

- Check to see what statistical office publications are in your library or the major research library near you. These publications are relatively inexpensive. Euromonitor suggests that you write to the applicable statistical office and offer to pay for charges, if any. It also warns that you may wait several months for answers from Spain, Portugal, Greece, and Italy; France and Germany send lists of publications unless you are very precise. Disadvantages are that the information is at a general level, will be in the language of the country, and in the less affluent countries, will not be current.
- Use market research agencies and reports, described in Chapter 10. They may already be publishing statistics based on their analysis of the official statistics.
- Online databases provide a wealth of valuable information. However, it may be necessary to access a wide range of international services.
- Contact a trade association. The data the associations provide are a measure of the present market. While some conduct their own studies, many rely on official publications. The available data are usually country-specific. Associations are readily identifiable in Gale's *International Associations.*

SELECTED ARTICLES ON INTERNATIONAL MARKETING

Advertising Theory

Fields, George. "Great Marketing Concepts Are Not Immutable." *Tokyo Business Today* 60 (March 1992): 35.

> Even major brands differ in one or more of the marketing elements, from positioning and application to distribution techniques. Coca-Cola's premier brand in Japan is Georgia Coffee, not Coke.

Onkvisit, Sak; and John J. Shaw. "Standardized International Advertising: A Review and Critical Evaluation of the Theoretical and Empirical Evidence." *Columbia Journal of World Business* (Fall 1987): 43–55.

> Includes a review of the literature, discussing standardization, localization, and compromise.

Silverstein, Michael J. "Companies That Meet Higher Ante Will Win Global Marketing Pot." *Marketing News* 26 (March 30, 1992): 13.

Primary research, information networks, broadly defined categories, acquisitions, and adapting the world brand to the local tastes are signs of a successful global company. Grand Metropolitan is given as an example.

Culture

Jarvis, Susan S.; and William W. Thompson. "Making Sure Your Canadian Advertisement Does Not Sink Your Sale." *Journal of Consumer Marketing* 12, no. 2 (1995): 40–46.

Before placing an advertisement in Canadian media, the business person must know about Canada's comprehensive advertising laws and social/cultural constraints.

Stephens, Gregory K.; and Charles R. Greer. "Doing Business in Mexico: Understanding Cultural Differences." *Organizational Dynamics* 24 (Summer 1995): 39–55.

Cultural differences such as values, behaviors, and expectations affect U.S.-Mexican business alliances.

Developing Markets for Western Products

Dominguez, Luis V.; and Carlos G. Sequeira. "Strategic Options for LDC Exports to Developed Countries." *International Marketing Review* 8, no. 5 (1991): 27–43.

Marketing to developing countries is complex and success is based not only on market conditions but, according to the authors' survey, the commitment and management focus of the exporting firm.

Guzek, Elizbeta. "Ways of Entering the Polish Market by Foreign Companies." *Journal of Business Research* 24 (January 1992): 37–50.

Changes are occurring in the Polish market that are relevant to foreign marketers. These include the role of intermediaries, marketing channels, and joint ventures.

Nasierowski, Wojciech. "Doing Business in India." *Business Quarterly* 56 (Summer 1991): 71–74.

India has an enormous potential market but complex regulations has made entry for foreign companies difficult.

Franchising

Gourlay, Richard. "Survey of Franchising: Demand Is Increasing." *Financial Times* 7 March 1996.

There are signs that established large businesses are increasingly adopting the franchise formula.

Tomzack, Mary E. "Ripe New Markets: Emerging Economies with Little Competition and Big Payoffs— International Franchising." *Success* 42 (April 1995): 73.

Includes a list of information sources.

Williamson, Garry. "Australia: Taking the Mystery out of Franchising." *Sydney Morning Herald* 4 June 1996.

The article includes a list of franchises that have survived 12 years.

Zeidman, Philip F. "Franchising in Russia: Sorting It All Out." *Franchising World* 27 (November/December 1995): 34–35.

Major franchisers should consider entering Russia, based on Russians' desire for Western goods and a potential upturn in the economy. Zeidman wrote about "Franchising in South Africa" in September/October 1995 *Franchising World*.

Japan

Conlan-Ayache, Gladys. "European Exports to Japan: Successes and Failures." *European Trends* no. 3 (1991): 66–69.

According to a 1990 survey, Consumer's Awareness of Imported Goods by the Manufactured Imports Promotion Organization of Japan, good taste, good quality, and good design are the 3 criteria essential for consumers in Japan. The greatest problem in exporting to Japan remains the distribution system.

Latin America

Lagniappe Letter (biweekly) and *Lagniappe Quarterly*. New York: Latin American Information Services.

Country by country economic, finance and company information. Available online on all systems that carry *PROMT* and *IAC* Newsletters files.

Pricing

Sherman, W. Richard; and Jennifer L. McBride. "International Transfer Pricing: Application and Analysis." *The Ohio CPA Journal* (August 1995): 29–35.

The U.S. Internal Revenue Service issued final regulations on international transfer pricing in 1994. This article examines the rules and provides an international case study.

Public Relations

Corbett, William J. "EC '92—Communicating in the New Europe." *Public Relations Quarterly* 36 (Winter 1991–92): 7–13.

The EC provides a market of 342 million people and a $4.8 trillion gross national product. This creates an opportunity for U.S. public relations practitioners who need to be better educated and more cultured than before.

Services

Bouchard, Micheline. "International Marketing of Professional Services." *Business Quarterly* 56 (Winter 1992): 86–89.

Three penetration strategies that professional services can use to enter a new market are opening an office, making an acquisition, and forming a strategic alliance.

Strategy

Buckley, Peter J.; C. L. Pass; and Kate Prescott. "Foreign Market Servicing Strategies and Competitiveness." *Journal of General Management* 17 (Winter 1991): 34–46.

A case study of three different approach strategies to gaining a foreign presence for a sample of U.K. manufacturing firms in pharmaceuticals, scientific instruments, and decorative paints.

King, Elliot. "At Ease Overseas." *Target Marketing* 15 (January 1992): 19–20.

Three successful global direct marketing successes are presented: (1) the *Economics Press*, (2) *Business Week International*, and (3) *Reader's Digest*.

Stonham, Paul. "A Conversation with Michael Porter: International Competitive Strategy from a European Perspective." *European Management Journal* 9 (December 1991): 355–60.

Porter's theory states that advantage arises when a company's home base is located in the nation, or even a city within a nation, when the most dynamic environment for innovation is present in the nation.

Trade Shows

Friedlander, Pat. "Flexing the Marketing Muscle of European Trade Shows." *Journal of European Business* 3 (January/February 1992): 10–14.

U.S. companies need to understand some key differences between exhibiting in the U.S. and exhibiting in Europe. While U.S. exhibitors are used to sending only sales people to shows, Europeans expect company senior executives. For example, U.S. attendees at the International Online Meeting in London immediately notice the difference in the level of both the attendees and the exhibitors.

Trademarks

Kunze, Gerd F. "The Trademark Law Treaty." *Managing Intellectual Property* no. 46 (February 1995): 23–27.

The article outlines the history and content of the Trademark Treaty.

Ojala, Marydee. "Trademarks for the Business Searcher." *Online* 20 (March/April 1996): 52–57.

Ojala offers business searchers basic trademark information and compares the trademark databases on DIALOG and DataStar. WWW access is also discussed.

Bibliographies

Cavusgil, S. Tamer; and John R. Nevin. *International Marketing, an Annotated Bibliography*. Chicago: American Marketing Association, 1992 and 1983.

NOTES

1. Theodore Levitt, "The Globalization of Markets," *Harvard Business Review* (May/June 1983): 1.

2. Vern Terpstra and Ravi Sarathy, *International Marketing* (Orlando, FL: Dryden Press, 1990): 5. This text was used by the author as background for this chapter.

3. Compiled from *Philadelphia Inquirer* (19 September 1992: D1); *Kommersant* (29 June 1992: 12); from DataStar, PROMT; and *Ecotass* (4 June 1990). DataStar, *Textline*.

4. Michael Porter, "Changing Patterns of International Competition," *California Management Review* 28 (Winter 1986): 9–40. Other related Porter titles are *Competition in Global Industries* (Boston: Harvard Business School Press, 1986) and *The Competitive Advantage of Nations* (New York: Free Press, 1990).

5. Francoise Bourguignon and Christian Morrisson, *External Trade and Income Distribution* (Paris: OECD, 1989).

6. *Foreign Economic Trends Thailand* (January 1993).

7. "The Discreet Charm of Provincial Asia," *Economist* 339, no. 7963 (27 April 1996): 85–86.

8. Baker and McKensie from Thomson & Thomson WWW page, June 1996, http://www.thomson-thomson.com.

9. "Broad, Deep, Long and Heavy," *Economist* 341 (16 November 1996): 72–75.

10. "Global Advertisers Should Pay Heed to Contextual Variation," *Marketing News* (13 February 1987): 18.

11. Milton Pierce, "How to Write Direct Mail Copy for Overseas Use," *Direct Marketing* (May 1988): 132–33.

12. Peter R. Klein, "Advertising: Does Research Find a Cross-Cultural Effect?" *Applied Marketing Research* 31 (Spring/Summer 1991): 17–26.

13. Terpstra, page 506.

14. "ICC Announces New Rules of Conduct to Fight Extortion and Bribery in Trade," BNA *International Trade Daily* 28 March 1996, from LEXIS-NEXIS Services.

15. Martin Mendelsohn, "Where Franchising Goes, Must Regulation Follow? (Parts I and II) *Franchising World* 27 (July/August 1995, September/October 1995): 34, 42.

16. "How Central and Eastern Europe Compares with EU and USA," Eurostat *News Release* 19/96 (1 April 1996), http://europa.eu.int/.

CHAPTER 10
International Marketing Research

TOPICS COVERED

- Introduction
- Issues in International Market Research
- Market Research Reports
- Worldwide Market Share
- Market Research as an Industry
- Demographics
- Real Estate
- Selected Articles on Market Research

MAJOR SOURCES DISCUSSED

- Euromonitor *Market Direction Reports*
- Datamonitor
- Frost & Sullivan
- Profound
- IAC Predicasts Files
- *Findex*
- *ULI Market Profiles*

INTRODUCTION

Marketing research involves gathering and analyzing the information needed to solve marketing problems. Large firms usually do their own marketing research and have the capability to collect their own primary data. Middle-sized firms may use marketing research firms to do the data collection and analysis for them. Smaller firms often rely totally on secondary data sources.

The specific tasks to be performed by a market researcher or information specialist are set out in Table 10.A. In the previous chapter, we examined the data needs and sources for the first three steps in Table 10.A. In this chapter, we will look at the more specific consumer and product information required for step four.

TABLE 10.A

The Tasks of International Marketing Research

Marketing Decision	Intelligence Needed
1. Go international or remain a domestic marketer? *Screen potential markets*	1. Assessment of global market demands and firm's potential share in it, in view of local and international competition and compared to domestic opportunities
2. Which markets to enter? *Assess targeted markets*	2. A ranking of world markets according to market potential, local competition, and the political situation
3. How to enter target markets?	3. Size of market, international trade barriers, transport costs, local competition, government requirements and political stability
4. How to market in target markets	4. For each market: buyer behavior, competitive practice; distribution channels, promotional media and practice, company experience there and in other markets

Source: Vern Terpstra and Ravi Sarathy, *International Marketing* (Orlando, FL: Dreyden Press, 1990): 207.

ISSUES IN INTERNATIONAL MARKET RESEARCH

There are several difficulties in collecting and using international market research data. Data are needed for many countries, but data items may not be available for individual countries. When data items are available, they may not be comparable across borders. There is often an absence of secondary data and difficulty gathering primary data. Data quality, data categories, and data consistency are all potential problems. Will we be able to find data in the demographic categories for the geographic level over the period of time that we need? Related questions are:

- What age breakdowns and income ranges are available?
- Are there data for regions, cities, or postal codes within countries?
- Are there time series and forecasts for the items we need?

Evaluating Secondary Information Quality

The key elements in evaluating secondary information quality are its timeliness, accuracy, comparability, and cost.

- *Timeliness* is data dependent. Current macroeconomic data may be two or more years old; useful consumer data should be more recent.
- *Accuracy* of the data depends on clarity and consistency in item definitions and objectivity of the collection organization.
- *Comparability* of data among countries is difficult at best. Even organizations such as the EU and OECD, which report data in standard formats, caution the user that the data have been collected by individual countries in nonstandard formats.
- *Cost* of the information is relative to the needs and budget of the organization. Generally, the less expensive the data, the older and less specific they are.

Difficulties with Primary Data Collection

In addition to being more costly than secondary data collection, primary data collection is also sensitive to environmental and cultural factors in individual countries. The following are some of the problems associated with international primary data collection.

- *Survey Design (phone, mail, door-to-door).* The same data collection instrument often cannot be used in different countries. Very few countries have as many household telephones as the United

States. Response rates will vary. Many people are reluctant to speak with market researchers using any method.
- *Questioning the Correct Individual and Getting the Correct Response.* An outsider may not know who the decision maker is in a culture. In some cultures, interviewees do not want to offend the interviewer with a critical response.
- *Language (meaning and translation).* An English-language firm first has to translate the survey instrument into the local language and then have the responses translated back. If the survey is being conducted in more than one country, the translations may not be consistent.

Differences also exist in conducting qualitative studies such as focus groups. Major differences in doing focus groups in other countries include: (1) time frame to bring together a focus group, (2) structure or number of people in the group, (3) method of recruiting and rescreening, (4) length of project, (5) facilities, and (6) cost.

The solutions for the problems of primary data collection will depend on the country. For example, a U.S. government report on Thailand suggested that an individual having an extensive knowledge of the Thai culture and its characteristics write the survey instrument. A solution for developing countries is to use macro-level data to build models based on known variables for similar products or countries. Improvisation is the technique in Eastern Europe, where strategies may include:

- Talking with official importing organizations
- Attending exhibitions and trade fairs
- Establishing local offices
- Participating in intergovernmental groups

MARKET RESEARCH REPORTS

The macroeconomic data used in country-level analysis are available and well documented in print and electronically. The data might not be as timely as we would like or in the categories we prefer, but we have a choice of sources and often can find time series data for one country or comparable categories of data for several countries.

However, information on market share, consumer demographics, or advertising expenditures is fragmented, often expensive, and of questionable reliability. We cannot access one international source and find comparable information for a range of data items across products, countries, and companies. Compiling this information from a variety of sources takes time, patience, money, and luck.

Print Sources

One way to get at the information and analysis we need is to use market research reports. Market research reports are written reports describing the market for a given product or service and its industry. These reports include analysis, forecasts, and recommendations. They describe the structure of the industry, size of the market, major players, characteristics of end-users or consumers, and external factors such as government regulations.

Commercially prepared market research reports for sale to the public are referred to as "off-the-shelf" reports. Off-the-shelf reports are provided by many publishers such as the Economist Intelligence Unit, Euromonitor, Financial Times, Mintel, ICC KeyNote Reports, and Frost & Sullivan. A non-commercial source is the U.S. International Trade Administration.

Market research reports may be expensive, costing from several hundred to several thousand dollars. Full reports can be purchased directly from the publisher. While the reports may provide excellent information, they are not tailored to the needs of the individual and they are often several months or years old.

Market research reports answer such specific questions as:

What is the size of the German beer market?

What are the consumption and purchasing trends in the Italian healthcare market?

What are future uses for lithium batteries worldwide?

Electronic Sources

Many of the print market research reports are available in full-text online databases. Table 10.B lists reports that appear on some or all of the major databank providers: DIALOG, DataStar, LEXIS-NEXIS, or FT Profile, or on Profound and Markintel, which focus on market research.

Researchers weigh the relative costs of purchasing an off-the-shelf report, accessing reports or parts of reports online, or conducting primary research. For example, one individual online record of a Euromonitor report may be a reasonable $20. But a full 200-page "World" Freedonia report is prohibitive both in terms of cost and time online.

Cost-saving tip: If you are retrieving reports online, narrow your search. Instead of retrieving the entire European Beer Report, only screen those records with information about consumer profiles, for example. Since most major vendors now divide reports into multiple records, just retrieve the specific records you need.

TABLE 10.B

ELECTRONIC SOURCES OF MAJOR MARKET RESEARCH REPORTS

Publisher	Content
Datamonitor	Analysis and forecasts for over 400 market sectors in U.K., Europe, and U.S.
Euromonitor	
Market Directions	Marketing information on consumer product sectors in UK, France, Italy, Japan, Germany, Spain and the U.S.
Market Reports	Full-text consumer product reports with an international focus; also surveys of emerging markets
Freedonia Industry & Business	Reports on industrial products
Frost & Sullivan	Analysis and forecasts of technical and market trends for Europe and U.S. markets
ICC Key Note	Detailed marketing information reports on consumer and industrial products, mainly in the U.K.
Investext	Company and industry reports produced by major international investment analysts
ICC International Business Research	Brokerage house reports from U.K. and rest of the world; primarily U.K. companies
MarketLine	International market research reports; also includes country reports

Euromonitor

In addition to publishing reference and statistical sources, Euromonitor publishes international marketing reports and will provide custom reports. There are a series of published reports on the world market for a wide range of consumer products from "Soft Drinks" to "Entertainment Software," costing as much as $9,990 in mid-1996.

Euromonitor Market Direction is an online file of full-text market research reports on consumer product sectors in the U.K., France, Italy, Germany, Spain, and the U.S. Many may also cover Japan. Examples of online titles include:

AIR FRESHENERS AND INSECTICIDES
ANALGESICS
AUDIO PRODUCTS
BABY CARE
BOOKS
DAIRY PRODUCTS
HEALTH, SLIMMING AND DIETETIC FOODS
MEN'S TOILETRIES

For ease of comparison, each report has a standard format with the following sections:

Market Overview
Sources of Supply
Consumption and Purchasing Patterns
Advertising and Promotion
Future Outlook
Total Market Size
Market Sectors
Prices and Margins
Brands and Manufacturers
Retail Distribution

Data are collected through interviews with manufacturers in all product sectors and countries. In addition, information is taken from trade journals, manufacturer and trade associations, and Euromonitor's original market analysis and forecasts. Each report is updated twice a year to incorporate the latest data. For example, all reports include advertising expenditure data complied from local sources, as shown below.

Country	Local Data Source
U.K.	MEAL
Germany	Media Analysen GmbH or Schmidt und Pohlmann
France	Trade press after Secodip
Italy	Distribuzione Organizzata/Agb Italia

Other Euromonitor report files are:

Emerging Markets
Market Reports
Market Journals
   Retail Monitor International
   Market Research International
   Market Research Europe
   Market Research Great Britain

In addition to online access, in mid-1996, Euromonitor released *Euromonitor Reports on CD-ROM*. The CD-ROM contains all of Euromonitor's current market research reports, listed above. There is a minimal registration fee to use and search the disc; users buy reports on a pay-as-you-go basis. Free information about each report includes the table of contents, a list of tables, and, in some cases, the introduction. Tables of contents can be printed or downloaded at no charge. For example, the free contents and introduction for "Snackfood Markets in South East Asia" is 10 pages and included several tables of country market data. Reports that you pay to view can be printed in rich text format but only 1,024 characters may be downloaded! Discs are updated quarterly. An entire world report may cost as much as $9,900 while one table costs $20. For information about Euromonitor products, check http://www.bookshop.co.uk.

Datamonitor

Datamonitor focuses on market research reports and does not provide the data and source materials associated with Euromonitor.

Topics Covered by Euromonitor and Datamonitor
Apparel
Automotive
Banking and Finance
Computers and Electronics
Demographics and Lifestyle
Entertainment and Leisure
Food and Beverages
Health Care
Household Products
Office Equipment
Packaging
Personal Care
Pharmaceuticals
Publishing and Media
Retail
Travel and Tourism

Topic Unique to Euromonitor
Tobacco

Topics Unique to Datamonitor
  Aerospace and Defense
  Chemicals
  Communications
  Energy
  Marketing Services
  Paper and Textiles
  Plastics
  Services
  Telecommunications
  Transportation

About a third of Datamonitor reports are for the U.K., but there are pan-European and world reports as well. Online, Euromonitor provides an individual report for an individual country. A Datamonitor pan-European report, in contrast, takes one product and divides it into individual segments. The segments are individual subjects, country, or company reports. Many of the European titles are divided into the following separate country records: Belgium, Netherlands, U.K., Spain, Italy, Germany, France. Sample subject records are entitled Competitive Analysis, Executive Summary, Market Opportunities, and Questionnaires.

The online file contains the full text of reports that cover a wide range of products from stockbroking to chewing gum. Each report analyzes the major changes that have occurred in the market during the previous year and provides detailed market forecasts. In addition, the reports provide recent historical data on market size, segments, brand shares, advertising, trade, distribution, and consumer profiles. They contain analysis based on business school and Datamonitor models.

Data are collected through trade interviews and exclusive surveys from Gallup. Additional data are gathered from published sources including stockbroker reports, trade press, government statistics, and MEAL, and from trade associations, consumer panels, and store checks. Sample Datamonitor titles include:

ASIA PACIFIC TV AND VIDEO
EUROPEAN AIRLINES
EUROPEAN BAKERY AND CEREALS
ITALIAN INSURANCE MARKETS
JAPAN PHARMACEUTICAL MARKETS
WORLD ANTI-CANCER AND IMMUNOLOGY
  MARKETS
WORLD BEER
WORLD GERIATRIC DRUGS—WORLD
  MARKET OPPORTUNITIES
50 PROFILES OF THE MAJOR GLOBAL PHAR-
  MACEUTICAL

Datamonitor Strategic Intelligence Reports are loaded along with the Market Reports on FT Profile and Profound. For information about Datamonitor products, see http://www.bookshop.co.uk/.

MarketLine International

MarketLine is part of the Datamonitor Group. Its market reports are designed primarily for the online market and cover 4,000 industrial, consumer, and business-to-business markets. The reports are divided into standard sections: executive summary, market size, market shares, competitive analysis, company profiles, market forecasts, and further sources. There are reports for the U.K., France, Germany, Italy, Spain, U.S., and Japan. Sample titles include "Italy Car Rental" and "Snapshots: Industrial Gas Market Spain." MarketLine has three CD-ROM products, *USA MarketLine, European MarketLine,* and *UK MarketLine.*

Frost & Sullivan

Frost & Sullivan reports are widely respected. About 75% of the records are evenly divided between the U.S. and Europe. Many of the reports cover specific hi-tech, industrial products. The cost of these reports will be prohibitive for many users. The online cost for a full report may be even more than for the print version. Representative titles are *European Wound Management Product Markets*, *World Satellite Ground Segment Equipment Markets*, and *Profiles of Companies in the World Drug Deliver Systems Market.* In 1996, Frost & Sullivan issued its own CD-ROM that contains the contents page and report summary for the 200 Frost & Sullivan reports on European markets. There are also company profiles for the over 1,000 companies covered in the reports. Abstracts of reports are also loaded at http://www.frost.com

Freedonia

Freedonia's Industry Studies, Business Research Reports and Corporate Intelligence is another, less familiar, source of market information. The file contains the full text of studies/reports published by the Freedonia Group, Inc. Geographically, 75% of the studies/reports deal with the U.S. The remaining reports cover all areas of the world, including countries, such as Iran or Nigeria, not indexed by the other publishers.

Each study/report contains analysis of economic environment, products and technology, end-use markets, marketing patterns, channels of distribution, competitive strategies, industry structure and market share, and company profiles of leading participants. Also included are analyses and tables of detailed product/ market data. Reports often contain product histories and forecasts to the year 2000. Selected major industry groupings covered are:

Advanced materials
Biotechnology
Building and construction
Environment
Industrial and manufacturing
Metal
Paper and textiles
Services
Telecommunications
Transportation

Examples of Freedonia reports on world markets include:

WORLD ALUMINUM
WORLD BEARINGS TO 2000
WORLD RUBBER AND TIRE TO 2000
WORLD FLAT GLASS TO 1998
WORLD ADVANCED CERAMICS TO 2000
WORLD HEALTH CARE TO 2000 (DEVELOPED COUNTRIES)
WORLD MAJOR APPLIANCES TO 2000
WORLD PREFABRICATED HOUSING TO 2000

For abstracts and prices, see Freedonia's Web site, http://www. freedoniagroup.com.

Mintel International Group Ltd.

Established in 1972, Mintel publishes around 300 consumer market research reports. Reports are available in hard copy, on Mintel CD-ROM, directly through Mintel online, via Lotus Notes, and on FT Profile. Reports cover specific products, such as bottled fish sauce or large cigars, and more general subjects, such as direct mail or customer retention. Market Intelligence Reports contain research on the U.K. consumer product market. International Information Services offers worldwide information on new products. Mintel also provides tailored research services covering global markets. In July 1996, the price of print reports ranged from £195 to £595. Pricing packages for the print and CD-ROM services are available. Mintel's WWW site is: http://www.mintel.co.uk.

Databanks

While most of the databases described above are on all databanks, most of the individual databanks have additional market research reports and have different ways of presenting the information.

Profound (formerly known as M.A.I.D; Market Analysis and Information Database)

Profound, a product of M.A.I.D plc, has the widest selection of market research providers in its Researchline database. Researchline has over 40,000 full-text reports from over 50 publishers, half of which are unique to Profound. Below is a brief list of publishers, with a sample international title and an off-the-shelf price. These reports are loaded in small sections on Profound to hold down the cost of retrieving full documents.

Publisher	Sample Title	Full Cost
ERC Statistics Intl	Toy Companies in Europe	£6950
	Spectacle Lenses in Latin America	£6000
Pyramid Research	Telecom Markets in the Newly Independent States	$2350
World Information Technology	Hard and Superhard Materials World Market, Applications and Opportunities	$2400
Yano Research Institute Japanese	Soft Drink Market	$2150

In December 1996, M.A.I.D announced that DRI/ McGraw-Hill World Market, U.S. Regional, and Energy Services publications would be available exclusively on Profound.

This high-end service uses WWW and client/server access for delivery. On the WWW, documents are displayed in Adobe Acrobat PDF format and contain color graphics. With the add-on "Premier Release" service, market research reports are available on Profound while they are still under embargo elsewhere. The WWW site is http://www.profound.com.

Markintel

Another databank focusing on market research and industry reports is Markintel, from Thomson Financial Services. In addition to the usual sources, market research contributors to Markintel are:

Beverage Marketing (New York, USA)—BEV
China Business Resources (Hong Kong)—CBR
Drewry Shipping Consultants (London, United Kingdom)—DRW
Global Trade Intelligence (Boston, USA)—GTI
Leatherhead Food Research (Leatherhead, United Kingdom)—LHD
Market & Business Development (Manchester, United Kingdom)—MBD

Nicholas Hall & Company (Southend-On-Sea, United Kingdom)—NHL

Nielsen Marketing Research (Markham, Canada)—NIE

Verdict Research Limited (London, United Kingdom)—VER

DIALOG

MARKETFULL is a collection of full-text market research files on DIALOG. The international files in MARKETFULL are the Datamonitor, Euromonitor, Frost & Sullivan, and Freedonia databases. Each record represents a part of the report. Records may be anywhere from one computer screen, to more than 10 screens. Reports vary from 10 records for a single-country Euromonitor Report, to more than 100 pages for a European Datamonitor report or more than 200 pages for Freedonia world reports. Each file may also be searched separately. In 1996, DIALOG MARKETFULL contained the databases listed below.

File 761: Datamonitor Market Research	current year
File 762: Euromonitor Market Research	1991–current year
File 763: Freedonia Market Research	1990–current year
File 764: BCC Market Research	1989–six-month delay
File 765: Frost & Sullivan Market Intelligence	1992–current year
File 766: FIND(R)/SVP Market Research Reports, including Packaged Facts and Specialists in Business	1993–current year
File 767: MarketLine Market Research	loaded in mid-1996

DataStar

Market Research Focus (RESFOCUS) is DataStar's menu-driven access to 11 files. In addition to the databases listed in Table 10.B, DataStar's RESFOCUS has the Italian Market Research database, Market Structure MAST, and MSI Industrial Market Reports (MSIR), which monitors industrial and business-to-business research in the U.K. and Europe. Sample MSI titles are "Security Equipment" for Spain, France, and Italy and "Furniture and Furnishings in Hotel Chains in Western Europe and Scandinavia." MSI reports are also on FT Profile.

Market research databases in DataStar but not in RESFOCUS include Euromonitor's research journals, MOJO, and the newest addition to DataStar's market research package, CIRE, Corporate Intelligence on U.K. and European Retailing. These are separate reports about retailing in 17 West European and 14 East European countries, plus specialist reports on topics such as discount food retailing in the U.K. or food distribution in Europe. Reports are loaded in sections.

Corporate Intelligence on Retailing has its own online network as well, *Euro*-RETAILNET.

LEXIS-NEXIS Services

At the end of 1995, LEXIS-NEXIS added Market Reports to its MARKET library and a market research report file (MARRPT). Nielsen and Collector Trends Analysis were not on the other systems. Nielsen Marketing Research (NILSEN) provides scanner data for U.S. and Canadian grocery markets, covering the food and beverages industry, the health and beauty aids industry, and the Canadian computer hardware market. Collector Trends Analysis (CTA) Reports focus on the marketing activity of themes or brand licensing or use of theme motifs, rather than on particular industries. Because of the length and cost of the reports, LEXIS-NEXIS provides two files for each of the research reports, a file with the reports and a file with just the table of contents. LEXIS-NEXIS also has the U.S. Trade Administration Market Reports that are found on NTDB.

FT Profile

FT Profile's Market Research Library includes all the standard market research reports described above, plus reports from other U.K. publishers. The primary unique provider is Mintel. Mintel International Intelligence (MII) file on FT Profile has structured reports for France, Germany, Italy, the Netherlands, Belgium, Spain, and the U.K. Each report includes a Country Profile; Clothing & Footware, Food, Drink & Tobacco, Household Goods & Services; Shopper Attitudes: Recreations, Entertainment & Culture, Media; Tourism & Eating Out; and Transport. Most reports are divided into sections for online searching and retrieval.

Investment Bank Reports as Market Research Reports

Another source for market information about both companies and industries is investment bank reports. Investment bank reports differ from market research reports in that their primary application is the financial analysis of quoted companies and the industries of which they are a part. Therefore, much of the information in these reports focuses on the financial and stock market performance of the companies analyzed. However, investment reports also contain information of value to the market researcher. The reports are good sources of competitive intelligence. They may include product market share information as part of their analysis.

Individual investment banks conduct research on the companies and industries they follow for their clients. Although available in print, these reports must be searched through full text databases online or on-disc.

Electronic Sources of Investment Bank Reports

Investext is a product of Thomson Financial Network. Coverage is worldwide. *Investext* is available on many time-sharing hosts, including Thomson's own network, as well as on a CD-ROM provided by the Information Access Company and on IAC's subscription academic WWW site, Searchbank: http://www.searchbank.com/searchbank/.

A second electronic source is *ICC Stockbroker Research,* which includes the full text of U.K. and international reports. "Italian Food Products: Listening to the Customer" is an example of a market research title. In addition to online access, including ICC's own network, the *ICC Stockbroker Research Reports* for U.K. traded companies are on the DIALOG OnDisc *U.K. Factfinder* CD-ROM. A second ICC source, ICC KeyNotes, provides market analysis of key U.K. industrial sectors.

The Research Bank offers full text image reports. Search software accompanies the image reports.

Industry Reports as Market Research Reports

Industry reports, discussed more fully in Chapter 14, are also excellent sources for the market researcher. The *Financial Times Business Reports* on FT Profile, DataStar, and LEXIS-NEXIS Services have market analysis for a wide range of industries such as biotechnology, telecommunications, and pharmaceuticals. The information comes from the *Financial Times* newsletters and management and conference reports. The individual reports are also available in *Financial Times'* special surveys, which often include useful information for the market researcher. For example, "The Survey of India" in 1992 had interesting information from Marg, India's largest market research organization, on the huge potential Indian market in rural and semi-rural areas. Marg predicated the rapid penetration of television into the rural areas as being the major factor behind greater product awareness.[1]

Other industry reports that are useful to the market researcher are the *ICC KeyNote Reports* and the industry reports from EIU.

The former are available on most major databanks, direct from ICC, via the WWW in 1997, and on CD-ROM. The EIU reports focus primarily on the automotive industry and are available electronically on FT Profile and Profound.

Newsletters

Specialized newsletters are another excellent source for the market researcher. Because of their expense and narrow focus, it is more efficient to search newsletters electronically if they are needed only occasionally. Sources for newsletters are the newsletter files on DIALOG, DataStar, and LEXIS-NEXIS Services.

Database Files

IAC Files

The former Predicasts files, now provided by Information Access Company (IAC), are an important source of market information. They contain excerpts from market reports in addition to abstracts and full text of newspapers, trade publications, and business magazines. Files such as PROMT and the F&S Indexes are available as print indexes, and electronically as CD-ROMs, online databases from commercial vendors and on the WWW, and directly from IAC. The breadth and depth of the information, covering thousands of individual products from hundreds of countries, make these sources an essential tool for marketing research. *Euromonitor* and *Datamonitor Reports* only report on consumer products. Investment bank reports cover broad industry groups consisting of public companies. IAC's *PROMT* has much broader coverage. It includes specific industrial as well as consumer products to a 7-digit product code level.

Sections of *Investext* and Euromonitor's *Market Research Europe* appear as part of the online *PROMT* file, as do references to other market research reports. *PROMT* also extracts material from "Eurofood" and "Research Studies Market Assessment" publications. Prior to 1994, *PROMT* records indexed individual tables from reports.

Business & Industry

The Business & Industry Database, developed to compete with the IAC files, includes fewer articles on any given subject, but has less duplication and, more importantly, also has the tabular data now excluded from most IAC full text offerings.

W-Two Publications (IBC)

Three interesting and informative print newsletters—*Market Europe, Market Asia Pacific,* and *Market Latin America*—are widely available online. Only the IAC Newsletter files have complete coverage. *Business & Industry Database,* unlike IAC, does include the tabular data. These newsletters contain specific marketing and demographic information not readily available elsewhere. A fourth title, *Market Africa/Mid-East,* was released in 1996. Also, the company was purchased in 1996 by IBC, producers of Political Risk Service. Exhibit 10.1 is an extract from an article from *Market Latin America.*

Special reports; for example, *Consumers in Italy,* are available in the "Dynamic Market Reprint Series."

BRAZIL'S YOUNG-ADULT CONSUMERS

Market Latin America May 1, 1996 p. N/A

Brazil's large young-adult market includes approximately 37 million people between the ages of 20 and 34—nearly 25 percent of the country's total population. While disposable income is scarce for young-adult Brazilians, they spend what they have on clothes and entertainment with their friends. Jeans and sneakers are a must, regardless of socioeconomic class, with brand names the only feature to distinguish a person's social status. Fast foods are popular, and beer is the most popular choice of beverage to go with the meal.

EXTRACT FROM *MARKET LATIN AMERICA* RECORD

EXHIBIT 10.1

Source: Market Latin America on *PROMT* on DIALOG, July 1996. Copyright Information Access Company, Predicast/IAC. Reprinted with permission.

ITA Market Reports

Throughout this book we discuss *National Trade Data Bank* (NTDB) and the Market Reports written by the U.S. International Trade Administration. Printed reports may be purchased or searched on the NTDB CD-ROM, on the WWW on the fee-based STAT-USA site, or through LEXIS-NEXIS Services. Thousands of reports have been published for individual products in individual countries.

Finding Aids for Market Research Reports

Findex: The Worldwide Directory of Market Research Reports (published annually, with midyear supplements, by Cambridge Information Group)

Findex has abstracts and indexes for about 20,000 off-the-shelf reports. Reports are of different types, including audits and syndicated and multiclient studies. The majority of the entries are market research reports. Reports are arranged under 12 major industry groupings, with a separate section for reports about companies. The reports come from more than 500 publishers. *Findex* is indexed by publisher, title, subject, country, and company name. *Findex* abstracts

are searchable on DIALOG (File 196), LEXIS-NEXIS Market Reports (FNDCAT), and directly from Cambridge Scientific through their subscriber WWW interface at http://www.csa.com.

Sample titles from *Findex* that indicate the range of prices and subjects include *China Drug Purchase Audit,* a quarterly publication on Western-type pharmaceuticals sold to a sample of hospitals and clinics in the People's Republic of China, costing $19,500; and the annual "Machine Tools and Metalworking Equipment Industry Analysis: Ecuador," which sells for $150.

Marketsearch (published annually by the Arlington Management Publications and the British Overseas Trade Board)

Formerly the *International Directory of Published Market Research, Marketsearch* has a brief summary of 20,000 published market research studies. Countries are in the summaries, but index access is to publisher and corporate author.

International Market Research Information (NSA Ltd.)

International Market Research Information is available on DataStar as IMRI. It contains over 40,000 records, which are a mix of abstracts to literature on market research, details of multiclient and syndicated studies, and a directory of market research agencies, with company name, address, telecommunications, and contact. Sources include the Market Research Society's abstracts and directory along with ESOMAR's directory plus yellow pages. The directory is available on the WWW at http://www. IMRIresearch.com. Most of the agency listings on the WWW are limited to name and phone number, listed by country. Some have specialty, address, and contact name, and a few have links to agency home pages.

Marketing Surveys Index

Published monthly by Marketing Strategies for Industry U.K., *Marketing Surveys Index* is a directory of published business research worldwide. The *Index* covers reports published since 1983 and is available on FT Profile.

WORLDWIDE MARKET SHARE

Many commonly asked marketing questions concern "market share." The question must be clearly defined to be answerable. A question such as "What is Nestle's market share?" is too ambiguous for an answer. Market share requires a defined product or service, a defined geographic region, and a defined unit of measurement. Market share is now expressed globally, regionally, nationally, or locally. It can be measured by sales or volume, consumption or production, value or quantity (e.g., dollars or pounds/barrels or bottles). To calculate a meaningful share, the entire market quantity should be known. The answer is usually expressed as a percentage.

Market share can be measured at the level of broad industry grouping:

> *What is Nestle's share of the world food market?*

For a product line:

> *What is Nestle's share of the European coffee market?*

For a specific line of business:

> What is Nestle's share of the U.S. decaffeinated coffee market?

For a specific brand:

> What share of the coffee market is held by Decaf Nescafe?

Because of the elusiveness of the definition of *market* for each situation, no one source, printed or online, can be relied upon to answer market share questions, nor is there one definitive "right answer."

World Market Share Reporter (Gale Research, 1st ed., 1995/96)

The *World Market Share Reporter* is subtitled "A compilation of reported world market share data and rankings on companies' products and services." It combines *European Market Share Reporter* and *European Business Rankings*. It is modeled after the U.S. *Market Share Reporter*. The *World Reporter* presents market data that have been published in other sources. There are about 1,650 entries, arranged by 2-digit U.S. SIC industry groupings. The data are selected from newspapers and general purpose trade and technical periodicals that were published between August 1992 and September 1994. The *Reporter* has five indexes. The first index is sources, including over 300 primary sources and 700 original sources in which the data were found. For example, in Exhibit 8-9, the *Economist* was the source of publication but *Food Business* was the source for the data. The other four indexes are Place Names; Products, Services and Issues; Companies, with references to 3,900 company names, as they appeared in the rankings; and Brands, with references to over 600 brands or "brand equivalents." There are three listings of standard codes: U.S. SIC, international ISIC, and a 2-digit Harmonized Commodity classification.

Exhibit 8.9 in Chapter 8 is a sample record that serves both as a "ranking" and a "share" report. Note that in many entries the editors have calculated a "percent of the group." However, you cannot say that Nestle has 21% of the worldwide food market because it has 21% of the sales of the 12 companies in the example.

Use the *Market Share Reporter* with caution and primarily as a finding aid. Its limitations include the highly selective nature of the entries, which often appear random; the lack of underlying market information; and the age of the information. The burden is on the user to determine the reliability of the source and to examine the source document.

Gale has been planning to release this product on CD-ROM and to include it on Gale's direct access subscription WWW site, http://galenet.gale.com.

Researchers with access to any online or CD-ROM databases mentioned below would be much better served searching for market share information directly. Searching electronic sources is often expensive, but there is also a cost attached to providing partial, dated, or misleading information.

Electronic Access to Market Share Information

To find other market share data in print, it is usually necessary to begin by searching online or on CD-ROM. In addition to market research and investment bank reports, multipurpose databases such as *Textline, PROMT, Business & Industry,* and *ABI/Inform* all contain worldwide market share data. Because many of the publications in these files may be unfamiliar, and because the original source of the data is often not included, much of this data should be used judiciously. Table 10.C lists selected databases that provide market share information.

Information Access Company (IAC) Files

A diverse range of articles with market share data appear in the online *PROMT* database and the *F&S Index Plus Text International* CD-ROM. The print versions of the F&S Indexes and *PROMT* cannot provide the same level of access to articles containing market share data. IAC made "Market Share" an event code (EC=604) in *PROMT* in January 1997, but they did not back-index any of the existing articles. Many of the international sources in these files are difficult to obtain. IAC has been adding more full text to its electronic files. However, the tabular data are often omitted. Exhibit 10.2 is an article from *PROMT* that includes examples of important marketing concepts.

TABLE 10.C

SELECTED DATABASES WITH MARKET SHARE INFORMATION

Company	Database
IAC Files	F&S Index + Text CD-ROM (International and U.S. discs) PROMT Newsletter Database MARS (Marketing and Advertising Reference Service)
RESPONSIVE DATABASE SERVICES	Business & Industry
UMI	ABI/INFORM

AN 3751725 PROMT 920511.
SO East-Europe-Agriculture-and-Food, March, 1992, PAGE N/A,
    ISSN 0263-3205.
DT 920300.
LG EN.
PN Bulk-Fluid-Milk (P2026100). Cheese (P2022000). Butter (P2021000).
EN Foreign-Trade (E64).
CN **Poland** (C6POL).
TI INCREASING IMPORTS AFFECTING POLISH DAIRY SECTOR.
AT Poland: Imports 137.8 mil L of milk in 1990, with further large imports in 1991; discusses taste for Western prods.
AV *FULL TEXT AVAILABLE IN FORMAT 'ALL'*.
LE WORD COUNT: 571.
TX Polish **consumers** have rapidly developed a **taste** for western dairy products, despite the higher **prices** which they attract on the retail market. Official statistics show that Poland imported as much as 137.8 million litres of milk in 1990, mostly from France, Belgium, Germany and Denmark, with further large imports in 1991. The reason for the increase in the huge difference in **product quality,...**
These include the **administrative barriers and customs duties** which, as from March 1 1992, have been adjusted in accordance with the Poland-EC Association Agreement. In addition, these is only a limited number of more **affluent consumers** in Poland who can afford to buy Western milk. Thus the **market share** of imported milk and dairy products in 1991 remained at 10%.
Overall consumption falling . . .
There is also a general tendency towards decreased **consumption** of
milk and dairy products in Poland...The **structure** of the Polish **dairy industry** is far from satisfactory...
Market prices rising... liquid milk sold in the shops for between 4 400 and 5 200 zlotys per litre ($1 = 13 200 zlotys)...
Polish dairy exports in Jan-Sep 1991
According to the latest available data from the **Central Statistical Office,** imports of milk and selected dairy products the end-September 1991 stood at:

Milk (hectolitres)		Cheese (tonnes)		Butter (tonnes)	
France	5 934	Holland	126.8	Germany	1 052.0
Belgium	821	Hong Kong	20.0	Austria	439.7
Switzerland	15.0	France	364.7		
France	12.0	Holland	315.0		
Germany	9.0	Czechoslovakia	86.4		

Source: Monthly Statistical Bulletin of GUS (Polish Central Statistical Office) 1992, No. 1
Table details Poland's imports of milk and selected dairy products as of end-Sept 1991 by type and country.
THIS IS THE FULL TEXT: Copyright 1992 Agra Europe (London) Ltd.

EXCERPTS FROM PREDICASTS *PROMT*

EXHIBIT 10.2

Source: F & S Index + Text International, SilverPlatter CD-ROM. November 1992. Copyright 1993 by Information Access Company. Reprinted with permission.

Other representative titles relating to market share in the beer market in PROMT include:

- Mahou adelanta a El Aguila en el mercado cervecero. Spain: According to Spanish *Brewers'* Assn, in 1995, Cruzcampo *beer* leads mkt w/ 25.08% *share* & sales of 6,348,196 hectoliters. *Expansion-Spain*, June 11, 1996,
- Chang brewer eyeing 50% market share. Currently holds 15% share of the 800 mil liter beer mkt in Thailand with its Beer Chang. *Nation*, June 5, 1996.
- Japanese wine and beer share taiwan market. Taiwan: Japanese beer & wine enjoy good share of taiwanese market. *Economic-Daily-News*, March 15, 1995.

Textline

Reuter *Textline*, a subset of Reuters Business Briefing, had well over 200,000 records with market share information. Some sample titles on market share for beer are presented below.

- JAPAN: JUNE*BEER*SHIPMENTS SHOW ASAHI AT 31%*MARKET SHARE.* Comline-News-Service, COMLN; Nihon-Keizai-Shimbun, 12/07/96.
- CZECH REPUBLIC: SMALL INDEPENDENT* BREWERIES*HAVE 7.5%*MARKET SHARE* IN 1995.BIPCE;C-S-T-K-Ecoservice-Czech, CTK 20/6/96 P6.
- HUNGARY: Sopron, Martfu*breweries*boost* market share.* Reuter-News-Service, Reuter-News-Service-Ussr-and-East-Europe, Reuter-Economic-News, LBA; 16/05/96.

Textline may not exist as a separate database apart from Reuters Business Briefing after 1997.

Business & Industry Database

At a time when most database producers are targeting end users, Responsive Database Services, run by the first owner of the Predicasts products, introduced a database for librarians. The database selectively includes articles from thousands of publications, eliminates duplication, and uses business concept indexing. "Market Share" is one concept. The database also tags records that have tabular data. *Business & Industry* is available on the major databanks and is a DIALOG CD-ROM product. Sample titles on market share for beer are presented below:

- BBH helps Guinness rival.
  Murphy*Brewery* Ireland will spend $8 mil over 6 mos as part of a three-year campaign to double its*share*of the Irish dark*beer market.*

Euromarketing;Volume: IX; Issue: 40; June 18, 1996

- Isenbeck se acerca al 10%.
  Brewery Cerveceria Argentina conquers 8%*share*in Argentinean*beer market* with its Isenbeck brand. *La-Nacion*; June 16, 1996
- Pilsner Urquell will not pay dividends.
  Plzensky Prazdroj to commission new 42,000 bottle/hr bottling plant as part of attempt to maintain its 20%*share*of Czech*beer market.* *Ekonomicke-zpravodajstvi*; June 7, 1996

IAC products, *Textline,* and *Business & Industry Database* are good sources for specific products. *ABI/Inform* references market share information on a more global scale or for less specific products. Examples of *ABI/Inform* citations are shown below:

- Menke-Gluckert, Wanda. Hidden champions: Little-known firms succeed abroad. *Europe* n356 p18-19 May 1996 ... companies and not giant corporations are more often than not the real winners on the **world markets**. In some industries, they have **global market shares** of 70%-90%...
- Shim Jae Hoon. Raising the tone. *Far Eastern Economic Review* v159n15 p72 Apr 11, 1996. South Korean entrepreneur Shim Jae Yup heads Shimro Musical Instrument...Shim claims he has cornered **25% share of the $21m global market** for medium-grade violins. ...DESCRIPTORS: Market shares
- Krzyzak, Krystyna. Optimus pursues telecoms ambition. *Corporate Finance* p. 48 Nov 1995 ... Rationalization and attrition in the Polish computer market have brought the number of companies down from 7,000 in 1989 to 4,000 in 1994, with Optimus controlling 41% of the **market, an uncomfortably large share**. ..

Market Research Reports

All the market research reports we have discussed are potential sources for market share data, down to the brand level. Market share information at the brand level is fragmented. Individual market research reports may report on one product for one market. For example, a Euromonitor report on beer in Germany provides the shares for low alcohol, alcohol-free, or low calorie beer for 1995. The source is Typologie der Wuensche.

MARKETING RESEARCH AS AN INDUSTRY

Marketing research is an industry in itself. It is estimated that in 1994 the market research market had a worldwide worth of around $9 billion. Research on the market research industry is conducted by ESOMAR, the European Society for Opinion and Marketing Research, which was founded in 1948. ESOMAR has over 3,000 individual members. ESOMAR started collecting data on the market for market research in 1988. The data are collected from national market research societies and trade associations and measure turnover (sales) only from external market research companies or institutes. Forty-two percent of the marketing research value in the world is centered in Europe, primarily in France, Germany, and the United Kingdom. This is followed closely by North America, with the U.S. alone accounting for 38% of worldwide sales. The European strength in this area is reflected in U.S. access to commercial secondary market research material, since much of it is from European firms.

Exhibit 10.3 gives estimates of the world market for market research. Data on the world's top 10 market research companies are compiled by ESOMAR, in most cases from data provided by the companies themselves. Exhibit 10.4 lists the largest market research companies in 1994.

	Turnover [1] (mil ECU)	% 1994/1993	Index
EU 12	2,884	37	107
Other Europe[2]	367	5	111
Total Europe [2]	**2,474**	**46**	**108**
USA	2,909	38	108
Japan	795	10	109[3]
Other[4]	801	10	106
Total World	**7,746**	**100**	**108[3]**

1. Excludes market research conducted in house...average calendar year exchange rates are used throughout this report. 1 ECU=US$1.18; 1ECU=120.8 yen.
2. Excluding Eastern European countries with the exception of Bulgaria, Slovenia and the Czech Republic.
3. Comparison with 1993 statistics takes account of revised estimate for the Japanese market in 1993..also high growth rate for Japan is partly due to currency fluctuations with the comparable exchange rate in 1993 being 1ECU=Yen 129.2...
4. No complete data are available for 'other' parts of the world; this analysis is based on an assumed annual growth rate of 6% for 1993/1994
(Sources: trade associations and estimates, J Honomichl/Marketing News)

MARKET RESEARCH MARKETS, 1994

EXHIBIT 10.3

Source: Permission to reproduce these tables from ESOMAR Annual Market Study on Market Statistics 1994 has been granted by ESOMAR, Amsterdam; TEL +31-20-664-2131; Fax +31-20-664-2922.

WORLD TOP MARKET RESEARCH COMPANIES, 1994

Research Company	Turnover (million ECU)[1]	Countries with Office[2]	Head Office	Ownership
1. A.C. Nielsen	1144	65	USA	Dun & Bradstreet USA
2. IMS International	585	71	UK	Dun & Bradstreet USA
3. IRI	319	26	USA	Public Company, USA
4. GfK	200	25	GER	Public Company, Germany
5. Sofrès Group	153	7	FRA	Finalac-led Group, France
6. Research International	145	46	UK	WPP, UK
7. Video Research	113	1	JAP	Dentsu et al., Japan
8. Infratest/Burke	104	12	GER	Public Company, Germany
9. Arbitron	103	1	USA	Ceridian Corp USA
10. IPSCS Group	102	8	FRA	Public Company, France

Sources: Major research companies, J Honomichl Marketing News
1 Excluding associates
2 Including associates

LARGEST MARKET RESEARCH COMPANIES 1994

EXHIBIT 10.4

Source: Permission to reproduce these tables from ESOMAR Annual Market Study on Market Statistics 1994 has been granted by ESOMAR, Amsterdam; TEL +31-20-664-2131; Fax +31-20-664-2922.

In 1996, ESOMAR published *Esomar Market Research Industry Turnover Trend Report 1990–1994.* Trends are given by country, for location of client (domestic or foreign), research clients, and data collection method, and also on the leading research companies featured in the World Top Ten.

The U.K. journal *Marketing* published a supplement, "Ranking—Market Research: Researcher Developments," with its issue dated June 13, 1996. Tables cover 80 market research companies ranked on a variety of factors, such as specialists in customer satisfaction. Total turnover is given as well as turnover for the specialty.

Sources of Information about Market Research Companies

Marketing News (Chicago: American Marketing Association) published a *Directory of International Marketing Research Firms* as a supplement to its July 15, 1996 issue. This slender publication arranges research firms by country. All entries include name, address, and phone numbers. Fax numbers and a contact name and title may also be provided. If companies have additional offices, the offices are shown under the main listing and also in a special table.

ESOMAR publishes a *Directory of Members and Research Institutes,* which lists more than 2,600 members from 65 countries. Members abide by the ICC/ESOMAR International Code of Marketing and Social Research Practice, adopted by over 50 associations in 26 countries. The ESOMAR *Directory of Research Organisations* is available free on the WWW at http://www:esomar.nl/directory.html. It includes

nearly 1,100 entries from all over the world, displaying information of market research organizations employing ESOMAR members.

The records give an outline of the functions of each organization and a detailed chart showing the methods and techniques used to supply their various services and specializations. You may search by function, country, or company name. Exhibit 10.5 is a sample entry from the WWW directory.

ESOMAR also publishes a quarterly journal, *Marketing & Research Today. Directories of Marketing Information Sources* from Euromonitor have sections on Leading Market Research Companies, arranged by country. Each entry has name, address, and telecommunications, and most also indicate research services available, while complete entries also have parent or subsidiaries, countries reached, turnover, and employees. The Washington Researchers *Market Guides* have limited lists of research organizations for some countries with name, address, telecommunications, and a one-line description. Individual *Country Commercial Guides* may discuss marketing research within a country and provide the names of some of the major firms.

The standard directory sources for U.S. market research firms include a few international market research companies as well.

International Directory of Marketing Research Companies and Services (published annually by the New York Chapter, American Marketing Association)

Known informally as the Green Book, the *International Directory* has a geographical index to the companies listed alphabetically in the body of the book. In

---

MBL Behaviour (Vietnam) Ltd.
Home
Back Address: 197c Cach Mang Thang Tam St., Ho Chi Minh City, Vietnam Postal Address: As above E-Mail Address:
Telephone: +84-8-839.0774 Fax: +84-8-832.6603 Established: 1994 Employees: 18 Interviewers: 70 Turnover: Managing
Directors: Mr Michael Potter, Mr. Christopher N. Robinson ESOMAR Member: M. Potter Parent
Company: MBL Asia Pacific Ltd. Member of: The MBL Group Plc

  Methods used and Services offered [chart omitted]

Market Behaviour (Vietnam) Limited is a full-service research and consultancy organization... The staff of the company are both locals and expatriates.... Clients include San Miguel, Cable & Wireless, Cathay Pacific, Shell, Coca Cola, Nestle...

Areas of research specialization include high quality qualitative research market tracking (Stochastic Reaction Monitoring), concept evaluation (IdeaMap), advertising pre-testing...

Market Behaviour (Vietnam) Limited is a subsidiary of The MBL Group Plc., based in the UK.

SAMPLE ESOMAR WWW DIRECTORY ENTRY

EXHIBIT 10.5

Source: http://www.esomar.nl/directory.html, July 13, 1996. Copyright 1996-97 ESOMAR. Permission has been granted by ESOMAR, Amsterdam. Tel. +31-20-664-2131, Fax: +31-20-664-2922.

addition to name, address, and telecommunications, several contacts are given and, more importantly, each entry has an abstract describing the company's activities. For those companies listed both by ESOMAR and the American Marketing Association, ESOMAR provides more information on services.

Bradford's Directory of Marketing Research Agencies and Management Consultants in the United States and the World (published biannually by Bradford)

Bradford's has a brief international section. Entries have the company name, address, contact, and telecommunications. Other than the company name, there is nothing to distinguish marketing firms from management consulting firms in this directory.

A final place to look for marketing research companies is in company online databases such as the KOMPASS files, which have a classification for "Market Research Organisations."

DEMOGRAPHICS

For U.S. marketers, accustomed to readily available data at zip code (postal code), city, country, and Metropolitan Statistical Area level, international demographic research can be tedious and frustrating. The type and detail of demographic data necessary for regional marketing, new business locations, or real estate investments is not readily available on the international scene. Almost all the printed demographic data we have located is at a country level.

Syndicated Data

Marketing analysts use demographic data to answer questions such as:

How many people live in Germany?

How many people living in Germany are between the ages of 18 and 34?

How many people living in Germany between the ages of 18 and 34 drink imported beer?

How many people living in Germany between the ages of 18 and 34 had a Budweiser in the last seven days?

Are people living in the postal code for the Sorbonne more likely to play tennis than average for a French postal code?

What is the median home value in Osaka?

Answers to similar questions are available for the U.S. market in publications that may be available to small businesspersons and business libraries. But for the rest of the world, the available data, if any, are scattered, and most often part of a market research report.

One exception is in the United Kingdom, where Target Group Index (TGI), the U.K.'s largest product and media survey, samples about 25,000 adults per year. TGI cross-tabulates brand usages and lifestyle against media consumption. Target Group Index results are included in marketing journals accessible through *Textline, PROMT*, and *Globalbase*. The data are published in conjunction with the British Market Research Bureau, a part of the international WPP group. Almost 400 ICC *KeyNote* market reports include TGI data, such as Breweries and the Beer Market, Restaurants, Business Travel, and Toys and Games. Demographic data include standard age and sex breakdowns, and also have tables by major geographic region and "Social Grade." Exhibit 10.6 is an extract from the report on the U.K. confectionery industry.

Table 32: PURCHASES OF CONFECTIONERY ACCORDING TO SOCIAL GRADE (%), 1995

	AB	C1	C2	D	E
Bars of chocolate	83.2	84.7	85.0	84.0	79.6
Chocolate assortments and other boxed chocolates	64.0	59.7	57.0	53.8	46.6
Other chocolate items	79.8	82.3	82.7	79.6	74.6
Sweets in tubes and sweets for children	56.5	61.0	66.7	65.2	61.5
Mints	65.5	66.3	67.1	66.2	61.8
Toffees and caramels	30.8	33.7	34.8	5.7	36.9
Chewing gum	29.2	39.5	43.9	45.4	33.6
All confectionery (average)	58.4	61.0	62.5	61.4	56.4

Source: Target Group Index, BMRB International, 1995.

TARGET MARKET INDEX DATA IN *ICC KEY NOTE REPORT:* EXTRACT FROM "KEY NOTE REPORT CONFECTIONERY"

EXHIBIT 10.6

4.10.1 CONSUMER PROFILES: Usage Analysis
To assist in deducing a consumer profile of beer drinkers in Great Britain, Euromonitor Market Direction has had access to data supplied by National Opinion Polls (NOP), which have been reproduced with its permission. This survey was conducted between the 29th of January and the 3rd of February 1992.

Table 4.35 CONSUMER PROFILE OF BEER DRINKERS 1992

	Sample	Ale	Lager
% of sample	100	21	18
Men	50	91	68
Women	50	9	32
By age			
18–24	16	11	28
25–34	19	21	29
35–44	19	21	20
45–54	15	17	10
55–64	15	16	7
65+	16	15	6
By socio-economic group			
AB	18	13	5
C1	23	20	19
C2	30	33	38
DE	29	34	37
By region			
London	21	18	18
South/South-west	12	9	12
Midlands/Wales/West	31	27	32
North	28	42	34
Scotland	10	6	5
By working status			
Full-time	42	55	55
Part-time	11	4	9
Not working	47	41	36

Source: NOP Omnibus Services Base: all Adults Sample: 1,667.

NATIONAL OPINION SURVEY ON BEER DRINKERS IN EUROMONITOR *MARKET FOR BEER*UNITED KINGDOM* 1996

EXHIBIT 10.7

Source: Market for Beer in the United Kingdom from Euromonitor, reprinted with permission from Euromonitor.

ICC *Key Note Reports* are available in hard copy and electronically on DIALOG, DataStar, FT Profile, LEXIS-NEXIS Services, and direct from ICC, both dial-in and on the WWW. They are also available on CD-ROM.

Euromonitor publishes data supplied by National Opinion Polls (NOP) in its U.K. beer and wine reports. Exhibit 10.7 is an example.

The NOP Research Group is one of the major market research agencies in the U.K. with revenues of over 50 million pounds sterling. The NOP Research Group is a subsidiary of the international media and information group, United News & Media. Excerpts from sample reports are available at NOP's WWW site at http://www.maires.co.uk/.

International organizations, regional organizations, and individual countries produce some demographic data of varying depth, scope, and quality. It is possible to find demographics in National Trade Data Bank *Market Reports*. For example, there is a 1995 report entitled "China—Consumer Lifestyle Trends," a study of the lifestyles and consumption patterns of young people in four major regions in China. The report includes text and data.

PRIZM Canada

PRIZM Canada adopts the CLARITAS U.S. cluster analysis product for Canadian neighborhoods. *PRIZM Canada* classifies every Canadian neighborhood in terms of several dozen Canadian lifestyle clusters, such as "Money & Brains" and "Middle Canada" (equivalent to "Middle America"). Data are available for Canadian postal codes.

We found no printed postal code demographic data such as CACI's *Sourcebook of Zip Code Demographics*. In Europe, EU privacy issues, discussed in more detail in our examination of direct mail in Chapter 11, affect the public dissemination of this type of data. Many of the databases listed in Chapter 6 can be used to create mailing lists of establishments by function at a postal code level, in a manner similar to the Dun's Market Identifier Files.

Consumer Confidence

Consumer confidence surveys question consumers on their buying intentions. Market researchers use the surveys as predictors of buying plans. The Conference Board publishes a *Consumer Confidence Survey* for the U.S., EU, Japan, and Canada. Present data and expectations are part of all the surveys. The EU and Canadian surveys also survey present buying conditions for major purchases. These data are available online on Datastream and WEFA, and results are referred to in news articles.

General Sources for Demographic Data

Demographic information is available at a general country level from international and regional organizations.

Demographic Yearbook (published annually by the Statistical Office of the United Nations, New York)

The United Nations collects and compiles demographic data for more than 160 countries. Data items include population by age, by sex, and by urban/rural designation. Each table is well documented, with the data items defined and the data quality issues enumerated.

Social Indicators of Development (published annually by the World Bank)

Though compiled by the World Bank to measure human welfare in more than 170 countries, including the U.S., EU, and Japan, the information given for each country on social indicators is also useful for the potential market entrant. In addition to a "Current Conditions Table" for the world, up to 94 indicators are prepared for each country, depending on time series availability. Each country has a two-page entry. A table gives the year of the last census and official estimates for each country included.

Per capita income and income distribution are supplemented with infrastructure data, including fuel and power, transport (population per car), road length, and population per telephone. Data on education includes percent of students beyond high school enrolled in science and engineering. Other pertinent data items are percent of population in urban areas, urban/rural growth and birth rate differentials, labor force participation information, and natural resources.

Social Indicators was issued annually in paper and on diskette. The paper version presented observations from 1970–1975, 1980–1985, and the most recent estimate. The diskettes contains time-series from 1965; however, for many indicators, data are only available for a few benchmark years. The data also appeared on the World Bank's *World Data* CD-ROM, continued by *World Development Indicators*. The indicators used correspond to the United Nations' recommended fields from the *Handbook of Social Indicators*. The data are compiled mainly from other international agency publications.

Demographics in the European Community

The European Union collects a vast amount of statistics. The *New Cronos* database, one of six Eurostat databases, has over 70 million statistical data items, covering the member states, Japan, the U.S., and other EU trade partners. Some of these data appear in Eurostat's print sources. To get a full sense of the data available from Eurostat, one needs to examine the catalog and also request an index disk, which has 5.6 megabytes worth of data elements! Some of these data measure demographic and social characteristics.

In 1991, the EU-12 conducted a census of population. Some macro-level data were released in 1992. Because of the EU's concern with individual privacy, print information is not released at the level of detail of a U.S. population census. The next census will be in 2000, if the member states choose to undertake one.

The EU has moved toward "Eurodemographics," a harmonized system of demographics used in *Eurobarometer*. *Eurobarometer* public opinion surveys have been conducted for the Commission of the European Communities each spring and autumn since September 1973. The results have been published since 1974. In research universities, *Eurobarometer* data are available from ICPSR.

An identical set of questions has been asked of a sample of people aged 15 and over in each EU-12 country. Most of the questions are about the respondents' attitudes toward the EU. The surveys are carried out by national institutes that are members of ESOMAR, the European Society for Opinion and Marketing Research.

Central and Eastern Eurobarometer: Public Opinion in Central and Eastern Europe began publication in 1990. The survey released in 1996 (Survey No. 6) measured public opinion on EU membership and the survey countries.

EU depository libraries receive these reports. Non-depository libraries have access to the results of the reports online. Online records come from *European Community Press Releases,* which precede the printed versions. The European Information Service's European Report is a primary source of survey results.

The newest addition to the *Eurobarometer* series will be *Eurobarometer—Flash Opinion Polls.* These will be targeted at the general public and also at specific targets (e.g., teachers, farmers, company directors, etc.), and will cover one, several, or all member states, as well as Cyprus and/or Malta.

ESOMAR has created a system of Harmonisation of Demographic Classifications, which is being adapted by the EU as a common classification system in *Eurobarometer* surveys. The "recommended questionnaire" and definitions and comments are available directly from ESOMAR (Central Secretariat J. J. Viottastraat 29, 1071 JP Amsterdam, The Netherlands; fax: 31-20-664-29-22).

One of the items it has developed is an "economic status scale" based on the number of households in a country owning each of 10 durable goods, from color TVs to second homes. This effort is supported by the EAAA, European Association of Advertising Agencies. The questions are available in English, French, and German.

Demographic Statistics (published annually by Eurostat, Luxembourg)

An example of a regional publication is Eurostat's *Demographic Statistics.* The 1996 edition includes the 15 member states plus Iceland, Liechtenstein, Norway, and Switzerland. The data are designed for inter-country comparisons. The contents in the 1996 edition include:

- Population Change
- Population Structure (including age pyramids for each country)
- European Union and Its Regions
- European Union in the World
- Fertility
- Marriage and Divorce
- Mortality
- Population by Citizenship
- Population Projections (in 1995 through 2020)
- Households and Families

The 1990 print edition gave detailed age data with country breakdowns for men and women within the EC. Exhibit 10.8 is a brief extract from that table in the 1990 *Demographic Statistics.* The most detailed breakdown in the 1996 edition is by age groups by sex, as shown in Exhibit 10.9.

B-5				
Population by sex and age on 1 January 1989 (1000)				
	B		DK	
AGE	Males Hommes	Females Femmes	Males Hommes	Females Femmes
0	60.8	57.8	30.3	28.5
1	60.3	57.2	29.1	27.3
2	60.6	57.1	28.6	27.1
3	58.8	55.9	27.8	26.7
4	59.5	56.9	26.9	25.7
0–4	**300.0**	**284.9**	**142.8**	**135.4 . . .**

EXTRACT OF TABLE FROM 1990 *DEMOGRAPHIC STATISTICS*

EXHIBIT 10.8

Source: *Statistiques Demographiques,* Eurostat, 1990: 112. Reprinted with permission from Office for Official Publications of the European Communities.

B-12 Population by age group on 1 January 1994—females				
				(1000)
	B	**DK**	**D**	**GR**
0–4	303.3	159.1	2 108.7	253.9
5–9	290.1	137.5	2 294.5	288.9
10–14	299.7	137.4	2 167.4	348.3
15–19...	299.7	165.9	2 038.8	375.6
0–14	893.1	433.9	6 480.7	889.1
15–24...	644.5	348.4	4 664.0	761.0
0–19	1 192.7	599.9	8 519.5	1 264.7
20–39...	1 501.9	756.9	12 342.8	1 509.1

EXTRACT OF TABLE FROM *DEMOGRAPHIC STATISTICS,* 1996

EXHIBIT 10.9

Source: *Statistiques Demographiques,* Eurostat, 1996: 112. Reprinted with permission from Office for Official Publications of the European Communities.

The detailed data are available electronically as part of the *New Cronos* database and can be accessed via subscription to WEFA (Wharton Econometric Forecasts) or on tape or diskette directly from an EU distributor.

Statistics in Focus: Population and Social Conditions (published irregularly by Eurostat, 1987–)

This series of reports, formerly called *Rapid Reports,* contains statistical information of interest to the market analyst. It uses the harmonized nomenclature of ESOMAR. Reports focus on different topics such as "Unemployment in the Regions of the EU 1995." *Population and Social Conditions* are one of nine different titles in the series. Other Eurostat reports are available on the Eurostat WWW site at http://europa.eu.int/.

European Union Regions

The European Union issues a variety of titles focusing on regions. The nomenclature of territorial units for statistics (NUTS) classifies regions at three levels: 77 Level I units, made up of 206 Level II units, made up of 1,031 Level III units. The print publications generally cover down to Level II. For example, Ireland, Luxembourg, and Denmark are only presented in print at Level I, the entire countries, while Great Britain has over 30 regions. An example of a regional breakdown at Level II for Belgium is:

BRABANT
REG. BRUXELLES-CAP/BRUSSEL
VLAAMS GEWEST
  Antwerpen
  Limburg
  Oost-Vlaanderen
  West-Vlaanderen
REGIONS WALLONNE
  Brabant Wallon
  Hainault
  Liege

Luxembourg
Namur

More detailed information is accessible through Eurostat's REGIO databank.

Regions Statistical Yearbook (listed as an annual publication, published by Eurostat)

Regions Statistical Yearbook contains comparable social and economic statistics, including demographics and living standards for the EU regions. The book publishes data for geographic Levels I and II. The 1993 *Yearbook*, the latest available in mid-1996, has 1989 or 1990 data. Demographic categories in the *Yearbook* are more aggregated than in the *Demographic Statistics* but with more geographic detail. Unlike the 1990 edition, there are no rankings by regions. Exhibit 10.10 is a brief extract of population by age data.

RegioMap (Eurostat and GeoInformation International)

RegioMap, copublished with GeoInformation International, is a GIS CD-ROM of regional information, with time series from 1970 to 1993. Another GIS initiative with GeoInformation International is *Euripides UK*, statistics of over 140,000 areas in the U.K. with 200 variables. Data are from the 1991 census. *Euripides UK* CD-ROM resembles the high-end U.S. demographic programs that allow users to create their own geographic areas.

1.33 **Population by age class**		1.1.1990			
			Women Femmes		
	Total	<15	15–24	25–34...	≥65
EUR 12	167 714.6	28 990.4	24 517.2	24 977.5	29 888.5
BELGIGUE-BELGIE	5 087.7	878.4	690.8	779.6	898.3
Vlaams gewest	2 995.2	501.8	400.0	454.1	481.3
Regions wallonne	1 671.3	294.7	227.2	245.2	303.4
Bruxelles/Brussel	510.5	81.9	63.7	80.3	107.9
Antwerpen	*810.0*	*138.2*	*108.7*	*127.7*	*139.1*
Brabant	*1 161.1*	*93.7*	*149.6*	*180.9*	*213.0*
Hainaut . . .					
Liege					
Limburg					
Luxembourg					
Namur					
Oost-Vlaanderen					
West-Vlaanderen					

EXTRACT FROM *REGIONS STATISTICAL YEARBOOK*

EXHIBIT 10.10

Source: Regions Statistical Yearbook 1993, Statistical Office of the European Communities, page 23. Reprinted with permission from Office for Official Publications of the European Communities.

Portrait of the Regions (Eurostat, 1993)

Portrait of the Regions is a three-volume work covering 200 major regions in the EU-12, arranged by region within country. For each region, there are colored photos, maps, and harmonized statistical tables and analysis. Each entry also includes a list of like regions throughout the EU and comparative data to other regions within the country. Useful demographic data are population by age and disposable household income.

Volume I covers the 16 German Lander (with two pages on each Regierungsbezirke), Denmark, the three Belgian regions (with two pages per province), the 12 Dutch provinces, and the Grand Duchy of Luxembourg. Volume II is on the 22 French regions and four overseas departments, the 11 standard regions of the United Kingdom, and Ireland. Volume III covers the 17 self-governing communities of Spain (with two pages on the enclaves of Ceuta and Melilla), the seven Portuguese regions (including the self-governing regions of the Azores and Madeira), and the 13 Greek regions. Volumes can be purchased separately or as a set. Sample pages are available on Eurostat's WWW site, using Adobe Acrobat as your viewer: http://europa.eu.int/.

Statistics in Focus: Regions

The EU's *Statistics in Focus: Regions* updates the other regional publications. The first issue in 1996, titled "Per Capita GDP in the European Union's Regions," highlights the richest and poorest regions in the EU. The report includes data for the EU-15 from 1993, with a GPD per capita reported in European Currency Units (ECU). It also has Purchasing Power Standard (PPS), with indexes for 1993 and 1980. Data are presented at NUTS 11, as in the example in the *Regions Statistical Yearbook*. Newsworthy announcements from the *Statistics in Focus* series appear in Reuter *Textline*.

The Book of European Regions: Key Facts and Figures for Business (Euromonitor, 1992).

This volume is no longer available and will not be updated.

European Country Sources

Following is a list of European country demographic databases for individual countries. It is derived from an article in *European Business Intelligence Briefing* by David Mort.[4]

Denmark

Kommunal Statistisk Databank (KSDB) contains demographic time series data from 1971, arranged by municipality. KSDB is available on CD-ROM or online with an annual subscription to *Danmarks Statistik*.

Finland

CD Finland—Regional Market Data covers consumption, expenditure, and household characteristics in the regions of Finland. Selected data can be produced in English.

Germany

Statistisches Jahrbuch, the German *Statistical Yearbook*, is available on CD-ROM. Subjects include demographic trends, education, and social conditions. A second German database, *Wirtschafstruktur-Datenbank*, available on FIZ Technik, includes economic and demographic statistics.

Spain

Tempus, the electronic database from the National Institute of Statistics in Spain, has historical time series for social and demographic trends. It is available on diskette and tape.

United Kingdom

Social Trends is a CD-ROM product from the Central Statistics Office. The disc contains social and demographic statistics on the U.K. and its regions. It corresponds to the annual print publication *Social Trends*, but includes up to 25 years of data.

Special Sources

Some specialized resources are either too narrow in scope or too expensive for most collections. Demosphere International Inc. is an example of a company offering expensive, specialized products. The company is located in Virginia and Japan. Demosphere offers a GIS program designed to help consumer marketers analyze markets, segment population, evaluate media, and target direct mail. *JapanSite* is a mapping program for 47 prefectures, 3,387 cities, and neighborhoods within prefectures. There are 85 population variables and 108 business variables. Main subject areas are households, labor force, population (by age and sex), and establishments by type, number of employees, and age of establishment. Demosphere should be considered by institutions needing detailed data on the Asian market. Another Demosphere product is *Market Mexico* which has the following data:

Geographic Level	Number at Geographic Level	Number of Attributes	
State	32		66
Municipality	2,403	Population	73
		Income &	
		Industry	87
		Households	17
Block Group	23,797	Population	41
		Employment	
		& Income	19
		Households	23

Commercial prices range from about $300 for one state to about $30,000 for the entire set. Data are also available for business locations in Mexico City, Monterrey, and Guadalajara, down to postal code level.

One of Demosphere's newest products is *IndiaMap*, which is available to academic institutions for around $500. Demosphere products are available through two GIS software platforms, ArcData and MapInfo.

ArcData, which provides a GIS platform for a variety of information providers, has a limited range of international products for marketing applications. Geographic information systems allow users to create maps of specific areas and see the underlying data. Establishment data are available for Canada from Compusearch, based on Dun & Bradstreet businesses. Compusearch census data for Canada, down to six-digit postal code level, are also available through ArcData. Compusearch has Canadian lifestyles cluster data for 70 categories, as well as a database called *Wealthstyles*. The other demographic data on ArcData are the Demosphere *JapanSite* and *Market Mexico*.

SUPERMAP Hong Kong 1991 is a CD-ROM product based on the 1991 official Hong Kong census. *SUPERMAP* creates tables, maps, and graphs of population characteristics for any area in Hong Kong, down to 2,757 street blocks. The CD-ROM is published by Huang Kwan & Associates.

Market Europe, Market Asia, Market Latin America, and *Market Africa/Mideast,* from W-Two Publications, mention companies that have compiled demographic information. For example, vol. 1, No. 1, of *Africa/Mideast* includes data supplied by the South African Advertising Research Foundation. Searches of the online databases suggested for other marketing topics will also retrieve demographic information.

MARKET RESEARCH AND THE WWW

Researchers refer to the WWW both as a market research tool and as a market research source. Certainly, the WWW is the best place to find surveys on Internet use. An April 1996 article in *Marketing* has an extensive list of free and fee-based WWW sites.[3] Throughout this chapter, we have mentioned WWW sites that support or enhance the resources under consideration.

In January 1997, the major market research houses have WWW sites. However, reports themselves are unavailable directly on the WWW, except through subscription services such as Profound. Use the market research houses' home pages to track titles of new reports. Table 10.D lists major market research publishers' home pages.

REAL ESTATE AND DEVELOPMENT

Information about space, availability, price, and utilization rates for the housing, retail, office, and industrial real estate markets are all important to the market researcher in determining site selection. One source of international information answers such questions as:

> *What is the standard land price per acre for an industrial park in Bangkok?*
>
> *How many condominiums are there in Frankfurt?*
>
> *What is the standard rent for a new two-bedroom apartment in Sydney?*

TABLE 10.D

WHERE TO FIND MARKET RESEARCH PROVIDERS ON THE WWW

Datamonitor	www.datamonitor.co	Just company home page
Euromonitor	www.bookshop.co.uk/euromonitor	Publications
FIND/SVP	www.findsvp.com	Search catalog; online ordering
Freedonia Group	www.freedoniagroup.com	Publications abstracts; list of online hosts
Frost & Sullivan	www.frost.com	Abstract of new reports; download catalog by major industry group with Acrobat
Markintel	www.investext.com	News releases; list of report providers

ULI Market Profiles (published annually by Urban Land Institute)

U.S. business researchers use ULI publications for real estate research and as a source for regional demographic data for cities and their metropolitan areas. Beginning in 1995, *ULI Market Profiles* was issued in three volumes: North America, Europe, and Pacific Rim. North America includes 73 markets, including four from Canada and one from Mexico. Table 10.E lists the non-U.S. cities for which there is a 1996 profile.

TABLE 10.E

ULI MARKET PROFILES—INTERNATIONAL MARKETS

Metropolitan Areas Profiled in ULI *Market Profiles* 1996

EUROPE	PACIFIC RIM
Amsterdam	Bangkok
Barcelona	Hong Kong
Berlin	Kuala Lumpur
Brussels	Manila**
Budapest	Seoul*
Copenhagen**	Singapore*
Frankfurt	Sydney
Lisbon	Taipei*
London	Tokyo
Madrid*	
Manchester*	
Milan*	**NORTH AMERICA**
Moscow	
Paris	Calgary* +
Prague	Mexico City
Rome*	Montreal
St. Petersburg**	Toronto* +
Vienna*	Vancouver*
Warsaw	
Zurich*	

* added since the 1993 edition
** new to the 1996 edition
\+ short (two page) report

A ULI report provides statistical data and analysis on the development environment, residential market, retail market, office market, and industrial market, with a map of developmental activities for the city, its central business district, and the greater metropolitan area. Two-page short profiles report on significant changes in the development environment and real estate market. Each city's report is written by a regional market expert following ULI's format and specifications. Table 10.F lists the standard format from an individual ULI Market Profile. Not all subtopics are included in all reports, and the section on hotel development is not included in all reports. Exhibit 10.11 is an extract of a report.

International Construction Costs and Reference Data Yearbook (published by John Wiley, New York, 1996)

For researchers using ULI for plant location, the specialty publication *International Construction Costs and Reference Data Yearbook* is a complementary title to consider for plant costs. The book has detailed information about 23 countries and abridged data from 7 emerging markets. For each country, there is a general overview, statistical information on the construction industry, fees for construction professionals such as architects, hourly labor rates, materials costs, and costs per square foot for different types of buildings, including factories.

CONCLUSION

International market research is both expensive and time consuming. Much of the information is collected locally and is not readily available to an international audience.

Off-the-shelf market research reports may be purchased, but often cost thousands of dollars, and the reports are rarely for the exact situation that the researcher needs. Primary data collection in host countries has problems as well. Market share and consumer demographic data are also hard to find at the level of specificity to which the U.S., Canadian, or U.K. marketer is accustomed.

Use finding aids from companies such as Euromonitor and Washington Researchers to identify marketing research services in the host country in conjunction with secondary data from research reports, trade publications, and newsletters.

SELECTED ARTICLES ON MARKET RESEARCH

Greenbaum, Thomas L. "Understanding Focus Group Research Abroad." *Marketing News* 30 (June 3, 1996): H14.

The article explains factors to consider when doing focus group research outside the U.S. or Canada.

Miller, Richard. "First Steps to Selling Abroad." *Target Marketing* 5 (February 1992): 39–40.

Basic international research steps and sources are presented: geopolitical, socioeconomic, and strategical-logistical.

Stacey, Robert T. "Canadians, Eh! Similar but Different." *Direct Marketing* 54 (December 1991): 68–69.

Despite the geographic proximity and some demographic similarities, Canadians are different from both Americans and Europeans.

TABLE 10.F

ORGANIZATION OF *ULI MARKET PROFILES*

Development Environment
Market Area
The Economy
Demographics
Public Policy Issues

Residential Market
Development/Investment
  Activity
Location
Single-family Housing
Condominiums
Infill/Rehabilitation
Multifamily Housing/
  Apartments
Public Policy Issues
Outlook

Map
Market Area

Retail Market
Development/Investment
  Activity
Regional Centers
Nonregional Centers
Rents/Lease Terms
Public Policy Issues
Outlook

Office Market
Development/Investment
  Activity
Downtown/Core Area
  Market
Suburban Markets
Multiuse Projects
Business Parks
Financing
Rents/Lease Terms
Public Policy Issues
Outlook

Industrial Market
Development/Investment
  Activity
Industrial and Hybrid
  Industrial/Office Space
  and Parks
High-Tech Space and Parks
Rents/Lease Terms
Public Policy Issues

Hotel Market
Trends
Outlook

Standard Tables
General Economic Conditions
Housing Market
Shopping Center Market
Office Market
Industrial Market

HOUSING MARKET (Monetary figures not adjusted for inflation)

	1990	1993	1994	1995[1]	
Total Households	1,838,000	2,400,000	2,586,675	—	
Housing Inventory					
Total Units	1,556,000	1,928,000	2,009,000	2,262,0000	. . .
Typical Rent for New Units					
One-Bedroom[f]	$680	$720	$760	$760	
Typical Price for Single Family Lots[h]	$267,300	$323,100	$343,000	$371,000	

Notes [1] Estimated and projected. [f] For a furnished 430 square-foot (40m^2) one-bedroom apartment. [h] For a 10,000 square foot improved lot.

Sources: Government Housing Bank; and Richard Ellis

INDUSTRIAL MARKET
(Monetary figures not adjusted for inflation)

Industrial Employment[a]	115,000	277,240	328,230	335,670
Vacancy Rate	-	24%	22%	14%
Typical Price for Land				
Industrial Parks	$403,600/ac	$454,200/ac	$474,350/ac	$525,000/ac

[a] Employment on industrial estates (i.e. zoned industrial land) only

Source: Industrial Estate Authority of Thailand, Board of Investments and Richard Ellis

ULI MARKET PROFILES 1996: PACIFIC RIM, EXTRACT FROM BANGKOK METROPOLITAN AREA

EXHIBIT 10.11

Source: ULI Market Profiles 1996: Pacific Rim: 7-8. Reprinted with permission of ULI.

Wyle, K. "100 Leading Research Companies." *Advertising Age* 67 (May 20, 1996): 39–45.
  Lists the U.S. leading market research companies, with related articles.

NOTES

1. David Housego, "Survey of India," *Financial Times* (June 26, 1992).

2. David Mort, "Electronic Sources of European Economic and Business Statistics II: National Official Statistics and Selected Pan-European Sources from Private Publishers," *European Business Intelligence Briefing* (March 1996).

3. M. Austin, "Turn on, Tune in . . . and Market," *Marketing* (April 25, 1996): supplement. Internet supplement with sites for market research information and directories.

CHAPTER 11
Advertising, Media, and Direct Marketing

TOPICS COVERED

- Advertising Agencies
- Advertising Expenditures
- Advertising Rates
- Advertising Regulations
- Advertising Organizations
- Broadcasting and Advertising
- Direct Marketing
- Selected Sources of Information
- Further Reading

MAJOR SOURCES DISCUSSED

- *Advertising Age*
- *Advertising Statistics Yearbook*
- *SRDS Business Publication Advertising Source*
- International Media Guides
- *Standard Directory of International Advertisers and Agencies*
- *Latin American Advertising, Marketing and Media Data: Directory and Sourcebook*

Advertising is an important part of international marketing and an important international service industry. We examine three facets of international advertising in this book. The first is advertising as a part of international marketing strategy.

> *How do you advertise internationally? Do you use the same ad in Singapore as in Chicago?*

The second is advertising as an international industry.

> *Who are the major advertising agencies?*

> *What is the structure of the local media?*

The third is advertising regulations.

> *What restrictions do governments put on advertising?*

The first facet of international advertising is discussed in Chapter 9, within the section titled "The International Four P's." The second and third facets are discussed in this chapter.

ADVERTISING AGENCIES

Estimates of the world advertising market place revenues at around $300 billion U.S. dollars. Growth of large multinational agencies, through mergers and acquisitions, and growth of multipurpose agencies, which perform advertising services as well as market research and direct mail, describe the current international advertising industry structure.

In 1996, the *Wall Street Journal* reported that industry giants were looking for hot little specialty firms, while smaller global agencies were trying to get bigger faster. Over two-thirds of respondents to a survey from the investment banker, AdMedia Corporate Advisors, of top executives at 350 agencies, expected the pace of mergers and acquisitions to rise in 1996. The AdMedia survey reports that 75% of all respondents were interested in an interactive-media deal, while others were looking at direct marketing, public relations, and other lucrative specialties.[1]

International Agencies

Advertising Age (published weekly by Crain Communications)

Advertising Age publishes a special report on the world's top advertising organizations each year in the spring. April 1996 was the 52nd Annual Agency Report. The report lists top agency groups, top agency brands, and top agencies by country. Data elements for each agency are worldwide and U.S. gross in-

TABLE 11.A

TOP AGENCY ORGANIZATIONS AND TOP AGENCY BRANDS

AGENCY ORGANIZATION	HEADQUARTERS COUNTRY	AGENCY BRAND	AGENCY ORGANIZATION
WPP Group	U.K.	Dentsu	Dentsu
Omnicom Group	U.S.	McCann-Erikson Wwd	Interpublic
Interpublic Group of Cos.	U.S.	J Walter Thompson	WWP
Dentsu	Japan	Hakuhodo	Hakuhodo
Cordiant	U.K.	BBDO Worldwide	Omnicom
Young & Rubicam	U.S.	Leo Burnett	Leo Burnett
Hakuhado	Japan	DDB Needham Wwd	Omincom
Havas	France	Grey Advertising	Grey
Grey Advertising	U.S.	Ogilvy & Mather Wwd	WWP
Leo Burnett	U.S.	Foote, Cone & Belding	Publicis Communications (FR)

Source: From *Advertising Age,* April 15, 1996.

come, volume, employees, offices, and change from the previous year. Agency groups, the parent organizations, which own "50% plus of themselves," are ranked by equity gross income. Agencies are also listed by "brand," the individual core agencies that make up the groups. For example, the April 15, 1996, issue ranks WPP Group as the number one advertising organization. WPP lists over 700 international offices, which include its major international agencies: J. Walter Thompson Co., Ogilvy & Mather Worldwide, and Conquest Europe. J. Walter Thompson and Ogilvy & Mather rank third and ninth on the list of "World's Top 25 Agency Brands." Table 11.A lists the top 10 agency organizations and the top 10 agency brands and their headquarters' country.

The same *Advertising Age* issue lists over 1,350 non-U.S. agencies in 104 countries. The issue ranks agencies by gross income in U.S. dollars in their respective countries. Gross income, percent change, billings, and the exchange rate used are entry items reported for each locally based agency as well as its affiliation, if any, with worldwide agencies. More than 90% of the non-U.S. agencies are connected to network agencies owned by the world's top 50 ad organizations. For example, the April 15, 1996, issue ranks McCann-Erickson number one in Mexico and Saatchi & Saatchi Advertising (part of Cordiant) number one in China. Rankings of agencies by gross billings by continent, taken from the April issue, are available on *Advertising Age's* WWW site at http://www.adage.com.

A second *Advertising Age* special report focuses on world brands, arranged by agency. For each agency, a chart indicates which brands the agency handles in which countries. The report includes only those agencies that meet country and billing criteria.

This listing indicates how worldwide advertising has become. It shows the countries in which an agency is located, lists the international brands it handles, and indicates the countries in which that brand is advertised. McCann-Erickson leads all agencies with accounts in 10 or more countries, running advertisements in over 100 countries and having clients in 49. Out of a total of 78 countries included in the November 1996 report, Grey Advertising handles advertising for Procter and Gamble in 70 of them, from Argentina to Vietnam. The Agency/Client summary cross-references the major advertisers and the agencies creating the ads.

In addition to limited data, *Advertising Age's* Web site has snippets of international daily advertising news. To get any information of substance, a subscription is necessary.

Agency Networks

Mergers and acquisitions within the advertising sector have resulted in a few large, dominant firms. To compete with these large multinational agencies, smaller agencies have set up independent agency networks called "indies." An example of an "indie" is Partners in the Pacific, formed by seven agencies in mid-1994. Partners has since expanded to Vancouver and is seeking member agencies in five more countries.

The EU encourages agencies to form European Economic Interest Groups (EEIG). Despite encouragement, indies such as Alliance International Group and the International Federation of Advertising Agencies, IFAA, have lost members. A May 15, 1995, *Advertising Age* article listed the 22 largest indies. The chart includes the network name; 1993 and 1994 worldwide gross income and capitalized volume, with the percent change; and the number of worldwide and U.S. agencies in 1993 and 1994.[2]

National Agencies

Campaign (published weekly by Haymarket Publishing Ltd.)

The British weekly *Campaign*, subtitled "the national weekly of the communications business, embracing advertising, marketing, newspapers and magazines, television, radios and posters," has two annual agency surveys. One is based on profit and the other on billings. The annual survey of the top 50 agencies and their groups, ranked on profit, appeared in September 1996. The report ranks agencies on profit, operating profit margins, and pre-tax profit. It has several rankings based on per-head (employee)

ratios, such as turnover per head and employee costs per head. It also ranks the top independents. Copies of the report are available from Willott Kingston Smith, 10 Bruton Street, London W1; phone: 0171-304-4646. Exhibit 11.1 is a brief extract from the "Profits" table.

Campaign bases a second ranking of the top 300 U.K. agencies on agency billings. This ranking appears in a late winter issue of *Campaign*. Campaign presents Register-MEAL's table of the largest players in British advertising. All agencies appear in alphabetical order and are then ranked by their Register-MEAL billings. This supplement also includes agency profiles for the top 50, a list of the top business to business agencies, and top media agencies. Weekly billing updates appear in each *Campaign*.

	Top Ten Groups	Operating profit pounds m		Gross income per head pounds	
		latest	previous	latest	previous
1	WPP Group plc	124.700	111.300	65.899	62.710
2	Cordiant plc	48.600	44.500	72.006	71.053
3	Aegis Group olc	36.100	29.900	89.491	84.807

U.K. AGENCIES RANKED BY PROFIT IN *CAMPAIGN*

EXHIBIT 11.1

Source: "UK: Agency Performance League," by Caroline Marshall, *Campaign*, September 27, 1996.

	BUSINESS PERFORMANCE LEAGUE—25 NOVEMBER 1996				
Rank this week	Rank last week	Agency	Latest account gain	Total billings gained pounds m	Total billings lost pounds m	Net billings gained pounds m
1	1	M&C Saatchi	Sovereign Lights	73.5	1.0	72.5
2	2	Abbott Mead Vickers BBDO	Wrangler	55.5	13.0	42.5
3	3	Euro RSCG Wnek Gosper	Iomega	40.6	5.0	35.6

U.K. AGENCIES RANKED BY REGISTER-MEAL BILLINGS

EXHIBIT 11.2

Source: Campaign November 29, 1996: 55 (wins reported in 15 December 1995 issue, or since). Queries to John Owen on 0171-413-4287 (searched in LEXIS-NEXIS).

Rank	Company	Fee Income 95	Head-quarters	% Change Income 94-95
1	**Entente International Comms**	25,624,000	Brussels	30
2	Worldcom	22,376,492	Arnhem	64
3	**Charles Barker International**	19,283,770	London	6
4	**PROI Limited**	14,505,000	Chicago	26
5	Ludgate	12,697,032	London	17
12	**European Communication Partners**	6,412,931	Dublin	-.042

TOP PR CONSULTANCY NETWORKS

EXHIBIT 11.3

Source: "Europe: Supplement—Top European Consultancies 1996; Networks - Network News," *PR Week*, July 26, 1996: 9, from *Textline* on DIALOG.

Public Relations Firms

Many companies seek promotion through public relations, nonpaid publicity, as well as advertising. Globalization of public relations firms has taken the shape of "voluntary networks" of firms, rather than the global agencies that exist in advertising. The U.K. publication *PR Week* publishes annual lists of top public relations firms. In its July 27, 1996, supplement, *PR Week* lists the top European public relations consultancy networks and top PR consultancies by country, for Belgium, France, Germany, Italy, the Netherlands, Spain, and Switzerland. Exhibit 11.3 lists the top European networks. Companies whose names appear in bold were in the 1992 listing.

ADVERTISING EXPENDITURES

Advertising Age is the standard source for worldwide agency and advertiser data. On its WWW site, it has a list of the "top 50 Global Marketers." When ranked by total spending outside the U.S., Procter & Gamble ranked number one in 1995, followed closely by Unilever. However, it does not provide data about the different advertising media used or provide data by individual countries.

The one standard international publication, *Survey of World Advertising Expenditures*, from INRA Hooper and the International Advertising Association, ceased publication with the 1990 edition. Therefore, as with so many of the other topics related to marketing, the data for advertising expenditures, rates, circulation, and readership are fragmented and available on a hit-or-miss basis in print and electronically.

Advertising Statistics Yearbook

What percent of U.K. advertising expenditures is spent in national newspapers?

What is the advertising-to-sales ratio for toilet soap?

The U.K.'s Advertising Association, in conjunction with NTC Publications Ltd., publishes the annual *Advertising Statistics Yearbook*. The *Yearbook* uses data collected in the Association's "Quarterly Survey of Advertising Expenditure," covering business and professional magazines, consumer magazines, direct mail, radio, national newspapers, posters, television, products sectors, and regional newspapers. The book includes a wealth of data on advertising expenditures and on advertising as part of the U.K. economy. Time series on advertising expenditure include 1938, 1948, and 1952 to date. There are data on newspaper, magazine, directory, television, outdoor and transport, radio, and cinema at current prices, constant prices, and as a percent of the total.

There are chapters for each type of media with charts, time series data, and a brief analysis. There is a sector on advertising by product sector, taken from Register-MEAL data (Media Expenditure Analysis Ltd.) and a table on the advertising-to-sales ratio for specific product classes. For example, the ratio for men's underwear is .01 while the ratio is 16.48 for toilet soap. The lower the ratio, the more sales per advertising dollar.

The book has rankings such as the top 50 advertisers in the U.K. In 1994, Procter and Gamble was number one. There is also a list of the top 50 brands and their agencies. There are listings for the top agencies in the U.K.

Finally, there is a chapter on "World Advertising Agency Statistics," with listings of the world's top 50 and individual European countries' top 10, taken from *Advertising Age*. The book concludes with a summary table of advertising expenditure in Europe, the U.S., and Japan. Table 11.B presents extracts of international data.

TABLE 11.B

TOTAL DISPLAY AND CLASSIFIED ADVERTISING EXPENDITURE BY COUNTRY

	Total Expenditure* 1993	% Expenditure on Total TV
Austria	1,179	20.5
Belgium	1,116	27.2
Denmark	849	18.1
Finland	590	18.4
France	6,974	31.2
Germany	14,501	19.1
Greece	642	61.5
Ireland	413	21.2
Italy	5,106	47.5
Netherlands	2,485	17.1
Norway	665	12.9
Portugal	533	49.3
Spain	8,104	51.1
Sweden	1,150	15.1
Switzerland	1,719	8.1
U.K.	8,689	32.7
Europe	54,715	
EC	52,331	
Japan	26,597	39.9
USA	65,424	34.7

* based on conversion to ECU

Source: Tables 26.1 and 26.3 in *Advertising Statistics Yearbook 1995.*

Market Research Reports

Information on expenditures for individual products in individual countries appears in the commercial market research reports discussed in Chapter 10. For example, the Euromonitor "Market for Beer—Germany" has a table on the percent of advertising expenditures on beer, by brand, for 1994–1995. The table shows that for all money spent on beer advertising from January to June 1995, Kombacher was the leading spender at 5.1%, and the leading 12 brands spent 44.1%. Data are from GfK/Horizont/Schmidt & Pohlmann.

In 1993, Datamonitor issued a report on "European Magazines" with in-depth analysis of advertising expenditure by year by type of media, along with readership by type of publication and by age of reader. At the end of 1996, there was no follow-up to this study. A table in this study shows total advertising revenue for seven European markets, through 1993.

Advertising and media data also appear in individual Datamonitor reports. A report on the biscuit market in the Philippines, for example, analyses the television market. It states that cable and satellite penetration is "nil and negligible" and then even gives advertising rates for a cable station. The same report lists the top 10 advertisers in the Philippines.

MEAL data is also reported, independent of market research reports, on Profound and as part of Reuter *Textline* services. Reports are arranged three ways: by product class, such as "soft drinks—carbonated"; advertising agency; and advertiser. Data include monthly total spending for the brand, usually combined for all media.

ADVERTISING RATES

How much does it cost for one full-page, black-and-white ad in the Asia/Pacific edition of the Economist?

SRDS Business Publication Advertising Source— Part 3 (published monthly by Standard Rate and Data Service)

Standard Rate and Data Service publications, the standard U.S. sources for advertising rates and circulation figures, now include sections on international publications. By 1996, *Business Publications* had over 1,000 titles in the international section arranged by subject groupings. The subject groups are the same as those used for the U.S. SRDS has been expanding the list as more publications conform to their format and policies. SRDS includes both audited and nonaudited publications. "International" covers non-U.S. publications and U.S. publications with international circulation. There is no geographical index to publications. Therefore, it is difficult to ascertain how many titles are actually published in the U.S. and circulate internationally, such as *Air Transport World*, and how many are published outside the U.S., for circulation outside the U.S., such as the Russian-language *Woodworking DBM*, published in Germany.

Entries for international publications are the same as for U.S. titles, with the addition of language of publication and currency of rates. All entries are uniform. Introductory material has journal title, address, frequency, publisher, and a brief content note. For audited journals, the insignia of the auditing agency is also in the entry. Each entry may contain any of these additional data items:

1. Personnel
2. Representatives
3. Commission and cash discount
4. General rate policy editions
5. Black/White rates
6. Color rates
7. Covers SRDS print media production data
8. Inserts

9. Bleed
10. Special position
11. Classified/Mail order branch offices
12. Split run
13. Special issue rates
13a. Geographic and/or demographic
14. Contract and copy regulations
15. General requirements; also see
16. Issue and closing dates
17. Special services
18. Circulation and establishment date, including geographical distribution

SRDS places the following warning in its "Index to International Publications."

CAUTION—CAUTION—CAUTION

Devaluation of the many national currencies now floating in relation to the dollar, such as the British pound sterling, German marks, Italian lire, Swiss and French francs, etc., suggests caution should be exercised in determining billing arrangements for space placed in International publications whose rate structures are reported in U.S. dollars.

SRDS recommends that buyers of media consult the nearest U.S. advertising sales office of each international publication for current procedures and arrangements.

Source: SRDS Business Publication Advertising Source—Part 3, SRDS, July 1996: 1685.

SRDS TV & Cable has an international section arranged by continent: Asia, Europe, and Latin America. For each continent, there is a map of the region, an annotated list of satellites, pan-regional cable, and satellite cable. For each station, entries give name, address (local or headquarters), telecommunications numbers, number of viewer households, personnel, and a "Position Statement," which is a description of business.

This volume also contains a list of the "peoplemeter services," i.e., the companies that measure program ratings and viewer patterns. Unlike the U.S., where A.C. Nielsen controls the market, some countries have several companies providing different services. A table presents the country, service name, date of the first meter, and methodology, such as diary or interview type. The list comes from the European Association of Advertising Agencies.

Consumer Magazine Advertising Source has a small section specifically on international magazines. There is a list of the magazines grouped separately by classification. Information for news weeklies is listed in the *Consumer* rather than *Business* publication. *Newspaper* also has an international chapter.

Information about Standard Rate and Data Service publications and links to audit bureaus and other ad-

vertising industry WWW sites can be found at its WWW site: http://www.srds.com.

International Media Guides (published annually, IMG)

IMG Inc. publishes a series of media guides covering 17,000 print publications in over 200 countries. Media covered are business management publications, industrial and technical publications, professional publications, and trade publications. The guides are divided into five separate titles:

Newspapers Worldwide	Over 2,000 newspaper profiles
Consumer Magazines Worldwide	Top 4,000 publications, in 24 subjects from 170 countries
Business/Professional Asia/Pacific-Middle East-Africa	3,000 publications
Business/Professional Europe	5,000 publications in 55 industry groups
The Americas	3,000 publications in 55 industry groups

Entries in these *Guides* include contact names, general rates, mechanical requirements, international representatives, and readership profiles. Exhibit 11.4. is an example of an entry from *International Media Guide Business/Professional Asia/Pacific-Middle East/Africa.*

Vietnam Business   **Vtm**
Vietnam Trade Information Ctr., 46 Ngo Nguyen St. Hanoi
Tel: 262319/262316   **Fax:** 263177
Ed-in-Chief Ho Hai Long
Freq: Biweekly, in English, Vietnamese & Chinese
Est 1991
Rate Card: 1/95
Rates quoted in US$
1 pg (b/w) $200
1 pg (4 color) $500
Trim sz: A4 **Circ:** 10,000
Readership: foreign traders & investors

INTERNATIONAL MEDIA GUIDE SAMPLE BUSINESS/PROFESSIONAL PUBLICATION

EXHIBIT 11.4

Source: Business/Professional Asia/Pacific-Middle East/Africa 1996: 18. Reprinted with permission of International Media Guide.

Other data elements that may be listed are publisher, advertising manager, advertising closing date, offset screen, type page, description, and distribution. The *Guides* are arranged by subject and then by country. The following additional information is included in each guide:

- A list of worldwide advertising representatives
- A two-page checklist for the small business person, "Checklist for International Media Planning from a U.S. Base"
- Annual holidays
- A table of the New York Foreign Exchange rates that were used
- A copy of the questionnaire sent to publishers

The *Newspaper Guide* also has a list of readership surveys that are available for individual countries, with survey organization, scope, cost, and order information.

The *Guides* contain advertising. The initial listing in a *Guide* is free, but there is a fee for cross listings and the inclusion of a logo.

International Media Guides are annual publications. The information they contain for any one entry is generally not as complete as a comparable listing from a Standard Rate and Data Service publication. The *Guides* are also much less expensive than Standard Rate and Data. They contain more entries from more countries and may be adequate for non-marketing or advertising library collections. In 1996, the set cost $695. Information about the guides and a sample record is available at IMG's WWW site: http://www.internationalmedia.com.

Canadian Advertising Rates & Data—CARD (published monthly by McLean Hunter Publishing)

CARD lists advertising rates; addresses, including e-mail addresses where available; personnel; and circulation for business publications, consumer magazines, daily newspapers, farm publications, and community newspapers printed in Canada. It also includes radio and TV stations. Special sections are "Canadian Market Data" in alternative issues, starting with January; "Ethnic Media & Markets Index"; and "International Media Representatives," arranged by country and media. There is directory information for Canadian advertising, marketing, and media associations, with addresses and executives and officers, and for advertising agencies. Finally, *CARD* maintains a WWW site, http://www/cardmedia.com, with links to Canadian publications and other media Web sites.

Audit Bureaus

Getting accurate circulation figures is important to advertisers. Audit bureaus verify newspaper and magazine circulation claims, to provide the same authority that a CPA provides for a company's financial filings. The first bureau was Audit Bureau of Circulation,

formed in the U.S. in 1914. International Federation of Audit Bureaux of Circulation (IAFBC), founded in 1963, is the voluntary cooperative representing audit bureaus. As of December 1996, 29 countries were members of IAFBC. At its most recent meeting in September 1996, the members agreed to set up a standards committee to develop minimum measurement and reporting standards for use by members when seeking World Wide Web verification.

The non-U.S. audit bureaus used in the SRDS publications include:		
ABC	Audit Bureau of Circulations Ltd.	U.K.
ojd	Bureau dé Controle de la Diffusion de la Presse Payante	France
IVC	Instituteo Verificador de Circulacao	Brazil
IVW	Informationsgemeinschaft zur Feststellung der Verbreitung von Werbertragen e.V.	Germany
CCAB	Canadian Circulations Audit Board	Canada
Other non-U.S. audit bureaus are:		
ADS	Accertamenti Diffusione Stampa	Italy
CAB	Circulations Audit Board	Australia
CIM	Centre d'Information sur les Medias	Belgium
DO	Dansk Oplagskontrol	Denmark

A complete list of IFABC members is posted on its WWW site at http://www.accessabc.com/ifabc.html.

ADVERTISING REGULATION

When we discussed accounting in Chapter 2, we examined the work of international and regional organizations toward harmonization. The development of advertising codes within a framework of international and regional organizations has met with limited success. There is no international code on advertising. It is therefore recommended that when advertising abroad, the home enterprise should seek legal advice from a host practitioner.

History of Regulation

Advertising regulation, taking the form of consumer protection, can be traced back to Roman law. In the U.S., advertising regulation dates from the Sherman Anti-Trust Act of 1890 and the formation of the Food and Drug Administration in 1906. The Federal Trade Commission (FTC) was created as part of the Federal Trade Commission Act of 1914 and had the authority to prohibit unfair practices, such as advertising that injured competitors. The FTC authority was extended in 1938 to include advertising adversely affecting consumers. In the late 1960s and early 1970s, legislation for consumer protection was enacted in Western

Europe. In the rest of the world, most advertising regulations, until the 1970s, were based on the prevailing colonial background.

Today, host countries regulate advertising within their borders, including advertisements originating outside their borders. As with accounting and financial practice, the underlying legal culture determines the direction of national advertising regulations. Advertising regulations can be categorized as civil law or common law; and also as socialist law; Islamic law; Confucian law, which is based on human rather than legal relationships; and traditional or unwritten law. For more on the distinction between code and civil law countries, see Chapter 2.

Regulation in the EU

As with other areas of regulation, much of the attempt at harmonization has been taking place within the European Union. The EU has passed directives that affect advertising. The two major ones are the Misleading Advertising Directive and the "Television without Frontiers" Broadcasting Directive. Despite these regulations, cross-border advertising within the European Union is difficult at best, with individual regulations and culture dictating the advertising environment. The EU issued a Green Paper in May 1996, "Commercial Communications in the Internal Market," which promises to end unreasonable restrictions.

The text of the 1984 directive concerning misleading advertising is printed in the EC *Official Journal* No. L 250, 19/09/84: 0017. The text is also online in *CELEX,* and updated information on implementation is in *CELEX* and *Spearhead* (84/450/EEC: Council Directive of 10 September 1984 Relating to the Approximation of the Laws, Regulations and Administrative Provisions of the Member States Concerning Misleading Advertising). For EU purposes, the following definitions are used.

> **Advertising** means the making of a representation in any form in connection with a trade, business, craft or profession in order to promote the supply of goods or services, including immovable property, rights and obligations; **Misleading advertising** means any advertising which in any way, including its presentation, deceives or is likely to deceive the persons to whom it is addressed or whom it reaches and which, by reason of its deceptive nature, is likely to affect their economic behaviour or which, for those reasons, injures or is likely to injure a competitor.

The Misleading Advertising Directive was passed in 1984, and all EU-12 countries enacted it by 1992. The Council justified involvement in advertising because misleading advertising impedes fair competition.

The Television Directive provides a limited harmonization of member states' laws in relation to television broadcasting activities, including advertising and the protection of children (*Official Journal* Reference L298 of 17 October 1989). Advertising restrictions concern:

- Duration of advertising
- The form of interruption
- Ethical considerations (particularly for children)
- Advertisements for alcohol (Council Directive 89/552/EEC of 3 October 1989 on the coordination of certain provisions laid down by law, regulation, or administrative action in member states concerning the pursuit of broadcasting activities).

The Council was required to reexamine Directive 89/552/EEC, and issued opinions in 1996 concerning percent of European programming and advertising to children.

In March 1992, the Council enacted a wide-ranging directive that addressed advertising of medicines, Council Directive 92/28/EEC on the advertising of medicinal products for human use. It appeared in the *Official Journal* Reference L113 of 30 April 1992. "Advertising" includes advertisements and information of any kind directed both to the public or health care professionals that may promote the prescription, supply, or sale of medicinal products. The activities of pharmaceutical company sales representatives are also subject to certain requirements. Enactment was scheduled for January 1993 (from *Spearhead*).

In March 1996, the European Council formally adopted its common position on comparative advertising, agreeing to amend Directive 84/450, *OJ* C219 27/07/96 p14. Some member states permit comparative advertising under various conditions, and four prohibit it: Italy, Belgium, Germany, and Luxembourg. The debate has centered on providing consumers with better information, improving competition, and facilitating cross-border advertising.

The council defines "comparative advertising" as advertising that either implicitly or explicitly identifies a rival or the goods and services provided by a rival. To be legal, comparative advertising must be objective, compare goods and services that meet the same needs, must not discredit or denigrate brands or trade names, and cannot profit from a competitor's brand or trade name. In the U.S., comparative advertising has been encouraged by the FTC.

The EU has been studying a series of draft directives concerned with privacy and data protection, issues that have been of concern to advertisers and direct marketers. In October 1995, Directive 95/46/ EC on the protection of individuals with regard to the processing of personal data and on the free movement of such data was passed, *OJ* L281 23/11/95 p 31. The directive is designed to balance the need for privacy against the need for data to move freely within the EU. It protects against misuse of the data. Member states have until October 1998 to implement the legislation into country law. The directive is worded to require the data subject to give consent to have personal data collected, stored, processed, and disseminated.

Finally, the Commission issued a directive on the Legal Protection of Databases in 1996, 96/9/EC, 1996 *OJ* L77 March 11, 1996. This Directive has been of interest to the information community as well.

Seven other key advertising areas are under consideration within EU countries:

1. **Alcohol:** Various restrictions exist in most member states. The "Loi Evin" banned a large proportion of alcohol and tobacco advertising in France as of 1 January 1993. The EU is taking legal action against France for banning the broadcast of sporting events at which alcohol and tobacco advertisements can be seen. Finland and Austria back France's proposal to impose a Europe-wide ban.

2. **Tobacco:** All television tobacco advertising has been banned in the U.K. and several other EU states since October 1991. Industry self-regulation under a voluntary code of conduct is present in the U.K. However, after suggesting industry self-regulation for the Union, the EU then introduced a draft regulation banning all tobacco advertising except that onsite where tobacco is sold. In early 1996, the U.K., the Netherlands, Greece, and Denmark were able to block passage of this directive. Compromise proposals are being addressed.

3. **Food:** The four main framework directives are labeling; food for particular nutritional purposes; additives; and materials and articles in contact with foodstuffs. The EU is also looking at a draft directive banning weight loss claims for slimming foods advertising and banning of ads for sweets, snacks, and soft drinks to children.

4. **Pharmaceuticals:** All EU member states prohibit the advertising of prescription-only pharmaceuticals. Most members permit advertising of nonprescription medicinal products.

5. **Distance Selling (Direct Mail):** A position on the proposed Directive, "Protection of Consumers in Regard to Distance Selling," was presented in 1995, *OJ* C288 30/10/95: Original concerns covered the following areas: information overload, right of refusal, inertia sales, contract terms, membership of a recognized guarantee fund, unaddressed offers, and confusion over delivery dates. The EU is now also looking at sales promotion techniques, presentation of solicitations, and financial security.

6. **Children and Toys:** In 1995, Sweden proposed a ban on all advertising to children. The EU is first looking at banning toy advertising. Greece, Norway, Sweden, and the Flanders region of Belgium already have such a ban.

7. **Sexual Stereotyping:** Spain introduced a draft resolution in 1995 to ban sexual stereotypes in advertising and editorial environments, *OJ* C296 10/11/95: 15. The possibility of such legislation ever succeeding is remote.[3]

Canadian Regulations

The Competition Act of 1991 is the only federal statute applying to all Canadian media advertising. Other federal statutes, such as the Food and Drugs Act, the Consumer Packaging and Labeling Act, and the Broadcasting Act, regulate style and content of advertisements. The major provision of the Competition Act relates to misleading advertisements. Advertisers should contact the Marketing Practices branch of the Bureau of Competition Policy, Consumer, and Corporate Affairs (Place du Protage, Phase II, 5th Floor, Hull, Quebec K1A 0C9) before running an advertisement in Canada.[4]

Individual provinces do have laws of their own. The province of Quebec has consumer-focused regulations for removal of names from lists and regulations on the use of the French language.

Other Advertising Regulations

Hong Kong has adopted a data protection law closely modeled after the EU's. A majority of OECD countries have also enacted data protection statutes. Those that have not include the United States, Australia, and Japan.

Many of the countries newly engaged in free enterprise are introducing advertising regulations. Some are based on the existing EU directives, while others meet the individual legal and cultural needs of the issuing country.

The countries in Eastern Europe and the former Soviet Union are implementing a range of advertising laws and restrictions. A brief country-by-country overview appears in the September 30, 1996, issue of *Media and Marketing Europe*. A good source for tracking changing advertising laws and regulations is *East European Business Law*, a Financial Times publication available in FTEE on DataStar and FTB on FT Profile. Sample recent articles from the publication have presented the following information:

Lithuania: Restricts alcohol advertising (95/05/00: 16).
Poland: The Unfair Competition Law specifies a long list of illegal advertising practices, such as advertising that violates law, good practice, or human dignity; appeals to emotions by arousing fear; or appeals to superstitions or children's credulousness (95/08/00 :9).
Romania: False advertising claims of quality and copying symbols or logos is illegal (95/08/00: 11).
Slovakia: Passed "The Act on the State Language of the Slovak Republic" (the Language Law), Act No. 270/1995, which requires that all advertisements be in the Slovak language (96/01/00: 4).
Ukraine: Passed legislation banning alcohol and tobacco advertising (96/05/00: 11).

The new Advertising Law for the **People's Republic of China** was passed in October 1994 and became effective February 1, 1995. It is based on the Interim Regulations on the Advertising Agency System and Interim Advertising Censorship Standards introduced in 1993. A translated version of the laws and regulations appears in EIU's *China Hand.*

> This Law is formulated in order to regulate Advertising activities, to promote the healthy development of the Advertising industry, to safeguard the lawful rights and interests of consumers, to maintain the social and economic order and to give full play to the positive role of Advertising in the socialist market economy.
>
> (*China Hand*, 1 June 1995: Appendix)

The law has over 30 articles, dealing with everything from truth in advertising, advertising to children, bans on tobacco advertisements, and agency billings, to moral issues such as respecting "socialist spiritualist civilization" (Article 3).

Various bodies of the United Nations have been active in areas related to advertising and consumer protection. The Transnational Corporations and Management Division of the United Nations Conference on Trade and Development (UNCTAD) has focused on consumer protection and has a draft Code of Conduct, while the World Health Organization and the Food and Agricultural Organization are examining the health affects of multinational activities. UNESCO is concerned with the cultural effects of global advertising. Advertising had been one topic in the GATT discussions and continues as an issue of concern to its successor, the World Trade Organization (WTO).

ADVERTISING ORGANIZATIONS

Self-regulation began in 1904 with the formation of the Associate Advertising Clubs of America. The group established a National Vigilance Committee which became the Better Business Bureau in 1915. Self-regulation took a step forward in 1938 when the International Chamber of Commerce issued a Code of Standards of Advertising Practice. Also in 1938, the Export Advertising Association of New York was founded and this grew into the International Advertising Association in 1954. The IAA held its 35th convention in Korea in 1996 with representatives from more than 45 countries attending.

Some industry associations have also created bodies to monitor advertising and marketing behavior. One example is the International Federation of Pharmaceutical Manufacturers. Selected organizations and their focus, when known, are presented in Table 11.C.

The Institute of Practitioners in Advertising (IPA) supported an agreement with the European Association of Advertising Agencies (EAAA) to set common standards for advertising production costs, the benchmark "European Production Contract,"[5] and IPA is presently working on an agreement for an airtime advertising code of radio shows.

The European advertising industry established a cross-border self-regulatory system in June 1992. It attempts to monitor and regulate media that originate in one country for consumption in another. The arrangement handles complaints from the public and from competitor companies. The framework is overseen from Brussels by the European Advertising Standards Alliance (EASA), an association of regulatory authorities that monitor the guidelines. Membership comes from the 15 EU members and five other European nations with the Advertising Standards Authority of South Africa a corresponding member. Member associations and their addresses are available on EASA's WWW site, http://www.easa-alliance.org.

TABLE 11.C

SELECTED GOVERNMENT AND INDUSTRY REGULATORY BODIES

ORGANIZATION	LOCATION	FUNCTION or FOCUS
Institute of Practitioners in Advertising (IPA)	Europe	Production costs
European Association of Advertising Agencies (EAAA)	Europe	
European Advertising Standards Alliance (ESEA)	Europe	Industry association
Advertising Standards Authority (ASA)	U.K.	Code of advertising regulatory
Committee of Advertising Practice (CAP)	U.K.	Guidelines on offensiveness
Advertising Standards Authority	South Africa	Arbitration of complaints
Hungarian Complaints Board-Regulatory	Hungary	Fines
Advertising Federation of Australia	Australia	
Australian Association of National Advertisers	Australia	
Advertising Standards Authority-Regulatory	New Zealand	
GCC Advertising Association	Bahrain & Gulf	
Advertising Department	China	Regulatory
National Advertising Council	Mexico	Industry Association

One issue facing EASA is varying tastes among countries and how to judge an advertisement originating in one country and disseminated in a country with different standards. For instance, in France, bare bottoms are acceptable, while in the U.K. the same ads draw complaints. The authorities in individual countries will continue to monitor internal complaints.

The U.K. Advertising Standards Authority (ASA) monitors advertisements to make sure they comply with the U.K. Code of Advertising Practice and rules on complaints within the U.K. For example, a Bacardi ad from Westbay showed a bar with the caption: "Don't be shy, who's first up for Karaoke? " The ASA agreed with the complainant that its code had been broken because the ad suggested that drinking could remove inhibitions in social situations.[6] The ASA lists U.K. advertising regulations on its WWW site, http://www.asa.org.uk.

Another current issue is advertising and children. The European Association of Advertising Agencies' Advertising and Children Committee has accepted a self-regulation code. The 12-point self-regulatory code allows children to appear in ads but not to endorse a product verbally or act as presenters.

Advertising and Media Organizations

There is an interdependence between advertising and media, which includes both TV and print publications (newspapers, consumer, and business publications).

Several organizations, called tripartite organizations, represent advertisers, advertising agencies, and the media in which they advertise. Some of these are shown in the list that follows.

International Advertising Association (IAA)	International
European Advertising Tripartite (EAT)	Europe
Advertising Association (AA)	U.K.
ZAW	Germany
Stuurgroet Reclame	Netherlands
American Advertising Federation (AAF)	
U.S. Interamerican Society for Freedom of Commercial speech (SILEC)	Latin America and Spain
Hungarian Advertising Self-Regulatory Board (HASB)	Hungary

The IAA is the global tripartite association representing the common interests of advertisers, agencies, and the media. Its principal objectives are to protect freedom of commercial speech and consumer choice, promote the value of advertising, encourage self-regulation, and foster professional development through education and training. It has 3,000 members in 87 countries. Its members account for 97% of global advertising expenditures. The World Secretariat is located in New York City. IAA coordinates its activities with the other major advertising tripartites listed above. More information about IAA is available at its WWW site, http://www1.usa1.com/~ibnet/iaahp.html.

The U.K. Advertising Association maintains a WWW site with information about all member organizations in the U.K. at http://www.adassoc.org.uk.

BROADCASTING AND ADVERTISING

The structure of a country's advertising expenditures depends on the availability of media. In the U.S., we take for granted the large number of television and radio stations, most of which survive on advertising revenue. In other countries, the government may regulate the number of stations, the programming, and the amount and content of advertising. In fact, until 1980, only three European countries—Great Britain, Italy, and Luxembourg—had privately owned TV stations.

Television has been a major factor in the globalization of the world market. Now the TV market itself is becoming global with the rapid growth of satellite TV.

- There are more than one billion TV sets in the world
- TV sets are more common than flush toilets in Japanese homes
- Most Chinese households have a TV, while less than 10% have telephones

The satellite dish has replaced the TV antenna. There are hundreds of satellite-delivered TV services worldwide. At the end of 1992, CNN was viewed in 137 countries. Satellite TV is viewed as the "holy grail" of marketing, making instant global advertising a reality.

Within recent years, there has been a move toward deregulation of television worldwide, resulting in more stations and more outlets for advertising. See Appendix I (at the end of this chapter) on TV availability in OECD countries which shows that countries, have different broadcast models. It also shows a trend toward liberalization.

DIRECT MARKETING

Direct marketing refers to both a distribution method and a promotion technique between supplier and customer. It describes the way some companies, e.g., L.L. Bean, do business, and the manner in which companies promote their products and services.

- Direct marketing: distribution
- Direct advertising: promotional technique
- Direct mail along with telemarketing: two types of direct marketing or direct advertising
- Direct contract: EU terminology

Direct mail alone is estimated to account for 25% of the world's total advertising budget.[7]

Though generally associated with direct mail or telephone contact, direct marketing is embracing new technologies for increased distribution. Direct marketers are using everything from fax, to email, to Internet, as well as interactive TV and CD-ROM catalogs.

There are many examples of international direct marketing:

- The Lands' End catalog is shipped to more than 100 countries. Most international sales come from Canada, Western Europe, and Japan. Lands' End has expanded its catalog availability to the Internet, with 20% of the visitors to its site coming from outside North America, mainly Japan.
- Harrods had three broadcasts on QVC, the U.S. home shopping network in December 1996. Harrods' owners have now announced plans to set up their own TV shopping network.
- Digital Equipment International established a European Customer Services Center to provide multilingual software ordering and support.

Direct marketing grew rapidly in the 1980s though it has flattened in the early 1990s in North America. NAFTA should open up the Canadian market and potentially the Mexican market as well. In Europe, the U.K. is accustomed to direct marketing. The Germans order through the mail and have begun ordering through toll-free telephone lines. The catalog business is no longer new to Japan. Despite limitations of an erratic postal service and lack of accurate mailing lists, direct mail volume has been growing in Russia.

Direct marketing will be limited in the EU by the new data protection regulations. Since Sweden has just become a member of the EU, it had not faced these restrictions. Direct mail had accounted for over 15% of Sweden's advertising expenditures, over twice as much as the percent that has been spend on television advertising. Cold calling is still also legal in Sweden, but not in neighboring EU countries such as Denmark and Germany.

Successful direct marketing campaigns depend on accurate contact lists. Two types of lists are available to the international direct marketer: multinational and indigenous. Multinational lists are files of list owners who have small quantities of names in many different countries. Presently, sources of consumer lists often come from U.S. magazines with subscribers abroad, such as *Business Week*, *Fortune*, or the *International Herald Tribune*. These may be useful for testing which foreign markets are interested in an offer. Indigenous lists are country-specific and are used for campaigns within a particular country.

Telemarketing and use of "800" and "900" numbers has been growing. The European Direct Marketing Association predicts that by the year 2000, telemarketing could command as much as 20% of Europe's $33 billion in direct sales. Much of the business today is by U.S. companies. Many of these calls go through multilingual call centers set up in Ireland. The large international outsourcing company Softbank (formerly UCA&L) operates one of the major telemarketing and fulfillment services in Dublin.

In the early 1990s, the percentage of catalog orders taken by phone in Europe varied greatly by country.

Country	Percent of Catalog Orders Taken by Phone
France	25
Italy	25
Germany	35
Sweden	60
United Kingdom	70

Some of the differences among countries can be explained by the more restrictive environments in France, Italy, and Germany. Also, credit card ownership varies and may be under 20%.

Direct Marketing Agencies and Organizations

In doing research for this chapter, we found an overlap between conventional advertising and direct marketing at one end of the scale, and direct marketing and sales promotion at the other. The traditional distinctions between marketing disciplines are breaking down.

This is reflected in the structure of the industry. While direct marketing services are provided by direct marketing agencies, many of these are now part of advertising agency groups. Prominent multinational agencies include Ogilvy & Mather Direct, Watson Ward Albert Varndell (WWAV), Rapp Collins, Wunderman Cato Johnson, Grey Direct, and Evans Hunt Scott (Eurocom).

The direct marketing industry is lobbying for more involvement in drafting regulations and prefers self-regulation to stem consumer criticism and potentially harsh legislation. The European Direct Marketing Association (EDMA), located in Brussels, has 600 members from 37 countries. EDMA is taking a strong position on self-regulation in response to the EU Directive on Data Protection. EDMA has a "Single Market Campaign," which includes a List Forum for list brokers and creation of EURODIP, a standard address layout. The U.K. has formed its own Direct Marketing Association.

The EU Directive, discussed above, is designed to give European citizens rights over use of personal data, even beyond the boundaries of the EU. In the U.S., anyone may use names and addresses unless individuals make the effort to have their names removed. The situation in the EU is reversed.

The United Nations established the Universal Postal Union (UPU), which in turn created the International Direct Mail Advisory Council, which met for the first time in 1995. The United States databank service

DATABASE AMERICA is a sponsor of the organization. During 1996 and 1997, Arthur D. Little will be conducting a global direct marketing study for the Universal Postal Union. In addition to examining strategic issues, the study will identify best practices, address structures, and standardization, and will also identify available lists. The United Nations UPU plans on using the results of the study to expand the direct mail business worldwide. It is estimated that the mail order response rate will be higher outside the United States, where many of the products are not available for sale and where catalogs will be a novelty.

NAFTA

Direct marketing is a new industry in Mexico, according to the Mexican Association of Direct Mail (Associacion Mexicana de Correo Directo). There is also a Mexican Association of Direct Marketing (Associacion Mexicana de Mercadotecnia Directa) with 150 members. One concern with direct mail is the Mexican postal system. Other problems include lack of zip codes, necessary for bulk mail, pirating of lists, and lack of updated lists. Market segmentation information is also lacking in Mexican lists. *Reader's Digest* has built its own proprietary list of eight million Mexicans.[8]

The Canadian Direct Marketing Association is a self-regulating body. Consumers can register to have their names removed from mailing and telephone lists. The Canadian Post Corporation maintains a WWW site with Canadian direct marketing information, including federal and provincial regulations: http://www.mailposte.ca/english/directmarketing/connexions/about.html.

SELECTED SOURCES OF INFORMATION

Directories of Advertisers and Agencies

Standard Directory of International Advertisers and Agencies (National Register Publishing: A Reed Reference Publishing Company, 1984; published annually, with updates)

International Advertisers and Agencies has profiles of 9,000 international advertisers and 3,000 agencies from more than 90 countries. This is a companion to the U.S. *Standard Directory of Advertisers* and *Standard Directory of Advertising Agencies* described in detail in the second edition of Michael Lavin's *Business Information*, pages 120–21.

In addition to extensive listings of advertisers and agencies, *International Advertisers and Agencies* has several informational features: listings of new agencies and advertisers; mergers, acquisitions, and name changes for advertisers and agencies; and international advertising associations.

Many of the advertisers are international divisions of U.S. firms. There is an alphabetical index to all company names. The body of the directory is arranged alphabetically by parent company. This arrangement is different from the U.S. version, which is arranged by broad product grouping.

A standard advertiser's listing may include the following elements, also present in the U.S. counterpart:

> Name, address, telecommunications
> Approximate sales
> Approximate number of employees
> Fiscal year-end
> Year founded
> Business description with SIC codes
> Advertising expenditures
> Total, by media
> Month of advertising budget
> Type of media used (coded)
> Key personnel
> Distribution of products/services, e.g., national, international, direct
> Subsidiary or parent information
> Computer system used
> Agency
> Possibly products advertised and account executive

There are geographic indexes of advertisers and agencies, U.S. SIC codes, a trade names index, and,

finally, "Who's Where in International Advertising and Marketing," a listing of personnel, their titles, company, and country.

Though designed for marketing applications, *International Advertisers and Agencies* provides long lists of subsidiaries, both domestic and foreign, which are also available in the publisher's international volume of *Corporate Affiliations* (1993–). The amount of actual advertising data for each company varies greatly from the name and address of one agency to a complete breakdown of advertising expenditures. Exhibit 11.5 shows an example of an advertiser record from Avon Thailand.

The second part of the book has agency information that again is similar to the U.S. Agency Red Book. The agencies that are included are all linked to one or more advertisers. Not all international advertisers' branches and subsidiaries included in agency listings are included in the company listings. A sample agency entry appears in Exhibit 11.6.The *Directory* is available electronically as a Reed CD-ROM product and on LEXIS-NEXIS Services as the SDA file in the MARKET library. The electronic record also includes: SDA Number; company type, such as parent or international company; and agency type, examples being outside or none. What is unique about the electronic advertiser record are links to the company's affiliates and links to the agency record. What is unique about an individual agency record is a link to the agency's parent group. The two publications recently came up on DIALOG as part of Files 177 and 178.

MEDIA TYPES INCLUDE:

1	Daily Newsp.
5	Outdoor
14	Network T.V.
15	Spot T.V.
16	Exhibits
17	Product Samples
18	Yellow Pages
19	Point of Purchase
20	Newsp. Dist. mags
23	Cable T.V.

AVON COSMETICS (THAILAND) LTD

Advertising Expenditures: $1,360,000
Consumer Mags. $720,000; Premiums, Novelties; $480,000; Network TV $160,000
Media: 3-9,14
Distr: Natl; Direct to Consumer

Advertising Agency:
Dentsu, Young & Rubicam Ltd (Bangkok)

STANDARD DIRECTORY OF INTERNATIONAL ADVERTISERS AND AGENCIES: EXTRACT OF AN ADVERTISER ENTRY

EXHIBIT 11.5

Source: Reprinted from *Standard Directory of International Advertisers and Agencies* 1996: 4. Reprinted with permission of Reed Elsevier.

BBDO Marketing
31 Staromonetny Preulok Moscow, 109017
    Russia
Tel: 7-520-222-2770
Fax: 7-520-222-2771

National Agency Associations: IAA
Agency specializes in: Marketing, Advertising, Public Relations & Direct Marketing & Merchandising
Breakdown of Gross Billings by Media
  Newsp. $1,100,000; Mags. $1,600,000; Pub Rels; $200,000; DM$300,000; Outdoor
Alexander TitovMktg Dir & Research
Tim Hennssey   Cient Services Dir.

Clients:
Delta Airlines, Atlanta, GA, Passenger & Freight
M&M
Wrigley GmbH, Unterhaching, Germany Chewing Gum

STANDARD DIRECTORY OF INTERNATIONAL ADVERTISERS AND AGENCIES: AGENCY ENTRY

EXHIBIT 11.6

Source: Reprinted from *Standard Directory of International Advertisers and Agencies* December 1996, on LEXIS-NEXIS Services. Reprinted with permission of Reed Elsevier.

---

le Dossier des Agences Conseil en Communication

(published annually by Publications Professionelles Francaises, Paris)

This French directory of advertising agencies is a glossy edition, with color examples of advertisements for each agency and a full page of information that includes establishment date, officers, major clients, prizes, associated agencies, and philosophy.

Media Directories

There is a fine line between the media directories listed here and the *International Media Guides* listed above. The directories include more media sources but may not have audited circulation information or any advertising rates. The *Guides* are targeted for a business audience while the directories listed here have more general-purpose applications.

Benn's Media (published annually by Miller Freeman, U.K., 144th ed. in 1996)

Benn's Media is a three-volume guide to newspapers, periodicals, television, radio, and cinema. The guides are divided geographically:

Volume 1: United Kingdom
Volume 2: Europe, including over 50 countries
Volume 3: World, including the Americas, Africa, Asia, and Australasia

Entries are arranged by country and subject within the country. The order of information within each country is: country editorial, useful contacts, national and regional newspapers, consumer periodicals, business and professional periodicals, reference publications, broadcasting, and cinema. Entries are further arranged by subject groupings in each country. There is a mas-

ter index by specific subject classification and a master alphabetical index.

A sample entry may include the following:

Title
Language
Address
Telecommunications
Frequency
Content
Readership
Establishment date
Circulation
Personnel
Annual subscription in U.S. dollars

A limited number of entries have basic advertising rates. There is no way to know which titles have advertising rates, except by scanning.

The inclusion of both contact names and reference publications, in addition to the media by specific subject, make this a useful publication. An individual volume costs £110 and the set costs £265.

Annuare de la Presse de la Publicité et de la Communication (Ecran Publicite published annually, in French)

1995 marked the 108th time Ecran published its guide to the French press, including newspapers, consumer and cultural publications, professional and business publications, newsletters, literary and scientific publications, radio, television, press agencies, public relations organizations, and photography, brochures, and other related media. Titles are arranged alphabetically by subject area. A sample entry may include name, address, telecommunications, personnel, cost for an individual issue or a subscription, and an ISSN. Television and radio are arranged by region. Companies may pay for logos.

Large academic libraries own this publication for general use. It may also be used by a marketer trying to locate media in France either by type or by subject.

Asian Overviews

Advertising in Asia (Iowa State University Press, 1996)

Advertising in Asia: Communication, Culture, and Consumption, edited by Katherine Toland Firth, covers the advertising environment in 11 Asian countries: Japan, Hong Kong, China, Taiwan, Korea, India, Philippines, Thailand, Malaysia, Indonesia, and Singapore. Each chapter is written by an author who either works in the country or is originally from the country. The content of the chapters is not standardized. Within each chapter you may find historical and economic background of the country, information about the different media, largest advertisers, advertising organizations, cultural environment, consumer behavior, and a bibliography. The amount of actual data varies from one table on leading national advertisers in the Taiwan chapter to many tables in the Thai chapter, including advertising rates in the major Thai newspapers.

Japan Marketing & Advertising (Dentsu, published annually)

Japan Marketing & Advertising, published by Dentsu, one of the world's largest advertising agencies, has a wide variety of information, from glossy photos of the Dentsu Advertising Awards of the year to a directory of Japanese publications with circulation and age of readership. The publication also includes data on advertising expenditure by industry and media, advertising volume by industry and media, and overviews of different media during the year. There are tables of radio and TV advertising rates. It also has marketing research data, with brief summaries of surveys. Finally, it includes a directory of Japanese market research and advertising agencies.

Finding Aids

International Advertising and Marketing Information Sources, edited by Gretchen Reed (SLA, 1995)

International Advertising and Marketing Information Sources is a publication from the Advertising & Marketing Division of the Special Libraries Association. The book has information from 42 countries. The entries were submitted by SLA Advertising Division members. For each country, the book may include agency/client directories, sources of media expenditures, periodicals, and sources of print and commercial advertising. A listing includes title, address, phone and fax numbers, and frequency.

Statistical Information and Sourcebooks— Print

Latin American Advertising, Marketing and Media Sourcebook, 1st ed.(London, U.K.: Euromonitor, 1995)

Although the 1992 *European Advertising, Marketing and Media Data* has not been updated, Euromonitor issued another title in this series, *Latin American Advertising, Marketing and Media Sourcebook* in 1995. The book is a mix of data and sources for Latin America's advertising and media markets. While some of the information is found in other Euromonitor titles, there is also unique media and advertising statistics. Eight countries are covered. For each, there are advertising data, media data, and directories of advertising agencies, leading newspaper and magazine publishers, television stations, radio, cable and satellite TV, cinema, and outdoor operators. National advertising associations and research firms are also listed.

A chart is given for each country, indicating advertising restrictions and regulations for selected categories of products. The categories include tobacco, spirits, beer and wine, pharmaceuticals, food, ads aimed at children, toys, records, travel services, and financial services. The restrictions vary by country, although usually advertising for tobacco and spirits is banned on TV and radio.

There is also some useful summary media data in Euromonitor's *European Directory of Marketing Information Sources*, described in more detail in Chapter 9. Not only are the standard numbers of TVs, radios, etc. included, but also the *Directory* presents legislation on television advertising and advertising regulations, newspaper circulation, and advertising expenditure by type.

Sources Available on the WWW

Canadian Dimensions

Statistics Canada has published a series of reports on the television industry. Ongoing reports include data on the private TV industry and the cable TV industry. There is also a special *Canadian Dimensions* report on the average hours per week of television viewing by age and sex for Canada and the provinces. *Canadian Dimensions* is available by searching the Statistics Canada WWW site at http://www.statcan.ca.

The U.K.'s Radio Advertising Bureau collects statistics and creates charts on radio advertising data, taken from the Advertising Association's Quarterly Survey, mentioned at the beginning of this chapter. Find this data at http://www.rab.co.uk/.

The U.K.'s Direct Marketing Association has a Web site under construction at http://www.dma.org.uk.

Sources for Advertising Regulations

International Advertising Handbook: A User's Guide to Rules and Regulations, Barbara Sundberg Baudot (Lexington, MA: Lexington Books, 1989)

Published in 1989, this handbook is still a useful treatment of the subject of international advertising regulations for business and much of it still accurately reflects the advertising regulatory environment.

The book is arranged in six parts:

1. Background
2. Industrialized Market-Economy Countries—United States, Europe by parts and Community, and Japan
3. Socialist Countries—Eastern Europe, China and Socialist Asia
4. Third World Countries—the Arab Middle East, Latin America and the Caribbean, Third World Asia, categorized by income level
5. Africa South of the Sahara
6. International controls with guidelines and standards

Each group of countries has a table called Regulatory Profile that includes, among other categories, legal system and ad regulation. For example, the profile for "High-Income Latin American" reports significant regulation of advertising while the table for "Low Income Asia" reports moderate regulation based on the British system.

Economist Intelligence Unit

Other sources for worldwide advertising regulations are the EIU publications discussed in Chapter 9. The August 19, 1996, *EIU ViewsWire*, formerly *Global Financial Markets*, reports on restrictions on alcohol and tobacco ads in 11 Central European countries, from Albania to Slovakia. Each brief report has a paragraph on country law and practice, legal restrictions, specific conditions, health warnings in advertising and on packaging, and pending legislation. For example, the Slovakia report stated that new legislation came into effect in September 1996, banning cigarette and alcohol advertising on TV, radio, in outdoor and print media, and in cinema. Other EIU reports address advertising regulations in individual countries.

Sources of Direct Marketing Information

In 1994, very little reference material was available on direct marketing outside the U.S. and U.K. Since then, several basic guides have been written.

Multinational Direct Marketing: Methods and Markets (McGraw Hill, 1995)

Multinational Direct Marketing includes a wide range of brief entries from the how-tos of direct marketing to the costs of major international lists. There are chapters on direct marketing in Europe, Asia, and North America, followed by 32 one- or two-page country profiles. Each country entry has three sections: general statistics; direct marketing infrastructure and statistics, such as association, lists, telemarketing, and sample address; and general observations and cultural sensitivities. Finally, there are a series of appendixes, with a list of other published sources, mailing lists, and paper and envelope sizes.

Asian Direct Marketing Handbook, (Singapore: World Publications Group, 1995)

Asian Direct Marketing Handbook is a useful volume for both experienced and new direct marketers who want to enter the Asian market. Part One of the Handbook covers regional strategy, with chapters on mailing lists, postal options, Asian names, and direct response. Part Two contains chapters for 11 Asia/Pacific countries. Each chapter is written by a local practitioner, but follows the same format. Section titles include:

- Vital Statistics
- Direct Marketing Associations and Agencies
- Regulatory Requirements
- Direct Mail
- Lists
- Postage
- Direct Response Advertising and Inserts
- Telemarketing
- Direct Response Radio and TV
- Databases

For some countries, there are lists of the top five direct response advertising media. The final section is local insights, a personal evaluation of the market.

Building and Maintaining a European Direct Marketing Database (Gower, 1994)

Building and Maintaining a European Direct Marketing Database is a unique book for a company that actually is compiling its own lists. The first part of the book is a how-to in creating lists. The second part of the book covers 33 Western and Central European countries, but excludes the former Soviet states. Chapters vary in length but all include information on how to format addresses, with information on thoroughfare types, postal codes, and administrative districts. For some countries, there are maps with postal regions and languages spoken.

Direct Mail List Rates and Data (Standard Rate and Data)

Direct Mail List Rates and Data has a brief section on established Canadian lists and established international lists. *Scientific American* and *Time* both provide international consumer lists. Many of the business lists are also based on circulation records or established databases.

Direct Marketing Marketplace (National Register, published annually)

The *Direct Marketing Marketplace* includes companies located in the United States and Canada. Entries do not indicate if a company markets outside these two countries.

Market Research Reports

Some of the market research firms discussed in Chapter 11 have reports on direct marketing. An example is the 1995 Datamonitor report "Direct Marketing 2000," which includes data on the industry, projections, and profiles of companies.

Online Databases

If you have access to LEXIS-NEXIS Services, a consistently good source of information on the media at a country level is the Walden Publishing Ltd. *Country Reports,* described earlier. Each country report has a section entitled "Communications and the Media," with a subsection "Broadcasting and the Press." A Walden *Country Report* also lists newspapers with their circulation, indicating which figures are audited.

For some countries, recent data is not available and for other countries no data is available. For example, the report for South Africa, updated January 1995, presents audited circulation figures from the Audit Bureau of Circulation for the calendar year 1992. In Pakistan, the government ceased including aggregated data on the country's print media in 1987. Newspapers do not announce their revenues. The Audit Bureau of Circulation (ABC) of the Ministry of Information and Broadcasting in Pakistan monitors

the circulation of newspapers to fix their advertising rates, but does not disclose the circulation figures.

Using online databases such as *Textline*, IAC *MARS* (Marketing and Advertising), or *ABI/Inform* is another good way to keep up on advertising regulations worldwide. Some examples of the direction regulation has been taking, based on online searches, are presented below:

> **Canada's** TV regulator conditionally opened the door for a return of liquor advertising on TV, simply mandating TV industry self-policing. A complete ban on all alcohol advertising on TV in Canada came to an end in 1995 when a federal court overturned a Canadian Radio-Television and Telecommunications Commission regulation.[9]
>
> **Ireland's** North Eastern Health Board is calling for all media, particularly RTE, to ban advertising for alcohol and alcohol related products.[10]
>
> The Interamerican Society for the Freedom of Commercial Speech (SILEC) urges self-regulation as the best way of upholding "freedom of expression in advertising." The society represents 14 countries in **Latin America and Spain.**[11]
>
> The **Vietnamese** government announced that it will set up an Advertising Institute to oversee the industry, and both Vietnamese and foreign agencies are hopeful that joint ventures may be allowed. Meanwhile, Vietnam's advertising industry grew 99% from U.S. $31.5 mn in 1994 to U.S. $62.8 mn in 1995 and is expected to grow further to almost U.S. $140 mn in 1997.[12]

Business and Industry Database is another place to look for advertising and media information. An article from *Cable and Satellite Express*, provided by Ipunkt, has a table on German TV market share for April 1996. The article reports that RTL is Germany's most watched TV station for all age groups, households with children, and for adult men and women during all time periods.[13]

CONCLUSION

Advertising in the host country is an important facet of international marketing. The choice of agency, message, and media are made by a company but affected by local custom and regulations. This chapter has provided information about the advertising industry worldwide and sources of agency information, advertising regulations, the role of the EU in regulating advertising, and the interaction between advertising and media. The WWW is referred to, both as a tool for advertising and as a source of advertising information. Standard advertising print sources are described and online databases are recommended as the best method of monitoring ongoing changes in regulations.

FURTHER READING

Advertising Regulations

Petty, Ross. "The Law of Misleading Advertising: An Examination of the Difference between Common and Civil Law Countries." *International Journal of Advertising* 15, no. 1 (1996): 33–47.

> The author presents a conceptual framework to analyze similarities and differences in advertising law and regulation of both common and civil law countries. Extensive references.

Reader, Thomas W. "Is Self-Regulation the Best Option for the Advertising Industry in the European Union? An Argument for the Harmonization of Advertising Laws through the Continued Use of Directives." *Journal of International Business Law* 16, no. 1 (1995): 181–215.

> An in-depth study with hundreds of citations to background articles.

Direct Marketing

Desmet, Pierre, and Dominque Xandel. Challenges and Pitfalls for Direct Mail across Borders: The European Example." *Journal of Direct Marketing* 10, no. 30 (Summer 1996): 48–60.

> This study describes logistical decisions, focusing on international mail.

EU Green Paper

Many articles were written in May 1996 with the release of the EU "Green Paper on Commercial Communications." Three that provide a clear discussion of the subject are:

Summers, Diane. "Management: Marketing and Advertising: Campaigns sans Frontiers," *Financial Times* (May 16, 1996): 11.

> The article discusses some of the obstacles to cross-border advertising that Brussels is attempting to remove.

"Industry Welcomes EC's Green Paper on Advertising," *Euromarketing* IX, no. 35 (May 14, 1996): 2 (in *Business & Industry Database*).

"Single Market Common Rules Planned for EU-Wide Advertising Campaigns," *Europe Environment* (May 14, 1996) .

> Spells out the Green Paper's proposals (in *PROMT*).

China

Ha, Louisa. "Concerns about Advertising Practices in a Developing Country: An Examination of China's New Advertising Regulations," *International Journal of Advertising* 15, no. 2 (1996): 91–102.

> Identifies four advertising issues facing developing countries, with China's 1993 draft regulations as an example.

NOTES

1. Sally Goll Beatty, "Marketing and Media Advertising: Big Agencies Are on a Buying Spree That Is Consolidating the Industry," *Wall Street Journal* (April 1, 1996): B8.
2. R. Craig Endicott, "New Markets Nurture Indie Agencies," *Advertising Age* (May 15, 1995).
3. Connor Dignam. "Ten Most Wanted; European Union Law Reforms Will Affect Advertising Freedom," *Marketing* (September 7, 1995): 14.
4. Susan J. Jarvis and William W. Thompson, "Making Sure Your Canadian Advertisement Does Not Sink Your Sale," *Journal of Consumer Behavior* 12, no. 2 (1995): 42.
5. "Europe: Institute of Practitioners in Advertising Welcomes European Deal on Product Costs," *Marketing* (November 6, 1992): 10. DataStar, *Textline.*
6. "UK: Advertising Standards Authority Upholds Complaints against Several Drinks Companies," *Off License News* (November 6, 1992): 8. DataStar, *Textline.*
7. Len Egol, "UPU is Talking Big on Streamlining," *Direct* 8 (March 1996): 84.
8. Ramirez, Stacey, "Hand Outs," *Business Mexico* 6 (May 1996): 12–15.
9. Walker, James, "Canada: CRTC Sets Out New Rules for Liquor Advertising," *Financial Post* (August 2, 1996) from Reuters *Textline.*
10. "Republic of Ireland: Health Board Set to Urge Ban on Alcohol Adverts," *Irish Times* (June 26, 1996) from Reuters *Textline.*
11. Jo Bedingfield, "Mexico: Silec Hails Benefits of Ad Self-Regulation; Latin American Group Boosts Expansion of Watchdog Units," *Advertising Age* (June 10, 1996).
12. "Vietnam Hints at Easing Rules for Joint Advertising Ventures," *AGRA Alimentation* (June 20, 1996): 2.
13. "German TV Market Share," *Cable and Satellite News* 11 (June 6, 1996): 14.

APPENDIX I
Broadcast TV Operators in OECD Countries

Country	Broadcast TV Operator(s)	Number of Over-the-Air Channels	Status of Service	Regulatory Body
Australia	ABC plus 52 commercial stations	n.a.	Competitive	Department of Transport and Communications Australian Broadcasting Tribunal
Austria	ORF	2	Monopoly	State Chancellor's Office
Belgium	BRTF; BRT; 3 commercial	4 (+1 scrambled)	Liberalized in mid 1980s	Regional governments
Canada	CBC; Other public broadcasters; 5 main commercial channels	n.a.	Competitive	CRTC
Denmark	Danmarks RadioTV2	2 plus local	Liberalized in 1986	Directorate General of P&T
Finland	Finnish Broadcasting Co.; Mainos-TV Co.	Kolmos-TV Co. 3	Liberalized in 1986 Competitive	Competitive Council of State
France	TFI,A2,FR3, ARTE, M6 (Canal Plus)	5 (+1 scrambled)	Liberalized in 1986	CSA
Germany	ADR, ZDF + Regional stations	3	Competitive	State governments (Länder)
Greece	ERT1,2,3+ foreign channels; re-broadcast	3	Liberalized since 1989	2 government bodies for "social" and "political " regulation
Iceland	RTE	2	Monopoly	Icelandic Government
Italy	RAI 1,2,3 Commerical channels incl. Canale 5, Rete 4, Italia I	6 main channels	Liberalized since 1976	P&T ministry plus local and district courts
Japan	NHK + 158 regional channels	n.a.	Competitive	Ministry of Posts and commerical Telecommunications
Luxembourg	CLT	4	Private monopoly	2 government commissions for technical and content issues
Netherlands	NOS	3	Open access monopoly	Ministry of Welfare, Health & Culture
New Zealand	TVNZ,TV# plust 7 private channels inc. Sky Network TV	Up to 10	Liberalized in 1987	Broadcasting Commission
Norway	NRK, TV2	2	Liberalized in 1989	National Advisory Council; Ministry of Culture
Portugal	RPT plus 2 commercial channels out to tender	2 (+2)	Liberalized in 1986	Institute of Communications in Portugal (technical) Directorate General for Social Communications (other)
Spain	RTVE plus private channels	Up to 8	Liberalized	Presidential Ministry
Switzerland	SSR Télécinéromanie and others	3 + 1 pay-TV Regional and local	Liberalized in 1992	Federal Council(Executive) Federal Dept. of Transports, Communications & Engery; Independent Authority for radio and TV broadcasts complaints (AIEP)
Turkey	TRT, Magic Box	3	Liberalized in 1989	Ministry of Transport
U. K.	BBC 1,2; Channel 3,4, 5 (in 1993); cable	4 (+1)	Competitive since 1950s	ITC Home Office

Source: Information Computer Communications Policy 29. "Telecommunications and Broadcasting: Convergence or Collision," OECD, 1992.

CHAPTER 12
Exporting and Importing

TOPICS COVERED

- Exporting and the Economy
- Referral Sources
- Exporting
- Importing
- Sources of Information for Exporting and Importing

MAJOR SOURCES DISCUSSED

- U.S. Government Agencies
- *Basic Guide to Exporting*
- *National Trade Data Bank (NTDB)*
- *Importing into the United States*
- *Directory of United States Exporters/ Directory of United States Importers*
- *Exporters' Encyclopaedia*

EXPORTING AND THE ECONOMY

Exporting is the sale of goods or services in another country; importing is the purchasing of goods or services from another country. As noted in Chapter 9, exporting is one type of market entry strategy. When a company decides to manufacture at home but sell abroad, this company is an exporter.

Exporting is important to the U.S. economy. According to the U.S. Department of Commerce publication *Business America* in May 1996, the goods from 1995 export shipments generated $574.9 billion, and along with revenue comes jobs.[1]

- 11 million jobs in the U.S. were directly or indirectly supported by goods and services exports in 1995.
- On average, the wages of workers in jobs supported by goods exports are 13% higher than the national average.
- The largest number of export-related manufacturing jobs were in the category of capital goods, including aircraft. Other important industries for exports include industrial supplies and materials and automotive goods.

In the U.S., the Department of Commerce and the Small Business Administration encourage small companies and entrepreneurs to consider exporting to improve business. The small business person is usually unfamiliar with library sources and research techniques and is least able to pay the price for published market research reports or online databases searches. This chapter is designed for this group of users.

I make specialty boxes for chocolates and I would like to start selling them abroad. Is Germany a good place to do this?

What's the market for push pins in South Africa?

How do I sell cosmetics in Thailand?

Why Export?

There are many reasons why companies of all size export. The U.S. Department of Commerce encourages exporting to improve the U.S. balance of trade and to create jobs in the U.S. The Commerce Department estimates that every $45,000 in exports creates one job—more than double the rate from domestic sales. For individual companies, exporting will:

- Broaden their market base
- Increase overall sales
- Improve profit/sales ratio by lowering costs through improved economies of scale
- Extend product life cycle

Who Exports?

It is difficult to get a good count of the number of companies actively involved in exporting. Less than 15% of U.S. companies export, and 15% of these account for 85% of the value of U.S. manufactured exports. The U.S. Commerce Department estimates that 104,000 U.S. companies export, and that of these, 37,000 are manufacturing companies. Half of the exporters sell to only one market. There is no complete list of U.S. exporters. The *Directory of United States Exporters* lists 28,000 exporters, and Duns Market Identifiers (File 516) has identified about 100,000 companies as exporters (1996).

This chapter is divided into four major parts. The first part lists referral sources, which in many cases are as important as in-house library resources. The second part describes the process of planning and financing export. The third part discusses importing, but in less detail. The fourth part describes library sources for the exporter and importer.

REFERRAL SOURCES

In all of our other chapters, understanding the topic and sources has been of primary importance. In this chapter, knowing where to send your clients is of primary importance.

U.S Government Sources

The U.S. government supplies a vast assortment of information on trade, in particular on exporting. The information is available in print, on CD-ROM, through telephone hotlines, through modem connection, by fax, and most recently through the WWW. A useful starting point for exploring the WWW is the *U.S. Business Advisor International Trade Section* site (http://www.business.gov/trade.html). Here you will find links to other U.S. government sites on international trade, arranged under broad headings (Exports, Imports, Financing Insurance and Investment, Laws & Regulations). Several of the sites are described below.

International Trade Administration

The International Trade Administration (ITA) is part of the Department of Commerce and the primary agency for promoting exporting and offering information on markets and trade practices worldwide. Their WWW site (http://www.ita.doc.gov) provides extensive information about the agency, as well as links to their services.

One arm of the ITA, the Trade Development Unit, promotes U.S. trade interests. It is arranged in seven major industry sectors: aerospace, automotive affairs and consumer goods, basic industries, capital goods and international construction, science and electronics, services and textiles, and apparel. Potential exporters can contact the appropriate industry desk officer.

Another arm, the Commercial Service (formerly called the U.S. and Foreign Commercial Service), has 83 domestic offices and 134 overseas offices in 69 countries. These offices help businesses through stages of the exporting process by offering individual counseling, seminars, and educational programming. Examples of Commercial Service programs are:

- Export Mailing List Service (EMLS): Provides custom mailing lists as labels or tape, and trade lists of companies by country or by product.
- Trade Opportunities Program (TOP): Commercial Service officers in over 60 countries seek out trade opportunities and disseminate the information daily or weekly through TOP.
- Agent/Distributor Service (A/DS): Provides custom searches for overseas import agents and distributors.

Another service, *Commercial News USA*, is published monthly for the Commercial Service by Associated Business Publications International Inc. U.S. providers of newly manufactured single products or services pay from $250 to $5000 to have their products promoted in overseas markets. Three programs are: New Product Information Service (NPIS)—product is described in *Commercial News* with pictures, sometimes promoted on Voice of America (VOA); International Market Search (IMS)—a special issue of *Commercial News U.S.A.* is devoted to one technology, product, or service; and Worldwide Services Program (WPS) for service firms. For more information on *Commercial News, U.S.A.* contact ABPI, Inc. at 212-490-3999.

Table 12.A lists the product groupings that are covered in *Commercial News*.

TABLE 12.A	
PRODUCT GROUPINGS PROMOTED IN *COMMERCIAL NEWS USA*	

1. Agricultural machinery equipment, supplies	17. Fishery & seafood
2. American handcrafts	18. Food processing/packaging equipment & supplies
3. Audiovisual	19. Forestry
4. Automotive	20. General industrial
5. Aviation	21. Health care
6. Business & Office	22. Housewares/hardware
7. Chemical & petrochemical	23. Laboratory & scientific
8. Communications	24. Land transportation
9. Computers, peripherals, software	25. Marine
10. Construction	26. Metalworking
11. Consumer goods	27. Mining & heavy construction
12. Consumer service supplies	28. Pollution control
13. Electronic components	29. Printing & graphic arts
14. Electronics industry production & test equipment	30. Production
	31. Restaurant, hotel, catering equipment & supplies
15. Energy: Electricity, fossil fuel	32. Safety & security
	33. Sports, recreation, hobby
16. Energy: Solar, wind-generated & other	34. Trade & technical literature

Other ITA Programs

Listed below are other important programs provided to exporters by the International Trade Administration.

- The ITA has Export Development Offices located abroad. The Commerce Department also has country desk officers, industry and country specialists.
- The Export Hotline (800-USA-XPORT). Business people can obtain country and industry reports directly from ITA by dialing the Export Hotline through a fax. The system is available 24 hours a day, seven days a week, from any fax machine anywhere in the world. The calls and reports are free.
- The *Export Hotline Directory*, an electronic yellow pages, was added to the fax service in January 1993 to facilitate the North American Free Trade Agreement. Companies in the U.S., Canada, and Mexico, may list themselves in the *Directory*. Access to company listings is through harmonized codes. Companies are not limited in the number of codes they assign themselves. There is a small fee for listing and no fee for fax retrieval.
- The Trade Information Center (800-USA-TRADE) is an interagency hotline, designed to assist the exporter in identifying programs from the 19 federal agencies that are members of the Trade Promotion Coordinating Committee. Information is available on topics such as how to export, where to find financing, and how to conduct foreign market research (http://www.ita.doc.gov/ita_home/itatic.html).
- Special assistance in exporting is provided for minority owned businesses through the Minority Business Development Agency (MBDA).
- Another listing of the government's programs is in *Export Programs: A Business Directory of U.S. Government Resources*, prepared by Trade Promotion Coordinating Committee (phone: 800-USA-TRADE).

Other Governmental Programs

Listed below are programs run by other U.S. government departments and agencies that assist exporters.

- Department of State provides commercial services in 84 embassies. It maintains regional bureaus and country desk officers (http://www.state.gov).
- Small Business Administration is another important contact agency. It, too, offers export counseling services, training, financial assistance, and legal advice (http://www.sba.gov).
- Foreign Agricultural Service of the Department of Agriculture has several major export programs (http://ffas.usda.gov/).
- Commodity and Marketing Programs (CMP) for six commodities
- Export Programs Division (EPD)
- Export Incentives Program (EIP)
- Agricultural Information and Marketing Services (AIMS) serves as the liaison between U.S. companies and foreign buyers of U.S. food and agricultural products. It provides trade leads, publicity, contacts, and statistical information.
- State and Local Governments are actively involved in supporting export development. For example, the state of California has a World Trade Commission with an office of Export Development and Export Finance.

Non-Governmental Sources

Private agencies also offer information and support for exporters. Among them are:

- More than 300 commercial banks with international banking departments.
- Chambers of Commerce both in the U.S. and abroad
- Trade associations
- Export intermediaries

Global Trade Point Network

The United Nations' Global Trade Point Network grew out of a UN international symposium on trade efficiency in 1994. Trade Point Network was designed to help cut trade barriers by linking trade centers in 60 countries. The Trade Points include information and information sources on trade leads, insurance, transportation, banking, and finance. They also provide electronic trading opportunities. For a fee, business people can establish their own sites on the Trade Point Network. As of early 1997, most of the Trade Point sites were not yet available on the WWW.

Trade Point USA (http://www2.tpusa.com/)

Under the heading "I-TRADE (International Trade Resources and Data Exchange)," the U.S. Trade Point site provides a rich assortment of free and for-fee services. Examples of the for-fee services include

- *Services*
  Advertise products on the site
  List your company (special exposure)
  I-TRADE Consulting—a service for
    international trade staff
  I-TRADE Research—customized research on
    specific topics
- *Electronic publications*
  D&B *Exporters' Encyclopaedia*
  Economist Intelligence Unit publications
  Graydon America—a source for international
    credit reports
  National Trade Data Bank
  Price Waterhouse *Doing Business* Guides
- *Databases*
  National Trade Data Bank

The fee structure on the database is complex, with several pages devoted to showing the options. Examples of free services include

- *Services*
  American Countertrade Association online
    referral service
  Bankers' Association for Foreign Trade online
    referral service
  I-TRADE Calendar—a searchable database
    of upcoming, global trade–related events, to
    which users can submit their own entries
  List your company (free listing option)—an
    online form enables users to add their firm to
    a standard listing in I-TRADE's online Inter
    national Business Directory

- *Electronic Publications*
  D&B's *How to Plan for Global Growth*
  D&B's *How to Target Your Best Global Prospects*
    Basic Guide to Exporting
  Exporting from the United States—technical
    export information
  NAFTA—A Guide to Customs Procedures
  NAFTA—Summary and Analysis
  *The North American Free Trade Agreement
    (NAFTA)*—full text
  U.S. Customs Guide to Importing
- *Directories*
  I-TRADE International Business Directory—
    global, online directory of over 250,000 firms,
    with links to individual company Web sites
  I-TRADE Opportunities—a searchable database of
    private sector trade leads and public procure-
    ment opportunities; users may submit leads
- *Metalinks*
  US DOC Global Export Market Information System (GEMS) provides access and links to regional information on Central and Eastern Europe, Russia and the Newly Independent States, Northern Ireland, the NAFTA members, and emerging economies

Trade Fairs

Trade fairs have long been an important element of European business, with the first recorded fair at St. Denis near Paris in A.D. 710. Today there are over 1,000 fairs in Europe each year. Probably the best known is the Hannover Industrial Trade Fair, held annually in the spring. In 1990, there were over 6,000 exhibitors from 51 nations.

In the U.S., the first World Trade Week observance was in 1926. Since then, a week has been designated every spring to focus attention on the importance of exporting to the U.S. economy. The objective is to make the American business community more aware of the opportunities in overseas markets, and the services offered by U.S. government agencies to help U.S. companies penetrate those markets. Some of those services include

- Certified Trade Fair Program: The Department of Commerce has a Certified Trade Fair Program that aids U.S. companies to participate in shows abroad. Organizers of trade fairs may receive certification if the fair organizer meets the Department's standards.
- Foreign Buyers Program: Foreign buyers are encouraged to attend U.S. shows through the work of the Commercial Service.

- Trade Missions: Planned visits to potential buyers and clients overseas, sponsored by the Commerce Department.

There are several sources of trade fair listings in print and in electronic form. A listing of Commerce Department–sponsored, approved, or certified trade promotion events around the world are listed monthly in *Business America*. Upcoming fairs for the next year are listed in *Business America*'s last yearly issue.

European Trade Fairs: A Key to the World for U.S. Exporters (Washington, DC: U.S. International Trade Administration, 1993)

European Trade Fairs lists major trade fairs by product and country and also provides information on successful participation in European fairs.

Trade Shows Worldwide: An International Directory of Events, Facilities and Suppliers (Detroit: Gale, published annually)

Information about upcoming trade fairs is published in *Trade Shows Worldwide*. The 1996 edition included more than 6,800 events worldwide, including the United States. U.S. contacts are given for shows held abroad.

A sample record, shown in Exhibit 12.1, has entry number; trade fair name; contact information, including the exhibit management and the U.S. contact; descriptive information such as frequency, date, audience, attendance, space rental, principal exhibits, number of exhibits, and exhibition space; and dates and locations for three years.

EventLine (EVNT), an online database available through DataStar, contains information on trade shows, exhibits, workshops, and public holidays worldwide. An organization requiring infrequent access to trade fair information or one that wants to scan for fairs meeting a variety of criteria would select *EventLine* in

---

2744 **HANNOVER FAIR—THE WORLD'S BIGGEST INDUSTRIAL FAIR**

Contact Information
Exhibition management company: Deutsche Messe AG Messegelande, D-30521 Hannover 82 Germany. Phone: 511 8933120. Telex: 922728. Facsimile: 511 8932626
U.S. Contact: Hannover Fairs USA, 103 Carnegie Center PO Box 7066, Princeton, NJ 08540. Phone: (609)987-1202. Telex: 5101011751. Facsimile: (609)987-0092.
Descriptive Information
Frequency: Annual. Always held at the Exhibition Centre in Hannover, Germany.
Founding date: 1947
Audience: Experts from industry, commerce, and general public.
Principal exhibits: Electrical engineering and electronic equipment, supplies and services; lighting equipment, supplies, and services; computer technologies for manufacturing; plant engineering equipment supplies and services; research and technology innovations; advertising and public relations information; energy, air conditions, and environmental technology; technical optics and laser technology; new materials, including metals , polymeters, and ceramics; surface treatment supplies; factory equipment; robotics; and handling technology.
Dates and Locations
1996 Apr 17-24; Hannover, Germany; Exhibition Centre

TRADE SHOWS WORLDWIDE: AN INTERNATIONAL DIRECTORY OF EVENTS, FACILITIES, AND SUPPLIERS

EXHIBIT 12.1

Source: Trade Shows Worldwide: An International Directory of Events, Facilities and Suppliers, 1996: 29.

EVNT
AN 351824 9601.
TI   20th European Congress Fair for Technical Communications - ONLINE 1997 Intl Exh.& Integrated Workshop Centers for Telecommunications & Information Technologies.
LO   Hamburg
     Congress Centrum Hamburg.
CN   Germany
     Western Europe.
DT   February 5-8, 1997.
AG   Albin L. Ockl
     ONLINE GmbH
     P.O. Box 10 08 66
     D-42508 Velbert
     Germany
     Tel: (2051) 2 8520
     Fax: (2051) 2 85219.
DE   59000 Communications
     59020 Telecommunications.
TE   Conf. + Trade.
NT   Participants: 10000
     Exhibition : Yes
     Exhibitors : 200
     Off. carrier: n/a
     Frequency : Biennial
     Deadline (call for papers): n/a
     Simult. Interpretation: Yes.
ED   951227.

EVENTLINE ON DATASTAR: TELECOMMUNICATIONS CONFERENCES IN 1997

EXHIBIT 12.2

Source: EventLine (DataStar) July 1996.

preference to the Gale's *Trade Shows Worldwide*. Exhibit 12.2 is a sample record from *EventLine*.

Trade Show Central is a WWW site (http://www.tscentral.com) that provides descriptions of trade shows, conferences, public shows, and seminars worldwide. The site allows searching by date, location, name, subject, and event type. A useful feature is the ability to correspond with event organizers through the site.

EXPORTING

Export Planning

Since exporting is one international marketing strategy, many of the same considerations discussed in Chapter 9 on international marketing apply to exporting. *A Basic Guide to Exporting* lists the different steps involved in creating an export marketing plan.

Basic Guide to Exporting (U.S. International Trade Administration, 1992)

Basic Guide to Exporting simplifies the process for potential exporters by recommending that they use third parties as sources of information. Such third parties can include U.S. government agencies, export intermediaries, and banks or freight forwarders.

The *Basic Guide* recommends that the exporter first define the market, which it breaks down into a four-step process that recommends use of many of the information sources discussed in the marketing, industry, and country chapters of this book. Many are also basic sources that many libraries already have in their collections. The four steps the *Basic Guide* recommends for defining a market are:

Step 1. Classify your product.

Use the U.S. SIC Code Manual; the United Nations' Standard International Trade Classification, Revision 3; or the Harmonized Commodity codes. Individual coding schemes are also available for Europe (NACE codes) and for individual countries.

Step 2. Research many countries using sources such as:
World Factbook (CIA)
U.N. Statistical Yearbook
World Bank Atlas
Exporters' Encyclopaedia (Dun's Marketing)
Export Trading Company Guidebook
U.S. Census export statistics
National Trade Data Bank (NTDB)
Private data retrieval files
Private market research companies

Step 3. Access a handful of markets you want to target with more specific information. Factors to consider are:
  a. Government regulations—patents, copyright, trademarks
  b. Political climate
  c. Socioeconomic factors
     Culture / taboos
     Population / densities
     Literacy Language
  d. Infrastructure
     Local transportation—packaging, shipping
     Ports, warehouses
     Distribution channels
  e. Trade terms for wholesaling/retailing; commissions, service charges
  f. Market Size
     Physical size, stability, "market life cycle"
  g. Competition
     International competitors, local competitors, market share, pricing, promotion

Step 4. Select the market you want to enter.

General sources discussed below, such as *Exporters' Encyclopaedia* or the *Official Export Guide*, provide basic information for most of the factors listed above. Once a market has been selected, the type of in-depth information available from the U.S. ITA's country desk officers or from expensive print or online services, such as the Business International's *IL&T* (*Investing, Licensing & Trading*) should be consulted.

Any library that receives export questions should own *Basic Guide to Exporting*. *Basic Guide* is available in print and electronically through the National Trade Data Bank (described below). Some libraries will be able to help the exporter in Step 1 in the process listed above through printed directories, such as *Directory of U.S. Importers* and *Directory of U.S. Exporters*. More specialized libraries and information centers with access to online databases, CD-ROMs, and WWW sites should be able to answer most research needs. Other recommended sources include trade associations, current customers, suppliers, and competitors.

Export Methods

The Commerce Department identifies several methods of exporting: (1) export directly; (2) export indirectly through intermediaries; (3) use foreign-based agents; and (4) fill orders for domestic companies who then export your product as part of their product line. The first three methods have many variations, which are presented in list form below.

- Export directly. A company can market directly overseas, although this method is not recommended for small businesses. It is the most expensive method and requires the most expertise on the part of the exporter, but gives the exporter the most control. The following distribution channels are available to the direct marketer:

  1. *Sales representatives* are the equivalent of the domestic manufacturer's representative; the rep often handles noncompeting complementary lines. He/she works on a commission and has no risk or responsibility.
  2. *Agents/Representatives* have authority to make commitments for the firms they represent.
  3. *Distributors* purchase merchandise from the domestic exporters (often at a discount). The distributor provides parts and servicing.
  4. *Foreign retailers* purchase directly from the domestic supplier; this requires use of a traveling sales force.
  5. *End users* who are identified through trade fairs, industry publications, or contract programs, are sold to directly.

- Export indirectly through intermediaries. This approach is recommended for small to medium-sized manufacturers who are new to exporting or who do not have the expertise or financial resources to cope with exporting on their own. Larger companies may use these intermediaries to break into new geographical areas. The disadvantage is that the company turns over control to the intermediary. There are many types of intermediaries.

  1. *Brokers and commission agents* set up deals.
  2. *Exporting service companies* specialize in marketing U.S. products and services abroad.

     U.S. export trading companies differ from French and Japanese companies, both in their smaller size and their focus just on exporting. There are two types of export intermediaries, though the distinctions are blurring and the terms are often used interchangeably.

     a. *Export management companies* (EMCs) are private firms that act as the export department for several companies, help with the overseas marketing functions on an exclusive basis, and arrange financing and shipping. EMCs work closely with the supplier. They generally specialize in a particular geographical region or country or a particular product category, and they provide individualized service. They may take title, work on commission, or on retainer. The EMC and the company develop a market-

ing plan and share the overseas marketing costs, with the supplier providing the product information. A usual contract is three years. There are about 2,000 in the U.S. *The Directory of Leading U.S. Export Management Companies* has more information about EMCs, in addition to listings.

> A Washington, DC, EMC deals exclusively with 10 U.S. suppliers of orthopedic equipment, marketing the products primarily in developed countries. It takes titles to 90% of the goods it sells.[2]

     b. *Export Trading Companies* (ETCs) are similar to EMCs but most take title to the goods and pay the exporter directly. They act as independent distributors and provide a broader range of services. They also work with a large range of products and may identify U.S. companies for overseas clients.

> A Chicago company identifies products in demand and buyers, then finds U.S. suppliers. It buys and sells a variety of industrial products, from several manufacturers.

     c. *ETC cooperatives*, a third method using intermediaries, are a network of export-oriented companies with similar products, primarily industrial and agricultural.
  3. *Piggyback arrangements* describes a situation in which one company uses the distribution channels of another, usually larger, company that often takes title to the goods.
  4. *Foreign trading companies* may provide the export services for a U.S. company. They are European, Japanese, and Korean. In Japan, they are extremely large conglomerates called *Sogoshosha*. For example, Mitsubishi, the world's largest, has offices in the United States.

- Use foreign-based agents or distributors.

  1. *Foreign agents* are like manufacturer's representatives working on commissions. They check local laws and develop a marketing strategy.
  2. *Foreign distributors* work either on commission or buy goods for resale. The product is kept in inventory and sold off the shelf. Marketing may be a joint effort, but the distributor handles service. When using a foreign distributor, you should define responsibilities and know the local laws.
  3. *State-controlled trading companies* still exist in some countries. For example, imports of such products as rice, medicines, building materials, and fishing equipment into the Maldives is through the State Trading Organization.

The U.S. government passed the Export Trading Act in 1982 to stimulate U.S. exports by encouraging the formation of EMCs and ETCs in the public as well as private sector, to facilitate export financing, and to remove antitrust disincentives to export. For example, as a result of this act, the New York–New Jersey Port Authority operates an ETC subsidiary, XPORT.

The government set up an Office of Export Trading Company Affairs (OETCA) within ITA to inform businesses of the benefits of exporting through intermediaries. To this end, OETCA publishes the *Export Trading Company* guidebook, which is for sale through the Government Printing Office. OETCA also maintains a database of more than 12,000 firms involved in foreign trade. The list of firms is published annually as Export Yellow Pages. Export Yellow Pages is also on the National Trade Data Bank.

Service Exporting

As noted in Chapter 9, most attention is given to the export of goods rather than services. The Department of Commerce has made the Office of Service Industries responsible for analyzing and promoting service trade. Divisions of the Office include: the Information Industry; Transportation, Tourism, and Marketing; and the Finance and Management Industries. Firms may list their services in *Commercial News USA*.

Export Financing

There are also many options for methods of payments and sources of funds. This section details the methods and describes some government programs.

The *Basic Guide to Exporting* (p. 45) lists the following items to consider when making the financing decision:

- The need for financing to make the sale: The exporter may need financing to produce; the importer may need financing to purchase.
- The cost of different methods of financing and the effect this has on the overall cost of the deal.
- The length of time that financing is required; the longer the time, the higher the costs.
- The risk involved.
- The company's financial resources.

Methods of Payment

There are a variety of payment methods. The first three methods involve a high level of risk. Therefore, new exporters, or exporters dealing with new clients, tend not to use them.

- Advance payment: The buyer pays before delivery; this method is rarely used because it is too risky for the buyer.
- Open account: The buyer pays after delivery without guarantees; this method is too risky for the seller (see Forfaiting and Factoring, below, as two means of handling open accounts).
- Consignment: The seller gets paid after resale; this method is riskier yet for the seller.

The next two methods, documentary collection and letters of credit, require a third party, often a bank, which acts as intermediary, or two banks, one in each country. The banks charge percentage fees for handling the payments. Usually the buyer is expected to pay the charges for the letter of credit.

Documentary collection (bill of exchange or draft) involves an unconditional written order from the *drawer* (seller) to the *drawee* (buyer), directing the drawee to pay a specified amount to the drawer at a fixed or determinable future date, analogous to a personal check. Title is transferred through the drawee's bank. The drawee pays the bank in his/her country and then receives the documents necessary to collect the goods. There are two types of drafts: *sight drafts* (payment before goods are released to the buyer) and *time* or *date drafts* (payment after goods are received by the buyer).

Letters of credit involve three parties: buyer, seller, and the buyer's bank, which guarantees payment. The following steps are part of the letter of credit transaction:

1. The buyer arranges to open a letter of credit at his/her bank after the terms of the deal have been set with the seller.
2. The buyer's bank prepares the letter of credit, including all shipping instructions and sends the letter to the seller's review.
3. The seller's bank prepares a letter of confirmation for the seller's bank.
4. The seller arranges with a freight forwarder for delivery, and the forwarder completes the necessary documentation.
5. The seller or forwarder presents the documents of compliance to the seller's bank. If the documents are in order, the bank issues the seller a check; the documents are forwarded to the buyer's bank.
6. The buyer or his/her agent gets the documents needed to claim the goods.

Table 12.B categorizes methods of payment.

<table>
<tr><td colspan="6">

TABLE 12.B

</td></tr>
</table>

TABLE 12.B

PAYMENT METHODS (IN ORDER OF DECREASING RISK TO EXPORTER AND INCREASING RISK TO IMPORTER)

Method	Goods Available to Buyers	Usual Time of Payment	Exporter Risk	Importer Risk
Open account	Before payment	As agreed	Riskiest; relies on importer to pay account	Least
Consignment	Before payment	After sold	Maximum; exporter retains title	Minor; inventory cost
Time draft	Before payment	On maturity of draft	High; relies on importer to pay draft	Minimal; check of quantity/quality
Sight draft	After payment	On presenting draft	Be careful of recourse	Little if inspection report required
Letter of credit	After payment	When documents are available	None	None if inspection report required
Cash	After Payment	Before shipment	Least	Most

Source: "Table 4-1 Payment Methods" from Carl A. Nelson, *Import/Export: How to Get Started in International Trade* (New York: McGraw-Hill, 1990).

Exporters or their representatives should do a credit check on the buyer. In addition to the private sources mentioned in the section on credit in Chapter 8, the Department of Commerce will provide a World Traders Data Report for a fee of $100. The reports include trade and financial references.

Sources of Funds

For the U.S. exporter and his/her import partner, the primary government funding agency is the Export-Import Bank of the U.S. (Eximbank), in existence since 1934. Eximbank supports exports by using loans, guarantees, and insurance programs. Since its inception, it has supported more than $300 billion in U.S. exports.

Programs are designed for lenders, overseas borrowers, or both. The bank reorganized in the spring of 1992 to offer more support to small business and to allow presidential discretion in opening up loans for deals in former Eastern bloc nations.

For example, the *Working Capital Guarantee* is for 100% of the principal and interest on commercial loans from certified banks to small and medium-sized companies with a 12-month repayment schedule. Loans can be up to $750,000.

Other loans go directly to foreign buyers of U.S. capital equipment and services. Not all countries are eligible for loans, and special conditions apply in many countries. For example, no coverage is allowed for Afghanistan or Albania; discretionary short term insurance is offered to Latvia and Lithuania; the al-

lowable coverage for new countries such as Slovenia and Tajikistan had not been determined as of July 1992; no special conditions exist in most industrialized countries and Asian NICS.[3]

Eximbank also works with 19 states, 2 cities, and Puerto Rico to facilitate use of its financing programs.

Eximbank had provided insurance policies to foreign buyers, protecting them against political and commercial risks resulting in economic deterioration in a buyer's market area, fluctuations in demand, shifts in tariffs, or technological change. The insurance had been written by a private agent, FCIA Management Companies Inc., but in January 1993, Eximbank began administering its own credit insurance program.

There are special policies for small businesses: *new-to export* program and the *umbrella program*. The former covers 95% of commercial risks and 100% of political risks. The umbrella policy is given to an administrator who acts as the exporter's representative.

The bank conducts one-day, two-day, and four-day seminars throughout the year in Washington, costing from $25 to $100, plus occasional three-day sessions outside of Washington. Any bank listed on its *Bank Referral List* must have had a representative attend a three- or four-day session. Both the World Bank and Inter-American Development Banks hold briefings to coordinate with Eximbank. Bank programs are outlined in Table 12.C. The publication *Ex-Im Bank of the United States,* which gives information on how the

---

TABLE 12.C

LOAN AND GUARANTEE PROGRAMS OF THE EXPORT-IMPORT BANK OF THE UNITED STATES

Exports	Appropriate Programs
Short-Term (up to 180 days)	
Consumables, small manufactured items, spare parts, raw materials	Working Capital Guarantee Credit Insurance (formerly FCIA)
Medium-Term (181 days to 5 years)	
Mining, refining, construction, and agricultural equipment; general aviation aircraft; planning and feasibility studies	Commercial Bank Guarantees Small Business Credit Medium-Term Credit Working Capital Guarantee Credit Insurance (formerly FCIA)
Long-Term (5 years and longer)	
Power plants, LPG and gas-producing Guarantees plants, other major projects, commercial jet aircraft or locomotives; other heavy capital goods	Direct Loans, Financial

Source: Basic Guide to Exporting, 14–16.

bank assists U.S. companies to increase sales of American goods and services overseas, is available on Trade Point USA (http://www2.tpusa.com/). The WWW site for the Eximbank is (http://www.exim.gov/mpub.html).

Other government-related funding sources include:

- Private Export Funding Corporation (PEFCO): This corporation is owned by commercial banks, industrial corporations, and an investment banking firm; it works with Eximbank to provide medium- and long-term loans of $1 million or more.
- State and local governments: Twenty-two states have laws permitting financial assistance.
- Small Business Administration: This agency offers an Export Revolving Line of Credit.
- U.S. Department of Agriculture: Contained within the USDA are the Export Credit Guarantee Program and Commodity Credit Corporation.
- Overseas Private Investment Corporation: This independent, financially self-supporting corporation is fully owned by the U.S. government. It facilitates investment in developing nations and Eastern Europe.

Contact numbers and Web addresses for U.S. government export funding sources are listed in Table 12.D.

Finally, when using *commercial banks* with international departments, the exporter should ask the following questions:

- How big is the department?
- Does it have foreign branches or use correspondents?

TABLE 12.D

CONTACT NUMBERS AND WEB ADDRESSES FOR
U.S. GOVERNMENT EXPORT FUNDING SOURCES

- U.S. Trade and Development Program (TDP) 202-875-4357
- Export-Import Bank of the United States (Eximbank) 202-566-8873; [www.exim.gov/mpub.html]
- Small Business Administration (SBA) 202-653-7794 Export Information System (XIS)—data reports based on SITC product codes for the 25 largest importing markets for each product [www.sba.gov/]
- Overseas Private Investment Corporation (OPIC) 202-457-7200
- Agency for International Development (AID) 202-663-1451; [www.info.usaid.gov/]
- U.S. Department of Agriculture (USDA) 202-447-8732 [www.usda.gov/]

- What are the charges for preparing documents?
- Does the bank provide credit reports?
- Has it worked with the government finance programs?
- What other services does it offer?

Alternative Means of Payment

Alternative means of payment to government-backed funding or commercial banks include:

- Countertrade: Payment through a transfer of goods and services.
- Factoring: Transfer title to the factor in exchange for immediate payment.
- Forfaiting: The exporter forfeits rights to future payment in exchange for immediate cash.

Countertrade: Countertrade involves an exchange of goods and services between buyer and seller. For example, Pepsi trades soft drinks for Russian vodka. Ten percent of world trade in 1989 was through countertrade, and 100 countries, including industrialized nations such as Australia, mandate countertrade. About half of the U.S. Fortune 500 companies participate in countertrade. The exporter is often from a developed country and the purchaser is from a less developed country (LDC) or nonmarket economy. However, as the former Eastern bloc moves toward more private enterprise, its use of countertrade may change.

Vienna is a key location to find countertrade intermediaries. The Department of Trade and Industry in London maintains a list of countertrade companies.

Five types of countertrade are identified by the U.S. International Trade Commission:

1. **Barter:** This type of countertrade involves a contractual direct exchange of goods or services between two principals without the use of currencies. Barter agreements often take place within a year. One contract is used. Barter is used when foreign currency is a problem. It is estimated that over 150,000 U.S. companies are swapping goods and services.[4] Several firms called "barter-brokers" or "matchmakers" have appeared to facilitate deals.

   Clearing agreements are barter agreements between governments. Two nations decide the types and quantities of goods to exchange at a predetermined exchange ratio. Any imbalance at the end of the contract, usually one year, is compensated for in cash.

   Switch trading involves a third party, usually a trading house. This method is used when the exporter wants nothing that the customer is supplying as payment.

2. **Compensation or Buyback:** The original export consists of plant and technology such as turnkey construction projects. Part of the payment to the exporter is the output from the project. It involves one contract. For example, an Australian company provided anthracite coal handling equipment to Vietnam and expertise to use it; in return, Vietnam's National Coal Export-Import & Material Supply Corp. will pay with the coal extracted, to be sold on international markets.[5]

3. **Counterpurchase (parallel barter):** This method involves reciprocal buying to be fulfilled over some time period in the future, with

flexibility as to the actual goods to be purchased. The products offered by the buyer are unrelated to the products being sold by the exporter. The majority of the price may be in cash. The time period is generally one to five years. The value of goods offered is usually less than the full contract amount. There is one contract for each product. For example, Beijing Capital Iron and Steel imports equipment from Northern Telecom Canada to build a 5,000-port, program-controlled telephone switchboard system valued at U.S. $12 million). Northern Telecom agrees to counterpurchase U.S. $8 million in Chinese steel products.[6] Exhibit 12.3 displays an example of a countertrade deal from *Countertrade Outlook*.

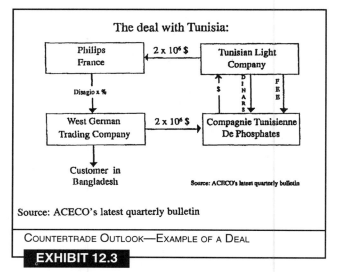

COUNTERTRADE OUTLOOK—EXAMPLE OF A DEAL

EXHIBIT 12.3

Source: Flow chart derived from *Countertrade Outlook,* Fairfax Station, VA 22039-7188, vol. X, no. 34, September 14, 1992: 3–4. Reprinted with permission.

a. Philips France, an electrical company in Europe, sold $10 million worth of equipment to an electrical utility in Africa, Tunisian Light Company.

b. The Light Company paid in dollars, which it purchased in local currency from a North African Mining Company, Compagnie Tunisienne de Phosphates.

c. Philips France purchased an equivalent amount of minerals to make up the hard currency account.

d. Philips France then transferred the obligation to the West German trading company that actually purchased the minerals and sold them to a company in Bangladesh.

4. Offset: This method is used in defense-related contracts, such as aircraft sales and other priority items for the buyer government. The supplier is required by the buyer government to assist in or arrange for the marketing of goods produced in the buyer country.

5. Evidence Accounts: This method is usually used in deals with East European countries and other countries without sources of foreign exchange. Use of these accounts implies a long-term relationship.

Countertrade is used when other more conventional means of finance are not available, e.g., if your foreign partner cannot get foreign exchange. It is also used to gain a presence in another country. For small businesses, countertrade is not recommended unless normal financing channels are not available. Barter is the most common form of countertrade used in Egypt while counter purchase is used in China.

The weekly newsletter *Countertrade Outlook* and the daily newspaper *Financial Times* are the major sources of information on global countertrade transactions. American Countertrade Association has an online countertrade assistance referral service, activated upon the completion of a form available on *Trade Point USA* (http://www2.tpusa.com/).

Countertrade Outlook and Offset (DP Publications; published weekly)

Countertrade Outlook and Offset, published in Fairfax Station, Virginia, covers countertrade deals by individual companies, country policy, meetings, and revisions to their *Directory of Organizations Providing CT Services*. This is a specialized and unique source for organizations that need to scan countertrade (http://www.access.digex.net/~dpub).

Factoring

Factoring is discounting a foreign account receivable that does not involve a draft. Factoring has been used commercially since 1790 but it did not appear on the international scene until the 1970s. According to Factors Chain International (FCI), an association of factors in 30 countries on five continents, export factoring growth is now exceeding domestic factoring growth. However, in 1991, international factoring accounted for only 6% of the $266 billion factoring business. Three of the leading export factoring countries, Netherlands, Germany, and Belgium, account for 30% of the foreign volume. Japan, which has had a relatively inactive domestic factor market, contributed 3.3% to the international factor market. Only seven firms offer international factoring services in Japan.[7]

Financing through a factor involves the following steps:

1. Sellers turn over goods to the factor who assumes full responsibility for credit and collection.
2. Seller receives cash at a 2% to 4% discount.
3. Seller's factor selects a foreign factor from FCI and gives the foreign factor information about the importer.
4. Foreign factor checks the buyer's credit and establishes a line of credit.
5. Seller's factor turns over receivables to foreign factor.
6. Foreign factor collects and remits funds to seller's factor by wire transfer.

Factoring is suitable for exporters who sell relatively small amounts of goods to the same customers on open account terms. It is not used in developing countries and non–market economies. The availability of export credit insurance, through Eximbank and FCI in the U.S. and the Export Credit Guarantee Department in the U.K., has reduced demand for factoring by small businesses in these countries.

Forfaiting

Forfaiting is derived from the French term *à forfait* which means "without recourse." The forfaiter buys from the exporter (at a discount) an importer's fixed rate letters of credit or bills of exchange. The seller receives immediate cash from the forfaiting institution. The forfaiting institution will collect from the buyer in the future. Forfaiting institutions may be subsidiaries of large international banks or companies specializing in international trade financing.

The deal is usually arranged between the seller's and buyer's banks. The seller's bank, or forfaiting institution, takes over the right to the seller's bills of exchange or buyer's promissory notes. Therefore, four parties are involved:

- Exporter, seller, or supplier of the goods or services
- Importer, buyer, or purchaser of the goods or services
- Guarantor for the importer
- Forfaiter

Forfaiting has been used in Europe for a long time, beginning with Finanz AG of Frankfurt and Union Bank of Switzerland. It only appeared in the U.S. and U.K. in the 1980s. There are 30 main providers of forfait finance in London. In 1995 it was estimated that less than 1% of world trade, some $20 billion, was financing with forfaiting.[8]

Financing through a forfaiter involves the following steps:

1. The seller makes a sale to a foreign buyer.
2. The seller receives bills of exchange or promissory notes for future payment at a fixed rate.
3. The seller sells the bills or notes to its bank at a discount from face value and receives immediate cash.
4. The bank assumes full responsibility for collection.
5. The notes or bills are guaranteed by the importer's forfaiting institution; the guarantee is often unconditional and irrevocable.
6. The importer pays for the purchase over time (2–5 years).[9]

Typical sales range from $200,000 to $5 million and carry a fixed rate of interest. Forfaiting is used most frequently in deals by capital goods manufacturers and distributors of commodities. The risk is on the exporter's bank.

The advantage of this type of deal is that the exporter receives payment immediately, while the buyer gets extended payment terms. The popularity of forfaiting as an export financing mechanism is sensitive to interest rates. Rising interest rates discourage forfaiting.

We have identified no one directory for countertrade, factoring, or forfaiting houses. However, these companies are listed in a variety of different databases, especially those covering the U.K., Germany, and Austria. A WWW site that specializes in information concerning factoring and forfaiting is Commercial Finance Online (http://www.cfonline.com/cfo/opps/opps.htm).

Financing Deals with Lesser Developed Countries (LDCs)

Many of the financing arrangements we have discussed require the participation of a bank and guarantees and insurance. Many U.S. banks no longer offer loans to LDCs because of defaults. Possible alternative forms of financing include:

- Confirmed Letters of Credit: Banks in many LDCs are not well known, but some U.S. banks will confirm the letter of credit for a fee. Some banks will confirm letters from one country, e.g., Thailand or Poland, but not others, such as Pakistan.
- Export Credit Insurance: This insurance was formerly unwritten by FCIA and by private insurers, but is now offered directly by Eximbank. Buyers might prefer this method.
- Forfaiting: This is a competitive finance method for short- to medium-range dealings with the less risky developing countries.
- Sales through Trading Companies: Certain trading companies specialize in less developed countries.

One way to determine the types of financing available in a country is through the monthly charts in Euromoney's *Project and Trade Finance* (London: Euromoney, 1993; published monthly; formerly called *Trade Finance*). Monthly reports are divided among Asia, Eastern Europe and the Middle East, and Latin America. Exhibit 12.4 displays an entry from *Project and Trade Finance*.

Export/Import Regulations

Goods and services leaving a country must comply with the export regulations of the home country, any international agreements, and with import regulations of the host company.

The following are some important U.S. requirements and regulations:

- Export Licenses: These licenses are necessary for all sales except those made under the North American Free Trade Agreement. Licenses are governed by the Export Administration Act as reported in the Export Administration Regulations. The type of license required depends on the type and destination of the product. Exporters should check with the Export Assistance Division of the Department of Commerce to determine the license needed.

In April 1992, President George Bush implemented new rules that eliminated the need for prior government approval to export more than 2,000 items that account for about $2.5 billion in export sales annually. Validated export licenses are no longer needed to sell semiconductor manufacturing equipment, materials technology, certain computers, and aircraft, helicopters, and their engines to nations that reexport those goods to other nations that had been under existing U.S. export controls.

Licenses still are required for the export of supercomputers, high-speed streak cameras, and flash discharge X-ray equipment, which can be used in developing nuclear weapons; cryptographic equipment, which can be used to encode and decode military and intelligence data; night-vision equipment, which can be used in combat systems; and items that are controlled to curb missile proliferation.

- Antidiversion, antiboycott, and antitrust requirements: Goods may go only to destinations legally authorized by the U.S. government. Goods may go to countries friendly to the U.S. that are being boycotted by other countries. U.S. antitrust rules apply to international as well as national trade. The Foreign Corrupt Practices Act has special relevance for international trade (see Chapter 9).

The Exporter's Guide to Eastern Europe and the Middle East			
Country/ population	**Remarks**	**Aid\ Credit lines**	**Consensus group**
Slovenia	The economy is still recovering from the shock of separating Yugoslavia. FX reserves are tight due to the loss to Belgrade $1.9bn in bank deposits. However, debt obligations are fairly small and it seems likely that as exports increase and tourists return the FX position should improve	Little information available at present	II

| **Exim short term/** Medium term No cover available | **NCM Credit Risk/ Private** Pre-credit Risk No credit cover available. MRA £0.15 pre-credit risks | **Transfer position** market Some cover now now available on secure terms (L/C Ljubjanska Bank). No long term cover | **Non-recourse** Paris Club date Little data available | finance-index A |

EUROMONEY'S *PROJECT AND TRADE FINANCE*

EXHIBIT 12.4

Source: Project and Trade Finance, 1993: 62-63; prepared by Jardine Insurance Brokers.

- FDA and EPA restrictions: An item for foreign export need only meet the standards of the importing country. While the EPA does not control any aspect of exporting, it requires notification of the export of hazardous waste.
- Tax incentives: Under provisions of the Tax Reform Act of 1984, special U.S. income tax treatment is given to Foreign Sales Corporations. An FSC is a corporation set up in certain foreign countries or U.S. possessions (except Puerto Rico) that shares tax information with the U.S. In 1991, 29 countries qualified, but most FSCs are incorporated in Guam or the U.S. Virgin Islands. The FSC must have both export sales and at least one foreign director. Fifteen percent of the profit attributable to export sales is not taxed in the U.S. There are separate incentives for small FSCs, which do not have to meet the same requirements.
- Drawback of customs duties: This specialized form of tax relief is available to U.S. firms that import materials and components that they process and then reexport. The import duties are refunded as drawbacks. Drawback is a refund of 99% of all ordinary customs duties and internal revenue taxes. Drawbacks were initially authorized by the first tariff act of the United States, in 1789. A *direct identification drawback* is given on imported merchandise that is partially or totally used in the manufacture of an exported article. A *substitution drawback* is given on designated imported merchandise upon exportation of articles manufactured or produced with use of substituted domestic or imported merchandise that is of the same kind and quality as the designated imported merchandise.
- Foreign trade zones: U.S. foreign trade zones are 180 domestic port sites that provide customs privileges. The zones are considered outside the United States. Exported goods become imports to the home country and face another set of regulations.
- Import regulations of destination's government: Every country has its own set of import regulations.
- Carnet: When bringing samples or professional equipment into another country for trade fairs, exhibits, demonstrations, or promotions purposes, arrange for an ATA Carnet, or Admission Temporariare / Temporary Admission. This is a special customs document for the business traveler that guarantees customs payments if the goods are not reexported.
- Intergovernmental regulations: The United Nations' Convention on Contracts for the International Sale of Goods became law in the United States in 1988. It applies automatically to all contracts between sellers and buyers in countries that have signed the Convention. Over 25 countries are signatories, in-

cluding most of the EU countries, a few of the newly independent republics, and China.

Transportation

Additional information is needed to arrange for transporting goods in an international deal. Issues include size of shipment, shipping terms, packaging, labeling, insurance, and documentation.

The size of the shipment may determine the method of shipment. Small shipments use air express or integrated carriers—air and ground service. Large shipments use ocean or regular freight. The daily *Journal of Commerce* provides a lists of shippers, rates, and individual ships arriving each month.

When negotiating the export sale, shipping terms are part of the agreement. Determine who pays for shipping costs and who is responsible for damage. There are two published sets of terms:

- *Guide to Incoterms, 1990* by Jan Ramberg (International Commercial Terms, International Chamber of Commerce, 1991)
- *Revised American Foreign Trade Definitions* (originally published in 1941 by the Chamber of Commerce of the United States, the National Council of American Council of Importers, and the National Foreign Trade Council)

INCOTERMS (A dictionary of trade terms and abbreviations) is available from Trade Point USA (http://www2.tpusa.com/).

Table 12.E lists 13 trading terms identified in *Guide to Incoterms* that specify the obligations of buyer and seller in an international transaction:

In addition to selecting the means and payment of transport, the exporter also has to use correct packaging, labeling, documentation, and insurance.

- Packing: Packing problems involve breakage, moisture, weight, and theft.
- Labeling: Labeling involves specific markings used to meet shipping regulations, assure proper han-

TABLE 12.E
INTERNATIONAL TRADING TERMS FROM *GUIDE TO INCOTERMS*
INCOTERMS 1990
EXW Ex Works
FCA Free Carrier
FAS Free Alongside Ship
FOB Freight on Board
CFR Cost and Freight
CIF Cost, Insurance, and Freight
CPT Carriage Paid To
CIP Carriage and Insurance Paid To
DAF Delivered At Frontier
DES Delivered Ex Ship
DEQ Delivered EX Quay (Duty Paid)
DDU Delivered Duty Unpaid
DDP Delivered Duty Paid

Source: International Chamber of Commerce Brochure, 1992.

dling, conceal the identity of the contents, help receivers identify shipments, and meet country requirements. Marks include port marks, customer identification, origin, weights, and dimensions. For example, products ranging from liquid gas to shampoo must be labeled in metric units to be imported into Thailand. Labels may show either Thai or Arabic numerals, but Thai script must be used.

- Insurance: Cargo insurance is arranged by buyer or seller depending on the deal.
- Documents: Table 12.F lists the 10 most common documents required in the movement of goods between countries.

Each country of destination has different requirements. Some requirements are listed in *Exporters' Encyclopaedia* or *Official Export Guide*. A more specialized source is *International Trade Report Export Reference Manual* (formerly *Export Shipping Manual*) from BNA (Bureau of National Affairs).

Freight forwarders are service companies that design and implement international shipping programs for exporters for compensation. They use common carriers and serve different roles based on the type of

TABLE 12.F			
DOCUMENTS REQUIRED FOR THE MOVEMENT OF GOODS BETWEEN COUNTRIES			
Transportation	*Government Control*	*Commercial Invoice*	*Banking/Payment Method*
Ocean bill-of-lading	Export declaration		Letter of credit (for example)
Dock receipt	Consular invoice		
Delivery instruction	Certificate of origin		
Insurance certificate			
Transmittal letter			

Source: Port Authority of NY/NJ in *World Is Your Market*, pages 68–69.[9]

carriers. For example, for ocean freight, the freight forwarders act as exporter's agent; for air freight, freight forwarders consolidate shipments and are licensed by the U.S. Civil Aeronautics Board (CAB) or International Air Transport Association (IATA).

The forwarders are also among the best sources of information and assistance on export regulations and documentation, foreign import regulations, and shipping methods.

Exporting in the United Kingdom

Many governments encourage and support export initiatives. In fact, the U.S. has been slow to export compared to many other countries. In the United Kingdom, the Department of Trade and Industry's (DTI) export promotion program provides practical help and support for exporters. Through the British Overseas Trade Services, which has over 200 business people helping exporters, and the Diplomatic Service Posts overseas, DTI provides services to British business.

DTI's Web site (http://www.dti.gov.uk) provides contact names and telephone numbers for specific projects. Examples include:

Metallurgical and chemical projects worldwide
Guidance on countertrade
Anglo-Japanese co-operation in third countries

As of 1997, 21 countries had separate Web pages. The pages for the U.S., for example, included separate help desks and fax numbers for consumer goods, capital goods, and service goods, as well as general market conditions.

Barclay's Guide to International Trade for the Small Business (Oxford, U.K. and Cambridge MA: Blackwell, 1990)

Barclay's Guide is an introductory source for U.K. potential exporters. In addition to the how to's and the contacts, the book also lists recommended online information providers and services in the U.K.. These recommended sources include Export Network Ltd. and Barclay's own Trade Development Service.

Chambers of commerce are important sources and facilitators of export and import throughout Europe. Those from France, Italy, and Spain are actively involved in soliciting business from the information industry. Chambers of commerce are also beginning to play major roles in newly independent countries. For example the Slovenian Chamber of Commerce has developed a floppy disk with a listing of potential partners.

IMPORTING

As we have seen, the U.S. government actively encourages exporting because it is viewed as vital to the health of the U.S. economy. The goal of any country is to become a net exporter. Exporting is therefore treated as a marketing tool.

Importing, on the other hand, is not encouraged. Therefore, the government does not allot resources to help companies import. Importing is treated as a legal issue centering on customs. Table 12.G diagrams the structure of the U.S. Customs Service.

There are also U.S. customs officers stationed in 16 countries, in Europe, Asia, and South America.

Customs invokes the same level of uneasiness as the Internal Revenue Service; both services are under the same U.S. agency, the Department of the Treasury, and both have collection and protection of revenue as their primary goal. However, U.S. Customs employs only 16,000 people, a small staff by government standards.

Import Laws and Regulations

Customs laws are found in Title 19 of the *United States Code* and customs regulations in Title 19 of the *Code of Federal Regulations*. Customs enforces not only its own laws and regulations, but also those of 40 other federal agencies who have interest in imported merchandise.

The customs employees who work most closely with importers and import brokers are the *import specialists*. These are the individuals who classify the goods, appraise them, determine import duties, and generally ensure that imports meet all other legal requirements.

There are six fundamental rules that importers into the United States are responsible for knowing.[10]

Rule 1. Goods that are allowed in: Importing is not a right, and certain goods may be excluded.

Rule 2. How revenue officers make decisions:
- Protect the revenue.
- Resolve all doubts in the government's favor. If two different rates might apply, the customs officers will always choose the higher.

Rule 3. Voluntary compliance (the burden rests with the importer): U.S. Customs assumes that importers have:
- Read the Customs rules and regulations and know which apply to their merchandise
- Done everything to ensure that they have complied with these laws and regulations.

TABLE 12.G

STRUCTURE OF THE U.S. CUSTOMS SERVICE

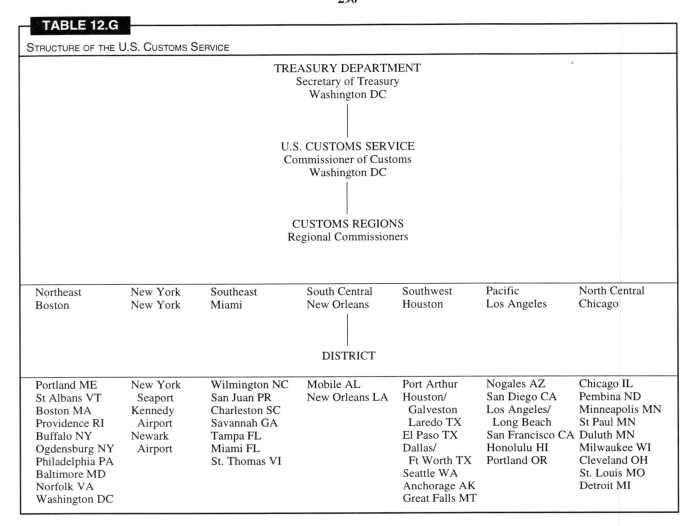

TREASURY DEPARTMENT
Secretary of Treasury
Washington DC

U.S. CUSTOMS SERVICE
Commissioner of Customs
Washington DC

CUSTOMS REGIONS
Regional Commissioners

Northeast Boston	New York New York	Southeast Miami	South Central New Orleans	Southwest Houston	Pacific Los Angeles	North Central Chicago

DISTRICT

Portland ME	New York	Wilmington NC	Mobile AL	Port Arthur	Nogales AZ	Chicago IL
St Albans VT	Seaport	San Juan PR	New Orleans LA	Houston/	San Diego CA	Pembina ND
Boston MA	Kennedy	Charleston SC		Galveston	Los Angeles/	Minneapolis MN
Providence RI	Airport	Savannah GA		Laredo TX	Long Beach	St Paul MN
Buffalo NY	Newark	Tampa FL		El Paso TX	San Francisco CA	Duluth MN
Ogdensburg NY	Airport	Miami FL		Dallas/	Honolulu HI	Milwaukee WI
Philadelphia PA		St. Thomas VI		Ft Worth TX	Portland OR	Cleveland OH
Baltimore MD				Seattle WA		St. Louis MO
Norfolk VA				Anchorage AK		Detroit MI
Washington DC				Great Falls MT		

Rule 4. Duty due on all imports, unless exempt: Importers should assume that they will pay duties on foreign and domestic items

Rule 5. Duty exemptions—burden of proof: Importers must prove, beyond doubt, that they qualify for exemptions.

Rule 6. Items purchased in the United States may be foreign made: This refers to situations where merchandise may be made in the U.S., assembled offshore, and reimported at reduced rates. There must be proof that the original item was indeed made in the U.S.

Importing, like everything else in business, begins at the planning stage. Potential importers in any country should take the same preliminary planning steps as the potential exporter.

Planning for Importing

Several factors have been identified as important to importing and importing research.

The Product

The importer must consider not only if there is a demand for the product in the country, but also if there will be special duties and/or restrictions and regulations.

- Is the product a raw material or component for the manufacturing process?
- Is it a finished product for resale?
- Is it a spare part?
- Is it subject to special import restrictions?

For example, fruits, vegetables, and nuts must meet United States import requirements relating to grade, size, quality, and maturity.

Volume

Not only do regulations vary based on what is being imported, but regulations also vary based on how much is being imported. When planning for importing, it is necessary to consider the size of the shipment. Formal international purchase agreements and entry procedures must be followed for the importation of large quantities

Country sourcing refers to finding the best place from which to import a product. Obviously, importing minerals and natural resources is limited to those countries where they are mined or grown. However, manufactured products are available in many countries. Identifying the low-cost countries based upon proximity to raw materials, labor costs of manufacturing, current exchange rates, or transportation costs may require considerable study and analysis. This information is not always easy to obtain. Since the U.S. government is more interested in promoting exports, they do not regularly collect and make available such information to U.S. companies wishing to import.[11]

Sources of local import information include:

- Foreign chambers of commerce in the importer's country
- Foreign trade associations
- Foreign banks operating in the U.S., or U.S. banks with foreign branches

Identification of Suppliers

Finding suppliers requires many of the same techniques as finding buyers, such as attending trade fairs, accessing listings of potential sellers, performing credit checks, and visiting facilities, which, if possible, is recommended by the American Management Association (AMACOM).

Compliance with Foreign Law

Suppliers often overlook some basics so the importer should check with a bank or attorney.

- Foreign export controls: The "Wassenaar Arrangement," is composed of 33 members, including the U.S., Russia, Japan, the EU, and 15 other industrialized nations. It replaced the Co-ordinating Committee for Multilateral Export Controls (COCOM) in 1996 and deals primarily with arms control.
- Exchange control licenses: Many countries control foreign exchange or control methods of payments.
- Export quotas: These quotas come generally from the importing country; however, the U.S. has brought pressure to bear on some countries to control exports through voluntary restraint agreements.

Compliance with Domestic Law

Importers should also check carefully the following domestic considerations:

- Customs Considerations—regulations and procedures
- Import quotas
- Antidumping, countervailing, and other special duties that apply to imports as well as exports.
- Classification—correctly categorizing a product using the Harmonized Tariff codes

An import quota is a quantity control on imported merchandise for a certain period that serves to protect domestic industries. There are two general categories: absolute tariffs and differential tariff rates. *Absolute tariffs* are quantitative; that is, only a fixed amount is allowed in per year. They may be worldwide or country dependent. Examples in the U.S. include certain types of chocolate, ice cream, textiles, and watches. These tariffs are administered by the Departments of Commerce and the Interior). Some quotas have *differential tariff rates*. There is no limitation to the amount of the product that may enter during the quota period, but quantities in excess of the quota for the period are subject to higher rates. Examples include tuna fish, certain sugars, brooms, and olives.

Import Marketing, Packaging, and Labeling

The issues are similar to export considerations. In the United States, customs laws require that articles produced abroad for import be marked with the country of origin. Some products, such as eggs, screws, or Christmas trees, are on an excepted list and do not require marking on the product itself, while other products, for example, watch movements, require additional markings.

Domestic Commercial Considerations

These considerations include:

- Prevailing market price
- Government policy, e.g., "Buy American"
- Industry standards, e.g., auto emissions

Shipping Terms

Since a good being imported has been exported from its country of origin, it bears the international trading terms listed in Table 12.E, such as FOB or CIT.

Tariffs

Goods leaving a country are subject to export controls and regulations. Goods entering a country are subject to tariffs. Tariffs are dependent on the good itself, its quantity, its country of origin, and what stage of processing it is in when it leaves and/or arrives in the destination country.

Restrictions are placed on some products to protect local industry. For example, U.S. sugar prices are kept well above market level through tight restrictions on the importation of sugar into the United States. In 1985, frozen Israeli kosher pizzas were stopped from entering the United States based on sugar regulations, although the pizzas contained less than 1% sugar! President Reagan later signed a law allowing packaged food items for retail sale into the United States if they contain less than 10% sugar, which released the 20,000 pizzas.

To facilitate the tracking of goods between countries, most nations of the world have adopted the Harmonized Commodity Coding System, which was introduced in 1988. The coding system is derived from the United Nations SITC codes and are in harmony with Schedule B of the United States and the European Community NACE codes. The code that a good receives when it leaves its home country should be the same as the one it receives when it reaches its destinations.

Just determining the tariff that will be placed on an item coming into the United States can be confusing and, as in the case of the Israeli pizzas, potentially bankrupting to a company that has failed to understand the laws. The new Harmonized Tariff is still providing problems for the textile industry, which falls under provision 9802 dealing with the duties paid on items fabricated in the United States but assembled in another country and then brought back into the United States.

The tariff schedule is used for the classification of imported merchandise for rate of duty and statistical purposes. An example of regulations is presented in Exhibit 12.5.

Exhibit 12.6 lists the different Harmonized Tariff codes for sugar.

The information in these tables is printed annually by the U.S. International Trade Commission and reprinted in the commercial source, Official Custom House Guide.

The tariff schedule for the different types of sugar is preceded by three pages of notes, and includes quotas for different country groupings.

The Customs Process

The Customs Service annually publishes *Importing into the United States*, which outlines the requirements and procedures for bringing goods into the United States. There is a four-step formal entry process for all goods valued at more than $1,000.

1. File documents (includes getting an Importer's Number).
2. Post bond. A Customs bond is purchased from a surety company. The importer pays a fee to the surety company to obtain the bond that guarantees that all duties and fees assessed by Customs will be paid. The importer has to go through a credit check to get bonded.
3. Undergo a Customs examination to determine tariff. The exam determines whether the goods are what they claim to be and the transaction value of the goods (price plus shipping, insurance, etc.): Valuation for importing has its own foreign exchange rule. U.S. Customs must use the rates of exchange determined and certified by the Federal Reserve Bank of New York, based on the first business day of each calendar quarter, except on days where rates fluctuate more than 5%. The date of exportation of the goods is the date used to determine the applicable exchange rate. The classification category is determined by the importer, based on Harmonized Tariff Codes.
4. Liquidation. This is the legal term used to indicate that Customs decisions regarding entry of the goods have been completed and the goods will be released to the importer after payment of the required duty.

To keep up with changes in Customs rulings, quota status, and daily exchange rates, you can access the *Customs Electronic Bulletin Board* at no charge either by phone (703-440-6236) or modem (703-440-6155). The U.S. Customs Service Web site (http://www.customs.ustreas.gov/) has several useful searchable texts including ruling letters, Title 19 of the *U.S. Code,* and the *Harmonized Tariff Schedule of the United States*.

The Guide to United States Customs and Trade Laws
(Kluwer, 1991)

The International Trade Reporter (BNA, 2/2/92) recommended this publication for use by customs brokers, freight forwarders, in-house legal counsel, and others who must deal with complex U.S. customs regulations. A second edition is due in 1997.

Import Support Companies

Parallel to the exporter's freight forwarder is the importer's customhouse broker. Customhouse brokers in the U.S. are regulated by the Treasury Department and must take a qualifying examination. They act as the importer's agent. The brokers prepare docu-

HARMONIZED TARIFF SCHEDULE of the United States (1997)
Annotated for Statistical Reporting Purposes

XV
83-2

Heading/ Subheading	Stat. Suf- fix	Article Description	Units of Quantity	Rates of Duty		
				1		2
				General	Special	
8301		Padlocks and locks (key, combination or electrically operated), of base metal; clasps and frames with clasps, incorporating locks, of base metal; keys and parts of any of the foregoing articles, of base metal:				
8301.10		Padlocks:				
		Not of cylinder or pin tumbler construction:.				
8301.10.20	00	Not over 3.8 cm in width............	doz.....	2.3%	Free (E,IL,J) 0.2% (CA) 1.3% (MX)	39.5%
8301.10.40	00	Over 3.8 cm but not over 6.4 cm in width............................	doz.....	3.8%	Free (E,IL,J) 0.3% (CA) 2.2% (MX)	29.5%
8301.10.50	00	Over 6.4 cm in width...............	doz.....	4%	Free (A,E,IL,J,MX) 0.4% (CA)	28.5%
		Of cylinder or pin tumbler construction:				
8301.10.60	00	Not over 3.8 cm in width...........	doz.....	6.1%	Free (A,E,IL,J,MX) 0.6% (CA)	27%
8301.10.80	00	Over 3.8 cm but not over 6.4 cm in width............................	doz.....	4.8%	Free (E,IL,J) 0.4% (CA) 2.8% (MX)	36%
8301.10.90	00	Over 6.4 cm in width...............	doz.....	4.2%	Free (A,E,IL,J,MX) 0.4% (CA)	29.5%
8301.20.00		Locks of a kind used on motor vehicles........	....	5.7%	Free (A,B,E,IL,J, MX) 0.5% (CA) 1/	45%
	30	Non-integral steering wheel immobilizer devices...............................	doz			
	60	Other................................	kg			
8301.30.00		Locks of a kind used for furniture...........	....	5.7%	Free (A,CA,E,IL,J, MX)	45%
	60	Cam locks and other locks suitable for use with chests, drawers and similar items...............................	kg			
	90	Other................................	kg			
8301.40		Other locks:				
8301.40.30	00	Luggage locks.......................	doz.....	4.3%	Free (A,E,IL,J,MX) 0.6% (CA)	45%
8301.40.60		Other................................	....	5.7%	Free (A,E,IL,J,MX) 0.5% (CA) 2/	45%
	30	Door locks, locksets and other locks suitable for use with interior or exterior doors (except garage, overhead or sliding doors)..............	kg			
	60	Other............................	kg			
8301.50.00	00	Clasps and frames with clasps, incorporating locks...................................	kg......	4.3%	Free (A,CA,E,IL,J, MX)	45%
8301.60.00	00	Parts....................................	kg......	4%	Free (A,B,E,IL,J, MX) 0.5% (CA) 3/	45%
8301.70.00	00	Keys presented separately....................	kg......	5%	Free (A,B,CA,E,IL, J,MX)	45%

1/ See subheading 9905.00.00.
2/ See subheading 9905.83.05.
3/ See subheading 9905.83.10.

EXHIBIT 12.5

```
SUGAR ........................................... Ch. 17, 17 US3 (a)-(ij)
    chemically pure, except sucrose, lactose,
        maltose, glucose, fructose ............................ 2940.00
    confectioneries ........................................... 1704.10-90
    raw ......................................................... 17-S1, 1701-1702
    refined .......................................................... 1701-1702
    wastes ...................................................... 2303.20
SUGAR BEET ...................................................... 1212.91
SUGAR BEET SEED ........................................... 1209.11
SUGAR BOWLS
    of plastics .......................................................... 3924.10
SUGAR CANE ...................................................... 1212.92
SUGAR CONFECTIONERY ................................. Ch. 17
    containing cocoa ......................................... 18-2, 1806
```

ALPHABETICAL LISTING OF THE TARIFF CODES FOR SUGAR

EXHIBIT 12.6

Source: Harmonized Tariff Schedule of the United States (1997): Annotated for Statistical Reporting Purposes, 3.

ments, obtain bonds, deposit duties, and arrange for the release and delivery of goods for the importer. A listing of these brokers appears in *National Directory of Customs Brokers*, published by Adele Falco in Red Bank, NJ (201-530-9668).

SOURCES OF INFORMATION FOR EXPORTING AND IMPORTING

U.S. Government Publications

Basic Guide to Exporting (Washington, DC: U.S. Dept. of Commerce, in cooperation with Federal Express Corporation, 1992)

Basic Guide to Exporting is an introductory source that is a must for any library with small business persons as patrons. The book is designed for companies who will be exporting either through intermediaries or directly. It emphasizes government sources and contacts and gives addresses, phone numbers, and prices of print government publications.

The importance of planning is stressed and a table containing management issues for the export decision, plus an outline for an export plan, are given in the first chapter.

Sections of the outline plus sample questions are in Exhibit 12.7. Additional planning tips from the *Basic Guide* are found in Appendix I. Table 1-2 of the *Basic Guide to Exporting* contains the "Sample Outline for an Export Plan," with the Table of Contents and a one- or two-page executive summary.

Basic Guide to Exporting is also available on the National Trade Data Bank. A new edition, published by World Trade Press, was announced in 1996.

TABLE 1-1 MANAGEMENT ISSUES INVOLVED IN THE EXPORT DECISION

I. **Experience**
  - With what countries has business already been conducted (or from what countries have inquires already been received)?
  - What general and specific lessons have been learned from past export experiences?

II. **Management & Personnel**
  - What in-house international expertise does the firm have?
  - Who will follow through after the planning is accomplished?

III. **Production Capacity**
  - How is the present capacity used?
  - What would be required to design and package products specifically for export?

IV. **Financial Capacity**
  - What amount of capital can be committed to export productions and marketing?
  - By what date must an export effort pay for itself?

BASIC GUIDE TO EXPORTING

EXHIBIT 12.7

Source: Basic Guide to Exporting, 1992: 1–5.

Business America (U.S. Department of Commerce, International Trade Administration; published biweekly)

Business America bills itself as the official U.S. government trade magazine. It was first published in 1880, under another name, by the U.S. State Department. Its mission has always been to help American companies sell their products overseas. In addition to articles, issues have listings of trade fairs in the U.S. for overseas traders and Commerce Department promotions abroad for U.S. traders. For the 1996 prices of $50 in the U.S. or $62.50 abroad, this publication is a good buy for any organization with clientele interested in U.S. exporting. Articles from *Business America* are available online in databases from IAC, in *ABI/Inform* and on *National Trade Data Bank* (NTDB). The WWW site (http://www.ita.doc.gov/bizam/) provides sample articles and ordering information.

U.S. Government Trade Information on CD-ROM

National Trade Data Bank (published monthly by the United States Department of Commerce)

Any discussion of United States import/export information sources must include the National Trade Data Bank—NTDB. We recommend NTDB for libraries throughout the world because it contains the complete text of many useful U.S. government publications. NTDB is available as a subscription database through STAT-USA (http://www.stat-usa.gov).

NTDB is also available as a two-disc CD-ROM database. A review of the database is in July 1991 *CD-ROM Professional*. A year's subscription to this comprehensive two-disc CD-ROM database is $585. Our description of NTDB is based on the CD-ROM version.

Access to information on disc one is by SOURCE, TOPIC, PROGRAM, SUBJECT, or ITEM. NTDB is made up of documents from about 20 different U.S. governmental SOURCES, all having some relationship to international trade or activity. Disc two has two directories: Export Yellow Pages and Commercial Service International Contacts, discussed under CONTACTS below.

NTDB uses menu-driven software. Exhibit 12.8 is the Source Menu and Exhibit 12.9 is the menu for the selection International Trade Administration.

The most efficient way to search this disc is not obvious. However, whether you begin in the SOURCE, TOPIC, PROGRAM, or SUBJECT menu, you will eventually arrive at the documents you need.

One of the strengths of NTDB is the series of more than 10,000 market reports. The reports have market information and data on selected products and industries in "countries offering opportunities for U.S. goods." Included are International Market Reports, Market Insight Reports, Industry Sector Analysis, and Best Prospect Industry Sectors. These reports can be called up by country or product and include a wide range of subjects. Some are directly related to trading, such as *Israel-Trade Statistics*-IMI960222. Others are related to individual products in regions or countries. One example is *Italy-Computer Printer Purchase*-IMI1960814. Most market research reports are kept on NTDB for 3 years. Some may stay 6 months to a year if they involve time-sensitive information.

COMMERCIAL SOURCES

Finding Aids

Listed below are important finding aids to import/export information.

Global Trade White Pages (Carroll Publishers, 1991)

Global Trade White Pages lists national, state, country, and international contacts, with contact names. The book looks a lot fuller than it is because its white pages contain so much white space! The book has not been updated but is still in print.

1	AFRICAN DEVELOPMENT BANK
1	ASIAN DEVELOPMENT BANK
5	BOARD OF GOVERNORS OF THE FEDERAL RESERVE SYSTEM
1	CENTRAL INTELLIGENCE AGENCY
1	EXPORT-IMPORT BANK OF THE UNITED STATES
3	OFFICE OF THE U.S. TRADE REPRESENTATIVE
1	OVERSEAS PRIVATE INVESTMENT CORPORATION
5	U.S. DEPARTMENT OF STATE
1	U.S. INTERNATIONAL TRADE COMMISSION
1	U.S. SMALL BUSINESS ADMINISTRATION
1	UNIVERSITY OF MASSACHUSETTS
1	USDA, FOREIGN AGRICULTURAL SERVICE
12	USDOC, BUREAU OF ECONOMIC ANALYSIS
8	USDOC, BUREAU OF EXPORT ADMINISTRATION
9	USDOC, BUREAU OF THE CENSUS
24	**USDOC, INTERNATIONAL TRADE ADMINISTRATION**
3	USDOC, NATIONAL INSTITUTE OF STANDARDS AND TECHNOLOGY
1	USDOC, OFFICE OF ADMINISTRATION
2	USDOC, OFFICE OF BUSINESS ANALYSIS
1	USDOE, ENERGY INFORMATION ADMINISTRATION
2	USDOL, BUREAU OF LABOR STATISTICS

SOURCE MENU FOR *NTDB*

EXHIBIT 12.8

Source: NTDB CD-ROM (October 1996).

24	A BASIC GUIDE TO EXPORTING
32	BISNIS BULLETIN (NEWLY INDEPENDENT STATES)
572	BUSINESS AMERICA
2051	COUNTRY COMMERCIAL GUIDES
24	DOMESTIC & INTERNATIONAL COAL ISSUES & MARKETS
5	EUROPE NOW: A REPORT
8	EXPORT PROGRAMS:A BUSINESS DIRECTORY OF U.S. GOVERNMENT RESOURCES
41	FOREIGN DIRECT INVESTMENT IN THE U.S. - ANNUAL TRANSACTIONS
13	INVESTMENT GUIDES
3	LEXICON OF TRADE TERMS
10945	**MARKET RESEARCH REPORTS**
29	NORTH AMERICAN FREE TRADE AGREEMENT INFORMATION
23	UNDERSTANDING U.S. FOREIGN TRADE DATA
540	U.S. FOREIGN TRADE HIGHLIGHTS
14	U.S. FOREIGN TRADE UPDATE - MONTHLY ANALYSIS
44	U.S. GLOBAL TRADE OUTLOOK
58	U.S. INDUSTRIAL OUTLOOK
30	U.S. MANUFACTURERS TRADE PERFORMANCE -QUARTERLY REPORT

USDOC, INTERNATIONAL TRADE ADMINISTRATION MENU

EXHIBIT 12.9

Source: NTDB CD-ROM (October 1996).

Trade Directories of the World (Fairfax VA: Croner; loose-leaf update)

For the most complete print listing of trade directories, by country, with access by trade or profession, use *Trade Directories of the World*. This also has an index to export and import directories arranged by country. What the Trade Directory cannot easily do is provide a list of directories of importers or exporters for a given product.

A WWW site that brings together a wide listing and description of trade publications, as well as other directories, is dNet (http://www.d-net.com). The site allows searching by name of publications, topic ("import & export—international trade"), advertising rates and data (whether a publication accepts advertising), and publisher name. The site provides a basic description of the publication or database, publisher, publication date, number of pages and listings, and price. It indicates the format of the information (print, online, CD-ROM, diskette) and indicates whether mailing lists are available. You can reach the publisher through e-mail, phone, or fax. You can also request dNet to find a publication for you.

Directories of Who Exports and Imports

Directory of United States Importers and *Directory of United States Exporters* (New York: Journal of Commerce; published annually)

The *Directory of United States Importers* and the *Directory of United States Exporters* are similar in form, content, and price. The stated purposes of the two directories are:

- To provide a geographical listing of *all* U.S. exporters and importers.
- To provide an alphabetical listing of products by Harmonized Commodity Codes.
- To provide information on customs regulations and export procedures.

Arrangement in both publications is the same. The main company entries are arranged alphabetically by company within states. There is an alphabetical company listing, an alphabetical product index using the harmonized tariff coding schedule, and listings of American consulates and embassies abroad, associations, banks, foreign consulates and embassies in the United States, foreign trade zones, trade commissions, and world ports. The banks are international banks in the United States that provide loan packages, letters of credit, and assistance with foreign exchange transactions. There is a lot of duplication of basic information in the two directories.

Banana Republic (S)   <——*
1 Harrison St. 1st Fl San Francisco, CA 94105
TEL: 415-777-0250
President-Robert J Fisher
Port of Entry - Oakland
Women's Leather Zipper Portfolios, Men's Wool Nylon Woven Jackets, Women's Leather Wallets, Textile Piece Goods, Women's Wool Jackets, Men's Shorts, Women's Cotton Pants, Men's Cotton T-Shirts, Men's Cotton Shirts, Women's Cotton Blouses, Cotton Readymade Garments, General Merchandise, Wearing Apparel, Container Cargo - Australia, Hong Kong, India, Indonesia, Japan, Korea, Macau, Malaysia, People's Republic of China, Philippines, Singapore, Sri Lanka, Taiwan, Thailand, United Kingdom

* Note: Designations of (S), (L), and (A) are used for mode of transportation - sea, land, or air.

DIRECTORY OF UNITED STATES IMPORTERS

EXHIBIT 12.10

Source: *Directory of U.S. Importers*, 1997: 322.

The information on how to export, in the *Exporters Directory*, is taken from *Basic Guide to Exporting*. Exhibit 12.10 displays an entry from the Directory of United States Importers.

Other information that may be in a record includes names of import manager, traffic manager, custom house broker, the establishment date, and the value of the import/export. This is not a list of *all* companies that import or export. Companies fill in questionnaires to be listed in the directory. Additional firms shipping goods via U.S. ports, identified in the PIERS (Port Import Export Reporting Services) database, have also been included.

Directory of U.S. Importers & Exporters CD-ROM (DIALOG OnDisc; semiannual)

Often books do *not* easily answer many of the more specific directory questions local libraries tend to get:

> *What companies in the Delaware Valley are exporting computer equipment to the Middle East?*

> *Who's importing T-shirts from Thailand?*

However, the DIALOG OnDisc *Directory of U.S. Importers & Exporters* does answer these questions—and many others—easily.

> *What New Jersey companies are exporting through the Port of Philadelphia?*

> *What customs house brokers are being used by companies exporting food products to countries in Asia?*

```
00004238
Record Last Updated On: 08/01/92

Banana Republic
1 Harrison St., 1st Fl.
San Francisco, CA  94105
USA

Telephone:  415-777-0250
Import/Export Indicator: IMPORTER

Import/Export Country:
Australia
Hong Kong
India
Indonesia
Japan
Korea
Macau
Malaysia
People's Republic of China
Philippines
Singapore
Sri Lanka
Taiwan
Thailand
United Kingdom

Shipment Information

Number of Shipments:  668
Aggregated Tonnage:  149,909
Ports:  New York, Port Everglades, Oakland, Long
Beach, Los Angeles, Tacoma

Officers

President: Robert J. Fisher

Products

966900   Container Cargo
621142   Cotton Readymade Garments
960100   General Merchandise
620520   Men's Cotton Shirts
620520   Men's Cotton T-Shirts
620349   Men's Shorts . . .
```

DIRECTORY OF IMPORTERS & EXPORTERS *CD-ROM*

EXHIBIT 12.11

Source: DIALOG OnDisc, searched May 1993.

The disc has over 45,000 U.S. companies. It incorporates shipping information from the *Journal of Commerce's* Piers databases (DIALOG Files 571–574, discussed in Chapter 15), with the directory information from the two print publications. Exhibit 12.11 is a sample record from the CD-ROM, with the product list shortened. Additional information on the CD-ROM is the number of shipments and tonnage and also the date of the last record update. Some records were three years old.

Many of the standard print sources discussed in Chapter 4 indicate if a company is an exporter or importer. Regional business directories also may include these designations.

International Directory of Importers (Pousbo, WA: Interdata)

International Directory of Importers is a series of volumes, arranged by continent. The entire set is eight volumes; see Table 12.H. Volumes are arranged by country and then by product. All countries have a classified list of importers and general and statistical information, while some countries also have an expanded company information section. Interdata uses its own product classifications.

The basic entry is company name and mailing address. The "expanded" company information adds a contact name, telecommunications numbers, establishment date, number of employees, and a list of products the company imports.

There are many other export and import directories that cover U.S. regional geographical areas such as the ones listed below.

International Trade Directory: A Guide to International Trade for the Delaware Valley and Mid-Atlantic Region
Wharton Export Network (Philadelphia: 1991)

Colorado International Trade Directory (Boulder, CO: Greater Denver Chamber of Commerce; published biennially in odd years)

California International Trade Register (Database Publishing Co., Inc.; published annually)

World Chamber of Commerce Directory (World Chamber of Commerce Directory; published annually)

Chambers of commerce are excellent sources for locating import/export information. In many European countries, such as France or Spain, they are the best source of information and offer online and CD-ROM databases. Chambers of commerce provide free or low cost print directories of members, and other publications as well. Use this directory to locate chambers of commerce.

Canadian Trade Index (Toronto: Canadian Manufacturers' Association; published annually)

Canadian Trade Index, published since 1900, is an example of an industry association publication. The three-volume directory itself contains Canadian manufacturing companies that have more than local distribution for their products. Exporters are indicated by a star in both the product and name volumes. Information includes address, telecommunications numbers, and geographic areas exported to, as shown in Exhibit 12.12.

TABLE 12.H

INTERNATIONAL DIRECTORY OF IMPORTERS COVERAGE

Region	No of Vols	No of Ed.	No of Companies	No of Countries	Latest Ed Date	Cost
Europe	2	6th	40,000	24	1991/92	275
North America	1	6th r	24,000	2	1992/93	150
Middle East	1	7th	14,000	17	1992/93	150
Asia/Pacific	2	5th r	30,000	14	1992/93	275
South/Central America	1	5th r	16,000	18	1991/92	150
Africa	1	5th r	12,000	40	1991/92	150

Source: Company brochure, January 1993

PAPERBOARDS ...
 Peterboro Cardboards Limited, Peterborough, Ont.
Tel. 705-742-8444
 (S.M.) Ian Blaiklock
 Export: N Central USA, S Central USA, N.W. USA, S.W.
 USA, China/Hong Kong, Australia, New Zealand, S.E. Asia, South America

CANADIAN TRADE INDEX

EXHIBIT 12.12

Source: Canadian Trade Index, 1992: D-142.

While there are a wide range of directories published, the countries they cover, their frequency of publications, and their availability are scattered at best. Most are arranged by country. Table 12.I lists a sampling of other titles from an RLIN search for export(ers/ing) and directories as subject words.

Few libraries have the resources needed to buy and store all the existing trade directories. Beyond the standard sources, it is difficult to anticipate what directories you need to stock. In addition, printed directories do not have the flexibility needed to answer specific questions concerning line of business and geographical regions. We recommend using the online databases listed in Table 12.J as a substitute for printed directories.

Selected Export/Import Directories. Listed below is a selection of important and useful export/import directories.

Directory of American Business in Hong Kong (Hong Kong: GTE, 1990).

For use in import/export trade with Hong Kong. Lists American holidays and services in Hong Kong, an overview of the Hong Kong economy, and an alphabetical listing of American companies. Entries include local English name, telecommunications, address, major products and services, parent company, parent headquarters, and sometimes a company logo. There are also product index and listings and service index and listings.

TABLE 12.I

RANGE OF DIRECTORIES OF EXPORTERS AVAILABLE

** PAPUA NEW GUINEA DIRECTORY OF PRODUCERS AND EXPORTERS.
* DIRECTORIO DE EXPORTADORES (MONTEVIDEO, URUGUAY)
* DIRECTORY OF TAIWAN'S LEADING EXPORTERS
* TAIWAN IMPORTERS DIRECTORY
* CHUNG-KUO WAI HSIANG HSING CHI YEH NIEN CHIEN. SHANG-HAI
* EXPORTERS' DIRECTORY OF NORTHERN GREECE
** PAKISTAN RED PAGES BUSINESS DIRECTORY.
* MEXICAN EXPORT REGISTER. American Chamber of Commerce of Mexico)
** THAILAND EXPORT-IMPORT MONITOR.
* MADE IN MALTA
** CARIBBEAN EXPORTERS, IMPORTERS, AND BUSINESS SERVICES DIRECTORY.
** - [Export and Import]

There are a few product-specific directories:
* AMERICAN FOOD AND AG EXPORTER. Vol. 2, issue 6 (Oct. 1990)-
* U.S. INDUSTRIAL EXPORT DIRECTORY.
* THE INTERNATIONAL DIRECTORY OF IMPORTERS. WORLDWIDE FASHION ACCESSORIES IMPORTING FIRMS.
* DIRECTORY OF PHILIPPINE GARMENTS & TEXTILE EXPORTERS.

Sample associations include:

Canadian Importers Association. MEMBERSHIP DIRECTORY.

American Association of Exporters and Importers. MEMBERSHIP DIRECTORY

Directory of Leading U.S. Export Management Companies, 3rd ed. (Fairfield, CT: Bergano Book Co. and Johnston International Publishing Co. 1991)

Arranged alphabetically by company within state; index by general product grouping and company name. Entries include company name, address, telecommu-

---

TABLE 12.J

DATABASES ON DATASTAR AND DIALOG WITH EXPORTERS/IMPORTERS

Label	Database	Field
EURE	ABC Europe:European Export Industry	RP
BDIE	BDI German Industry	RP
BUSI	Business Opportunities	MJ,MN
DBZZ	D & B Market Identifiers -European Files	HI
F 518, F521,F522	D & B International, Europe, Asia-Pacific	SF
FRIE	French Import/Export	CN
ABCE	German Business & Industry Directory	RP
E1X1	German Buyers' Guide	
HOAU, HOEA, HOPE	Hoppenstedt Austria, East Germany, Germany	IE
BNLU	Hoppenstedt Benelex	EX, IM, FT
ITIE/SDOE	Italian Trading Companies	IE
JPCO	Japanese Company Directory	DE
JORD	JordanWatch -UK Companies	RE
F590, F591	KOMPASS Europe, UK	FT
F592	KOMPASS Asia/Pacific	PX
KOIS	KOMPASS Israel	PN,EX
KSVA	Kreditschutzverband -Austrian Companies	RC
UKIM, UKIA	UK Importers	
WGZW	wer gehört zu wem	CC
WLWE	Who Supplies What?	
ZVIE	ZVEE	RP

---

nications, principal, geographic areas covered, languages spoken, and product area.

General Trade Index & Business Guide, Poland
(Toronto, Canada: Business Foundation Co., 1993).

Directory of 3,500 Polish businesses and firms seeking trade opportunities; section on Polish economy and laws, banking and finance, culture; entries include trade names, full name, address, year of establishment, contact person and language spoken, line of business, number of employees, estimated turnover; uses EU classification codes; includes advertising.

Trading Company Sourcebook (National Federation of Export Associations, 1992)

The sourcebook is both a yearbook, which has articles and information about export management and export trading companies, and a directory for those companies that are members of NFEA. Each directory entry has name, address, contact, telecommunications, and products handled.

World Business Directory (Detroit: Gale and World Trade Centers Association)

Includes companies associated with the World Trade Centers Association. The emphasis is on import/export firms and the number of companies per country is proportionate to that country's participation in world trade (see Chapter 4 for a complete description of this publication).

Sources on How to Export and Import

Several valuable sources of information on how to import and export are detailed below.

Exporters' Encyclopaedia (Dun & Bradstreet; published annually, with semimonthly updates)

Dun and Bradstreet's *Exporters' Encyclopaedia* is a comprehensive guide to all phases of exporting. It includes the standard export information similar to *A Basic Guide*. It also has communications data, transportation information, and contacts. The majority of the *Encyclopaedia* consists of information about export markets. The Market section is divided into: Country Profile, Communications, Key Contacts, Trade Regulations, Documentation, Marketing Data, Transportation, and Business Travel.

The Country Profile overview includes a section on Best U.S. Export Prospects, shown in Exhibit 12.13.

Trade Regulations includes summary information on import licensing and exchange regulations and controls, taxes, and countertrade. Guidelines are given for necessary documentation.

Thailand
COUNTRY PROFILE

Best U.S. Export Prospects: Computers and peripherals, medical equipment, and supplies; food processing and packaging equipment, and agricultural products.

SAMPLE OF BEST U.S. EXPORT PROSPECTS FROM *EXPORTERS' ENCYCLOPAEDIA*

EXHIBIT 12.13

Source: Exporters' Encyclopaedia 1995/1996: 1384.

Marketing Data includes legal requirements regarding importer/agents. For example, in Thailand there are four categories:

1. Expatriate firms; strong resources, large turnover.
2. Smaller importers specializing in one line of business and/or more government departments.
3. New companies that have technical and modern marketing know-how; recommended for medium-sized exporters.
4. Private Thai international trading companies; generally granted special privileges.

Also in this section is information on procurement, standards, environmental protection/pollution control, food/health, safety regulation, marking and labeling, patents and trademarks, advertising, media, and market research. Business travel includes a section on business etiquette.

Official Export Guide and U.S. Customs House Guide (Philadelphia PA: North American Publishing; published annually, with updates)

The *Official Export Guide* and the *U.S. Customs House Guide* are two additional standard library sources. Each costs about $300.

The *Official Export Guide* contains the exporting information from *Basic Guide to Exporting*; a country profiles section that includes the U.S.; service directories, with transport, automation, and financial services, as well as free-trade zones. The *Guide* is useful, too, for its listing of the telephone numbers of Commerce Department desk officers for countries and regions, and for individual industries. The listing in the *Guide* is more comprehensive than what is available from the International Trade Administration's WWW site.

The unique feature of this resource is that it contains the official U.S. Export Administration Regulations, with the product coding schedule B, the actual regulations, and additional regulations on hazardous materials and export documents.

The country profiles in this book are divided into seven sections:

1. Documentation—marking, labeling
2. Trade Data—tariff rates, licenses, prohibited goods distribution channels, trade agreements
3. Best Export Opportunities (see Exhibit 12.13)
4. Profile—country level statistical data
5. General Information—business hours, etc.
6. Key Contacts
7. Shipping Information

The U.S. Custom House Guide is the companion to the *Export Guide*. Its 133rd annual edition was published in 1996. It claims to "provide all the information you need—whether it's a HTSUSA number, a government import regulation, a sample document, or port information." It includes a guide on how to import, with information on the North American Free Trade Agreement, customs audits, and insurance.

Other informational chapters include preferential tariff treatment, trade agreements, marking, insurance, quotas, ports, and services. The *Guide* also includes the Harmonized Tariff Schedules sample import documents.

The Ports section is arranged alphabetically by port. The volume also includes U.S. government agencies, chambers of commerce, airports, rail service and seaports, free-trade zones, and a listing of companies serving the port.

Both the U.S. Export Regulations and the Harmonized Tariff Schedule are available through the U.S. Government Printing Office:

- *Export Administration Regulations* (Washington, DC: United States Office of Export Administration). Kept up-to-date by supplement, *Export Administration Bulletin*.
- *Harmonized Tariff Schedule of the United States* (Washington, DC: United States International Trade Commission). Kept up-to-date between editions by sequentially numbered supplements. The U.S. Customs Service Web site (http:/www.customs.ustreas.gov/) has the searchable text of the *Harmonized Tariff Schedule of the United States*.

Investing, Licensing & Trading Conditions Abroad (New York: Business International; published annually, loose-leaf)

For those who can afford it, a useful service for potential exporters and investors is Business International's *Investing, Licensing & Trading Conditions Abroad*. IL&T is divided into four loose-leaf volumes, which may be purchased separately: Americas, Asia, Europe, and Africa/Middle East. The entire set costs close to $4000. For each country it covers, it lays out most of the basic regulations necessary for trading in countries throughout the world. In 1992, Eastern European countries were added to this valuable service.

Reports are divided into 13 sections with a number of subsections:

1.00	Introduction
	1.09 Official Sources of Business Information
	1.10 Other BI Sources of Information
2.00	State Role in Industry
3.00	Organizing Requirement of a Joint-Stock Company
4.00	Rules of Competition Advertising regulations
5.00	Price controls
6.00	Licensing Patents and trademarks
7.00	Remittability of funds
8.00	Corporate Taxes
9.00	Personal Taxes (with a tax table)
10.00	Incentives
11.00	Capital sources
12.00	Labor
13.00	Foreign Trade

IL&T is also available on many online systems, such as LEXIS-NEXIS Services (INLITR), as part of the regional libraries, and on DIALOG File 627. IL&T is also published in CD-ROM format. An advantage of using the electronic version is that you can find those countries whose reports discuss specific issues; for example, misleading advertising.

Export Profits: A Guide for Small Business (Upstart Publishing, 1992)

Export Profits, by Jack Wolf, is an example of the many basic books designed for the small business person, building on uncopyrighted material from government sources. *Export Profits* is fairly well done. In some ways, it is arranged like our book. It discusses a topic, for example "Finding and Choosing Intermediaries," and also has an annotated list of sources for each topic. It has many of the same lists, i.e., ports, government contacts, chambers of commerce, and sample documents, as well as many more expensive sources.

This type of book is appealing because it is about one-tenth the price of any of the individual reference sources we cite. It is very readable, but ages rapidly. The rules and regulations are modified, desk officers are replaced, new sources are added and old sources modify their names and prices, and the way in which the government is offering information is changing. All libraries' first choice for a introductory export guide should be the *Basic Guide to Exporting*. A book such as *Export Profits* is a good $20 investment today for small business people who want to own their own source.

Journal of Commerce (New York: Knight-Ridder; published weekdays)

Journal of Commerce, published since 1827, is a daily commercial source of export information. It includes articles of interest to international trade, announcements of trade fairs, a major section on shipping, and listings of business opportunities.

Electronic Sources

Only online databases, WWW sites, and CD-ROM products, often from foreign chambers of commerce, can provide very specific levels of company detail. Many of the databases we discussed in Chapters 4 and 6 have fields that identify companies that export or import. Some also give the geographical areas in which companies are active. Dun & Bradstreet's *Market Identifiers* (in different versions on DIALOG, Dow Jones News/Retrieval, and DataStar) can be used to identify importers and/or exporters.

Who are some very small U.S. companies who are exporting? What are their lines of business?

Use File 516 on DIALOG to generate a list of companies with sales under $100,000 that list themselves as importers. Results are shown in Exhibit 12.14, sorted in ascending order.

The following databases have searchable fields that indicate if a company is an importer or exporter.

Table 12.K gives us a sense of how many import and export companies are listed in DIALOG directory databases. Note the high number of European companies.

Companies are not necessarily exclusively engaged in exporting or importing. In the D&B Europe file, for example, about 135,000 companies identify themselves as both importers and exporters.

Some databases identify the countries with which a company deals, as well as the names of exporters and importers. Exhibit 12.15 is an example of this type of database from the *European Export Directory*, *ABC Europe* on DataStar.

Are there any European companies importing chocolate from the United States?

Company Name	City	State	Primary SIC
Ajram Trading Co Inc	Escondido	CA	5084
Arte Nova Limited (inc)	Fort Lee	NJ	5099
Broadbent Selections Inc	San Francisco	CA	5921
Carran Chemical Company	Tucson	AZ	5169
Carron, Michael C	Bedminster	NJ	5199
Central American Records	Union City	NJ	3652
Continental Venture Trading, I	Park Ridge	IL	5136
Dante Trading Co	Santa Rosa	CA	5136
Diversified Trading	Dallas	TX	5199
Globus Trade Co	Detroit	MI	5014
Golden Beverage Company (inc)	Denver	CO	5181
Hawaii Jewelry & Gift Trading	Honolulu	HI	5094
Intermex Import Export Company	National City	CA	5149
Jal Enterprises, Inc	Houston	TX	5031
Jaytex International Inc	Manchester	NH	5051
Newell Systems	Tustin	CA	5199
Park, Joe	Rowland Heights	CA	5065
Piff Trading Inc	Floral Park	NY	5023
Pyramid Inc	Newark	DE	5137
Quality Products Enterprises	Las Vegas	NV	5031
Ramsey, Trisha	Friendswood	TX	5199
Rodriguez, Harvey	Tempe	AZ	8748
S & J International	Alhambra	CA	5199
Saimol International Inc	Hopkins	MN	5169
Sunbrook Enterprises Group & C	Los Angeles	CA	5085
Universal Trading, Ltd.	Brooklyn	NY	4731
Zita Corporation	New Providence	NJ	5199

DUN & BRADSTREET FILE 516—U.S. COMPANIES LISTED AS IMPORTERS WITH SALES OF $100,000 (AUGUST 1996)

EXHIBIT 12.14

Source: Dun and Bradstreet Market Identifiers, File 516 on DIALOG, October 1996.

TABLE 12.K

NUMBER OF EXPORTERS AND IMPORTERS ON DIALOG DATABASES

File	Database Label	Date	Exporters	Importers
516	D & B United States -DMI	6/96	101,201	9,665
518	D & B International -IDMI	4/96	350,676	379,851
521	D & B Europe	4/96	265,424	265,854
529	Hoppenstedt German Companies	4/96	21,764	9,925
590	KOMPASS Western Europe	5/96	158,083	68,260
591	KOMPASS UK	4/96	14,446	1,883
592	KOMPASS Asia/Pacific	6/96	53,041	15,098
593	KOMPASS Cent/Eastern Europe	5/96	16,509	15,953

Source: DIALOG, July 1996.

Selected Online Export/Import Sources

CD-Export (Telexport, Cerved, ICEX)

CD-Export contains the databases on exporting companies supplied by five organizations:

- French chambers of commerce and industry (Telexport)
- Cerved, the EDP branch of the Italian chambers of commerce
- ICPE, the Portuguese institute for foreign trade
- ICEX, the Spanish institute for foreign trade
- WKÖ, the Austrian Economic Federal Chamber

Each company profile includes the following information: company name, registration number, address, telephone and fax, industry codes, NACE product codes, turnover, employees, products exported and imported, and export and import countries. The database is searchable in each language, using Database DOS or Windows software.

```
                 1 EURE _
   DB    EURE, FIZ Technik Frankfurt: ABC Europe,
         ABC-Verlag.
   AN    E40784740; Update: 19960507
   AS    Annoni & Figli, S.a.s., Attilio, di Luigi Annoni & C.
         Via N. Bettoni, 2.
         I-20125 Milano
         Italy.
   TL    Telephone: (02) 6709309
         Telex: 311271
   PE    Non-alcoholic beverages.
         Beer.
         Dietetic preparations.
         Chocolate.
         Soya bean products.. . .
   RP    Exports to: Spain, Germany, Malta, Turkey, Cyprus
         United Arab. Emirates, Libya, Australia, Singapore.
         Imports from: Europe, USA.
```

ABC EUROPE ON DATASTAR

EXHIBIT 12.15

Source: *ABC Europe* from DataStar, July 1996.

Firmimport/Firmexport (Chambre de Commerce et d'Industrie de Paris; quarterly updates with annual revision)

Firmimport/Firmexport provides information on 30,000 French companies and businesses that export or import. Entries includes company's full name, address, telecommunications numbers, manager, legal status, broad industry grouping, list of products using EU harmonized tariff codes, countries traded with and (where available) sales, values for imports and exports, and number of employees. Available from Telexport and DataStar.

TELEXPORT (Chambre de Commerce et d'Industrie de Paris)

The Paris Chamber of Commerce and Industry (CCIP) represents over 270,000 French companies. It is part of a network of over 175 organizations collecting business and economic information on French companies and opportunities. CCIP-Business Information compiles this information and makes it available in a variety of databases. Those that are of most interest to the exporter or importer are Telexport and Export-Affairs Plus. Telexport comprises 37,000 French companies involved in international trade. Export and import products and countries are part of each of the company records. Telexport is available on DataStar as file FRIE and as part of the CD-EXPORT CD-ROM.

Export-Affaires-Plus is designed to identify export or import partners. This database is available electronically as part of the IBCC network of information complied by world chambers of commerce (http://www1.usa1.com/~ibnet/).

ABC der Deutschen Wirtschaft Verlagsgesellschaft mbH (Darmstadt)

ABC Europe: European Export Industry (EURE) and ABC West Germany: German Buyers' and Sellers' Guide (ABCE) are the online equivalents of ABC *Europe Production* and ABC *de Deutschen Wirtschaft*. The publications have records for about 150,000 exporting manufacturers in Western and Eastern European countries. Entries include address and contact numbers, product types, industry classification, association memberships, sales representatives, banks, management names, number of employees, incorporation year, commercial registration, and capital. Records also provide export destinations. They are online on DataStar and FIZ Technik, and a subset is on CD-ROM.

BDI-The German Industry-Made in Germany (Mindelheim, Germany: Verlag W. Sachon GmbH & Co.)

BDI can be searched in English or German. The database has records on 22,000 German manufacturers that are involved in export trade. Data items include address and contact numbers, numbers of employees, names and addresses of subsidiaries, and business data (e.g., capital, sales volume). The print equivalent is *BDI-Die Deutsche Industrie*. The database is available on DataStar and the German databanks FIZ Technik and GENIOS.

Selected WWW Sites and Online Bulletin Boards

When we think of online services, we generally think of the commercial time-sharing systems or Web sites. However, there are several services that have both voice and electronic access for export and import information. We have mentioned three U.S. government services: *Economic Bulletin Board* (U.S. Department of Commerce), *U.S. Customs Electronic Bulletin Board* (U.S. Customs Service), and *Eximbank Bulletin Board*. Check with your state to see if they provide bulletin board access. There are also private sources, which are generally repackaging government information. Test these services before entering a subscription.

Business Opportunities

In addition to directories that identify importers and exporters, there are sources that are designed to identify specific business opportunities. Governments put out bids for projects, or individual companies advertise themselves as potential trade patterns. They answer such questions as:

We would like to invest in Thailand, especially in a resort. Are there any projects needing financial or technical assistance?

Are there any library construction projects in Europe?

Which Slovenian shoe manufacturers, if any, are looking for foreign partners?

There are several sources of online information that list potential partners for the exporter or importer and their representative. Table 12.L lists sources of business opportunities.

Foreign Trade Opportunities—the Trade Opportunity Program, TOP (U.S. Department of Commerce)

TOP covers sales opportunities and leads compiled by U.S embassies abroad for specific products, projects, government tenders, representation, joint ventures, direct sale for resale or end users, and barter arrangements being sought by foreign companies, governments, or organizations. Information provided includes a description of the opportunity, a contact name, address, phone, fax and telex numbers, and a five-digit harmonized tariff code. Over 100 countries contribute to TOP.

The Trade Opportunity Program is disseminated in several different forms. The daily leads are available online, along with over 700 other files, through the Commerce Department's Economic Bulletin Board, EBB (modem access: 202-482-3870). Each day at approximately 1:00 PM, Eastern Time, two files are made available for downloading by subscribers. One file contains private-sector opportunities and the other contains government tender opportunities. A one-year subscription is $35, including a $12 credit for connect time with the system. An EBB fax (900-786-2329) is also available.

District offices of the Commerce Department also receive the leads daily and have them on file for the public. Government tenders are printed in the *Commerce Business Daily* (Chicago: Dept. of Commerce), the source of U.S. government procurement announcements. Corporate requests are published in the commercial *Journal of Commerce*. TOP is also online on LEXIS-NEXIS in the *Business Reference Library*, file name FTO.

Commercial Service International Contacts (U.S. Department of Commerce)

Formerly called *Foreign Traders Index*, this source lists foreign companies, organizations, government entities, banks, associations, and institutes in about 60 selected countries served by the U.S. and Foreign Commercial Service that have some interest in importing goods or services from the U.S.

Information for each entry includes the name of the organization or business, year established, a contact name and address, number of employees, and description of the product or service needed with a four-digit code. *Contacts* is available electronically through NTDB on the STAT-USA WWW site, on NTDB CD-ROM disc 2 (see Exhibit 12.17), and on the LEXIS-NEXIS Services in the *Business Reference Library*.

TABLE 12.L

SOURCES FOR BUSINESS OPPORTUNITIES

PROGRAM	Compiling Body	Target Countries	Availability
Foreign Trade Opportunities TOP	U.S. Dept of Comm	Worldwide government and commercial	Commerce Business Daily; Journal of Commerce; L/N; D-S; WWW
Foreign Traders Index	U.S. Dept of Comm	Worldwide companies	NTDB; L/N
Overseas Private Investment Corporation - OPIC	U.S. OPIC	Worldwide projects	Direct; L/N
Tenders Electronic Daily TED	EC	EC, GATT, US, Japan, Canada	L/N; D-S; Echo
DunsContract	D & B	U.K., private contractors, Eastern Europe	Fee-based; DunsNet
Business - BUSI	European Banks	Worldwide commercial	D-S; F-T; online direct; WWW
Advertise - ADVE	Germany	Mainly European Commercial	D-S
Scan-A-Bid	UN	Noncommerical construction	United Nations; D-S
Bisnis	US Dept of Comm	Eastern Europe	[FAX; WWW; E-mail]

L/N - LEXIS/NEXIS Services; D-S - DATA-STAR; F-T - Fiz Technik

Copyright (c) 1993 Commission of the European Communities
TED (Tenders Electronic Daily)
April 21, 1993

TYPE OF DOCUMENT: Invitation to tender
LENGTH: 880 words
TITLE OF DOCUMENT: F-Poitiers: multimedia library (Only the original text is authentic)
AWARD AUTHORITY: Local authorities
KEYWORDS: 5011 - GENERAL BUILDING CONTACTORS; 5031 - GENERAL INSTALLATION WORK;
5041 - GENERAL BUILDING COMPLETION WORK

BODY:
Doc. No: 17319-93; Cite: JO S 077; Page: 0007; Date: April 21, 1993
Type of Procurement: Open procedure
Regulation of Procurement: EEC
Type of Bid Required: Not specified
Award Criteria: Not specified

1. Awarding authority: Ville de Poitiers, service des batiments communaux, hotel de ville, F-86021 Poitiers. Tel. 49 88 82 07.
2. (a) Award procedure: Public invitation to tender. National legislation applicable: CMP art. 295-300, RPAO. (b)
3. (a) Site: Poitiers. (b) Works: Multimedia library. 6 floors. Total surface: 10 209 m**2. 31 lots. (c) (d)
4. Completion deadline: 17 months.
5. (a) Documents from: Applications in writing. As in 1, direction generale des services techniques, M. le Maire. (b) Fee: Deposit in the form of a cheque. FF 800. Payee: Mme le Tresorier principal municipal de Poitiers. Fee will be refunded to bona fide tenderers.
6. (a) Deadline for receipt of tenders: 4. 6. 1993 (17.00). (b) Address: As in 1, secretariat de la direction generale des services techniques. Tenders must be submitted in a double sealed envelope. Tenders to be submitted by registered post with form for advice of receipt or by hand, in which case a receipt will be issued. (c) Language (s): French.
7. (a) (b)
8. Deposits and guarantees: 5 %.
9. Financing and payment: Progress payments as indicated in contract documents.
10.
11. Qualifications: See notice in original language.
12. Tenders may lapse after: 120 days.
13.
14.
15. Other information: M. Tourneboeuf ou M.Masse, tel. 49 88 82 07.
16.
17. Notice postmarked: 13. 4. 1993.
18. Notice received on: 13. 4. 1993.
DATE RECEIVED: April 13, 1993
DEADLINE FOR TENDER: April 13, 1993
COUNTRY: FRANCE

TENDERS ELECTRONIC DAILY FROM LEXIS-NEXIS

EXHIBIT 12.16

Source: TED on LEXIS-NEXIS Services, May 1993.

Another useful feature of the NTDB file is its "Country Directories of International Contacts," which describes print and electronic directories for 21 countries. Included in the description are price and publishers' addresses.

OPIC (Overseas Private Investment Corp. Opportunity Bank)

The Overseas Private Investment Corporation, a U.S. government corporation chartered by Congress, provides political risk and other insurance and investment services to U.S. corporations. OPIC operates an "Opportunity Bank" as part of its effort to promote U.S. direct investment in the developing world. The data bank enables U.S. firms and overseas project sponsors to register their respective investment interests and requirements and "find each other." At present, there are approximately 2,400 records from 100 countries. The Opportunity Bank contains two types of information:

- U.S. company profiles: Descriptions of companies interested in investing overseas.
- Investment project profiles: Descriptions of projects worldwide that are seeking U.S. investment.

Application forms to register a company or project with OPIC are available directly from Opportunity Bank Project Profile, 1516 M Street NW, Washington, DC, 20527; phone 202-457-7010; fax 202-331-4234; telex 493-8219.

Tenders Electronic Daily (Office for Official Publications of the European Communities, BP 2373 L-1023 Luxembourg B-1049)

Governments, local authorities, and utilities are required by an EU directive to advertise contracts in excess of about $150,000. The information appears in TED, *Tenders Electronic Daily*, the official publication of the European Communities. TED contains the full text of requests for bids that are published in supplement "S" of the *Official Journal* of the European Communities. TED is available from the ECHO web site. A password is required.

In addition to EU countries, about 60 participants in WTO, the U.S., Japan, and Canada, submit tenders exceeding $300,000. Tenders cover electrical and mechanical engineering, consumer goods, catering, hotel management, printing, fuel supply, and a wide array of other items. The EU maintains TED on its own databank, ECHO, and other online services access it, including the British Export Network Limited, Cerved, DataStar (TEDA), Dun & Bradstreet, and LEXIS-NEXIS Services in the Business Reference Library, file name TED.

BUSINESS (BUSINESS Datenbanken GmbH, Heidelberg, Germany)

BUSINESS (International BUSINESS Opportunities Service), on DataStar, FIZ Technik, and GENIOS, is a European database with worldwide business opportunities. It is a joint venture among European banks, information providers, and the EU. It contains worldwide trade opportunities and business contacts in such areas as imports and exports, sales, services, representation (e.g., general, agency, distributorship), research and development, technology, and cooperative ventures in manufacturing, marketing, and investment. Includes activity and interest profiles of firms, research institutes, and service organizations. Sources include published exchanges, bulletins from trade promotion agencies, manufacturers' lists, exhibition catalogs, directories, new product announcements, and original company entries.

ADVERTISE (Munich: Deutscher Sparkassenverlag, the publisher for German Savings Banks)

ADVE contains business opportunities for small to medium-sized companies. Companies pay to be listed. Information is valid for one year. Non-German companies often include a German contact. The database is in German. *ADVE* uses *Predicasts* country codes and shortened *Predicasts* product codes. There are 10 types of opportunities:

- Gesuch—Wanted
- Angebot—For sale/On offer
- Vertretung—Representation
- Lizens—License
- Production Handelsvermittlung—Trade Opportunity
- Importanfrage—Import Request
- Vertrieb—Distribution/Sale
- Abnehmer—Customers
- Ankauf —Buying
- Verkauf—Selling

In addition to being offering on commercial time-sharing systems, it is available in Germany as part of S-Database Services, a fee-based information system offered by German savings banks and state banks. Available as ADVE on DataStar.

Scan-a-Bid (New York: United Nations, Development Business/ Development Forum)

Scan-a-Bid is the online version of "Development Business," a twice monthly procurement newspaper published by the United Nations. The file contains requests for quotations on major construction projects worldwide, financed by international organizations. Included are the name of the project, country, type of project (e.g., highway), building materials required, amount of money allocated for the project, and name of person and organization to contact for further information. A companion database, *Summary of Proposed Projects*, is also available. It contains a description (operational summaries) of projects (by region, country, and sector) that are pending approval at the World Bank, the Inter-American Development Bank, and the African Development Bank. Both *Scan-a-Bid* (SCAN) and *Summary of Proposed Projects* (SOPP) are available on DataStar.

BISNIS (U.S. Dept. of Commerce)

BISNIS is the acronym for the Commerce Department's Business Information Service for the Newly Independent States. BISNIS provides information in several formats. *BISNIS Bulletin* contains news and practical advice on doing business in the former Soviet Union. Sample article titles are:

- *Media Use in Kazakstan*
- *Moving Your Money in Russia*

BISNIS Bulletin is available in print, through the BISNIS Web site, as well as on the National Trade Data Bank CD-ROM and NTDB through the STAT-USA Web site.

BISNIS Search for Partners is a newsletter designed to help U.S. companies find business opportunities in the states of the former Soviet Union. In order to publish business leads quickly, the main form of distribution is via biweekly e-mail broadcast. To receive *Search for Partners* in this format, send an e-mail to bisnis@usta.gov, providing contract information and requesting receipt of the *Search for Partners* biweekly e-mail report. *Search for Partners* is also available on BISNIS Online (http://www.itaiep.doc.gov/bisnis) and through the BISNIS fax retrieval system (800-872-8723). A selection of

Search for Partners opportunities will continue to be printed and mailed each month. Exhibit 12.17 is an example of a *Search for Partners* business lead.

Each issue focuses on long and medium-term trade leads in one country. Exhibit 12.18 is an example of an entry dealing with Armenia.

BISNIS Trades and Tenders is an electronic newsletter designed to help U.S. companies find business opportunities in the newly independent states. See Exhibit 12.19.

National Trade Data Bank
```
ITEM ID         :     IT CSIC  12204004226
DATE            :         Sep 23, 1996

AGENCY          :     USDOC, International Trade Administration
PROGRAM         :     Commercial Service International Contracts
TITLE           :     E.D. Sagman Trading Reg'd.

Program         :     IT CSIC
Update          :     :Monthly
End year        :     1996
Date of record  :     19950320
```

<ADDRESS>
Mr. Edward Sagman
President
E.D. Sagman Trading Reg'd.
940 D'Alencon
Laval, QC H7W 3W4
Canada

<OTHER COMPANY INFORMATION>
PHONE: 514/682-5550
YEAR ESTABLISHED: 1986
NO. OF EMPLOYEES: 1
RELATIVE SIZE: SMALL
INFORMATION DATE: 03/20/95
FAX: 514/681-9241

<PRODUCT INFORMATION>

HARMONIZED CODE	PRODUCT SERVICE DESCRIPTION
1702904500	Sugars and syrups, nesoi, deriv fr sgr cane/ beets Int. in handling as Agent
220300	Beer made from malt Int. in handling as Agent
2402200000	Cigarettes containing tobacco Int. in handling as Agent
61	Apparel articles and accessories, knit or crochet Int. in handling as Agent
S505	METALS & MINERALS, EXCEPT PETROLEUM Sales Agent
S6793	COMMODITY TRADERS Sales Agent

COMMERCIAL SERVICE INTERNATIONAL CONTACTS INDEX ON NTDB: SEARCH FOR BEER

EXHIBIT 12.17

Source: Commercial Service International Contracts on NTDB (CD-ROM), January 1997.

Product: Consumer Goods
Company: Arsenal Corporation
Established in 1994 by a group of entrepreneurs, Arsenal Corporation encompasses seven enterprises and assists in managing a state company soon to be privatized. Arsenal's diversified activity includes production of stone and concrete building materials, office furniture and apparel. The company also operates livestock farms, grows vegetables, and processes and sells agricultural production. Arsenal will soon operate its own television station and newspaper in the city of Hrazdan. The company has several foreign business partners and an annual turnover of US$1 million. With its significant assets and available capital, human resources, and excellent trade links in the NIS, Arsenal seeks U.S. partners to assist with design, production, and marketing of general consumer goods, furniture, or agri-products.
Contact: Edik Gharibyan, President
378550 Yerevan
Central Post Office, Building #10
Arsenal corporation
Tel: (374-2-67)2-13-02
Fax:(374-2-67)2-68-01
Source: BISNIS Rep Yerevan

BISNIS SEARCH FOR PARTNERS

EXHIBIT 12.18

Source: *BISNIS Search for Partners*, December 1996.

PACKAGING EQUIPMENT AND TIN-PLATE

CONTACT:
GARRIMAN VOROBYEV, GENERAL DIRECTOR, NAKHODKA CAN MANUFACTURING PLANT, 1 ASTAFIEVA STREET, NAKHODKA, RUSSIA 692911.
TEL: (7-42366) 234-84; FAX: (7-42366) 236-67.
TELEX: 213828 CAN RU

PRODUCT CODES:
HS 842240 PACKAGING EQUIPMENT
HS 800400 TIN-PLATE (MUST CORRESPOND TO RUSSIAN STANDARD GOST 13345-85)

PRODUCT SPECIFICATIONS/TECHNICAL DATA:
HS 843930: PACKAGING EQUIPMENT FOR CEMENT PRODUCTS; VOLTAGE 220-250
HS 800400: 1) THICKNESS OF PLATE - 0.22 MM, WIDTH OF ROLL - 820 MM, TYPE OF HARDNESS - B, TYPE OF
SURFACE - DLLL; 2) THICKNESS OF PLATE - 0.22 MM, WIDTH OF THE ROLL - 724
MM, TYPE OF HARDNESS - A2, TYPE OF SURFACE - DLLL.

QUANTITY:
HS 843930: 1 SET; HS 800400: 2,604 TONS OF EACH TYPE

PURCHASE NEEDED BY:
EARLY 1997

OTHER INFORMATION:
FOR HS 843930: WILL CONSIDER LEASING

BISNIS TRADES AND TENDERS

EXHIBIT 12.19

RESPONSE DATA:
RESPONSE LANGUAGE: ENGLISH
BEST WAY TO RESPOND: FAX, TELEX

INFORMATION DESIRED FROM U.S. FIRMS::
PRICE-LIST, CATALOGS, TERMS OF PAYMENT AND DELIVERY
PRIMARY BUYING FACTOR:
PRICE, QUALITY, TERMS OF PAYMENT AND DELIVERY

COMPANY DATA:
TYPE OF BUSINESS: MANUFACTURING. YEAR ESTABLISHED: 1953. NUMBER OF EMPLOYEES: 1,189
ANNUAL SALES: MORE THAN $10 MILLION. THE COMPANY MANUFACTURES TIN, PLASTIC, PAPER PACKING MATERIALS FOR FISHERY, FOOD-PROCESSING, AND OTHER INDUSTRIES OF THE RUSSIAN FAR EAST AND SIBERIA.

BANK NAME AND ADDRESS:
VNESHTORGBANK, 19 SHKOLNAYA STREET, NAKHODKA, RUSSIA

POST REMARKS:
THE COMPANY IS PARTICIPATING IN DEVELOPMENT OF AN INDUSTRIAL PARK WITHIN
THE NAKHODKA FREE ECONOMIC ZONE AND SEEKS OPPORTUNITIES FOR JOINT MANUFACTURING OF PACKING MATERIALS. PARTNER SOUGHT TO CONVERT ST. PETERSBURG PALACE INTO HOTEL

BISNIS TRADES AND TENDERS

EXHIBIT 12.19 (continued)

Source: *BISNIS Trades and Tenders*, December 1996.

NOTES

1. "U.S. Trade Facts," *Business America* 117 (May 1, 1996): 5.

2. Richard Barovick and Patricia Anderson, "EMCs/ETCs: What They Are, How They Work," *Business America* 113 (July 13, 1992): 2–5. Includes some cases.

3. "Eximbank Targets Small Business: Seeks Charter Changes to Help Exports," *BNA International Finance Daily* (April 16, 1992); from LEXIS-NEXIS search. Outlines changes to three major Eximbank programs: Working Capital Guarantee, New-to-Exporting Insurance and Umbrella Insurance.

4. Nigel M. Healey, "A Beginner's Guide to Corporate Barter," *Illinois Business Review* 48 (Spring 1991): 13–15.

5. Aspy Pailia and P. Shenkar, "Countertrade Practices in China," *Industrial Marketing Management*, 20 (February 1991): 357–65. Includes examples from *Countertrade Outlook* 6, no. 5 (1988) and analyses of 80 countertrade transactions with China

6. Aspy Pailia and P. Shenkar, "Countertrade Practices in China," pp. 357–65.

7. Charles Batchelor, "Survey of Factoring," *Financial Times* (April 1, 1992): 16; LEXIS-NEXIS search. Statistics and state of international factoring.

8. Frank Gray, "Forfaiting Market Looks to Further Expansion," *International Trade Finance* (October 20, 1995), 4–6. The article explains how forfaiting is done.

9. Adapted from R. Michael Rice, "Four Ways to Finance Your Exports," *Journal of Business Strategy* 9 (July/August 1988): 30–33. This article provides brief description of forfaiting, factoring, the Export-Import Bank, and insurance underwriting.

10. Michael J. Horton, *Import and Customs Law Handbook* (New York: Quorum Books; 1992). This book provides guidance to those whose jobs make them responsible for handling U.S. customs matters. Although the book deals with the legal aspects of Customs, it is understandable to a layperson.

11. Thomas E. Johnson, *Export/Import Procedures and Documentation* (New York: AMACOM, 1994). Published by the American Management Association Communications Division this is another introductory guide to importing and exporting basic. It has extensive sample documents.

PART IV
Industrial and Economic Statistics

CHAPTER 13
Economic Statistics

TOPICS COVERED

- Country Classifications
- National Accounts
- Comparative Economic Statistics
- Sources for Economic Statistics
- Measures of Price Levels
- Labor Statistics
- Financial Data
- Additional Sources

MAJOR SOURCES DISCUSSED

- *National Accounts Statistics*
- *National Accounts ESA*
- *World Economic Outlook*
- *Monthly Bulletin of Statistics*
- *Bulletin of Labour Statistics*
- *International Financial Statistics*
- *Monitoring the World Economy 1820–1992*

INTRODUCTION

Economic statistics are the basic indicators of a nation's economic well-being. They include measures of national income, employment, price levels, and industrial output. They are used to gauge an economy's performance and to predict future conditions. In this chapter, we examine some of the issues concerning the use of economic statistics in an international setting and describe general sources of economic data. We use "economic statistics" in a broad sense and include in our discussion national finance, labor statistics, and energy. Trade statistics are discussed separately in Chapter 15.

Economic data are available in three basic forms. The first form is a time series, numbers reported at a regular interval over time. The monthly consumer price index for Canada for the past three years would be a time series. The second form is cross-sectional, several economic characteristics described for a particular time. An example would be a country's industrial production by industry group for the current year. The third form for economic data is text. An example would be a news story that describes Japan's trade surplus. In practice, these forms of data are often combined. Cross-sectional data frequently include historical (time series) as well as current data. Text often combines descriptions of economic variables with tables and graphs of the data.

COUNTRY CLASSIFICATIONS

The individual country is the basic unit for the presentation of comparative international data. Countries are grouped in several ways for analysis.

- By geographic region (e.g., Asia)
- By type of economy (e.g., market)
- By stage of economic development (e.g., "developing countries")
- By political organization (e.g., EU)

Economic Classifications

There is no standard economic classification scheme for countries. Recent publications by the International Monetary Fund (IMF) categorize countries by economic development into three groups: "industrial countries," "developing countries," and "countries in transition."

Industrial countries include those in North America, Southern and Western Europe (excluding Cyprus, Malta, and the former Yugoslavia), along with Australia, Japan, New Zealand, and South Africa. Developing countries are found in Latin America and the Caribbean, Africa (other than South Africa), Asia, and the Pacific (excluding Australia, Japan, and New Zealand), Cyprus, Malta, and the former Yugoslavia. Countries in transition include the former USSR and socialist countries of Eastern Europe (excluding the former Yugoslavia).

Other country classifications that are frequently used include:

- Group of Seven (G-7): These are the seven largest developed market economies: Canada, France, Germany, Italy, Japan, U.K., and the U.S. Since 1994, the annual G-7 Summit has included Russia in its political meetings. The expanded G-7 is referred to as the P-8—"Political Eight." The G-7 Information Centre at the University of Toronto has a WWW site devoted to describing this group (http://www.g7.utoronto.ca/). It includes the G-7 communiques, news stories, and research about the organization.

   There are several other "groups" of countries; the Group of 10 (G-10), for example, which consists of the 10 wealthiest countries in the IMF. In 1997, a newly formed group of Muslim countries met for the first time: the D-8 ("D" for developing) consists of Turkey, Iran, Pakistan, Bangladesh, Indonesia, Nigeria, Malaysia, and Egypt.

- Newly Industrializing Economies: "Newly industrializing economies" (NIEs) is a category widely used in economic analysis. It describe countries with rapidly expanding market economies that are heavily engaged in international trade. There is some disagreement on which countries should be included. Hong Kong, Singapore, South Korea, Taiwan, Argentina, Brazil, and Mexico are the countries most commonly identified with the term. An older term referring to this category is "newly industrializing countries" (NICs).

There are a host of informal names for other country groups. For example, Hong Kong, South Korea, Singapore, Taiwan are sometimes referred to collectively as the "Four Dragons" or the "Four Tigers." The U.S., Japan, and the EU are often called the "Triad" in discussions of international trade.

Formal Economic Groups

There are a number of formally constituted economic country groups. The following groups are among the most important:

- EU (European Union): The members of the EU are Austria, Belgium, Denmark, France, Finland, Germany, Greece, Ireland, Italy, Luxembourg, Netherlands, Portugal, Spain, Sweden, and the United Kingdom. The EU is a supranational body, and it ranks with the U.S. and Japan as one of the world's leading economic powers. The EU's goal is to join its member nations in a political, economic, and monetary union.

Europa (http://europa.eu.int/) is maintained by the European Commission for EU institutions. It includes information on the history, institutions, policies, and news of EU. Some useful links include EUROSTAT (statistics), ECHO, CORDIS (R&D Information), EUR-OP (office for EU official publications), as well as sites for individual governments in the EU.

- EFTA (European Free Trade Association): EFTA was set up in 1960 as a common market. It has eliminated all customs duties and quota restrictions on industrial products between members and with the EU. Members of EFTA are Iceland, Liechtenstein, Norway, and Switzerland.

- OPEC (Organization of Petroleum Exporting Countries): OPEC is a group of countries that are net exporters of petroleum. All the countries in the group are "developing countries." Several important oil exporting countries, such as Bahrain and Mexico, are not part of OPEC. The category "net energy exporters" is sometimes used to include all oil exporting nations. The members of OPEC are Algeria, Gabon, Indonesia, Iran, Iraq, Kuwait, Libya, Nigeria, Qatar, Saudi Arabia, United Arab Emirates, and Venezuela.

- OECD (The Organization for Economic Cooperation and Development): The OECD is an international organization for industrialized market-economy countries. It is a forum where officials from member countries exchange information and coordinate policy. As of 1997, there were 29 members of the OECD. They include the EU member states plus Australia, Canada, the Czech Republic, Hungary, Iceland, Korea, Japan, Mexico, New Zealand, Norway, Poland, Switzerland, Turkey, and the U.S. The organization gathers a wide range of statistical information from member states, processes it for comparability, and distributes it to the public. The OECD Web site (http://www.oecd.com) provides statistical compilations (for example, *OECD in Figures* and *OECD Leading Economic Indicators*), as well as descriptions of OECD programs and publications.

A useful source for descriptions of country groups is the CIA's *World Factbook,* described below. Eurostat's *Europe in Figures* gives a clear description of the evolution and present situation of the EU.

NATIONAL ACCOUNTS

National accounts are compilations of the data that are needed to estimate the monetary value of goods and services produced by a country. This measure is usually expressed as gross national product (GNP) or gross domestic product (GDP).

Gross national product (GNP) is the market value of all goods and services produced during a particular period by the residents of a country. In the United States, for example, GNP is the sum of the market value of all goods and services produced by individuals, businesses, and government. GNP *includes* income earned by U.S.-owned corporations overseas and U.S. residents working abroad. For example, U.S. GNP includes income earned by General Motors in the United Kingdom. GNP *excludes* income earned in the U.S. by residents of the rest of the world. U.S. GNP excludes, for example, income earned by the Honda Corporation in the United States.

Gross domestic product (GDP) is the market value of all goods and services produced by people in a country whether or not they are citizens. For example, profits earned by foreign-owned businesses in the U.S. are included in U.S. GDP but not in U.S. GNP. In contrast, profits earned by U.S. firms abroad are included in U.S. GNP but not in GDP. GDP has become the standard form of reporting national accounts for countries, as well as for international organizations. Until 1991, the U.S. used GNP as its main measure of national economic output; it now uses GDP.

Because GDP is a key variable in the analysis of a country's economy, there is interest in several aspects of this measure. In addition to examining the trend in GDP over time and determining differences in GDP by region and country, researchers often want details such as the following:

- GDP at constant prices. GDP is measured in a country's currency. Because currencies are subject to changes in value, GDP must be adjusted for inflation. GDP price deflators (general measures of an economy's inflation rate) are used to convert GDP measured in current prices to constant prices.
- The contributions of economic sectors to GDP. One method of calculating GDP is to add up the value-added contribution of a country's economic sectors. As a result, it is possible to determine each sector's contribution to total GDP. One could, for instance, determine the share of the Italian service sector in the total Italian GDP.
- GDP by type of expenditure. GDP represents the use of goods and services produced by an economy. GDP is used by consumers (households), by governments, and by businesses (investment). Determining the changes in final uses of GDP over time, or the differences in final uses among countries, is often of research interest. For example, the expenditures by households is one indication of a country's standard of living.
- The relation of GDP to other economic variables. A nation's per-capita GDP is calculated by dividing its GDP by its population. This measure allows a direct comparison of the economic strengths of countries with unequal populations. A nation's expenditures or debt is sometimes expressed as a percentage of GDP. Examples would be defense expenditures as a percentage of GDP (Expenditures/GDP) or budget deficit as a percentage of GDP (Debt/GDP). Deficit as a percentage of GDP is a crucial measure for countries of the EU. The Maastricht Treaty has as a goal annual government deficits of not more than 3% of GDP as a condition for participation in the European Monetary Union in 1999.
- The effect of the underground economy on GDP. Not all income in an economy is recorded by governments. Underground economic activity ranges from unreported fees collected for child care to the income of organized crime. There are no firm statistics for the underground economy; estimates in the U.S. range between 5% and 15% of GDP.[1] Some estimates of the underground economy in developing countries are as high as 50% of reported GDP.[2]

Sources for National Accounts

National Accounts Statistics (published annually by the UN)

The United Nations System of National Accounts (SNA) was first formulated in 1952. It provides the framework for the display of the national accounts of more than 180 countries and areas. It is used extensively by individual countries and by international organizations in their national accounts reporting. The EU's European System of Integrated Economic Accounts (ESA) is based on the UN system. The U.S. is adopting features of the United Nations system of national accounts.

The UN's annual two-part *National Accounts Statistics* is an essential resource, particularly for its coverage of countries not part of the OECD or the EU. Part One of the series *(National Accounts Statistics: Analysis of Main Aggregates)* gives general measures of GDP for 184 countries for the past 12 years. The measures include total and per capita GDP, and GDP by type of expenditure and by kind of economic activity. The overall GDP figures are given in current prices using the national currency. Details of economic activity and type of expenditures are given as percentages of total GDP.

Part Two of the series *(National Accounts Statistics: Main Aggregates and Detailed Tables)* gives detailed breakdowns of GDP expenditures in both current and constant national currency prices. The notes that begin each country's entry give the source of information for the accounts. In most cases, this consists of the name of the statistical office in the country together with the name of the published vol-

---

1.2 Expenditure on the Gross Domestic Product, in Constant Prices

Million Austrian schillings

	1980	1983	1984	1985	1986	1987	1988	1989	1990	1991	1992	1993
					At constant prices of:1983							
1 Government final consumption expenditure	212270	226891	227378	231800	235652	236594	237369	239241	242087	249481	255494	263212
2 Private final consumption expenditure	651890	694839	694309	710861	723426	746147	773044	799812	828622	852981	869581	871153
3 Gross capital formation	328498	263729	295709	301289	307534	316390	344021	358497	385111	398876	402887	395642
A Increase in stocks a	29170	-5821	20467	12277	7885	7394	16354	10615	17279	7805	6773	7693
B Gross fixed capital formation b	299328	269550	275242	289012	299649	308996	327667	347882	367832	391071	396114	387949
Residential buildings	62993	61577	61114	60086	61447	62866	68182	67902	68806	76613	86029	95910
Non-residential buildings	98185	83412	85031	87936	91503	98376	103356	111952	121398	125010	125786	120472
Other construction and land improvement etc.												
Other	121238	107977	112828	124208	128995	130220	137557	148983	157419	167593	161570	148330
4 Exports of goods and services c	404606	449686	477069	509958	496138	507911	553725	610644	659913	699154	718744	711700
5 Less: Imports of goods and services c	428601	433928	476898	506366	500451	523817	572885	621770	670405	712611	731305	727212
Statistical discrepancy	.	.	.	.	.	.	.	.	.	.	.	.
Equals: Gross Domestic Product	1168663	1201217	1217567	1247542	1262299	1283225	1335274	1386424	1445328	1487881	1515401	1514495

a) Item 'Increase in stocks' includes breeding stock, draught animals and a statistical discrepancy. These estimates are shown separately as 'Statistical discrepancy' in tables 2.7, 2.8, 2.9, 2.10 and b) Item 'Gross fixed capital formation' includes value added tax on investments of investors not 2.11. entitled to deduct invoiced value added tax. This component is not included in the sub-items. For c) The estimates on transit trade are on a net basis. years 1973-1975, 1977 and 1978 of the current prices table, special investment tax is included.

1.3 Cost Components of the Gross Domestic Product

Million Austrian schillings

	1980	1983	1984	1985	1986	1987	1988	1989	1990	1991	1992	1993
1 Indirect taxes, net	132774	161686	180154	186728	187997	197773	209808	226304	240026	249343	264667	275048
A Indirect taxes	162828	197080	216087	225931	234044	245154	254887	271413	287880	305779	325823	338559
B Less: Subsidies	30054	35394	35933	39203	46047	47381	45079	45109	47854	56436	61156	63511
2 Consumption of fixed capital	116098	149238	158193	167526	176195	183870	194114	205630	218486	235173	252575	270063
3 Compensation of employees paid by resident producers to:	545631	642438	676330	717091	761254	792734	821941	874476	940062	1020817	1088971	1135998
4 Operating surplus	200201	247855	262098	277080	297051	307011	340576	366490	402735	422981	439867	436732
Statistical discrepancy	.	.	.	.	.	.	.	.	.	.	.	.
Equals: Gross Domestic Product	994704	1201217	1276775	1348425	1422497	1481388	1566439	1672900	1801309	1928314	2046080	2117841

1.4 General Government Current Receipts and Disbursements

Million Austrian schillings

	1980	1983	1984	1985	1986	1987	1988	1989	1990	1991	1992	1993
						Receipts						
1 Operating surplus	...	...	...	...	...	...	...	...	...	...	...	...
2 Property and entrepreneurial income	18493	22400	23058	26153	25909	29436	30724	33339	38069	40787	45733	42772
3 Taxes, fees and contributions	418681	502925	549418	591184	617660	635784	665260	694568	752338	816876	890971	928701
A Indirect taxes	162828	197080	216087	225931	234044	245154	254887	271413	287880	305779	325823	338559
B Direct taxes	128390	156637	173768	193628	203767	203357	214461	214465	238931	267125	297765	304938
C Social security contributions	124578	145462	155463	167804	175993	183339	191817	204269	220619	238882	262307	279759
D Compulsory fees, fines and penalties	2885	3746	4100	3821	3856	3934	4095	4421	4908	5090	5076	5445
4 Other current transfers	24444	31737	33668	36190	38508	40491	42019	44422	47055	51104	54314	57482
Total Current Receipts of General Government	461618	557062	606144	653527	682077	705711	738003	772329	837462	908767	991018	1028955
						Disbursements						
1 Government final consumption expenditure	178697	226891	237759	254999	270655	280436	288356	302881	319888	349632	377059	405598
A Compensation of employees	119658	152695	160925	171732	182910	191440	195816	205391	218514	238794	257802	277476
B Consumption of fixed capital	7481	9596	10095	10690	11310	11561	11803	12218	12770	13502	13809	14468
C Purchases of goods and services, net	49617	62265	64269	69932	73568	74525	77823	81919	85032	93485	101327	108964
D Less: Own account fixed capital formation	...	...	...	...	...	...	...	...	...	...	...	...
E Indirect taxes paid, net	1941	2335	2470	2645	2867	2910	2914	3353	3572	3851	4121	4690
2 Property income	24739	36618	43069	47847	51880	58355	61792	66410	73118	82130	87928	93023
A Interest	24739	36618	43069	47847	51880	58355	61792	66410	73118	82130	87928	93023
B Net land rent and royalties	...	...	...	...	...	...	...	...	...	...	...	...

SAMPLE PAGE FROM *NATIONAL ACCOUNTS STATISTICS*

EXHIBIT 13.1

Source: United Nations National Accounts Statistics: Main Aggregates and Detailed Tables.

ume containing the account. Exhibit 13.1 displays a sample page from *National Accounts Statistics*.

National Accounts of OECD Countries (published annually by the OECD)

Similar to the UN's *National Accounts Statistics*, but much more limited in scope, are national accounts published by the EU and by the OECD. The OECD's *National Accounts* is published in two volumes. The first volume gives for each country the main GDP aggregates, calculated on the basis of the UN System of National Accounts. The OECD publication is unique in presenting constant dollar GDP figures calculated on the basis of both market exchange rates and purchasing power parity rates. The series go back to 1960 (exchange rate basis) and to 1970 (purchasing power parity basis).

The second volume gives detailed national accounts for each country in its national currency.

The information is updated in the publication *Quarterly National Accounts*.

National Accounts ESA (published annually by the EU)

EU national accounts publications have more detail than the publications of the UN or OECD. There are four annual publications:

- *National Accounts ESA—Aggregates*
- *National Accounts ESA—Detailed Tables by Branch*
- *National Accounts ESA—Detailed Tables by Sector*
- *General Government Accounts and Statistics*

The EU defines "sectors" as economic units such as households or businesses that have similar economic behavior. Statistics for the EU as a whole are given in ECUs. Individual nations' accounts are in their national currency. The data is available online through the EU's statistical databank CRONOS.

Table 13.A compares some of the main features of the national account statistics prepared by the UN, the EU, and the OECD.

COMPARATIVE ECONOMIC STATISTICS

Researchers are often interested in comparing the economic statistics of countries.

- Compare the growth of GDP in France with Germany.
- Compare the unemployment rate in Mexico with the U.S. unemployment rate.
- Compare the consumer price index of the U.K. with Japan's CPI.

In Chapter 8, we discussed the problems associated with the international ranking of companies and their products. These problems include foreign exchange conversions, the definition of products, and the frequency of data collection. A similar set of problems is involved in making economic comparisons among countries. The *Statistical Abstracts of the United States*, in its section on international statistics, gives a succinct statement of the pitfalls of using economic statistics for international comparisons.

> The bases, methods of estimating, methods of data collection, extent of coverage, precision of definition, scope of territory, and margins of error may vary for different items within a particular country and for like items for different countries.[3]

Economic data come from such a variety of sources that international comparisons should be undertaken with caution. Economic data are usually collected by individual countries. International agencies such as the UN often simply report the data they receive from national sources. An example of this reporting is seen in the *Bulletin of Labour Statistics'* summary of unemployment statistics. The figures vary by country in frequency, currency, and detail. Every country's entry is footnoted to show the variations in the definition of "unemployed."

TABLE 13.A

NATIONAL ACCOUNTS PUBLICATIONS OF INTERNATIONAL ORGANIZATIONS

	UN	EU	OECD
Publication Lag	3 Years	4 Years	2 Years
Currency Used	National & US Dollar	National & US Dollar	National & US Dollar
Update	NA	Quarterly	Quarterly
Countries Reported	184	12	24
Years Covered (Main Aggregates)	12	17	30
Years Covered (Detailed Tables)	NA	17	12

The states of the former Soviet bloc present the researcher with a special set of problems. The former Soviet Union and most of the other socialist countries of Eastern Europe were not members of several key international organizations including the International Monetary Fund, the OECD, and GATT. Consequently, the long annual time series of economic and financial variables we find in such sources as the *IMF Yearbook* do not include most of the countries of Eastern Europe. "Country pages" for Russia in the IMF's *International Financial Statistics* began only in April 1996, with retrospective coverage for most series beginning in 1993.

When statistics are available, they are often sketchy. For example, in the UN's *National Account Statistics*, Russian national accounts take up 3 pages, while the U.S. accounts occupy 60 pages. A further complication is that the Soviet Union and other centrally planned economies reported their national accounts as "Net Material Product" rather than as GNP or GDP. The NMP measure, among other things, excluded most services from national accounts.

With a few exceptions, such as the former Yugoslavia, the socialist countries of Eastern Europe regarded most economic data as state secrets. In the U.S., the CIA made estimates of basic economic production statistics for Eastern Europe—with low accuracy, as it turned out. Even basic economic statistics such as GNP were estimates. Published GNP per capita estimates for the USSR in 1989 ranged from $1,780 by the World Bank to $9,230 by the CIA.

Although much less secretive than in the past, Russia is still not forthcoming in its publication of data. The *Economist* notes that Russian statistical services do not publish tabular data, but instead issue monthly textual bulletins within which numbers pertaining to economic data are sprinkled. There seems to be little consistency or reason for the numbers chosen. Mayonnaise prices may be available every month, but statistics on foreign exchange are not.[4] However, all the countries that made up the USSR are now members of the International Monetary Fund, so we can expect to see increasing consistency in data collection and presentation from these nations.

Data on foreign direct investment in Central and Eastern Europe is available in Volume 2 of the *World Investment Directory,* covering Central and Eastern Europe. This source also supplies lists of the largest foreign affiliates in the host countries and the largest transnational corporations abroad, together with some information on sales and exports. The *World Investment Directory* is described in more detail in Chapter 15.

In 1992, the IMF began publishing reports on the individual states of the former Soviet Union. Two additional sources of information on the "economies in transition" are the monthly reports of *PlanEcon* and the quarterly *Russian Economic Trends*. Both are described below.

Currency Conversion

A central issue in the use of international data is how to compare statistics denominated in national currencies. We are often required to compare the wages, prices, or output of one country with another. Examples might be comparing the average wage in Japan to that in the U.S., ranking the countries of the world by their per-capita GDP, or comparing the price of gasoline in Japan with the price in the U.S. Making these kinds of comparisons depends fundamentally on comparing the values of currencies. For example, to compare the wages of Japanese and American workers, we must convert the wages to a common currency, such as dollars or yen. The market exchange rate frequently is used to make the conversion. Let's assume that the average hourly Japanese wage in 1992 was 1,535 yen per hour and that the average U.S. hourly wage was $10.34. Assume further that the wage rates were calculated for the same period and for the same group of occupations. We can use the exchange rate to find the average Japanese wage in terms of dollars. If the exchange rate was 133 yen per dollar, then Japanese workers made the equivalent of $11.54 per hour, $1.20 more than their U.S. counterparts.

However, market exchange rates often do not reflect accurately the purchasing power of a currency within a country. An alternative method of comparing currencies is with purchasing power parities (PPP). Purchasing power parities are the rates of currency conversion that equalize the purchasing power of different currencies. This means that a given sum of money, when converted into different currencies at the PPP rates, will buy the same basket of goods and services in all countries.

As an example of how purchasing power parities operate, look at the "Big Mac purchasing power parity," devised by the *Economist*.[5] The "Big Mac" exchange rate is the rate that makes the price of a Big Mac the same in all countries. Here, our basket of goods and services is reduced to one item, a McDonald's Big Mac hamburger. In April 1996, the average price of a Big Mac in 4 American cities was $2.36. In Japan, a Big Mac cost 288 yen ($2.70 at the market exchange rate of 107 yen per dollar). If we divide the yen price of a Big Mac by the dollar price, we get an exchange rate of $1 = 122 yen. If the actual (market) dollar foreign exchange rate was $1 =107 yen, then the dollar was undervalued by 14% against the yen.

Obviously, purchasing power parities that are used for currency conversion require the analysis of more than the price of Big Macs. The OECD calculates purchasing power parities for 24 member countries. In 1990, this involved collecting data on 2,150 consumer goods and services; 30 government, education, and health services; 350 types of equipment goods; and 23 construction projects.[6]

When we rank countries on such economic measures as GDP, investment, or wages, the results will depend on whether we use purchasing power parities or exchange rates to convert currencies. When purchasing power parities first began to be used extensively by international organizations to calculate national output, there were many published examples showing the difference in rankings of country GDP obtained by using PPP and exchange rates.

For example, Tables 13.B and 13.C show the difference in country rankings of GDP per capita as a result of using exchange rates or purchasing power parity rates. Table 13.B shows the ranking of countries by their per capita GDP or GNP in 1989 U.S. dollars (exchange rate basis).[7]

TABLE 13.B

COUNTRIES RANKED BY PER CAPITA GDP/GNP (EXCHANGE RATE BASIS)

Rank		per Capita GDP/GNP U.S. dollars, 1989
1	Switzerland	$30,050
2	Luxembourg	$26,220
3	Japan	$24,240
4	Finland	$22,120
5	Sweden	$21,580
6	Iceland	$20,940
7	Norway	$20,940
8	United States	$20,850
9	Denmark	$20,740
10	West Germany	$20,450

Source: "How the Nations Rank," *Fortune* (July 27, 1992).

Table 13.C shows GDP per capita adjusted for purchasing power U.S. dollars in 1989. The differences in the lists are striking. All the rankings have changed and only 4 of the 10 nations in Table 13.B are in Table 13.C.

TABLE 13.C

COUNTRIES RANKED BY PER CAPITA GDP/GNP (PPP BASIS)

Rank		per capita GDP/GNP adjusted for purchasing power U.S. dollars, 1989
1	United Arab Emirates	$23,798
2	United States	$20,998
3	Canada	$18,635
4	Switzerland	$18,590
5	Norway	$16,838
6	Luxembourg	$16,537
7	Kuwait	$15,984
8	Australia	$15,266
9	Hong Kong	$15,180
10	Singapore	$15,108

Source: "How the Nations Rank," *Fortune* (July 27, 1992).

The International Monetary Fund began publishing GDP calculated with purchasing power parities in the 1993 edition of *World Economic Outlook*. The OECD adopted the PPP method of measuring GDP in the December 1993 *OECD Economic Outlook*. However, the World Bank and the United Nations have not yet adopted the new method.

The different methodologies used by international organizations have resulted in multiple figures being published for a country's GDP. The disparity is most pronounced for China. In 1994, published figures for China's per capita GDP ranged from $425 to more than $3,500.[8] The lower figure would make China's economy the ninth-largest in the world. If the larger figure is accepted, China would have a GDP equal to Japan's and second only to the United States. The CIA's 1995 *World Factbook* gave China's GDP as $2.9788 trillion for 1994, but note that this figure may overstate China's GDP by as much as 25%.

Robert Summers and Alan Heston are the experts most closely associated with developing purchasing power parity methodology. See their article, "The Penn World Table (Mark-5): An Expanded Set of International Comparisons, 1950–1988," *Quarterly Journal of Economics* 106, no. 2 (1991): 327–68. Subsets of the Penn World data (Summers-Heston data) can be retrieved from WWW site http://nber.org.

SOURCES FOR ECONOMIC STATISTICS

There are thousands of economic data series. Table 13.D lists a few of the series that are generally available for many countries. The series are available as pure number databases in electronic format; as printed statistical publications, often accompanied by graphs; and as part of textual reports on a broad range of topics. Economic statistics are published in confusing abundance by national governments, international organizations, and commercial publishers. The most authoritative sources of statistics are usually the official national statistical reports of a country. The practical problems of language barriers, multiplicity of sources, and the need to compare series from several countries over time make using primary sources difficult. Fortunately, various agencies of the UN, the EU, and the OECD collect and make available thousands of economic data series in scores of serial publications, as well as through electronic media. Basic data on national accounts, labor statistics, trade, and finance can be found in the publications of all three groups. The series frequently overlap among the organizations, and even within one organization. A statistical series gathered by one agency may appear in several publications. For example, expenditure on the gross domestic product in purchasers' values at current prices is furnished by the United Nations Statistical Office and is published in the Statistical Office's *Yearbook of National Accounts Statistics*, the *Statistical Yearbook,* and the *Monthly Bulletin of Statistics*. In addition, these data appear in the publications of other agencies such as the IMF's *International Financial Statistics*.

```
┌─────────────────────────────────────────┐
│  TABLE 13.D                             │
├─────────────────────────────────────────┤
│  ECONOMIC TIME SERIES                    │
│                                          │
│    Business Failures                     │
│    Capacity Utilization                  │
│    Capital Appropriations                │
│    Consumer Confidence                   │
│    Consumer Credit                       │
│    Consumer Price Index                  │
│    Distribution of Income                │
│    Employment/Unemployment               │
│    Flow of Funds                         │
│    Government Budget and Debt            │
│    Gross Domestic Product                │
│    Housing Starts                        │
│    Import/Export Price Index             │
│    Industrial Production Index           │
│    Interest Rates                        │
│    International Investment Position      │
│    Manufacturer's Orders                 │
│    Money Supply                          │
│    Personal Income and Savings           │
│    Plant & Equipment Expenditures        │
│    Producer Price Index                  │
│    Productivity                          │
│    Unit Labor Cost                       │
└─────────────────────────────────────────┘
```

The data are often expressed in different units by the various agencies. A series may be presented as an index number by the UN, in dollars by the OECD, and in ECUs by the EU. When series are expressed as index numbers, the base years used by the agencies are often different. The *Index to International Statistics (IIS)*, described in Chapter 1, is a general index to the statistical publications of international organizations.

To make our discussion of economic statistics sources more coherent, we have divided the sources into several categories.

- Current and forecast time series
- World, regional, and national summaries
- Special subject
- Computer-readable data

Because of their importance, we pay particular attention to the topics of national accounts, price indices and labor statistics.

Current Statistics

Economic statistics usually appear at less frequent intervals than do financial statistics. A nation's GDP figures, for example, usually are published quarterly. The foreign exchange value of a nation's currency, however, changes continuously. Despite the slower pace at which economic statistics appear, we want to be able to secure the most recent data that is available.

Three useful monthly publications for general economic data are the UN's *Monthly Bulletin of Statistics*; the OECD's *Main Economic Indicators*, and the EU's *Eurostatistics*. These publications all give country breakdowns for the current year in months or in quarters. They typically provide annual statistics for the past four or five years. In general, the greater the country coverage (as in the publications of the UN), the less detailed the data. Table 13.E shows the principal economic series they present. In the table, "currency" refers to the currency of individual countries. Table 13.E is designed to show the variety of data presentations, as well as gaps in coverage among these publications. *Eurostatistics* gives data for the U.S. and Japan, in addition to the EU member countries.

Because they depend on statistics-gathering by individual countries, the data in these publications vary greatly in timeliness. The *Monthly Bulletin of Statistics* has the greatest variability, with some series being two or more years out of date. Consumer price indexes for many countries, in contrast, are current within one month.

Forecasts

Economic forecasts are used by governments and industry to estimate the effect of policy changes and to project capital and labor requirements. The forecasts may be based on mathematical models of an

TABLE 13.E

MONTHLY ECONOMIC PUBLICATIONS OF THE UN, OECD, AND EU

	UN Monthly Bulletin	OECD Main Economic Indicators	EU Eurostatistics
Agricultural Products	Index		ECUs
Balance of Payments		Currency	
Business Failures			Index
Business Surveys		Percent	Percent
Consumer Price Index	Index	Index	Index
Employment	Number	Index	Index
Exchange Rates		Dollars	ECUs & Dollars
Exports	Currency	Dollars	ECUs
GDP		Index	Index
GDP Deflator		Index	
Hourly Earnings			Index
Hours Worked	Number		
Housing Starts		Number	
Imports		Dollars	
Industrial Production	Index	Index	Volume
Interest Rates	Percent	Percent	Percent
International Reserves	Dollars		
Leading Indicators		Index	
Money Supply	Currency	Index	Currency
National Accounts		Currency	Index
Passenger Cars Produced		Number	Index
Producer Prices	Index	Index	Index
Retail Sales		Index	
Share Prices	Index	Index	Index
Trade Balance	Dollars	Dollars	
Unemployment		Percent	Percent

economy. The most detailed econometric models are available on time-sharing systems such as WEFA and DRI. In Table 13.E, we give brief summaries of print sources of international economic forecasts.

International Economic Outlook (published twice a year by Basil Blackwell)

The forecasts contained in the journal *International Economic Outlook* are based on the global model maintained by the London Business School and the U.K's National Institute of Economic and Social Research. Eight-year forecasts are given for output and demand of the industrialized countries. A narrative description of the outlook for the world's economy is a useful feature in each issue.

World Economic Outlook (published annually by the International Monetary Fund)

World Economic Outlook gives an overview of the performance and prospects for the global economy. It includes approximately 50 tables of 10-year time series of economic variables with short-range (one-year) projections. Medium-range (two- to four-year) projections are given for a few measures such as GDP.

The tables are divided into industrial countries and developing countries. Country detail is available only for the G-7 industrial nations. *World Economic Outlook* includes a series of "annexes" that contain brief discussions of specialized economic topics. The 1996 report, for example, contains an article on the effects of debt reduction in all industrial countries.

OECD Economic Outlook (published twice a year by the Organization for Economic Cooperation and Development)

This publication gives analyses of the latest economic trends and approximately 50 tables of short-term (one-year) projections for OECD countries. The projections include components of GDP, public debt, balance of payments, employee compensation, and unit labor costs. Additional tables of "reference statistics" give 20-year time series for national accounts, prices, unemployment, balance of payments, and exchange rates.

Economic and Financial Outlook (published monthly by the National Westminster Bank)

This newsletter published in the U.K. gives up to four-year projections for several key economic and financial variables including GDP, consumer prices, balance of payments, interest rates, stock exchange indices, commodity prices, exchange rates, and bond yields. The number of countries for which projections are made varies; typically they include OECD members. A difficult-to-find piece of information also provided by this publication is purchasing power parity estimates for major currencies. The purchasing power parity estimates are compared against exchange rates, and currencies are shown as under- or overvalued against the U.S. dollar, the German mark, the Japanese yen, and the British pound.

Global Forecasting Service. (published quarterly by the Economist Intelligence Unit)

The service gives five-year forecasts for 55 countries. Forecasts include GDP and its components, population, consumer prices, exchange rate, external trade, and foreign indebtedness.

The Book of European Forecasts (Euromonitor, 1996)

This is a 400-page compendium of forecasts on every facet of European life. It includes an extensive array of forecasts for macroeconomics, labor force, industrial development, trade, and energy. Most of the forecasts are to the year 2000. The sources are a combination of published data and Euromonitor's own estimates. Many of the sources are described in a final section of the book. The book's main subject divisions are listed below.

OVERVIEW
Macroeconomic Prospects
The Demographic Revolution
Employment and Labour Issues
Policy Trends
Environmental Issues
Industry Profiles

SOCIO-ECONOMIC
Population
Economic Growth
Government Budgets
Employment
Industrial Growth
Foreign Trade
Exchange Rates
Interest Rates
Inflation

INDUSTRY SECTORS AND SERVICES
Automotives
Car Rental
Catering
Chemicals
Construction

MARKETING PARAMETERS
Households
Housing
Retailing and Retail
 Structure
Advertising and Media
 Access
Consumer Expenditure

SPECIAL TOPICS
Environment
The European Union
Health
Transport

Consumer Electronics
Multimedia
Energy
Farming
Personal Finance
Pharmaceuticals, Cosmetics and Toiletries
Steel
Telecommunications
Cable
Satellite
Textiles
Tourism
Transport

SPECIAL TOPICS
Environment
The European Union
Health
Transport

Country Data Forecasts (published twice a year by Bank of America)

Twenty-three key economic variables are presented for 80 countries. Six years of historical statistics, the current year, and five years of forecasts are also included. Variables include income per capita, growth and size of the economy, inflation rates, trade performance, indebtedness, and exchange rates.

Consensus Forecasts (published monthly by Consensus Economics, Inc.)

Consensus Forecasts surveys 200 financial and economic forecasters each month for their estimates of key variables. The forecasters constitute the world's major investment banking and economic research centers. The projections are for the next six quarters. Individual country forecasts are given for 35 countries (industrialized countries plus several newly industrialized countries). Detailed forecasts are given for the U.S., Japan, Germany, France, the U.K., Italy, Canada, and Australia. The detailed forecasts include the specific forecasts of individual institutions. For all countries, forecasts are made for GDP, consumer prices, current account, and exchange rates. In addition, detailed forecasts include projections of private consumption, business investments, industrial production, unemployment, and both short-term (three-month) and long-term (10-year) interest rates. The bimonthly *Latin American Consensus Forecasts* surveys some 60 prominent Latin American economic and financial forecasters for their estimates for the countries of Central and South America.

World and Regional Summaries

The world and regional summaries of economic data produced by the UN and other international bodies are useful for their consistent presentation of long time series. However, the data they provide are limited in detail and frequently dated.

World Tables (published annually by the World Bank)

World Tables gives 20-year economic time series data for more than 130 countries. The series are presented both by subject and by country. The data are derived mostly from national account statistics. The topical pages are updated semiannually. In the basic volume, the latest year of data is usually two years behind the date of publication. The information in the semiannual update is one year behind the publication date.

World Bank STARS (published annually by the World Bank)

STARS stands for Socio-Economic Time-Series Access and Retrieval System. This CD-ROM combines information from several World Bank publications including *World Tables* and *World Debt Tables*. It presents 730 economic annual time series from as early as 1960. The 1995 edition had data through 1993. The disk lists 200 countries, although data for many of them are very sparse. The software is easy to use and allows the construction of customized three-way tables (country by series by year, or series by country by year) that can be downloaded as a spreadsheet.

Statistical Yearbook (published annually by the United Nations)

The UN's *Statistical Yearbook* presents country data and world and regional aggregates on a broad range of economic, demographic, and social topics. It includes 10-year time series on national accounts, balance of payments, international trade, industrial production, agriculture, and energy. Most of the world aggregates are expressed as index numbers. The latest information is about three years behind the date of publication. For example, the 40th issue of the *Yearbook* appeared in late 1995 with statistical series covering, in general, 1983–92 or 1984–93.

World Bank Atlas (published annually by the World Bank)

This is a compact reference to basic economic and social statistics on 185 countries. Statistics included are GNP, GNP per capita, growth rates of GNP, population, fertility rates, illiteracy, life expectancy, and daily calorie supply. Each country is ranked on the variables. The information is also presented in color-coded maps. The data are about one year behind the publication date.

Basic Statistics of the European Union (published annually by Eurostat)

Eurostat's *Basic Statistics* contains 300 tables of annual data on all aspects of the EU's economy. Included are data on national accounts, balance of payments, labor statistics, energy, agriculture, foreign trade, environment, and demographics. Some of the tables include information on the U.S., Canada, Japan, and selected non-EU European countries. The 1995 edition had data as current as 1993.

Eurostat Yearbook (published annually by Eurostat)

The 1995 *Yearbook*, subtitled "A Statistical Eye on Europe, 1983–1993," compares significant features of each country of the EU, U.S., Canada, and Japan. It presents 10-year time series in tables and graphs of a wide range of economic, financial, social, and demographic data. Most of the 650 tables and 200 graphs are for the period 1983 to 1993. They cover the countries of the EU prior to its enlargement in January 1995. The *Eurostat Yearbook* is available on CD-ROM, but the publication is preferable in print. The CD has poor software; it does not allow tables to be downloaded to a spreadsheet and has a primitive search engine.

Country Statistics

Publications of central banks and country statistical abstracts are excellent sources of data, if you can read the language in which they are written. Clearly, the publications of the U.K. Central Statistical Office will not be a problem, though the publications of the Statistisches Bundesamt may be. Some countries publish their statistics with English overlays. Three examples of statistical sources that attempt to bridge the language gap are given below.

Economic Statistics Monthly (published monthly by the Bank of Japan)

Despite its name, this publication contains mostly financial data. All the material in this publication, including the introduction, table of contents, and all the statistical tables plus their notes, are in both Japanese and English.

Census of Commerce (published triennially in Japan, by the Ministry of Internal Trade and Industry)

Japan's *Census of Commerce* has been conducted every three years since 1976. From 1952 to 1976, it was conducted every two years. It reports on all Japanese wholesale and retail establishments with the exception of eating and drinking places. Eating and drinking establishments are covered in a separate volume released in 1990. The *Census of Commerce* has many points in common with the U.S. *Census of Wholesalers* or U.S. *Census of Retailers*. It reports the number of establishments, number of employees, and total annual sales. It gives breakdowns by Japanese industrial classification and geographically (cities, towns, and villages). General table headings are given both in Japanese and in English. Detailed headings are in Japanese only, but English language templates are provided in the introduction.

Statistisches Jahrbuch (published annually by the Federal Statistical Office, Federal Republic of Germany)

The *Statistisches Jahrbuch*—the Statistical Yearbook for the Federal Republic of Germany—is a compendium of economic and social statistics. To help those who do not read German, it is accompanied by a booklet that translates the table headings (*Where to Find What: Statistical Yearbook for the Federal Republic of Germany*). Although this booklet will lead you to the appropriate table, translating the subheadings and table breakdowns will still be a problem.

Central Banks Annual Reports in the Joint World Bank–International Monetary Fund Library: A Resource Guide (http://jolis.worldbankimflib.org/JL/annualre.htm)

This WWW site gives a list of annual reports of central banks, monetary authorities, and related institutions from some 190 countries. It was design to provide staffs of the International Monetary Fund and the World Bank with a tool to simplify access to the Joint Bank–Fund Library's collection of reports. The *Guide* is arranged alphabetically by country. Under each country's name is the name of the central bank, the title of its annual report, and the call number of the report. If the bank has a site on the World Wide Web, its address (URL) is listed and an active link is provided. About one-third of the countries have Web sites. The *Guide* links to Central Banks Online at the Center for the Study of Central Banks, NYU School of Law (http://www.law.nyu.edu/centralbanks). The Center publishes the *Central Bank Bulletin*.

Country Reports

Compendiums of statistical data are the raw material of analysis. Often we want data that has been shaped by analysis. Economic analysis of countries is abundantly available in books and journals. The material in books tends to be two or more years out of date. Journal articles are more timely but often have a narrow focus. The country analyses in both books and journals will be scattered. The country report series we describe below overcome these problems. They are timely, provide an overview of the economies, and analyze all countries in a consistent fashion.

Country Profiles and Country Reports (published annually with quarterly updates by the Economist Intelligence Unit)

An excellent example of timely economic analysis from a commercial source, the *Country Profiles* series organizes data from national and international sources into a standard 40-page format. The series contains 92 reports covering 165 countries. They include basic macroeconomic, political, and demographic data, as well as details of national accounts, wages, prices, employment, industrial production, and foreign trade. They are updated by quarterly *Country Reports* that presents the most recent economic data available and provide short-term forecasts. The Economist Intelligence Unit also publishes *World Outlook*, an annual compendium of forecasts of political and economic trends in over 180 countries. The full text of all the publications in the series are available from LEXIS-NEXIS Services, DIALOG, and DataStar. They are also published on CD-ROM.

Walden Country Reports (published twice a year by Walden Publishers)

Walden Country Reports were formerly distributed by Reuters as part of its country reports service. The series contains 60-page reports on 100 countries. The reports give less emphasis to macroeconomic data than do the EIU *Country Profiles*. They are a much better source of information on a country's major industries and companies, its labor profile, and its banking and finance. They also include extensive information on demographics, customs, and culture. The *Walden Country Reports* are available on LEXIS-NEXIS Services.

IMF Occasional Papers (published by IMF, Washington; frequency varies)

Many of the *IMF Occasional Papers* are studies of individual countries. Examples of recent titles include *India: Economic Reform and Growth*; *United Germany: The First Five Years*; and *Singapore: A Case Study in Rapid Development*.

OECD Economic Surveys (published biannually by OECD)

The OECD publishes separate economic surveys of each of its member countries on a two-year cycle. It has been publishing, in addition, surveys of some East European countries including Hungary, Poland, and the former Czechoslovakia. The *Surveys* review the most important economic developments for the past few years and give short-term projections. They include extensive statistical appendixes.

Key Economic Indicators (published weekly by OECD)

Each issue contains one page of statistical information for each of the 26 OECD countries. In general, the coverage parallels the OECD's *Main Economic Indicators*. Also known as the *OECD Hot File*, the publication is made available exclusively through the WWW as a subscription service.

Regional Reports

EIU Regional Newsletters (published by the Economist Intelligence Unit; publication interval varies)

EIU Regional Newsletters are a series of reports designed to provide practical and current business information. They are 12-page reports that highlight business economic trends, short-term country forecasts, regulatory and policy changes, and specific company and industry developments. Table 13.F lists the specific regional newsletters published and their approximate price. The full text of all the publications in the series are available on the LEXIS and NEXIS Services, DIALOG, and DataStar. They are also published on CD-ROM.

TABLE 13.F

EIU REGIONAL NEWSLETTER

TITLE	ISSUES PER YEAR	APPROX. PRICE 1996
Business Africa	24	$ 845
Business Asia	26	$ 695
Business Russia	12	$ 675
Business Eastern Europe	51	$ 1,175
Business Europe	50	$ 1,150
Business Latin America	50	$ 975
Business China	26	$ 695
Business International	50	$ 675
Business Middle East	24	$ 845
Business South Asia	12	$ 450

Social Indicators

Measures such as GDP are good indicators of a nation's economic strength but may be misleading when used to estimate a nation's quality of life. Social measures, such as literacy, healthcare availability, and political freedom are often combined with economic measures to analyze a country's welfare. We describe two compendiums of social indicators below.

Human Development Report (published annually by the UN Development Programme, New York Oxford University Press)

The United Nations Development Programme has developed a Human Development Index (HDI) that attempts to measure a nation's social as well as economic strength. The HDI combines per capita GDP with measures of educational attainment and life expectancy. The annual *Human Development Report* includes a table ranking 160 countries on human development. In addition to the Index, the *Report* contains more than 40 tables of national data on education, poverty, and health, with area and world aggregates.

Social Indicators of Development (published annually by the World Bank)

Social Indicators provides data for assessing human welfare in more than 170 countries, including both members and non-members of the World Bank. Up to 94 indicators are reported for each country, depending on the availability of information. Country data are presented in two-page tables that describe income, poverty levels, human capital investment (such as medical care and education), natural resources, labor force statistics, and vital statistics. The volume is particularly useful for its long (25-year) time series.

Developing Economies

Economically, most of the nations of the world fall into the category of "developing countries." Statistical compendiums on developing economies emphasize such measures as GDP growth and the amount of external debt. We describe two important publications below.

World Development Report (published annually by the World Bank)

World Development Report provides economic, social, and natural resource indicators for 185 economies and various analytical and geographical groups of economies. Each *Report* has a distinctive title, e.g., *From Plan to Market in 1996*. The reports are useful for their estimates of world totals of series such as GDP, average annual growth rate of GDP, purchasing power parity estimates of GDP per capita, and per capita energy consumption.

World Debt Tables: External Debt of Developing Countries (published annually by the World Bank)

The *World Debt Tables* are a two-volume annual on external public and private debt and debt flows of 107 developing countries, including totals by region and economic groups. It includes data on debt outstanding, debt service projections, loan disbursements, payments, amortization, and interest, expressed in U.S. dollars.

MEASURES OF PRICE LEVELS

In the U.S., the Consumer Price Index, the Producer Price Index, and the GDP deflator are standard measures of inflation. Similar price indexes are used worldwide to measure changes in the purchasing power of money. Measures of inflation have several purposes. They are used to gauge the success of economic policy, to adjust wages and pensions for changes in prices, and as a deflator in the calculation of national accounts. Price indexes are also used to compare inflation among countries. Comparing inflation rates across borders raises familiar problems of differences in definitions and data collection methods.

For example, a consumer price index requires data to be collected on a fixed market basket of goods and services. The specific items to be priced are determined by a survey of consumer buying patterns. There is great variation among countries in the population included and in the number of items covered in household income and expenditure surveys.[9]

Once a consumer price index has been constructed, there are again major differences among countries in survey methods. Table 13.G gives the name of the consumer price index for EU countries. The number of items priced in the survey is given in parentheses. As some of the titles indicate, the population surveyed is often different in the various countries. France, for example, surveys urban households, while the Netherlands surveys the entire population. There are many differences among the indices, including sampling procedure, frequency of survey, and index construction. The EU is attempting to harmonize its consumer price index, but this procedure has yet to be completed.

TABLE 13.G

CONSUMER PRICE INDEXES IN THE EC

Belgium	Consumer Price Index (401)
Denmark	Consumer Price Index (523)
France	Consumer Price Index for Urban Households (296)
Germany	Cost of Living Index for all Private Households (755)
Greece	Consumer Price Index (386)
Ireland	Consumer Price Index (722)
Italy	National Consumer Price Index (878)
Luxembourg	Consumer Price Index (255)
Netherlands	Consumer Price Index for the Whole Population (690)
Portugal	Consumer Price Index (500)
Spain	Consumer Price Index (428)
U.K.	General Index of Retail Prices (394)

Source: Consumer Price Indices in the European Community 1989: 48.

Sources for Price Level Data

Consumer price indices (CPIs) for most countries of the world are available in the UN's *Monthly Bulletin of Statistics*. The indices have a common base year. The gap between the date of the reported figures and its publications varies, with a three-month lag typical. The UN reports both a general CPI (all items) and a CPI for food. More detailed consumer price indices are reported by the OECD and the EU. The EU's monthly *Eurostatistics* gives CPI broken down by eight categories of consumption.

Note that in comparing the consumer price indexes of two or more countries, we are comparing the rate of inflation for the countries, not the relative costs of living in the countries. For example, in July 1992, the consumer price index for Japan was 128.2 and for the U.S. 170.5 (1980=100). The figures tell us that the cost of goods and services increased 28.2% in Japan between 1980 and 1992 and increased 70.5% in the U.S. during the same period. However, they do not tell us anything about the costs of living in Japan compared with the U.S.

U.S. Department of State Indexes of Living Costs Abroad, Quarters Allowances, and Hardship Differentials (published quarterly by the U.S. Dept. of State)

For U.S. citizens, this is the standard source for comparing living costs among countries. It is used to establish allowances to compensate U.S. government civilian employees for costs and hardships related to assignments abroad. The information is also used by many business firms and other private organizations to assist in establishing private compensation systems. The indexes are computed at the currency exchange rate in effect as of the date of the survey. The index for Washington, D.C., is set at 100. For example, the July 1992 *Indexes* show that the local index for Tokyo was 192. This tells us that it cost about 92% more for an American family to live in Tokyo than in Washington, D.C. The indexes can be adjusted to reflect changes in the exchange rate.

The publication warns that the indexes cannot be used for measuring cost changes over time at a foreign location. In addition, the indexes should not be used to compare living costs of Americans in the U.S. with the living costs of foreign nationals living in their own country, since the indexes reflect only the expenditure pattern and living costs of American families. The *Indexes* are also available through the U.S. State Department's Web site (http://www.state.gov/) under "U.S. Foreign Per Diem Rates."

Retail Price Indexes Relating to Living Expenditures of United Nations Officials (published quarterly by the UN)

Appearing four times a year in the *Monthly Bulletin of Statistics*, the publication uses New York City as the base (100), and gives two sets of figures, a total index and an index that excludes housing. The information is keyed to specific cities in more than 160 countries. These indexes relate to United Nations officials, whose consumption patterns may differ from the general population of their countries.

The UN also publishes a monthly Schedule of Daily Subsistence Allowance Rates. It gives, in dollars and in local currency, the daily amounts required by UN officials in some 800 cities around the world. Before March 1995, the Schedule was published quarterly in the *Monthly Bulletin of Statistics*.

Prices and Earnings Around the Globe (published triennially by the Union Bank of Switzerland)

Executive Living Costs Worldwide (published twice a year by Business International)

These two commercial publications compare living costs across borders. *Prices and Earnings Around the Globe* compares price levels, wages, working hours, are purchasing power in more than 50 cities. It also gives dollar prices for purchases of a variety of items including clothing, appliances, and food. *Executive Living Costs Worldwide* gives an index of living costs for 102 cites, as well as pricing information for goods, services, transportation, and housing.

Sources for Producer Price Data

Producer price or wholesale price indexes are less available than are consumer price indexes. Annual producer price indexes (wholesale price index) for most countries of the world are included in the *UN Statistical Yearbook*. Unfortunately, they will be at least three years out of date. The details of the indices will vary by country. For example, France reports one index only (for agricultural products). Japan reports 12 producer price indices, including indices for raw material, intermediate products, finished goods, and capital goods. Except for the price of exported goods, producer price information is not updated in the UN's *Monthly Bulletin of Statistics*. Wholesale price indices are reported for some countries in the IMF's *International Financial Statistics*. This publication also includes monthly commodity prices for about 50 products. Monthly producer price indices are reported for most OECD member countries in *Main Economic Indicators*. More detailed producer price indices are reported in the OECD quarterly *Indicators of Industrial Activity*. The EU reports producer prices in the monthly *Industrial Trends*.

LABOR STATISTICS

The size and quality of a country's labor force is crucial to its economy. Labor force statistics are used to gauge an economy's efficiency and to measure a country's standard of living. Some of the important labor statistics series are described below:

- Economically active population (all persons who furnish the supply of labor for the production of goods and services)
- Employment (all persons above a specified age who were, for a certain period, either self-employed or a paid employee)
- Unemployment (all persons above a specified age who, during a particular period, were without work and currently available for work and seeking work)
- Hours of work (hours actually worked)
- Earnings (wages, salaries, bonuses, and gratuities)
- Labor cost (cost incurred by the employer in the employment of labor)
- Occupational injuries (deaths, personal injuries, and disease resulting from work accidents)
- Strikes and lock-outs (temporary work stoppages by workers or employers attempting to enforce or resist a demand, or to express grievances)

In addition, we often require breakdowns by sex, age, industry, or occupation for many of these variables. For example, we may be interested in employment categorized by sex or unemployment broken down by age group.

There is great variation among countries in the timeliness, availability, and detail of labor statistics. Some of the gaps in reporting may seem surprising. The general definitions of labor terms have been framed by the International Labour Organization and are in wide use. However, the details of these definitions vary among countries. For example, the age that people are included in the "economically active population" vary from 6 years and older in countries such as Egypt and Peru to 15 or 16 years and older in many industrialized countries. The ILO's *World Labour Report* for 1995 has a chapter that discusses the problems in collecting and reporting international labor statistics.

Methods and frequency of data collection vary as well. Collecting data on unemployment according to the ILO definition requires labor force surveys. Many countries do not conduct labor force surveys but calculate unemployment (if at all) based on registrations at an employment office. The registration method invariably undercounts the unemployed. Among OECD countries, for example, monthly labor force surveys are carried out in Canada, the U.S., Japan, Australia, Finland, and Sweden. Quarterly surveys are carried out in New Zealand, Italy, Norway, Portugal, and Spain. Annual surveys are used in the U.K., Ireland, Switzerland, France, Germany, and Austria. The OECD estimates quarterly unemployment figures for the countries that use annual surveys.

As in the case of national accounts reporting, the UN (through the International Labour Organization), the OECD, and the EU all publish extensive data on labor. The International Labour Organization's *Year Book of Labour Statistics* and its update *Bulletin of Labour Statistics* have the broadest coverage and are described below in some detail. The OECD's annual *Labour Force Statistics* and its update *Quarterly Labour Force Statistics* give more detailed statistics for its members.

Year Book of Labour Statistics (published annually by the ILO)

Published by the ILO since 1936, the *Year Book* presents labor statistics for more than 180 countries and territories for the preceding 10 years. The subjects covered include employment, unemployment, wages, hours of work, industrial disputes, and price indices. Data by industry are grouped by major divisions of International Standard Industrial Classification (ISIC) code. Data for occupations are arranged by the major groups of the International Standard Classification of Occupations.

Bulletin of Labour Statistics (published quarterly by the ILO)

Issued in March, June, September, and December of each year, the *Bulletin* gives recent time series on employment, unemployment, hours of work, wages, and the consumer price index. Information is given for the most current year and three previous years. The *Bulletin* is updated four times a year by a *Supplement*. The information in each *Supplement* is then incorporated in the following issue of the *Bulletin*. The data in the *Supplement* often is surprisingly current. For example, the third quarter supplement for 1992 (published in October 1992) had consumer prices for countries such as Chile, Sri Lanka, and Thailand through August 1992. Compared with many statistical publications of the UN, this is almost "real time" availability.

Each October, a separate issue of the *Bulletin* is published called the "October Inquiry Results." It contains the results of an annual worldwide (150-country) survey of wages, hours of work, and retail prices. In the survey published in 1991 with data for 1989 and 1990, the wages and hours reports included details from 159 occupations in 49 industries. The retail prices reports covered 93 food items. For some countries, the prices are given for individual cities. We can find details such as the price of a kilogram of oranges in Bangkok (17.6 baht in October 1990). Prices and wages are reported in national currencies.

Foreign Labor Trends (published annually by the U.S. Department of Labor)

Foreign Labor Trends is prepared by the embassies in 80 countries. It provides key labor statistics (including employment, prices, and wages), as well as description of the labor market and union organization. This source is useful for addresses of foreign unions, labor market organizations, and government offices.

Monthly Labor Review (published monthly by the U.S. Bureau of Labor Statistics)

Although the *Monthly Labor Review* is primarily a source for U.S. labor, it does include foreign labor statistics as part of its coverage. Annual data with 10 years of historical data are provided for G-7 countries plus Australia, Sweden, and the Netherlands. The series are:

- Civilian labor force (number)
- Employment participation rate (percent)
- Employment (number)
- Participation rates (percent)
- Unemployment (percent)

Annual indexes of manufacturing productivity and related measures are given for G-7 countries plus Belgium, Denmark, the Netherlands, Norway, and Sweden. The series are:

- Compensation per hour (index)
- Output per hour (index)
- Total hours (index)
- Unit labor cost (index)

FINANCIAL DATA

Financial and economic data overlap to some extent. Economic measures such as consumer prices and national income frequently are included with financial data. Financial measures such as money supply and interest rates often are included with economic data. However, the economic researcher often has a different focus than the financial researcher. The economist is usually interested in longer-range trends and in data that are available with, at most, monthly frequency. The financial researcher is often concerned with daily or intra-day changes in data.

International Financial Statistics (published monthly by the International Monetary Fund)

Published since January 1948, this is the principal statistical publication of the IMF. It contains country tables for each of the approximately 150 members of the IMF. It includes data on a country's exchange rates, international liquidity, money and banking, interest rates, production, prices, international banking, and trade. In addition, it includes data on both GNP and GDP. It also presents world and area tables listing major data series broken down by country. The series include exchange rates, interest rates, consumer prices, imports, exports, and industrial production. The most recent data is two months behind the publication date. For most series, monthly data is given for the current year, quarterly data is included for the previous six quarters, and annual data is presented for the previous seven years. The *International Financial Statistics Yearbook* presents the same data as 30-year annual time series.

Although its emphasis is on financial data, *International Financial Statistics* is a convenient source of current information on several standard economic series, including consumer prices, discount rates, and both GNP and GDP. The data series in the publication are available on CD-ROM and through commercial time sharing systems such as Datastream. Exhibit 13.2 displays a sample page from *International Financial Statistics*.

Government Finance Statistics Yearbook (published annually by the International Monetary Fund)

The *Yearbook* gives data on the income and expenditures of central governments. It has three parts. "World Tables" lists IMF member countries and shows in detail the components of income and expenditures as percentages of GDP and of total expenditure. The data are for the most current available year. "Statistical Tables for Individual Countries" presents additional details as a 10-year time series for each country. Expenditures are given in the national currency. "Institutional Tables for Individual Countries" describes the units of government, lists government accounts and funds, and supplies a list of reports that form the source of the data.

Money and Finance (published quarterly by Eurostat)

Money and Finance summarizes the various financial statistics covering the countries in the EU, the U.S., and Japan. The first part presents a 10-year time series set of indicators, such as money supply and interest rates, designed to show basic trends. Part two deals mainly with current information on the working of the European monetary system and the private use of the ECU as an instrument of investment. The third part groups financial indicators that are used in current economic analysis.

Risk Assessment

Estimating the risk associated with lending or investing in a foreign country is essential for doing business abroad. Country risk assessment is a combination of economic and political analysis. The economic analysis includes examining a country's economic performance, its access to bank lending and capital markets, and its past repayment of debt. Political analysis requires an estimation of a country's future stability and its openness to foreign investment.

Euromoney (published by Euromoney PLC)

The March and September issues of *Euromoney* give country risk rankings for about 175 countries based on nine political and economic factors. The same issues includes "Global Economic Projections," a table that estimates real GNP growth for the coming year for 165 countries.

Finland

172

	1990	1991	1992	1993	1994	1995	1996	1994 I	1994 II	1994 III	1994 IV	1995 I	1995 II	1995 III	1995 IV
Exchange Rates															*Markkaa per SDR:*
Official Rate ... aa	5.1699	5.9120	7.2119	7.9454	6.9244	6.4790	6.6777	7.7238	7.6914	7.1434	6.9244	6.7665	6.6984	6.3909	6.4790
															Markkaa per US Dollar:
Official Rate ... ae	3.6340	4.1330	5.2450	5.7845	4.7432	4.3586	4.6439	5.4678	5.3104	4.8681	4.7432	4.3361	4.2699	4.2427	4.3586
Official Rate ... rf	3.8235	4.0440	4.4794	5.7123	5.2235	4.3667	4.5936	5.6028	5.4420	5.1030	4.7463	4.5853	4.2929	4.3069	4.2816
															Index Numbers (1990=100):
Official Rate ... ahx	100.0	94.7	85.5	66.9	73.4	87.5	83.1	68.1	70.1	74.8	80.4	83.3	88.9	88.6	89.1
Nominal Effective Exchange Rate ... neu	100.0	96.3	83.9	73.4	79.2	87.2	84.3	77.0	77.1	79.0	83.7	85.2	87.5	88.3	88.0
Real Effective Exchange Rate ... reu	100.0	91.5	75.1	63.5	66.6	73.9	....	65.5	64.9	66.1	70.0	71.4	74.0	75.5	74.8
Fund Position															*Millions of SDRs:*
Quota ... 2f.s	574.9	574.9	861.8	861.8	861.8	861.8	861.8	861.8	861.8	861.8	861.8	861.8	861.8	861.8	861.8
SDRs ... 1b.s	152.5	157.7	78.4	83.8	222.7	241.6	201.6	84.6	85.5	86.2	222.7	238.5	191.6	224.3	241.6
Reserve Position in the Fund ... 1c.s	151.0	192.3	241.0	220.4	196.1	259.5	292.8	216.0	198.9	196.1	196.1	196.1	213.5	243.1	259.5
International Liquidity															*Millions of US Dollars Unless Otherwise Indicated:*
Total Reserves minus Gold ... 1l.d	9,644.1	7,608.7	5,213.4	5,410.8	10,662.0	10,038.3	6,916.3	7,395.9	9,519.3	10,468.9	10,662.0	11,099.0	10,819.3	10,201.4	10,038.3
SDRs ... 1b.d	216.9	225.6	107.8	115.1	325.1	359.2	289.9	119.5	123.8	126.5	325.1	372.2	300.5	337.9	359.2
Reserve Position in the Fund ... 1c.d	214.8	275.1	331.3	302.7	286.3	385.8	421.1	305.1	288.1	287.8	286.3	306.1	334.9	366.1	385.8
Foreign Exchange ... 1d.d	9,212.4	7,108.0	4,774.3	4,993.0	10,050.6	9,293.4	6,205.3	6,971.2	9,107.4	10,054.6	10,050.6	10,420.7	10,183.8	9,497.3	9,293.4
Gold (Million Fine Troy Ounces) ... 1ad	2.002	2.002	2.002	2.002	2.003	1.600	1.600	2.002	2.003	2.003	2.003	1.600	1.600	1.600	1.600
Gold (National Valuation) ... 1and	599.9	527.5	415.6	376.9	459.6	399.7	375.1	398.7	410.5	447.8	459.6	401.7	408.0	410.6	399.7
Monetary Authorities: Other Assets ... 3..d	20.6	8.2	....	....	....	....	....	....	....	....	....	....	....	....	....
Other Liab. ... 4..d	270.6	11.2	452.7	33.4	27.5	278.6	201.2	26.0	17.2	31.8	27.5	55.7	169.4	226.0	278.6
Deposit Money Banks: Assets ... 7a.d	27,000	24,272	21,499	21,608	22,295	24,169	26,986	20,534	20,543	22,546	22,295	26,442	23,254	23,599	24,169
Liabilities ... 7b.d	59,906	53,452	40,169	31,854	30,679	29,269	25,884	31,918	31,751	30,922	30,679	33,337	31,353	28,685	29,269
Monetary Authorities															*Millions of Markkaa:*
Foreign Assets ... 11	37,678	34,095	29,928	33,478	52,752	48,916	36,461	42,619	52,732	53,144	52,752	53,547	51,476	48,403	48,916
Claims on Central Government ... 12a	1,314	1,376	2,447	1,788	1,806	1,882	1,907	1,793	1,819	1,847	1,806	1,763	1,793	1,797	1,882
Claims on Private Sector ... 12d	3,793	3,054	2,921	4,404	3,951	3,302	2,462	4,259	4,145	4,124	3,951	3,822	3,714	3,619	3,302
Claims on Deposit Money Banks ... 12e	13,075	15,648	11,547	7,575	1,718	8,415	13,301	4,080	2,922	3,723	1,718	2,939	3,257	6,774	8,415
Reserve Money ... 14	32,410	35,976	37,803	38,031	57,463	58,377	39,250	44,988	53,446	58,732	57,463	59,402	57,281	58,779	58,377
of which: Currency Outside DMBs ... 14a	9,555	8,813	9,404	10,394	10,810	12,401	13,645	10,241	10,446	10,535	10,810	10,824	11,088	11,116	12,401
Time Deposits ... 15	9,925	7,057	3,362	2,087	1,549	994	574	1,804	1,758	1,705	1,549	1,337	1,218	1,169	994
Restricted Deposits ... 16b	—	—	—	—	—	—	—	—	—	—	—	—	—	—	—
Foreign Liabilities ... 16c	983	46	2,375	193	130	1,214	934	142	91	155	130	242	723	959	1,214
Central Government Deposits ... 16d	1,321	4	90	784	93	75	—	251	526	60	93	68	555	76	75
Capital Accounts ... 17a	6,904	6,607	6,790	6,895	6,749	6,691	6,716	6,879	6,850	6,788	6,749	6,731	6,716	6,691	6,691
Other Items (Net) ... 17r	4,317	4,483	-3,577	-745	-5,756	-4,836	6,658	-1,314	-1,053	-4,601	-5,756	-5,708	-6,255	-7,081	-4,836
Deposit Money Banks															*Millions of Markkaa:*
Reserves ... 20	22,400	27,162	29,983	27,638	46,653	45,976	25,604	34,747	43,000	48,197	46,653	48,578	46,193	47,664	45,976
Foreign Assets ... 21	98,117	100,316	112,765	124,993	105,751	105,344	125,320	112,276	109,092	109,758	105,751	114,656	99,292	100,123	105,344
Claims on Central Government ... 22a	1,993	I3,426	7,568	11,117	15,630	37,442	30,796	9,629	12,115	12,351	15,630	26,693	26,988	31,252	37,442
Claims on Private Sector ... 22d	449,853	467,798	437,016	398,932	360,408	350,038	347,768	393,041	385,491	370,722	360,408	368,646	367,908	363,994	350,038
Demand Deposits ... 24	34,837	I121,832	125,425	131,365	143,547	163,521	191,188	138,666	142,919	140,657	143,547	149,106	153,777	150,543	163,521
Time and Savings Deposits ... 25	228,976	I158,200	154,861	153,618	145,670	142,710	104,963	145,856	146,069	145,077	145,670	145,192	144,509	144,538	142,710
Foreign Liabilities ... 26c	217,697	220,917	210,685	184,260	145,519	127,572	120,204	174,523	168,611	150,532	145,519	144,553	133,874	121,702	127,572
Central Government Deposits ... 26d	14,237	4,280	2,911	3,358	4,644	12,859	14,299	3,247	4,367	9,655	4,644	11,440	7,237	8,020	12,859
Central Govt. Lending Funds ... 26f	6,820	7,034	6,933	6,816	6,607	6,198	5,581	6,859	6,798	6,829	6,607	6,614	6,485	6,467	6,198
Credit from Monetary Authorities ... 26g	12,419	I15,648	13,132	7,576	1,718	8,415	13,301	4,080	2,922	3,723	1,718	2,939	3,257	6,774	8,415
Other Items (Net) ... 27r	57,377	I70,791	73,387	75,686	80,737	77,526	79,951	76,463	78,014	84,556	80,737	98,728	91,241	104,990	77,526
Monetary Survey															*Millions of Markkaa:*
Foreign Assets (Net) ... 31n	-82,886	-86,552	-70,367	-25,982	12,854	25,474	40,643	-19,770	-6,878	12,216	12,854	23,408	16,170	25,866	25,474
Domestic Credit ... 32	434,574	I464,336	440,018	405,283	370,451	373,532	363,052	398,365	391,880	372,501	370,451	382,801	386,125	386,099	373,532
Claims on Central Govt. (Net) ... 32an	-19,072	I-6,516	81	1,947	6,092	20,192	12,821	1,066	2,244	-2,345	6,092	10,333	14,503	18,486	20,192
Claims on Private Sector ... 32d	453,646	470,852	439,937	403,335	364,359	353,340	350,231	397,300	389,636	374,846	364,359	372,468	371,622	367,613	353,340
Money ... 34	44,428	I130,645	134,829	141,759	154,357	175,921	204,834	148,907	153,365	151,193	154,357	159,929	164,865	161,659	175,921
Quasi-Money ... 35	238,901	I165,257	158,223	155,705	147,218	143,704	105,537	147,660	147,827	146,781	147,218	146,529	145,727	145,707	143,704
Restricted Deposits ... 36b	—	—	—	—	—	—	—	—	—	—	—	—	—	—	—
Other Items (Net) ... 37r	68,360	81,881	76,599	81,836	81,730	79,381	93,324	82,028	83,810	86,743	81,730	99,750	91,703	104,599	79,381
Money, Seasonally Adjusted ... 34..b	44,473	I129,995	134,158	141,054	153,589	175,221	204,018	147,287	151,546	154,752	153,589	158,503	162,750	165,464	175,221
Unused Overdrafts ... 39b	10,500	....	....	....	....	....	....	....	....	....	....	....	....	....	....
Interest Rates															*Percent Per Annum*
Discount Rate *(End of Period)* ... 60	8.50	8.50	9.50	5.50	5.25	4.88	4.00	5.25	5.25	5.25	5.25	5.25	5.25	5.25	4.88
Money Market Rate ... 60b	14.00	13.08	13.25	7.77	5.35	5.75	3.63	4.94	5.29	5.66	5.51	5.97	5.95	6.05	5.03
Deposit Rate ... 60l	7.50	7.50	7.50	4.75	3.27	3.19	2.35	3.33	3.25	3.25	3.25	3.25	3.25	3.25	3.00
Lending Rate ... 60p	11.62	11.80	12.14	9.92	7.91	7.75	6.16	7.99	7.88	7.94	7.83	7.85	7.88	7.84	7.42
Government Bond Yield ... 61	....	....	....	8.8	9.0	8.8	....	6.9	8.8	10.3	10.2	10.2	9.0	8.3	7.6
Prices, Production, Labor															*Index Numbers (1990=100):*
Industrial Share Prices ... 62	100.0	73.1	68.9	116.3	179.5	199.0	208.1	175.0	172.0	182.6	188.5	180.4	186.7	230.7	198.3
Prices: Domestic Supply ... 63	100.0	100.3	101.4	104.4	105.8	106.5	105.5	104.7	105.5	106.4	106.7	106.9	107.7	106.1	105.4
Producer, Manufacturing ... 63ey	100.0	99.8	102.4	106.1	107.7	111.4	111.5	106.1	107.0	108.7	109.1	109.9	111.1	111.9	112.6
Consumer Prices ... 64	100.0	104.1	106.8	109.1	110.3	111.3	112.0	109.1	110.0	111.0	111.0	111.0	111.5	111.5	111.3
Wages: Hourly Earnings ... 65ey	100.0	106.4	108.7	....	....	....	....	....	....	....	....	....	....	....	....
Industrial Production, Seas.Adj. ... 66..c	100.0	90.3	92.3	97.4	107.6	115.6	....	102.3	107.0	109.0	112.0	114.3	116.0	115.9	116.3
Industrial Employment, Seas.Adj. ... 67eyc	100.0	90.4	81.5	76.2	76.7	82.2	....	72.3	77.0	81.0	76.5	76.9	84.2	84.3	83.2
															Number in Thousands:
Labor Force ... 67d	....	....	....	2,507	....	....	....	....	....	....	....	....	....	....	....
Employment ... 67e	2,488	2,366	2,199	2,041	2,024	2,068	2,096	1,952	2,048	2,078	2,018	1,993	2,105	2,124	2,049
Unemployment ... 67c	88	193	328	444	456	430	408	487	464	447	425	437	446	424	411
Unemployment Rate (%) ... 67r	3.4	7.6	13.0	17.9	18.4	17.2	16.3	20.0	18.5	17.7	17.4	18.0	17.5	16.6	16.7
International Transactions															*Millions of Markkaa*
Exports ... 70	101,380	93,088	107,471	133,962	153,690	172,380	176,592	34,831	38,970	37,814	42,075	40,307	45,962	39,576	46,535
Newsprint ... 70ul	2,917	2,875	2,656	2,955	2,915	3,187	3,342	764	749	735	668	729	680	852	926
Imports, cif ... 71	103,066	87,821	94,984	103,162	119,897	122,428	134,422	25,057	29,850	29,179	35,811	28,793	31,096	29,626	32,913
Imports, fob ... 71.v	98,628	84,039	90,894	98,720	114,734	117,156	128,633	23,978	28,565	27,922	34,269	27,553	29,757	28,350	31,496

SAMPLE PAGE FROM *INTERNATIONAL FINANCIAL STATISTICS*

EXHIBIT 13.2

Finland

172

		1996 I	II	III	IV	1997 I	1996 July	Aug	Sept	Oct	Nov	Dec	1997 Jan	Feb	Mar	Apr
Exchange Rates		*End of Period*														
Official Rate	aa	6.7693	6.7026	6.5799	6.6777	6.9271	6.5725	6.5073	6.5799	6.5439	6.6512	6.6777	6.7976	6.9790	6.9271	*7.1120*
		End of Period (ae) Period Average (rf)														
Official Rate	ae	4.6327	4.6438	4.5714	4.6439	4.9947	4.4847	4.4642	4.5714	4.5248	4.6041	4.6439	4.8740	5.0392	4.9947	*5.2082*
Official Rate	rf	4.5322	4.7197	4.5353	4.5871	4.9412	4.5888	4.4777	4.5393	4.5714	4.5500	4.6398	4.7765	4.9757	5.0716	*5.1307*
		Period Averages														
Official Rate	ahx	84.2	80.9	84.2	83.2	77.3	83.2	85.2	84.1	83.5	83.9	82.2	79.9	76.7	75.2	*74.4*
Nominal Effective Exchange Rate	neu	84.8	82.7	85.0	84.6	....	84.2	85.6	85.2	85.0	84.4	84.4	84.1	83.8	....	....
Real Effective Exchange Rate	reu	70.2	68.1	....	....	....	68.7	69.5	68.9	68.5	67.8	67.4	66.9	66.3	....	....
Fund Position		*End of Period*														
Quota	2f.s	861.8	861.8	861.8	861.8	861.8	861.8	861.8	861.8	861.8	861.8	861.8	861.8	861.8	861.8	*861.8*
SDRs	1b.s	171.6	185.7	214.2	201.6	219.1	180.1	181.7	214.2	155.4	157.1	201.6	201.0	221.3	219.1	*166.8*
Reserve Position in the Fund	1c.s	265.6	285.1	292.5	292.8	279.2	285.2	292.4	292.5	292.7	292.7	292.8	284.2	284.2	279.2	*279.3*
International Liquidity		*End of Period*														
Total Reserves minus Gold	1l.d	8,265.1	6,461.7	6,771.0	6,916.3	11,098.1	6,568.9	6,770.4	6,771.0	7,169.8	7,103.3	6,916.3	11,844.4	11,453.6	11,098.1	*10,180.8*
SDRs	1b.d	250.8	268.1	308.3	289.9	303.8	264.0	264.8	308.3	224.8	227.0	289.9	280.3	306.5	303.8	*227.8*
Reserve Position in the Fund	1c.d	388.1	411.5	421.0	421.1	387.3	417.9	426.3	421.0	423.3	422.8	421.1	396.4	393.6	387.3	*381.4*
Foreign Exchange	1d.d	7,626.2	5,782.1	6,041.7	6,205.3	10,407.0	5,887.0	6,079.3	6,041.7	6,521.8	6,453.6	6,205.3	11,167.8	10,753.5	10,407.0	*9,571.6*
Gold (Million Fine Troy Ounces)	1ad	1.600	1.600	1.600	1.600	1.600	1.600	1.600	1.600	1.600	1.600	1.600	1.600	1.600	1.600	*1.600*
Gold (National Valuation)	1and	376.0	375.1	381.1	375.1	348.8	388.4	390.2	381.1	385.0	378.4	375.1	357.4	345.7	348.8	*334.5*
Monetary Authorities:Other Assets	3..d	....	....	....	....	....	....	....	....	....	....	....	....	....	....	....
Other Liab.	4..d	98.4	241.0	195.0	201.2	68.1	264.1	382.4	195.0	218.4	260.4	201.2	77.6	86.0	68.1	....
Deposit Money Banks: Assets	7a.d	23,842	23,618	26,050	26,986	....	25,508	25,253	26,050	25,382	26,508	26,986	*25,693*	*27,082*	....	....
Liabilities	7b.d	26,706	24,700	26,326	25,884	....	24,669	24,925	26,326	26,368	26,308	25,884	*28,319*	*28,768*	....	....
Monetary Authorities		*End of Period*														
Foreign Assets	11	43,528	34,772	35,368	36,461	59,766	33,904	34,638	35,368	36,762	37,046	36,461	62,059	62,062	59,766	*58,836*
Claims on Central Government	12a	1,874	6,460	5,998	1,907	1,907	6,460	6,297	5,998	5,982	5,987	1,907	1,907	1,907	1,907	*1,904*
Claims on Private Sector	12d	3,213	2,711	2,653	2,462	2,430	2,694	2,684	2,653	2,626	2,469	2,462	2,445	2,435	2,430	*2,216*
Claims on Deposit Money Banks	12e	3,582	9,625	11,865	13,301	19,803	8,278	11,711	11,865	12,372	9,443	13,301	15,933	13,752	19,803	*18,696*
Reserve Money	14	46,438	40,885	43,657	39,250	68,730	38,899	42,521	43,657	45,346	41,755	39,250	68,111	64,514	68,730	*64,481*
of which: Currency Outside DMBs	14a	12,195	12,996	12,674	13,645	*13,672*	12,632	12,928	12,674	13,026	13,263	13,645	13,312	13,404	*13,672*	....
Time Deposits	15	875	767	697	574	278	746	735	697	665	606	574	400	341	278	*213*
Restricted Deposits	16b	—	—	—	—	—	—	—	—	—	—	—	—	—	—	—
Foreign Liabilities	16c	456	1,119	891	934	340	1,184	1,707	891	988	1,199	934	378	434	340	*273*
Central Government Deposits	16d	40	—	—	—	—	—	—	—	—	—	—	—	—	—	—
Capital Accounts	17a	6,732	6,719	6,705	6,716	6,751	6,705	6,696	6,705	6,698	6,712	6,716	6,737	6,760	6,751	*6,779*
Other Items (Net)	17r	-2,344	4,078	3,934	6,658	7,808	3,801	3,672	3,934	4,045	4,673	6,658	6,717	8,108	7,808	*9,905*
Deposit Money Banks		*End of Period*														
Reserves	20	34,243	27,889	30,983	25,604	*55,058*	26,267	29,593	30,983	32,321	28,492	25,604	54,799	51,110	*55,058*	....
Foreign Assets	21	110,453	109,677	119,083	125,320	....	114,395	112,733	119,083	114,847	122,047	125,320	*125,228*	*136,471*	....	....
Claims on Central Government	22a	31,297	39,403	31,878	30,796	....	37,538	42,892	31,878	33,347	30,917	30,796	*34,259*	*33,942*	....	....
Claims on Private Sector	22d	347,660	349,212	346,868	347,768	....	346,469	347,049	346,868	347,117	348,062	347,768	*343,875*	*346,518*	....	....
Demand Deposits	24	166,715	176,335	178,107	191,188	*192,114*	175,391	176,336	178,107	182,567	183,368	191,188	*193,644*	*186,977*	*192,114*	....
Time and Savings Deposits	25	128,185	119,614	114,081	104,963	....	117,801	115,824	114,081	110,636	107,849	104,963	*103,575*	*104,665*	....	....
Foreign Liabilities	26c	123,723	114,700	120,347	120,204	....	110,632	111,272	120,347	119,308	121,124	120,204	*138,026*	*144,966*	....	....
Central Government Deposits	26d	14,412	16,829	16,789	14,299	....	13,845	17,415	16,789	15,820	14,473	14,299	*17,062*	*21,178*	....	....
Central Govt. Lending Funds	26f	6,061	5,826	5,844	5,581	....	5,834	5,838	5,844	5,636	5,597	5,581	*5,569*	*5,569*	....	....
Credit from Monetary Authorities	26g	3,582	9,625	11,865	13,301	19,803	8,278	11,711	11,865	12,372	9,443	13,301	15,933	13,752	19,803	....
Other Items (Net)	27r	80,975	83,252	81,778	79,951	....	92,888	93,872	81,778	81,293	87,666	79,951	*84,353*	*90,935*	....	....
Monetary Survey		*End of Period*														
Foreign Assets (Net)	31n	29,802	28,630	33,213	40,643	....	36,482	34,392	33,213	31,313	36,771	40,643	*48,883*	*53,134*	....	....
Domestic Credit	32	363,531	375,132	364,764	363,052	....	373,481	375,669	364,764	367,615	367,366	363,052	*359,855*	*358,055*	....	....
Claims on Central Govt. (Net)	32an	12,658	23,209	15,243	12,821	....	24,318	25,936	15,243	17,873	16,834	12,821	*13,535*	*9,102*	....	....
Claims on Private Sector	32d	350,873	351,923	349,521	350,231	....	349,163	349,733	349,521	349,743	350,531	350,231	*346,320*	*348,953*	....	....
Money	34	178,910	189,332	190,781	204,834	*205,786*	188,022	189,264	190,781	195,593	196,631	204,834	*206,956*	*200,381*	*205,786*	....
Quasi-Money	35	129,060	120,381	114,778	105,537	....	118,547	116,558	114,778	111,301	108,455	105,537	*103,975*	*105,006*	....	....
Restricted Deposits	36b	—	—	—	—	—	—	—	—	—	—	—	—	—	—	....
Other Items (Net)	37r	85,363	94,049	92,417	93,324	....	103,394	104,239	92,417	92,035	99,051	93,324	*97,807*	*105,802*	....	....
Money, Seasonally Adjusted	34..b	177,314	186,718	195,272	204,018	*204,153*	187,087	190,024	195,272	198,572	200,439	204,018	*204,907*	*198,397*	*204,153*	....
Unused Overdrafts	39b	....	....	....	....	....	....	....	....	....	....	....	....	....	....	....
Interest Rates		*Percent Per Annum*														
Discount Rate *(End of Period)*	60	4.50	4.50	4.25	4.00	4.00	4.50	4.50	4.25	4.00	4.00	4.00	4.00	4.00	4.00	*4.00*
Money Market Rate	60b	4.16	3.77	3.48	3.09	3.07	3.63	3.54	3.28	3.10	3.08	3.08	3.07	3.07	3.07	*3.08*
Deposit Rate	60l	2.58	2.50	2.33	2.00	2.00	2.50	2.50	2.00	2.00	2.00	2.00	2.00	2.00	2.00	*2.00*
Lending Rate	60p	6.72	6.31	6.01	5.59	*5.36*	6.12	6.04	5.87	5.67	5.62	5.48	5.39	*5.36*	*5.32*	....
Government Bond Yield	61	7.5	7.4	....	....	....	7.1	....	....	....	....	....	....	....	....	....
Prices, Production, Labor		*Period Averages*														
Industrial Share Prices	62	180.8	201.5	213.3	236.8	....	205.5	214.7	219.7	224.9	235.3	250.2	....	....	....	....
Prices: Domestic Supply	63	105.7	105.4	105.2	105.8	*106.2*	105.0	105.0	105.5	106.0	105.5	105.9	106.0	106.3	*106.3*	....
Producer, Manufacturing	63ey	112.8	111.9	110.5	110.7	*110.7*	110.8	110.3	110.4	110.8	110.5	110.7	110.6	110.8	*110.8*	....
Consumer Prices	64	111.6	112.1	112.1	112.1	*112.2*	112.1	111.9	112.1	112.4	112.0	112.0	112.0	112.1	*112.5*	*113.1*
Wages: Hourly Earnings	65ey	....	....	....	....	....	....	....	....	....	....	....	....	....	....	....
Industrial Production, Seas.Adj.	66..c	115.8	119.6	121.5	....	....	120.4	119.6	124.4	....	....	....	....	....	....	....
Industrial Employment, Seas.Adj.	67eyc	....	....	....	....	....	....	....	....	....	....	....	....	....	....	....
		Period Averages														
Labor Force	67d	....	....	....	....	....	....	....	....	....	....	....	....	....	....	....
Employment	67e	2,027	2,126	2,146	2,083	....	2,228	2,135	2,075	2,093	2,090	2,067	I2,051	....	....	....
Unemployment	67c	427	422	398	384	....	421	403	370	377	395	379	I411	....	....	....
Unemployment Rate (%)	67r	17.4	16.6	15.6	15.6	....	15.9	15.9	15.1	15.3	15.9	15.5	I16.7	....	....	....
International Transactions		*Millions of Markkaa*														
Exports	70	41,225	46,117	41,208	48,042	....	12,783	13,813	14,612	15,040	18,383	14,619	....	....	....	....
Newsprint	70ul	962	885	723	771	....	261	240	223	176	273	322	....	....	....	....
Imports, cif	71	32,185	32,791	31,743	37,703	....	9,610	10,318	11,815	12,680	12,259	12,764	....	....	....	....
Imports, fob	71.v	30,799	31,379	30,376	36,079	....	9,196	9,874	11,306	12,134	11,731	12,214	....	....	....	....

SAMPLE PAGE FROM *INTERNATIONAL FINANCIAL STATISTICS*

EXHIBIT 13.2 (continued)

Finland

172

Finland 172									1994				1995			
		1990	1991	1992	1993	1994	1995	1996	I	II	III	IV	I	II	III	IV
																1990=100
Volume of Exports	72	100	91	99	117	133	....	....	124	134	129	144	....	....	....	....
Newsprint	72ul	100	96	95	103	105	91	84	110	105	105	98	90	86	91	96
Volume of Imports	73	100	83	81	78	93	....	....	78	93	90	113	....	....	....	....
Unit Value of Exports	74	100	100	106	113	113	....	....	110	114	116	114	....	....	....	....
Newsprint	74ul	100	102	96	98	95	120	136	95	97	96	93	111	108	128	132
Unit Value of Imports	75	100	102	113	129	125	....	....	126	123	126	123	....	....	....	....
Import Prices	76.x	100	101	108	119	119	118	120	118	119	119	118	119	119	118	117
Balance of Payments														*Millions of US Dollars:*		
Current Account, n.i.e.	78ald	-6,962	-6,696	-4,945	-1,123	1,273	5,385	4,178	14	398	813	48	741	1,232	1,244	2,169
Goods: Exports f.o.b.	78aad	26,531	22,969	23,942	23,478	29,731	40,515	40,412	6,228	7,167	7,414	8,922	9,177	10,918	9,419	11,001
Goods: Imports f.o.b.	78abd	-25,829	-20,738	-20,165	-17,217	-22,241	-28,169	-29,465	-4,294	-5,238	-5,454	-7,255	-6,390	-7,242	-6,797	-7,739
Trade Balance	78acd	701	2,231	3,777	6,261	7,490	12,346	10,946	1,934	1,929	1,960	1,667	2,787	3,675	2,622	3,262
Services: Credit	78add	4,649	4,300	4,943	4,490	5,754	7,553	7,508	1,238	1,325	1,587	1,604	1,729	1,879	1,987	1,959
Services: Debit	78aed	-7,627	-7,546	-7,405	-6,481	-7,187	-9,655	-9,190	-1,543	-1,652	-1,802	-2,191	-2,269	-2,475	-2,347	-2,564
Balance on Goods & Services	78afd	-2,276	-1,014	1,315	4,270	6,057	10,245	9,264	1,630	1,602	1,745	1,080	2,246	3,079	2,262	2,657
Income: Credit	78agd	3,505	2,546	1,457	1,098	1,748	3,021	2,484	393	497	363	494	638	881	638	863
Income: Debit	78ahd	-7,239	-7,248	-6,923	-6,063	-6,078	-7,283	-6,472	-1,799	-1,623	-1,203	-1,453	-1,958	-2,410	-1,486	-1,429
Balance on Gds, Serv. & Inc.	78aid	-6,010	-5,716	-4,152	-695	1,727	5,982	5,276	224	476	906	122	926	1,550	1,414	2,092
Current Transfers, n.i.e.: Credit	78ajd	288	345	427	475	410	1,536	1,144	94	96	98	122	232	248	386	671
Current Transfers: Debit	78akd	-1,240	-1,326	-1,221	-903	-863	-2,133	-2,242	-304	-174	-191	-195	-417	-567	-557	-593
Capital Account, n.i.e.	78bcd	—	-71	—	—	—	66	51	—	—	—	—	—	-24	—	90
Capital Account, n.i.e.: Credit	78bad	—	—	—	—	—	114	125	—	—	—	—	—	—	—	114
Capital Account: Debit	78bbd	—	-71	—	—	—	-48	-74	—	—	—	—	—	-24	—	-24
Financial Account, n.i.e.	78bjd	12,405	4,196	3,071	374	4,093	-4,468	-7,657	2,687	1,472	504	-569	-790	-1,315	-1,877	-486
Direct Investment Abroad	78bdd	-2,782	120	757	-1,401	-4,354	-1,678	-3,538	-964	-884	-960	-1,547	-482	-347	-238	-610
Dir. Invest. in Rep. Econ., n.i.e.	78bed	812	-233	396	864	1,496	1,044	1,227	686	557	465	-212	572	-290	35	726
Portfolio Investment Assets	78bfd	-469	-334	-622	-604	826	243	-4,118	34	1,417	164	-789	146	533	-226	-210
Equity Securities	78bkd	1	87	-10	-151	-78	-209	-712	-64	-18	8	-4	28	-87	-107	-43
Debt Securities	78bld	-470	-421	-612	-452	904	452	-3,406	97	1,436	156	-785	118	620	-119	-167
Portfolio Investment Liab., n.i.e.	78bgd	5,696	8,610	8,243	6,836	6,186	-1,179	1,442	1,325	2,112	3,746	-996	-261	-1,468	728	-177
Equity Securities	78bmd	96	20	89	2,216	2,541	2,027	1,915	783	442	1,015	301	95	811	683	448
Debt Securities	78bnd	5,600	8,590	8,154	4,620	3,645	-3,206	-472	542	1,670	2,731	-1,297	-347	-2,280	45	-625
Other Investment Assets	78bhd	719	-2,964	-3,286	-1,833	-668	-2,863	-4,450	1,095	-929	-1,789	954	-1,989	1,300	-1,008	-1,166
Monetary Authorities	78bod	151	-1	-416	-29	99	146	27	-6	—	-4	109	-13	63	45	51
General Government	78bpd	-82	-83	-275	-344	-445	-366	-635	-199	-110	-13	-123	-196	-216	-19	66
Banks	78bqd	935	-1,899	-896	-987	-511	-1,926	-3,811	853	-106	-1,776	519	-2,033	1,851	-813	-932
Other Sectors	78brd	-284	-981	-1,698	-472	189	-717	-30	447	-712	5	450	254	-399	-222	-351
Other Investment Liab., n.i.e.	78bid	8,428	-1,003	-2,418	-3,488	607	-35	1,779	511	-802	-1,123	2,020	1,225	-1,042	-1,167	949
Monetary Authorities	78bsd	96	-251	1,244	-298	-107	92	-96	-2	-9	18	-114	25	49	10	8
General Government	78btd	-104	257	255	983	965	-331	764	-466	297	238	896	209	-636	21	75
Banks	78bud	4,764	-414	-5,034	-4,970	-1,088	869	-965	881	-1,092	-1,054	177	1,278	-500	-372	463
Other Sectors	78bvd	3,672	-595	1,118	796	837	-666	2,076	98	2	-324	1,061	-288	44	-826	404
Net Errors and Omissions	78cad	-1,511	685	-276	1,041	-652	-1,354	393	-866	—	-548	763	416	-194	265	-1,841
Overall Balance	78cbd	3,931	-1,886	-2,150	291	4,714	-372	-3,035	1,835	1,869	768	241	367	-301	-369	-68
Reserves and Related Items	79dad	-3,931	1,886	2,150	-291	-4,714	372	3,035	-1,835	-1,869	-768	-241	-367	301	369	68
Reserve Assets	79dbd	-3,931	1,886	2,150	-291	-4,714	372	3,035	-1,835	-1,869	-768	-241	-367	301	369	68
Use of Fund Credit and Loans	79dcd	—	—	—	—	—	—	—	—	—	—	—	—	—	—	—
Exceptional Financing	79ded	....	....	....	....	....	....	....	....	....	....	....	....	....	....	....
International Investment Position														*Millions of US Dollars*		
Assets	79aad	45,048	44,118	39,957	40,838	51,570	58,153	65,395	....	....	....	....	....	....	....	....
Direct Investment Abroad	79abd	11,227	10,845	8,565	9,178	12,534	15,177	17,830	....	....	....	....	....	....	....	....
Portfolio Investment	79acd	2,582	2,803	3,257	4,144	3,520	3,613	7,676	....	....	....	....	....	....	....	....
Equity Securities	79add	210	103	89	308	418	738	1,539	....	....	....	....	....	....	....	....
Debt Securities	79aed	2,372	2,700	3,168	3,835	3,101	2,875	6,137	....	....	....	....	....	....	....	....
Other Investment	79afd	20,994	22,333	22,510	21,729	24,395	28,153	32,050	....	....	....	....	....	....	....	....
Monetary Authorities	79agd	729	659	928	874	969	911	830	....	....	....	....	....	....	....	....
General Government	79ahd	1,411	1,415	1,521	1,841	2,481	2,966	3,511	....	....	....	....	....	....	....	....
Banks	79aid	10,997	12,164	11,301	10,933	12,021	14,203	17,809	....	....	....	....	....	....	....	....
Other Sectors	79ajd	7,857	8,095	8,759	8,081	8,924	10,073	9,900	....	....	....	....	....	....	....	....
Reserve Assets	79akd	10,245	8,137	5,626	5,788	11,122	11,210	7,839	....	....	....	....	....	....	....	....
Liabilities	79lad	84,362	86,073	83,423	85,949	107,281	111,245	118,411	....	....	....	....	....	....	....	....
Dir. Invest. in Rep. Economy	79lbd	5,132	4,220	3,689	4,217	6,714	8,465	9,160	....	....	....	....	....	....	....	....
Portfolio Investment	79lcd	34,243	40,475	44,974	52,820	68,416	69,762	76,100	....	....	....	....	....	....	....	....
Equity Securities	79ldd	1,390	1,004	979	5,251	12,767	14,625	23,457	....	....	....	....	....	....	....	....
Debt Securities	79led	32,853	39,471	43,995	47,569	55,649	55,137	52,643	....	....	....	....	....	....	....	....
Other investment	79lfd	44,987	41,378	34,760	28,913	32,151	33,018	33,151	....	....	....	....	....	....	....	....
Monetary Authorities	79lgd	876	558	1,301	908	996	1,176	1,018	....	....	....	....	....	....	....	....
General Government	79lhd	1,412	1,551	1,689	2,767	4,016	3,886	4,299	....	....	....	....	....	....	....	....
Banks	79lid	27,789	25,905	19,348	12,708	12,620	13,824	12,196	....	....	....	....	....	....	....	....
Other Sectors	79ljd	14,909	13,363	12,423	12,530	14,519	14,133	15,638	....	....	....	....	....	....	....	....
Government Finance														*Millions of Markkaa:*		
Deficit (-) or Surplus	80	945	-34,096	-70,346	-64,554	-58,781	....	....	-16,939	-15,515	-15,750	-16,650	-22,939	-24,817	-6,887	-4,264
Revenue	81	160,241	154,141	156,114	160,235	168,307	....	....	31,801	31,702	31,834	33,260	29,159	36,927	36,063	42,419
Grants Received	81z	3,867	4,173	5,881	5,585	5,520	....	....	....	....	....	....	....	....	....	....
Expenditure	82	158,673	184,225	203,201	218,612	223,119	....	....	46,945	46,355	41,273	48,300	50,865	53,049	41,914	48,806
Lending Minus Repayments	83	4,490	8,185	29,140	11,762	9,489	....	....	1,795	862	6,311	1,610	1,233	8,695	1,036	-2,123
Financing (By Residence of Lender)																
Domestic	84a	-4,377	11,301	19,449	15,431	26,024	....	....	....	....	....	....	....	....	....	....
Foreign	85a	3,432	22,795	50,897	49,123	32,757	....	....	....	....	....	....	....	....	....	....
Debt: Domestic	88a	27,444	30,216	51,956	97,288	123,434	....	....	....	....	....	....	....	....	....	....
Foreign	89a	29,210	57,699	119,974	175,490	190,851	....	....	....	....	....	....	....	....	....	....
Debt: Domestic	88b	....	....	....	....	....	....	....	112,495	118,945	130,728	143,261	171,273	174,778	183,201	199,304
Foreign	89b	....	....	....	....	....	....	....	157,783	175,588	179,307	176,562	183,648	178,641	....	....

SAMPLE PAGE FROM *INTERNATIONAL FINANCIAL STATISTICS*

EXHIBIT 13.2 (continued)

Finland 172

	1996 II	III	IV	1997 I	July	Aug	1996 Sept	Oct	Nov	Dec	1997 Jan	Feb	Mar	Apr		
I																
1990 = 100																
94	86	77	80	....	80	77	74	65	94	81	....	....	....	....	Volume of Exports	72
....	....	....	....	....	....	....	....	....	....	....	....	....	....	....	Newsprint	72ul
....	....	....	....	....	....	....	....	....	....	....	....	....	....	....	Volume of Imports	73
140	141	129	132	....	135	128	124	112	120	163	....	....	....	....	Unit Value of Exports	74
....	....	....	....	....	....	....	....	....	....	....	....	....	....	....	Newsprint	74ul
119	121	121	121	*121*	121	120	121	122	120	120	121	121	*120*	....	Unit Value of Imports	75
															Import Prices	76.x
Minus Sign Indicates Debit															**Balance of Payments**	
465	1,146	1,277	1,290	....	....	....	....	....	....	....	....	....	....	....	Current Account, n.i.e.	78ald
9,577	10,345	9,396	11,093	....	....	....	....	....	....	....	....	....	....	....	Goods: Exports f.o.b.	78aad
-7,156	-7,140	-6,833	-8,335	....	....	....	....	....	....	....	....	....	....	....	Goods: Imports f.o.b.	78abd
2,421	3,205	2,563	2,757	....	....	....	....	....	....	....	....	....	....	....	*Trade Balance*	78acd
1,783	1,813	2,008	1,903	....	....	....	....	....	....	....	....	....	....	....	Services: Credit	78add
-2,351	-2,211	-2,203	-2,425	....	....	....	....	....	....	....	....	....	....	....	Services: Debit	78aed
1,853	2,807	2,368	2,235	....	....	....	....	....	....	....	....	....	....	....	*Balance on Goods & Services*	78afd
656	687	557	584	....	....	....	....	....	....	....	....	....	....	....	Income: Credit	78agd
-1,618	-2,057	-1,354	-1,444	....	....	....	....	....	....	....	....	....	....	....	Income: Debit	78ahd
891	1,438	1,571	1,376	....	....	....	....	....	....	....	....	....	....	....	*Balance on Gds, Serv. & Inc*	78aid
190	315	169	470	....	....	....	....	....	....	....	....	....	....	....	Current Transfers, n.i.e.: Credit	78ajd
-616	-607	-464	-555	....	....	....	....	....	....	....	....	....	....	....	Current Transfers: Debit	78akd
-13	—	—	64	....	....	....	....	....	....	....	....	....	....	....	Capital Account, n.i.e.	78bcd
—	—	—	125	....	....	....	....	....	....	....	....	....	....	....	Capital Account, n.i.e.: Credit	78bad
-13	—	—	-61	....	....	....	....	....	....	....	....	....	....	....	Capital Account: Debit	78bbd
-2,838	-2,279	-940	-1,600	....	....	....	....	....	....	....	....	....	....	....	Financial Account, n.i.e.	78bjd
-1,190	-1,413	-827	-108	....	....	....	....	....	....	....	....	....	....	....	Direct Investment Abroad	78bdd
385	150	585	107	....	....	....	....	....	....	....	....	....	....	....	Dir. Invest. in Rep. Econ., n.i.e.	78bed
-1,543	-914	-527	-1,133	....	....	....	....	....	....	....	....	....	....	....	Portfolio Investment Assets	78bfd
-127	-221	-161	-203	....	....	....	....	....	....	....	....	....	....	....	Equity Securities	78bkd
-1,416	-694	-366	-930	....	....	....	....	....	....	....	....	....	....	....	Debt Securities	78bld
1,207	447	-1,081	869	....	....	....	....	....	....	....	....	....	....	....	Portfolio Investment Liab., n.i.e.	78bgd
268	1,302	82	262	....	....	....	....	....	....	....	....	....	....	....	Equity Securities	78bmd
939	-855	-1,163	607	....	....	....	....	....	....	....	....	....	....	....	Debt Securities	78bnd
-1,825	-738	-590	-1,297	....	....	....	....	....	....	....	....	....	....	....	Other Investment Assets	78bhd
9	-37	11	44	....	....	....	....	....	....	....	....	....	....	....	Monetary Authorities	78bod
-188	-181	-197	-70	....	....	....	....	....	....	....	....	....	....	....	General Government	78bpd
-2,049	-265	-416	-1,082	....	....	....	....	....	....	....	....	....	....	....	Banks	78bqd
403	-256	12	-189	....	....	....	....	....	....	....	....	....	....	....	Other Sectors	78brd
128	190	1,500	-38	....	....	....	....	....	....	....	....	....	....	....	Other Investment Liab., n.i.e.	78bid
-178	177	-61	-35	....	....	....	....	....	....	....	....	....	....	....	Monetary Authorities	78bsd
112	277	217	158	....	....	....	....	....	....	....	....	....	....	....	General Government	78btd
-250	-921	930	-724	....	....	....	....	....	....	....	....	....	....	....	Banks	78bud
443	657	413	562	....	....	....	....	....	....	....	....	....	....	....	Other Sectors	78bvd
784	-659	-87	355	....	....	....	....	....	....	....	....	....	....	....	Net Errors and Omissions	78cad
-1,602	-1,792	249	109	....	....	....	....	....	....	....	....	....	....	....	*Overall Balance*	78cbd
1,602	1,792	-249	-109	....	....	....	....	....	....	....	....	....	....	....	Reserves and Related Items	79dad
1,602	1,792	-249	-109	....	....	....	....	....	....	....	....	....	....	....	Reserve Assets	79dbd
—	—	—	—	....	....	....	....	....	....	....	....	....	....	....	Use of Fund Credit and Loans	79dcd
....	....	....	....	....	....	....	....	....	....	....	....	....	....	....	Exceptional Financing	79ded
Millions of US Dollars															**International Investment Position**	
....	....	....	....	....	....	....	....	....	....	....	....	....	....	....	Assets	79aad
....	....	....	....	....	....	....	....	....	....	....	....	....	....	....	Direct Investment Abroad	79abd
....	....	....	....	....	....	....	....	....	....	....	....	....	....	....	Portfolio Investment	79acd
....	....	....	....	....	....	....	....	....	....	....	....	....	....	....	Equity Securities	79add
....	....	....	....	....	....	....	....	....	....	....	....	....	....	....	Debt Securities	79aed
....	....	....	....	....	....	....	....	....	....	....	....	....	....	....	Other Investment	79afd
....	....	....	....	....	....	....	....	....	....	....	....	....	....	....	Monetary Authorities	79agd
....	....	....	....	....	....	....	....	....	....	....	....	....	....	....	General Government	79ahd
....	....	....	....	....	....	....	....	....	....	....	....	....	....	....	Banks	79aid
....	....	....	....	....	....	....	....	....	....	....	....	....	....	....	Other Sectors	79ajd
....	....	....	....	....	....	....	....	....	....	....	....	....	....	....	Reserve Assets	79akd
....	....	....	....	....	....	....	....	....	....	....	....	....	....	....	Liabilities	79lad
....	....	....	....	....	....	....	....	....	....	....	....	....	....	....	Dir. Invest. in Rep. Economy	79lbd
....	....	....	....	....	....	....	....	....	....	....	....	....	....	....	Portfolio Investment	79lcd
....	....	....	....	....	....	....	....	....	....	....	....	....	....	....	Equity Securities	79ldd
....	....	....	....	....	....	....	....	....	....	....	....	....	....	....	Debt Securities	79led
....	....	....	....	....	....	....	....	....	....	....	....	....	....	....	Other investment	79lfd
....	....	....	....	....	....	....	....	....	....	....	....	....	....	....	Monetary Authorities	79lgd
....	....	....	....	....	....	....	....	....	....	....	....	....	....	....	General Government	79lhd
....	....	....	....	....	....	....	....	....	....	....	....	....	....	....	Banks	79lid
....	....	....	....	....	....	....	....	....	....	....	....	....	....	....	Other Sectors	79ljd
Year Ending December 31															**Government Finance**	
-10,648	-9,851	....	....	....	-3,262	768	....	....	....	....	....	....	....	....	Deficit (-) or Surplus	80
44,166	39,652	....	....	....	12,067	12,433	....	....	....	....	....	....	....	....	Revenue	81
															Grants Received	81z
53,880	48,214	....	....	....	15,214	11,427	....	....	....	....	....	....	....	....	Expenditure	82
934	1,289	....	....	....	115	238	....	....	....	....	....	....	....	....	Lending Minus Repayments	83
															Financing (By Residence of Lender)	
....	....	....	....	....	....	....	....	....	....	....	....	....	....	....	Domestic	84a
....	....	....	....	....	....	....	....	....	....	....	....	....	....	....	Foreign	85a
....	....	....	....	....	....	....	....	....	....	....	....	....	....	....	Debt: Domestic	88a
213,695	230,500	231,259	....	....	233,793	240,641	231,259	....	....	....	....	....	....	....	Foreign	89a
....	....	....	....	....	....	....	....	....	....	....	....	....	....	....	Debt: Domestic	88b
....	....	....	....	....	174,375	172,292	172,161	....	....	....	....	....	....	....	Foreign	89b

SAMPLE PAGE FROM *INTERNATIONAL FINANCIAL STATISTICS*

EXHIBIT 13.2 (continued)

Finland
172

National Accounts		1990	1991	1992	1993	1994	1995	1996	1994 I	II	III	IV	1995 I	II	III	IV
																Billions of Markkaa
Exports of Goods & Services	90c	118.83	109.29	128.27	159.44	182.53	207.52	....	41.41	45.90	45.60	49.62	49.56	54.52	48.66	54.78
Government Consumption	91f	108.54	118.72	118.45	112.19	114.00	119.14	....	26.35	27.66	29.52	30.47	26.75	29.01	30.96	32.43
Gross Fixed Capital Formation	93e	139.14	110.06	87.95	71.19	74.19	82.60	....	17.06	17.10	18.58	21.45	20.64	19.31	21.10	21.55
Increase/Decrease(-) in Stocks	93i	5.77	-19.49	-8.14	-2.23	4.83	.75	....	-1.98	1.88	2.36	2.56	1.10	-1.03	1.74	-1.05
Private Consumption	96f	269.75	274.71	272.11	275.25	284.43	295.85	....	67.67	70.44	70.98	75.33	70.71	74.66	73.16	77.33
Imports of Goods & Services	98c	-126.60	-112.42	-121.88	-133.45	-150.04	-160.14	....	-32.27	-37.03	-36.45	-44.29	-38.54	-40.74	-38.18	-42.69
Gross Domestic Product (GDP)	99b	515.43	480.87	476.78	482.40	509.92	545.73	....	118.24	125.95	130.59	135.15	130.22	135.73	137.43	142.34
Gross Dom. Prod. 1990 Prices	99b.p	515.43	479.01	462.00	456.57	476.66	496.91	....	112.26	117.82	120.29	126.29	120.51	123.53	124.00	128.86
						Millions: Midyear Estimates										
Population	99z	4.99	5.01	5.04	5.07	5.09	5.11	....	....	....	....	Population				99z

Date of Fund membership: January 14, 1958

Standard Sources:

B: Bank of Finland, *Monthly Bulletin*

N: Ministry of Finance, *Economic Survey*

S: Central Statistical Office, *Bulletin of Statistics*

Exchange Rates: *Official Rate (End of Period* and *Period Average):* Central bank midpoint rate.

International Liquidity: Beginning March 1979, data on gold and foreign exchange holdings exclude the deposits made with the European Monetary Institute (EMI) of the gold and gross U.S. dollar holdings; the holdings of European currency units (ECUs) issued by the EMI against these deposits are included in *line 1.d.d. Gold (National Valuation) (line 1and)* is obtained by converting the value in national currency terms, as reported in the country's standard sources, using the prevailing exchange rate, as given in *line de, line ae,* or *line we.* In December 1979 gold was revalued at the average daily quotations in London during November 1979 less a discount of 25 percent.

Monetary Authorities: Comprises the Bank of Finland only.

Deposit Money Banks: Comprises seven commercial banks (including the central bank of the cooperative banks and the central bank of the savings banks), the Post Office Bank, cooperative banks, and savings banks. I Beginning January 1991, data are based on improved sectorization.

Monetary Survey: In the monetary survey (see Introduction for the standard method of calculation), *Central Government Lending Funds (line 26f)* is included as a liability in *line 32an.* I See note to section 20.

Interest Rates: *Discount Rate (End of Period):* Source B. Rate provides the basis for determining the interest rates charged by commercial banks.

Money Market Rate: Source B. Rate refers to the three-month Helibor rate. Monthly data are the average of daily figures for the month.

Deposit Rate: Rate on twenty-four-month time deposits with deposit money banks (mean of end-month rates).

Commercial Bank Lending Rate: Data are from source B. Mean value of the end-of-month lending rates weighted by credit outstanding.

Government Bond Yield: Data are period averages of quotations for a fixed rate serial bond with an average remaining maturity of 10 years. The 1992 yearly average is based only on data for November and December.

Prices, Production, Labor: *Industrial Share Prices:* Source S index, base 1990, refer to the average of daily buying quotations. *Prices: Domestic Supply:* Source B basic price index of domestic supply, base 1985. *Producer Manufacturing:* Source B producer price index for manufactured products, base 1985. *Consumer Prices:* Source B index of consumer prices, base 1985. *Wages: Hourly Earnings:* Source B index of salary and wage earnings in mining, quarrying, and electricity, base 1985. From January 1985 this index covers manufacturing only.

Industrial Production. Seasonally Adjusted: Source B index of industrial production, base 1990. *Industrial Employment:* Index constructed from source S data on employment in mining, manufacturing, electricity, gas, and water.

International Transactions: *Exports* and *Imports:* Total exports and imports, c.i.f. are from source B; newsprint export value is from source S data. *Imports, f.o.b.* are calculated from *Imports, c.i.f.* by applying a freight and insurance factor estimated for IFS.

Volume of Exports: Source B Paasche index of volume of exports, base 1980. Newsprint export volume is from source S. *Volume of Imports:* Source B Paasche index of volume of imports, base 1980.

Unit Value of Exports: Source B Laspeyres index of unit value of exports, base 1980. *Newsprint:* Source S value of exports of newsprint divided by quantity of newsprint exports. *Unit Value of Imports:* Source B Laspeyres index of unit value of imports, base 1980. *Import Prices:* Source B basic price index of domestic supply of imported goods, base 1985.

Government Finance: Monthly data are as reported by the Bank of Finland; debt data do not include the outstanding debt of the social security funds and selected extrabudgetary funds. Annual data are as reported in the *Government Finance Statistics Yearbook (GFSY)* and cover consolidated central government.

National Accounts: Source N. *Line 93i* includes a statistical discrepancy.

SAMPLE PAGE FROM *INTERNATIONAL FINANCIAL STATISTICS*

EXHIBIT 13.2 (continued)

| | 1996 | | 1997 | | | | 1996 | | | | 1997 | | | | | Finland |
I	II	III	IV	I	July	Aug	Sept	Oct	Nov	Dec	Jan	Feb	Mar	Apr		172

Billions of Markkaa — **National Accounts**

49.26	56.07	....	....	....	....	....	....	....	....	....	....	....	....	....	Exports of Goods & Services 90c
28.33	30.12	....	....	....	....	....	....	....	....	....	....	....	....	....	Government Consumption.................. 91f
21.48	19.67	....	....	....	....	....	....	....	....	....	....	....	....	....	Gross Fixed Capital Formation........ 93e
4.30	-2.50	....	....	....	....	....	....	....	....	....	....	....	....	....	Increase/Decrease(-) in Stocks 93i
74.04	76.55	....	....	....	....	....	....	....	....	....	....	....	....	....	Private Consumption 96f
-40.73	-39.56	....	....	....	....	....	....	....	....	....	....	....	....	....	Imports of Goods & Services 98c
136.68	140.34	....	....	....	....	....	....	....	....	....	....	....	....	....	Gross Domestic Product (GDP)....... 99b
122.24	125.50	....	....	....	....	....	....	....	....	....	....	....	....	....	Gross Dom. Prod. 1990 Prices...... 99b.*p*

Gabon
646

								1996			
	1990	1991	1992	1993	1994	1995	1996	II	III	IV	

Millions of US Dollars: Minus Sign Indicates Debit — **Balance of Payments**

	1990	1991	1992	1993	1994	1995	1996	II	III	IV	
78ald	167.7	74.8	-168.1	-49.1	319.7	....	....	....	....	....	Current Account, n.i.e.................... 78ald
78aad	2,488.8	2,227.9	2,259.2	2,326.2	2,349.4	....	....	....	....	....	Goods: Exports f.o.b.................... 78aad
78abd	-805.1	-861.0	-886.3	-845.1	-756.5	....	....	....	....	....	Goods: Imports f.o.b.................... 78abd
78acd	1,683.7	1,366.9	1,372.9	1,481.1	1,592.9	....	....	....	....	....	*Trade Balance* 78acd
78add	241.6	324.0	347.6	311.1	219.6	....	....	....	....	....	Services: Credit 78add
78aed	-1,006.6	-881.6	-924.8	-1,022.7	-812.1	....	....	....	....	....	Services: Debit 78aed
78afd	918.7	809.3	795.6	769.5	1,000.4	....	....	....	....	....	*Balance on Goods & Services....* 78afd
78agd	20.1	28.0	47.2	32.1	11.9	....	....	....	....	....	Income: Credit 78agd
78ahd	-636.7	-642.7	-868.9	-658.3	-569.0	....	....	....	....	....	Income: Debit 78ahd
78aid	302.0	194.6	-26.1	143.4	443.3	....	....	....	....	....	*Balance on Gds, Serv. & Inc....* 78aid
78ajd	58.9	44.0	51.4	48.0	59.3	....	....	....	....	....	Current Transfers, n.i.e.: Credit... 78ajd
78akd	-193.3	-163.8	-193.4	-240.5	-182.8	....	....	....	....	....	Current Transfers: Debit.............. 78akd
78bcd	—	—	—	—	....	....	....	....	....	....	Capital Account, n.i.e.................... 78bcd
78bad	—	—	—	—	....	....	....	....	....	....	Capital Account, n.i.e.: Credit... 78bad
78bbd	—	—	—	—	....	....	....	....	....	....	Capital Account: Debit................ 78bbd
78bjd	-398.3	-306.7	-218.7	-389.2	-506.7	....	....	....	....	....	Financial Account, n.i.e............... 78bjd
78bdd	-28.8	-14.9	-25.7	-2.5	-.7	....	....	....	....	....	Direct Investment Abroad........... 78bdd
78bed	73.5	-54.6	126.9	-113.7	-102.8	....	....	....	....	....	Dir. Invest. in Rep. Econ., n.i.e. . 78bed
78bfd	—	—	—	—	....	....	....	....	....	....	Portfolio Investment Assets 78bfd
78bkd	—	—	—	—	....	....	....	....	....	....	Equity Securities 78bkd
78bld	—	—	—	—	....	....	....	....	....	....	Debt Securities 78bld
78bgd	—	—	—	—	....	....	....	....	....	....	Portfolio Investment Liab., n.i.e.. 78bgd
78bmd	—	—	—	—	....	....	....	....	....	....	Equity Securities 78bmd
78bnd	—	—	—	—	....	....	....	....	....	....	Debt Securities 78bnd
78bhd	-285.1	-14.2	-27.2	-7.8	-258.8	....	....	....	....	....	Other Investment Assets 78bhd
78bod	....	....	....	....	....	....	....	....	....	....	Monetary Authorities................ 78bod
78bpd	—	—	—	—	....	....	....	....	....	....	General Government................. 78bpd
78bqd	10.0	.7	6.8	4.6	-40.9	....	....	....	....	....	Banks 78bqd
78brd	-295.0	-14.9	-34.0	-12.4	-217.9	....	....	....	....	....	Other Sectors 78brd
78bid	-157.8	-223.0	-292.8	-265.2	-144.3	....	....	....	....	....	Other Investment Liab., n.i.e. 78bid
78bsd	-31.8	-2.9	1.9	-6.4	-26.3	....	....	....	....	....	Monetary Authorities 78bsd
78btd	-187.7	-149.2	-236.1	-174.1	-133.1	....	....	....	....	....	General Government 78btd
78bud	29.0	11.3	-2.6	1.8	7.7	....	....	....	....	....	Banks 78bud
78bvd	32.6	-82.2	-55.9	-86.5	7.4	....	....	....	....	....	Other Sectors 78bvd
78cad	-38.0	8.6	-55.1	-13.6	6.7	....	....	....	....	....	Net Errors and Omissions 78cad
78cbd	-268.6	-223.3	-442.0	-451.9	-180.2	....	....	....	....	....	*Overall Balance*.......................... 78cbd
79dad	268.6	223.3	442.0	451.9	180.2	....	....	....	....	....	Reserves and Related Items 79dad
79dbd	-219.3	-54.0	246.3	67.5	-167.4	....	....	....	....	....	Reserve Assets............................ 79dbd
79dcd	-5.9	-19.4	-36.3	-35.9	40.9	....	....	....	....	....	Use of Fund Credit and Loans ... 79dcd
79ded	493.8	296.7	232.0	420.3	306.7	....	....	....	....	....	Exceptional Financing 79ded

Billions of Francs: Year Ending December 31 — **Government Finance**

	1990	1991	1992	1993	1994	1995	1996	II	III	IV	
80	50.9	-25.2	....	....	....	....	....	....	....	....	Deficit (-) or Surplus............................ 80
81	373.3	441.7	....	....	....	....	....	....	....	....	Revenue 81
81z	5.0	6.0	....	....	....	....	....	....	....	....	Grants Received 81z
82	326.7	465.5	....	....	....	....	....	....	....	....	Expenditure..................................... 82
83	.7	7.4	....	....	....	....	....	....	....	....	Lending Minus Repayments............ 83
											Financing
84a	-94.0	25.5	....	....	....	....	....	....	....	....	Domestic.. 84a
85a	43.0	-.3	....	....	....	....	....	....	....	....	Foreign... 85a

SAMPLE PAGE FROM *INTERNATIONAL FINANCIAL STATISTICS*

EXHIBIT 13.2 (continued)

Source: IMF *International Financial Statistics.*

Country Risk Service (published quarterly by Economist Intelligence Unit)

Country Risk Service gives two-year economic projections and risk assessments for more than 80 of the world's most highly indebted and developing countries. Its emphasis is on predicting growth, budget deficits, and current accounts. *Country Risk Service* is available online through LEXIS-NEXIS Services in the WORLD library (and several regional libraries) with the file name EIUCRS.

International Country Risk Guide (published monthly by Political Risk Services)

Written and edited in the U.K., *International Country Risk Guide* examines the politics, economic policy, financial conditions, and economic trends for 130 countries. It provides a current assessment and one-year forecast of political, financial, and economic risk. It is available online through LEXIS-NEXIS Services in the MARKET library with the file name

IACNWS. Historical data from the statistical tables is available on diskette.

Political Risk Yearbook (published annually by Political Risk Services)

Political Risk Services is the source of several publications on political risk including *Political Risk Yearbook*, *International Country Risk Guide* (described above), and *Country Forecasts*. *Political Risk Yearbook* is a six-volume set (in print or CD-ROM) covering 100 countries. It gives extensive economic, demographic, and social background for each country, with 18-month and five-year forecasts of risk to international business. *Country Forecasts* is a single volume published twice each year, summarizing current forecasts for 100 countries. Samples of Political Risk Services country forecasts are available on their Web site (http://www.polrisk.com or http://www.countrydata.com).

Competitiveness

International competitiveness is the ability of a national economy to achieve sustained high rates of economic growth, as measured by annual change in per-capita gross domestic product. Measuring competitiveness is difficult because it is a multifaceted concept involving both hard data such as balance of trade and soft data such as quality of management. Two current annual surveys of international competitiveness are the *World Competitiveness Yearbook* and the *Global Competitiveness Report*.

Global Competitiveness Report (published by the World Economic Forum, Geneva, Switzerland)

From 1989 to 1995, the World Economic Forum published their report in cooperation with the international Institute for Management Development (IMD) under the title *World Competitiveness Report*. In 1996, they assumed sole responsibility for the publication of *Global Competitiveness Report*.

The *Report* is based on quantitative data and survey data (2,000 responses from business leaders in 49 countries) collected and combined into one overall "Competitiveness Index" ranking by country. The information is arranged by eight factors of competitiveness:

- Openness of the economy to international trade and finance
- Role of the government budget and regulation
- Development of financial markets
- Quality of infrastructure
- Quality of technology
- Quality of business management

- Labor market flexibility
- Quality of judicial and political institutions

The information is further subdivided into 155 variables.

In addition to its "Competitiveness Index," the *Report* gives two additional indexes: a "Growth Ranking Index" that takes into account the country's initial income in predicting growth rates, and a "Market Growth Index" that predicts the share of the total world economic growth that will be accounted for by each country.

The *Report* contains country profiles that give individual country rankings on the eight factors of competitiveness, and a "national competitiveness balance sheet" that presents factors and subfactors in the form of assets and liabilities. It further provides country rankings on all 155 variables used in the study. The "technical notes and sources for quantitative data" given in an appendix provide insight into the methodology.

The World Competitiveness Yearbook (published by the Institute for Management Development, Lausanne, Switzerland)

The *Yearbook* is based on quantitative data and survey data (3,000 responses from CEOs and economic leaders representing 46 countries) collected and combined as a "World Competitiveness Scoreboard" ranking by country. The *Yearbook* information is also arranged by eight factors of competitiveness:

- Domestic economy
- Internationalization
- Government
- Finance
- Infrastructure
- Management
- Science and technology
- People

It is further subdivided into 230 variables.

The *Yearbook* provides competitiveness rankings by subgroups (OECD, non-OECD, European, G-7), by individual factors, and by individual variables. It also gives competitiveness profiles for all 46 countries. There are extensive appendixes listing sources and describing the methodology. Summary results from the *Yearbook* are available from the Institute for Management Development Web site (http://www.imd.ch).

Although the *Global Competitiveness Report* and the *World Competitiveness Yearbook* employ similar methodology, they use different factors and different weights to arrive at their rankings. It is not surprising that their rankings differ, as shown in Table 13.H. But there is often substantial agreement. Canada, ranked 8th by *Global* was ranked 12th by *World*. The two reports were in agreement in placing Russia in last place in the country rankings.

TABLE 13.H

COUNTRY RANKINGS IN *WORLD COMPETITIVENESS YEARBOOK 1996* (WORLD) AND *GLOBAL COMPETITIVENESS REPORT 1996* (GLOBAL)

Rank	*Global*	*World*
1	Singapore	United States
2	Hong Kong	Singapore
3	New Zealand	Hong Kong
4	United States	Japan
5	Luxembourg	Denmark
6	Switzerland	Norway
7	Norway	Netherlands
8	Canada	Luxembourg
9	Taiwan	Switzerland
10	Malaysia	Germany

Energy

The consumption and production of energy affects all aspects of economic life, but transportation and industry in particular. Statistics of energy typically include the following categories:

- Energy sources (e.g., coal, petroleum, natural gas, nuclear)
- Energy produced and consumed
- Energy prices
- Energy imports and exports

A confusing feature in the presentation of energy statistics is the variety of units used to express energy consumption and production. In addition to familiar units such as barrels of oil, energy use is expressed variously in quadrillion BTUs, tetra joules, and thousands of metric tons of coal equivalent. The UN, the OECD, the EU, and the U.S. Energy Information Administration all publish multinational data on energy.

Energy Statistics Yearbook (published annually by the UN)

This comprehensive compendium of energy statistics is designed to provide a global framework of comparable data on the supply of commercial forms of energy. Data for each type of fuel and aggregate data for all fuels are shown for individual countries and areas and are summarized into regional and world totals. The data are two years behind the date of publication.

Energy Prices and Taxes (published quarterly by the International Energy Agency)

The International Energy Agency is an autonomous body established within the OECD. In addition to OECD member countries, it includes statistics from the Czech Republic, Hungary, India, Poland, South Korea, and Taiwan. The publication contains country statistics on energy prices and taxes for all energy sources and main consuming sectors. Detailed country statistics are given in national currency. General country statistics are given in U.S. dollars. The publication is a convenient source of spot prices for oil and gasoline. It gives the most recent 18 months of data and annual data for the previous 17 years. The International Energy Agency also publishes the annual *Energy Statistics of OECD Countries*.

International Energy Annual (published annually by the U.S. Energy Information Administration)

This U.S. government publication presents current information on world energy production and consumption for petroleum, natural gas, coal, hydroelectric, and nuclear power. Trade and reserves are shown for petroleum, natural gas, and coal. Prices are given for major petroleum products. Country breakdowns are given by regions and for the 50 largest energy producers and consumers. In addition to its data, *International Energy Annual* is useful for its list of international sources of energy information. Data are one year behind publication date.

World Energy Outlook (published annually by the International Energy Agency)

Appearing since 1994, this work gives an overview of world energy markets, along with selected sectoral and regional analysis. Studies include the long-term outlook for countries of the former Soviet Union in the Middle East. *World Energy Outlook* contains extensive statistical appendixes that include historical data as well as projections of energy demands to 2010.

Electronic Sources

Many of the print sources for economics that we have described have electronic counterparts. The OECD, the UN, and the World Bank make much of their data available on magnetic disk and on diskettes. The International Monetary Fund publishes its data on CD-ROM as well as magnetic tape. Some of the risk services and country profile services have their text online through commercial databanks such as LEXIS-NEXIS Services and DataStar.

The EU provides access to more than one million macroeconomic time series through their CRONOS databank. Another EU databank is COMEXT, which contains statistics on trade between the member states and their trade with non-EU countries. Both the CRONOS and COMEXT databases are available in the U.S. through the WEFA system. A small part of the WEFA database is available on DIALOG as *EconBase* (File 565). It has economic time series, as well as some projections on key variables, from about 15 countries. The EU-sponsored ECHO (European Commission Host Organization) databases are accessible through the Internet. Their Internet address is http://www2.echo.lu/echo/lu/home.html. There is no charge for access, although you must obtain a password. ECHO has about 20 databases, most of which deal with research and development issues.

The data sets of the OECD, the UN, the World Bank, and the IMF are retrievable online through commercial time-sharing systems. A comprehensive source of this material is Data Resources (DRI). DRI makes available the data series from the OECD's *National Accounts* and *Main Economic Indicators*, and the IMF's *Direction of Trade* and *International Financial Statistics*. In addition, DRI maintains several regional and country economic databases based on data from national sources, central banks, and trade organizations. These include the Nikkei macroeconomic statistics database from Japan, the DRI developing countries database, and the DRI European database. DRI also makes available economic forecasts, with quarterly updates for 50 countries and seven regions, including a world forecast.

Another commercial source for online economic data is Datastream. Datastream includes national government series from each of the G-7 countries plus Australia, Hong Kong, and Taiwan, as well as IMF and OECD statistics. These series include statistics on labor, trade, prices, industrial activities, finances, exchange rates, balance of payments, and national accounts. Datastream has the entire data set of the Deutsches Bundesbank (the German central bank), some 15,000 individual series of data from this source alone.

ADDITIONAL SOURCES

Numerous additional sources of international economic statistics are described below.

Europe in Figures, 4th ed., 1995 (published by Eurostat)

A compendium of statistics and narrative descriptions on all aspects of the EU: history, political organiza-

tion, finances, demographics, industry, economics, and international relations.

OECD Economies at a Glance: Structural Indicators (OECD, 1996)

Presents data illustrating the structure and performance of economies of OECD members. The report draws on a wide array of OECD data sources to present statistics on specific structural areas (e.g., labor markets, public finance, and social services), as well as general indicators of living standards and price levels. It is a convenient source of some unusual or difficult-to-find time-series data. These include:

- Measures of income inequality (using Gini coefficients and the Atkinson Index)
- Non-employment rates
- Real compensation per employee (using purchasing power parities)
- Survival rates of new firms
- Import penetration rates and export intensities for manufacturing industries

IBIS Briefing Service (published monthly by Charles D. Spencer & Associates)

IBIS (International Benefits Information Service) publishes a 50-page monthly newsletter that gives brief descriptions of news relating to benefits worldwide. Arranged by country, the service includes stories on medical benefits, labor relations, social security, payroll taxes, pension plans, unemployment insurance, and retirement.

International Economic Trends (published quarterly by the St. Louis Federal Reserve Bank)

International Economic Trends presents economic data for the G-7 countries. It gives annual rates of change for GDP, GDP deflator, and CPI for the previous 20 quarters. In addition, the publications includes tables of cross-country comparisons for interest rates, stock market indexes, employment growth, unemployment rates, and indexes of leading indicators.

International Economic Scoreboard: Long-Term Outlook (The Conference Board)

This newsletter features a section (International Survey of Long-Term Economic Forecasts) that gives three-year projections of real GDP, consumer prices, and short-term interest rates for approximately 25 nations.

Monitoring the World Economy 1820–1992 (Angus Maddison, OECD, Paris, 1995)

For the researcher who needs the "big picture" in economics, *Monitoring the World Economy 1820–1992* will provide the data. Here you will find a statistical overview of the whole period of modern capitalist development, from 1820 to 1992. The book develops the data for 56 countries accounting for 93% of world output and 87% of world population in 1992. Statistical series include population, GDP and per capita GDP, world trade, employment, working hours, labor production, births per 100 population, life expectancy, and educational levels. In addition, it gives estimates of GDP, population, and per capita GDP for 143 non-sample countries for the period from 1950 to 1990. The work provides a detailed description of its methodology together with sources of information.

Table 13.I will give an indication of the time range of the economic statistics presented.

TABLE 13.I

HISTORICAL WORLD ECONOMIC PERFORMANCE

	1500	1820	1992
World GDP (billion 1990 $)	240	695	27,995
GDP Per Capita (1990 $)	565	651	5,145
World Exports (billion 1990 $)	n.a.	7	3,786

Russian Economic Trends (published quarterly by Whurr, with monthly updates)

This analysis of the Russian economy is produced by the Centre for Economic Reform, Government of the Russian Federation, with the assistance of the Centre for Economic Performance, London School of Economics. Based on Russian published and unpublished sources, it provides a discussion of Russian economic strategy and of the main measures of economic activity (e.g., budget, money, prices, wages, consumer expenditures, production and investment, foreign trade, employment, and privatization). The statistical appendix contains data on economic variables that is difficult to find elsewhere. These include industrial production, money expenditures of the population, retail sales, capital investment, consumer price indices, wages, and daily exchange rates.

PlanEcon Report (published irregularly by PlanEcon, Inc.)

Subtitled *Developments in the Economies of Eastern Europe and the Former USSR*, this weekly report combines official data sources with estimates by the PlanEcon staff. Each quarter, the publication presents a comparative risk assessment for the emerging markets of Eastern Europe and the former Soviet republics. PlanEcon also publishes two annuals (*Review* and *Outlook*), which include four-year forecasts of economic developments in Eastern Europe and the former Soviet Republics. The data series in *PlanEcon* are available through the DRI database system.

World Factbook (published annually by the U.S. Central Intelligence Agency)

The *World Factbook* includes one-page economic, social, political, and demographic descriptions for every nation in the world, plus descriptions of dependent areas (e.g., Puerto Rico). The *World Factbook* also describes areas such as the West Bank and Antarctica. Particularly useful is the one-page summary for "The World." Here are estimates of many hard-to-find economic and demographic aggregates, including "gross world product" (an estimated $31 trillion in 1994), world unemployment, world inflation, world literacy, and world infant mortality. In an appendix, the *World Factbook* includes capsule descriptions of formal and informal international organizations. The *World Factbook* is available in print, microfiche, magnetic tape, and diskettes. It is available as a time-sharing database through the Internet. It is also included in the *National Trade Data Bank*.

NBER Macrohistory Database (National Bureau of Economic Research)

This extensive data set is useful for its coverage of pre–World War One and the interwar period. It includes monthly, quarterly, and annual statistics for many economic series, including prices, foreign trade, income and employment, security markets, interest rates, money and banking, and leading indicators. The data set has some coverage of the U.K., France, and Germany, although it predominantly covers the United States. An example of the depth of coverage is its series of monthly statistics from 1866 to 1969 of total United States exports. The *NBER Macrohistory Database* is available from http://www.nber.org.

OECD Input-Output Database (OECD, 1995)

Presents the input-output database of the OECD covering 10 OECD member countries (Australia, Canada, Denmark, France, Germany, Italy, Japan, the Netherlands, the United Kingdom, and the United States). It gives statistics for several time points from the early 1970s to 1990, using a common industrial classification based on the ISIC revision 2 (36 sectors).

CONCLUSION

In this chapter, we have examined some of the issues concerning the use of international economic statistics. We included in our discussion national finance, labor statistics, and energy, as well as standard macroeconomic topics such as national accounts. Economic data are usually collected by individual countries. The methods of data collection and definitions of terms vary greatly among nations. International organizations, such as the World Bank and the IMF, are beginning to change their methods of comparing national output. For these reason, use caution when making cross-border economic comparison.

NOTES

1. Joel F. Houston, "The Underground Economy a Troubling Issue for Policymakers," *Business Review* (Federal Reserve Bank of Philadelphia), (September/October 1987): 3–12.

2. "No Room for the Faint-Hearted," *Euromoney* (March 1989): 71.

3. *Statistical Abstracts of the U.S.,* 1995: 836.

4. "Russian Statistics: Magic Numbers," *The Economist* (August 29, 1992): 63.

5. "McCurrencies: Where's the Beef?" *Economist* (April 27, 1996): 82.

6. *Purchasing Power Parities and Real Expenditures,* Paris: Organization for Economic Co-operation and Development, 1992: 5.

7. "How the Nations Rank," *Fortune* (July 27, 1992): 68.

8. "For Richer, for Poorer," *The Economist* (March 18, 1995): 9.

9. *ILO Statistical Sources and Methods,* vol. 6: "Household Income and Expenditure Surveys," Geneva: International Labour Office, 1990.

CHAPTER 14
Industry Information

TOPICS COVERED:

- Coding and Structure of Industries
- Researching Industries
- Sources of Industry Statistics
- Industry and Country Average: Ratios
- Selected Supplemental Sources

MAJOR SOURCES DISCUSSED

- *Encyclopedia of Associations—International Organizations*
- *Panorama of EU Industry*
- *International Yearbook of Industrial Statistics*
- *Industrial Structure Statistics*
- *Services: Statistics on Value Added and Employment*
- *FAO Yearbook: Production*

In preceding chapters, we discussed product codes, rankings, and market share. These aspects of industry analysis focus on individual companies. This chapter examines the concepts and sources that address industries and their structure. Practical applications for industry analysis include company intelligence, financial and economic analysis, exporting, and marketing.

We may be interested in a global industry:

What is the structure of the steel industry?

We may be interested in many industries in many countries:

What service industries are growing fastest in the EU?

We may be interested in one industry in one country:

What is the outlook for the British plastics industry?

In this chapter, we use the term "industry" to refer to all categories of economic activity. Described on the basis of the U.S. Standard Industrial Code (SIC), we are interested in industries grouped under major categories (one-digit level), major groups (two-digit level), industry groups (three-digit level), and finally industries themselves (four-digit level).

The definition of an industry for U.S. SIC classification is a group of establishments primarily engaged in the same activity, that meets a criterion of economic significance based on number of establishments, employment, payroll, value added, and value of shipments or receipts.

According to Michael Porter, "an industry (whether product or service) is a group of competitors producing products or services that compete directly with each other."[1]

Older descriptions of industry centered on "manufacturing." The EU gets around this double meaning of industry by using the term "sector" in its classification scheme, NACE. NACE, established by Eurostat in 1970, is the official general industrial classification of the economic activities within the EU. The NACE system divides economic activity into 10 broad sectors (one digit), subdivided into more detailed classes (two digits), and further divided into groups (three digits) or subgroups (four digits), and finally into items (five digits). NACE is most often applied at the enterprise level.

| Sector—Transport equipment | NACE 35/36 |
| Subsector—Aerospace equipment | NACE 364 |

The manufacturing sectors often are covered more completely in sources listing "industrial" statistics. It is far easier to find worldwide statistics on the steel industry than the recreation industry. However, as non-manufacturing economic activity continues to grow in value and employment, the statistical collection and reporting mechanisms probably will improve.

When we are evaluating sources of industry information, we need to be aware of three general concepts.

1. At what level of business activity is the data being collected; for example, establishment or enterprise?
2. At what level of aggregation is the industry being defined? one-digit? four-digit?
3. What is being measured?

In gathering and reporting data, agencies make distinctions between physical entities such as "establishments" (local economic units), and "enterprises" (legal entities). They also make distinctions between industry data and product data. These distinctions are based on how the data is collected and reported.

In the U.S., the Economic Census data is collected at the establishment or local unit level. An establishment is usually one physical location engaged predominately in one type of economic activity. For example, consider a U.S. textile manufacturing establishment (U.S. SIC 23) that produces both men's shirts (2321) and women's shirts (2322). If 60% of the value added in the manufacturing of the products comes from women's shirts, this establishment is classified in industry 2322, and *all* value added and employment from this establishment is included in SIC 2322.

Product level data refers to the total value of the product, wherever the activity occurs. For example, if the sale of meat (SIC 5411) is 11% of a grocery establishment's sales and 67% of a butcher store's sales (5421), the sales from both establishments will be included in the product level value of meat sales. Statistics from official bodies are often at the enterprise or establishment level, rather than the product level.

CODING AND STRUCTURE OF INDUSTRIES

Coding of Industries

Coding systems usually group industries in a hierarchy. At the top of the hierarchy are the "major industry groups." Some sources of industry data divide companies into three groups: manufacturing, service, and trading. "Trading" companies are in either wholesale or retail trade.

A more detailed industry classification is seen in the Worldscope and CIFAR financial services. They group companies by industry class according to differences in accounting practices. Groups such as industrials, transportation, utilities, banking, and insurance each have a distinct financial template. Worldscope further subdivides industries by group (e.g., aerospace) and then by U.S. SIC Code. An example of a classification for an individual company in Worldscope would look like the listing below.

AMSTRAD PLC

INDUSTRY CLASS: INDUSTRIAL

MAJOR INDUSTRY GROUP: ELECTRONICS

MINOR INDUSTRY GROUP: DIVERSIFIED ELECTRONICS

INDUSTRY AVERAGE CATEGORY: ELECTRONICS—UNITED KINGDOM

Three standard coding systems are used by most providers of international industry data: the U.S. SIC Codes and the two major international systems, the EU's NACE and the UN's International Standard Industrial Classification (ISIC). Outlines for these systems are given in Table 14.A. Note the similarity between NACE and the ISIC. Many countries also have their own individual systems.

NACE classifies economic activity on the basis of the goods and services produced, or by the nature of the production process employed. NACE was officially revised in late 1990. The revision will be used for data collection within the next few years.

The original version of the International Standard Industrial Classification of All Economic Activities was adopted in 1948. It is used by the United Nations to classify data according to kind of economic activity in fields such as production and employment. The latest revision was 1989.

These coding schemes are designed to describe the business activity within a country; therefore, they differ from the Harmonized System of Codes (HS Codes) and the SITC system described in Chapter 15 on international trade, which classify goods traded among countries. Annex IV in the 1991 *Industrial Statistics Yearbook* (published in 1993) is a preliminary table of correspondence among ISIC-based codes, SITC, and HS Codes.

Table 14.B illustrates the different codes assigned by SIC, NACE, and ISIC to two product classes. Definitions differ among the coding systems for "Spinning and Weaving."

TABLE 14.A

INDUSTRY CLASSIFICATION SCHEMES

U.S. SIC Division		EU NACE Sector		UN ISIC Major Division	
01	Agriculture, forestry & fishing				
10	Mining	1	Energy and water	1	Agriculture, forestry & fishing
15	Construction				
20–39	Manufacturing	2	Extraction & processing of non-energy-producing minerals & derivatives	2	Mining and quarrying
		3	Metal Manufacture	3	Manufacturing
40	Transport, communications electric, gas & sanitary services	4	Other manufacturing	4	Electricity, Gas and Water
50	Wholesale Trade	5	Building & Civil engineering	5	Construction
52	Retail Trade				
60	Finance, insurance & real estate	6	Distributive Trade, hotel catering, repairs	6	Wholesale & Retail Trade; Restaurants and Hotels
70–80	Services and	7	Transport & Communication	7	Transport, Storage Communication
		8	Banking & Finance: Insurance, business services, renting	8	Financing, Insurance Real Estate and Business Services
90	Public Administration and	9	Other Services	9	Community, Social Personal services
9999	Nonclassifiable				

TABLE 14.B

SAMPLE CODING WITH U.S. SIC, NACE, AND ISIC

	SIC	NACE	ISIC
Textile Mills	22	43	321
Spinning & weaving *	228	434	3211
Chemicals	28	25	35
Industrial Chemicals	281	251	351
Pharmaceutical	2834	257	3522

*Definitions differ

The level of coding used by a researcher should be appropriate to the needs of the analysis. Economist Michael Porter, for one, believes that a grouping such as "banking" or "chemicals" is too broad to be useful strategically or for practical applications.

The definitions of industries and products are different for each of the international and national classification schemes. Euromonitor warns that comparisons among product classification codes are difficult. While trade statistics now conform to an international classification scheme, product statistics do not and are not compatible, either with the country's own trade statistics or with industry figures for other countries.[2]

Table 14.C lists the codes used by European countries for industries and products. An extensive classification concordance is available on the WWW (http://intrepid.mgmt.purdue.edu/Jon/Data/Trade Concordances.html#FromSITC). This concordance includes cross classifications of ISIC, SITC, U.S. SIC, Canadian SIC, HS Codes, and NACE.

Structure of Industries

The structure of an industry is often of interest to researchers. Some of the questions concerning industry structure are:

> *What is the scope of the industry? Is it global or domestic?*
>
> *How does the industry contribute to the GNP/ GDP of a country?*
>
> *What is the relationship between large and small enterprises in the industry?*

When companies in an industry compete worldwide, the industry is described as "global." Automobiles and semiconductors are in this category. Other industries, because of the nature of their products or services, are domestic. Competition among companies in a domestic industry is within the nation. When we examine industry structure, we often are using data that measure an activity within one country. European sources, however, include trade data as a part of their industry data.

One point of interest in examining industry structure is the contribution of the industry to the economy. Table 14.D measures the percent each industry group contributed to total manufacturing in four countries.

TABLE 14.C

INDUSTRY AND PRODUCT CLASSIFICATION SYSTEMS USED IN SELECTED EUROPEAN COUNTRIES

Country	Industry Code	Product Code
Belgium	NACE	Import/Export:HS
Denmark	ISIC	Import/Export:HS
	DSE (Danmarks Statistiks Occupational Classification	
France	A.P.E. (Activité Principale Exercée) Production: NAP (Nomenclature des Activités et Produits)	Import/Export:HS
Germany	WZ (Systematik der deutschen Wirtschaftszweige - Statistishes Bundesamt) Production:GP (System-atisches Guterverzeichnis fur die Produktion)	Import/Export:HS
Ireland	Production:NACE	Import/Export:SITC
Italy	Repertorio Merceologico Codice Attivita	Import/Export:HS
Netherlands	SIC Codes	Import/Export:HS
Spain	NACE	Import/Export:HS
UK	UK SIC	Import/Export:HS

Source: Karen Beesley, "Researching European Markets," presented at the London Business School, December 11, 1992.

TABLE 14.D

STRUCTURE OF MANUFACTURING INDUSTRIES (1990)

	Percent of contribution to total manufacturing			
	U.S.	Japan	U.K.	W. Germany
Food	14.5	10.2	15.8	11.7
Textiles	4.9	4.2	5.0	4.4
Wood	3.1	2.5	3.1	2.8
Paper	9.9	6.6	8.7	NA
Chemical	19.9	14.2	18.9	NA
Nonmetal	2.3	3.3	3.9	2.8
Basic metal	4.7	7.4	5.4	5.5
Machinery	39.5	50.2	38.2	47.5
Other	1.2	1.4	1.0	0.5

Source: From OECD *Industrial Structure Statistics* 1990 and unpublished data in *Statistical Abstracts of the U.S.* 1995, Table No. 1395, 865.

Another useful concept for industry analysis is "industry concentration." It shows the degree to which large companies dominate an industry. Industry concentration is measured by a "concentration ratio," the percentage of total business in an industry that is handled by a specified number of the largest firms. Concentration ratios are often expressed as the percentage of sales, assets, or profits accounted for by the 3–20 largest firms in an industry.

For example, the top 6% of the companies in the European transport equipment sector account for 94% of the sales. For the precast concrete industry, however, small to medium-size production units still dominate.[3]

A knowledge of the geographical distribution of establishments helps us understand the structure of an industry, especially on a global scale. Some industries are concentrated in particular countries. For example, more than 85% of EU production of transport equipment is concentrated in four countries.[4]

Table 14.E shows the geographic concentration of several industries (based on export value in 1985).

TABLE 14.E

GEOGRAPHIC CONCENTRATION OF INDUSTRIES

Industry	Country	Share of Total World Exports
Aircraft	USA	77.5
Building Stones	Italy	62.6
Motorcycles	Japan	82.0
Rotary Printing Presses	Germany	51.1
Rough Unsorted Diamonds	Switzerland	89.3

Source: Michael Porter, *Competition Among Nations;* appendix.

RESEARCHING INDUSTRIES

Research for U.S. industry information might begin with Gale's *Encyclopedia of Associations* for its list of industry organizations and publications. For aggregate industry data, the "Industrial Outlook" tables in the *U.S. Statistical Abstract* is a good source. For major U.S. industries with large publicly traded companies, we might turn to Standard & Poor's *Industry Surveys.* For detailed industry statistics, we could use the quinquinnial Economic Census data or the *Annual Survey of Manufacturers.* International industry research could follow a similar path.

Encyclopedia of Associations—International Organizations (published annually by Gale)

Multinational and non-U.S. national associations can be found in Gale's *Encyclopedia of Associations—International Organizations,* which lists more than 11,000 associations located in more than 180 geographical areas. It is available as a two-volume set, as part of File 114 on DIALOG, and on the CD-ROM produced by Gale Research. Table 14.F gives some examples of the range of associations and publications represented in this source.

Industry information is available in a variety of statistical sources and in scattered analytic reports written by international government bodies, private publishers, or investment banks.

Statistical information is compiled and published by such international organizations as the UN, the World Bank, the Organization for European Cooperation and Development (OECD), and the EU, as well as by industry associations, individual countries, and private organizations. The best source to locate statistics from international organizations is the *Index to International Statistics,* described in Chapter 1.

Several useful measurements that are in any industry source, regardless of the publisher and the countries described, include:

- How many (number of establishments)
  Total number
  Number by size, arranged by employees or value
  Number by geographic breakdown
  Number of employees
- How much (value of shipments/receipts)
  Value added
  Payroll
- How good (production indexes)
  Price indexes
  Productivity measures

Panorama of EU Industry (published annually by the Office for Official Publications of the European Communities)

Panorama of EU Industry is the key source to EU industry information and should be owned by all libraries that receive questions about European indus-

TABLE 14.F

SAMPLE INDUSTRY ASSOCIATIONS AND PUBLICATIONS IN GALE'S *ENCYCLOPEDIA OF ASSOCIATIONS—INTERNATIONAL ORGANIZATIONS*

INDUSTRY	PUBLICATION
INTERNATIONAL:	
International Federation of Fruit Juice Producers	*International Directory of Fruit Juices, periodic
REGIONAL:	
East African Tea Trade Association	* East African Trade Assn. biennial. Directory.
Caribbean Assocation of Industry and Commerce	* *Business Wave* (in English) Quarterly
COUNTRY:	
Bangladesh Jute Spinners Association	* Annual report (Bengali) Spinners News (English), monthly
Government of Israel Economic Mission	* *Business Opportunities from Israel,* Monthly

try and services. Prepared by Eurostat, the Statistical Office of the European Union, and first published in 1989, *Panorama* covers 125 major industry sectors. It gives an overview of manufacturing and service sectors in the European Union. The special issues chapter examines the global scene. Industry reviews provide microeconomic surveys for each sector, covering production, employment, trade, and structural changes, with detailed statistical data and forecasts. The 1994 edition was written during the second and third quarters of 1993. Time series cover the period 1983–1992. There are bimonthly supplements.

Panorama of EU Industry uses the NACE coding system. However, some of the service sectors do not have codes. *Panorama* is primarily focused on the 3-digit level. The three main sources of data and analysis are Eurostat, DEBA (Data for European Business Analysis), and professional trade associations.

Transport Equipment is an example of a sector described in *Panorama*. It covers the following subsectors shown below.

	NACE numbers
Motor Vehicles	351–352
Motor Vehicle Parts & Accessories	353
Shipbuilding	361
Railway rolling stock	362
Mopeds and motorcycles	363
Aerospace equipment	364

Manufacturing industry tables in general include main indicators, trends in EU exports and imports, share of employment and production by country, largest companies in the EU, and a five-year forecast.

Table 14.G lists the tables that are included in the *Panorama of EU Industry* for the 1994 Aerospace equipment sector:

TABLE 14.G

STATISTICAL TABLES IN *EU PANORAMA*

Table	Time	Data Element
1: Main indicators	1983-92 1993 estimate	Apparent consumption Net export Trade balance Employment
2: Breakdown of sales	1991	Aircraft+missles Engines Equipment Space Total
3: Average and real annual growth rates		Apparent consumption Production Extra-EC exports Extra-EC imports
4: EC external trade (current prices)	1983-92	Extra EC-exports Extra EC-imports Trade Balance Ratio exports/imports Terms of trade Index Intra EC-Trade Share of total imports(%)
5: Labor productivity and unit costs	1983,1992	Productivity (thousands ECU) Productivity Index Unit labor cost index Total unit costs index
6: 10 Leading European companies	1992	Ranked by sales Aerospace Sales Total sales Net Profit Aerospace employees Total employees
7: Expected real annual growth rates		Apparent consumption Production Extra-EC exports

Industry and Development: Global Report (Vienna: United Nations Industrial Development Organization, 1985; published irregularly)

UNIDO's *Industry and Development: Global Report* provides an overview of industrialization and industrial performance in 10 regions of the world, as well as industry surveys for manufacturing industry groups. The 1993/94 report analyzes the industries listed below.

A.	Cocoa processing
B.	Seafood processing
C.	Market pulp
D.	Copper processing
E.	Petrochemicals
F.	Fine chemicals
G.	Higher value-added steel
H.	Advanced materials
I.	Semiconductor industry
J.	Power generating equipment
K.	Fertilizer equipment
L.	Industrial lift trucks
M.	Numerically controlled machine tools

The industry surveys are based on ISIC codes. For example, "Market pulp" covers ISIC 341101–341116 and draws on data from industry publications, in this case Pulp and Paper International's *Fact and Price Book*. Data includes production by country, prices, international trade, capacity and capacity utilization, worldwide market share, and environmental considerations. A separate table lists recent and proposed company capacity expansions. For the industries included, these are useful summary surveys.

Industry and Development contains a Statistical Annex, "World Industry Development Indicators." It provides full-page reports on 104 countries. Each report contains a diagram of industrial structural change, graphs of GDP and MVA (manufacturing value added) growth, and tabular data. The tables include manufacturing value added (in millions of dollars) for 28 industries, manufacturing profitability, productivity, and structural indices.

Unfortunately, there is no good international parallel to Standard & Poor's *Industry Surveys*.

SOURCES OF INDUSTRY STATISTICS

International Sources

For over 30 years, the United Nations has supplied detailed annual compilations of statistics on world industry. The first seven editions were entitled *The Growth of World Industry*, the 1974–81 editions were called *Yearbook of Industrial Statistics*, and the 1982–94 editions were called *Industrial Statistics Yearbook*. Formerly a two-volume set, the series was continued in 1995 by two single-volume publications: the *Industrial Commodity Statistics Yearbook* and the *International Yearbook of Industrial Statistics*.

Industrial Commodity Statistics Yearbook (published annually by the United Nations)

The *Industrial Commodity Statistics Yearbook*, published in 1995, contains 10-year time series of annual quantity data on production of 530 industrial commodities by country, geographic region, economic grouping, and for the world. Most refer to the 10-year period 1984–93 for about 200 countries. Part two presents data by country on apparent consumption of about 200 industrial commodities for 1985–93.

International Yearbook of Industrial Statistics (published annually by the United Nations Industrial Development Organization)

The *Yearbook* provides statistical indicators of the manufacturing sector for more than 100 counties. The *Yearbook* answers such questions as:

> *What is the average number of employees engaged in the rubber industry in Malaysia?*
>
> *How are "wages and salaries" defined in Israel?*
>
> *What is the share of women employed in the textile industry in Kenya?*

The *Yearbook* consists of two parts. Part I deals with the manufacturing sector as a whole, presenting such statistics as the distribution of worldwide manufacturing value added and rankings of countries by value added for individual products. Part II consists of country tables presenting data on manufacturing production and employment arranged by three- and four-digit SITC number. Number of establishments, number of employees, wages and salaries, output, value added, index numbers of industrial production, and gross fixed capital formation are the typical data items reported.

Each measurement is defined in the introduction. For example, the United Nations makes a distinction among number of persons engaged, employees, and operatives.

The coding system used in the present version is a three-digit ISIC, supplemented by several four-digit groups. For most countries, data is collected at the establishment level while in East European countries, it is collected for the enterprise.

The data has been collected by questionnaire from a central agency in each country in the survey. For example, the data from Malaysia, except the indices, is based on the *Annual Survey of Manufacturing Industries* supplied by the Jabatan Perangkaan (Department of Statistics), Kuala Lumpur (see Exhibit 14.1). The concepts, definitions, and classifications by branches of industry are generally according to United Nations standards.

ISIC-BASED CODE
3844-04   Bicycles—Cycles

Unit:Thousand Units   unite:en milliers

Country or area	1984	1985	1992	1993
America North	6 241	6 197	6 310	6 314 Amérique du Nord
Asia	44 591	449431	75 195	77 702 Asie
Bangladesh (2)	26	20	17	13 Bangladesh
China	28 614	32 277	40 836	41 496 Chine
Bulgaria	94	90	65	24 Bulgarie
Belarus			724	603 Bélarus

(2) Twelve months ending on June 30 of year stated

INDUSTRIAL COMMODITY STATISTICS YEARBOOK

EXHIBIT 14.1

Source: Industrial Commodity Statistics Yearbook 1993, Commodity Production Statistics: 856; annual data from 1984-93: 272.

Millions of MK	Table FN.2	FINLAND		(Current Prices) p48 VALUE ADDED	
		1984	1985	1992	1993
31	Food, Beverages & Tobacco	9,940	8,899	13,087	13,601
311,2	Food	8,345	7,331	10, 166	10,548
313	Beverages	1,263	1,280	2,363	2,518
314	Tobacco	332	287	559	536
32	Textiles,Apparel & Leather	5,197	4,869	2,772	2,837
321	Textiles	1,889	1,766	1,306	1,404
3213	Knitting mills	688	621	469	517
322	Wearing Apparel	2,431	2,316	1,027	987
323	Leather & Products	246	234	155	158
324	Footwear	621	554	283	288
33	Wood Product & Furniture	5,985	5,623	5,844	6,518
39	Other Manufacturing nes	612	630	697	769
3901	Jewelry	153	128	175	164
3000	Total Manufacturing	79,772	80,003	90,926	98,867
1000	Agri., Hunt.,Forest.,Fish	—	—	—	—
2000	Mining & Quarrying	1,341	1,262	1,392	1,313
3000	Total Manufacturing	79,772	80,003	90,926	98,867
4000	Electricity,Gas & Water	9,387	9,319	12,485	12,619
5000	Construction	—	—	—	—
6.90	Services	—	—	—	—
0000	Grand Total	90,500	90,584	104,803	112,798

EXTRACT FROM OECD INDUSTRIAL STRUCTURE STATISTICS

EXHIBIT 14.2

Source: OECD Industrial Structure Statistics, 1993: 44.

Manufacturing Worldwide (edited by Arsen J. Darnay and published by Gale Research, 1995)

Subtitled *Industry Analyses, Statistics, Products, and Leading Companies and Countries*, this source derives the bulk of its data from the United Nations, the same data that is used to prepare the UN's *International Yearbook of Industrial Statistics* and *Industrial Commodity Statistics Yearbook*. An advantage for the U.S. researcher is that country currencies are translated into U.S. dollars.

Regional Sources

Industrial Structure Statistics (published annually by OECD)

The 1993 edition was published in 1995 (see Exhibit 14.2 for an extract). Classification is by ISIC, Revision 2. The annual is supplemented by the quarterly *Indicators of Industrial Activity*. It can answer the following type of questions:

How many person-hours were employed in the Norwegian chemical industry in 1989?

How does that compare with Germany?

The data are presented in two sections. Section one contains industrial survey data collected from national statistical organizations' samples. It also includes foreign trade data derived from customs figures. Twenty-one member states are represented in this section.

Section two gives estimates from national accounts, disaggregated by industry. OECD refers to this as the "top down" approach. Eight member states are represented in this section. Only five countries, Denmark, Iceland, Finland, Norway, and Sweden, are represented in both.

Industrial Structure Statistics contains an individual listing for each country, giving the country's industrial classification system and sources of industrial data. All series published are available on magnetic tape and on a $350 diskette.

As many as 15 data items are presented for each of the OECD countries, with up to 10 years of data. However, not all items are reported for each country, and very few countries have 10 years' worth of data. The data items collected from 1984–93 are shown below.

```
    PRODUCTION
    VALUE ADDED
    EMPLOYMENT
    EMPLOYEES
    INVESTMENT
    INVESTMENT - m&e
    WAGES & SALARIES
    SUPPLEMENTS TO W & S
    SOCIAL COSTS
    ESTABLISHMENTS*
    MANHOURS*
    EXPORTS - current prices
    IMPORTS - current prices
    EXPORTS - 80 prices
    IMPORTS - 80 prices

    *Collected from 1985–1989
    m&e - machinery and equipment
```

Industry Statistical Yearbook (published annually by the Statistical Office of the European Communities)

First published in 1985, this Eurostat compilation covers industries in EU, U.S., and Japan. The object of the yearbook is to provide a "clear and comprehensive" overview of industry in the EU, to present a picture of industrial activity and structure in the community and its member states, and compare it with the U.S. and Japan. The questions it can answer include:

What has been the trend in motor vehicle production in France between 1970 and 1988?

How many workers in Stuttgart are employed in the food, drink, and tobacco industry?

Data is derived from a variety of sources, such as social statistics, Integrated Economic Accounts, and OECD publications.

The publication is divided into 8 chapters, each of which has several tables, arranged by country. Chapter headings are:

Industry in the European Community, the USA and Japan
Employment in Industry
Structure and Activity of Industry
Data by Size of Enterprise
Industrial Products: Production and External Trade
Regional Industrial Statistics
Energy and Raw Materials

The *Yearbook* is updated monthly by *Industrial Trends*. These EU industry publications are based on data supplied by member states. Part A has harmonized statistics on the following sectors: textiles; leather and footwear; pulp, paper, and board; data-processing equipment; domestic electrical appliances; mechanical engineering products; and electric and electronic construction. Part B has non-harmonized data from the mining, chemical, transport equipment, food, and drink industries.

Industrial Trends includes macro-level data and graphs for the EU and for countries in the EU, with the U.S. and Japan included for comparison. It has production and price indices for capital goods, intermediate goods, and consumer goods. It also has production indices, turnover, and number of employees for major industry sectors.

Results of the Business Survey Carried out among Managements in the Community (published monthly by the Commission of the European Community)

This survey measures the expectations of members of the EU manufacturing and mining community. Started in 1962, the publication surveys 20,000 enterprises each month, using a harmonized questionnaire across the EU.

Each month, respondents are asked whether they expect production trends, production expectations, and selling price expectations to go up, down, or to be unchanged. They are also asked if they expect order-books, export order-books, and stocks of finished products to be normal, above normal, or below normal. Additional questions about employment, new orders, and capacity are asked quarterly. This survey does not publish industrial statistics and presents survey responses as percentages.

For example, in November 1995, 59% of the Dutch respondents thought production trends would be unchanged. Of the remaining 41%, 22% expected production trends to go up while 19% expected it to go down, for a net balance of 3% up.

Selected Industry-Specific Sources from International Organizations

We will examine several examples of specific industry sources from a variety of governmental organizations including Eurostat, UNCTAD, and the OECD.

Steel is an industry that is monitored by both the United Nations and the European Union. In fact, the United Nations publishes two serials specifically about steel.

Steel Market in . . . and Prospects for . . . has been published annually since 1953 by the United Nations Economic Commission for Europe (ECE). It is a review of the steel market, with analysis of international developments and national developments. Information is based on statistics from governments, oral statements, and the work of the ECE Steel Committee. There are more than 20 individual country reports and regional and worldwide data.

> *What is the trend in steel consumption in the Czech Republic?*
>
> *How many tons of steel were used in the manufacture of private cars in Czechoslovakia in 1993?*

At the country level, there are four years of data with general economic trends, trends in iron and steel production, foreign trade, trend by demand (sectors), and deliveries by sectors and products. Also provided are employment figures, cost indexes, and base prices. Text supports the data.

Statistics of World Trade in Steel is also published by the United Nations Economic Commission for Europe. The purpose of this publication is to provide basic data on exports of semi-finished and finished steel products from European and other steel exporting countries in the world.

> *How many tons of Japanese steel does the United States import?*
>
> *How much of this is used for railway track material?*
>
> *What country is the world's largest importer of semi-finished steel products?*

A third source, *Iron and Steel: Yearly Statistics,* is compiled by the Statistical Office of the European Union. This publication differs from the other two in that it is purely statistical and covers only the EU countries. Data items include production, consumption, prices, and trade.

> *How many tons of steel were consumed in the manufacture of wire rods for the EU countries?*
>
> *Which EU country employed the most foreign workers in the iron and steel industry in 1990? Has the pattern changed since 1970?*

The Steel Market in 1995 and the Outlook for 1996 and 1997 is an OECD publication that has appeared since 1978. It is a 50-page analysis of the world steel market with two year projections of production and consumption. It examines the market for both OECD and non-OECD countries. It includes a brief chapter on employment in the steel industry in OECD countries.

Prospects for the World Cocoa Market Until the Year 2005 (1991) is an example of a United Nations Conference on Trade and Development (UNCTAD) report. Prepared in conjunction with the International Cocoa Organization, an active industry association, this has in-depth analysis of trends in world supply of, and demand for, cocoa at world and country levels.

> *What country had the highest per capita chocolate confectionery consumption in 1987?*
>
> *What percent of Swiss chocolate sales are filled chocolate?*
>
> *How much chocolate was it estimated that Ukraine would produce in 1990?*

ECE and UNCTAD also publish more technical reports, which provide comprehensive analysis of a few industries. One example from the ECE is *World Engineering Industries and Automation: Performance and Prospects.* First published in 1979 under the title *Annual Review of Engineering Industries and Automation,* the 1994 edition analyzes developments in the ECE region, with reference to the United States, Japan, and Eastern Europe for the period 1989–92, with estimates for 1993 and forecasts for 1994. Data is based on a questionnaire sent out jointly by ECE and OECD.

The work has three sections. The first is a structural analysis of the engineering industries. The second is an analysis of production and trade of selected engineering products. This section describes 21 separate products (e.g., electric motors, semiconductors, and telecommunications). The final section gives estimates and forecasts.

Country level data, as well as company-specific information, is included. For example, the chapter on computers and information technology provides market share data for the world's largest information technology suppliers in 1992. The time series data is often useful. An example is the chapter on industrial robots, which provides data on the world stock of industrial robots with breakdowns by country for the period 1981–92.

The Chemical Industry In..., also from the Economic Commission for Europe, is arranged by country overview, and then by some 80 specific chemicals for which production and import/export data are given.

A third publication of the ECE is *Food-Processing Machinery,* which includes information about the food industry and packaging techniques. This is an excellent analysis of the industry, containing analyses of the structure and trends in selected countries.

UNCTAD (United Nations Conference on Trade and Development) is another arm of the United Nations that issues industry studies. *Structural Changes in the Automobile and Components Industry During the 1980s with Particular Reference to Developing Countries* and a companion *Structural Changes in the Electronic Industry...* are two examples of recent titles. These studies grew out of the UNCTAD Committee on Manufacturers' decision to consider supply, demand, trends, comparative advantage, and market access to specific sectors of export of interest to developing countries. These two reports are primarily analytical, based on data from other UN published sources, OECD, and the *Panorama of EU Industry.*

Other recent titles from UNCTAD include *Contribution of Transnational Mining Corporations to the*

Asia-Pacific Region and the quarterly *International Tin Statistics,* which gives, by country, tin production, current prices, consumption, stocks, trade, mining activity, and employment.

The main problem for librarians regarding UNCTAD publications is finding them. We located these titles by using the *Index to International Statistics.* Some are on microfiche and some in paper. Libraries often do not catalog these publications.

UNCTAD http://www.unicc.org/unctad does include selected full text items. Examples are *Least Developed Countries Report 1996* (UNCTAD) and *Globalization and Liberalization (UNCAD9 Report).*

Sources for Commodities

The Commodities Yearbook is the standard source for commodities information in the United States. It examines commodities primarily from the perspective of the futures trader.

A very different source is the World Bank's *Price Prospects for Major Primary Commodities 1990–2005,* a two-volume publication giving forecasts of production, consumption, and prices.

Volume I: Summary, Energy, Metals and Minerals

Volume II: Agricultural Products, Fertilizers, Tropical Timber,

Sample data appear in Exhibit 14.3.

Table 1. Commodity Prices and Price Projections in 1985 Constant Dollars[a]

| | | Actual | | | Projections | | |
		1970	1980	1989	Short-term 1990	1995	Long-term 2000	2005
Energy								
Petroleum	$/bbl	3.6	29.1	11.8	14.7	12.3	15.2	14.5
Coal	$/mt	n.a. 29	29	29	28	30	30	
Food								
Coffee	¢/kg	314	328	172	135	164	207	207
Cocoa	¢/kg	185	248	90	86	94	109	126
Tea	¢/kg	300	213	146	139	153	147	166
Sugar	$/mt	222	602	204	188	200	223	227
Beef	¢/kg	357	263	186	174	179	189	160

a Computed from unrounded data and deflated by MUV(1985=100) manufacturing unit value

EXTRACT FROM *PRICE PROSPECTS FOR MAJOR PRIMARY COMMODITIES 1990–2005*

EXHIBIT 14.3

Source: Price Prospects for Major Primary Commodities 1990–2005.

Chapters in Volume I include a summary, demand and supply outlook, and price outlook. Chapters in Volume II have a summary, consumption and price history, and outlook. For example, the price of sugar is given annually in constant and current U.S. dollars per ton between 1950 and 1989, with projections for 1990–2005. Sources of information include the commodity's international organization, FAO, and the World Bank. The annual *Price Prospects* is supplemented by the periodical *Quarterly Review of Commodity Markets*.

Sources for Services

According to Eurostat, services accounted for about 63% of GDP of the EU in 1992 (based on 12 countries). Approximately 10.5 million firms in the EU (EUR-12) are engaged in service activities. Most of the service firms engage in commercial activities. The relative importance of services in the EU, compared to the U.S. and Japan, can be seen from the following figures (1992).

Contribution of Services to Economy		
	TOTAL EMPLOYMENT	VALUE ADDED
Europe	61%	63%
United States	74%	69%
Japan	56%	59%

Despite their growing importance in the world economy, information about services is hard to obtain. Eurostat states that enterprise-level data is most significant at the small to medium enterprise level, especially for service industries. Yet this is the area for which the least data is available.

Services: Statistics on Value Added and Employment (published by OECD, 1996)

The purpose of this publication is to document the growth and changes in the structure of the service sector in OECD countries over the past two decades. Annual data is given from 1970 through 1993. Data are derived from member countries' national accounts and are shown at the most detailed level available. The service sector is defined as all activities in major division 6 through 9 of the International Standard Industrial Classification code (ISIC Revision 2).

6: Wholesale and retail trade; restaurants and hotels

7: Transport, storage, and communication

8: Financing, insurance, real estate, and business services

9: Community, social, and personal service

The publication includes data on both market and non-market services. The main part of the publication is a country listing of services for total employment and gross value added (in national currency).

A summary table showing the available data on service activities from OECD member countries highlights the many information gaps. For example, only the U.S. supplies information on "banking" in their national accounts. Several countries (e.g., Mexico, Japan, Italy, and Ireland) provide little or no detail beyond the single-digit ISIC level.

Statistics in Focus: Distributive Trades, Services, and Transport (published monthly by Eurostat)

Distributive Trades is a 10-page newsletter that describes one service area in each issue. Examples in 1996 include "Telecommunication Services in Europe," "Insurance Service Statistics," and "European Statistics on Financial Services Enterprises." The type of data presented and its currency varies greatly by the type of service being discussed. Number of enterprises, employment, and personnel costs for each of the EU countries and the EU as a whole, plus comparative figures for Japan and the U.S., are standard in each publication.

Sources of Agriculture

An important source of worldwide agricultural statistics is described below.

FAO Yearbook: Production (published annually by Food and Agricultural Organization of the United Nations)

The principal agency publishing worldwide agricultural statistics is the Food and Agricultural Organization (FAO) of the United Nations. The 1993 *FAO Yearbook: Production*, published in late 1994, is the 47th edition. The date range for the data is from 1979–81 to 1993. Data are compiled from FAO questionnaires to national governments.

As with many of our data providers, FAO warns the user that definitions of categories differ among participating countries. There are 90 different crops and more than 200 different geographical entities. The number of countries varies per crop. Data for individual crops are given by country, region, continent, and world. The aggregated totals include only those countries listed for that particular crop.

What countries in the world provide buffalo meat?

What country in Europe has the highest percent of its economically active population engaged in agriculture?

Table Tableau 17 Cuadro	Rice, Paddy		Riz, Paddy		Arroz En Cascara	
	Area Harv 1000HA Sup Recoltee Sup Cosechad		Yield KG/HA Rendement Rendimento		Production 1000MT Production Production	
	1979-81	1993	1979-81	1993	1979-81	1993
Asia	128237	131665	2807	3665	359786	482549
Afghanistan	210	175F	2182	1714	415	300*
Bangladesh	10310	10900	1952	2569	20125	28000*
Bhutan	28	26F	2017	1654	56	43F
Thailand	8986	8972	1887	2128	16967	19090
Turkey	67	45	4706	5017	314	225
Viet Nam	5579	6466	2116	3449	11808	22300

* Unofficial figure; F-FAO estimate

FAO YEARBOOK: PRODUCTION

EXHIBIT 14.4

Source: *FAO Yearbook-Production* 1993: 70-71.

How has the world's per capita production of food changed over the past 10 years?

Exhibit 14.4 is an extract containing data from the *FAO Yearbook: Production*. Reports on over 20 individual fruits and vegetables, ranging from apples to kiwis to unshelled walnuts, are published by the OECD in its *International Standardization of Fruit and Vegetables* series.

Country Statistics

All of the previous examples have come from international and pan-regional sources. Most of the data have been drawn from the data collected by the participating countries. These countries also have their own statistical publications.

Norway is an example of a country with a set of industry data that is available to the public. *Industristatistikk* comprises two volumes of manufacturing statistics and commodities statistics. Volume 1 includes figures by industry, group of employees, and county. The purpose of the set is to give detailed structural figures. Another set of industry data, *Regnskapsstatistikk*, contains retail trade data. Norway also provides quarterly, monthly, and weekly data.

The international publications generally list the country level agencies or publications with industry statistics that they have used. Researchers needing more information can use this as a finding aid to locating more specific country level sources. Some of these sources are listed in Table 14.H.

Commercial Sources of Industry Information

In addition to the data and analysis from international, regional, and national agencies, there are commercial sources of industry information.

D&B Europa (published annually by Dun's International, Ltd.)

D&B Europa provides a breakdown of the 60,000 companies in the directory (see Chapter 4) arranged by size in terms of sales range and by 2-digit U.S. SIC code, shown in Exhibit 14.5. Over 50% of the companies fall into the 10–49.9 million ECU range. The largest industry groupings are for wholesale trade, with a total of 22% in durable and nondurable wholesaling. Similar data is provided for each country in the directory. For example, over half the 910 Turkish companies in the 1996 edition of the directory are in the 1–9.9 million ECU range, and the largest number of companies is in SIC 22, textile mill products. The companies in *Europa* have been selected for their size and their importance to international trade.

TABLE 14.H

OFFICIAL COUNTRY SOURCES OF INDUSTRIAL STATISTICS

Agency Collecting Industry Information

COUNTRY	INDUSTRIAL STATISTICS	BUSINESS SURVEYS
Belgium	Institut national de Statistique, from VAT and Social Security	Banque Nationale de Belgique
Denmark	Danmarks Statistik; VAT and workplace registers	Danmarks Statistik
Greece	National Statistical Service from 78 and 84 censuses	IEIR: Institut of Economic and Industrial Research
Spain	Instituto National de Estadistica; internal such as 1980 census and private sources and other governmental sources	MIE: Ministerio de Industria y Energia
France	Institut national de la Statistique et des Etudes economiques (INSEE); 3 enterprise level surveys	INSEE
Ireland	Central Statistical Office; 1986 census Istituto	CIL: Confederation of Irish Industry
Italy	Centrale di Statistica; 1981 economic census; generally enterprise level	ISCO: Insitiuto Nazionale per lo Studio della Congiuntura
Luxembourg	Service central de la Statistique et des Etudes economicques; from registery and 1975 census	STATEC
Netherlands	Central Bureau voor de Statistiek; annual sample surveys	CBS
Portugal	Instituto Nacional de Estatistica; 1982 census or enterprises; annual hotel survey	INE AECOPS : Associacao de Empresas de Construcao e Obras Publicas do Sul
United Kingdom	Business Statistics Office; various sources	CBI: Confederation of British Industry BSO: Business Statistics Office

Many of the commercial sources of industry information are specialized. One example is *World Motor Vehicle Data,* published by the American Automobile Manufacturers Association. In 1996, the 32nd edition was published; it reports data up to 1994. Vehicle production for individual manufacturers in 50 countries, vehicle registration in 120 countries, and import/export movements are the important features of this volume. *World Motor Vehicle Data* can answer such questions as:

> *What is General Motors' share of the Japanese market for imported passenger cars?*

> *What was the world total and the U.S. total of motor vehicle registrations by year, from 1935 to 1994?*

Individual investment bank reports, available through Investext or in the ICC Brokerage Reports database, provide in-depth information for many industries. Although the focus of these reports is often on the financial performance, of individual companies, they frequently include industry analysis, performance, and forecasts. Online investment bank reports are expensive, a fact that limits their usefulness.

ICC provides *KeyNotes*, which analyzes 175 U.K. industry sectors. Information includes industry structure, market size and trends, major companies, market and brand shares, advertising expenditures, and recent and future developments. A feature that makes these reports more valuable is an extensive list of additional sources, including industry associations, periodicals, directories, general sources, government publications, and non-U.K. sources. Chapter 10 contains a more detailed description of *KeyNotes*.

McCarthy cards have been providing an industry "clipping service" to U.K. libraries for many years and continue to do so even in an electronic age. A sample industry grouping is "Beer & Lager Brewing & Sales."

The cards dated January 10, 1992 are numbered 603–605, indicating that 602 cards have gone before. A sample card appears to be a cut-and-paste photocopy of articles from U.K. papers: *Daily Telegraph* of December 23, 1991; *Times* from December 31, 1992; and *Financial Times* from January 2, 1992. The articles cover an increase in sale of full-bodied beers at Christmas, as well as the U.S. action against Canadian beer. *McCarthy* is also available online through FT Profile.

	1-9.9	10-49.9	50-74.9	75-99.9	100-249.9	250-499.9	500-749.9	750-999.9	1,000+	Total
01 Agricultural Production - Crops	5	81	5	6	6	1	1		1	106
02 Agricultural Production - Livestock	1	77	15	5	13	5	2		4	122
07 Agricultural Services	1	29	11	3	4	1	1			50
08 Forestry	1	15	4	4	4	2	3			34
09 Fishing, Hunting & Trapping		29	3	1	2					35
10 Metal Mining	3	33	4	4	7	5			1	57
11 Anthracite Mining		4	2		4	1				11
12 Bituminous Coal & Lignite Mining	1	12	4	1	4	3	1		5	31
13 Oil & Gas Extraction	3	47	17	10	38	17	11	10	27	180
14 Non-Metallic Mineral Mining, Except Fuels	2	81	31	13	21	6	2	2	1	159
15 General Building Contractors	24	883	232	93	184	61	16	10	20	1523
16 Construction other than Bldg Contractors	8	361	99	65	80	31	16	2	20	682
17 Special Trade Construction Contractors	17	465	101	44	71	19	9	5	13	744
20 Food & Kindred Products Manufacturers	38	2104	590	357	608	231	77	40	92	4137
21 Tobacco Manufacturers	1	21	12	4	13	9	9	3	16	88
22 Textile Mill Products	47	849	150	53	77	12	6	1	3	1198
23 Apparel/Other Finished Fabric Pdts Mfrs	45	514	99	51	61	11	7	1	3	792
24 Lumber & Wood Product Mfrs, Ex. Furniture	7	290	65	39	44	10	3	3	1	462
25 Furniture & Fixtures Manufacturers	4	377	69	33	35	4	1	1		524
26 Paper & Allied Product Manufacturers	10	504	136	95	169	65	11	3	14	1007
27 Printing, Publishing & Allied Industries	11	618	173	88	130	54	13	8	15	1110
28 Chemical & Allied Product Manufacturers	41	1204	412	208	436	171	58	18	80	2628
29 Petroleum Refining & Related Industries	2	64	23	12	42	14	9	4	39	209
30 Rubber & Misc Plastics Product Mfrs	18	668	160	63	117	36	11	6	14	1093
31 Leather & Leather Product Manufacturers	16	262	35	15	21	2	2	2	1	356
32 Stone, Clay, Glass & Concrete Product Mfrs	21	668	151	97	135	45	15	4	15	1151
33 Primary Metal Industries	14	597	173	94	200	75	22	13	37	1225
34 Fabricated Metal Pdt Mfrs, Ex Machinery	24	1013	263	100	143	43	16	6	11	1619
35 Machinery MFRs, Except Electrical	17	1531	373	167	342	120	51	16	66	2683
36 Electrical Equipment & Machinery Mfrs	40	1119	253	171	285	100	45	28	53	2094
37 Transportation Equipment Manufacturers	20	488	149	92	175	64	27	20	65	1100
38 Measuring & Photo/Medical Equip & Clocks	4	353	83	31	85	21	11	1	14	603
39 Miscellaneous Manufacturing Industries	2	270	42	26	32	7	3		1	383
40 Railway Transportation	4	22	5	4	9	2		2	9	57
41 Local Public Transprt & Intercity Buses	21	204	22	16	28	7	1		8	307
42 Haulage & Warehousing	14	420	99	53	76	12	11	7	14	706
43 Postal Services		2			3	4			9	18
44 Water Transportation	9	207	58	29	68	30	3	3	9	416
45 Air Transportation	4	99	27	12	50	26	13	6	18	255
46 Pipe Lines, Except Natural Gas		11			2					13
47 Transportation Services	8	532	157	84	152	43	16	3	21	1016
48 Communication	2	58	27	22	34	17	5	5	15	185
49 Electric, Gas & Sanitary Services	6	380	120	83	202	116	44	25	66	1042
50 Wholesale Trade - Durable Goods	31	3517	1036	472	876	265	88	34	96	6415
51 Wholesale Trade - Nondurable Goods	19	3623	1006	526	930	272	108	48	119	6651
52 Building & Garden Supply Retailers		56	18	7	19	13	5	1	5	124
53 General Merchandise Retailers	8	593	106	54	104	51	28	15	57	1016
54 Food Retailers		191	45	25	61	32	12	10	32	408
55 Motor Vehicle Dealers & Petrol Stations	2	965	141	59	92	42	9	7	16	1333
56 Clothing & Accessory Retailers	2	172	52	32	65	24	4	4	5	360
57 Home Furnishings/Equipment Retailers	2	170	55	24	47	19	5	1	6	329
58 Eating & Drinking Establishments	8	157	26	19	31	14	5	4	5	269
59 Miscellaneous Retail Trade	4	267	72	40	70	35	8	5	17	518
62 Security & Commod Brokers/Dealers/Svcs	3	78	31	20	36	12	5	3	5	193
64 Insurance Agents, Brokers, & Services	4	106	23	16	44	8	6	2	4	213
65 Real Estate	8	525	166	75	155	41	13	5	12	1000
66 Comb of Real Estate/Insurance/Loans/Law		21	4	3	10		1		2	41
67 Holding & Other Investment Offices	30	372	177	129	276	140	42	34	126	1326
70 Hotels/Rooming Houses/Camps/Lodgings	9	133	27	17	24	6		2	2	220
72 Personal Services	21	163	31	13	13	7	5		2	255
73 Business Services	145	1582	368	212	419	131	29	24	73	2983
75 Automotive Repair, Services & Garages		138	39	16	40	12	7	1	5	258
76 Misc Repair Services	4	28	9	4	9	2			1	57
78 Motion Pictures		83	19	12	8	6	2	1	5	136
79 Amusement & Recreation Svcs, Ex Cinemas	6	124	28	12	15	8	4	5	5	207
80 Health Services	14	244	29	11	19	6				323
81 Legal Services		6	2	1	3	1				13
82 Educational Services	2	38	10	2	8				1	61
83 Social Services	4	55	2	5	3					69
84 Museums/Art Galleries/Bot. & Zool. Gdns			1						1	2
86 Membership Organisations	1	32	7	10	12	4	3	2	3	74
89 Misc Services	5	377	87	54	138	38	9	4	15	727
Total	848	31382	8071	4218	7739	2692	950	471	1421	57792

SIZE OF COMPANIES IN *D&B EUROPA* STATISTICAL PROFILE FOR EUROPE

EXHIBIT 14.5

Source: *D&B Europa*, 1997, vol. 4: 47.

Selected Sources of Commercial Industry Reports

Jordan & Sons Limited

Jordan & Sons is a British information company. It collects U.K. company information that it makes available in a variety of print and electronic formats. In conjunction with individual consultants, it also provides a series of industry reports.

One example is the 1990 *British Plastics Industry*, priced at £150. It extracts establishment and enterprise data from the U.K. 1987 Census of Production and from the industry association, Plastics Processing Industry Training Board, with limited comparative data from other EU countries and the U.S.

Different types of plastics are defined and the major participants are named. Concentration ratios are not calculated; however, the reader can determine that the six establishments with 1,000 or more employees account for less than 8% of net output. Geographical distribution is also given: 26.7% of total employment is in southeastern England. Individual company data is also provided for both listed and unlisted companies. There are no calculated ratios.

British drinks, sporting goods, airlines, and franchises are other industries analyzed by Jordans. The surveys cost under $500 and are also available on diskette.

Another source of reports is the *Financial Times Business Reports*. Covering a wide range of issues, some of the reports are organized around individual industries such as banking, pharmaceuticals, and hazardous waste management. The *Reports* are targeted for top management and are nontechnical. They are designed to fill the gap between a book and a detailed consultants' report. An individual report costs approximately $300.

The *Financial Times Business Reports* are also available online. On DataStar, there is one database for energy and the environment (FTNV); one for technology and communications (FTTC); one labeled "industry reports," covering industries such as biotechnology and pharmaceutical (FTIN); and one including all the FT reports (FTBR). Coverage begins in 1992 and is updated weekly.

Economist Intelligence Unit (EIU), another U.K. information provider, has a series of industry reports on major groupings including:

Automotive
Commodities
Consumer Goods
Energy
Textiles
Travel and Tourism

For example, for the automotive industry, EIU has a monthly *Automotive Intelligence Service*, quarterly publications such as *Japanese Motor Business,* and many special topics such as *The Motor Industry of South-East Asia: Prospects to 2000*. Report cost varies but typically ranges between $500 and $1,000.

Online Sources of Industry Information

Table 14.I lists some commercial databases on DIALOG or DataStar that cover industries. The codes are DIALOG file numbers and DataStar mnemonics.

TABLE 14.I

ONLINE DATABASES WITH INDUSTRY INFORMATION

Code	Name of File	Type
AINS	Automotive Information and News	AB
CBNB or 319	Chemical Business Newsbase (75% Europe)	AB
CISS	Computer Industry Software and Services	TX
CNEW	European Chemical News	TX,D
EECM	East European Monitor—Chemicals	TX
269	Materials Business File	AB
240	Paperchem	AB
PLST or 328	CHEM-INTELL Trade & Production Statistics	TX,D
VWWW	Volkswagen- Vehicles Technology & Management	AB(German)
67	World Textiles	AB
GENERAL DATABASES WITH INDUSTRY INFORMATION		
	Globalbase	AB
	Predicasts	AB,TX,EX
	Textline	TX
	Trade and Industry	AB,TX

AB-Abstract; TX-Full text; D-Directory; EX-Extract

Industry-Specific News from Reuters

Reuters Insurance Briefing is an online end-user product for the individual who needs up-to-date worldwide information on the insurance industry. It is menu driven and runs in a Windows environment. The service is divided into two parts, current and archives. "Current" includes articles published within the past two to three days (with a few minutes' delay) that may be accessed by country or by the following general subjects: all news, economic news, political news, general news, sports news, insurance news, and risk news. The annual archives of articles may be searched by countries, industries, companies, topics such as acquisitions or contracts, and sources such as insurance publications like *Lloyd's List* or *Reinsurance*.

Users may combine menu choices with a keyword, for example "typhoon," and also select a date range: one week; one, three, or six months; one year; or a specific time.

Articles are translated from 15 languages into English and presented in full text or as an abstract. Two or more translated articles may be integrated into one story by Reuters' editors; all sources will be listed.

INDUSTRY AND COUNTRY AVERAGES: RATIOS

Researchers often require country or industry financial "averages." For U.S. industries, this type of information is available in print sources such as Dun & Bradstreet *Industry Norms and Key Business Ratios* or the Robert Morris & Associates *Annual Statement Studies*. Often this information is used to compare a company with its peer group. Here are examples of typical requests for average balance sheet ratios:

- For all companies worldwide in the aerospace industry
- For all U.K. companies
- For all companies in the aerospace industry in the U.K.

There is no global equivalent to D&B's *Industry Norms* or Robert Morris's *Annual Statement Studies*. However, global industry ratios are available for major traded companies. In Chapter 5, we described CIFAR's *Global Company Handbook* as a source for worldwide company financial information and rankings. Volume 1 also includes 12 industry averages for up to 20 industries in 48 countries. All reports include:

- Profit margin (OPMG)
- Debt to equity ratio (D/E%)

- Price/earnings ratio (P/EX)
- Price to book value ratio (PBVSx)
- Market value to cash flow (PCF%)
- Market value to sales (P/Sx)
- Dividend yield (DY%)
- Return on assets (ROA%)
- Return on shareholders' equity (ROE%)
- Shareholders rate of return
- Current ration (CR%)

Two additional ratios are calculated for industrials, banks, insurance, and other financial services. A weighted average technique is used, based on sales in U.S. dollars for industrials and total assets for financial companies.

Listed below are four examples of tables using ratios from the *Global Company Handbook*. They illustrate the differences in performance standards among countries, among industries, and by year. Exhibit 14.6 provides samples of Examples 1–4.

Example 1: Table R.1. Ratios for one industry in one country for several years

Example 2: Table R.2. Using ratios to compare two industries in one country

Example 3: Table R.3. Comparing the same industry in different countries

Example 4: Table R.4. Comparing all industries in different countries

How should we evaluate this information? Many of the same problems we have encountered before in evaluating the comparability of data apply here as well. Two important issues are these:

1. *Fiscal year end differences among countries.* The data from which the country averages are calculated represent different time periods. For example, the fiscal year for the U.S. is usually January to December. In Japan, the reporting year runs from April 1 to March 31.
2. *Classification of a company within a product grouping.* There is surprisingly little agreement among information providers on assigning industry classification codes to individual companies.

In Table R.1, shown in Exhibit 14.6, notice how the figures for the U.K. Utilities/Transportation industry vary from year to year. Shareholders' rate of return (ROR) went from more than 50% in 1989 to below 13% in 1990. The debt-to-equity ratio (D/E) increased 230% in the five-year period, while the current ratio (CR) remained the same. When the figures are this volatile, it is risky to compare current year figures with published industry averages.

Table R.1 UK Utilities/Transportation
Averages of Key Financial Ratios

	Year	OPMG	D/E%	P/Ex	PBVSx	PCFx	P/Sx	DY%	ROA%	ROE%	ROR%	CR%
UNITED KINGDOM												
Industry related	1990	12.4	66.4	10.0	2.8	7.0	0.92	4.6	6.4	27.9	-13.6	1.2
Averages in	1989	14.0	64.8	11.5	3.5	11.5	0.89	3.5	7.5	34.9	50.4	1.1
a country	1988	13.8	61.9	9.4	2.6	6.2	0.63	3.3	8.1	32.1	28.0	1.1
Utilities/Trans	1987	12.7	52.6	14.0	2.5	5.7	0.44	3.6	7.6	21.8	26.6	1.3
# of companies: 19	1986	10.8	20.1	14.3	2.2	6.7	0.39	3.9	5.8	23.2	27.1	1.2

Table R.2: UK Construction and Electronics
Comparing Two Industries in a Country

	# Cos	Year	OPMG	D/E%	P/Ex	PBVSx	PCFx	P/Sx	DY%	ROA%	ROE%	ROR%	CR%
Construction	45	1990	4.1	50.2	12.3	1.3	5.2	0.28	6.1	2.2	9.3	-26.3	1.4
Electronics/ Elec Equip.	51	1990	10.5	23.8	10.0	2.9	5.9	0.71	3.8	6.9	24.5	-17.6	1.5

Table R.3 Utilities/Transportation 1990
Comparing the Same Industry in Different Countries

	U.K.	JAPAN	GERMANY	U.S.
Country Averages				
No. of companies	19	81	35	248
Debt/Equity (D/E%)	66.4	246.8	94.4	112.0
Return on Equity (ROE)	27.9	5.1	-1.6	9.1
Price Earnings (P/EX)	10.0	66.8	81.7	14.2

GLOBAL COMPANY HANDBOOK—INDUSTRY AVERAGES

EXHIBIT 14.6

Source: Global Company Handbook, 1992, vol. 1, IV Industry and Country Averages.

Also notice in Table R.2 the differences among industries within the same country. Generally, the industry average profile for the U.K. construction industry, especially in profit margin, market value to sales, and return on equity, is different from either the utilities or electronics groups.

Finally, in Table R.3 there are large differences in country norms, even for the same industry. The U.K. debt/equity ratio for the utilities industry is less than 25% of that for Japan, while its return on investment is five times greater. National differences are less pronounced for all industries, but finally notice that the country averages for all industries also differ from the country averages for an individual industry.

Worldscope and CIFAR products calculate industry averages, country averages, and some industry averages for individual countries. There is one record for each country and industry on Worldscope and additional industry records if there are enough companies in an individual country, as in Exhibit 14.7.

The average records are a separate section in Cifarbase. Select the specific data items you want and receive an individual report for each one. There is no single record for all data items. Selection choices include: Country/Worldwide; Industry—33 groupings, including NONE and OTHER; and Type of Account—Each individual line item. Exhibit 14.8 is an example of one time for one industry in one country.

AEROSPACE / FRANCE

INDUSTRY AVERAGE RECORD
AEROSPACE
FRANCE

CURRENT EXCHANGE RATE: 0.20446 US Dollars per French Francs

INDUSTRY CLASS: INDUSTRIAL
MAJOR INDUSTRY GROUP: AEROSPACE
MINOR INDUSTRY GROUP: AEROSPACE
INDUSTRY AVERAGE CATEGORY: AEROSPACE - FRANCE
NUMBER OF EMPLOYEES: 10,458 (SOURCE:12/31/94)

FISCAL YEAR END: 12/31
LATEST ANNUAL FINANCIAL DATE: 12/31/94

PROFITABILITY RATIOS - ANNUAL
INDUSTRY AVERAGE RECORD

PROFITABILITY RATIOS - ANNUAL

FISCAL YEAR ENDING	12/31/94	12/31/93	12/31/92	12/31/91	12/31/90
CASH FLOW/SALES	14.44	12.17	13.61	12.77	13.56
COGS/SALES	75.25	79.59	78.58	82.97	86.45
GROSS PROFIT MARGN	15.83	11.29	11.78	7.45	3.96
PRETAX MARGIN	-1.26	-1.52	-2.12	0.57	1.09
EFFECTIVE TX RATE	NA	NA	NA	25.41	62.75
NET INCOME MARGIN	-2.00	-1.73	-2.42	0.71	0.71
SALES/EMPL (MIL)	0.96	0.93	0.97	0.94	0.86
EFFECT INT RATE	9.44	9.41	8.94	8.10	7.28
OPER INC/TOT CAP	-4.20	-7.12	-9.31	-10.58	-14.37
RET ON INVST CAP	-0.13	0.88	-0.52	5.58	4.99
ROE PER SHARE	-12.49	-9.34	-12.07	3.88	3.96
RETURN ON EQUITY	-12.03	-10.10	-14.09	4.20	3.81
RETURN ON ASSETS	-0.05	0.33	-0.21	2.21	1.88
OPER PROFIT MARGN	-2.06	-3.39	-3.81	-3.78	-5.46
CASH EARNINGS ROE	87.03	70.89	79.08	75.41	73.18

EXTRACTED *WORLDSCOPE* INDUSTRY AVERAGE RECORD

EXHIBIT 14.7

Source: Worldscope CD-ROM, November 1995.

YEARLY AND 5-YEAR AVERAGES

COUNTRY/WORLDWIDE	FRANCE
INDUSTRY	Aerospace
TYPE OF ACCOUNT	RETURN ON EQUITY
YEAR	AVERAGE VALUE

90:	0.000
89:	16.171
88:	10.716
87:	-3.698
86:	7.231
85:	14.623
84:	10.242

5 YR. AVER./ANNUAL GROWTH

90:	6.084
89:	9.009
88:	7.823
87:	5.825
86:	7.410

CIFARBASE CD-ROM—SAMPLE AVERAGE RECORD RETURN ON EQUITY FOR THE FRENCH AEROSPACE INDUSTRY

EXHIBIT 14.8

Source: CIFAR CD-ROM February 1992.

ICC Information Group calculates 30 ratios for the individual companies in its database. Ten of these are also calculated for the 4-digit U.K. SIC Code industry grouping, presenting lower, median, and upper quartiles.

The ratios are published in the U.K. as special industry reports. Users can also access these ratios from the ICC British Company Financial Database, available on DataStar, DIALOG, and direct from ICC, as well as in the ICC financial records on DIALOG OnDisc's *UK Company Factfinder*. Ratio categories are: profitability (4), revenue (4), credit (5), gearing (debt) (4), productivity (7), value added (4), and auditor's fee (2).

The example in Exhibit 14.9. compares Cadbury Schweppes with the confectionery industry in the U.K.

ICC INDUSTRY COMPARISONS
SIC Code: 4214 (Cocoa, chocolate and sugar confectionery)

Year to : 31.12.91		Lower Quartile	Median	Upper	CADBURY SCHWEPPES PLC
Profitability:					
Profit/Capital Emp.	%	1.5	10.6	24.1	19.5
Profit/Total Assets	%	.0	4.8	11.1	11.9
Profit/Sales	%	.1	3.3	7.9	9.8
Revenue					
Sales/Total Assets	%	120.8	160.9	203.9	121.8
Credit					
Credit Period	Days	66.7	50.4	31.6	48.5
Liquidity	R	.8	1.1	1.8	1.2
Value added					
Value Added/Employee	UKL	NA	NA	NA	2909.6
Productivity					
Average Remuneration	UKL	6,102.2	7,216.6	8,609.0	14257
Sales/Employee	UKL	24,604.7	37,263.2	48,994.6	91390.2
Wages/Sales	%	26.8	22.0	17.1	15.6

ICC *BRITISH COMPANY FINANCIAL DATABASE*

EXHIBIT 14.9

Source: ICC File 561 on DIALOG.

Other even more specialized databases, such as the financial CD-ROMs *Amadeus, Diane,* and *Fame,* using Bureau van Dijk software, have ratio information and the capability to compare companies with their industries (peer group analysis) or companies with any set the user creates.

SELECTED SUPPLEMENTAL SOURCES

Other sources of industry information are published regularly by both governmental and private organizations. The United Nations Statistical Office publishes such annual titles as *Construction Statistics Yearbook, Energy Statistics Yearbook* and *Energy Balances and Electricity Profiles.* For a full range of Statistical Office publications, check the United Nations Publications Catalog.

The United Nations Industrial Development Organization publishes special reports on industries and countries. One set of reports is in the Industrial Development Review Series, which examines the state of industry in developing countries. Blackwell began publishing this series for UNIDO in 1992.

GATT (General Agreement on Trade and Tariffs) and its successor organization, the World Trade Organization (WTO), publishes analyses of agricultural markets. One example is the annual *International Markets for Meat* (Geneva: GATT, 1995/96; 12th annual report), an in-depth analysis prepared by the GATT secretariat, based on the work of the International Meat Council. Each annual includes data for publication year and forecasts for the following year; along with numbers for slaughter levels, production, prices, imports, consumption, and exports in the bovine meat sector. There is summary data on pigs, poultry, and sheep. Information also comes from OECD, IMF, and industry and private sources. *Meat* covers 18 countries and the EU. GATT (now WTO) also publishes the *World Market for Dairy Products,* based on the International Dairy Arrangement.

Individual countries publish a wide range of statistical data. *Statistics Canada* is an example. *Quarterly Financial Statistics for Enterprises* presents industry level data for more than 30 industry groupings, including financial services, that are part of the business sector. It uses vertical integration of industry categories; i.e., food and food retailing, electronic equipment, and computer services, collected at enterprise level. A Canadian coding scheme, the Standard Industrial Classification for Companies and Enterprises 1980 (SIC-C) is used. Detailed information is available on request. Data is collected from questionnaires and sampling. Data include balance sheets for 5 quarters, income statement, and 5 selected ratios: return on capital employed, ROE, profit margin, debt/equity, and working capital ratio.

ICC annually publishes *Industrial Performance Analysis and ICC Business Ratio Report: An Industry Sector Analysis.* The *Report* calls itself the guide to profitability and efficiency in British industry. It is a U.K. equivalent of Dun & Bradstreet's *Industry Norms and Key Business Ratios.* The series includes one industry-wide compilation plus individual industry reports. Data items include balance sheet and profit-and-loss statistics for the industry and its sector; graphic representation of return on capital by sector; key ratios and statistics for industry and sector; and employee-based ratios in matrix format for sectors. The ratios are also available in ICC online British company database (see Exhibit 14.7).

CONCLUSION

This chapter describes the basic tools for industry research. Most of the sources that we present are compilations of data about industry groups and come from governmental and non-governmental organization such as the United Nations, the EU, and the OECD. Some of these sources compile data for all industries in specific regions. Industry data are used heavily in conjunction with the market research data discussed in Chapter 9 and 10.

NOTES

1. Michael Porter, *The Competitive Advantage of Nations* (New York: Free Press, 1990): 33.
2. *European Directory of Marketing Information Sources* (Euromonitor, 1992): 14.
3. *EU Panorama* 1994: 11–5; 5–19.
4. *EU Panorama* 1994: 11–6.

APPENDIX J
International Coding Systems

Table 14.A outlines existing coding schemes, which have been used for data collection during the 1990s. The EU has published its NACE-1 codes, which have been adopted by some European countries and are being phased in for data collection. The U.K. has adapted NACE-1 and some information providers have begun to use them.

In 1989, the United Nations resolved to use Revision 3 of its ISIC codes. These, too, are still being phased in. In 1997, the U.S., Canada, and Mexico will begin collecting data using NAICS codes.

Therefore, over the next few years, we will be seeing all or any of these coding systems in our establishment and industry data presentations.

	U.S. SIC Division	EC NACE -1 SECTOR	ISIC - Rev 3 MAJOR DIVISION	NAFTA NAICS US, Canada, Mexico
01	Agriculture, Forestry, & Fishing	Agriculture, Hunting, & Related Services	Agriculture, Hunting, & Forestry	
02		Forestry, Logging, & Related Services		
03				
04				
05		Fishing, Operation of Fish Hatcheries & Fish Farms; Services	Fishing	
06				
10	Mining	Mining...	Mining and Quarrying	
11				Agriculture, Forestry, Hunting, Fishing
15	Construction	Manufacturing	Manufacturing	
20	Manufacturing			
21				Mining
22				Utilities
23				Construction
30	Manufacturing			
31-33				Manufacturing
40	Transportation and Public Utilities	Electricity, Gas, Steam, Hot Water	Electricity, Gas, and Water Supply	
41				Wholesale Trade
44-45				Retail Trade
45		Construction	Construction	
48-49				Transportation
50	Wholesale Trade	Sale, Maintenance, and Repair of Motor Vehicles; Retail Sale of Auto Fuel	Wholesale and Retail Trade...	
51		Wholesale Trade ex. Motor Vehicles		Information
52	Retail Trade	Retail Trade		Finance & Insurance
53				Real Estate, Rental, Leasing
55		Hotels and Restaurants	Hotels and Restaurants	
56				Professional, Scientific, and Technical Services
57				Mgmt, Support, Waste Mgmt
60	Finance, Insurance, and Real Estate	Transport	Transport, Storage, and Communications	
61				Educational Services
62				Health & Social Assistance
65		Finance, Insurance	Financial Intermediation	
70	Services	Real Estate, Leasing	Real Estate, Renting, and Business Activity	
71				Arts, Entertainment, & Recreation
72				Accommodations & Food

Code				
75			Public Administration and Defense...	Service
78				
80	Services	Education	Education	
81				Other Services, Except Public Administration
85		Health and Social Work	Health and Social Work	
86				
90	Public Administration		Other Community, Social, & Personal Service	
91				Public Adminstration
95		Private Households with Employed Persons	Private Households with Employed Persons	
96				
9999	Nonclassifiable	Extra-Territorial Organizations & Bodies	Extra-Territorial Organizations & Bodies	

PART V
International Transactions

CHAPTER 15
International Trade and Payments

TOPICS COVERED

- Balance of Payments
- Foreign Trade
- Services
- Capital Flows
- Sources for Balance of Payment Statistics
- Sources for Merchandise Trade Statistics
- Sources for International Trade in Services
- Sources for Capital Flow Statistics
- Caveats for Researchers
- Additional Sources

MAJOR SOURCES COVERED

- *Balance of Payments Yearbook*
- *Direction of Trade Statistics*
- *Commodity Trade Statistics*
- *World Trade Annual*
- *International Trade Statistics Yearbook*
- *Trade Policy Review*
- *TradStat*
- *PIERS Imports/Exports*
- *World Trade Atlas*
- *WTO Trade Policy*
- *World Investment Directory*

The world economy is fueled by trillions of dollars of international investments and international purchases of goods and services. In tracing these international economic transactions, the researcher is faced with the problems of multiple monetary systems, economic policies, government regulations, and languages. In this chapter, we present the main concepts for international economic transactions. We use the categories of the balance of payments as the framework for our discussion.

BALANCE OF PAYMENTS

International economic transactions involve payment by the residents of one country to the residents of another. The payment may be in one of three forms:

- Barter (goods or services exchanged for other goods or services).
- The exchange of goods or services for money or other financial instruments.
- The exchange of financial claims (e.g., stocks exchanged for money).[1]

"Residents" includes governments, companies, and individuals. "U.S. residents," for example, includes persons residing and pursuing economic interests in the U.S. Corporations are considered to be residents of the country in which they are incorporated. In contrast, the foreign branches and subsidiaries of corporations are considered the residents of the country in which they are located.

International economic transactions are often divided into four types:

1. Merchandise trade (international transfer of physical goods).
2. International service transactions (international transfers of intangibles such as transportation and insurance).
3. Capital flows (international financial transfers such as direct foreign investment and purchase of financial instruments).
4. Official reserves transactions (transfers by governments of foreign exchange, special drawing rights, and monetary gold).

Together, merchandise trade, service transactions, capital flows, and official reserves transactions make up the economic series called the balance of payments.

The balance of payments provides a useful framework for understanding several economic concepts, including foreign trade, foreign direct investment, and international debt. The balance of payments is a statistical statement for a given period (usually a year) showing transactions between one economy and the rest of the world. The transactions are usually presented in the national currency of the compiling country. Payments are "balanced" in the sense that every transaction is entered on both sides of the balance sheet, as a debit and a credit based on double-entry bookkeeping. Debits are transactions that either increase a country's assets (items owned) or decrease its liabilities. Credits are transactions that either decrease assets or increase liabilities.

For example, here is the effect on the U.S. balance of payments when a resident of the U.S. purchases a car manufactured in Japan.

1. The transaction is recorded in the U.S. balance of payments as a debit. The acquisition of the automobile increases U.S. assets. The U.S. now has an additional automobile.
2. The transaction is also recorded in the U.S. balance of payments as a credit. The payment of dollars to the Japanese manufacturer increases U.S. dollar liabilities to Japan. The U.S. owes Japan several thousand dollars in payment for the car.

The effect on the Japanese balance of payments is the opposite.

1. The export of the automobile is recorded in Japan as a credit. Japan has one less automobile, a decrease in its assets.
2. The payment received in dollars is recorded as a debit. Japan has decreased its foreign currency claim liabilities.

We can better understand how the transaction is recorded by examining the balance of payments concept in more detail. Exhibit 15.1 shows the main categories of the balance of payments.

The balance of payments is often arranged into three subaccounts.

1. The *current account* groups all international transfers of goods and services, as well as unilateral transfers. Unilateral transfers by governments and private individuals refer to transfers of money for which there is no direct economic benefit. An example of a private unilateral transfer would be a Turkish worker in Germany sending money to her family in Turkey. An example of a public unilateral transfer would be the Canadian government sending aid to Somalia. Unilateral transfers are described as "unrequited transfers" in IMF publications.

    We frequently see more detailed subdivisions of the current account balance. The *merchandise trade balance* (the balance of trade) is a country's total export of merchandise minus its total merchandise imports for a given period. The *balance on goods and services* is a country's total export of both merchandise and services minus its total imports of merchandise and services.

	CREDITS	DEBITS
Current Account	Merchandise Exports	Merchandise Imports
	Service Exports	Service Imports
	Private Unilateral transfers (nonresidents)	Private Unilateral transfers (residents)
	Official Unilateral transfers by foreign governments	Official Unilateral transfers by national governments
Capital Account	Foreign Direct Investment (by nonresidents)	Foreign Direct Investment (by residents)
	Portfolio Investment by nonresidents	Portfolio Investment abroad by residents
	Other Long-term capital inflow	Other Long-term capital outflow
	Short-term capital inflow	Short-term capital outflow
Reserve Account	Net change in reserve	

BALANCE OF PAYMENTS CATEGORIES

EXHIBIT 15.1

Source: World Bank.

2. The *capital account* includes all financial transactions, with the exception of reserve transfers. It consists of direct foreign investment, portfolio investment, and short-term capital flows. *Foreign direct investment* is the ownership of enterprises located in one country by the residents of another country. *Portfolio investment* includes cross-border loans, bank deposits, and the purchase of stock. *Short-term capital* is capital payable on demand or with a maturity of one year or less.

3. *Reserve transfers* are the official financial transfers of a nation's monetary authority. A nation's monetary authority (frequently, the central bank) has the exclusive right to use gold, special drawing rights from the IMF, and foreign exchange to finance balance of payments transactions.

Let's return to our example of the effect on the balance of payments of a Japanese export of an automobile to the U.S.

- The balance of payments for the U.S. would record the transaction as both
  —a debit in the current account
  —a credit in the short-term capital account
- The balance of payments for Japan would record the transaction as both
  —a credit in the current account
  —a debit in the short-term capital account

In practice, individual international transactions are not recorded in a country's balance of payments ledger. However, total transactions are represented in the manner we have described. Thus, all imports of automobiles into the U.S. would be represented as both a debit in the U.S. current account and a credit in the short-term capital account.

Because the balance of payments is a key economic series, there is much interest in its components: merchandise trade, trade in services, and capital flows. Extensive detailed data are available on merchandise trade. The quality of these data is mixed; the import data for a country are generally of higher quality than its export data. For trade in services, the data are sketchy and often of poor quality. Capital flow data are described by many economists as positively misleading.

FOREIGN TRADE

Foreign trade is the physical movement of merchandise across international borders. Exports are goods shipped from a country. Imports are goods shipped into a country. Foreign trade is an important component of a country's balance of payments. For many countries, foreign trade constitutes a critical part of the economy. Import and export data are used by governments to assess their economic policy and by companies to evaluate foreign competition and to identify market opportunities. Merchandise trade is highly concentrated; about 80% of world trade is generated by 25 countries.

Trade between countries is profitable for both when one country can produce a particular product more efficiently than another country. Economic theory demonstrates that this efficiency does not have to be absolute but only comparative. For example, Japan may be more efficient than all other countries in producing both automobiles and airplanes. If Japan is relatively more efficient in producing automobiles than airplanes, Japan will maximize its gains by producing automobiles exclusively and purchasing airplanes from other countries.

The dollar value of world trade has increased 60-fold since 1950. The increase is the result of international agreements designed to improve world trade. Economists agree that the prosperity of individual nations improves with an increase in international trade. The degree to which trade can be improved depends on the following conditions:

- Stable exchange rates
- Improved employment and production in less developed countries
- Removal of trade barriers

Following the collapse of trade in the depression of the 1930s and the destruction of World War II, the international community created three key agencies that affected world trade: the International Monetary Fund (IMF), the International Bank for Reconstruction and Development (the World Bank), and the General Agreement on Tariffs and Trade (GATT). GATT was replaced by the World Trade Organization (WTO) in 1995.

The IMF and the World Bank were established at the Bretton Woods Conference in July 1944. The purpose of the IMF was to reduce the disruption in trade caused by unstable exchange rates. The nation members of the IMF agreed to peg their exchange rates to either the U.S. dollar or to gold. A country was not allowed to change the value of its currency except to correct a severe problem in its balance of payments. Since 1973, currencies of IMF member countries have been allowed to "float." The currencies no longer need to be pegged to the U.S. dollar or to gold. Market forces of supply and demand set a currency's value. The IMF helps nations maintain their currency's exchange value by allowing members to borrow the currencies of other countries.

The International Bank for Reconstruction and Development (the World Bank) was created to provide short-term capital for postwar reconstruction and long-term policies for providing a larger flow of international private investments. The World Bank was established to operate with the IMF. Each member of the IMF subscribes to the World Bank's stocks, and each member is given 250 votes and an additional vote for each share held. The World Bank promotes international private investments by providing guarantees, or by participating in loans when there is a need and private capital is not forthcoming. Loans are made for specific projects. Borrowers must be able to repay the loans.

GATT was a multilateral agreement drafted in 1947. It set rules of conduct for trade among signatory countries and provided a forum for trade negotiations and dispute resolution. Each GATT member sought to gain greater access to foreign markets by allowing more foreign access to domestic markets. Originally signed by 12 developed and 11 developing countries, GATT membership reached 125 members in 1994.

GATT members engaged in a series of eight negotiations called "rounds" between 1948 and 1995. The successive rounds of negotiations slowly and steadily lowered the barriers obstructing free trade. The first round led to GATT's establishment. The most recent round, called the Uruguay round, began in 1986 in Punta del Este with the object of expanding and improving multilateral trading. Finally signed in 1995, the Uruguay round went on for so long that pundits began referring to the GATT as the "General Agreement to Talk and Talk."

As part of the Uruguay round, GATT created a successor organization called the World Trade Organization (WTO), with expanded rule-making and enforcement responsibilities. Under GATT, trade disputes could run for years and countries involved in disputes could block the adjudication process or refuse to comply with rulings. The WTO process allows a maximum of 18 months for the settlement of all trade disputes. The International Trade Law Project at the University of Tromso, Norway, has texts of GATT and WTO documents, plus a list of current members of WTO. Their WWW site is http://itl.irv.uit.no/trade_law/documents/freetrade/wta-94/nav/toc.html.

GATT coexisted with the WTO in 1995 and ceased to exist on December 31, 1995.

In addition to the WTO, several other international organizations deal with trade issues. They include the Organization for Economic Cooperation and Development (OECD), the United Nations Conference on Trade and Development (UNCTAD), and the EU.

Trade Data

World merchandise trade involves over 200 countries, tens of thousands of product categories, and $5 trillion annually. With this level of complexity, it is not surprising that trade data are sometimes incomplete and often inconsistent. One inconsistency in merchandise trade data are that exports are usually underreported. For example, exports of merchandise from the U.S. to Canada should equal Canada's imports of merchandise from the U.S., but they seldom do. Canada's imports are usually higher than the corresponding export figures from the U.S. On a worldwide basis, there are about $150 billion less exports reported than imports. There are several reasons for this. Customs officials may be less diligent about reporting exports than imports. Exporting companies do not report transactions that are restricted or banned under law. Exporting companies also have incentives to understate export sales to reduce taxable income and to pay lower duties to importing countries.

Trade Classification

For nations to compare their international trade, they must agree on a classification scheme. The UN created the Standard International Trade Classification (SITC) in 1950. All member nations must submit their own foreign trade statistics to the UN based on this system, which uses five-digit codes grouped into 10 major categories. The SITC, with about 3,000 headings, is a useful classification system for international comparisons of trade. However, it may not be detailed enough to serve as a substitute for an individual country's import and export classification schedule. To meet the need for detailed and consistent schedules, many countries adopted the Harmonized Commodity Description and Coding System developed in 1985. The U.S. adopted the Harmonized System (HS) in 1989. It is important to realize that the SITC and the Harmonized System are completely different classification schemes. The *National Trade Data Bank* (CD-ROM) has cross-classification tables that give equivalent numbers for the Harmonized System, the SITC, and U.S. SIC numbers. An extensive classification concordance is available on the WWW (http://intrepid.mgmt.purdue.edu/Jon/Data/TradeConcordances.html#FromSITC). It includes cross-classifications of ISIC, SITC, U.S. SIC, Canadian SIC, Harmonized Codes, and NACE.

Developed by the Customs Cooperation Council, the HS classification consists of approximately 5,000 six-digit numbers arranged in 96 categories. Most countries, as well as the EU, have modified the HS classification for their own use. The EU uses the Combined Nomenclature, which contains about 16,000 headings.

The U.S. has extended the classification to the 10-digit level and uses separate classifications for imports and exports. The classifications are the same for the first six digits. Table 15.A shows the import and export classifications for computer printers. The import schedule gives a specific 10-digit code for laser printers. The export code has only an eight-digit code for printer units (and it is different from the import code).

TABLE 15.A

COMPARISON OF U.S. EXPORT AND IMPORT CLASSIFICATIONS

Imports
8471   Automatic data processing machines and units thereof
     8471.92   Input or output units
       8471.92.65   Printer units
         8471.92.6560   Laser printers
Exports
8471   Automatic data processing machines and units thereof
     8471.92   Input or output units
       8471.92.75   Printer units

Countries often use different codes beyond the basic six digits. For example, the U.S. and Canada both compile their merchandise trade statistics according to the Harmonized System. About 80% of the U.S. Schedule B Export Classification is directly comparable to Canadian import classifications. There are a few cases where U.S. and Canadian customs do not agree on the first six digits of the code.[2]

Regulation of International Trade

"Free Trade" is the unrestricted exchange of goods and services between countries. No country allows completely free trade. Signatories to the GATT agree to provide one another with most favored nation (MFN) status. MFN treatment requires that any tariff concession granted by one country to any other country is automatically extended to all other countries. The negotiations of GATT have sharply reduced the average tariffs worldwide, as can be seen from Table 15.B.

TABLE 15.B

URUGUAY ROUND REDUCTION IN AVERAGE TARIFFS ON IMPORTS FROM DEVELOPING COUNTRIES

All Sectors	Average MFN Rate Before	After
Canada	12.4	7.4
EU	9.8	6.9
Japan	7.4	4.7
United States	7.6	5.5

Source: World Economic and Social Survey: Current Trends and Policies in the World Economy (United Nations, New York, 1995): 117.

For the U.S., MFN treatment is the norm. As of 1996, only six countries (Afghanistan, Cuba, Kampuchea, Laos, North Korea, and Vietnam) were not given this status. Although Libya, Iran, and Iraq have MFN status with the U.S., trade embargoes against these countries make their MFN status irrelevant.

Exhibit 15.2 is a page from the Harmonized Tariff Schedule of the United States. It shows the rates of duty. In Column 1, "General" is MFN rates, and "Special" means rates below MFN rates. Column 2 is for countries given MFN status. In spite of their international agreements to improve the flow of trade, all governments attempt to regulate the international trade of their countries. Some of the principal reasons for this policy are:

- To improve their balance of trade. The "balance on merchandise trade" (imports minus exports) is an important component of balance of trade statistics. When exports exceed imports, countries are said to be running a positive trade balance. A positive trade balance often makes a country's currency more valuable abroad. This fact, in turn, can help reduce interest rates domestically.

- To protect national industries. Import protection can be designed to help industries survive, to prevent unemployment, or to counter "dumping" by foreign competitors. Dumping occurs when foreign suppliers sell imports at less than their home market price. The practice can drive domestic firms out of business.

- To respond to national pressure groups. Interest groups within a country often view imports as an economic threat. For example, the EU imposes import duties on imported agricultural products to protect internal farm prices, in response to a strong EU agricultural bloc.

HARMONIZED TARIFF SCHEDULE of the United States (1997)
Annotated for Statistical Reporting Purposes

Heading/ Subheading	Stat. Suffix	Article Description	Units of Quantity	Rates of Duty		2
				1		
				General	Special	
2203.00.00		Beer made from malt..............................	....	1¢/liter 1/	Free (A,E,IL, J) 1/ 0.1¢/liter (CA) 1/ 0.9¢/liter (MX) 1/	13.2¢/ liter 1/
		In containers each holding not over 4 liters:				
	30	In glass containers.....................	liters			
	60	Other...................................	liters			
	90	In containers each holding over 4 liters......	liters			

1/ Imports under this subheading are subject to Federal Excise Tax (26 U.S.C. 5051).

HARMONIZED TARIFF SCHEDULE OF THE UNITED STATES (1997)

EXHIBIT 15.2

- To protect national security. Countries restrict the export of products they believe to be vital to their national defense. The United States government, for example, will not allow the export of "stealth" technology.

Trade Restrictions

Governments use several techniques to control foreign trade. The most common device is the tariff, which is a tax on goods imported into a country. Bilateral treaties, multi-country trading arrangements such as the EU, and GATT have sharply reduced tariffs worldwide. However, countries use a variety of nontariff barriers. They include:

- Import quotas (quantitative restrictions on imports). For example, Canada has annual global import quotas for chickens, turkeys, and table eggs.
- Import licensing. Countries may prohibit imports without a license and then restrict the issuance of licenses.
- Export subsidies. The EU grants export subsidies on many agricultural products. This allows EU agricultural producers to sell on the world market below world market prices.
- Voluntary export restraints. A country may ask a trading partner not to export a particular product. For example, the U.S. has asked Japan to restrict its exports of automobiles to the U.S.
- Customs valuation procedures. By valuing imports at a higher price than market price, customs increases the duty payable.
- Local content regulations. Countries may require imported manufactured products to contain a certain percentage of domestic parts to escape tariffs.

SERVICES

Merchandise trade deals in tangible goods such as machinery, food, and textiles. Services, in contrast, are intangible. They have been described as ". . . the things that one can buy and sell, but not drop on one's foot."[3] Services include such activities as wholesale and retail trade, transportation, communication, banking, finance, insurance, real estate, and business services. According to the WTO, world trade in commercial services in 1995 was more than $1.2 trillion. The United States was the both the largest exporter and importer of commercial services, with 16% of world services exports and 12% of service imports.

Trade in services is much more difficult to measure than is merchandise trade. Although services are recorded by all countries as part of their balance of payments statistics, comparison between countries and between types of services is difficult for the following reasons:

- There is no detailed international classification of trade in services.
- The methods used to value services are not identical in all countries.
- There is little agreement on valuing certain services, such as insurance operations.
- Certain transactions are not regarded as services by all nations. For example, construction operations

carried out abroad and lasting more than a year are treated by some countries as direct investment rather than services.[4]

Despite the problems of data collection and comparison, some information concerning international transfer of services is available.

CAPITAL FLOWS

Capital flows are transactions in financial assets between residents of different countries. Capital flows include foreign direct investment, portfolio investment, and short-term capital investment.

- Foreign direct investment is the ownership of enterprises located in one country by the residents of another country. Countries often use some percentage of foreign ownership of a business to define foreign investment. In the U.S., foreign direct investment is defined as the ownership of 10% or more of the voting securities of an incorporated business enterprise or an equivalent interest in an unincorporated business. A U.S. firm meeting this criterion is considered a domestic affiliate of a foreign investor. All investment transactions between parent organizations and their foreign affiliates are direct investment flows. For example, Honda's establishment of a manufacturing plant in the U.S. is an example of a foreign direct investment. *Flows* of foreign direct investment refer to the amounts invested by foreign parent companies in affiliates during a period, usually a year. A *stock* of foreign direct investment refers to the cumulative outstanding value of direct investment at any point in time, usually the end of a year. Most countries report only flows of direct foreign investment.
- Portfolio investment includes cross-border loans, bank deposits, drafts, and the purchase of security equities. Portfolio investments are, by definition, not large enough to qualify as direct foreign investment. An example of a portfolio investment would be the purchase of 100 shares of IBM stock by a citizen of Germany.
- Short-term capital is capital payable on demand or with a maturity of one year or less. Short-term capital includes the cross-border transfer of currency (cash).

With the explosion in direct and portfolio investments across national boundaries in the 1980s, the values of capital flows have come to surpass those of trade flows. The measurement of capital flows is important for a nation in several respects. For example, such measurements allow a country to assess the impact of foreign direct investment on the domestic economy and to estimate the amount of foreign indebtedness.[5]

Of all data on international economic transactions, capital flow statistics are most subject to errors and gaps. Clive Crook, the economics editor of the *Economist*, refers to "lies, damned lies, and capital flows"[6] and notes that any attempt to measure capital flows quickly runs into acute difficulties. For example, the IMF reports that in 1990 all countries contributed $229 billion to direct investment, but only $179 billion is reported as received by countries in which the money was invested. Fifty billion dollars appears to have been lost in transit. Instant cross-border electronic transfer of funds makes it difficult for nations to keep track of capital flows.

Moreover, countries use different methods to measure flows and may have different definitions of foreign direct investment. For example, the U.K. defines foreign investment as ownership of 20% or more voting shares of all directly and indirectly owned subsidiary companies. The U.S. uses 10% ownership as its criterion. In addition, the two countries use different accounting principles to compile financial data and have different methods of collecting the data. The definition of foreign direct investment may change over time. Australia's definition of foreign direct investment was 25% ownership until 1986 when the threshold was lowered to 10%.

John Dunning and John Cantwell were the first to deal systematically with capital flow statistics in their work *IRM Directory of Statistics of International Investment and Production,* described below.

SOURCES FOR BALANCE OF PAYMENT STATISTICS

Balance of Payments Yearbook (published by the IMF)

We begin our discussion of sources with a description of balance of payments statistics. The most comprehensive general source of balance of payments statistics is the IMF's *Balance of Payments Yearbook*. The data are based on reports sent to the IMF by member countries.

Volume 1 consists of country sections, containing both a general (aggregated) presentation of the transaction data, as well as a detailed presentation. Figures are in U.S. dollars. Annual and quarterly data are given if available. Data are shown for the eight or nine most recent periods. For some of the industrialized countries, stock data are given for the capital and reserve accounts, in addition to transactions data.

Volume 2 of the *Yearbook* aggregates the data by balance of payment category and breaks down the data by country group.

Volume 3 of the *Yearbook* contains technical reviews describing methodologies, compilation practices, and data sources used by countries in compiling their balance of payments statistics.

In addition to print, the *Yearbook* is also available on CD-ROM and computer tape. An excerpt is shown in Exhibit 15.3. Summaries of balance of payments data can also be found in the IMF publication, *International Financial Statistics*.

The Balance of Payments Yearbook began to include data from Russia and some of the states of the former Soviet Union in its 1996 edition. The IMF publication *Economic Review: Russian Federation* gives estimates of summary balance of payments statistics for both Russia and the former USSR for 1990 and 1991.

The OECD and the EU also publish detailed balance of payments statistics for their member nations. We briefly describe their publications below, under "Additional Sources."

The primary sources for balance of payments statistics are the publications of individual countries. A useful listing of these publications can be found in the *Balance of Payments Yearbook* "notes" to the country sections. Often a country's central bank is responsible for collecting balance of payments data.

Current estimates of international transactions of the U.S., including estimates of merchandise and service trade, are reported quarterly in the *Survey of Current Business*. Estimates of the international investment position of the United States appear in the *Survey* annually. The *Survey of Current Business* is available through STAT-USA at least a week before the printed version. The electronic version (in PDF format) is available at least a week before the printed version. There is a fee to access STAT-USA (http://www.stat-usa.gov).

Balance of payments data for individual countries are available as well in several online (time-sharing) databases, including WEFA and Datastream. *Econbase*, a subset of the WEFA database that is available on DIALOG, can sometimes be used as an inexpensive substitute for the more specialized economic online sources. *Econbase* contains current account balance and capital account balances for about 20 nations from 1970. Forecast data are available for the current account balances of many of these countries.

France
132

Table 1. ANALYTIC PRESENTATION, 1988–95
(Millions of U.S. dollars)

	Code		1988	1989	1990	1991	1992	1993	1994	1995
A. Current Account [1]	4 993	Y .	−4,619	−4,671	−9,944	−6,518	3,893	8,990	7,033	16,443
Goods: exports f.o.b	2 100	. .	161,586	172,186	208,932	209,172	227,442	199,044	224,726	270,400
Goods: imports f.o.b	3 100	. .	−169,242	−182,491	−222,186	−218,886	−225,071	−191,528	−217,677	−259,225
Balance on Goods	4 100	. .	−7,656	−10,305	−13,253	−9,714	2,371	7,516	7,049	11,175
Services: credit	2 200	. .	54,523	59,940	76,457	80,100	91,765	86,377	90,390	97,770
Services: debit	3 200	. .	−43,836	−46,342	−61,052	−63,690	−72,647	−69,536	−71,103	−78,530
Balance on Goods and Services	4 991	. .	3,031	3,293	2,151	6,696	21,489	24,357	26,336	30,415
Income: credit	2 300	. .	34,016	41,287	55,736	69,771	87,596	98,992	110,034	130,033
Income: debit	3 300	. .	−34,969	−41,566	−59,632	−75,503	−96,210	−108,158	−120,972	−137,479
Balance on Goods, Services, and Income	4 992	. .	2,078	3,013	−1,745	964	12,875	15,191	15,398	22,969
Current transfers: credit	2 379	Y .	13,012	11,524	14,795	18,756	20,726	16,743	15,857	19,351
Current transfers: debit	3 379	. .	−19,709	−19,208	−22,994	−26,238	−29,707	−22,944	−24,222	−25,877
B. Capital Account [1]	4 994	Y .	−186	−211	−4,133	−27	661	27	−4,641	−115
Capital account: credit	2 994	Y .	217	235	219	252	929	305	271	301
Capital account: debit	3 994	. .	−403	−446	−4,352	−279	−268	−278	−4,912	−415
Total, Groups A Plus B	4 010	. .	−4,805	−4,882	−14,077	−6,545	4,555	9,016	2,391	16,329
C. Financial Account [1]	4 995	X .	−1,307	10,361	24,764	−3,066	−8,035	−16,675	−3,934	−20,484
Direct investment abroad	4 505	. .	−14,496	−19,498	−34,823	−23,932	−31,269	−20,605	−22,801	−18,734
Direct investment in France	4 555	Y .	8,490	10,304	13,183	15,153	21,840	20,754	16,628	23,735
Portfolio investment assets	4 602	. .	−4,152	−6,653	−8,409	−15,716	−18,463	−31,499	−24,659	−22,901
Equity securities	4 610	. .	−1,164	−1,455	501	−2,979	−1,550	−2,522	−1,952	606
Debt securities	4 619	. .	−2,988	−5,198	−8,910	−12,737	−16,912	−28,977	−22,706	−23,507
Portfolio investment liabilities	4 652	Y .	11,945	32,045	43,219	29,535	52,500	34,516	−30,109	9,700
Equity securities	4 660	Y .	1,746	6,999	5,898	7,663	5,407	13,579	4,807	7,070
Debt securities	4 669	Y .	10,199	25,046	37,322	21,873	47,093	20,937	−34,916	2,630
Other investment assets	4 703	. .	−28,178	−62,794	−61,543	151	−61,086	−13,380	26,316	−25,604
Monetary authorities	4 703	. A	. . .	. . .	. . .	. . .	. . .	. . .	. . .	. . .
General government	4 703	. B	−5,157	−4,468	−1,574	−5,125	−4,961	−3,911	1,683	−1,349
Banks	4 703	. C	−23,525	−52,303	−52,831	8,739	−65,086	−46,688	22,630	−46,719
Other sectors	4 703	. D	504	−6,023	−7,138	−3,463	8,961	37,219	2,002	22,464
Other investment liabilities	4 753	X .	25,084	56,956	73,136	−8,257	28,444	−6,460	30,689	13,320
Monetary authorities	4 753	XA	−4,104	3,541	−325	644	22,022	−1,070	−9,910	2,713
General government	4 753	YB	−231	−17	−556	−135	112	231	328	465
Banks	4 753	YC	27,355	57,505	80,259	−5,074	10,394	−5,688	32,499	15,217
Other sectors	4 753	YD	2,063	−4,072	−6,242	−3,692	−4,084	66	7,772	−5,076
Total, Groups A Through C	4 020	. .	−6,112	5,479	10,687	−9,611	−3,481	−7,658	−1,543	−4,155
D. Net Errors and Omissions	4 998	. .	953	−6,336	262	4,416	1,905	2,652	3,991	4,868
Total, Groups A Through D	4 030	. .	−5,159	−857	10,949	−5,194	−1,576	−5,006	2,448	712
E. Reserves and Related Items	4 040	. .	5,159	857	−10,949	5,194	1,576	5,006	−2,448	−712
Reserve assets	4 800	. .	5,159	857	−10,949	5,194	1,576	5,006	−2,448	−712
Use of Fund credit and loans	4 766	. .	. . .	. . .	. . .	. . .	. . .	. . .	. . .	. . .
Liabilities constituting foreign authorities' reserves	4 900	. .	. . .	. . .	. . .	. . .	. . .	. . .	. . .	. . .
Exceptional financing	4 920	. .	. . .	. . .	. . .	. . .	. . .	. . .	. . .	. . .
Conversion rates: French francs per U.S. dollar	0 101	. .	5.9569	6.3801	5.4453	5.6421	5.2938	5.6632	5.5520	4.9915

[1] Excludes components that have been classified in the categories of Group E.

BALANCE OF PAYMENTS YEARBOOK

EXHIBIT 15.3

Source: Balance of Payments Yearbook, IMF.

SOURCES FOR MERCHANDISE TRADE STATISTICS

Foreign trade data are compiled by individual countries, by several international organizations, and by commercial database producers. The international organizations include the EU, the OECD, and the UN, with its specialized agencies such as the International Monetary Fund.

The foreign trade publications of international organizations have several common characteristics. The first is long delays before the information is published. In general, the more commodity and country detail we require, the longer we must wait for it.

A second characteristic of foreign trade data published by international organizations is lack of product detail. The EU's annual *External Trade Statistics* with eight-digit harmonized code product description is an exception. The details of product descriptions in the other sources vary from none at all (in the publications of the IMF) to five-digit SITC descriptions in some UN publications. In comparison, the Harmonized System used by many countries in their individual foreign trade reports gives 7- to 10-digit classifications of products. The lack of product detail is not necessarily a shortcoming. We often want aggregate statistics. In addition, detailed product listings of trade among many countries are cumbersome in a book format. The eight-digit detail presented by the EU requires 26 volumes a year, in minuscule print.

A final characteristic of the publications of international organizations is that they provide a consistent format and valuation method over time. With the exception of the EU, they use the SITC classification. Although the SITC system was revised in 1960, in 1976, and again in 1988, its main features are constant. All the publications use the U.S. dollar as the measure of value, with the exception of the EU, which uses the ECU.

Table 15.C shows the characteristics of several standard foreign trade publications of international organizations.

One of the complications of finding import/export statistics is the variety of variables that may be used to present the data. The variables include:

- Product type
   Ranging from "all products" to 10-digit code detail
- Measurement
   Price (for individual units of products)
   Quantity (such as kilograms)
   Value (price times quantity)
- Classification variety
   Standard International Trade Classification
   Harmonized Code
- Country/geographic area/political group
   Japan
   EU
   Non–oil exporting nations
   Central America
   Massachusetts
- Time period
   Current month
   Year-to-date
   Annual trade
- Valuation
   CIF
   FOB
   FAS

In addition, we may want reports in a particular format, such as a ranking by value, or as an import/export matrix of countries. We may want quantities expressed in nonstandard forms (e.g., export volume expressed as pairs of shoes rather than weight of shoes). We may be interested in the details of "re-exports" and "re-imports," or in the volume of trade passing through a particular port.

TABLE 15.C

CHARACTERISTICS OF FOREIGN TRADE PUBLICATIONS

Publication	Lag	Numeric Detail	First Published
Direction of Trade (IMF)	1 Yr	-	1964
Direction of Trade Annual (IMF)	2 Yrs	-	1962
Eurostat Annual External Trade (EU)	2 Yrs	8	1964
Eurostat Monthly (EU)	1 Yr	2	1964
Foreign Trade by Commodities (OECD)	1 Yr	2	1960
Monthly Stats of Foreign Trade (OECD)	4 Mths	2	1960
Commodity Trade (UN)	2 Yrs	4	1951
International Trade Statistics (UN)	3 Yrs	5	1952
World Trade Annual (UN)	5 Yrs	5	1963

An important consideration is the different methods of measuring the value of trade. The value of imports for most countries is recorded as CIF (the cost of the item plus the cost of insurance and freight required to ship the item to its port of entry). The value of exports for most countries are recorded as FOB (Free on Board). This includes the cost of the item plus the cost of loading, but does not include insurance or ongoing freight charges. An exception to this rule is the United States, which values its exports FAS (Free Alongside Ship). This includes the cost of the commodity plus all costs associated with getting the product to a shipping point.

The IMF and the UN both publish merchandise trade data. The IMF statistics are general trade figures between countries that are IMF members. The UN statistics give detailed commodity descriptions of trade between UN member countries. The World Trade Organization publishes detailed studies of the trade practices of individual countries. We discuss the major trade publications of the IMF, the UN, and WTO in some detail.

The EU and the OECD also publish trade statistics for their member states. We outline these publications in the "Additional Sources" section of this chapter.

IMF Trade Publications

Direction of Trade Statistics (published quarterly by the International Monetary Fund)

Direction of Trade Statistics (DOT) was first published in 1964. It gives current figures on the value of merchandise exports and imports in dollars for more than 150 countries, including details of trade with their major trading partners arranged by country and area. The reported data are supplemented by estimates whenever the data are not current or are unavailable. In addition to tables for individual countries, *DOT* publishes the following aggregate tables:

- "World Aggregates," comprising all countries including about 37 small countries for which individual country tables are not presented.
- "Industrial Country Aggregates," 22 countries.
- "Developing Countries Aggregates."

Trade data are made available monthly with a delay of four months or less by 43 countries representing about 80% of recorded world exports and imports. Reported data, including data published in *International Financial Statistics,* are the basis of all estimates. The data have a lag of about five months—the December quarterly has figures up through July.

A companion IMF publication, the *Direction of Trade Statistics Yearbook,* presents seven-year time series of merchandise trade for about 180 countries. For each country, the *Yearbook* gives dollar value of trade for major trading partners and percent distribution and annual percent change for individual countries' trade by geographic area. It also includes aggregate tables for the world, geographic regions, the EU, and oil exporting countries. The *Yearbook* was first published in 1962.

United Nations Trade Publications

Commodity Trade Statistics (published annually by the UN)

This publication combines product detail (mostly four-digit SITC) with comprehensive country coverage (almost all UN members are included). The information is reported to the UN annually by member countries and converted to a common format that allows direct comparisons to be made between countries over time. Values are in thousands of U.S. dollars; the lowest published value is $100,000. The conversion into U.S. dollars has been made using weighted exchange rates. Quantities, when available, are expressed in metric units.

Exhibit 15.4 shows the general form of the statistics. In this table, 885 is an SITC number. The numbers following areas and countries are values in thousands of U.S. dollars. The abbreviation "EC" stands for "economies." Other tables may include measures of quantity; e.g., weight in kilograms.

World Trade Annual (published annually by the UN)

Published annually since 1963, the *World Trade Annual* provides detailed and summary trade statistics by commodity by nation for 23 industrial countries, using SITC classifications to the five-digit level. The *Supplement to the World Trade Annual* gives trade of the industrialized nations with developing countries. It is arranged by country. The *World Trade Annual* and its *Supplement* are very slow in publication. The 1987 edition, for example, appeared in 1992.

International Trade Statistics Yearbook (published annually by the UN)

The *Yearbook* is published in two volumes. It provides trade statistics on more than 150 countries. The first volume contains:

- The total value of imports and exports by country for each year since 1954.
- Imports and exports expressed as a percentage of total value for broad industry groups for the previous seven years.

885 WATCHES AND CLOCKS	
WORLD	152452
DEVELOPED EC	114209
DVELOPING EC	37924
OTHER	318
NORTHRN.AMER	647
N.AMER.DEVPO	647
USA	645
ASIA	47318
ASIA DEV'PED	9568
JAPAN	9564
ASIA DEV'PNG	37749
OTHER ASIA	37745
CHINA	5062
HONG KONG	28787
KOREA REP.	901
•	•
•	•
EUROPE	104354
EUROPE DEVPD	103990
EEC	36284
BELGIUM-LUX	406
•	•
•	•

IMPORTS OF AUSTRIA JANUARY–DECEMBER 1991

EXHIBIT 15.4

Source: *Commodity Trade Statistics* (Austria), Jan-Dec 1991: 165.

- Trade by principal countries of origin and last destination for the previous five years.
- The value of the country's trade for the previous 10 years, reported as a percentage of their world trade for major trading partners, political group, and geographic areas.
- General exports and imports by commodity group in U.S. dollars and in weight for the previous four years. Up to five-digit SITC detail is given.
- Several special tables, including world exports by commodity classes and by regions, and export price index numbers of primary commodities.

The second volume contains:

- Import/export value by product, broken down by country, political group, and geographic area for the past five years. The product detail is three-, four-, and five-digit SITC groups.
- The value of the product's trade for the previous 10 years, reported as a percentage of the product's world trade for major industrial countries, political groups, and geographic areas.
- Commodity matrix tables for the year of publication. They show the trade between countries for specific three-digit SITC product groups. Twenty-

two exporting countries and 20 importing countries are ranked for value for each commodity.

The *International Trade Statistics Yearbook* is useful for time series of trade by product or by country. It is less complete than the *UN Commodity Trade Statistics* or *World Trade Annual* in providing details of product trade among countries.

WTO Publications

Trade Policy Review (published by the WTO, frequency varies)

Under GATT, the trade policies of all contracting parties were subject to periodic review. The policy is being continued by the WTO. The four largest "trading entities" (countries and trading blocs such as the EU) by world market share, counting the European Union as one, are reviewed every two years. WTO reviews the next largest 26 trading entities every four years, and others every six years. Reviews are conducted by the WTO council on the basis of two reports, one presented by the contracting party under review and another drawn up by the WTO secretariat. Following each review the reports are published.

Trade Policy Review: Switzerland (1996) is a typical WTO review. It is in two sections (called "volumes"). Volume 1 consists of a description of Switzerland's role in world trade, a description of its economic environment, and its trade policy regime. Most of the volume is devoted to a detailed description of Switzerland's trade policy. The second volume is written by the government of Switzerland. Its purpose is to answer questions raised by the WTO in the first volume and to supply additional information concerning Switzerland's trade policies.

The annual *WTO International Trade, Trends and Statistics* provides a broad overview of world trade and its impact on individual economies. It is useful for the general picture it gives of world trade and its product composition for the past 20 years.

The WTO Web site (http://www.wto.org/) has executive summaries of *Trade Policy Reviews* as well as excerpts from *WTO International Trade, Trends and Statistics*.

Trade Statistics from Individual Countries

The foreign trade statistics published by individual countries are more accessible than most country-specific data sources. Language differences may not be a serious problem in using an individual nation's printed trade statistics. There is little text, and the sources often use the Harmonized Code to categorize products. In addition, the trade statistics of many non–English-speaking countries include English translations. The main drawback to the use of these sources for purposes of comparison will be the lack of a standard currency unit.

The main sources for U.S. import/export statistics are described clearly in Michael Lavin's *Business Information: How to Find It, How to Use It*, 2nd ed. (Oryx Press, 1992). Several electronic sources for U.S. trade data have appeared after the publication of *Business Information*. Examples of such products are described in the next section.

Online Sources for Merchandise Trade Statistics

The printed sources we have described often have electronic equivalents. *Direction of Trade*, for example, is available on CD-ROM and on magnetic tape. The electronic formats will have the same shortcomings as the printed products; namely, lack of product detail and lack of timeliness. The trade publications of international organizations are useful mainly as economic indicators and for historical research. The identification of trade opportunities, the monitoring of specific product imports and exports, and the identification of potential trade partners require electronic sources that are timely and detailed.

TradStat (DataStar)

TradStat is a world trade statistics database that provides official government import/export information on all reported commodities traded by 24 countries. In addition, the database can create aggregate import or export reports for the European Union. Available through the DataStar online system, *TradStat* includes about 90% of world trade. *TradStat* obtains its data tapes directly from official government statistical or customs offices. The monthly data are usually received within 4–10 weeks of the trading month. The data are stored by detailed customs product code representing more than 60,000 traded commodities. Monthly data for the latest 25 months are stored online for all reporting countries. Annual data are available from 1982 for many of the countries in the file. Table 15.D lists the countries in the database, the year from which data are first available, and the year in which the data can be searched by harmonized code number.

The product codes for individual countries can be searched online, but there are several complications. The Harmonized Code is used only from 1988/89 to date. Before this date, countries used their national

TABLE 15.D		
COUNTRIES AND YEARS OF COVERAGE IN *TRADSTAT*		
Country	*Beginning Year Online*	*Harmonized Code*
Argentina	1986	1990
Austria	1982	1988
Belgium/Lux	1982	1988
Brazil	1985	1989
Canada	1982	1988
Denmark	1982	1988
Finland	1988	1988
France	1982	1988
Germany*	1982	1988
Greece	1985	1988
Hong Kong	1985	1988
Ireland	1981	1988
Italy	1982	1988
Japan	1982	1988
Netherlands	1982	1988
Norway	1981	1988
Portugal	1986	1988
Spain	1984	1988
Sweden	1981	1988
Switzerland	1981	1988
Taiwan	1986	1989
Venezuela	1981	1990
United Kingdom	1982	1988
United States	1982	1989

*East Germany included from 1/1/91

trade classifications. The amount of product detail varies. Some countries do not use English for their product descriptions. Product classifications vary in detail over time and among countries. For example, the U.S. uses a 10-digit code after 1989 and a 7-digit code before that date.

An insight into the problems of trade data quality and availability is given by *TradStat*'s attempt to use trade figures from Mexico and India in 1992. The data provided by the Mexican authorities were poor (e.g., product codes with extra characters and symbols, and no corresponding descriptions). The Indian authorities would only publish data for 50 commodities out of several thousand commodities traded. Consequently, *TradStat* was unable to make the data from the two countries available.

TradStat allows flexibility in the selection and presentation of data. The database has 24 formats for the creation of import/export reports. The currency of any of the 22 countries in the database can be used to display price and value. The unit of quantity can be requested in the units used by each country or can be converted to a unit of your choice. You can search the database for a product or product group using either the harmonized code or natural language. Some examples of reports include:

- Import/export figures for the current month and year-to-date trade between a reporting country and all its trading partners.
- Year-to-date trade between a reporting country and its key trading partners (quantity value and price), by imports or exports.
- Ranking of the value of imports or exports between a reporting country and its partners for a product.
- Ten-year annual trend reports between a country and selected trading partners.

Exhibit 15.5 is an example of a *TradStat* report. It ranks the first 10 countries importing shampoo into Spain based on quantity. Currency is shown in U.S. dollars.

An important feature of the database is its ability to produce "deduced reports" for countries that do not supply figures to *TradStat*. Imports and exports are mirror images of trade. One country's imports are another's exports. For example, the figures for Poland's import of shampoo can be estimated from the export figures for shampoo reported for the 23 countries in the database. China's exports of plastic dolls can be deduced from the corresponding import figures of plastic dolls from China. It is also possible to produce deduced trade reports for each of the newly emerged states created after the breakup of the Soviet Union and Yugoslavia.

For the U.S., *TradStat* includes the names of the ports through which products were exported or imported. The U.S. port data should be identical to the information available on CD-ROM (*U.S. Exports and Imports of Merchandise*). It includes reporting district (e.g., New York City), the product, and the country of destination or origin.

TRADSTAT World Trade Statistics
R3 - IMPORT RANKING

PAGE 1
MONTH : 12/92
RUN DATE: 10/05/93

PRODUCT : (HS)33051000
   (HS) SHAMPOOS
REPORTING COUNTRY : SPAIN

COUNTRY IMPORTED FROM	YEAR TO DATE QUANTITY	PERCENTAGE OF TOTAL QUANTITY	YEAR TO DATE VALUE	PRICE
001 FRANCE	5404184	56.39	13737382	2.54
006 U.K.	1514423	15.80	4760175	3.14
331.95			14340	88.66
010 PORTUGAL	888785	9.27	927293	1.04
004 GERMANY	700927	7.31	2875589	4.10
2396.32			1200	7.42
400 U.S.A	363940	3.80	1547048	4.25
12086.31			128	0.79
003 NETHERLANDS	349226	3.64	909005	2.60
005 ITALY	180167	1.88	733386	4.07
48892.41			15	0.09
002 BELGIUM-LUXEMBOURG	72317	0.75	240096	3.32
404 CANADA	30000	0.31	89418	2.98
007 IRELAND	16124	0.17	117955	7.32
OTHER COUNTRIES	62753	0.65	292034	4.65
	492	3.04		593.57
CALCULATED TOTALS	9582846	100.00	26229382	2.74
	16175	100.00		1621.60

***** QUANTITY OPTIONS : PRIMARY QUANTITY IS SHOWN IN KILOGRAMS
                                              NO CONVERSION FACTOR WAS USED
                                              A FILTER WAS USED FOR TOP 10 TRADING COUNTRIES
                                              LINE 2 SHOWS QUANTITY IN SUPPLEMENTARY UNITS
***** CURRENCY OPTIONS : CURRENCY IS SHOWN IN US DOLLARS
                                              CONVERSION FACTOR FROM ORIGINAL UNITS WAS 112.48391

TRADSTAT REPORT—SPANISH IMPORTS OF SHAMPOO

EXHIBIT 15.5

Source: TradeStat—DataStar.

PIERS Exports/Imports (Journal of Commerce)

PIERS (Port Import Export Reporting Service) collects data from bills of lading and ship manifests of vessels loading international cargo at 62 U.S. seaports. *PIERS* covers all maritime movement into and out of the continental U.S., Alaska, and Puerto Rico. The records contain the details of each shipment—approximately 8.5 million transactions a year. They make the information available in several formats: as a time sharing system directly from *PIERS* or as a DIALOG database, as a CD-ROM database, and as hard-copy reports. *PIERS* is planning to expand its database to cover international air cargo transiting the nation's leading airports. Exhibit 15.7 is a record from *PIERS* showing the level of detail available for a single shipment of Chilean wine.

PIERS also collects similar data for its Latin American Trade Database with comprehensive coverage of Brazil, Chile, Colombia, Ecuador, Mexico, Peru, and Venezuela. The file is available as hard copy or on CD-ROM, tape, or diskette.

Exhibit 15.6 is a sample record from the *PIERS Imports* database.

```
14456118
  Product Imported: WINE FROM GRAPES
  Product Code: 1673000 (WINE; NOS)
    Weight of Cargo:      43982 POUNDS
    Number of Units of Cargo:    1300 CASES
  Date of Arrival (YY/MM/DD): 951214
  Exporter: VINA CHONCHA & TORO
    Company Location: SANTIAGO, CHILE (337)
  U.S.-Based Importer: BANFI PRODUCTS
    Company Location: FARMINGDALE, NY
  Point of Origin: VALPARAISO (33797), CHILE (337)
  U.S. Port of Discharge: NEW YORK (1001)
```

SAMPLE RECORD FROM *PIERS IMPORTS* DATABASE

EXHIBIT 15.6

Source: Sample data supplied by PIERS.

World Trade Atlas: U.S. (Global Trade Information Services, CD-ROM)

World Trade Atlas: Japan (Global Trade Information Services, CD-ROM)

Global Trade Information Services, Inc. (Columbia, SC; 803-765-1860), produces several compilations of trade data on CD-ROM. Their databases are distinguished by their completeness, currency, and ease of use.

World Trade Atlas software uses an ingenious solution for the problems of searching merchandise trade data. They provide a default table of trade data that can be modified to find the specific answer you need. Exhibit 15.8 shows the default table from *World Trade Atlas: Japan*. The table ranks Japanese exports by country of destination. Clicking on a country name will display a table of export trade with that country ranked by two-digit harmonized code category. For Japanese data, up to nine-digit harmonized code detail will be displayed, if available (Exhibit 15.9). For U.S. data, 10-digit code detail is given.

The software allows extensive revision of the tables, including toggling between export and import data, downloading to a spreadsheet, displaying graphs, sorting, and switching from volume to unit pricing.

World Trade Atlas: U.S. uses official U.S. export and import merchandise trade data from the Census Bureau. *World Trade Atlas: Japan* uses official Japanese export and import merchandise trade data from the Japan Tariff Associations. Both CD-ROMs are updated monthly.

Other GTI publications include *Waterborne Trade Atlas* and *Customs District Series of the World Trade Atlas*. These databases enable users to determine trade by product and country of destination or origin for all U.S. ports or U.S. customs districts at two-, four-, or six-digit level of the Harmonized Code.

National Trade Data Bank (published monthly by the United States Department of Commerce, ITA)

The *National Trade Data Bank* is described in detail in Chapter 12. One of the features of the database is its detailed U.S. trade statistics. The statistics are arranged in four groups.

Imports by Commodity (with country breakdowns)
Exports by Commodity (with country breakdowns)
Imports by Country (with commodity breakdowns)
Exports by Country (with commodity breakdowns)

For example, choosing "Imports by Country" and then "Japan" would retrieve a table similar to Table 15.E. It will give trade statistics for all two-digit harmonized code categories. It will then give statistics for 10-digit code categories. Table 15.E was downloaded as a spreadsheet file (comma delimited). It has been truncated to save space. Only the first four columns of numeric data are shown.

IMPEX (OECD, CD-ROM)

IMPEX is a database containing import and export data for members of the OECD. Trade information is available by commodity for reporting countries and their trade partners. Statistics are available annually from 1980 on. There is a two-year lag in the availability of data. Commodity detail is available to the five-digit SITC level. IMPEX is designed to download data to Excel spreadsheets. Table 15.F is a matrix showing total exports among four OECD members in 1992.

IMPORTER: (COMPANY NUMBER: 00080068013000)
  BANFI PRODUCTS
  21 BANFI PLAZA

  FARMINGDALE, NY 11735

SHIPPER: (COMPANY NUMBER: 00229925000000)
  VINA CHONCHA & TORO
  FERNANDO LAZCANO 1220

  SANTIAGO, CHILE

NOTIFY NAME : (COMPANY NUMBER: 00002449002000)
  FEDWAY ASSOC
  HACKENSACK AVE
  PO BOX 519
  KEARNY, NJ 07032

COMMODITY DETAILS
  MANIFEST COMMODITY DESCRIPTION: WINE IN BOTTLES
  JOC STANDARD COMMODITY DESCRIPTION AND CODE
    7 DIGIT : WINE; NOS (* 1671/1674) (1673000)
    4 DIGIT : STILL WINES (1673)
  HARMONIZED COMMODITY DESCRIPTION AND CODE
    6 DIGIT : WINE, FR GRAPE NESOI & GR MUST WITH ALC, NESOI (220429)
    4 DIGIT : WINE OF FRESH GRAPES; GRAPE MUST NESOI (2204)

  DIRECTION : I   SHIP LINE: SEAL VESSEL : SEA LAND HAWAII
  VOYAGE NUMBER : 122   VESSEL CODE: 7233278
  ARRIVAL DATE AT U.S. PORT: 97/06/11
  U.S. PORT & CODE   : NEW YORK (1001)
  FOREIGN PORT & CODE : HAINA (24741)
  ORIGIN POINT & CODE : SANTIAGO (33776)
  COUNTRY & CODE   : CHILE (337)
  US FINAL PORT CODE: 0000   FOREIGN FINAL PORT CODE: 00000

  CARGO PARTICULARS
  PACKAGING QTY/TYPE :   1,292 CS   0 CU FT
  CONFLAG: C   CONTAINER QTY/SIZE: 1   40
          2.00 TEU S   19.51 METRIC TONS
          $25,240 ESTIMATED VALUE THIS TRANSACTION
  BILL OF LADING: 229014211   MANIFEST NUMBER: 2709
  RECORD NUMBER: 40811618   AVAILABLE FROM PIERS AS OF: 97/07/18

REPORT FROM *PIERS IMPORTS* DATABASE

EXHIBIT 15.7

Source: Sample data supplied by PIERS.

World Trade Analyzer (Statistics Canada, International Trade Division)

This WWW site (http://www.tradecompass.com/trade_analyzer/) will display merchandise trade for 190 countries and 2,200 four-digit SITC for the years 1980–95, based on UN statistics. The database will display several preformatted reports, including:

- Importer Market Share Report. For a specific commodity and exporter country or region, this report shows the top 30 countries that import the commodity from the exporter country or region.

- Exporter Market Shares. For a specific commodity, this report shows which countries export the most to the market you choose (importing country or region).

- Top 30 SITCs Report. For a specific country or region of export and country or region of import pair, the Top 30 SITC Report shows which two-digit SITCs were most actively traded during a particular year.

Global Trade Information Services
World Trade Atlas

Total JAPAN Exports

CALENDAR YEAR
Billions of Yen

		% Share				% Change		
Rank	Country	1993	1994	1995	1993	1994	1995	95/94
	—WORLD—	40,202	40,498	41,531	100.00	100.00	100.00	2.55
1	USA	11,735	12,036	11,333	29.19	29.72	27.29	-5.84
2	KOREAN REP	2,124	2,489	2,928	5.28	6.15	7.05	17.61
3	TAIWAN	2,456	2,434	2,710	6.11	6.01	6.52	11.31
4	HONG KONG	2,525	2,632	2,600	6.28	6.50	6.26	-1.24
5	SINGAPORE	1,844	2,006	2,158	4.59	4.95	5.20	7.55
6	CHINA	1,911	1,914	2,062	4.75	4.73	4.96	7.75
7	GERMANY	2,021	1,823	1,908	5.03	4.50	4.59	4.63
8	THAILAND	1,365	1,502	1,850	3.40	3.71	4.45	23.13
9	MALAYSIA	1,070	1,263	1,573	2.66	3.12	3.79	24.59
10	UNITED KING	1,342	1,305	1,323	3.34	3.22	3.19	1.41
11	INDONESIA	667	783	935	1.66	1.93	2.25	19.30
12	NETHERLAND	830	858	932	2.06	2.12	2.24	8.67
13	AUSTRALIA	858	890	759	2.13	2.20	1.83	-14.67
14	PANAMA	511	599	672	1.27	1.48	1.62	12.09

REPORT FROM *WORLD TRADE ATLAS* (JAPAN)

EXHIBIT 15.8

Source: World Trade Atlas Japan. Reprinted with permission from Global Trade Information Service.

1995 Japanese vehicle exports		
Maker	Volume	Change from 1994
Toyota	1,202,420	-20.1%
Nissan	598,070	-1.8%
Mitsubishi	506,155	-9.1%
Mazda	440,392	-28.7%
Honda	433,937	-14.9%
Suzuki	200,527	+5.2%
Isuzu	208,280	-10.9%
Daihatsu	76,000	-15.4%
Fuji (Subaru)	71,344	-27.2%
Hino	31,256	+5.7%
Nissan Diesel	22,395	+8.2%
Total	3,790,778	-15.0%

EXPORT DATA FROM *PROMT*

EXHIBIT 15.9

Source: Japan Automobile Manufacturers Association.

Import/Export USA (CD-ROM produced monthly by Gale)

This title was published too late for us to examine. The publisher's brochure indicates that the CD allows you to search and display U.S. trade statistics as well as retrieve full-text articles relating to trade.

PROMT (Predicasts)

The online version of *PROMT* is primarily a bibliographic/full-text file, but it can often be used as a

convenient source of merchandise trade data that appear in trade publications. *PROMT* is available on several time-sharing systems including DIALOG and DataStar. Here is a search for tabular information about Japan's exports of automobiles. The database has the useful feature of allowing us to search for all information in tables. In the DIALOG system, the command is S SF=TABLE.

SOURCES FOR INTERNATIONAL TRADE IN SERVICES

The World Trade Organization estimated that the worldwide value of trade in services was $1.2 trillion in 1995, about 20% of the value of merchandise trade. Unlike merchandise trade, the details of international trade in services are scarce. For many countries, the only information concerning trade in services is given in their balance of payments figures. It consists of these three items:

- Transport
- Travel (tourism)
- Other services

For the U.S., international services transaction statistics are published annually in the *Survey of Current Business*. The *Survey* provides data in 25 broad categories for some 40 countries and areas. The detailed information presented in the *Survey* is then highly

TABLE 15.E

MERCHANDISE TRADE—U.S. IMPORTS BY COUNTRY IMPORTS FROM JAPAN

National Trade Data Bank (Web Version)

0 .	0 U 0	Commodity		
1 $	3 U 0	Gen: Customs	($1,000):	Jan-Aug, 1996
2 $	3 U 0	Gen: Customs	($1,000):	Jan-Aug, 1995
3 $	3 U 0	Gen: Customs	($1,000):	1995
4 $	3 U 0	Gen: Customs	($1,000):	1994
5 $	3 U 0	Gen: Customs	($1,000):	1993
6 $	3 U 0	Gen: C.i.f.	($1,000):	Jan-Aug, 1996
7 $	3 U 0	Gen: C.i.f.	($1,000):	Jan-Aug, 1995
8 $	3 U 0	Gen: C.i.f.	($1,000):	1995
9 $	3 U 0	Gen: C.i.f.	($1,000):	1994
10 $	3 U 0	Gen: C.i.f.	($1,000):	1993

Note: 2nd, 4th, etc. numeric columns are in addition to those shown above and indicate footnotes for the data. 0=valid zero, 1=rounds to zero

		0	1	2	3	4
	All commodities		75935965	84351811	123577419	119149367
01	Live Animals		873	5265	5618	1021
02	Meat And Edible Meat Offal		303	248	425	482
03	Fish And Crustaceans, Mollu		73425	70718	103346	127130
04	Dairy Produce; Birds' Eggs;		45	35	55	234
05	Products Of Animal Origin,		1470	2464	3195	2027
06	Live Trees And Other Plants		608	510	1100	1163
07	Edible Vegetables And Certa		4278	5641	7885	6393
08	Edible Fruit And Nuts; Peel		313	119	2322	2311
09	Coffee, Tea, Mate And Spice		2383	2438	3777	3925
10	Cereals		44	31	53	110
11	Milling Industry Products;		825	762	1305	1392
12	Oil Seeds And Oleaginous Fr		17475	20363	26839	26322
13	Lac; Gums; Resins And Other		10092	4890	8967	5844
14	Vegetable Plaiting Material		254	67	124	473
15	Animal Or Vegetable Fats An		12540	13557	20935	20594
16	Edible Preparations Of Meat		16054	16297	25043	27106
97	Works Of Art, Collectors' P		33759	55954	73095	71984
98	Special Classification Prov		878973	688146	1056494	1031206
99	Special Import Reporting Pr		502312	560024	831803	786572
8473301000	Prts Of Adp Mch, No		1202059	1423944	2225363	2063267
8703230044	Pass Mtr Veh,Nesoi,		1492851	1647336	2091072	2947517
8703230046	Pass Mtr Veh,Nesoi,		956098	1523304	2050422	3843481
8471935000	Storage Units, Neso		0	1192628	1924157	1431465
8703230068	Pass Veh,Spark Ign,		439624	1520328	1838817	2215061

TABLE 15.F

TRADE MATRIX FROM IMPEX

IMPEX	(OECD Trade Statistics)
Product	Total trade
Year	92
Flow	Exports
Currency	US Dollar

Units ('000)	Canada	U.S.	Japan	Germany	Total
Canada		96,959,447	6,128,939	1,788,699	104,877,085
U.S.	82,726,196		45,697,732	19,825,271	148,249,199
Japan	7,072,844	96,558,910		20,309,032	123,940,786
Germany	2,689,193	27,369,521	9,399,200		39,457,914
Total	92,488,233	220,887,878	61,225,871	41,923,002	416,524,984

condensed for reporting as part of the quarterly U.S. balance of payments. The U.S. has exceptionally detailed information on service trade.

International Trade in Services: EUR 12, from 1979–1988 (Eurostat, 1991)

Eurostat has produced the following classification for trade in services:

Transport
  Sea freight
  Sea passenger transport
  Air freight
  Air passenger transport
  Other transport

Travel/Tourism

Other Services
  Insurance
  Trade earnings (merchandising fees)
  Banking (financial institution fees)
  Advertising
  Business services (e.g., engineering, legal, management)
  Construction
  Communications (postal and telecommunication services)
  Films/television
  Income from patents
  Miscellaneous services

Eurostat has developed data for each of these categories for all EU countries, Japan, and the U.S. for the period 1979 to 1988. Eurostat warns that the figures they have developed should be interpreted with caution and trends should be analyzed rather than absolute figures.

Services: Statistics on International Transactions 1970–1993 (OECD, 1996)

The OECD has complied and assessed data for member countries' international trade in services. The series represent balance of payments data between residents of the reporting countries and nonresidents. Section A of the report presents data for the whole OECD area and for the main services categories. The structure of this section is derived from the standard components of the balance of payments. Section B presents data for individual countries. Data are shown in both national currency and U.S. dollars.

SOURCES FOR CAPITAL FLOW STATISTICS

Worldwide, foreign direct investment totals over $315 billion annually and represents an investment stock of about $2.7 trillion. The investment is highly concentrated; about three-fourths of world investment flows take place among developed countries; in particular, the U.S., the EU, and Japan. About two-thirds of all investment flows to developing countries are directed to just 10 countries.

The source for the above information is the annual *World Investment Report* a publication of the United Nation's Transnational Corporations and Management Division. Published since 1991, each *World Investment Report* has a distinctive title and theme. The 1996 edition was subtitled "Investment, Trade and International Policy Arrangements." "Annex Tables" in the 1996 edition provide information concerning international comparisons of direct foreign investment. Some examples of the tables include:

- Foreign direct investment inflows, outflows, and stock, by host region and economy, 1984–95.
- Cross-border merger and acquisitions sales, 1988–95.
- Cross-border merger and acquisitions, by industry 1988–95.
- Foreign direct investment inflows and outflows in infrastructure-related industries (various years).
- Bilateral investment treaties concluded from 1994–96).

A related series by the U.N.'s Transnational Corporations and Management Division are the six volumes of the *World Investment Directory*. The volumes in the series are:

Volume 1. *Asia and the Pacific*
Volume 2. *Central and Eastern Europe*
Volume 3. *Developed Countries*
Volume 4. *Latin America and the Caribbean*
Volume 5. *Africa and West Asia*
Volume 6. *Global Trends*

Collectively, the series has data for approximately 100 countries. The directories give data on foreign direct investment, basic data on businesses, the legal framework for investment, and extensive bibliographic sources. Each directory cautions that foreign direct investment statistics suffer from a lack of comparability and advise us to read the technical introduction and explanatory notes carefully.

The detail of the data presented varies by country. The following series are often available for a country:

- Number of foreign affiliates
- Sectoral distribution for foreign investment
- List of largest foreign affiliates in country
- Largest transnational corporations abroad

The data on direct investment flows are presented as 10-year time series, although for many countries most of the series may be absent. Exhibit 15.10 is an example of a summary table for Poland.

The *World Investment Directory* is designed to be an update and an extension of the *IRM Directory of Statistics of International Investment and Production* by John Dunning and John Cantwell. The *IRM Directory* assembled data on the international direct investment position of 80 countries in a systematic and comparable way. Although now outdated (1985), the *IRM Directory* was the first source that addressed issues of data quality and comparability of balance of payment statistics.

In the U.S., the Bureau of Economic Analysis (BEA) has the major role in collecting data on foreign direct investment. The BEA conducts quarterly, annual, and benchmark surveys of U.S. direct investment abroad and of foreign direct investment in the U.S. The information often appears initially in the *Survey of Current Business*. Here are the major information series on foreign direct investment and the month they appear in the *Survey*.

- The direct investment position and flows of capital, income, royalties, and license fees between parent companies and affiliates (June issue).
- Capital expenditures by majority owned foreign affiliates of U.S. companies (March and September issues).
- The financial structure and operations of U.S. parent companies and their foreign affiliates (month varies).
- The financial structure and operations of U.S. affiliates of foreign companies (May issue).
- U.S. business enterprises acquired or established by foreign direct investors (May issue).

In 1992, the Bureau of Economic Analysis in cooperation with the Bureau of the Census published highly detailed establishment level data on foreign direct investment in the United States. The data give the number, employment, payroll, and sales of the establishments of U.S. affiliates of foreign companies in 1987. In 1993, expanded information was published for 1989 and 1990 on the manufacturing establishments of U.S. affiliates. The information was published in summary form in the October 1992 *Survey of*

Table 1. Summary of international investment position (Millions of dollars)		
Variable	Inward	Outward
1. Flow of foreign direct investment '86 -'91 (annual av.)	111.7[b]	2.7[c]
2. Flow of foreign direct investment as percentage of GDCF	-	-
3. Foreign direct-investment stock 1991	670.0[b]	146.1[d]
4. Foreign direct-investment stock as percentage of GDP	-	-
5. Employment in foreign affiliates, 1990	85249	27[e]
6. Sales of foreign affiliates, 1990	1380.8[f]	4200.8
7. Number of foreign affiliates, 1991	15100	202[g]
8. Number of transnational corporations	-	58

Source: United Nations, Economic Commission for Europe, ECE database on East-West joint ventures; United Nations Department of Economic and Social Development, Transnational Corporation and Management Division, the *East-West Business Directory 1991/1992* (United Nations publication, Sales Nol. E.92.II A.20); and Carleton University, East-West Project database.

a Excludes "Polnia" investments.
b As of the end of the third quarter 1991.
c Includes only 1980-1990 annual average investment in developed countries.
d Includes only investments in operational foreign affiliates in developed countries, end-1990.
e Average estimated employment in foreign affiliates located in developed countries, per company, 1990.
f Sales of 1,119 operational foreign affiliates, end-1990.
g Number of operational foreign affiliates only, end-1990.

POLAND'S INTERNATIONAL INVESTMENT POSITION

EXHIBIT 15.10

Source: World Investment Directory, 1992.

Current Business and as a 650-page publication *(Foreign Direct Investment in the United States: Establishment Data for 1987).*

The *Survey of Current Business* is on the Internet. The electronic version (in PDF format) is available at least a week before the printed version on STAT-USA (http://www.stat-usa.gov), described below.

The *U.S. Treasury Bulletin* is a comprehensive source for information on foreign purchases and sales of long-term securities by type and country. The information provided includes country details as well as aggregate data (e.g., Asia).

The *U.S. Treasury Bulletin* is available in PDF format at http://www.ustreas.gov.

International Direct Investment Statistics Yearbook (OECD)

The OECD countries account for 90% of worldwide direct investment outflows and 80% of inflows. At the end of 1993, these figures represented $1.58 trillion for outward stock and $1.09 trillion for inward stock. The *Yearbook* (first published in 1993) is a joint effort of the OECD and Eurostat to harmonize foreign direct investment data collection and processing. The data are based on balance of payments statistics published by central banks and statistical bureaus. The 1995 *Yearbook* is organized in three parts. Part 1 includes summary tables in U.S. dollars on flow data for 1983–94 and stock data from 1982–93. Part 2 presents country data in national currencies. Part 3 includes a series of technical notes with detailed information on statistical sources and data collection methods for each country. This section is particularly valuable for its definitions of foreign direct investment for individual countries.

The *OECD Reviews of Foreign Direct Investment* is another important source for analysis of trends and foreign investment policies of OECD countries. Appearing since 1993, *OECD Reviews* concentrates on three or four countries each year.

CAVEATS FOR RESEARCHERS

The balance of payments and its components can generate many research questions. Before beginning research, be aware of the issues of data comparability between countries and data availability from individual countries. For example, comparing the amount of direct foreign investment of one country with another may involve differing definitions of "direct foreign investment." Other questions represent gaps in the collection of data. For example, the amount of a country's national currency circulating abroad is not

part of balance of payment statistics. The United States estimates this statistic as $200 to $250 billion in 1996.

ADDITIONAL SOURCES

Balance of Payments

Balance of Payments Manual, 5th ed. (IMF, 1993)

This is a guidebook for member countries reporting balance of payments statistics. It is also used as a model by the OECD and the EU. It is a convenient source for definitions of the components of the balance of payments.

Merchandise Trade

Handbook of International Trade and Development Statistics (published annually by the UN)

The *Handbook* presents merchandise data analytically. The tables emphasize growth rates, rank order, and extended time series.

Foreign Trade by Commodities (published annually by the OECD)

Published in multiple volumes, each containing import/export data at the two-digit SITC level for six OECD member countries. A final volume contains data arranged by country groups (the OECD, North America, Europe, and the EU).

External Trade Analytical Tables (published annually by Eurostat)

The *Tables* give breakdowns by eight-digit harmonized code category by country for EU member countries for imports and exports. A second breakdown of country by two-digit code is also presented. The EU began using the harmonized code to report trade statistics in 1988. Before 1988, they used the Nomenclature of Goods for the External Trade Statistics of the Community (NIMEXE). Eurostat publishes CD-ROM versions of its annual and monthly trade, and of historical data *(External Trade 1976–1987).* The newsletter *Statistics in Focus: External Trade*, published 10 times a year, discusses trade with important EU trading partners and blocks.

National Trade Estimate Report on Foreign Trade Barriers (published annually by the Office of the U.S. Trade Representative)

The *Report* supplies an inventory of the most important foreign barriers to U.S. exports of goods and services and barriers affecting U.S. investment and intellectual property rights. The publication gives quantitative estimates of the impact of these foreign practices on the value of U.S. exports. The trade barriers include laws, regulations, and policies that either protect domestic products from foreign competition or artificially stimulate exports of particular domestic products. It covers more than 40 countries and the EU.

The Year in Trade: Operation of the Trade Agreements Program (published annually by the U.S. International Trade Commission)

This report provides factual information on U.S. trade policy and its administration, together with a historical record of major trade-related activities of the past year. It is an excellent source of information on the activities of GATT and of other trade-related organizations such as the OECD, the Customs Cooperation Council, and the UN Conference on Trade and Development. It gives a good overview of existing U.S. trade agreements (such as the U.S.-Canada Free Trade Agreement) and NAFTA—the North American Free Trade Agreement. Chapters are devoted to developments with the major U.S. trading partners (the EU, Canada, Japan, Mexico, the Republic of Korea, Taiwan, and Brazil).

CONCLUSION

This chapter discussed the concepts and sources of information for international trade and payments. The balance of trade was used as a framework to discuss merchandise trade, international service transactions, and capital flows. There is great variation in the quantity and quality of data available for international trade and payment. A country's import data, for example, are often detailed and of good quality. Capital flow data, in contrast, are typically sketchy and of poor quality.

NOTES

1. Franklin R. Root, *International Trade and Investment* (Cincinnati: South Western Publication, 1990): 349.

2. *U.S. Merchandise Trade: Exports, General Imports, and Imports for Consumption*, U.S. Dept. of Commerce, May 1992: 5.

3. *Foreign Direct Investment and Transnational Corporations in Services*, United Nations, 1989: 4.

4. *International Trade in Services: EUR 12, from 1979 to 1988*, Offices for the Official Publications of the European Communities, 1991: 9.

5. *Behind the Numbers: U.S. Trade in the World Economy*, Washington, DC: National Academy Press, 1992: 156–57.

6. Clive Crook, "Fear of Finance," *Economist* (September 19, 1992): 6.

CHAPTER 16
International Financial Markets

TOPICS COVERED

- Foreign Exchange Markets
- The World's Financial Exchanges
- Sources of Information for Financial Markets
- Additional Sources

MAJOR SOURCES COVERED

- Datastream
- *European Directory of Financial Information Sources*
- *LGT Guide to World Equity Markets*
- *Emerging Markets Factbook*
- *Moody's International Manual*
- *Morgan Stanley Capital International Perspective*
- *Quarterly Review of Emerging Stock Market*
- *Tradeline International*
- *World Financial Markets*
- *World Currency Yearbook*

INTRODUCTION

Financial markets are concerned with the purchase or sale of one or more types of financial instruments, such as stocks or bonds. International financial markets are involved with financial transactions that cross national frontiers. Financial markets sometimes operate through exchanges—physical locations, such as the New York or London stock exchanges. Financial exchanges involve members who purchase the right to trade securities. Alternatively, financial markets may be communication networks (computer links and telephones) between buyers and sellers. Financial instruments not traded on exchanges are said to be traded OTC (Over the Counter). The globalization of financial markets may be making physical exchanges obsolete as electronic networks allow 24-hour trading around the world.[1]

Table 16.A summarizes the chief types of international financial markets, gives brief descriptions of their purposes, and lists a typical financial instrument.

International financial markets use many of the same financial instruments employed in domestic markets, including stocks, bonds, options, and futures. However, international markets may denominate these instruments in foreign currencies, in

Eurocurrencies, or in composite currencies such as the ECU (European Currency Unit). In addition, there are specialized instruments of international financial markets such as currency and interest rate swaps and foreign exchange forwards. The market for foreign currency is, by its nature, international in scope.

Specific factual questions about financial markets are often of two types. The first type concerns the operations and characteristics of the markets as a whole. For example:

> *What is the name, address, and principal officers of the Amsterdam exchange?*
>
> *What are the types and number of financial instruments traded on the London stock exchange?*
>
> *What has been the overall performance of the Tokyo Stock Exchange?*
>
> *How do the world's stock markets rank by size?*

The second type of question concerns the characteristics and performance of specific financial instruments. For example:

> *What was the high, low, and close of Sumitomo Corporation's stock on the Tokyo exchange on July 2, 1991? during 1990? for the past 10 years?*

TABLE 16.A

INTERNATIONAL FINANCIAL MARKETS AND INSTRUMENTS

Type of Market	Purpose	Typical Financial Instrument
Stock Market	Purchase or sale of equities	Common Stock
Bond Market	Purchase or sale of long-term debt obligations	Bonds
Money Market	Purchase or sale of short-term debt obligations	Commercial Paper
Foreign Exchange Market	Exchange of one country's currency for another country's	Forward
Commodity Market	Purchase or sale of agreements to take delivery of a commodity often at some date in the future	Future
Options Market	Purchase or sale of rights to buy or sell securities on or before a future date	Put/Call

What types of options, if any, are available on Sumitomo Corporation stock?

What is today's U.S. dollar to Japanese yen exchange rate?

What is a current rating for the bonds of the Tokyo Electric Power Company?

In this chapter, we will briefly describe the principal types of international financial markets and financial instruments and discuss sources of information for both.

FOREIGN EXCHANGE MARKETS

Central to all transactions in financial markets is the value of a country's currency in terms of other currency. Consequently, the market that has the greatest effect on all other financial markets is the foreign exchange market. Foreign exchange involves the buying and selling of currencies. A foreign exchange rate is the price of one country's currency in terms of another country's currency. Foreign exchange markets are mechanisms to transfer currencies between countries. They allow the free flow of goods and services among countries by providing a medium of exchange. In addition, exchange rates are important as economic indicators and as a means for the cross-border comparison of industries and companies.

Although there are no precise statistics on the volume of foreign exchange trading, we know that it is immense, perhaps a trillion dollars a day. Only about 5% of foreign exchange transactions are conducted by traders in goods and services.[2] Most transactions are the result of businesses hedging against fluctuations in currency values, or speculators attempting to profit by the same fluctuations. London is the leading center of foreign exchange transactions, with about 25% of the business. About 15% is handled in New York and 10% in Tokyo. The remainder of foreign trade transactions are spread among several cities including Frankfurt, Singapore, and Hong Kong.[3] A central part of the foreign exchange mechanism is the computer system of the Clearing House Interbank Payments System (CHIPS). Described as "the heart of global capitalism," CHIPS is owned by 11 large New York banks. When currency is converted into or out of dollars, it is often processed through the CHIPS computers because of their speed and low cost.[4]

In the spot foreign exchange market, currencies are purchased and sold for immediate delivery within two business days after the day that the transaction is agreed upon. In the forward market, foreign currencies are purchased and sold for future delivery (usually 30 or 90 days). A foreign exchange swap combines a spot purchase of a currency with the simultaneous sale of a forward on the same currency. A swap reduces the risk of switching from one currency to another and back again.

Although there are more than 150 currencies in the world, only about 50 countries have currencies that are actively traded. In addition to national currencies, there are two important composite currencies. These are the ECU (European Currency Unit) and the SDR (Special Drawing Right).

The ECU is the official currency unit for the European Monetary System, established in 1979. It is a weighted average of the currencies of countries that are members of the EU. Its value relative to the U.S. dollar is calculated daily. January 1999 is the proposed starting date for the European Monetary Union, at which time the ECU in its present form will cease to exist and be replaced by a common European currency.

The SDR is an artificial currency created by the International Monetary Fund (IMF). It is a weighted average of the U.S. dollar, the German mark, the French franc, the Japanese yen, and the British pound. Both the ECU and the SDR are used as a means of payment and loan. The ECU may be held by private individuals. Ownership of the SDR is confined to governments, although individuals may own financial instruments denominated in SDRs. The ECU is much more widely employed than the SDR.

Countries sometimes link or peg their currency to that of another country or to a basket of currencies. For example, several African nations (Niger, Senegal, and Togo) peg their currency to the French franc. These "exchange rate arrangements" are listed in the IMF's monthly *International Financial Statistics*.

Currency Quotations

Currencies can be quoted in terms of the number of units of currency A to currency B (for example, the number of U.S. dollars required to "buy" one German mark), or in terms of the number of units of currency B to currency A (the number of German marks required to "buy" a U.S. dollar). The two exchange rates are reciprocals. For example, if there are 1.55 German marks (DM) per U.S. dollar (if one dollar will buy 1.55 DM), there are $1 \div 1.55$ or .64817 U.S. dollars per DM (i.e., the DM is worth about 65 cents).

The relative value of two non-U.S. currencies is usually determined by comparison of the value of each against the U.S. dollar. These exchange rates are called "cross rates." If you know the exchange rate of two currencies to the dollar, you can calculate the cross rate. For example, if a U.S. dollar is worth 1.2590 Australian dollars and 1.4646 New Zealand dollars, the exchange rate of the Australian to the New Zealand dollar is:

$$1.4646 \div 1.2590 = 1.1633$$

Thus, the Australian dollar is thus worth 1.1633 New Zealand dollars. Exchange rates are usually quoted to four decimal places. Transactions in these currencies usually involve one million units of currency. Exchange rates may be expressed as a bid price (the price at which a bank is willing to buy the currency) and an asked price (a higher price for which banks are ready to sell a currency). The difference between selling and buying rates is called the spread. Occasionally, rates will be reported as midpoint rates (the midpoint between the bid price and asked price).

When one price is given as the exchange rate, it is usually the selling price (the asked price).

There are several potential pitfalls in interpreting foreign currency exchange rates. Some issues to be aware of are:

- How was the rate quoted? For example, a weekly U.S. dollar to Japanese yen exchange rate may be calculated as an average of the week, or it may be the closing rate at the end of the week. A daily rate may be calculated at different times of the day.
- Where was the rate quoted? An exchange rate that represents the daily close in New York may be different from the closing rate for the same day in London.
- What does an exchange rate represent? Exchange rates may be expressed as bid rates (the rate at which a dealer is willing to buy a currency), asked rates (the rate at which a dealer is willing to sell a currency), or midpoint rates (the average of the bid and asked rate).

To clearly define what its exchange rates represent, the *Federal Reserve Bulletin* uses the following footnote in its table of monthly and annual rates: "Averages of certified noon buying rates in New York for cable transfers."

In addition, exchange rates may expressed as "trade weighted" or as "real exchange rates." Trade weighted exchange rates take into consideration the importance of a country's trading patterns in determining the value of its currency. For the United States, changes in the value of the Canadian dollar (a leading trading partner) would be of more importance (would have a greater weight) than changes in the Italian lira. Real exchange rates adjust nominal exchange rates for the difference in inflation among countries. Trade weighted and real exchange rates are expressed as index numbers. The relation between the price of goods and exchange rates is known as purchasing power parity. Purchasing power parities are described in more detail in Chapter 13.

Be aware of devaluations or revaluations of currency rates that you are reporting. Countries with high inflation frequently devalue or revalue their currencies. For example, on January 1, 1993, Mexico introduced a "new peso" worth 1,000 pesos. The exchange rate of the Mexican peso before the devaluation was about 3,100 to the dollar.

The February 1993 issue of *International Financial Statistics* reported the following figures for the Mexican exchange rate.

> **Example 1:**
> Mexico: Exchange rate per U.S. Dollar
>
> | 1990 | 1991 | 1992 |
> |------|------|------|
> | 2,945.4 | 3,071.0 | - |

After the revaluation took place, the March 1993 issue of *International Financial Statistics* retroactively calculated the exchange rate for previous years.

> **Example 2:**
> Mexico: Exchange rate per U.S. Dollar
>
> | 1990 | 1991 | 1992 |
> |------|------|------|
> | 2.9454 | 3.0710 | 3.1149 |

The purpose of recalculating the exchange rate is to represent the rate of change over time accurately. For example, the value of the Mexican peso declined about 6% against the U.S. dollar between 1990 and 1992. We can determine this change from the figures in Example 2. The historical exchange rates by themselves would indicate that the peso had increased in value by 1,000% during this period. However, recalculated exchange rates can be misleading if we need the historical exchange rates for accounting purposes, or if we are unaware that a revaluation has occurred. This is one instance in which printed sources may be superior to electronic numeric databases. Printed sources typically explain the details of currency revaluations. Machine-readable sources usually give the numbers without explanation.

When you are reporting the value of a currency that does not "float" (that is not freely convertible into other currencies and has an exchange rate set by a government), there will be a parallel market ("black market") rate of exchange, in addition to an official rate. There also may be more than one official rate. For example, Iran in 1992 was using three different official exchange rates for its currency, the rial. In addition, there was a black market rate. At the official exchange rate, the dollar was worth around 70 Iranian rials in January 1992. Iran also used two other rates, one for travelers and one for certain business transactions; these rates valued the rial more closely to its black market rate of about 1,400 rials to the dollar.

Information Sources for Foreign Exchange

Business newspapers are a good, if limited, source for foreign exchange rates. For example, each issue of the *Wall Street Journal* includes currency cross rates for 10 major currencies. In addition, the *WSJ* gives the exchange rates of 50 currencies for the previous two days. The equivalents are given both as U.S. dollar equivalents per foreign currency, and foreign currency per U.S. dollar. In addition to exchange rates, the table gives forward rates (for 30, 90, and 180 days) for major world currencies. A weekly table ("World Value of the Dollar") gives the current and previous exchange rate of the dollar against 200 currencies. The same tables are also available online through the Dow Jones News/Retrieval system described below.

Foreign Exchange Rates for the Week Ending...
(published weekly by the Federal Reserve Board)

Foreign Exchange Rates for the Month Ending...
(published monthly by the Federal Reserve Board)

The Federal Reserve Board's two statistical releases, *Foreign Exchange Rates*, are widely quoted sources of exchange rates. The weekly release gives rates against the dollar for 31 currencies plus the ECU for each day of trading during the week. In addition, it gives an index of U.S. trade weighted exchange value against the currencies of the G-10 countries. The monthly release gives rates for the same group of currencies for the current month and previous two months. The statistical releases are available from the Federal Reserve Board's Web site (// www.bog.frb.fed.us/). Exhibit 16.1 shows an extract from the weekly listing.

International Financial Statistics (published monthly by the International Monetary Fund)

International Financial Statistics gives several time series of exchange rates per U.S. dollars and in terms of SDRs. The publication will print market values if available, otherwise it gives official rates. The time series give figures for each of the most current seven months, quarterly figures for the past three years, and annual figures for the preceding seven years. In addition to actual exchange rates, the IMF provides indexes of exchange rates adjusted for inflation and for trading patterns. The *International Financial Statistics Yearbook* gives 30 years of annual statistics for many of the same statistics that appear in the monthly publication. Older editions of the *Yearbook* will give series as far back as 1949. The *International Financial Statistics Yearbook* is described in more detail in Chapter 13.

Electronic Sources for Exchange Rates

Printed sources of exchange rates are awkward to use if we are dealing with several countries' rates over an extended period. Online databases not only simplify gathering exchange rates, they are essential for much foreign exchange data retrieval. Although many of the printed sources of exchange rates exist as well in electronic form, much foreign exchange data is exclu-

---

Federal Reserve Statistical Release December 6, 1996
FOREIGN EXCHANGE RATES FOR THE WEEK ENDING NOVEMBER 22, 1996

The Board of Governors of the Federal Reserve System is advised that the Federal Reserve Board of New York has certified for customs purposes the following noon buying rates in New York City for cable transfers payable in foreign currencies

Country	Monetary Unit	(Currency Units per Dollar)		
		Nov. 18	Nov. 19	Nov. 20
*Australia	Dollar	0.7916	0.7940	0.7995
Austria	Schilling	10.566	10.586	10.533
Belgium	Franc	30.950	31.000	30.840
Canada	Dollar	1.3419	1.3426	1.3420
China, P.R.	Yuan	8.3302	8.3302	8.3301
Switzerland	Franc	1.2673	1.2705	1.2653
Taiwan	Dollar	27.520	27,520	27.520
Thailand	Baht	25.420	25.430	25.410
*United Kingdom	Pound	1.6700	1.6760	1.6780

*Value is U.S. Dollars

U.S. FEDERAL RESERVE STATISTICAL RELEASE: CURRENCY VALUES

EXHIBIT 16.1

Source: Federal Reserve Statistical Release. Reprinted with permission.

Fixed Page 804 06/07 10:57 EDT
World Foreign Exchange Cross Rates, US, UK, DM, SF & JY

Currency	US-1	UK-1	DM-1	SF-1	JY-1000
US	1.6720-.6735	.5655-.5658	.6594-.6598	7.1235-.1266	
UK	.5976-.5979		.3379-.3383	.3940-.3945	4.2567-.2617
DM	1.7675-.7785	2.9561-.9596		1.1642-.1656	12.587-.599
FF	5.9840-.9855	9.980820.0167	3.3946-.3874	3.9459-.9495	42.627-.653
SF	1.5165-.5165	2.5347-.5479	.8572-.8582		10.806-.817
IL	1308.0-10.0	2188.3-92.9	739.8-41.2	862.6-4.2	9317.6-35.1
CD	1.1469-.1484	1.9191-.9111	.6486-.6491	.7660-.7674	82.705-.770
JY	139.33-44800	234.60-.936	79.37-.45	92.54-.53	
AD	1.3289-.3301	2.2226-.2260	.7516-.7528	.8763-.8877	9.466-.479
BF	36.34-.35	.6080-.6085	20.68-.59	23.96-.98	259.81-.28
NG	1.9910-.9925	3.3209-.3354	1.1261-.1273	1.3130-.3144	14.283-.199
DK	6.7340-.7890	11.367-.379	3.8360-.8410	4.4785-.4835	48.363-.419
NK	6.8825-.8875	1.1526-.1541	3.8999-.9049	4.5363-.5426	49.017-.070
HK	7.7325-.7355	13.035-.048	4.4754-.4796	5.0972-.1026	55.055-.116
NZ	1.7218-.7232	2.8707-.8840	.9741-.9755	1.1451-.1365	12.362-.376
SD	1.7800-.7810	2.9776-.9814	1.0157-.0175	1.1738-.1749	1.2680-.2692

DIALOG/MONEYCENTER REPORT

EXHIBIT 16.2

Source: DIALOG/MoneyCenter Report.

---

sively electronic. Because exchange rates are constantly in flux, to determine a currency's rate as it changes throughout the day requires access to an online system that is continuously updated. Professional foreign exchange dealers use systems such as Telerate and Globex. Access to real-time quotes or intra-day quotes is also available through such general time-sharing systems as DIALOG and Dow Jones News/Retrieval.

DIALOG/MoneyCenter (DIALOG)

This real-time menu-driven financial database from Knight-Ridder Financial Information includes not only foreign exchange quotes, but also news from all major U.S. and international cash, futures, and options markets. Exhibit 16.2 is a report on foreign exchange as it appears on DIALOG/MoneyCenter. The two rates given are bid and asked.

Dow Jones News/Retrieval

Dow Jones News/Retrieval reports the spot and future prices of major currencies hourly on the Dow Jones Futures database. Exhibit 16.3 shows the format Dow Jones uses for presenting currency spot prices. The exchange rates in Exhibit 16.3 require interpretation. The 7834 figure given for the opening Australian dollar quote indicates that the exchange is .7834 U.S. dollar per Australian dollar. Spot currency prices are available daily on Dow Jones News/Retrieval from April 1991 to date.

AUSTRALIAN DOLLAR-SPOT (IMM), $ PER AD$
DATE: 7/2/96

	OPEN	HIGH	LOW	LAST	CHANGE
INDX	7834	7834	7825	7827	- 43

FRENCH FRANC SPOT (IMM), $ PER FRANC
DATE: 7/2/96

	OPEN	HIGH	LOW	LAST	CHANGE
INDX	19394	19394	19352	19373	- 36

CURRENCY RATES ON DOW JONES FUTURES DATABASE

EXHIBIT 16.3

Source: Dow Jones News/Retrieval Futures Database.

Econbase (DIALOG)

DIALOG's *Econbase* is a convenient online source for monthly and annual time series of foreign exchange rates of major currencies against the dollar. The database also contains one-year forecasts for annual exchange rates. *Econbase* can be searched by series codes or with natural language. The database contains exchange rates for 21 currencies. Exhibit 16.4 shows the first few entries for the record of the monthly exchange rate of the Japanese yen.

Other Time-Sharing Sources

Long time-series of daily data for currencies can be retrieved from several online systems. They include Reuters (http://www.reuters.com), Bloomberg (http://www.bloomberg.com), and IDD's Tradeline database. Tradeline, for example, gives historical reports (daily, weekly, monthly, quarterly, or yearly rates) for 154 currencies. In addition, Tradeline allows retrieval of comparison reports (multiple currencies for a single day) and reports showing percent change over time. IDD's database consists of calculated cross rates from the British pound.

The Datastream online system (http://www.datastream.com) is an example of a time-sharing database designed to retrieve multi-year time-series of daily financial data. The system gives daily rates from major markets worldwide. In addition, the systems are designed to download large quantities of data directly into spreadsheets. Datastream is described in more detail later in this chapter.

WWW Sources

There are scores of currency converters on the Web. They are a convenient source of data if you need rates for a few currencies. They usually do not give long time-series of daily rates in spreadsheet-ready formats. We list the URLs for several converters:

Series Code:	MF8117
Corp Source:	FRB ; TABLE 3.28, FEDERAL RESERVE BULLETIN
Start Date:	JANUARY, 1971 (7101)
Frequency:	MONTHLY
Units:	JAPANESE YEN PER US DOLLAR

1996	JAN	105.7500	FEB	105.7900	MAR	105.9400
	APR	107.2000				
1995	JAN	99.7700	FEB	98.2400	MAR	90.5200
	APR	83.6900	MAY	85.1100	JUN	84.6400
	JUL	87.4000	AUG	94.7400	SEP	100.5500
	OCT	100.8400	NOV	101.9400	DEC	101.8500
1994	JAN	111.4400	FEB	106.3000	MAR	105.1000
	APR	103.4800	MAY	103.7500	JUN	102.5300
	JUL	98.4500	AUG	99.9400	SEP	98.7700
	OCT	98.3500	NOV	98.0400	DEC	100.1800
1993	JAN	124.9900	FEB	120.7600	MAR	117.0200
	APR	112.4100	MAY	110.3400	JUN	107.4100
	JUL	107.6900	AUG	103.7700	SEP	105.5700
	OCT	107.0200	NOV	107.8800	DEC	109.9100

ECONBASE—JAPANESE YEN PER U.S. DOLLAR

EXHIBIT 16.4

Source: Econbase (DIALOG File 565).

Bloomberg World Currency Values
  http://www.bloomberg.com/markets/wcv.html
Daily Exchange Rates
  http://www.dna.1th.se/cgi-bin/kurt/rates
TravelFinder.com Currency Conversion
  http://travelfinder.com/currency.html
Olsen & Associates Currency Converter
  http://www.oanda.com/cgi-bin/ncc
Pacific Exchange Rate Service
  http://pacific.commerce.ubc.ca/xr/
Universal Currency Converter
  http://www.xe.net/currency/
World Exchange Rates
  http://www.rubicon.com/passport/currency/
    currency.htm

THE WORLD'S FINANCIAL EXCHANGES

Most of the world's exchanges have transactions in stock. In addition to equities, stock exchanges are often involved with the trading of fixed interest instruments such as bonds. However, most bonds are traded OTC and not on exchanges. Some stock exchanges trade options on stocks (so-called "equity options"). Futures and commodity options are usually traded on exchanges that specialize in these instruments. Foreign exchange transactions in the spot and forward markets and Eurocurrency transactions are conducted among banks and not on formal exchanges.

Stock Markets

The world market value of outstanding equity issues in 1995 was about 18 trillion dollars. There are more than 100 stock markets on which equities are traded. However, the market value of stocks (the value of stock traded on the exchange) is highly concentrated in a few markets. For example, the New York Stock Exchange and the Tokyo exchange together control about 40% of the value of stocks traded worldwide. The 10 largest exchanges ranked by value of outstanding equity issues account for 80% of the value of all equity issues.

In addition to being listed on national exchanges, large companies sometimes list their shares on foreign exchanges as well. A company such as Royal Dutch Shell, for example, is traded on a dozen markets. The requirements for foreign share listing vary greatly among the world's exchanges. In the U.S., a company must meet the requirements of both the exchange (such as the New York Stock Exchange) and the U.S. Securities and Exchange Commission. The expense and reporting requirements that foreign share listing requires has the effect of restricting direct listing in the U.S. to a few hundred companies.

20-F Filings

Foreign companies that list their shares on U.S. exchanges are required to file annual reports with the Securities and Exchange Commission within six months after the end of their fiscal year. These reports, called 20-F, are functionally equivalent to the 10-K reports required by U.S. companies. There are approximately 370 companies that file 20-F reports. At the beginning of 1996, 589 companies filed 20-F reports. A comprehensive list of companies filing 20-F reports, together with extensive extracts from the reports, is available from Disclosure/SEC on CD-ROM or Disclosure online. Table 16.B lists Canadian companies listed on the New York Stock Exchange.

TABLE 16.B	
CANADIAN COMPANIES ON THE NEW YORK STOCK EXCHANGE FILING 20-F REPORTS	
Company Name	**Net Sales ($000s)**
BCE INC	21,670,000
ROYAL BANK OF CANADA	15,306,000
BANK OF MONTREAL	9,108,000
CANADIAN PACIFIC LTD	7,053,400
TRANSCANADA PIPELINES LTD	5,204,200
PETRO CANADA	4,581,000
WESTCOAST ENERGY INC	3,712,000
MAGNA INTERNATIONAL INC	3,568,500
HORSHAM CORP	2,492,944
ROGERS COMMUNICATIONS INC	2,250,233
DOMTAR INC	2,141,000
ABITIBI PRICE INC	2,111,000
ROGERS CANTEL MOBILE COMMUNICA	750,420
PREMDOR INC	744,256
POTASH CORP OF SASKATCHEWAN IN	596,731
RANGER OIL LTD	158,629
GOLDCORP INC	140,943
KINROSS GOLD CORP	125,837
AGNICO EAGLE MINES LTD	76,562
NORTHGATE EXPLORATION LTD	2,280

Source: Disclosure/SEC, February 1996 Disk.

The complete texts of 20-F filings are available from Disclosure, Inc. on microfiche, in CD-ROM image format, and from their WWW site (http://www.disclosure.com).

American Depositary Receipts

Companies sometimes trade their stock in foreign markets without direct listing on an exchange. In the U.S., foreign shares can be listed as American Depositary Receipts (ADRs). U.S. banks accept deposits of foreign shares and issue ADRs in the name of the foreign company. The Bank of New York, the leading issuer of ADRs, lists these benefits to an investor:

- ADRs are quoted in U.S. dollars and pay dividends in U.S. dollars.
- ADRs overcome the obstacles (such as currency conversation and tax treatment) that result from owning foreign securities directly.
- ADRs are as liquid as the underlying securities.

About 1,500 companies trade ADRs in the U.S. For example, Broken Hill Proprietary Co., Ltd., an Australian company, trades American Depositary Receipts on the New York Stock Exchange. The ADRs were issued by Morgan Guaranty Trust. Each ADR issued after May 28, 1987, represents four shares of Broken Hill Proprietary stock. Many companies trading ADRs are listed in *Standard & Poor's Corporation Record* and *Moody's International Manual*. These sources give the details of the initial ADR offering, the price when issued, and the trading range of the ADRs. The Bank of New York provides an *American Depositary Receipt Directory* at its Web site (http://www.researchmag.com/company/alpha.htm). The *Directory* provides the name of the issue, CUSIP number, exchange, symbol, ratio, sponsorship, country, and industry group.

Hoover's Handbook of World Business provides a list of non-U.S. company stocks available through U.S. stock markets.

Investment Companies

Another way to invest in foreign stocks and bonds is through investment companies. There are many U.S.-based mutual funds that invest in non-U.S. markets. The Lipper Analytical Service, which tracks these funds, has defined several types based on their objectives.[5]

- *Global fund:* A fund that invests at least 25% of its portfolio in securities traded outside the U.S. and may own U.S. securities as well.
- *International fund:* Invests its assets in securities whose primary trading markets are outside the U.S.
- *European region fund:* A fund that concentrates its investments in equity securities whose primary trading markets or operations are concentrated in the European region or a single country within this region.
- *Pacific region fund:* A fund that concentrates its investments in equity securities whose primary trading markets or operations are concentrated in the Western Pacific region or a single country within this region.

Questions about mutual funds are often concerned with the names and portfolios of funds that have a particular international objective. A related question is, What funds hold particular non-U.S. bonds and equities?

A useful source for both these questions is Morningstar on CD-ROM. The CD gives performance data and portfolio holdings on 6,500 mutual funds. The software allows detailed screening. For example, one can screen for funds that have Europe or Pacific as investment objects, an annual return of more than 10%, and a beta (risk factor) of 1 or less.

Exhibit 16.5 is an extract of a table showing the holdings of Vanguard International Equity Emerging Market Fund. Exhibit 16.6 is an extract of a list of funds that own the Australian company Broken Hill Proprietary.

VANGUARD INTL EQTY EMERG MKT
PORTFOLIO HOLDINGS
AS OF 12/31/94

Total Net Assets $MM:142:2 **No. of Securities:244**

Shares	Share Change	Value $000	%Net Asset	Ticker
8092541 ELECTROBRAS	2769241	2860.0	3.43	———
1229550 TELEFONOS DE MEXICO CL L	320500	2622.0	3.14	———
383000 TELEKOM MALAYSIA	130000	2593.0	3.11	———
614000 TENAGA NATIONAL	224000	2427.0	2.91	———
1038800 HONG KONG TELECOMMUNICATIONS	426400	1980.0	2.37	———
86424 YPF SOCIEDAD ANONIMA	33400	1819.0	2.18	———
206100 HANG SENG BANK	74100	1478.0	1.77	———
261050 TELEFONICA DE ARGENTINA	87900	1347.0	1.62	———
312800 BANK OF AYUDHYA (FOR)	46200	1284.0	1.54	———
98000 SIME DARBY (MALAYSIA)	-189000	1140.0	1.37	———
18800 SIAM CEMENT (FOR)	12300	1126.0	1.35	———
189000 RESORTS WORLD	76000	1109.0	1.33	———

TABLE FROM MORNINGSTAR MUTUAL FUNDS CD-ROM

EXHIBIT 16.5

Source: Morningstar Mutual Funds CD-ROM. Reprinted with permission.

BROKEN HILL PROPRIETARY

Ticker:——

Number of Funds:182

Fund Names	#Shares Held	Share Change	Value $000	% Net Assets	Date
59 Wall St Pac Basin Equity	84000	17000	1287.0	1.07	10/31/94
Accessor Intl Equity	2526	N/A	38.0	0.51	12/31/94
AIM Constellation	425000	0	6511.0	0.17	10/31/94
AIM Global Growth A	1416	N/A	22.0	0.70	10/31/94
AIM Global Growth B	584	N/A	9.0	0.70	10/31/94
AIM International Equity A	363329	72520	5569.0	0.79	10/31/94
AIM International Equity B	2480	N/A	38.0	0.79	10/31/94
AIM Value A	120996	-13834	1837.0	0.14	12/31/94
AIM Value B	60565	16164	920.0	0.14	12/31/94
AIM Weingarten	425000	0	6511.0	0.16	10/31/94
Alliance International A	46558	46558	707.0	0.40	12/31/94
Alliance International B	13040	13040	198.0	0.40	12/31/94
Alliance International C	7680	7680	117.0	0.40	12/31/94
American Cap Global Equity A	7277	-15	105.0	0.19	11/30/94
WPG International	5000	0	77.0	0.42	10/31/94
Wright Intl Blue Chip Equity	37000	0	530.0	0.26	12/31/94
Zweig Managed Assets A	6878	6878	104.0	0.07	12/31/94
Zweig Managed Assets C	25417	25417	386.0	0.07	12/31/94

PORTFOLIO FROM MORNINGSTAR MUTUAL FUNDS CD-ROM

EXHIBIT 16.6

Source: Morningstar Mutual Funds CD-ROM. Reprinted with permission.

Money Markets

The money market is a wholesale market for low-risk highly liquid short-term IOUs. It is a market for debt securities rather than equities (such as stocks). The money market provides a mechanism by which the surplus funds of cash-rich corporations and financial institutions such as pension funds can be channeled to banks, corporations, and governments that need short-term money (money that must be repaid in less than one year). The "money market" is not one market but a collection of markets for several distinct and different instruments, including commercial paper, certificates of deposit, banker's acceptances, and government agency bills and notes.

Eurocurrencies are an important part of the international money market. Eurocurrencies are currencies of one country that are held by the citizens of another country. For example, Eurodollars are U.S. dollar balances held on deposit in a bank located outside the United States. The prefix "euro" is derived from the evolution of the market's London origins. During the 1950s, interest grew in borrowing and lending offshore dollars free from U.S. government interference.

The Eurocurrency Market (the Euromarket) deals with borrowing and lending Eurocurrencies. It is closely linked with the foreign exchange market. For example, in May 1992, banks would lend Spanish pesetas for three months at 12.5% interest. During the same period, banks were prepared to pay 12% interest to borrow Spanish pesetas for 90 days. The *Financial Times* would list this information in a daily table (Euro-Currency Interest Rates) as shown below.

	Three Month
Spanish peseta	12-12 1/2

Closely allied to the Eurocurrency Market is the market for Euro-notes. Euro-notes take various forms such as Euro-commercial paper, banker's acceptances, and certificates of deposit.[6]

The interest rate for lending on the Euromarket is often based on the London Interbank Offered Rate (LIBOR). This is the interest rate for loans made by banks in London to other London banks. It is calculated as the average of rates quoted by several reference banks. The rate is usually for three- or six-month loans. Rates for Eurocurrency are expressed as LIBOR plus an additional percentage. Other major financial centers often calculate their own interbank offering rates. They include NYBOR (New York), HKIBOR (Hong Kong), and MIBOR (Madrid).

Bond Markets

There are about $1.5 trillion of international bonds outstanding. About $250 billion in new bonds are issued each year.[7] The predominant currency for bonds is the U.S. dollar, followed by the Japanese yen. International and domestic bond markets are closely related. There are important bond markets in Zurich, New York, Tokyo, Frankfurt, London, and Amsterdam. However, most bonds are traded OTC.

There are two general types of international bonds, foreign bonds and Eurobonds. Foreign bonds are issued by foreign borrowers in another country's capital market using that country's currency. For example, a bond issued by a Japanese company in the U.S. denominated in U.S. dollar is a foreign bond. In the U.S., as in most countries, foreign bonds have different registration and disclosure requirements than do domestic bonds.

Eurobonds are usually issued simultaneously in the capital markets of several countries. Eurobonds differ from foreign bonds in that most countries do require pre-offering registration or disclosure requirements for them.

Futures

A futures contract is a commitment (a legally binding agreement) to buy or sell a fixed quantity of a commodity or an underlying financial instrument (such as a group of stocks) during a specified month in the future. For example, on March 4, 1992, dealers on the London Futures and Options Exchange would pay 147.8 pounds sterling for the delivery of a ton of potatoes at the end of May. Futures are traded on formal exchanges. Most of these exchanges are so-called "floor traded" markets, in which brokers and traders in trading pits shout out the price and quantity at which they want to buy or sell. Other exchanges are "electronic markets." For example, only members of the Osaka Securities Exchange have access to terminals for trading Nikkei futures. Buy and sell orders appear on the screen, and all buyers and sellers are anonymous.[8]

There are two types of futures: commodity and financial. Commodity futures are based on such items as agricultural products, metals, and petroleum. Financial futures have as their underlying instruments groups of stocks (represented by a stock index), a currency, or fixed income securities.

Options

There are two general types of options. The owner of a so-called "American" option has the right to buy or sell a specified amount of a financial instrument for a specified price on or before a particular date. A "European" option, in contrast, can only be exercised on a specific date. Unlike a futures contract, the owner of an option is not obligated to exercise it. Options are sold on stocks, stock indexes, currencies, and on interest rate instruments. Example: On March 4, 1992, common stock in the Guinness Company closed at 584 pence per share. On the same day, an option to purchase Guinness stock (a call option) at 600 pence on May 31 cost 19 pence per share. On the same day, an option to sell Guinness stock (a put option) on May 31 cost 30.5 pence. This information appeared in the *Financial Times* in the form shown below.

Guinness (584)	May	Aug.	Nov.
Call 600	19	32.5	45.5
Put 600	30.5	36.5	41.5

Other Derivatives

Futures and options are often called derivative financial instruments. An equity option, for example, is derived from an underlying stock. Another important group of derivatives are interest rate and currency rate swaps. The world value of outstanding swaps is estimated to be $3 trillion. Swaps are customized financial arrangements that allow two parties to trade streams of interest payments. They allow corporations to better manage risks associated with interest rates and foreign currency rate fluctuation.

Here is an example of an interest rate swap. A corporation has issued a floating rate note, the interest rate of which is tied to the six-month LIBOR. The corporation is afraid that interest rates will rise and wants to exchange its floating rate note for a fixed rate note. The corporation makes an agreement with a bank to trade (swap) floating rate payments for fixed rate payments. The corporation pays the bank a fixed rate per year (say 10%), and the bank pays the corporation the prevailing floating rate.

In an currency rate swap, two institutions trade interest rate payments associated with borrowing foreign currency.

FINDING AIDS AND DIRECTORIES FOR FINANCIAL MARKETS

LGT Guide to World Equity Markets (published annually by Euromoney/LGT Management)

This useful worldwide directory of stock markets has been published by Euromoney and LGT Management (an international investment management company) annually since 1985. The *Guide* profiles the equity markets of 50 countries. For each country, the following information is given:

- Market performance of the exchange for the past five years
- Market indices and their constituents
- Brief history and structure of the market
- Principal exchanges' addresses
- Market size (as measured by number of listings and market value)
- Largest quoted companies
- Types of shares, trading systems
- Lists of principal brokers and their commissions
- Reporting requirements and shareholders' protection codes

The Handbook of World Stock and Commodity Exchanges (published annually by Basil Blackwell)

Another source of current information about world stock exchanges, the *Handbook* covers 86 countries and 254 exchanges. It includes information about such nascent exchanges as the Moscow Stock Exchange and the Moscow Commodity Exchange.

- Brief history and structure
- Trading hours
- Number of securities traded
- Market capitalization
- Main indexes
- Type of securities traded
- Trading system
- Settling and clearing process
- Commission rates
- Investor protection details
- Taxation and regulations of foreign investors
- Exchange holiday schedule
- Prospective developments

World Stock Exchange Fact Book: Historical Securities Data for the International Investor (published by Electronic Commerce Inc., Morris Plains, NJ, 1995)

The World Stock Exchange Fact Book provides statistical data on the exchanges in 42 countries covering up to 20 years of monthly index values, trading volumes, market capitalization, P/E ratios, and dividend yields.

In addition, it provides data on country GDP, CPI, imports/exports, and interest and exchange rates, in both tabular and graphic formats. The entry for each country gives a description of the principal stock exchange, the number of listed companies, information on commissions and fees, disclosure requirements, listing requirements, foreign investor restrictions, a description of investor protection for shareholders, and merger and acquisition regulations. A list of component stocks in the index is given,

together with descriptions of index computation methodology. A diskette of data is provided that provides the monthly index values.

Tradeline International

The Tradeline International database includes brief description of stock exchanges worldwide. Exhibit 16.7 is the output from a search on the DIALOG version of Tradeline International for information about the Madrid Stock Exchange. We first request the stock exchange symbols for Spain, and then enter the symbol for Madrid.

Stock Exchange Snapshot		
Stock Exch Code	**Exchange Name**	**Country**
EEB	Barcelona	Spain
EEM	Madrid	Spain
EEA	Bilbao	Spain
EEV	Valencia	Spain

Exchange Name: Madrid, Spain (EEM)

Hours of operation: 10:00AM-1:00PM
9:00AM-12:00PM GMT
4:00AM-7:00AM EST

Days of operation: Monday-Friday

Usual quotation convention: High-Low-Close

Major market index: Madrid S.E. Index (SEDOL 128817)

Issues in database: 578

TRADELINE INTERNATIONAL STOCK EXCHANGE SNAPSHOT

EXHIBIT 16.7

Source: IDD Information Services/Tradeline Interenational. Reprinted with permission.

Individual Exchanges

Individual financial exchanges often publish English-language versions of their annual reports and other descriptive materials. The reports typically gives such facts as listing requirements, volume of sales, number of issues, and market index composition. Often the material can be obtained for little or no direct cost. We list examples of stock exchange reports and fact books. Sometimes the text is included in WWW sites of the exchange (see description below).

Athens Stock Exchange—*Annual Statistical Bulletin*
Brussels Stock Exchange—*Statistics*
Federation of German Stock Exchanges—*Annual Report*
Kuwait Stock Exchange—*Trading Report*
Ljubljanska Stock Exchange—*Statistics*
Madrid Stock Exchange—*Annual Report*
Montreal Exchange—*Monthly Review*
Oslo Bors—*Key Figures*
Paris Bourse—*Fact Book*

Santiago Stock Exchange—*Facts and Figures*
Stockholm Stock exchange—*Annual Report*
Taiwan Stock Exchange—*Status of Securities*
Tehran Stock Exchange—*General Information*
Tel Aviv Stock Exchange—*Annual Report*
Tokyo Stock Exchange—*Annual Securities Statistics*
Vienna Stock Exchange—*Yearbook*
Warsaw Stock Exchange—*Quarterly Bulletin*
Zurich Stock Exchange—*Facts and Figures*

Web Sites for Stock Exchanges

The World Wide Web is a rich source of information on stock markets, exchanges, and the movements of individual stocks. Listed below are English language sites available as of June 1996. It is difficult to generalize about the characteristics of the sites. Some are mega sites: the Qualisteam site, for example (http://www/qualisteam.com/amarche.html) lists 22 countries and 50 exchanges. In addition, it includes sites for bonds, mutual funds, and options/futures. The information at WWW sites for exchanges ranges from comprehensive (e.g., current prices on listed companies) to sketchy (week-old stock price index). Some sites include stocks, bonds, futures, options, exchange rates, and ADRs. Some include news stories as well.

Bloomberg (World Markets)
  http://www.bloomberg.com/
DBC Online (Global Market Data)
  http://www.dbc.com/
FISH Supersite (Stock Exchange of Singapore)
  http://www.infront.com.sg/
Qualisteam
  http://qualisteam.com/amarche.html
Africa African Stock Exchange Guide
  http://africa.com/pages/jse/page1.htm
Asia Asian Stock Markets
  http://www.euro.net/chinacom/STOCKS1.html
Asian Stock Market
  http://www.qualisteam.com/aactas.html
Asian Stock Market Closings
  http://www.asia-inc.com/lippo/index.html
Europe Stock Exchanges in Europe
  http://www/qualisteam.com/aacteu.html
Australia
  http://www.asx.com.au/
Brazil Rio de Janeiro Stock Exchange
  http://www.embratel.net.br/infoserv/bvbrj/
Chile
  http://www.bolsasatiago.cl/bolsain.htm
Canada Montreal
  http://www.vse.com/
Costa Rica
  http://www.cool.co.cr/usr/bolsa/bolsa.html

Croatia Zagreb Stock Exchange
  http://ksaver208zse.com.hr/
Finland
  http://www.money.com/exchanges/e_hel.htm
France
  http://www.fastnet.ch/NETFUND/bors.html
  http://www.bourse-de-paris.fr/;
  [In French] http://apollo.wu-wien.ac.at/cgi-bin/boerse1.pl
Hungary Budapest Stock Exchange
  http://www.fomax.hu/mon/index.html
Israel
  http://www.tase.co.il/; (Tel Aviv)
  http://www.globes.co.il/EngReports/631.html
Italy Geneva Stock Exchange
  http://www.bourse.ch/
Jamaica
  http://www.infochan.com/jamex/jam-lite/jxt-hp.htm
Japan
  http://www.nikkei.co.jp/enems/
Nagoya Stock Exchange
  http://www.iijnet.or.jp/nse-jp/e-home.htm
Malaysia
  http://www.jaring.my/star/klse/klse.html
Mexico Mexicana de Valores
  http://quickllink.com/mexico/bmv/bmv1.html
Netherlands
  http://wwwaeb.econ.vu.nl/English/home.html netherl
Norway
  http://nettvik.no/financen/oslobors/
Peru
  http://www.money.com/exchanges/e_lim.htm
Prague
  http://info.eunet.cz:5555/bulsa/bulsa_e.html
Russia Nikko Stock Performance Index
  http://www.fe.msk.ru/infomarket/rtsb/ewelcome.html
Singapore Stock Market
  http://snoopy.asia1.com.sg/cgi-bin/realstk/star
Business Times Singapore
  http://www.asia1.com.sg/biztimes/
Slovenia Ljubljana
  http://www.ljse.si/
Spain
  http://www.bolsamadrid.es/
  http://www.bolsamadrid.es/homepin.htm
Taiwan
  http://www.tse.com.tw/ (Taiwan)
UK
  http://www.liffe.com/ (london int financial futures and options)
UK
  http://www.stockex.co.uk/aim/index.htm

Internet Securities information from Poland, Russia, Ukraine, the Czech Republic, the Baltic States, Hungary, China, and India. Expansion plans for Bulgaria, Turkey, Colombia, and the former Soviet Union.

Market Measures

Every financial market has one or more index or average that describes the movement of the market. For example, the most widely quoted German stock market index is the DAX (the Deutscher Aktienindex). It is an index of 30 large German companies, weighted by market capitalization, representing all the country's stock exchanges.

Large stock exchanges, such as the Tokyo and London exchanges, often have several indexes. For example, the Tokyo Stock Exchange calculates a broad general market index (the TSE Stock Price Index), as well as a "blue-chip" index (the Nikkei-Dow Index). Nikkei (Nihon Keizai Shimbun Inc.) also computes stock indices for over 30 industry and special subgroups, such as the Nikkei Automobile Stock Index.

In addition to measuring the movement of individual stock markets, market indices are available that track the performance of stock exchanges aggregated by geographic area and by special groups such as "emerging markets." Two examples of "world indices" are the Morgan Stanley Capital International Indices and the FT Actuaries Index. They measure the movement of the stock market worldwide.

Several other aggregate measures of market performance and size frequently are of interest to researchers:

- Price-earnings ratio
- Price–book value ratio
- Dividend yield
- Value of stocks traded
- Number of companies listed
- Index of total return

Market indices for important markets are reported daily in major financial newspapers such as the *Wall Street Journal* and the *Financial Times* (London). The *Financial Times*, for example, gives one or more market measures for 25 exchanges. Information is included for the four previous days, plus the high and low for the year. More extensive information is given for the *Financial Times'* own stock indices, including hourly changes.

The "Special Features Section" of volume one of *Moody's International Manual* is a convenient source for long time series of monthly and annual stock exchange indices. In Table 16.C we list the indices in the 1995 edition. Most of the indices give monthly data.

TABLE 16.C		
STOCK MARKET INDEXES IN *MOODY'S INTERNATIONAL MANUAL*		
Country	**Current Index**	**Approximate Coverage**
Australia	All ordinaries	20 years
Austria	Vienna Share Index	30 years
Belgium	Brussels SE Index	10 years
Brazil	Sao Paulo Stock Exchange	20 years
Canada	Toronto 300 Composite	40 years
France	CAC General Index	10 years
Germany	Commerzbank Index	20 years
Hong Kong	Hang Seng	25 years
Italy	Banc Commerciale Index	10 years
Japan	Tokyo Stock Exchange Index	50 years
Netherlands	All Share Index	25 years
Norway	Oslo stock exchange index	10 years
Singapore	Stock Exchange	10 years
South Africa	Johannesburge SE Industrials	10 years
South Korea	Composite Stock Price Index	15 years
Spain	Madrid SE Index	10 years
Sweden	Affarsvarlden General Index	30 years
Switzerland	SBC Index	30 years
Taiwan	SE	25 years
United Kingdom	FT/SE 100	10 years

Index Composition

The names of the companies that make up market indexes and averages are often a point of interest. Two sources of this information are described below.

Hoover's Handbook of World Business (published annually by Reference Press)

The 1995–1996 edition of *Hoover's Handbook* lists the names of the companies that make up the following major market indexes:

Nikkei Index 225 (Japan)
DAX Index (Germany)
FT-SE 100 Index (UK)
CAC Index (France)
SBF 120 (France)
Hang Seng Index (Hong Kong)
Straits Times Index (Singapore)
All Ordinaries Index (Australia)

The names of the companies that make up the individual market indices usually change slowly, but they do change as companies merge, change their names, or become financially weak. The Datastream online system, which lists the names of companies that comprise the major stock indexes, is a more current source. We discuss Datastream in some detail below.

Morgan Stanley Capital International Perspective

(published monthly and quarterly by Morgan Stanley)

Morgan Stanley indices measure the performance of the stock markets of the U.S., Europe, Canada, Mexico, Australia, and the Far East. Their indices consist of 7 international indices, 20 national indices, and 38 international industry indices. They are published in *Morgan Stanley Capital International Perspective* both monthly and quarterly (16 issues a year).

FT-Actuaries World Indices

The *FT-Actuaries World Indices* are complied by the Financial Times, Goldman, Saches and County NatWest Securities Limited. Their indices consist of one world index, 11 regional indices, 24 national indices, as well as 7 economic sectors and 36 industry groups. They appear daily in the *Financial Times*. In addition, they appear in the monthly publication *World Market Review*. The *Morgan Stanley Index* began over 20 years ago. The *FT-Actuaries* made its appearance in 1987 and is calculated from 1986. The *FT-Actuaries Index* is more broadly based (2,500 stocks) than the *Morgan Stanley Index*.

Both *Morgan Stanley Capital International Perspective* and *World Market Review* give measures of valuation in addition to performance for the groups of stocks that comprise their various indices. The *World Market Review*, for example, gives measures such as price-earnings ratio and dividend yield for country and industry groups.

Stock Exchange Quarterly (published quarterly by the London Stock Exchange)

The *Stock Exchange Quarterly* is a good source for the comparisons of international markets. Each issue contains several statistical tables detailing the size, activity, and composition of stock, commodity, and option markets. Included is a table showing the daily close for 11 major stock market indices for the previous quarter.

Annual Report of the Bank for International Settlements

The Bank for International Settlements (BIS) is a private company that is owned jointly by the central banks of most industrialized countries. Dating from 1930, it is the oldest international financial organization. The BIS is a bank for central banks. Its annual report includes chapters on domestic and international financial markets. In addition, it discusses issues relating to international trade, the monetary systems, and economic development. It is a good source for detailed descriptions of trends in international markets.

Emerging Stock Markets Factbook (published annually by International Finance Corporation)

The International Finance Corporation (IFC) was established in 1956 to promote the growth of developing countries through private sector investment. The *Emerging Stock Markets Factbook* brings together fundamental market data on the leading stock markets of the developing world. The *Factbook* is based on the IFC's *Emerging Stock Markets Data Base,* begun in 1981. Using a sample of stocks in each market, the database includes weekly and monthly statistics going back as far as 1975. The IFC has created several indexes of price and returns for the stocks in its database. Table 16.D lists the countries in the IFC Global Indexes. It also publishes details of valuation and performance by region and by individual country.

TABLE 16.D		
COUNTRIES IN THE IFC GLOBAL INDEXES		
Argentina	Jordan	Portugal
Brazil	Korea	South Africa
Chile	Malaysia	Sri Lanka
China	Mexico	Taiwan
Colombia	Nigeria	Thailand
Greece	Pakistan	Turkey
Hungary	Peru	Venezuela
India	Philippines	Zimbabwe
Indonesia	Poland	

In addition to the *Emerging Stock Markets Factbook*, the IFC publishes *Quarterly Review of Emerging Stock Markets*. The IFC makes its information available as well on diskette and magnetic tape. Online access to market indexes are available in several financial databases including Tradeline International and Datastream. These system are described below.

Bond Indexes

Bond indexes (indexes that chart the movement of bond markets) are not as numerous and are less widely published than are stock indexes. International bond indexes include the J. P. Morgan Government Bond Index, which gives total return performance and 10-year constant maturity yields for 12 major industrial countries. The J. P. Morgan Government Bond Index is published in *World Financial Markets*. The *Wall Street Journal* gives daily bond index total rates of return for Eurodollar bonds. The *Financial Times* also publishes daily quotes on benchmark bonds representative of major markets worldwide. Another sources of bond indexes are the Salomon Brothers bond index published in *Euromoney*. Monthly, quarterly, and annual interest rates on government bonds is one of the time series in *International Financial Statistics*.

The Datastream time-sharing system is an excellent online source for bond indices. Datastream has devised indices covering major government bond markets for 13 European countries, Australia, Japan, and the U.S. The indices are updated daily. In addition to its own indices, Datastream reports a wide variety of other bond measures including J. P. Morgan World Indices, ECU bonds, and Credit Suisse bond performance indices.

Bond Ratings

Moody's monthly *Bond Record* includes a section that features ratings on 6,000 international corporate and convertible bonds. In addition, Moody's includes information on interest dates and the amount outstanding in millions when issued. Exhibit 16.8 is an extract from *Moody's Bond Record* showing the first few entries for Tokyo Electric Power Company bonds. The first Eurobond described was issued in Canadian dollars. The second was issued in German marks. The two numbers following the listing of the bond are the interest rate paid by the bond (e.g., 7.625%) and the date the bond matures (e.g., 1997). The rating of Aaa given to the Tokyo Electronic Power Company bonds is Moody's highest. These bonds have the smallest degree of investment risk.

Moody's Annual Bond Record describes new issues of bonds and changes in corporate and municipal bond ratings during the previous year. Exhibit 16.9 shows entries for Tokyo Electric Power from the 1992 edition.

Standard & Poor's Corporation Records (published annually by Standard & Poor's Corporation, with updates)

S&P includes descriptions of about 200 foreign bonds in the statistical section of its *Corporation Records*. The information provided includes bond ratings, redemption provisions, underwriting provision, amount outstanding, yield to maturity, and prices. Three types of prices are given: a 10-year high and low, a current year high and low, and a month's end price.

ISSUE	MOODY'S RATING	INTEREST DATES	AMT OUTST. MIL$	ISSUED	CURRENCY
TOKYO ELECTRIC POWER CO.					
eurobonds 7.625 1997	Aaa	AUG 6	500.0	7-6-92	C$
eurobonds 7.625 2002[3]	Aaa	NOV 6		10-13-92	DM
japan bonds 6.10 2004	Aaa	MAY 25		5-14-92	YEN
japan bonds 5.80 2004	Aaa	JUL 14	100.0	7-14-92	YEN
japan bonds 5.375 2004[4]	Aaa	J&D 26	100.0	11-26-92	YEN

LISTING FROM *MOODY'S BOND RECORD*

EXHIBIT 16.8

Source: Moody's Bond Record.

CUSIP	TITLE	ACTION (SEE FOLLOWING SECTION)	DATE OF ACTION	MOODY'S RATING	PREVIOUS
	TOKYO ELECTRIC POWER CO.				
1>	eurobonds 7.625 8/6/1997	New Issue	7/6	Aaa	
1>	eurobonds 7.625 11/6/2002	New Issue	10/13	Aaa	
1>	japan bonds 6.10 5/25/2004	New Issue	5/14	Aaa	
1>	japan bonds 5.80 7/14/2004	New Issue	7/14	Aaa	
1>	japan bonds 5.375 12/26/2004	New Issue	11/26	Aaa	

LISTING FROM *MOODY'S ANNUAL BOND RECORD*

EXHIBIT 16.9

Source: Moody's Annual Bond Record.

Financial Times Credit Ratings International
(published quarterly by Financial Times)

This service gives credit ratings for issuers of internationally traded bonds, CDs, and commercial paper. The publication reports the ratings of 12 credit agencies as well as an average rating on about 6,000 company and government issuers. It is arranged both alphabetically and by 37 industrial groups. The rating services are:

Australian Ratings, Melbourne
Canadian Bond Rating Service, Montreal
Dominion Bond Rating Service, Toronto
Duff & Phelps, Chicago
Fitch Investors Service, New York
Japan Bond Research Institute, Tokyo
Japan Credit Rating Agency, Tokyo
McCarthy, Crisanti & Maffei, New York
Moody's Investors Service, New York
Nippon Investors Service, Tokyo
Standard & Poor's Corporation, New York
S&P-ADEF, Paris

A useful feature of the service is its detailed descriptions of the methodology used by the various rating agencies.

PRICES OF INDIVIDUAL FINANCIAL INSTRUMENTS

Hundreds of thousands of financial instruments are traded daily in world markets. Finding price and related information about individual stocks, bonds, options, or futures can be difficult if we are limited to printed sources. Newspaper listings of quotations may be adequate if we need only a few current prices for widely traded issues, but newspapers have several limitations. They typically report only the previous day's transactions. Understandably, financial newspapers concentrate on covering their domestic financial markets and use their local language and currency.

The *Wall Street Journal*, for example, gives quotations for companies on the New York, American, and NASDAQ exchanges (about 6,000 companies), but reports the prices of only a few hundred non-U.S. stocks. Virtually no quotes are given for non-U.S. options, bonds, and futures. The Canadian paper *The Globe and Mail* gives good coverage of U.S. securities in addition to its comprehensive coverage of Ca-

nadian financial markets. The *Financial Times* (London) is a good source of price information for foreign (i.e., non-U.K.) securities. About half the volume on the London International Stock Exchange is for non-U.K. stock.

Financial newspapers are best used as a source of news stories rather than as a data sources for prices. As a practical matter, following the price movements of several financial instruments on a variety of markets requires access to an online financial database.

The automation of the world's financial markets has not only made price information available virtually instantaneously, but has allowed the creation of historical files of data. Online databases of securities prices include real-time and historical data. The major supplier of international stock price data is Extel Financial Ltd. There are several online systems that supply historical financial pricing data. They include IDD, Reuters, and Datastream. We first examine IDD's Tradeline database which is available on Dow Jones, DIALOG, and directly through IDD. The following description is based on the DIALOG version of Tradeline International.

The Tradeline International database contains historical price quotes for more than 38,000 active and inactive equities and over 1,000 indexes traded on over 90 overseas stock exchanges. Historical price quotes for Canadian companies are included with U.S. companies in separate Tradeline databases. Historical price information can be obtained on a daily, weekly, monthly, quarterly, and yearly basis. This information dates back approximately two years. Quotes for active issues are current through the previous day's close. A standard Tradeline report provides price data and volume. Three prices are usually present which can be either ask; bid and mid; or high, low, and close, depending on how a specific security exchange records. Tradeline uses SEDOL numbers (described in Chapter 3) as unique identifiers of securities. The system has an online directory of SEDOL numbers. The default report will be the currency as originally reported by the exchange. The user can change this setting to convert prices into any major currency. For example, Exhibit 16.10 shows a report giving the price and volume of Sumitomo Bank stock on the Tokyo exchange in Japanese yen, and the same information converted to U.S. dollars.

685852 SUMITOMO BANK   Y50
Tokyo
Equity

Daily adjusted prices 4/20/92 to 5/01/92
Prices in currency as reported by exchange

Date	Volume	High	Low	Close
4/20/92	992000	1440.000 JPY	1380.000 JPY	1380.000 JPY
4/21/92	1360000	1410.000 JPY	1330.000 JPY	1370.000 JPY
4/22/92	1190000	1410.000 JPY	1340.000 JPY	1370.000 JPY
4/23/92	1155000	1440.000 JPY	1370.000 JPY	1440.000 JPY
4/24/92	1409000	1450.000 JPY	1380.000 JPY	1390.000 JPY
4/27/92	839000	1400.000 JPY	1380.000 JPY	1390.000 JPY
4/28/92	623000	1400.000 JPY	1380.000 JPY	1390.000 JPY
4/29/92	NA	NA	NA	1390.000 JPY
4/30/92	805000	1400.000 JPY	1380.000 JPY	1400.000 JPY
5/01/92	597000	1390.000 JPY	1370.000 JPY	1370.000 JPY

685852 SUMITOMO BANK   Y50
Tokyo
Equity

Daily adjusted prices 4/20/92 to 5/01/92
Unit of currency is the U.S. dollar

Date	Volume	High	Low	Close
4/20/92	992000	10.709 USD	10.263 USD	10.263 USD
4/21/92	1360000	10.519 USD	9.922 USD	10.220 USD
4/22/92	1190000	10.514 USD	9.992 USD	10.216 USD
4/23/92	1155000	10.706 USD	10.186 USD	10.706 USD
4/24/92	1409000	10.793 USD	10.271 USD	10.346 USD
4/27/92	839000	10.500 USD	10.350 USD	10.425 USD
4/28/92	623000	10.524 USD	10.374 USD	10.449 USD
4/29/92	NA	NA	NA	10.404 USD
4/30/92	805000	10.509 USD	10.358 USD	10.509 USD
5/01/92	597000	10.441 USD	10.291 USD	10.291 USD

REPORT FROM *TRADELINE INTERNATIONAL*

EXHIBIT 16.10

Source: IDD Information Services/Tradeline International.

TABLE 16.E

PRICE OF CEMENTOS (CEMEX A) STOCK IN MEXICAN PESOS

	Unadjusted Price	Adjusted Price
12-28-92	47000.00	47.00
12-29-92	46900.00	46.90
12-30-92	46900.00	46.90
12-31-92	46900.00	46.90
1-4-93	47.50	47.50
1-5-93	49.30	49.30
1-6-93	49.00	49.00
1-7-93	48.50	48.50

Source: Datastream (1993).

Tradeline International's coverage of individual financial instruments is confined to stock prices for the past two years. The DIALOG and Dow Jones versions of the database will not allow the users to download information in a spreadsheet format.

Tradeline adjusts stock prices for stock splits, stock dividends, and currency revaluations. Stock splits and stock dividends dilute stock. If a stock that is selling for $100 splits two for one, the stock should sell for $50 after the split. The effect of a currency devaluation can be seen in Table 16.E. It shows the unadjusted and adjusted price in Mexican pesos for the Cementos company. The Mexican peso was revalued 1,000 to 1 at the beginning of 1993.

Datastream is an example of a time-sharing system that has broad coverage of financial instruments and long time series of data. Such systems typically can supply 10 years or more of daily data on equities, fixed income securities (bonds), money markets, options, mutual funds, and commodities on markets worldwide. Other important international financial systems include Reuters (http://www.reuters.com), Bridge Information Systems (http://www.bridge.com), and Bloomberg (http://www.bloomberg.com). The WWW addresses are given here primarily as an aid to describing their products. The bulk of the financial information of these companies are not yet distributed through the WWW. Bloomberg financial information, in fact, is distributed through proprietary terminals. However, the WWW sites of these companies often do supply current-day statistics. For example,

the Datastream WWW site (http://www.datastream.com) gives the daily closing prices and other information relating to 32,000 world equities.

Datastream has broad coverage of stocks, bonds, money market instruments, options, and commodities. Datastream can often supply financial information that is difficult to find elsewhere. Examples of specialized financial data on Datastream are:

- Betas (measures of stock volatility) for non-U.S. stocks and industry groups.
- Lists of the companies that make up standard stock indices.
- Dividend yields, price earnings ratios, and total returns for equity markets.

NAME	CODE	MNEMONIC	CUR	NOTES
TOKYO ELECTRIC 2.2% 03-29-02	CV	799964	Y	
TOKYO ELEC.POWER 11% 06-05-01	1991	596230	£	
TOKYO ELEC.POWER 10 1/2% 06-14-01	1991	596342	C$	
TOKYO ELEC.POWER 7 5/8% 08-06-97	1992	381623	C$	
TOKYO ELEC.POWER 9 5/8% 12-20-96	1989	560938	CU	
TOKYO ELEC.POWER 8 3/4% 08-28-98	1991	599025	U$	
TOKYO ELEC.POWER 8 3/4% 08-23-96	1989	560163	U$	
TOKYO ELEC.POWER 10 5/8% 12-20-96	1989	561133	C$	
TOKYO ELEC.POWER 9 3/4% 09-29-93	1988	798629	U$	
TOKYO ELEC.POWER 4 1/2% 08-10-93	1988	796592	SF	

DATASTREAM LISTING OF TOKYO ELECTRIC COMPANY BONDS

EXHIBIT 16.11

Source: Datastream International. Reprinted with permission.

301V TOKYO ELEC.POWER 1992 7 5/8% 11-06-02		5-3-93		
HIGH VALUE 106.00 4-15-93		**LOW VALUE** 103.85		4-30-93
WEEK COMMENCING	**MONDAY**	**TUESDAY**	**WEDNESDAY**	**THURSDAY**	**FRIDAY**
3-15-93					105.40
3-22-93	105.15	104.95	104.85	104.95	105.10
3-29-93	105.05	105.00	104.80	104.75	104.50
4-5-93	104.70	104.60	104.70	104.90	104.90
4-12-93	104.90	105.35	105.50	106.00	105.45
4-19-93	105.55	105.55	105.40	105.00	105.25
4-26-93	105.00	105.05	104.60	104.25	103.85

DATASTREAM LISTING OF BOND PRICES

EXHIBIT 16.12

Source: Datastream International. Reprinted with permission.

Datastream can be used to screen for financial instruments that meet certain criteria. For example, international bonds can be screened to select those that have particular combinations of interest payment type, amortization features, and yields. Exhibit 16.11 shows the first 10 entries of Datastream's listings of Tokyo Electric Company Bonds. Exhibit 16.12 shows Datastream's listings of daily prices for Tokyo Electric's 7-5/8% bond issued in 1992.

In addition, the Datastream system has several other useful features. These include a statistical analysis package, a graphics package, and the ability for users to load and integrate their own data series with Datastream files.

Securities Data Corporation

Securities Data Corporation (SDC) has several unique international financial databases. We discussed their Merger and Joint Venture files in Chapter 7.

The U.K. Domestic New Issues database provides information on all equity and convertible issues offered in the U.K. domestic market since 1988. More than 500 data items are available on each issue type, including rights issues, institutional placing, vendor placing, offers of sale, and subscription offers. The database is updated daily from London Stock Exchange filings covering the listed, unlisted, and overseas markets.

The Euroequity and Eurobond Databases provide information on nearly 19,000 euro and foreign market transactions dating back to 1983. The databases cover public and private debt, common stock, and preferred stock securities offers.

The Warrants Database was created in association with IFR Securities Data Company in London. It provides users with information on over 2,600 international warrant issues since 1989. Coverage includes warrants exercisable into corporate equities, as well as a warrants linked to stock indexes, commodities, currency values, debt instruments, and stock baskets. A concise summary of the issue and its exercise provisions includes: total value of the issue, warrant price and repayment value, exercise premium, and market price of underlying stock. Details included about the structure of the issue feature relevant dates, issue minimums, and style of the issue.

A complete description of SDC databases and sample reports are given on their WWW site (http://www.secdata.com).

ADDITIONAL SOURCES

World Currency Yearbook (published irregularly by International Currency Analysis, Inc.)

Formerly titled *Pick's Currency Yearbook*, the *World Currency Yearbook* is a convenient source of historical information about currencies. The 27th edition, published in 1996, gives the history, currency developments, transferability, and currency administration for some 184 nations. Included in each description is a 10-year currency history, official and "black market" exchange rates, and a photograph of the currency. In addition to its descriptions of national currencies, the *World Currency Yearbook* provides useful descriptions and statistics on the Eurocurrency market, currency and trade areas, currency control categories, and the international black market for currency. The appendix include statistics on currency circulation and money supply per capita, a table showing the devaluation of paper money, and a directory of central banks. *World Currency Yearbook* is updated by the monthly newsletter *Global Currency Report* (e-mail: curncydata@aol.com).

International Capital Markets Statistics 1950–1995 (OECD, 1996)

This source gives annual data on issues of international bonds since 1950 and syndicated bank loans since 1972. It is a comprehensive compilation of data complied by the OECD and published in *Financial Statistics Monthly: International Markets* and in *Financial Market Trends*.

A Guide to Financial Times Statistics (Financial Times Business Information, 1991)

The *Financial Times (FT)* has few equals in its coverage of international markets. This guide describes how to read the financial and economic statistics that appear in the *FT*. It contains brief chapters with tables on equities, commodities, futures, options, currencies, equity indices, and British economic statistics. An appendix describes how financial averages, indexes, and percentage changes are calculated.

The international edition of the *Financial Times* that appears Monday through Friday is different than the British version. The international edition is printed in Germany, France, the U.S., and Japan. It has greater emphasis on international economic and financial developments, as well as more comprehensive prices of non-U.K. stocks.

Euromoney (published monthly by Euromoney Publications)

Euromoney describes itself as "the journal of the world's capital and money markets." In addition to its articles and columns, *Euromoney* issues several supplements each year. Ranging between 40 and 120 pages, the supplements are an excellent current source of information on the details of financial markets in Europe. Examples of supplements issued by *Euromoney* include:

Guide to Currencies
Guide to European Domestic Bond Markets
Guide to European Domestic Money Markets
Guide to Offshore Financial Centres
Borrower's Guide to Financing in Foreign Markets
Guide to the World's Best Credits

CONCLUSION

International financial markets are involved with financial transactions that cross national borders. This chapter describes the principal types of international financial markets and financial instruments and discusses the sources of information for both. Financial instruments familiar to us from domestic markets (such as stocks, bonds, options, and figures) are used internationally. In addition, there are specialized instruments of international financial markets such as currency swaps and foreign exchange forwards. Price and related information for individual financial instruments are best obtained from online databases. The large number of financial instruments and their constantly changing characteristics limit the usefulness of print sources.

NOTES

1. Peter A. Abkin, "Globalization of Stock, Futures, and Options Markets," *Economic Review* (July/August 1991): 19.

2. Roland Leuschel, "Fixed Exchange Rates or Financial Bust," *Wall Street Journal* (June 29, 1991): A14.

3. "The Last of the Good Times," *Economist* (August 5, 1992).

4. Peter Passell, "FAST Money," *New York Times Magazine* (October 18, 1992): 41.

5. *Lipper-Mutual Fund Performance Analysis*, Lipper Analytical Service (June 30, 1992): 2–3.

6. Bruno H. Solnik, *International Investments* (Reading, MA: Addison-Wesley, 1991): 87.

7. *Annual Report of the Bank for International Settlements* (Basle, 1992): 137.

8. Julian Walmsley, *The Foreign Exchange and Money Market Guide* (New York: Wiley, 1992).

Index

by Linda Webster

Page numbers in boldface refer to WWW sites.